W9-DIR-392

Peru

LATIN AMERICAN HISTORIES

Thomas E. Skidmore, Series Editor

James R. Scobie	*Argentina: A City and a Nation,* SECOND EDITION
Brian Loveman	*Chile: The Legacy of Hispanic Capitalism,* SECOND EDITION
Franklin W. Knight	*The Caribbean: The Genesis of a Fragmented Nationalism,* SECOND EDITION
Herbert S. Klein	*Bolivia: The Evolution of a Multi-Ethnic Society,* SECOND EDITION
Louis A. Perez, Jr.	*Cuba: Between Reform and Revolution,* SECOND EDITION
Ralph Lee Woodward, Jr.	*Central America: A Nation Divided,* THIRD EDITION
Thomas E. Skidmore	*Brazil: Five Centuries of Change*
Peter Flindell Klarén	*Peru: Society and Nationhood in the Andes*

Peru

*Society and Nationhood
in the Andes*

Peter Flindell Klarén

New York • Oxford
OXFORD UNIVERSITY PRESS
2000

Oxford University Press

Oxford   New York
Athens   Auckland   Bangkok   Bogotá   Buenos Aires   Calcutta
Cape Town   Chennai   Dar es Salaam   Delhi   Florence   Hong Kong   Istanbul
Karachi   Kuala Lumpur   Madrid   Melbourne   Mexico City   Mumbai
Nairobi   Paris   São Paulo   Singapore   Taipei   Tokyo   Warsaw

and associated companies in
Berlin   Ibadan

Published by Oxford University Press, Inc.,
198 Madison Avenue, New York, New York 10016
http://www.oup-usa.org

Oxford is a registered trademark of Oxford University Press

Library of Congress Cataloging-in-Publication Data

Klarén, Peter F., 1938–
    Peru : society and nationhood in the Andes / Peter Flindell
Klarén
        p. cm. — (Latin American histories)
    Includes bibliographical references (p. 439–477) and index.
    ISBN 0-19-506927-7 (cloth). — ISBN 0-19-506928-5 (pbk.)
    1. Peru—History.   I. Title.   II. Series.
F3431.K53   1999
985—dc21   99-20062
                                                                      CIP

Printing number: 10 9 8 7 6 5 4 3 2 1

Printed in the United States of America
on acid-free paper

*To Ali, for all those wonderful years we shared as you grew up,
and to Sara, for her wisdom, understanding, and encouragement*

Contents

List of Maps, Tables, and Charts   ix

Preface   xi

Chapter 1:   Geography and Incas/Pre-Incas   1

Chapter 2:   Clash of Empires and Formation of Colonial Society,
1532–1600   31

Chapter 3:   Transition and Consolidation of the Colonial Order,
1600–1730   69

Chapter 4:   From Imperial Reform to Reluctant Independence,
1730–1824   99

Chapter 5:   Republican Utopia and Postindependence Instability,
1824–40   134

Chapter 6:   From Rags to Riches: The Age of Guano, 1840–79   158

Chapter 7:   War of the Pacific and Reconstruction, 1879–95   183

Chapter 8:   The Aristocratic Republic, 1895–1919   203

Chapter 9:   Populist Challenge, 1919–45   241

Chapter 10:   Democracy and Dictatorship, 1945–63   289

Chapter 11:   From Reform to "Revolution from Above," 1963–75   323

Chapter 12:   Return to Orthodoxy, Redemocratization, and
Populism Redeux, 1975–90   359

Chapter 13: Fujimori, Neoliberalism, and Peru's Progress, 1990–95   **399**

Chronology   **425**

Tables and Charts   **431**

Bibliographical Essay   **439**

Index   **479**

Maps, Tables, and Charts

Maps

Map 1   Peruvian Cities, Departments, and Regions   facing page 1
Map 2   Physical Features of Peru   3
Map 3   Pre-Spanish Settlements and the Inca Empire   6
Map 4   Colonial Latin America: Political Organization   102
Map 5   Peru circa 1830   135
Map 6   Guide Map to Chilean Expansion   184

Tables

Table 1   Economic and Other Data   431
Table 2   Total Population and Annual Population Change in Peru, 1530–1995   433
Table 3   Total Population and Annual Population Change in Lima, 1614–1996   434
Table 4   Export Quantum Index and Growth Rate, 1830–1989   436
Table 5   Long-Term Trends in Exports   436
Table 6   Governments since Indepencence, 1821–1995   437

Chart

Chart 1   Registered Silver Production in Peru and Mexico, 1581–1810   435

Preface

Peru, a country of 25 million people (1997) occupying a half-million square miles of territory on the west coast of South America, is a country with a rich, if painful and torturous history. As the cradle of South America's most advanced native American civilizations, it has a unique heritage among the nations of the southern continent. Unlike the countries of the Southern Cone (Argentina or Chile) or, for that matter, North America (Canada and the United States), Peru encompasses a past that reaches back over 10,000 years in one of the most harsh and inhospitable, if spectacular, environments in the world—the high Andes of South America. A series of sophisticated pre-Columbian civilizations sprang up along the lush coastal river valleys and in the fertile, highland intermontane valleys and plateaus of the high Andes to the east. The culmination of Andean civilization was the construction by the Incas, in little more than a hundred years, of an empire that spanned a third of the South American continent and achieved a level of general material well-being and cultural sophistication that rivaled and, indeed, surpassed many of the great empires in world history.

Paradoxically, Peruvian history is also unique in other, less glorious ways. The Andean peoples engaged the invading Spaniards in 1532 in one of the first clashes between Western and non-Western civilizations in history. The ensuing Spanish conquest and colonization rent the rich fabric of Andean society and created the enormous gulf between the victors and vanquished that continued to reverberate through the centuries. The country, like its geography, became divided economically, socially, and politically between a "semifeudalized," largely native American, highland and a more modernized, capitalistic, urbanized, and mestizo coast. At the apex of its social structure, a small, wealthy white elite came to dominate the vast majority of Andeans, whom they systematically excluded from their narrow, Europeanized conception of the nation. The upshot was a chronic inability of the modern state to overcome the legacies of colonialism and underdevelopment that has effectively inhibited the integration and consolidation of the Peruvian nation to this day.

Writing the history of Peru has posed numerous obstacles and problems. Westerners have typically viewed this former land of the Incas from the vantage point of distance and deep cultural differences that Edward Said called "orientalism." That is, they have perceived Peru as a country not only shrouded in mystery and the exotic, a mirror of their own dreams and desires, but of extremes. Thus, for Western observers—travelers, journalists, businessmen, and others—Peru down through the years was a country of fabulous legendary wealth (El Dorado), of bloody conquest (Pizarro versus Atahualpa); of lost Inca cities (Machu Pichu); of a seignorial Spanish, Catholic nobility (colonial Lima); of violent, fanatical revolutionaries (the Shining Path guerrillas); and of drug traffickers pursuing the "white gold" of the international cocaine trade. The most recent manifestation of this "orientalism" is perhaps the perceived inscrutability of Alberto Fujimori, Peru's neopopulist president of Japanese ancestry who proclaims democracy, but closed down the elected Congress in a so-called autocoup in 1992.

Although such fabled images may contain a mixture of truth and legend, of distortion and contradiction, Peru's history, when examined up close and in depth, is, in fact, different. The epic stories of the construction of the Inca Empire and civilization, the sixteenth-century Spanish invasion, or Simón Bolívar's final liberation of the continent from three centuries of Spanish rule at the Battle of Ayacucho in 1824 still, of course, hold our attention and grip our imagination. But the telling of that story today centers more on how a suppressed, ethnically heterogeneous Peruvian population tenaciously managed to survive the conquest and domination of a small Europeanized creole elite in the midst of periodic, often horrific, natural and man-made disasters that have afflicted the country down through the ages. One need only point to the biological holocaust of demographic disaster caused by the uncontrollable spread of European diseases that were unleashed on the indigenous population at the time of the conquest or the panapoly of wars—civil and cross border—that have beset the country since independence (for example, against Spain, Chile, and the Shining Path). Each time, Peruvians have picked themselves up from the economic and human wreckage of these disasters and contrived a survival that cannot but elicit the admiration of readers of the country's long and contorted history.

Another problem for the historian is how to deal with a far-flung territory the size of England, France, and Spain and a heterogeneous population that is well known for its geographic, climatic, and ethnic diversity. In reality Peruvian history, like the "vertical archipelagos" that each Inca community, or *ayllu*, worked at different altitudes and climatic niches to cultivate a variety of crops, is a mosaic of microregions in which the tapestry of human history has unfolded in a myriad of different ways. This plural history was typically ignored by historians, mostly the country's elites, who, for a long time, imposed an artificial unity on the country's past from Lima, a narration from the center and the capital, where the history of the nation state, in European terms, was presumed to have taken place. This produced a double bind or distortion: history written from the perspective of the elites, who rarely ventured forth into the indigenous interior and therefore did not know the "real" Peru, and the past viewed from the commanding heights of the viceregal state and then its republican successor, both faced decidedly toward Europe.

It took a historiographical revolution, beginning in the 1970s with the new methodologies of social and economic history, to begin to change all that. A new generation of historians emerged who were trained in ethnohistory and what has come to be known as history "from the bottom up." This was history about and from the perspective of the powerless—workers, peasants, slaves, women, and so forth—the so-called subaltern classes that increasingly populate the postcolonial history of Latin America now being written in the United States. The upshot of these historiographical trends has been to begin to "decenter" the writing of Peru's history, on the one hand, away from the perspective of the ruling elites to the subaltern classes and, on the other hand, from Lima to the various regions and subregions that form the heart of Andean space. In short, the history of Peru went from the projection of the "history of Lima" and the elites onto the entire country to a greater approximation of what historian Jorge Basadre referred to as "el Perú profundo."

In this book I have taken a number of approaches that I hope effectively incorporate these changes, as well as overcome some of the aforementioned obstacles in writing the country's history. First, I endeavor to present the country's history as an ongoing debate between scholars by reporting controversies and divergent interpretations. My intention is to deepen and, in a sense, "complexify" the understanding of what Andean history is about. Second, I have pursued a strategy of treating most topics with relative brevity to leave more space for an in-depth treatment of one or two themes per chapter that I see as especially significant. There is, of course, a price to pay for this approach, but I believe that the contrast between a fairly speedy march through some themes and more luxury of detail and amplification on others will better illuminate the country's history and engage the interest of my readers.

Third, in approaching the long sweep of Andean history—the *long durée* if you will—I have concentrated on economic structures and change, on formal politics and power constellations, and on social structures and change. If there is a predominant issue underlying my approach, it is the struggle between Hispanic elites and indigenous, mestizo and Afro-Peruvian "masses" over power and inclusion, a struggle that I explore in both its ethnic and class dimensions. Broadly speaking, this sociopolitical approach (as well as space limitations) has meant that I have had to give lesser attention to cultural and intellectual issues. While I have tried to touch, however briefly, on some of these issues, they really deserve another book. Similarly, the new postmodern revisionism of the 1990s has only now begun to appear in the scholarship of a new generation of historians and therefore can just be glimpsed here and there in the following pages.

In the chapters that follow, I begin with an examination of the rise and decline of various pre-Hispanic Andean polities, starting with the Chavín culture in 800 B.C. and concluding with the rise and fall of the Incas. What is significant about the Incas, I think, is the curious mix of a peasant society at the local, communitarian level with the extraordinary superstructure of the state centered in Cuzco, as well as the importance of reciprocity, redistribution, and ancestor worship that characterized the empire.

From the Incas, I move on in succeeding chapters to the conquest and colonization of the Andes, focusing on the centralization of political power, initiated by the Spanish Hapsburgs through a system of bureaucratic patrimonialism and mercantilism. The ensuing economy was based on "Spain's treasure house in the Andes"—the rich silver mining districts of Potosí in Upper Peru (present-day Bolivia) that became the foundation of the transatlantic trade—as well as a far-flung internal Andean system of production and exchange. Hapsburg rule was followed by the Bourbon dynasty, whose reformers established more efficient and centralizing administrative and fiscal controls during the eighteenth century, which, in turn, elicited a broad range of Indian rebellions that shook the very foundations of imperial rule and led, in time, to independence from Spain.

Turning to the nineteenth century, I examine how the new creole elites narrowly "imagined" their new community, systematically excluding the indigenous masses, during a period characterized more by continuity with than change from the colonial era. Why Peru was unable to turn the enormous bonanza of the guano boom in the middle decades of the century into sustained economic development forms yet another part of my postindependence inquiry. What did begin during the guano era, however, was an opening of the Peruvian economy dating from the 1850s, which although interrupted by war and depression, initiated a long wave of export-led growth up to the 1960s. This export-led growth constituted the basis for the formation of an oligarchy—Peru's so-called forty families—who managed to rule the country until the late 1960s, although not unchallenged by insurgent populist forces that necessitated an alliance of the elite with the military.

In the book's final chapters, I analyze Peru's "time of troubles," which began in the "lost decade" of debt, governmental mismanagement, international recession, and civil strife during the 1980s and ended in the worst depression in more than a century. For one thing, export-led growth stalled in the mid-1960s while internal migrations that began after World War II continued to intensify and to shift the center of gravity of the population from the sierra to the coast and the city of Lima. By the 1990s, fully half the capital's 7 million inhabitants, a third of the country's total population, lived in shantytowns, called *pueblos jóvenes*, or young towns. Moreover, more than half the total population was classified as living in poverty or near poverty. In a city that historically prided itself on its European origins and cosmopolitan culture, this tidal wave of migrants from "the other" Peru signified no less than the Andeanization of the capital and redefinition of the country away from "lo criollo" and toward an inclusive autochthonous national identity.

I show how this trend was recognized and assimilated by the military reformers of the early 1970s into their effort to restructure and develop the country, only to flounder ultimately on the shoals of world recession and administrative mismanagement. The military's difficulties led to a return to democracy in the 1980s, which paradoxically, along with a spiraling economic decline, created opportunities for the emergence of the most radical guerrilla insurgency in the hemisphere. More recently, while the Shining Path was finally being defeated, Peru's fledgling democracy was jolted in 1992 by President Alberto Fujimori's self-coup, suggesting to some that the deeply rooted authoritarian tradition of the country remained in place. Certainly, that tradition and the persistence of violence are threads that run through the Andean past—from the rise and fall of pre-Inca polities, Inca expansionism, the Spanish conquest, and the three-century colonial domination—punctuated by Indian rebellions and their suppression—to the struggle for independence in the 1820s; the War of the Pacific (1879–83); and, on a deeper level, the long-term nature of neocolonialism and contemporary underdevelopment itself.

And yet, such a conclusion is overdrawn. On closer inspection, violence in Peru never approached that of the Mexican Revolution (1.5 million dead) or the genocide of Chile or Guatemala in the 1970s and 1980s. Nor was General Juan Velasco Alvarado anything approaching a fascist military dictator like Augosto Pinochet in Chile. As for the Incas, they were certainly undemocratic, like most empires, but they managed to achieve a level of development and welfare that has not been matched by any other government that has ruled Peru since. Finally, Peru did not seek or desire the war with Chile in 1879, and independence in 1824 was imposed from the outside more than constructed by Peruvians themselves.

And there are other aspects of Peru's recent past that suggest a better future. The hold of the old oligarchy has been broken; the imagined Peruvian community has broadened and deepened; women are increasingly emerging as central actors in the country's social movements and politics; and the subaltern classes, long suppressed and manipulated, have increasingly stamped their imprint on the country's culture, institutions, and future possibilities. Democratization, although incomplete and fraught with the problems of chronic institutional weakness, became more of a reality than a promise over the past decade, at least until the 1992 autocoup (arguably the longest stretch of uninterrupted civilian rule since 1895–1914). There are, then, reasons for optimism as Peru crosses the threshold of the twenty-first century. I hope that the following history, made possible, above all, by the Peruvian and international scholars who have provided the essential bricks and mortar for this work, will contribute to a deepening understanding of the processes that have brought this fascinating Andean country to the cusp of a new millennium.

The preparation of this book has been a labor of love that culminates more than thirty years of work on Peru's history ever since I first went to the country to do field research for my doctoral dissertation in 1965. I am extremely grateful to numerous colleagues who have read various portions of the manuscript and offered many helpful corrections, suggestions, and revisions. For the chapters on the pre-Columbian and colonial periods, these colleagues include Catherine Allen, Anita Cook, Steve Stern, Manuel Burga, and Nils Jacobsen, and for the chapters on the modern period, Peter Blanchard, Florencia Mallon, Dan Masterson, Cynthia McClintock, and Chuck Walker. I also want to thank the two anonymous peer reviewers who made several invaluable suggestions and prevented me from making more than one egregious error. Of course, I take full responsibility for the pages that follow.

I would also like to thank Tom Skidmore, the editor of the series, for his constant encouragement and advice and Yale historian and friend Frank Turner for his helpful council. Sara Castro-Klarén deserves a special *abrazo* not only for enduring the long hours that this book took away from family responsibilities, but for generously offering her scholarly wisdom, special insights, and professional advice. Stacie Caminos, Christine D'Antonio, and the staff of Oxford University Press have cheerfully dealt with all the foibles of editing the text, which often required the patience of Job, for which I sincerely thank them. Thanks also go to my research assistants Estelle McKinnie, Johana Ayers, and Max Skolnick for their good work and to Michael Weeks for getting me out of all those computer jams. Finally, I would like to thank George Washington University for providing me with a generous university research grant to cover much of the travel, research, and other expenses incurred in writing the book.

Peru

Map 1. Peruvian Cities, Departments, and Regions. *Sources:* Henry E. Dobyns and Paul Doughty, *Peru: A Cultural History* (New York, 1976), 24–25, and *Peru: A Country Study,* edited by Rex A. Hudson (Washington, DC, 1992), xxviii.

1 Geography and Incas/Pre-Incas

Geography

To understand Peru's history, one needs to begin with Peru's environment and ecology. And its environment and ecology start with the most dominant feature of its landscape, the spectacular, snow-capped Andean mountains that rise precipitously from the Pacific coast to towering heights. The highest, El Huascarán, peaks at 22,205 feet above sea level, commanding the majestic, 200-kilometer-long range of the Cordillera Blanca. Glaciers exist at these altitudes, and there is a line of permanent snow beginning at 5,000 meters. The runoff from this snowpack drains mostly westward into the Pacific or eastward into the Amazon Basin.

Below these heights facing west are hundreds of small, sparkling crystalline lakes that were carved out by the glacial ice flows of a past age. In pre-Columbian times, many were used for irrigation storage, while in this century their waters have generated hydroelectric power. But they and their higher glacial companions have also been the cause of sinister events. In 1941 heavy rains caused the lake barriers to rupture, producing a catastrophic flood that struck the city of Huaraz and drowned 5,000 people. In 1962 and again in 1970, avalanches, precipitated by falling ice from El Huascarán, buried the towns of Ranrahirca and Yungay, killing over 10,000 people.

Part of the great chain of mountains stretching from Alaska to Cape Horn, the Andes were formed by the "compacting" movement of the great Tectonic Plates off the Pacific coast beginning more than 200 million years ago. The resulting geological movement of the earth's crust buckled the so-called South American Plate during the Jurassic age to form the first of the three main *cordilleras*, or ranges, of the Andes.

One major consequence of this long period of formation of the Andes is its extraordinary climatic and ecological variety. In this respect, Peru is truly a land of contrasts. Its diverse terrain includes lifeless deserts; teeming rain forests; precipitous intermontane valleys; and high, windswept plains. Characteristic of the intermontane valleys is the breathtaking Callejón de Huaylas, through which flows the Santa River that empties into the Pacific after a precipitous journey from its watershed some 4,000 meters above the sea. Here, in what is known as *puna*, verdant grasslands serve as pasture for Andean camelids (llamas, alpacas, guanacos, and vicuñas) in cool temperatures that never rise above 65°F.

Farther below at the middle altitudes of sierra valleys like the Callejón de Huaylas, the climate is more benign, varying between 40°F and 75°F. Here both temperate and subtropical crops can be grown with the aid of irrigation, since the rainy season from November to March is followed by a long dry season. During the rainy season, the sierra experiences frequent landslides that block roads and damage irrigation canals. Yet at this more temperate level, peasants on small holdings, known as *chacras*, grow wheat, barley, quinoa, and rye at the higher elevations and maize, alfalfa, and various vegetables at the lower levels. Finally, at 2,000 meters near the city of Caráz, warmer, if drier, temperatures prevail, necessitating more extensive irrigation to produce oranges and other fruits.

In the southern sierra, the high *puna* broadens into an expansive plateau, or *altiplano*, where most of Peru's cattle and camelids graze. Stretching hundreds of miles from 130 miles south of Cuzco to Bolivia, the dry, cold temperatures of the *altiplano* are moderated somewhat only around Lake Titicaca, the world's largest navigable high-altitude lake. In the harsh, barren *altiplano*, life is complicated by the fact that two out of every five crops are destroyed by drought or frost.

Perhaps the most unique feature of the Andean highlands is the multiplicity of different microenvironments that prevail on the eastern and western slopes of the mountains. According to Dobyns and Doughty, "they are determined by complex variations in oxygen content in the air, degree of slope relative to sunlight, soil quality, mineral content, water availability, night and day wind patterns and air humidity" (1976, p. 17). As a result, an enormous diversity of flora and fauna have adapted and thrived in these different environmental and climatic niches. It is here above 3,000 meters, for example, where the potato and other tubers were first domesticated by prehistoric cultivators, along with other plants that adapted to the high altitude. Eventually, this colorful and flavorful vegetable (over 4,000 varieties have been identified) spread around the world to enrich and expand existing food supplies. Indeed, among other things, the Andean potato is credited with having contributed to the European Industrial Revolution by stabilizing the population and thus the labor supply for the factories of Manchester, England, and elsewhere from the seventeenth century on.

Coming down the west side of the Andes, one encounters a different landscape, the long, arid coastal strip that stretches between the Pacific ocean and the foothills from Tumbez in the north to Arica in the south. Because of the climatic effects of the Pacific's Humbolt Current, Peru's coast, constituting 12 percent of the country's territory, is mostly desert. Off-shore the current's cold water lowers the temperature of the air, which is carried eastward in the prevailing wind pattern over the warmer mainland. The resulting collision of cold and warm air prevents rain from falling and sucks moisture from the ground.

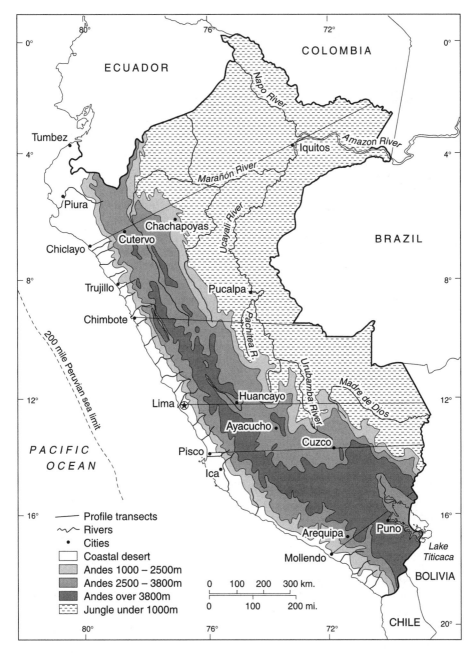

Map 2. Physical Features of Peru. *Source:* Henry E. Dobyns and Paul Doughty, *Peru: A Cultural History* (New York, 1976), 12–13.

While mostly desert, this barren coastal landscape is nevertheless interrupted by twenty-one rivers that flow down from the Andes, producing lush, green oases where they empty into the sea. It was in these green river valleys that early Andean settlement first developed and then evolved into the great coastal civilizations, such as the Moche, Nazca, and Chimú. The diet of these early coastal dwellers was also enriched by the fish life off shore that proliferated in the Humbolt Current's cold, mineral-and-plankton-rich waters. These fish, in turn, sustained the flocks of sea birds whose droppings on off-shore islands over the millennia produced mountains of guano that was used as a fertilizer even in pre-Columbian times.

Meanwhile, the water-laden air mass from the sea continues its eastward movement, crossing the mountains, where it is finally released onto the eastern slopes of the Andes. These slopes eventually flatten out into the sweltering, tropical expanse known as Amazonia. In Amazonia, a scattering of ancient Americans and their ancestors adapted to the biological rhythyms and life cycles of the great Amazonian rain forest. It spreads out, as one observer noted, like a dark, green carpet embracing 60 percent of the nation's territory.

A formidable barrier to penetration, with its dense jungle and army of stinging insects and lethal reptiles, the Amazon has nevertheless exerted a strong attraction to outsiders who have imagined it as something of a "paradise," even a potential panacea for the problems of underdevelopment. Its extraordinary range of exotic flora and fauna, together with a plethora of medicinal plants, have contributed to such an image. Indeed, pharmaceutical companies have only recently discovered the region as a potential source of new drugs and other products for markets in the West. The lure of finding El Dorado led more than one Spanish conquistador into ultimately futile expeditions into its interior, but the discovery of rubber did serve as a source of great wealth, as you shall see, at the turn of the century. Early inhabitants, however, tended to cling to its rivers and meandering streams that could be readily fished for sustenance and used for transportation and whose banks could easily be cleared for crops.

The region is actually divided into two regions, the high *"Ceja de la Selva"* ("Eyebrow of the Jungle") of the easter slopes of the mountains and the lower, flat expanse of jungle. The climate and soils of the *Ceja de la Selva* were particularly suitable for raising coca leaves that ancient Andeans and their descendants have masticated with lime and chewed for its mildly narcotic effect for millennia. Perhaps the origin of Andean civilization, the lower rain forest today is populated by some fifty Amazonic tribes, totaling an estimated 250,000 inhabitants.

From the great peaks of the Andean range, then, one can clearly discern the three major geographic regions of Peru: coast, sierra, and jungle. They include a total area of 1,285,121 square kilometers, in addition to the 95 square kilometers of Pacific Islands. This makes Peru the third largest country in South America, behind Brazil and Argentina.

Pre-Inca Cultures

The first great conquest of this Andean space began some 20,000 years ago, when the descendants of the original migrants, who crossed the land bridge over what is now the Bering Straits between the Asian and American continents, reached northern South America. Over the next several millennia, hunter-gathers fanned out from their bridgehead at Panama to populate the whole of South America. Between 11,000 and 8000 B.C., camps were established in the Piura-Chira Valleys of northern Peru by people who collected shellfish in nearby mangrove swamps. Farther south in the near-desert region around present-day Trujillo, fishermen, using finely carved stone points, speared their quarry in the streams and inlets that emptied into the Pacific between 10,000 and 7000 B.C.

To the east in the Andes at the Guitarrero Cave near the Santa River overlooking the Callejón de Huaylas, early Peruvians consumed viscacha, tinamou (a South American bird), dove, and deer, as well as tubers, squash, and lúcuma (a fruit). They also wove twined mats and mesh containers, may have domesticated beans and peppers, and hunted vicuña on the high *puna* at 4,000 meters above sea level. Most striking, these early cave dwellers created the earliest Peruvian art on the walls of their camps, pictoral renderings of the hunt, as well as red-and-black geometric designs.

Between 5700 and 2800 B.C., inhabitants of Paloma, just south of Lima, lived in semisubterranean, oval huts made of cane poles and reeds. They consumed fish from the sea; raised tubers, squash, and beans; and hunted in the nearby *lomas*, or meadows, using a variety of implements. Infant mortality rates were high (42%), and average life expectancy ranged between twenty and thirty-five years. In an early case of overexploitation of the environment, the Paloma inhabitants cut down the trees of the *lomas*, depriving them of moisture and drying them up.

By about 2500 B.C., small villages inhabited by farmers and fishermen began to spring up in the fertile river valleys of the north coast of Peru. These villages signaled a shift away from the hunter-gatherer encampments to more permanent settlements. These ancient Peruvians now lived in simple adobe houses, cultivated potatoes and beans, fished in the nearby sea, and grew and wove cotton for their clothing. The catalyst for the development of the more complex civilizations that followed was the introduction of a staple annual crop—maize (corn) from Meso-America—and the development of irrigation, both dating from 3000 to 1800 B.C. Both developments served to stabilize the food supply and produce surpluses that, in turn, stabilized the population and freed up labor to undertake more specialized tasks like constructing elaborate ceremonial buildings and making various crafts.

The spread of irrigation enabled the coastal peoples to move their settlements inland from the shoreline up the river valleys to the foothills of the Andes. Building their irrigation canals there enabled them to plant and har-

Map 3. Pre-Spanish Settlements and the Inca Empire, with Its Main Divisions and Roads. *Source:* Magnus Mörner, *The Andean Past: Land, Societies and Conflicts* (New York, 1985), 18.

vest more than one crop a year. In addition to corn and beans, new crops appeared, such as avocados, potatoes, sweet potatoes, and peanuts, as well as cotton. Moreover, with an expanding supply of labor, large ceremonial centers containing pyramids and other monumental buildings were constructed. Finally, at about this time (1800 B.C.) ceramic pottery making was introduced and developed, the technology for which probably came from the Amazon region or northern South America. In this increasingly specialized environment, an important strata of craftsmen emerged, weaving cotton textiles and turning out pottery on a large scale.

Similar developments in what came to be known as the Early Ceramic period also appeared in the highlands, although less imposing than on the coast and more dependent upon a mix of agriculture, herding, and hunting. The camelids that populated the high *altiplano* not only provided important proteins to highlanders' diets and fibers for their garments, but served as pack animals that could traverse the difficult mountain terrain.

At around 500 B.C. a major catastrophe caused the ceremonial centers of the Early Ceramic period along the coast to be suddenly abandoned. Evidence suggests that this catastrophe was caused by a major weather change known today as El Niño. The normally cold waters of the Pacific in this region (the Humbolt Current) are warmed from time to time by deep currents that cause heavy rains in the north and drought in the south. Archaeologists speculate that fish, deprived of deep-water nutrients, disappeared off the coast and that torrential rains damaged irrigation and field systems, causing famine, disease, and depopulation.

THE CHAVÍN

Three centuries after this catastrophe, around 800 B.C., a major new cultural center emerged in the northern highlands of Ancash at Chavín de Huantar. Located on a major trade route between the coast and the tropical Amazonian forests, the city's main temples were elaborately carved with religious symbols drawn from both the coast and the Amazonian rain forest. Chavín proceeded to develop into one of the largest religious and ceremonial complexes in the Americas. Although it was originally thought by Julio C. Tello, the father of Peruvian archaeology, to have been "the womb of Andean civilization," it now appears to have had Amazonian roots.

Chavín's impressive ceremonial center was carefully selected by its architects at the confluence of two rivers whose waters originated in the glaciers of the sacred mountain of Huantsán in the spectacular Cordillera Blanca. Underground canals were constructed beneath its main temple, apparently so that pilgrims could hear the roar of the rushing water under the imposing fifteen-foot stone oracle of the Snarling God that stood in the temple. The unusual sound effects added to the mystery and mystique of this sacred place. Oriented to the cardinal points of the compass, the great temple was perceived by the people of the Andes to be the center of the world—

the most holy and revered place of the Chavín culture. This concept of God and his priestly elite, tied to a geographic location at the center of the cosmos, a sort of spatial mysticism, persisted in the Andes and was fundamental to later Inca beliefs (Cameron, 1990, 41).

The Cult of Chavín, which included a particular set of ideas, rituals, and art styles, eventually encompased a large geographic space. Centered in Ancash, it reached north to Cajamarca and as far as Port Eten on the coast while extending south to the Mantaro Valley and to Huancavelica and Ayacucho in the highlands and to Nazca on the coast. Diffusing important innovations in metallurgy and weaving, along with the religious cult, Chavín for the first time united previously unrelated cultures throughout Peru in a shared religion and technology. Regional cults to Chavín sprang up over a wide area in the same way as they did in the early sixteenth century to Pachacamac, the imposing pre-Columbian ceremonial complex located in the Lurín Valley south of Lima.

Five hundred years after its rise, Chavín began to languish, eventually fragmenting into various parts. In its place, a variety of new regional cultures, both on the coast and in the highlands, arose during the next thousand years to fill the vacuum. On the coast, these cultures included the Recuay, Vicus, Moche, Paracas, and Nazca, two of which deserve special mention.

THE MOCHE

The Moche civilization was centered near Trujillo in the Moche Valley and reached its apogee around A.D. 400. It occupied a 600 kilometer-long expanse of the coast from Huarmey in the south to Piura in the north, an area containing several hundred thousand inhabitants. The Moche people built an impressive irrigation system of canals and aqueducts that transformed kilometers of barren desert into fertile and abundant fields that were capable of sustaining a population considerably larger than any between the Spanish conquest and the early twentieth century. Without benefit of the wheel, the plough, or a developed writing system, the Moche nevertheless achieved a remarkable level of civilization, as witnessed by their highly sophisticated ceramic pottery, lofty pyramids, and clever metalwork. They fertilized their fields with guano bird droppings, fished in the Pacific in their unique *totora*-reed boats, and developed an elaborate sea and overland trade network that extended along the coast and up into the highlands.

In 1987 near Sipán, archaeologist Walter Alva and his wife unearthed an extraordinary cache of Moche artifacts from the tombs of a great Moche warrior-priest and his retinue. Apparently the site of a regional Moche court, the tombs also contained finely crafted gold and silver ornaments; large, gilded copper figurines; and wonderfully decorated ceramic pottery. Indeed, the Moche artisans portrayed such realistic and accurately detailed depictions of themselves and their environment that we have a remarkably authentic picture of their everyday life and work.

THE NAZCA

Contemporaneous with the Moche culture was the smaller Nazca society that flourished from 100 B.C. to A.D. 600 along the south coast and highlands. Its heartland was located in the Ica Valley whose agricultural expanse was much less extensive than that of the north coast, as was its population. Water was scarce, droughts were common, and much of its main river ran underground, leading the Nazca to devise an ingenious underground filtration system to tap the water table. The Nazca people were renowned mainly for their colorful and elaborately embroidered textiles and finely painted, stylized ceramic pottery, but did not erect pyramids on the massive scale of their Moche counterparts to the north.

However, perhaps the most striking artifact of this culture is the now-famous Nazca lines. These lines, or geoglyphs, crisscross the desert for miles around Nazca and are shaped in a variety of geometric, animal, and human forms. They were apparently created by removing a strip of the manganese and iron oxide pebbles deposited over the millennium on the desert floor. The subject of much speculation, the Nazca lines have produced a number of hypotheses concerning their purpose. Perhaps the earliest, but the least supported by concrete evidence, was that suggested by Paul Kosok and his disciple María Reiche, who argued that the desert markings were a giant astronomical calendar designed to coincide with the agricultural cycle. More plausible is the idea supported by J. Reinhard that they formed part of a ritual associated with bringing water to the Nazca Valley.

TIAHUANACO-HUARI

Beginning in the 5th century A.D., the center of gravity of ancient Peruvian civilization shifted from these coastal cultures up into the high Andes. Two major imperial states emerged with large urban centers, one at Tiahuanaco (Tiwanaku) near Lake Titicaca and another at Huari (Wari), near the modern city of Ayacucho. Both represented a new synthesis in Andean society that had previously fragmented after the demise of Chavín. They both also heavily influenced the rise of the two later empires of Chimor on the north coast and the Incas at Cuzco. The exact chronology of the development of these two Andean cultures is unknown.

The city of Tiahuanaco near Lake Titicaca was the highest-known capital in the ancient world at some 12,630 feet above sea level. It was a ceremonial and administrative city whose population may have reached as high as 40,000 inhabitants, which, in global terms, was enormous for its times. Moreover, its religious and political influence extended over a vast area containing millions of people. Befitting its importance, the city of Tiahuanaco was laid out on a monumental scale, covering more than two square miles with great stone structures. Its stone building materials, some blocks as large as 130 tons, were hauled by a large army of laborers from quarries some distance from the city, using ramps and skids.

To sustain this large population center, the Tiahuanaco peoples developed a sophisticated and intricate system of raised fields above the marshy lake shore. The high crop yields from these fields supplemented the usual Andean diet of potatoes, quinoa (a protein-rich grain) and meats from camelid herds. Little is known, however, about the imperial system of the Tiahuanaco people, that is, the methods of trade and exchange, labor and exploitation, and administration and control they used to rule their empire. Two competing theories of exchange, for example, suggest that specialization and a developed network of trade between regions served to circulate products in the empire or that, alternatively, a system of colonies, tribute collection, and redistribution by the ruler assured access to products and goods of different Andean ecological zones. In any event, Tiahuanaco's imperial power seems to have been based more on religious and economic than military means.

The relationship between these two more or less chronologically coincidental empires—the Tiahuanaco and the Huari—is uncertain. Both shared a number of similar societal features and characteristics and indeed seemed to overlap administratively in some areas. Huari, at a lower elevation near Ayacucho, did display some important differences from its counterpart in the high *puna* of Lake Titicaca. For example, its field system was oriented to the lower slopes and intermontane basins of the Andes that could be configured for irrigation and terracing. Moreover, Huari's main crop was maize, which could be easily stored and transported and used for the production of *chicha* beer—an important Andean beverage, used for feasts and rituals and to seal the personal transactions of everyday life. In contrast, maize was absent from the colder, semiarid *puna* and had to be imported from lower elevations.

The Huari peoples also exhibited characteristics that became hallmarks of the later Inca state. For example, they may have resorted, as indicated earlier, to complementary ecological zones to vary their production and consumption, just as the Incas were to do. They also developed an early form of the *quipu* as a recording device, but used colors rather than knots. Finally, like the Incas later, the Huari empire built state installations in provincial areas to better administer and control them.

In sum, both Tiahuanaco and Huari developed large urban settlements and wide-ranging state systems in the Andes between A.D. 500 and A.D. 1000. Each also exhibited many of the aspects of the engineering ingenuity that later appeared with the Incas, such as extensive road systems and architectural styles. Between A.D. 1000 and A.D. 1450, however, a period of fragmentation shattered the previous unity achieved by the Tiahuanaco-

Huari stage. During this period, scores of different ethnic-based groups, both small and large, dotted the Andean landscape. In the central and southern Andes, for example, the Chupachos of Huánuco numbered some 10,000 and the Lupacas on the west bank of Lake Titicaca comprised over 100,000 and controlled large herds of camelids on the *puna*. One of the settlements of the Huancas, another such ethnic group in the central Andes, was located at Tunamarca near present-day Jauja, with a population estimated at 8,000 to 13,000 inhabitants.

These relatively small warring groups were spread over the highlands, sometimes separated from each other by large empty spaces or sometimes sharing the lands of more contiguous territories. The resources they controlled, based essentially on agriculture and herding, were often scattered and dispersed and harder to manage than, say, the richer, more developed river valleys of the coastal cultures. For this reason, the development of more centralized political units and, indeed, empires was much more difficult in the highlands than on the coast. To construct a viable empire in the highlands, these obstacles needed to be overcome. But once they were, as was the case with the Incas, the political and administrative skills they developed may have given them an advantage over their counterparts on the coast. Consequently, this ability to control and manage scattered territories and resources may explain why the successful highland empires were able to achieve a greater degree of dominance and influence over the coastal cultures than vice versa.

THE KINGDOM OF CHIMOR

In any event, with the decline and fragmentation that occurred in the post-Tiahuanaco-Huari period, once again the center of gravity of ancient Andean civilization shifted, this time back to the north coast. On the ruins of the Moche culture, a new kingdom called Chimor and its capital city Chan Chan, near today's Trujillo, arose around A.D. 850 or 900. The Kingdom of Chimor eventually extended the entire length of the central and north coast between Tumbez and Chincha, a distance of more than 800 miles. Chan Chan itself, located at the mouth of the Moche River, covered about 8 square miles, with a population at its apogee of more than 100,000 people. The city was the largest pre-Hispanic city in South America at the time and was divided into nine or eleven *ciudadelas*, or compounds, each apparently the residence of a local lord and sometime palace of the kingdom's ruler.

In addition to its ceremonial and administrative functions, Chan Chan was also a center of craft production. A quarter of the city's population was composed of artisans who turned out the metallurgical goods and textiles that were the crowning artistic achievements of the Chimú. Indeed, Chan Chan was a major "manufacturing" center. Goods were produced in large compounds; subdivided into a maze of small, individual workrooms within the *ciudadelas*; and stored in sizable storage buildings located throughout the city. A busy caravan site near the city center received shipments of raw materials and loaded finished products for transport throughout the empire. The redistribution of these goods, a common practice in the political economy of the Andes, served to extend and enhance the power of Chimor's ruler.

Chan Chan's precisely symmetrical urban space was surrounded by a lush garden oasis of agricultural fields that supported the city's dense population. Dependent on a complex irrigation system linked to the nearby Moche River, the heartland of the Chimor Kingdom was vulnerable, like the Moche before it, to periodic natural disasters, such as flooding from the effects of El Niño or earthquakes. Similarly, over time salt leaked into the system from the nearby Pacific, reducing agricultural productivity, which, in turn, may have given the Chimú the impetus to acquire more land through imperial expansion. Indeed, by A.D. 1200, they had gained control of the Zaña Valley in the north and the Santa Valley in the south, and by A.D. 1400, they had reached their imperial limits. It appears that Chimú hegemony over this region, however, was not based solely on military means, but rather on economic power and control of its crucial hydraulic systems. Paradoxically, the latter also made the Chimú, like their predecessors, vulnerable to the cutoff or diversion of their water resources by expanding highland polities, namely, the Incas in the middle of the fifteenth century.

The Inca Empire

The apogee of the Andean pre-Columbian civilizations was the construction by the Incas of an empire that spanned a third of the South American continent and achieved a level of general material well-being and cultural sophistication that rivaled, perhaps even surpassed, many of the other great empires in world history. Our knowledge of this great civilization, although better than the mainly archaeologically based information of the pre-Inca period, is nevertheless still problematic. It is problematic because of several factors, not the least because it is based almost entirely on the Spanish chroniclers who gathered information on the empire after the conquest in 1532. Unlike the Aztecs who had pictographs or the Maya who had hieroglyphics, the Incas had no such form of writing. They did, of course, possess the *quipu* system, a unique quantitative method of compiling data and keeping records that enabled the state to administer its far-flung empire from its capital in Cuzco. As for the Spanish chroniclers, they were dependent on the recollections of the native, Hispanized Inca elite at Cuzco for much of their information on the empire and its history.

Another problem is that the Inca dynasties did not develop a single official version of their past, as might have been expected in such a highly centralized, state-centered society. Rather, there existed different and competing histories derived from the households, or *panacas*, of the various royal

Incas and their descendants who ruled the empire and conspired to assert their dynastic claims on political power. Thus control of the historical past and its different versions was a central aspect of the struggle for power. These versions of history also reflected the different power relations of various groups in a highly stratified society. As a result, many historians view the narratives of Inca history "as constructions, constituted in the early years of the empire to explain and legitimate the practices and patterns of social relations that had been instituted" (Patterson, 1991, p. 45). This view stands in contrast to those of other historians who treat such accounts as approximating historical reality. Be that as it may, beginning in the 1960s, historians working in the Spanish colonial archives discovered a valuable new source on the Incas—the reports of *visitas* by colonial officials who made fact-finding trips to various provinces to gather information for the purposes of administration.

Perhaps the most difficult problem to overcome in constructing an accurate and coherent history of the Incas derives from an Andean worldview that was different from the West. Therefore, to understand the Inca past, historians must ask the question, as R. Tom Zuidema did, how the Incas themselves conceived of their own history. Europeans, at least since the enlightenment, saw history as linear, a chain of events in which each event was the product of its predecessor. Andeans, on the other hand, believed that history was cyclical, "an alternation of imperial and anti-political ages that followed one another in succession; the transitions from one age to the next were marked by cataclysms" (*pachacuti*; Patterson, 1991, 44). Furthermore, the Spanish chroniclers, many of them churchmen who saw the native Americans as infidels to be converted to Christianity, interpreted what they saw from a strictly Eurocentric and religious perspective. This bias more often than not obscured, rather than revealed, any meaningful understanding of their subjects.

With this said, it appears that the Incas or Quechuas were just one of the scores of different ethnic-based groups of various sizes that were scattered about the Andean landscape after the fall of the Tiahuanco-Huari civilizations around the first millennium A.D. This period, the so-called Late Intermediate, or pre-Inca, period of Andean history, lasted from roughly A.D. 1000 to A.D. 1400. It was characterized by a relative fragmentation and dispersal of the population and the absence of any large, urban concentrations that had been the hallmark of the previous Middle Horizon period from A.D. 600 to A.D. 1000.

ORIGINS

There are different interpretations of the origins of the Incas and the rise of their kingdom at Cuzco. A traditional school holds that the Incas originated in the region of Lake Titicaca, from which they began to expand, eventually entering (perhaps invading) the Valley of Cuzco as early as A.D. 1200. The prevailing opinion, however, is that the Incas were not invaders of the Valley of Cuzco at all, but had actually lived there for several hundred years. Then the Incas began to subdue and incorporate various other peoples who were also established in the Cuzco region. These groups included the Huallas, Sausirays, Alcavizas, and Ayarmacas whose elites were granted the title of "Inca by privilege." In this way, they were incorporated, through a system of royal *ayllus*, into the functioning of the incipient Inca state.

The *ayllus* constituted the basic, microlevel unit of Andean society. They were composed of endogamous kin groups whose most important function was dominion over specific lands on which members (couples) were allowed to cultivate parcels for subsistence. In return for the right to hold land, members of the *ayllus* were obligated to hold office and carry out certain religious functions in the community. In the *ayllu*, grazing land was held in common (private property did not exist), whereas arable land was allotted to families in proportion to their size. Labor tasks in the community were carried out on a communal basis, with the division of labor based on age and gender. Thus, community members would gather collectively to tend each member's fields, build a house, or repair irrigation systems while being given *chicha* beer, food, tools, and seeds by the host or beneficiary for the task. Such collective, community-based work parties still survive in the Andes and are called *mingas*. The age-gender division of labor had teenagers working as shepherds; men plowing; and women planting, spinning thread, weaving cloth, and brewing *chicha* beer. Some members of the community also produced crafts, such as pottery and silver objects, perhaps during slack time.

The aforementioned division of labor should not be construed as male dominance in Andean society, at least at the level of community. Rather, there existed an interdependence and complementarity between the sexes, and gender equality was the norm, just as it was among all members of the community. This gender equality was best expressed in the marriage ceremony, which celebrated the union of equals and was expressed in the ritual exchange of clothing. Nevertheless, in time Inca imperialism and conquest placed a premium on the male soldier, which began the process of creating a gender-based hierarchy. Moreover, as the empire expanded, its administration was placed in the hands of noblemen who became the real power brokers of the empire.

Still, another feature of gender equality in the Andes was the custom of parallel lines of descent—that is, women descended from their mothers and men from their fathers. Therefore, women, like men, were accorded a portion of the resources of the *ayllu* and thus independent access to the society's means of subsistence (including rights to community land, water, and herds). At the same time, inheritance was also gender based, so that women passed some of these resources down to their daughters (Silverblatt, 1987). This gender-based inheritance, like the communal versus individual ownership of land, proved to be a point of contention later when the Spaniards imposed their patriarchal notions of primogeniture in inheritance onto colonial society after the conquest, just as they did the concept of private property.

Because self-sufficiency was a fundamental ideal of ancient Andean society, communities often farmed parcels of land in different ecological niches in the rugged Andean terrain. In this way, they achieved what John Murra called "vertical complementarity," that is, the ability to produce a wide variety of crops—such as maize, potatoes, and quinoa—at different altitudes for household and community consumption.

In the early Inca period, Cuzco was probably no more than a village, and Inca "conquests" prior to the beginning of the fifteenth century were limited and probably more like raids. According to Rowe, "in early times, neither the Inca nor any of their neighbors thought of organizing their conquests as a permanent domain. A defeated village was looted, and perhaps a tribute was imposed on it, but otherwise it was left alone until it recovered sufficient strength not to be a menace again" (quoted in Davies, 1995, p. 38).

EXPANSION

During this formative period of gradual expansion (A.D. 1200–1400), the Incas were governed by a series of rulers whose names have been identified from the chronicles and other sources and whose reigns constitute a kind of official history. The pace of conquest expanded dramatically under the rule of the ninth of these Inca rulers, Pachacuti Inca Yupanqui, who ruled from 1438 to 1471. Hemming described Pachacuti as "one of those protean figures, like Alexander or Napoleon, who combine a mania for conquest with the ability to impose his will on every facet of government." (quoted in Cameron, 1990, 58) Another leading scholar said that he was not only a great ruler, "but [a] . . . primordial cultural hero, creator of both city and empire" (Davies, 1995, 40).

It should be noted here that, broadly speaking, two schools of thought have emerged in recent years purporting to explain the expansion of the Inca state during the fifteenth century. The traditional view, based on a careful analysis of the Spanish chronicles by Rowe (1946) and others, attributes it to the charismatic figure of Pachacuti and his organizing and leadership genius. A second group questions this event-based view of history that sees one individual, Pachacuti, as the prime agent of historical change among the Incas. This school sees the development of the Inca state as deriving from broader processes of social change, but is divided over the specific causes. For example, on the issue of expansion, Rostworowski de Diez Canseco (1988) stressed the manipulation of institutionalized exchange relationships, rather than military conquest; Lumbreras (1978) emphasized class conflict, as well as traditional animosities between Cuzco and the Chancas; Murra (1980) and others have pointed to economic management and systems of redistribution; and Conrad and Demorest (1984) and others have placed importance on the Inca system of inheritance.

Under Pachacuti's rule and that of his son Túpac Inca Yupanqui (1471–93), the Incas came to control upwards of a third of the South American continent, with an estimated population of 9 million to 16 million inhabitants under their rule at the time of the Spanish conquest. The springboard for this explosive expansion under Pachacuti was his victory over the Chancas, a fierce rival ethnic group that apparently threatened his incipient chiefdomship. Invading the valley in the fifteenth century, the Chancas tried

Túpac Inca Yupanqui (1471–93), son of Pachacuti Inca who was the architect of the great thirteenth century expansion of the Inca Empire. Reproduced courtesy of The Brooklyn Museum.

to capture Cuzco, but were repelled by a heroic, last-ditch defense of the city organized by Pachacuti and then crushed by his pursuing Inca army.

Once defeated, the Chancas accepted, as was customary in the Andes, the authority of their conqueror. Having exhibited their prowess in war, the Chancas were then integrated into Pachacuti's growing imperial army, a practice that the Incas would follow with other conquered peoples. In subsequent military campaigns, the emperor extended the radius of Inca power into Huamanga, Huánuco, and the region around Lake Titicaca. After Pachacuti's death in 1471, his son Túpac Inca Yupanqui extended the radius of conquests north to Cajamarca and Quito and south into present-day Chile. These conquests also included the advanced kingdoms along the coast, such as Chimor, which, as I said earlier, were vulnerable to the cutoff of the irrigation canals on which they depended for their food supply. On the other hand, the successor kingdoms to the Nazca and Chincha nations along the south coast accepted or opposed Inca intrusion, depending on the degree of political complexity from valley to valley.

After his great victory over the Chancas, Pachacuti transformed Cuzco into a resplendent, imperial city and consolidated his political hegemony. Using the loot seized from the defeated Chancas, Pachacuti rewarded surrounding local chiefs with lavish gifts in return for their loyalty to Inca rule. Such notions of reciprocity were characteristic of Andean politics and signified the acceptance of suzerainty by local chiefs to a higher authority. The key to this uniquely Andean arrangement was economic—the accumulation and distribution of wealth, in this case booty, in the form of foodstuffs and other sumptuary produced from land and labor and stored in large warehouses throughout the kingdom.

RELIGION

Pachacuti also instituted changes in the established, polytheistic religion of the Incas. These changes not only served to reinforce his temporal power, but were an expression of incipient Inca imperialism. In Cuzco, Pachacuti rebuilt the palace of Coricancha, formerly the residence of past Inca rulers, into a great shrine dedicated to the worship of Inti, the god of the sun. In the palace, he placed resplendent golden statues of the former Inca kings and ordered the priests to compose new chants and rituals to honor their memory. When the Spaniards later captured Cuzco in 1533, they were dazzled by this glittering monument to the sun god whose walls were elaborately covered with gold and silver and whose treasures were subsequently melted down for shipment back to Spain. Garcilaso de la Vega reported that the interior gardens of the Temple of the Sun were also sumptuously adorned with gold and silver and contained five golden fountains where sacrificial victims were washed before meeting their demise. Under Pachacuti, the Temple of Coricancha became the symbol of a new imperial cult of the Incas.

Inti was only one of a triad of gods in the Incas' religious pantheon. The other two were the creator god Viracocha and the weather or thunder god Illapa. Other important gods were Mama-Quilla, the moon, and Pacha-mama, mother earth. It was Viracocha who, on the eve of the great battle of Cuzco, appeared in a dream to Pachacuti as a bearded, white-faced figure promising victory over the Chancas. As a result of the Incas victory, Vira-cocha's position in the religious pantheon was also subsequently enhanced by a grateful Pachacuti as part of the general reform of the Inca state religion. The aim, like the upgrading of Inti, was to use the official religion as a means of legitimating Inca conquests. Since the gods' functions often seemed to merge or overlap indistinguishably and no Inca god was considered supreme (monotheism being unknown), scholarly opinion is divided as to which of these two gods, Inti or Viracocha, was more important to the Incas. However, the prevailing interpretation holds that a process of "solarization of the state religion" as an expression of the cult and ethos of imperialism clearly occurred during the reign of Pachacuti (Pease, 1978).

The religious life of the common and subject peoples of the empire, however, had little to do with the abstract and universalizing expressions of the official state religion. Rather, at the local level worship centered on sacred beings or spirits that resided in places or objects known as *huacas*, or holy sites. These sites included mountains, springs, lakes, rock outcrops, ancient ruins, and caves, as well as objects, such as effigies, mummies, oracles—anything human made. As holy sites or objects, *huacas* were revered by the people who showered them with gifts, such as llama and guinea pig meat, brilliantly colored mineral powders, clothing, coca leaves, and maize beer. Often *huacas* became the sites of temples and were served by priests who were supported by the production of village fields set aside for such a purpose.

In addition to instituting the cult of the sun, Pachacuti formalized and standardized the calendar by which the state established the dates for certain rituals, pageants, and other societal activities. This was another mechanism for state dominance over the conquered peoples, establishing the times when phases of the agricultural cycle were carried out, the census was taken, taxes were collected, labor was due, and even when marriage ceremonies could take place. Such a timetable was part of the development of an official cosmology called the *ceque* system, by which the Incas created a complex geographic representation of the country and the universe.

According to Zuidema (1986, p. 73), the system comprised forty-one imaginary lines or vectors radiated out from the center of Cuzco toward the horizon, somewhat like spokes in a wheel. Located on the *ceque* system were 328 *huacas*, mostly springs, mountains, or hills. Each sacred place was the object of a special ritual carried out by an assigned cult on a designated day. In addition to ordering the days of the year by way of each *huaca*, something similar to a rosary, the *ceque* system also helped codify Inca astronomical observations.

ORGANIZATION

Pachacuti was a great innovator in other ways. He initiated an ambitious program of public works. For example, the two main rivers of Cuzco, which often flooded the city during the rainy season, were canalized with labor mobilized by local *curacas*, or chiefs from the surrounding valley. Pachacuti also apparently began the construction of the massive fortress of Sacsahuamán to protect the city, mobilizing perhaps 20,000 laborers in a task that spanned the rule of subsequent kings. In addition to its military functions, Sacsahuamán also became the main storehouse of the capital, containing arms, clothing, and precious jewels and metals. Finally, the emperor began the construction of the great Inca road system, which would eventually radiate out of the central square of the capital in the four directions of the compass, dividing the city into four *suyus*, or sections. Eventually, as Inca territory was expanded, these four roads served as the main axis that divided the empire, like the capital, into four *suyus*, or quarters. In all respects, "the city thus became the very navel of its nascent empire" (Davies, 1995, p. 51), an empire that the Incas called Tawantinsuyu, or the four divisions.

To carry out these great public works, Pachacuti introduced a corvee system of labor, the core of which were *yanas* (serfs) and *mitimae* (settler groups). The latter were composed of contingents drawn from conquered peoples whose loyalty to the Incas was now ensured and who were therefore transferred en masse to reside and work in other parts of the empire. They replaced rebellious groups and others whose loyalty was suspect and had been deported to other settled regions for re-education and integration into the empire. *Mitimae* occupied their lands and might be employed in other tasks, such as building roads, temples, and canal works or producing foods and crafts for the state. They might also be used for the establishment of permanent garrisons to maintain control and order on the expanding Inca frontier. In either case, their removal and resettlement in recently conquered areas were a device to establish control and to integrate the new groups into the imperial order. The *yanas* were also drawn from recently conquered or rebellious communities and sent to Cuzco as servants or laborers. At first, they were apparently used to construct irrigation works in Cuzco and to cultivate the lands of the *panacas*. Already the *panacas*, the royal households of earlier Inca rulers and their assimilated counterparts (Incas by privilege), were being transformed into a hereditary aristocracy to man the growing administrative apparatus of the state. The *yanas* also worked on royal estates, in the households of local chieftains, or in the shrines of the state religious cults.

The *sapa*, or supreme Inca, stood at the apex of the Inca state; indeed, he was the state. Considered by the Incas as the son of the sun god Inti, the Sapa Inca was, in effect, both man and god and his subjects were the "children of God." The original importance of the sun god Inti is believed to derive from the beginnings of the cultivation of maize in the Andes that thrived only at low altitudes where the heat of the sun was most intense and the danger of frost less severe. Anthropologists also believe that the cultivation of maize was crucial to the Incas, since maize was easily produced and transported to sustain the imperial armies. The coincidence of imperialism, "solarization," and maize production was not accidental.

The Sapa Inca married one of his sisters, who became the *coya*, or queen. Just as her husband was the son of the sun, she was the daughter of the moon and the representative of all womankind. This gender-based duality masculine/feminine—sun/moon—day/night—formed part of the organizing principal that was the basis of Inca cosmogony and society. In social terms, this duality translated into the broader terms of reciprocity and complimentarity. There is some evidence that the *coya* had some political authority in the empire, ruling, for example, in the absence of the Inca or advising her husband on important matters. Nevertheless, as the "queen of woman," the *coya*'s authority was exercised principally over women in the empire. This authority was expressed in official ceremonies in Cuzco in which women kissed the hand of the queen, just as men paid similar obeisance to the king. Some sense of the authority of the *coya* can be gleened from this description of her by a chronicler:

> The Palace of the queen was located in this enormous construction, and it was almost as large as the Inca's; and since she held a preeminent office, she went about dressed with ornaments of *cumbi* (finely woven cloth) which represented the position she held in the palace. She had shrines, baths, and gardens, both for herself and for her *ñustas*, who were like ladies-in-waiting, of which there were more than two hundred. She was responsible for marrying them to lords who achieved honorable offices under the Inca. It was truly marvelous when the great queen walked about; she was served, in every way, with the majesty shown toward the Inca. (Murua, quoted in Silverblatt, 1987, 60)

The method of selecting the Sapa Inca is obscure. The Spanish chroniclers, accustomed to the rules of primogeniture or succession of the eldest son of the Spanish kings, assumed a similar system existed among the Incas. However, Viceroy Toledo, reporting to Philip II in 1572, stated rather that the son who exhibited the greatest capacity to rule rose to become the emperor. Such a method opened the way for opinion and intrigue in the imperial succession, and, indeed, the history of the Incas is replete with stories of numerous struggles for power. In fact, Pachacuti usurped power in a coup d'état against another heir or pretender to the throne. As the empire grew larger, with rulers spending longer periods away from the capital, factionalism and power struggles became more common. Indeed, the legendary civil war between Huáscar and his allegedly illegitimate brother Atahualpa that opened the way for the Spanish conquest was just such a struggle over imperial succession.

The absolute power of the Sapa Inca was not based only upon his spiritual authority. Theoretically the Sapa Inca was the owner of all land, mines, and herds in the empire. Communities were required to allot a portion of their fields and pastures, to be worked by *mit'a*, or draft labor, for the support of the state and the official religion. Ideally, this system meant the division of community lands into thirds (state, religion, community), although in practice the portions allotted to each sector varied from place to place. The production from these state lands was stored locally or sent to Cuzco or other administrative centers.

In the case of the herds—llamas, vicuñas, and alpacas—pastured on community lands in the higher elevations, they were valuable as transport, for religious sacrifice, and for the production of fine wool for the elaborate clothing worn by the Inca and the elite. The Sapa Inca reportedly wore garments only once and changed clothes several times a day. Mining also occupied an important place in the material wealth of the Sapa Inca. Precious metals, particularly gold and silver, were greatly valued by the Incas, who used them elaborately in the decoration of their temples.

Just below the Sapa Inca in the social pyramid was the inner elite, which was composed exclusively of descendants of the Inca rulers. The *orejones* or big ears, as they were called by the Spaniards, along with the high priests, resided exclusively in the center of Cuzco. They sent their sons to a special school, were allowed to wear sumptuary clothing, were exempt from taxes, and may have even spoken a distinct dialect of Quechua. While supported by revenues from the state, they were expected to give part of the revenues back in the form of gifts to the king. It was from among the *orejones* that the Sapa Inca recruited many of his top commanders and administrators. The Inca elite was served by the class of *yanas*, who were brought from the provinces to the capital for this purpose. They may have been the equivalent of slaves in other societies, although they seem to have been less oppressed and could attain a certain status, such as artisans.

ADMINISTRATION

The administration of such an immense empire must have been an awesome task, one that in the absence of writing—the basis of all modern bureaucracies—stretches the limits of credulity. Central to this process was the recording device called *quipus*, which consisted of strings or ropes, colored and knotted in meaningful ways. *Quipus* were the preserve of experts called *quipocamayos*, premodern accountants who kept records of everything in the empire, from food stores to herds to the movement of troops and people. Educated at special schools, the *quipocamayos* worked at every level of administration, from the center in Cuzco to the local and provincial level. Their prodigious feats of meticulous imperial record keeping astounded the conquering Spaniards and still defy the imagination.

While one risks, in the absence of adequate information, imposing Western concepts of organization, one can imagine an administrative apparatus and caste organized along judicial, fiscal, military, and transportation lines, with the latter two perhaps the most important. In a society geared for imperial expansion, the army and transport were paramount. What is truly remarkable is the extent and complexity of constructing a functional and efficient system of transportation across the Andes, a problem that has defied modern solution. The construction of bridges and roads to traverse this mountainous terrain called for the greatest degree of originality and technique, skills in which Inca engineers excelled. Scholars have been further impressed by the fact that Inca bridges and buildings were constructed without resorting to the arch, a concept used for 2,000 years in the West. The mystique of Inca engineering is further enhanced by the fact that the imperial communications infrastructure was centrally planned without resort to charts and maps, at least as they are known in the West. How such a system was "tracked" from the center, without such devices and perhaps relying largely on memory, again defies modern understanding. The *quipus* no doubt played some role, but exactly what is still a mystery.

Although its full extent will probably never be known, much of the Inca road system has been mapped in recent years in a notable project directed by archeologist John Hyslop. It may have comprised as much as 14,000 kilometers. Although used for religious and military purposes, its major function was administrative and economic. The central artery of the empire was the Cuzco–Quito road, along which lay many large Inca administrative centers. Lateral roads connected the highlands with the eastern and western valleys and facilitated the exchange of produce from different ecological zones. Along the roads, at intervals of a day's walk, stood *tampus*, lodging and storage structures containing arms, clothing, fuel, and foodstuffs. There were also *chasqui* stations at various intervals, where relay runners who were charged with carrying messages passed on their contents to fresh replacements. One of the more unique features of the road system were suspension bridges made of ropes and fibers that spanned some of the more spectacular heights in the Andes and amazed the first Spaniards who crossed them with great trepidation.

Military organization was equally crucial to the functioning of the empire, although the Inca conquest was often achieved as much through demonstrations of power and careful negotiation, accompanied by elaborate pomp, ceremony, and dancing. When military force was deployed, of course, the Incas depended upon efficient communications. In addition to ample storage facilities (*tampus* and the like) and roads, the Inca armies relied upon well-constructed fortifications throughout the empire. Strategically located forts were used to control lands already conquered. Often far from imperial centers, they were manned not by professional soldiers, but by *mitimae* settlers, who also cultivated the surrounding lands, thereby providing both security (from attack and rebellion) and local production.

The imperial armies, which apparently were not standing armies, were drawn from a compulsory draft of all men aged twenty-five to fifty. They were composed mainly of peasant farmers and included the ever-expanding populations of conquered areas, whose peoples the Incas converted into loyal and dependable subjects. The advantage these armies had over local adversaries proved to be their numbers, which could run as high as tens of thousands, with a seemingly endless supply of reserves who reportedly could wear down their numerically smaller opponents. Their weapons, which differed little throughout the Andes, included stone-hurling slings, bows and arrow, stone clubs fitted with spikes, and wooden lances. It is interesting that although the Incas had a sophisticated metallurgical industry, it was not deployed in weapons manufacture.

Inca armies seemed to have been highly trained and disciplined, not the least taught to respect the peoples through whose territories they passed. Their commanders were known for their ability to cooperate and coordinate troop movements, to achieve surprise, and to apply the principle of the concentration of force at a decisive point to achieve victory. Superior logistics kept their armies in the field during long campaigns. Since the Inca armies were always on the offensive, they held the advantage against the defenses of their opponents.

The problem of the deployment of troops and the exact timing of their arrival called for extraordinary organization and central administration from Cuzco. Indeed, as one expert has shown, the vast territorial domain of the Incas called for the construction of a system of command and control in which the periphery could relate efficiently with the center. Otherwise the empire would have been subject to constant rebellion and fragmentation. When we add to these feats the fact that the Incas were also renowned for the construction of great works of agricultural terracing and irrigation, we can begin to appreciate the magnitude of their achievements and their contributions to American civilization.

The construction of these and other public and community works, as well as the production of goods for delivery to the king, was undertaken by a draft labor system called the *mit'a*. This system constituted the principal form of taxes levied on the subject population and its individual households. Census takers, operating on an accounting system based on decimal groupings of households and communities, kept track of the *mit'a* system. Whether this was actually a labor or tribute system (a tax in kind) is unclear. What is certain is that every male subject was obligated to serve a determined number of days per year in the service of the state. Such service could be performed in road building; temple construction; mining precious metals; or producing a product, such as maize or feathered objects, for the king. Local *curacas* could also call upon *mit'a* labor for the performing of local tasks and the army for the recruitment of soldiers.

While preforming their *mit'a* labor, whether for the state or local leaders, *mitayos* were generously provided food, drink, and music by their hosts. Work, as with the communal *minga* within the community, was always carried out in a festive, ritualized manner. As Morris and Von Hagen (1993, p. 170) aptly put it, "in this way economics, politics and religion were wrapped in an elaborate package of work, ritual and festival."

GOVERNANCE

The Inca system of governance, like its class system, was pyramidal, with the emperor, who ruled by divine right and was worshiped as divine, at the top. Below the emperor were the *apo*, prefects who were in charge of the four quarters into which the empire was divided. Below them were the governors, selected from the elite, at the provincial level and the *curacas*, traditional ethnic lords loyal to Inca rule, at the local level. The governors resided in the main provincial centers, strategically located throughout the empire. They had judicial and administrative functions and oversaw the *curacas*, traveling about in litters to oversee their jurisdiction.

The domain of a *curaca* varied from a village of a couple of hundred inhabitants to a much larger concentration or territory. The most important task of the *curaca* was the mobilization of *mit'a* labor to carry out the military and civilian functions of the state. The *curaca* also had rights to the use of land and could call upon community labor to cultivate this land. Finally, he was responsible for the assignment of community lands to inhabitants according to family size. As a traditional ethnic lord, the *curaca* retained the loyalty of his community while ruling at the behest of the Incas. In this sense, *curacas* were intermediaries in the imperial system, articulating relations between the Inca ruling class and the state, on the one hand, and their own kin and community, on the other hand.

One way that the Inca secured the loyalty of these local lords was to marry their daughters, who became secondary wives in his household, and to require that their sons be educated in Cuzco. In the latter instance, the emperor not only acquired a useful hostage to ensure compliance, but assured the loyalty of the next generation of *curacas*. The king also plied the *curacas* with gifts of land and servants to ensure such loyalty. The activities of both the provincial governors and the local *curacas* were checked periodically by *tocricoc* (literally "those who see all"), or inspectors. Faithful men whom the emperor could trust, their job was to see to it that these officials were carrying out their obligations properly and that they were not hatching any rebellions or conspiracies against the state.

The Incas imposed the cult of the sun god Inti on all conquered ethnic groups as a symbol of their power and authority. Temples dedicated to the worship of Inti were erected in all the main provincial centers of the empire. At the same time, the Incas allowed the conquered peoples to retain their local rites and deities, even reportedly taking their images to Cuzco to occupy a place of honor (and hostage) in the temples. This was typical of the general Inca practice of allowing the continuation of many local traditions and customs in their expanding multiethnic empire, while establishing the dominance of the center over the periphery.

In addition to imposing the sun god Inti, another mechanism of "Incaization" of the conquered peoples was through language and culture. Quechua became the official language of the empire, and at the least, the provincial elites were expected to learn it. Other symbols of Inca culture spread throughout the empire, conveying important codes and meanings to the incorporated population. For example, administrative centers were laid out and buildings constructed and decorated in uniquely Incaic architectural forms and designs. These structures were usually built of finely cut stone and used trapezoidal doors and windows. At the same time, cities were divided into the customary four sections emanating from a spacious central plaza for public gatherings.

These and other everyday objects of material culture were decorated in special ways to convey information and meaning. For example, clothing was carefully designed with patterns, colors, and symbols to indicate the position and status of the individual and where he or she was from. According to one chronicler,

> The men and women of each nation and province had their insignias and emblems by which they could be identified, and they could not go around without this identification or exchange their insignias for those of another nation, or they would be severely punished. They had this insignia on their clothes with different stripes and colors, and the men wore their most distinguishing insignia on their heads. (Cobo, quoted in Morris and Von Hagen, 1993, p. 175)

Belts, slings, and bags often stood out with such special decoration and meaning. Ceramic vessels and tableware, particularly those used for state-sponsored public ceremonies, likewise exhibited particular shapes and patterns indicative of the event being celebrated. All these and other trappings of Inca culture, such as music and ritual performances, served as an important means by which the state conveyed its image and authority to the people in the expectation that they would reciprocate with work and loyalty.

These trappings were needed because the Incas generally ruled in an indirect manner through the existing power structure whose loyalty and allegiance were assured through force, negotiation, gift giving, and the like. When they took over highly centralized coastal polities such as Chimor, the Incas made little effort to impose their culture on such highly sophisticated and developed societies. Rather, they simply established themselves at the top of the political pyramid of power.

The crucial mechanism for the integration and control of the conquered peoples into the empire was the uniquely Incaic institution of *mitimae*. As I mentioned earlier, this was a system of mass resettlement whereby the Incas deported a portion of the defeated peoples to another province within the empire and replaced them with loyal colonies of *mitimae* from established parts of the realm. The function of the *mitmae* was mainly strategic and economic. They worked to educate and convert the local inhabitants into becoming loyal Inca subjects and, at the same time, served as military garrisons to protect against outside invasion or internal rebellion. They also worked the fields left by those who had been deported and claimed new land by applying more efficient Inca technology and know-how. Without the institution of the *mitimae*, it is unlikely that the Incas could have achieved a measure of unity and control over such a vast and distant territory containing such a variety of different ethnic groups so far from the imperial heartland (Davies, 1995, p. 168).

The state exerted control over conquered territories in other ways, some gender related. For example, after each new conquest, the defeated group was required to construct a temple to the sun and provide *aqllakuna*—chaste, prepubescent girls from the communities who were assigned to it. There they lived with other specially chosen women called *mamakuna*, who were wives of the sun and, like the *mamakuna*, also spun and wove cloth and prepared food and beer for the state. Maintained by the state to which they were taught to serve, the virginity of the *aqllakuna* was also strictly protected. The state used the *aqllakuna* for a variety of purposes: Some were sacrificed at religious ceremonies; some became wives of the sun god, like their mentors, or of the Sapa Inca; and others were given as wives to important officials or soldiers as rewards for their services to the state. As pawns of the state, as Silverblatt (1987) showed, the *aqllakuna* symbolized its total dominance over the conquered peoples. It was also their production of cloth, foods, and *chicha* beer for ceremonial and ritualistic purposes that helped maintain Inca power throughout the empire.

> By claiming the right to appropriate and redistribute *akllakuna*, the Inca ruler asserted his control, in principal if not in practice, over both the social and demographic reproduction of the groups incorporated into the empire. The *akllakuna* were political pawns, emblems of the state's power to control the reproduction of the communities incorporated into the web of social relations it dominated. (Patterson, 1991, p. 82)

Finally, in addition to the army, *mitimae*, and *tocricoc*, an extensive legal code ensured the obedience of the peasant classes. Severe penalties were ordered for noncompliance with imperial laws. These penalties ranged widely from corporal punishment for infractions, such as lying to census takers or moving field boundaries, to torture for not meeting *mit'a* requirements to execution for state theft or intercourse with the sexually forbidden *aqllakuna*.

Like preindustrial societies everywhere, the possession of land constituted the main economic and social resource of Inca society. As I noted, all land was theoretically owned by the Sapa Inca and held in usufruct by its inhabitants. Nevertheless, the conquering Inca did not expropriate carte blanche all conquered lands. On the contrary, intent upon establishing good relations, the emperor respected local rights and customs and generally upheld the prevailing economic system. Typically this meant that peasants continued to cultivate their traditional crops on community fields while local lords retained most of their holdings. However, the Incas did expropriate some conquered lands and brought new lands into cultivation to assign them to the church, the state, or new *mitimae* settlers. Some individuals were also given rights to the use of land by the Inca as a reward for distinguished military or administrative services.

THE PRINCIPAL OF RECIPROCAL EXCHANGE

The principal of reciprocal exchange and redistribution underpinned the politicoeconomic system of the Incas. Trade, commerce, and markets as we know them did not exist. In their place, the Incas built enormous warehouse facilities into which flowed the tribute collected from the populace (in the form of labor) for the operation of the state. Gathered and stored in large provincial centers or Cuzco itself, part of this tribute (food, cloth, and other goods) went to support the army, the civil administration, and the royal household. The remainder was redistributed back to the leaders of communities and conquered groups to ensure their loyalty and obedience to the Inca. In this way, the surplus production of the empire, in the absence of markets and currency, circulated throughout the realm. In effect, what "went to Cuzco . . . [would] then come *from* Cuzco" (Davies, 1995, p. 172).

One of the largest storage centers for tribute was at Huánuco Pampa in the central Andes, 375 miles north of Cuzco. There, more than 500 warehouses with a capacity of over 50,000 cubic yards were constructed to store food, cloth, and other supplies. Huánuco Pampa also served as an administrative center for the control of several conquered groups. The leaders of these groups would apparently come to the city for great public feasts and receive gifts from the Inca or his representatives. Such state hospitality and beneficence served to cement their loyalties to the Inca rulers.

Similarly, a large portion of tribute also went directly to the Sapa Inca in Cuzco, who, in turn, used it generously to bestow gifts on important visitors, including the local elites of incorporated groups, who came to the capital from outlying areas. These visitors were regaled with food and *chicha* beer on the occasion of great public ceremonies and festivals sponsored by the Inca himself. Conversely, when the Inca traveled throughout the empire, he invariably took with him huge stores of cloth and other goods to bestow as gifts on local leaders. In addition to cementing loyalties and conferring prestige on his guests, this hospitality and gift giving by the Inca served to enhance his own respect and authority.

This unique and fundamental principal of Inca redistribution and exchange was interpreted by scholars earlier in the century as forming the basis of a benign socialist regime. The notion was that the state used its tribute "revenues" to support an extensive welfare system in which the old and infirm were provided for. Anthropologist John Murra refuted this notion of a giant welfare state. Goods were collected in giant storage facilities and carefully counted by the *quipocamayos*, but what ever was left over after state functions were supported went to support the lavish lifestyles of the royal household, the *panacas*, the Cuzco elite, and the local *curacas*. This account leaves us with a typical picture of a preindustrial society ruled by a small, privileged elite and supported by the surplus production of a large, subservient mass of peasants.

"VERTICAL ARCHIPELAGOS"

In the absence of markets, the Incas and their ancient predecessors developed a system of self-sufficiency that Murra called "vertical archipelagos." The object was to diversify production and thus consumption according to different Andean ecologies and climates. Under this system, highland centers developed a series of settlements at different altitudes and microclimates, often by colonies of *mitimaes*, to produce foodstuffs and goods to "complement" community production. These settlements consisted of both farmers and llama herders who transported the produce to the centers. Ideally, then, a highland center might draw on production from the coast, say, cotton, maize, and fish; tropical products from the eastern slopes of the Andes and Amazon region; and produce from intermontane Andean Valleys, slopes, and niches.

This system of vertical archipelagos seems to have been most highly developed in the southern Andes, particularly the Lake Titicaca region. It does not seem to have been practiced by the great coastal empires of Chimor or Nazca or in other apparently unsuitable areas. According to Murra and Wachtel, however, verticality seems to have been expanding and undergoing fundamental changes prior to the Spanish conquest. As they noted:

> One particular Andean feature is that these complementary outliers were frequently multi-ethnic. Representatives of polities quite distinct from each other in the mountains found themselves in close, if tense, proximity at the periphery. These settlements were five, ten and sometimes even more days' walk distant from their respective power centers . . . the vertical archipelagos thus implied a rather closed economic circuit, linking several tiers through ties of kinship and political subordination (Quoted in Davies, 1995, p. 175)

Despite the prevalence of the principal of verticality in the Inca empire, there is evidence that some form of commercial exchange involving trade and barter also existed. A large number of merchants apparently travelled between Chincha and Cuzco as well as to Ecuador. They may have carried shells and dried fish from the coast and used pieces of copper as a form of currency. In addition, Pizarro's pilot reportedly saw a great raft, with a cabin and cotton sails, off the coast of Ecuador carrying a large cargo. Evidence also exists of merchants and markets in Quito (Salomon). Until more evidence is uncovered, however, it appears that commerce and trade was largely marginal to the Inca Empire (Murra).

In assessing the Incas and their achievements, one cannot help but be struck by the rapidity of their conquests (in less than a hundred years) and the remarkable way they asserted their control over a vast and geographically tortured empire. The rule of Tawantinsuyu—the land of the Four Quarters—was the largest and, to some extent, the most complex that the South American continent had ever seen. From a compact core of no more than a couple of hundred kilometers around the Valley of Cuzco, where their most elegant stone masonry buildings, impressive terracing and irrigation works, and elaborately decorated temples were located, the Incas extended their domain to embrace scores of different ethnic groups comprising as many as 12 million people, some 4,000 kilometers along the Andean spine of South America. They did so by employing not only sophisticated military and diplomatic means, but a flexible centralism that allowed their subjects to retain much of their local culture and traditions. To control and manage effectively such a far-flung, diverse empire, moreover, the Incas constructed a complex polity that included a vast bureaucracy and system of taxation, a complicated system of resettlement and integration, and a common "lingua franca" over a linguistically diverse area.

At the same time, despite these formidable achievements, we must recognize that the realm of the Incas was not the socialist paradise that an earlier generation of scholars romantically depicted. On the contrary, the Incas constructed an exploitative, hierarchical society in which a small, privileged ruling class benefited from the extraction of tribute, labor, and services from their subject peoples. To achieve this level of domination, the Incas imposed a system of control that included a repressive legal code, a militarized state, and the uses of religion as a means of legitimating political power and control.

Although united by their common interest in dominating and extracting surplus from the Andean peasantry, the Inca ruling class was often divided over questions of succession and competition for power. When such divisions became extreme, the empire, still relatively new and in the process of formation, became vulnerable to civil war and popular uprising, not to mention outside conquest. Just such a moment occurred in 1525 when the death of the Sapa Inca Huayna Capac divided the ruling class and plunged the empire into a bloody civil war over the royal succession.

One of Huayna Capac's sons, Huáscar, was subsequently proclaimed the twelfth Inca and duly crowned in Cuzco. However, he was shortly challenged by Atahualpa, another, purportedly illegitimate, son, but with strong backing in Quito and the northern part of the empire. Rostworowski argued that the ensuing struggle was a contest more between opposing factions or cliques than between two rival royal houses. Pease went further, saying that the civil war pitted the political ascendancy of the armies of the north, which backed Atahualpa, against the Cuzco politicoreligious establishment that favored Huáscar. The aim of the backers of Atahualpa was no less than to shift the political center of the empire north to Quito.

Be that as it may, there is little doubt as to the ferocity of the war that Atahualpa won. Cruelty and vandalism abounded on both sides, including the apparent slaughter of the entire *panaca*, or royal household, of Túpac Inca and the burning of its sacred mummy by the forces of Atahualpa. After succeeding in capturing Huáscar and seizing Cuzco, Atahualpa apparently unleashed merciless vengeance on the supporters of his defeated rival.

Atahualpa's triumph, however, was short lived. While celebrating the capture of Huáscar at Huamachuco, the new Inca king received news of a small expedition of strangers that had landed on the north coast and seized the town of Tumbez. A curious Atahualpa immediately sent emissaries to locate the newcomers and invited them to meet him in Cajamarca, where he was journeying to bathe at its famous thermal baths after his great victory. The expedition's captain, a Spanish adventurer named Francisco Pizarro, readily agreed, sending the Inca a fine shirt made in Holland and two Venetian glass goblets as the customary gifts to seal the arrangement. And so began the historic collision of two worlds that would dramatically alter the course of Andean history from that moment forth.

2 Clash of Empires and Formation of Colonial Society, 1532–1600

The arrival of Francisco Pizarro's small but intrepid band of conquistadors into the heart of the Inca empire in 1532 was a defining event not only in the history of Andean South America, but of the world. On the one hand, it represented an early stage in the developing clash between Western and non-Western peoples that has been a dominant theme in world history over the past four centuries. At the same time, it incorporated the Andes, which had stood in isolation for millennia, into the broad currents of world development. It did so, however, with devastating consequences for the native peoples who, by chance, lacked biological immunities against the viruses introduced by the invaders from the Old World. On the other hand, the Spanish invasion of Peru radically altered the course of Andean history. The lightning capture of the Inca emperor Atahualpa by Pizarro in the main square of Cajamarca on a fateful November afternoon in 1532 and the bloody massacre of his large military retinue effectively decapitated the leader of a divided empire that had not yet completely consolidated its hold over an enormous swath of Andean South America. The result was to open up the empire to the forces of radical change and "destructuration" whose repercussions are still resonating across the Andes today.

The Iberian Background

While the Inca empire expanded and flourished, Christian Spain was moving to expel the Moors who had occupied the Iberian peninsula for several hundred years since they invaded from Africa in 711. During the long period known as the *reconquista*, or reconquest (711–1492), the remaining Christian kingdoms, led by Castile, gradually pushed the Moors south, opening up huge tracts of conquered land to a warrior caste drawn from the nobility and organized into three great military orders. The continuous warfare represented by the reconquest, together with the fact that only through conquest and plunder could one hope to improve one's condition in the rigid Iberian social structure of the late Middle Ages, infused Spanish society with a strong military outlook and ethos. To make one's way through great deeds in battle against the Moors in the service of the king came to define a segment of the lower nobility—the so-called *hidalgos*—who were ambitious for land, power, and status and who became the prototypical societal heroes in Spain of the reconquest.

Late medieval Spanish values were also shaped by a distinctly aristocratic ethos derived from the great noble families who dominated Castillian society. It was this nobility, also in the service of the king, who organized and led the reconquest. In return for their services, the crown of Castile rewarded the *hidalgos* and grandees with huge land grants from seized Moorish territory. By the end of the fifteenth century, 2 percent to 3 percent of the population of Castile owned 97 percent of the land, more than half of which was in the hands of the great noble families of the kingdom. With a growing scarcity of labor, which was due, in part, to the lingering effects of the Black Death in the fourteenth century, the great landowners of the center and south had converted their lands to sheep raising, and the wool trade had become the backbone of the Castillian economy.

A third major contributor to the formation of Spanish society during the reconquest was the Catholic Church. The Church provided the enterprise of military expansion with a spiritual impulse and ideological justification that cloaked the more basic economic and political motives that underpinned the movement. Driven by the desire to defeat and convert the heathen Moslems to Christianity, the Church, increasingly in alliance with the state, infused and energized the reconquest with a crusading spirit that came to permeate all strata of the population.

Despite this largely "feudal" picture of late, medieval Spanish-Castillian society, commercial and bourgeois values were not absent from the peninsula. A bourgeois strata of merchants and shopkeepers had developed in Castile's towns and cities that would begin to challenge the aristocracy's political dominance by the late fifteenth century. Moreover, a strong class of merchant-traders, particularly in Aragón and the Levant region, had long been engaged in trade and commerce in the Mediterranean, as had the port of Seville in the south, which would be incorporated into Castile with the defeat of the Moors. While harbingers of the developing Iberian mercantile capitalism, the urban bourgeoisie and merchant-traders of Spain nevertheless still remained largely in the shadow of the great Castillian landed aristocracy for predominance. However, their entrepreneurial endeavors were never entirely eschewed by the grandees, many of whom realized that the accumulation of wealth served as the foundation for noble and aristocratic status.

Military, aristocratic, religious, and incipient commercial values, then, combined during the later phases of the long reconquest to shape late medieval Spanish society on the eve of Columbus's encounter with the New World. At the same time, the modern state began to form out of the diverse milieu of Christian Kingdoms that, led by Castile, were engaged in the drive to expel the Moors from the Iberian peninsula. Aided by tax revenues from the towns and urban classes, the state gradually expanded its authority and drew the aristocracy into its developing administration. The expansion of a new national state was further enhanced by the unification of the Kingdoms of Castile and Aragón through the royal marriage of Queen Isabel and King Ferdinand in 1479. Gradually, the other Christian Kingdoms were brought into the union, so that by 1492, when the last Moorish stronghold in Granada fell to the invading Castillian army, the fledgling political unification of Spain was virtually complete.

A final impetus for unification occured in 1492 with the order by the crown to expel and confiscate the properties of all Jews and Moors who did not convert to Christianity. Ostensibly aimed at achieving ethnic purity through religious conformity, the expulsion had several significant consequences. It removed a commercially dynamic segment of the population with adverse implications for the development of incipient Iberian capitalism and reinforced the old medieval notion of "purity of blood," or Christian descent, as a requisite for good citizenship in the emerging Spanish nation. Carried to the New World, "purity of blood" would later be tranformed into a racial bias against Indians and other people of color. Moreover, to enforce the new religious conformity, the state established the institution of the Inquisition, which was founded in Castile in 1483. The Inquisition not only represented a further reinforcement of the link between crown and church, but was one of the first attempts of a modern state to police the thoughts of its citizens.

The year 1492 was a watershed year in Spain for still another reason. It was the same year that Christopher Columbus, after a perilous thirty-two-day trans-Atlantic voyage of discovery, landed on a Caribbean island that he erroneously believed was located on the outer fringe of the great empire of China. The "discovery" of what later was perceived to be a "New World" in 1492 offered an outlet for the material, military, and religious ambitions of the newly victorious and united Spanish nation. In short, it was, in Steve Stern's words, a "symbol of exclusionary salvation, political unification, and imperial expansion condensed into one" (*JLAS*, 1992, 2).

Pizarro and the Enterprise of Conquest

Francisco Pizarro, a hollow-cheeked, thinly bearded *hidalgo* from Trujillo in Extramadura, was typical of the arriviste adventurers who came to America in the wake of Columbus's "discovery" to seek their fortunes. According to Varon Gabai (1997), he was the illegimate son of a not-too-rich Trujillan *hidalgo* and a woman, perhaps a servant, of low origin. Pizarro embarked for the Indies, like many fellow Extremadurans, in 1501 in the fleet of Nicolás de Ovando, governor of Hispañiola. Although the details of his early career in the Indies are little known, in 1513 he was second in command to Vasco Núñez de Balboa when Balboa discovered the Pacific Ocean.

Upon the founding of Panama a year later, Pizarro became one of its most prominent citizens and a member of the *cabildo*, or city council.

Panama soon became a hotbed of rumors about a rich land that lay to the south, which the Spaniards called Biru. These rumors led Pizarro to form a "company" with two other partners to mount expeditions of exploration and conquest south along the west coast of South America. Pizarro's associates were Diego Almagro, who managed his estates, and Hernando de Luque, a priest who apparently represented a local judge. Such expeditions of discovery and conquest in the Americas were considered speculative commercial ventures in which the organizers borrowed and/or invested their own capital to outfit their projects. Recruits were required to bring their own horses, equipment, and arms and received a previously stipulated share of the spoils instead of a salary. Pizarro provided the ships and other supplies.

In 1529 Pizarro received a *capitulación*, or agreement, from Charles V (1516–56) that appointed him to the rank of governor and captain-general of all territory 270 leagues from south of Tumbez on the north coast of Peru. This turned out to be a vague geographic designation that, according to Hemming (1970), would later call into question whether Pizarro or his partner Almagro had jurisdiction over Cuzco. He was also given the right to grant land and *encomiendas* (control over conquered Indians) and to organize a new colony on the model of the Canary Islands, the first Spanish overseas territory.

There were few professional soldiers on Pizarro's expeditions, but most were experienced Indian fighters, a skill acquired elsewhere in America before they arrived in Peru. Their leaders were mainly in their thirties and forties, the exception being Pizarro who was fifty-four. They included Sebastián de Benalcázar, the later conqueror of Quito, who brought thirty veterans from Nicaragua, and the dashing Hernando de Soto. The educational background of the recruits spanned the spectrum from illiterates to lawyers and *hidalgos* (although none belonged to the high nobility). The best educated were clerks, accountants, notaries, and a few merchants, whereas the least educated were artisans, seamen, and farmers. According to Lockhart, "the group had an overall plebeian flavor [but] its main strength, numerically and qualitatively, was in capable, literate commoners, lower-ranked professionals, and marginal hidalgos" (1972, p. 42). Most were motivated not, as is commonly believed, by a spirit of adventure, but by poverty, rivalry, and the opportunity for gain.

On his third expedition in 1530, Pizarro learned of the bitter civil war that had been raging throughout the empire since the premature death, probably from smallpox, of the Sapa Inca Huayna Capac in Quito sometime between 1525 and 1527. The disease had spread rapidly south after the initial Columbian encounter, ravaging the Amerindian populations of the Caribbean and Meso-America as the conquest proceeded.

While at Tumbez Pizarro received emissaries from Atahualpa and learned of his encampment outside Cajamarca, where he was relaxing in its renowned thermal baths and awaiting news from his generals about the final defeat of Huáscar's forces in the battle for Cuzco. Shortly thereafter, Pizarro's small force, consisting of 62 horsemen and 106 foot soldiers, set out for the long march up into the Andes. When they entered Cajamarca on November 15, 1532, the city was virtually deserted. "To our Indian eyes," wrote Felipe Guamán Poma de Ayala, the author of a later chronicle, "the Spaniards looked as if they were shrouded like corpses. Their faces were covered with wool, leaving only the eyes visible, and the caps which they wore resembled little red pots on top of their heads" (quoted in Dilke, 1978, p. 108). While their appearance and certainly their horses seemed curious, there was little else about the small party of strangers to cause anything more than a minor distraction to the mighty Inca whose armies had now defeated his rival and taken Cuzco. Encamped with a huge army, perhaps numbering as many as 80,000 troops, the Inca was probably thinking about the events of Cuzco and his plans to go to the city in triumph.

Underestimation was not the only advantage that Pizarro and his force possessed at Cajamarca. They also had knowledge of the Inca civil war and a tested battle plan—to repeat Cortés' tactic in Mexico of capturing the emperor and allying with his enemies in a divide-and-conquer strategy. Furthermore, they could also count on superior military technology—cavalry; cannon; muskets; and, above all, swords made of Toledo steel, the finest in all Europe. Elsewhere in the Americas, these weapons had proved far superior in the open field against a force, however large, of Amerindians armed only with stone-age battle axes, slings, and cotton padded armor. In particular, the horse, unknown in the Americas, gave the Spaniards a highly mobile cavalry force that was capable of breaking up native formations and generally wrecking havoc on lightly protected foot soldiers.

In any event, the deserted central plaza of Cajamarca, where Pizarro bivouacked his troops, was an ideal place to spring an ambush. In fact, the Inca later admitted to Pizarro that he himself had, paradoxically, planned to overwhelm and capture the Spaniards at their fateful rendezvous in the plaza. Leaving his army encampment late that Saturday afternoon of November 16, Atahualpa made a ceremonial entrance into the square. Such pomp and ritual were not uncommon in Incan encounters with ethnic groups outside the empire, a calculated demonstration of power that often led to negotiations and a peaceful takeover.

> Soon the first people began to enter the plaza; in front came a group of Indians in colored uniforms with checks; They came removing straw from the ground and sweeping the road. Another three groups came after them, all singing and dancing, dressed in a different way. Then many people advanced with armor, medallions, and crowns of gold and silver. Among them Atawalpa entered, and after this came two other litters and two hammocks in which two other important people rode. Then many groups of people entered with gold and silver crowns. As soon as the first entered the plaza, they went to the side and made room for the others. Upon arriving in the

middle of the plaza, Atawalpa made a sign for silence. (Jeréz, quoted in Morris and Von Hagen, 1993, p. 151)

Upon finding no Spaniards, who were drawn up in full battle gear out of sight in the surrounding buildings waiting to spring their trap, Atahualpa expressed surprise, apparently believing that they were hiding out of fear of his huge army.

Then the priest Valverde and a young translator approached the Inca from the buildings and proceeded to deliver, in a rambling fashion, the famous royal Requirement, a legalistically worded appeal for the Indians to accept Christianity or suffer "just war." He also handed the Inca a Bible that Atahualpa examined and then, as a gesture of displeasure with the claim

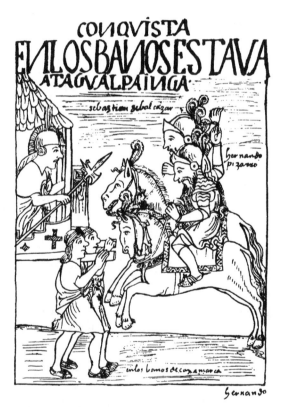

First encounter at Cajamarca between Pizarro (and Benalcázar) and Atahualpa in 1532, imagined by Felipe Guamán Poma de Ayala (1615) in a drawing entitled *Conquista/En Los Banos Estava Ataqvalpa Inga . . .* from his *El primer nueva crónica y buen gobierno*, vol. 2, edited by John V. Murra and Rolena Adorno, Quechua translations by Jorge L. Urioste, (Mexico City, 1980), p. 355. Reproduced courtesy of Siglo Veintiuno Editores, Mexico City.

that the Bible represented the word of God, furiously threw to the ground. When the Inca stood up and told his men to make ready, Valverde shouted to Pizarro to commence the attack. According to the account of the Spanish chronicler Zarate:

> He [Pizarro] ordered a gun to be fired, and the horsemen attacked the Indians from three sides. The Governor himself advanced with his infantry in the direction from which Atahuallpa was coming, and on reaching his litter they began to kill the bearers. But as fast as one fell several more came with great resolution to take his place . . . seizing Atahuallpa by the hair (which he wore very long) and dragging him roughly towards him till he fell out. Meanwhile, the Christians were slashing the litter—which was of gold—so fiercely with their swords that they wounded the Governor in the hand and, though many Indians rushed forward to rescue [Atahuallpa, the Christians] took him prisoner. When the Indians saw their lord lying on the ground a prisoner, and themselves attacked from so many sides and so furiously, they turned round and began to flee in panic. (Zárate, quoted in Morris and Von Hagen, 1993, p. 152)

In the ensuing stampede, hundreds of Indians were crushed trying to escape their attackers by scaling the six-foot-high walls of the plaza, while others were hacked to death by the sword-wielding Spaniards. When the walls collapsed, the horsemen pursued the fleeing Indians onto the surrounding plain, cutting them down and routing other native units, reportedly killing hundreds. Although Pizarro was slightly wounded by one of his own soldiers, the Spaniards suffered no casualties.

Aside from the great slaughter inflicted on his troops, the stunning capture of Atahualpa signified that the conquest had begun with a decisive checkmate. Once he was a prisoner, Atahualpa soon discovered the Spaniards' obsession for precious metals, and he therefore offered to trade a treasure in gold and silver in ransom for his freedom. The offer apparently surprised the Spaniards, but Pizarro agreed. Over the next few months, a fabulous cache of Inca treasure—some 11 tons of gold objects alone—was delivered to Cajamarca from all corners of the empire. The total loot, after being melted down, would amount to more than 1.5 million pesos, the equivalent of more than $75 million in 1998 dollars. Pizarro distributed 90 pounds of gold and 180 of silver to each horseman and about half that to the foot soldiers, keeping thirteen shares for himself, but allotting less to his partner, Almagro, who had arrived after the battle with reinforcements from the coast.

Once enriched by the Inca's treasure, the Spaniards reneged on their ransom agreement to free Atahualpa. There were rumors of an imminent attack from one of Atahualpa's commanders—allegedly secretly ordered by the imprisoned Inca himself. The Spaniards panicked and accused Atahualpa of treason. Although the charge later proved groundless, the Inca was quickly executed, without a trial, by garroting. The Spaniards had wanted to burn the emperor as a heretic, but offered the latter form of execution if Atahualpa agreed to be baptized a Christian. Atahualpa may have agreed to preserve his body for the traditional Inca custom of ancestor worship of the mummies of their dead kings. Pizarro was later censured for the act by the king, who did not take kindly to the idea of regicide.

Atahualpa's death now left the empire virtually leaderless and in political turmoil, enabling Pizarro to follow his strategy of divide and conquer by allying with the Huáscar faction. He did so by elevating Túpac Huallpa, Huáscar's younger brother, as the new emperor in an elaborate, if hurriedly, staged ceremony. The Spaniards then undertook the march to Cuzco, gaining allies along the way among the Huáscar faction for their showdown with Atahualpa's northern army of Quitans who still controlled the capital. Other ethnic groups, such as the Huancas who harbored anti-Inca sentiments, came to the assistance of the Spaniards at Jauja when they were threatened by Atahualpa's forces.

Inflicting a series of defeats on the retreating Quitans, the Spaniards and their Indian allies culminated the advance to Cuzco by routing their adversaries in the mountains above the city in mid-November 1533 (a whole year after the events at Cajamarca). Disheartened, the northern army disintegrated and vanished, allowing the Spaniards to enter the capital. In the meantime, Pizarro had been forced to replace his puppet emperor Túpac Huallpa who died suddenly, apparently by poisoning, en route to Cuzco. He selected another brother of Huáscar, the popular and able Manco, and together they both entered Cuzco at the head of their victorious army. Greeted as liberators in a thunderous welcome by the city's 100,000 inhabitants, Pizarro then had Manco formally crowned emperor in an elaborate ceremony.

In assessing the Spaniard's victory at Cuzco and elsewhere, where they often faced a numerical disadvantage of a thousand to one, the Inca civil war can hardly be underestimated. Writing in his memoirs years later, Pedro Pizarro, the conquistador's brother, stated "had Wayna Qhapaq been alive when we Spaniards entered this land it would have been impossible to win it. . . . Also if the land had not been divided by the war between Washkar and 'Ataw Wallpa we could not have entered or conquered it" (quoted in Bauer, 1992, p. 128). Other factors, such as the Spanish strategy of total war as opposed to the heavy ritualistic and ceremonial content of Inca warfare, also help explain the outcome. Finally, because of the Spanish cavalry, the Inca armies were invariably defeated when they operated out in the open on plains or fields. By contrast, when the Andeans caught their European enemies in narrow spaces, such as ravines and mountain passes, where their adversaries' horses lacked maneuverability, they often inflicted heavy casualties.

After the capture of Cuzco, the Spaniards were quickly able to assume control of the core of the empire, roughly corresponding to the boundaries of modern Peru. Once Cuzco had fallen and the Quitans were vanquished, other subjugated ethnic groups, in customary Andean fashion, welcomed the chance to ally with the new European contenders for power. Such a tactic could facilitate their access to a privileged place in the new colonial order. As for the other parts of the former Inca realm in the north and south, their conquests would be carried out by later arriving conquistadors, such as Benalcázar near Quito and Almagro in Chile.

With the capture of the capital of Tawantinsuyu, the Spaniards proceeded to loot the city's magnificent temples and royal palaces. A huge cache of gold and silver objects was melted down, actually exceeding the value of Atahualpa's initial enormous ransom. Part of it was dispatched as the royal fifth (actually about 40 percent) to Spain, where it filled the coffers of Charles V and his dreams of imperial expansion in Europe. The rest was distributed to Pizarro's soldiers and to some influential leaders of the native ruling class. Aside from making instant millionaires, this second bounty, together with the first, set off a virtual "gold rush" to Peru that threatened to depopulate the Caribbean Islands and other less lucrative parts of the colonies.

While the arrival of the newcomers served to reinforce the European invasion, it also brought about a deterioration in the Spanish treatment of the native population, for the expectations of the newcomers and others who had been left out of the distribution at Cajamarca and Cuzco were bound to fall short as Inca treasure quickly became exhausted. Increasingly angry and frustrated, this new group of immigrants was responsible for the sharp deterioration in relations with the natives whom they ruthlessly began to exploit for personal gain. These same feelings also contributed to growing conflicts and quarrels among the Spaniards over the remaining spoils of the conquest. The upshot was rising Indian discontent and resistance that came to a head in the rebellion of Manco in 1536. These conflicts also led to the outbreak of a bloody civil war between the followers of Pizarro and those of Almagro. Both events became intertwined and, for a time, severely complicated the Spanish enterprise in Peru.

Indian Revolt and Civil War

Pizarro soon left Cuzco for the coast where, among other things, he founded the City of the Kings, or Lima, on January 18, 1535. Located on the banks of the Rimac River near the Pacific Ocean, Lima gave the new colony both strategic access to the sea lanes and a climate more amenable to the Europeans than the high-altitude Andes. It also dislocated, although not necessarily totally eclipsed, Cuzco's centrality, becoming the administrative and institutional center, based on writing, that would constitute Spanish hegemony throughout the Andes. In its initial gridiron organizational layout, with streets radiating out from a central plaza, moreover, Lima became the model for urban development in the Andes and all Spanish South America. Surrounding the *plaza de armas* and facing each other in grand, if silent majesty, arose the key structures of colonial rule—an immense cathedral, *audiencia* (judiciary), ornate viceregal palace (executive), and ominous public pillory, or *picota*—which together came to symbolize the new imperial order.

In the meantime, in Cuzco the puppet ruler Manco was increasingly the subject of harassment and insult by the city's growing number of Hispanic residents. Everywhere, it seems, the natives were being unlawfully impressed into labor gangs or personal servitude, robbed of their produce and goods, and forced to turn over their women to become Spanish concubines. As a result of this worsening behavior by the Spaniards, as well as personal slights by Pizarro's brothers, Hernando, Gonzalo, and Juan, who had been left in charge of Cuzco, an increasingly humiliated Manco suddenly abandoned his collaborationist role and rebelled against his former allies. Mobilizing a huge force, estimated at between 100,000 and 200,000 men, in early 1536, Manco coordinated an attack and subsequent siege of Cuzco that came perilously close to overwhelming the 190 Spaniards who occupied the city. The rebellion also spread quickly throughout the highlands, with a number of unexpected Indian victories.

To make matters worse for Pizarro, a disgruntled Almagro now returned to Peru from a disastrous expedition to New Toledo, or present-day Chile. Relations between Pizarro and Almagro had long been strained, largely over the issue of the division of the conquest's spoils. Vagueness about who actually had legal jurisdiction of Cuzco had led Pizarro to persuade Almagro to lead a new expedition to conquer Chile, where it was hoped he would find sufficient treasure to satisfy his ambitions and those of his followers. The organization of *entradas*, or new expeditions of discovery and conquest, was a common method devised by the authorities in the New World to assuage such malcontents. Playing upon the commonly held European myths that the New World harbored numerous El Dorados, *entradas* sought to defuse and redirect to outlying areas the frustrated, unruly, and often dangerous late arrivals to Peru and elsewhere. Many of these expeditions turned out badly (Lope de Aguirre's murderous foray into the Amazon in 1562 being one of the most spectacular examples), and Almagro's expedition to Chile proved no exception.

Almagro marched out of Cuzco on July 3, 1535, with 570 cavalry and foot soldiers and 12,000 natives provided by Paullu, another surviving son of Huayna Capac. After twenty months, Almagro and his Men of Chile, as they came to be called, returned to Peru deeply disillusioned. Not only had they suffered severe privation and defeat at the hands of the natives, but they had failed to discover the anticipated treasure. Upon hearing of Manco's rebellion, Almagro saw his chance to unseat Pizarro, take what he believed was rightly his, pacify Manco whom he saw as a potential ally, and thus save Peru for the crown. Events proved otherwise. Although Almagro arrived in time to save and then take control of the besieged garrison at Cuzco, imprisoning the Pizarro brothers in the process, the alliance with Manco failed to materialize.

In the meantime, Pizarro led his forces up toward Cuzco from Lima to defeat Almagro at the Battle of Salinas on April 26, 1538, shortly after which Almagro was captured, tried, and executed for treason. This act, with no attempt by Pizarro to assuage Almagro's followers through negotiation or cooptation, only ensured that a vendetta between the two factions would ensue. Three years later, Almagro's son Diego, in an elaborate plot, succeeded in gaining a measure of revenge by assassinating Pizarro in June 1541.

As for Manco's rebellion, Manco came to believe that his revolt was doomed as he watched Almagro's army enter Cuzco. Ending his seige of the city, he gathered the remnants of his mainly peasant army, a large part of which had already dispersed to tend their fields, and retreated to the virtually impregnable high selva of the eastern slopes of the Andes. There he established a neo-Inca kingdom at Vitcos in the Vilcabamba region. Since it posed no real threat to Spanish Peru and could be taken only with great difficulty, Vitcos continued to exist, complete with a miniture, but elaborate court, for the next couple of decades. Why it did not become an effective center for organizing a coherent Indian opposition to the Spaniards is unclear.

As for the civil turmoil in Spanish Peru, the crown now intervened to try to restore order. However, it had contributed to roiling the waters of discontent itself by decreeing in 1542 the New Laws that called for the abolition of the *encomienda*. This uniquely Spanish institution was a trusteeship granted by the crown over large numbers of Indians as a reward for services rendered in the conquest and colonization of the New World. The grantees, or *encomenderos*, could collect tribute in the form of goods or labor in the name of the crown. In return, they assumed the responsibility for looking after the material and spiritual welfare of the Indians, that is, for protecting and Christianizing their charges.

Given the original size of the Indian population and its bountiful production, *encomiendas*, aside from Inca treasure, proved to be the greatest source of wealth and upward mobility that could be acquired in Peru. In 1536 there were about 500 *encomenderos* out of a total Spanish population of about 2,000. Ten years later, there were the same number of *encomenderos*, but they represented only 12.5 percent of the total Spanish population, a proportion that dropped to 6 percent by 1555. Moreover, after the initial reward of *encomiendas* to the men of Cajamarca, most of the later grants went to Spaniards of high social and political rank or influence, thereby excluding the great majority of newcomers of modest circumstances and backgrounds who were pouring into the Andean colony.

The crown had ample reason to move to reform the *encomienda*, but the issue was complex. For one thing, accounts of abuses by *encomenderos* against the Indians entrusted to their charge had become so numerous that humanitarian calls for its abolition, first raised in Hispañiola by the Dominican friar and former *encomendero* Bartolomé de Las Casas (1484–1566), had become intense. The charges had touched off a learned, but heated debate at court over the whole issue of the treatment of the Indian population in the New World. In Peru the issue was joined by various humanitarians, including Fray Domingo de Santo Tomás (1499–1570), a Dominican friar who had arrived in Peru in 1540. Quickly sizing up the deteriorating human rights of the natives, he petitioned the king to regulate what he and others believed to be its cause—the excessive demands on and other abuses of the Indians by the *encomenderos*.

In addition to the deteriorating conditon of the Indians in the emerging colonial order, the crown was alarmed by reports of the high rates of mortality among the indigenous population. Opponents of *encomienda* attributed the cause of native depopulation to settlers' widespread abuses of the institution. Madrid realized only too well that without Indians, to quote the adage, there would be no Indies. A sharp decline in the labor supply threatened to put the whole colonial enterprise at risk.

On the other hand, the crown also knew that the *encomienda* had been one of the main mechanisms that had driven the enterprise of conquest. In the absence of state funding, it had provided concrete material incentives for the expeditions of conquest by private individuals and groups. Even more important, the foundation of the entire early colonial "economy of plunder," was based, as you shall see, on the *encomienda* system. The 500 *encomiendas* that had been granted in Peru also gave rise to the formation of a privileged, seigneurial elite that theoretically had the power to challenge royal authority. The centralizing struggles of the emerging state in Spain of the fifteenth and early sixteenth centuries had made the crown particularly sensitive to this issue.

So, in the end, ruling against the *encomenderos* for pragmatic reasons of state, the crown, after considerable deliberation and vacillation, agreed to reform the *encomienda*. Rather than abolish the insitution, it decided to turn the *encomienda* into a onetime, nonhereditary privilege and thereby clear the way for its abolition within a generation. However, the crown then faced the tricky problem of how to enforce its decision in a distant colony thousands of miles from Madrid. As it turned out, it chose precisely the wrong moment, when Peru continued to be wracked by the repercussions of the factional conflict between the followers of Pizarro and Almagro, to try to institute a reform that would restrict and undermine the *encomienda*.

The New Laws were brought to the country in 1544 by its first appointed viceroy, the stiff-necked, intemperate, and unpolitic Blasco Núñez Vela who totally misjudged the mood of the settlers and foolishly tried to enforce them. The *encomenderos* promptly rebelled behind the figure of Gonzalo Pizarro, the slain leader's brother, who defeated and killed the new viceroy in a battle near Quito on January 18, 1546. The ensuing arbitrary and brutal rule by Gonzalo Pizarro, however, quickly degenerated, alienating his former allies among the colonial population. So, when another royal official, Pedro de la Gasca, arrived in Peru in 1547 to restore the authority of the crown, he wisely made a tactical retreat on the issue of the *encomienda*. This momentary reprieve for the *encomienda*, in addition to the confiscation and division of the Pizarro faction's large *encomiendas* among potential allies, enabled de la

Gasca to rebuild the settlers' support and gain further allies for the crown. As a result, a little over a year later he succeeded in organizing a proroyalist force that defeated and executed the mutinous Gonzalo Pizarro and his followers.

De la Gasca also skillfully regained the settlers' allegiance by using the financial bonanza from the recently discovered Potosí silver mines (1545) to appoint settlers to newly created colonial offices and thus co-opt them. This action inaugurated the royal practice of buying the political loyalty of colonists through the device of state patronage, heretofore accomplished by granting new *encomiendas* that were no longer available. By the time his term ended in 1551, de la Gasca had largely restored order and royal control in Spanish Peru.

The Andean Alliance and the Economy of Plunder

SILVER MINING

In the midst of the rebellion of Gonzalo Pizarro in 1545, an Indian named Diego Gualpa discovered what was to become "Spain's great treasure house in South America," the silver mines of Potosí. In search of a native shrine high in the mountains at the southeast end of the *altiplano* of Charcas, Gualpa was purportedly thrown to the ground by a high wind, uncovering a slab of silver ore in the process. A few years later, the five extraordinary veins of silver discovered at Potosí were producing 150,000 to 200,000 pesos worth of silver a week, yielding a royal fifth to the crown of 1.5 million pesos a year. During its first ten years, according to von Humbolt, Potosí produced some 127 million pesos that fueled the Hapsburg war machine and Spanish hegemonic pretensions in Europe. Equally significant, silver from Potosí would, over the next half century, also dinamize and articulate a far-flung Andean internal economy of production and exchange that included Northern Argentina, the central valley of Chile, and coastal Peru and Ecuador. This extraordinary development would lead one Peruvian viceroy to say that "if there are no mines, there is no Peru."

During the first or early stage of development of the Potosí mines, from 1545 to 1565, the production of silver was carried out largely by native Indians. The Incas had engaged in silver mining, mainly for decorative purposes, and had developed an effective metallurgical technology. Indigenous technology and tools, such as a smelting process, worked far better in the altitude than initial Spanish techniques. Foremost was the *guayra* smelting furnace (Quechua for "wind" or "air"), a small, three-foot-high, conical shaped furnace that melted the crushed ore, enabling the silver to run. Holes were pierced in the side of the *guayra* so that the wind would provide a blast-furnace effect on the fire, which was fueled with llama dung or charcoal. During the heyday of the *guayra*, so many wind ovens operated on the slopes of

Potosí at night, perhaps as many as 15,000, that Garcilaso de la Vega likened the scene to a dazzling new celestial galaxy (Padden, 1975, p. xv).

A boomtown of 14,000 inhabitants quickly sprang up at Potosí, a figure that would burgeon to an apogee of 160,000 in 1650. That would make it one of the largest cities in the Western world at the time and served to stimulate agricultural production in the surrounding valleys of the *altiplano* (then in Upper Peru and today the Bolivian plateau), for all foodstuffs had to be brought up the mountain to the enclave from the outside. Despite the considerable wealth that was generated in these early years, living conditions at Potosí remained primitive:

> Houses and buildings were cramped; ceilings were made low and rooms small to conserve heat. Windows were few and unglazed. Even rich miners lived in wretched shacks that were cruelly ventilated by cracks and fissures. Severe cold was expected in winter, but on the balmiest of summer days the temperature never rose above fifty-nine degrees Fahrenheit. The burning of charcoal in poorly vented fireplaces or simple braziers was the principal protection from the eternal chill and offered its own peril in the form of carbon monoxide poisoning, which was chronic. So rigorous was life in the early period that during the first fifty years not one child born in Potosí of European parents survived for more than two weeks. Women learned to go down to the lower valleys for confinement and to stay there with the child for its first year of life before returning to the High Place. (Padden, 1975, p. xvii)

After an initial spurt, the silver output at Potosí slowed because of the depletion of the easy-to-get-at surface veins, the diminishing silver content of the extracted ores, and the continuing political factionalism that plagued the country. Production would not pick up until the discovery of mercury mines in 1563 at Huancavelica, which enabled Potosí miners to switch to the more efficient patio refining process just being perfected in Mexico. Thus, once the patio process was installed in Peru in the early 1570s, silver became the engine for colonial development. Until then, the Spanish "economy of plunder" continued to be based largely on the *encomienda* system.

THE *ENCOMIENDA*

Tribute from the *encomienda* consisted of the basic necessities that the Spanish colonists needed to support themselves: food (typically eggs, maize, and honey); the transport of water, wood, and merchandise (woolen garments); and the construction of houses and public works, such as churches, roads, and bridges. Under the Incas, tribute had been collected only in the form of labor, not in kind, which now cut into village subsistence and had to be met regardless of good or bad harvests. The case of Pedro de Hinojosa, whose extremely rich *encomienda* or *repartimiento* in Upper Peru, was not atypical in terms of the Indians' tribute obligations. In addition to labor, Hinojosa collected 1,200 *fanegas* (at 1.6 bushels each) of maize and silver ore mined in various mines, including Potosí, valued at 27,300 pesos in 1559.

While there were rules or laws regulating the *encomienda*, specific relations between the *encomenderos* and their charges tended to be worked out over time. According to Spalding, these "relationships were hammered out between the 1530s and 1550s as the *encomenderos'* demands were accepted by the people or resisted until a modus vivendi—often an uneasy one—was reached. In the course of that often violent and brutal bargaining process, a rough political system emerged that lasted for more than three decades" (1984, 125). As a result, the *encomienda* tended to vary from place to place, and its efficiency in appropriating goods and labor depended, to a great extent, on the skills of the *encomenderos* in dealing with the natives.

To facilitate these relations and effectively organize an *encomienda*, the conquistador-*encomendero* entered into alliances with *curacas*, the principal Indian chieftains who had served as intermediaries between the Inca state and the local ethnic communities. The *curacas* would serve the same function in the new European order, with responsibility for overseeing and administering the Indians, as well as for collecting and delivering the assigned tribute and labor to the *encomenderos*. In return, the *curacas* took a cut of the tribute for themselves and received other Spanish goods and privileges from the *encomenderos*. As a result, the *curacas* preserved much of their former elite status and gained an important niche for themselves in the postconquest society. The *encomenderos*, on the other hand, by forging such alliances with the *curacas* and placing themselves in the positions of the representatives of the old Inca state, succeeded in taking over for themselves the existing Andean apparatus for surplus extraction.

To maximize profits from this system of decentralized, indirect rule, *encomenderos* were quick to realize that a good working relationship with the *curacas* ensured a bountiful flow of goods and labor. Therefore, they sought to cement such relations with favors and gifts to their Indian allies. For example, Diego Maldonado in Huamanga literally showered gifts—a black slave, mules, horses, livestock, and fine Inca and Spanish clothes—on his *curacas* because, according to one, "[Maldonado] owed it to them for the services they would render him" (Stern, 1982, p. 31). A similar generosity was also evident in the abundant quantities of corn, coca, salt, aji, meat, sheep, and wool received by Maldonado's Indians in payment for field work. In this way the shrewd *encomendero* applied "Andean rules of 'generosity' to create dependencies and 'reciprocal' exchange obligations."

This does not mean that conflict, violence, or abuse, such as whipping, looting, and rape of *encomienda* Indians by the *encomenderos'* hired hands—Spaniards, blacks, or mestizos—were not also part of the *encomienda* system. Nor does it mean that some Spaniards, often those seeking quick gains so they could return to Spain, did not harshly exploit their Indians when renting out their labor, a common practice in the early years. Thus, "early relations between the Andean native peoples and the Europeans displayed an uneasy mixture of force, negotiation, and alliance" (Stern, 1982, p. 34).

By virtue of their wealth in tribute and control over the native labor force, the *encomendero* class came to dominate the immediate, postconquest society in a system that resembled feudalism. Although the *encomienda* did not constitute a grant of property, it did allow for the establishment of effective sovereignty over the native population, with the lord-*encomendero* acting as the main arbiter and dispenser of justice. In this sense, the *encomendero's* word was law among his Indians.

The main political vehicle of *encomendero* power was the *cabildo*, or town council, which was formed to lay out and govern the first Spanish municipalities in the Andes and that the *encomenderos* quickly came to control. When the crown finally began to send out *corregidores*, or chief district magistrates, and Indian agents from Lima in the late 1560s, they were usually co-opted by *encomenderos* and other *cabildo* members into alliances of mutual interest. Such collusion blunted the extension of royal authority and worked to entrench further the power of the *encomendero* class at the local level. By the middle of the century, for example, the dozen or so *encomenderos* of Trujillo, north of Lima, formed, according to Ramirez, a tight-knit elite with a common economic base, shared interests, and close kinship ties. Having virtually converted the *cabildo* into their own exclusive club, they were able to exert almost total dominance over early Trujillo society.

One of the most important functions of the *cabildo* was to apportion town lots and grant lands (*mercedes*) for farming and grazing to the settlers. Gradually, with the growth of urban centers and markets, such as Cuzco, Lima, and the mining encampments, the possibilities of commercial agriculture became apparent to many settlers, including *encomenderos*. Therefore, the *encomenderos* began to acquire—by grant, sale, or forced usurpation—suitable farm and ranch land in order to produce and sell to the growing urban population. Although initially fragmented parcels—accessible to nearby markets and in generally fertile zones—these *mercedes* were consolidated over time into larger estates or haciendas. This was the origin of the hacienda, an institution that became a hallmark of colonial Peru, but during the sixteenth century remained small and undeveloped. The acquisition of these small estates was also facilitated by the demographic collapse of the Indian population, which left large tracts of fertile bottom land vacant and easy to take over by the European newcomers. As commercial agriculture spread with the growth of urban markets by the 1550s, the value of land, which during the first three decades had been insignificant in comparison with *encomiendas*, began to rise and take on increasing importance.

The expanding market demand for agricultural products, both Indian and European, by midcentury, then, was met by the *encomienda* system *and* the developing small haciendas. The former "collected" primarily, but not exclusively, Indian foodstuffs to sell for profit in towns, particularly at the mines where Indian laborers not only consumed large quantities of coca and indigenous foods, such as *chicha* beer, yerba mate tea, and jerky meat, but also rough-hewn clothing. The latter were manufactured in rudimentary workshops called *obrajes*, often established by *encomenderos* and about which I will have more to say later. As for the haciendas, they tended to specialize in the production of newly introduced Spanish products, such as wheat, cooking oils, wines, and meats, that were more palatable to European tastes and appropriate for urban resale. The transport and trading functions of this developing colonial economy were carried out by a growing number of muleteers and petty merchants who traveled the main commercial circuits of the developing Lima–Cuzco–Potosí mercantile axis.

Many Spaniards and not a few Indians proved adept at combining indigenous production with Spanish manufacturing, organizational, and distribution methods to turn a profit in this economy. This was particularly true for the most successful *encomenderos*, who exhibited commercial and entrepreneurial skills that belie their earlier image as simply rentiers living seignorial lifestyles as feudal barons. That they constituted great urban households in the seigneurial tradition, consisting of family members and kinsmen, as well as a large number of clients, retainers, and employees, there is no doubt. In fact, a considerable number of the artisans, notaries, majordomos, accountants, and other professionals who arrived from Spain attached themselves to these great *encomendero* households. The *encomenderos* also spent lavishly on conspicuous consumption, not only to validate their aspirations for aristocratic lifestyles and status, but to display their "power" as grandees in the colonial society. While the incomes that sustained these great families came in the form of "rents" from Indian tribute, these goods required processing and marketing skills that suggest an entrepreneurial bent that was readily present among early Spanish immigrants in Peru. For example, it was a common practice among *encomenderos* to reinvest their profits in trade and commerce. The *encomendero* Lucas Martínez Vegaso, for instance, used the income from the sale of tributary goods from his *encomienda* to markets in Potosí to sustain his large household in Arequipa and to mount extensive business interests, including mining, milling, vineyards, manufacturing, ranching, and shipping.

Similarly, many Indians—communities and individuals, commoners and ethnic lords—also reacted in innovative, entrepreneurial ways and sought advantage in the new conditions. *Curacas*, with their unique access to Indian land and labor, led the way. They were followed by Indian miners, artisans, merchants, and farmers, who began to adapt to and engage the new European commercial economy in a myriad of creative and profitable ways. For example, in 1588 Don Diego Caqui, the son of a *curaca* in Tacna, owned four vineyards and a winery, a llama train to transport wine to Potosí, and two frigates that operated commercially between Arica and Callao. According to Stern, this practice was commonplace as "ethnic groups, led by their chiefs, sold and occasionally bought services; rented, bought and sold lands; produced, marketed, and bought commodities of Andean and European origins; and invested in mines, obrajes, and trading companies" (1995, p. 77).

Those who adopted these new commercial practices also proved open to adaptation to aspects of European culture and religion, although they interpreted and assimilated them in terms of their own Andean frame of reference. Many, also, adopted, to various degrees Spanish dress, customs, language, and foods and embraced Christianity, even if they continued surreptitiously to follow old practices and to worship their own *huacas*, or holy places. This tendency toward acculturation, like its biological counterpart, set in motion the forces that would produce the mestizo or *casta*, a new ethnic category between Spanish and Indian in the postconquest, Andean society.

The early Andean economy of plunder, based on an alliance between the *encomenderos* and the natives, with *curacas* playing a crucial intermediary role as collaborating allies, worked relatively well in extracting Andean wealth and funneling it to an incipient colonial elite and to metropolitan Spain. However, the system was fundamentally vulnerable and flawed for the longer-term development of colonialism for two reasons.

First, from the point of view of Madrid, the rise and consolidation of the *encomenderos'* power was ultimately unacceptable, for it would invariably mean the diversion of Andean wealth away from the metropolis to an emerging local elite. Madrid's increasing dependence on the royal fifth from Andean silver for its European adventures made such an arrangement intolerable and dictated the taking of a different course whereby the state would control much more directly the course of colonial development. Second, the Andean alliance itself as a basis for colonialism was ultimately flawed because, as Stern suggested, it was dependent upon the Indians' compliance with the exploitative demands of the *encomenderos*. The *curacas* and their Indian clients cooperated in those demands for the moment, not only because of the demonstrated power of Spanish armed force, but because there were advantages in doing so—for the *curacas* who could retain their privileged positions and for the ethnic groups who could call upon the *encomenderos'* assistance against their enemies and rivals in other communities.

What upset this modus vivendi over time, however, was the Spanish tendency to increase steadily the tribute burdens, particularly large-scale labor demands for the mining boom, on an Indian population that was constantly falling. In other words, three decades after their defeat, overexploitation in the context of the demographic disaster caused the Indians to question their initial accommodation with their conquerors. Increasingly unable and unwilling to meet their oppressors' tribute demands, the Indians would break the Andean alliance on which the entire edifice of colonialism rested and, in the 1560s, would turn instead to forms of resistance and outright rebellion against that system.

THE DEMOGRAPHIC COLLAPSE

The burden of increasing tribute demands fell on a native population that was being ravaged by the spread of lethal diseases introduced by the Europeans. As a result, throughout the Americas, the natives experienced a catastrophic demographic collapse. Even before the appearance of Pizarro on the Peruvian coast, smallpox, malaria, measles, typhus, influenza, and even the common cold had spread to South America, perhaps carried by native traders, and begun to wreak havoc among the biologically defenseless inhabitants of Tawantinsuyu. Indeed, the death of Huayna Capac, which touched off the disastrous dynastic struggles between Huáscar and Atahualpa, is believed to have been the result of a smallpox epidemic that struck Quito sometime between 1523 and 1525.

Estimated between 4 and 15 million people (perhaps as high as 30 million) before the arrival of the Spaniards, Peru's Indian population, according to Cook (1981), fell to about 1.3 million in 1570 (48.5 percent) and to only around 700,000 in 1620. The decline was particularly precipitous during the first half century after Cajamarca, but varied from place to place, generally higher on the coast (96 percent between 1525 and 1575) than in the highlands (67–75 percent). Unlike Mexico, where the Indian population reached a low point in the 1620s, the nadir in Peru did not come until the mid- to late seventeenth century [although estimates for Peru are complicated by the difficulties in counting the large number of natives who left their communities (called *forasteros*) in order to avoid paying the tribute taxes and forced labor drafts to the silver mines (*mita*)].

The causes of this demographic disaster, which is without parallel in modern world history, were numerous. They ranged from the various calamities of war to the hardships caused by the exploitative nature of the new colonial regime to the widespread psychological demoralization of the conquered population. All these factors worked to intensify the spread of the killer diseases in a population without immunity. Whereas the warfare unleashed by the Spanish invasion was of relatively short duration, the longer-term confiscation of native food supplies through the exaction of tribute by the invaders severely undermined a society based on subsistence production. So did the draining off of *encomienda* labor from the villages to a wide variety of enterprises, both public and private. As manpower in the villages was diverted from indigenous production to other pursuits, the sophisticated and intricate Andean terracing and irrigation systems quickly fell into a state of decay and disrepair. It is hardly surprising, then, that a sharp drop in harvests occurred, contributing to growing food shortages and widespread hunger in the Indian sector. All this produced a vicious cycle of famine and death in the native communities.

The introduction of some European agricultural and pastoral techniques to the Andes contributed to this cycle of disease and death. Not content to continue living off the expropriation of Indian foodstuffs (*encomienda*), the conquistadors and their successors soon began to produce, as I said earlier, their own accustomed foods—various meats, bread, wine, sugar, and olive oil—on depopulated Indian lands. The colonists also introduced cattle and sheep to the Andes for the first time in millennia, with devastating effects on native agriculture. Left unfenced and roaming freely, Spanish cattle and sheep, which multiplied with astonishing rapidity, indiscriminately invaded and damaged the fields of neighboring Indian villages. In short, Spanish cattle and sheep ate men, by destroying native production and contributing to widespread hunger. Or put another way, "the more European crops and livestock there were, the fewer [the] Indians" (Sánchez Albornoz, 1984, p. 10). A countervailing argument to this destruction of indigenous production is that the introduction of new tools, metal plow tips for example, or the concentration of production on the most fertile lands actually raised agricultural productivity, even as the population declined dramatically.

The psychological trauma of defeat and colonization further intensified the Indians' decline. "The surrender that those who have been conquered have to make to the victor of self-esteem, wealth, prosperity, and comfort inevitably has repercussions on the raising of children, whom they can no longer afford to support," wrote Viceroy Marques de Castelfort about the depopulation of the province of Santa (quoted in Sánchez Albornoz, 1984, p. 11). Indeed, declining fertility rates, as much as rising mortality caused by malnutrition and disease, worked to reduce the Andean population. For example, in Huánuco in the central Andes, the size of the average family dropped from six before the conquest to 2.5 in 1562, as much from the lower rate of reproduction as to the breakup of the family. Reports of abortion and infanticide, not to mention suicide, are numerous in the chronicles and official documents of the period. Ethnohistorian Nathan Wachtel drew on an early government report, for example, that "tells of Indians driven to suicide by despair and the desire to escape ill-treatment; some hang themselves; some fast to death; others take poisonous herbs; and women even kill their babies at birth 'to free them from the torments they suffer' " (1977, p. 94).

Wachtel argued that the generalized demoralization of the Indian population at seeing the collapse of their traditional life, the powerlessness of their gods, and the general disorganization of the Inca state led them to utter despair. In particular, he cited reports of widespread drunkenness by Indians as an indication that they were trying to escape from a world that no longer held meaning for them. Under Inca rule, drunkenness in the home or workplace was strictly forbidden, except in connection with religious festivals, and severely punished. These and other signs of social disintegration, Wachtel concluded, were the result of the conquest and demographic disaster.

In the end, all these factors—war, exploitation, socioeconomic change, and the generalized psychological trauma of conquest—combined to intensify the spread of epidemic disease. Numerous killer pandemics swept down from the north, laying waste to entire communities where they often killed nine out of every ten inhabitants. Occurring in 1525, 1546, 1558–59, and 1585, these epidemics did not allow the population time to recover and impaired its ability to reproduce itself. The most serious epidemic, which occurred from 1585 to 1591, seems to have been a combination of several diseases. The chronicler Arriaga observed that "the victims' bodies were covered with boils; they blocked the throat, preventing the passage of food, and they attacked the eyes; the sick gave off a fetid smell and were so disfigured, that they could be identified only by their names" (quoted in Wachtel, 1977, p. 96).

In time, these pandemics gave way to more localized, but still lethal, epidemics during the seventeenth century. For example, on the coast, which endured a higher ratio of population loss than the highlands, yellow fever became endemic. It was transplanted there by incoming African slaves and flourished in a tropical climate similar to the dark continent. Ironically, it also took a heavy toll on the European population, which by this time clustered in the cities.

Spanish Peru

As the news of the conquest of the Incas spread in the Americas and across the Atlantic, Spanish immigration to Peru accelerated. The settlers, like their counterparts elsewhere in the Americas, came from a broad geographic, social, and occupational cross section of ordinary Spaniards from many occupations and ranks—artisans, professionals, merchants, and women. They represented the entire social spectrum of Spanish society and every region of the Castillian heartland and included not an insignificant number of African slaves and Europeans. Mostly ordinary people, they had heard about Peru from the enthusiastic letters that their friends and relatives sent home and decided to migrate. Contrary to later stereotypes, they were also not adverse to commerce and, in fact, most engaged in the range of entrepreneurial activities common to developing commercial capitalism in Europe.

The newcomers congregated in the new towns and cities being founded in the Andes. Indeed, from the outset Spanish Peru was urban centered, perhaps more so than in Spain itself. While there was much travel to the countryside, residence there was generally held in low esteem and left to miners, tribute collectors, and rural priests (*doctrineros*), who taught Christianity to the natives. The major purveyors of Spanish civilization in Peru were the *encomenderos*, artisans, Spanish women, and Hispanized blacks who resided in the cities.

To take one example, black Africans served as particularly valuable auxiliaries not only in defeating the native population, but in acculturating the Indians to Spanish ways of living and doing things, not to mention becoming a key ingredient to the supply of labor. Slaves had accompanied Pizarro on all his expeditions from Panama, and one purportedly helped save the life of his associate Diego de Almagro, who later took 150 blacks on his expedition to Chile. Soon African slaves were being imported in large numbers, in the context of the virtual disappearance of the indigenous population on the coast, to supply labor for the coastal *repartimientos*, the *encomiendas*, and the great houses in the Spanish towns. By 1586, Lima contained 4,000 African slaves to 2,000 non-Africans, a figure that jumped to 15,000 versus 9,000 non-Africans by 1640. Given their considerable utility, slaves drew high prices for the balance of the century, as exemplified by Gonzalo Pizarro's purchase of "a slave and some merchandise" for 500 pesos.

During the early years, most blacks were brought to Peru from other parts of the colony or from Spain itself, where slavery had a long history. As a result, they were thoroughly Hispanized and tended to identify with their masters in the alien and foreign environment of the Andes. In fact, acting as intermediaries and emulating their masters, they often terrorized the natives and treated them harshly, resulting in strong mutual antipathy between the two groups. Prized for their loyalty, skills, and know-how in a frontier setting, blacks generally were considered above the Indian population in the social stratification of the postconquest society.

Although social origins and occupation worked to stratify Spanish Peru as they did in the mother country, seniority in the conquest and possession of an *encomienda* also conferred prestige and contributed to the evolving new Andean hierarchy. Participation in the conquest of Cajamarca and Cuzco, which often carried with it the reward of *encomienda* grants, accounted for much of the social mobility that occurred in the first few years of the conquest. Thereafter, mobility was more difficult, particularly since *encomiendas* were increasingly acquired by late-arriving peninsulars, who came directly from Spain with money, status, and influence. At the same time, from the beginning, the possession of an *encomienda* conveyed to Peru the seignorial ethos that was the prevailing ideal in Spain. Indeed, as you have seen, *encomenderos* lived as lords and became the economic and social focal point in their new land:

> They were the principal customers of artisans and merchants; their lands and livestock fed the cities; their Indians worked the mines; their followings of relatives, guests, servants, employees, and Negro slaves made them the leaders of independent bands of men; in their large compound city houses were not only their residences, but stores, shops, and the dwellings of a good part of the population over all of whom the *encomenderos* wielded a patriarchal influence. (Lockhart,1968, p. 230)

In demographic terms, the first thirty years of Spanish occupation drew some 5,000 to 10,000 Spaniards to Peru. Women constituted a distinct minority of migrants, only 5 percent to 17 percent during this period, a figure that rose to around 28.5 percent between 1560 and 1579 as conditions stabilized. Their motives in coming varied, but most "came to settle, to be protected, to carve out a better future for themselves" (Lavrin, quoted in Bethell, 1984, p. 323). Not all were successful, however, as indicated by the numerous letters that many destitute widows and penniless daughters of conquistadors and early settlers wrote to the royal authorities requesting pensions and financial aid. Marrying predominantly other compatriots, they formed households and were particularly important as "transmitters of Hispanic domestic and material culture and of religious and social values."

Of these 5,000 to 10,000 immigrants, perhaps 2,000 to 4,000 were marginal transients, vagabonds, beggars, and rapscallions. They were reminiscent of the *pícaros* of Spain and a source of constant trouble and instability, leading the authorities to organize the numerous *entradas* mentioned earlier as safety valves of social control. The total number of Spanish inhabitants was matched by Hispanized black slaves. They were joined by a large number of Hispanized Indians, who were initially brought from Nicaragua and other parts of the Indies. But by the 1560s they were surpassed in number by acculturated Indians residing near or in the major urban areas. The overwhelming majority of this population lived in towns and cities, with about half residing in 1569 in Lima and Potosí.

The social and racial configuration of this society was both complex and ambiguous. Blacks stood at the bottom of the Spanish world, but on top of the Indian majority over whom they exerted some power. Spanish commoners counted black slaves and Indian servants in their households, but were treated as inferiors by other Spaniards who were their superiors. And an entirely new ethnic category—the mestizo, or *casta*, of mixed blood—was rapidly emerging from both the biological and cultural encounter between the Spanish victors and the Indian vanquished. The colonial administration tried in vain to classify this diverse multitude for the purposes of collecting taxes and establishing social categories of stratification. But the "reality of an uncontrollable 'mestizaje' eventually gave the lie to a racist nomenclature developed as a control mechanism for fixing the population in geographical space as well as in rigid social and economic niches" (Castro-Klarén, "Lima: A Blurred Centrality," in Valdés, 2000).

THE CHURCH AND THE SPIRITUAL CONQUEST

The establishment of Spanish Peru, of course, not only implied a continuous stream of immigration from the homeland and the implantation of Iberian civilization in the Andean heartland. It also involved the transfer of Hispanic institutions, and none was more important in the establishment of European control in the Andes than the Catholic Church. Indeed, if, on one level, the conquest represented the clash between opposing military forces that was decided on the battlefields of Cajamarca and elsewhere, on another level, it represented the longer-term struggle between two opposing religions, ideologies, and worldviews. As in all such colonial conflicts, the ultimate outcome hinged upon the struggle to replace one set of beliefs with another—Andean deities and traditions with European Christianity.

History and tradition had uniquely prepared the Spanish Catholic Church for the spiritual conquest of the Andes. For one thing, as was noted earlier, the Church had played a significant motivating and justifying role in the reconquest of Spain by mounting a crusade, or holy war, against the infidel Moors. For another, the unification of the peninsula into the fledgling Spanish nation under the crown of Castile at the end of the fifteenth century owed much to the immense power and wealth of the Catholic Church that the crown was able to harness to its political ends. This unification of church and state was largely accomplished by a series of papal bulls at the end of the fifteenth and early sixteenth centuries which conferred on the crown the *patronato real*, or royal patronage, over the church in Spain. In effect, Rome legitimated Spain's claims to newly discovered or conquered territories and granted the state control over the Church in exchange for the obligation to convert their inhabitants (Moors, later Indians) to Christianity. By virtue of royal patronage, the crown gained the right to confirm or nominate all ecclesiastical appointments and assumed the obligation to pay salaries and build churches out of revenues received from tithes levied on agrarian production.

Finally, as a common set of universally accepted values, orthodox Christianity provided the ideological glue for the centralizing tendencies of the Castillian monarchy in its efforts to unify the geographically and politically diverse kingdoms that made up the Iberian peninsula. Of no little assistance in the task of national unification, of course, was the Holy Office of the Inquisition, first established in Castile under crown control in 1483 to ensure religious orthodoxy among the *converso* population of converted Jews. Its role expanded with the external threat of heretical Protestant reformism that emerged in northern Europe to challenge Rome and the church universal during the early sixteenth century. The struggle between Protestantism and Catholicism during the Reformation, of course, became a political, as well as a religious, conflict. As Hapsburg Spain assumed the role of defender of the faith, the Church, spearheaded by the Inquisition, became increasingly militant and orthodox.

It was in this context of militant orthodoxy during the Counter Reformation in Europe that the Spanish, led by Pizarro and accompanied by a few priests, arrived at Cajamarca in 1532. Unlike the missionary fervor that imbued the early Church in Meso-America with a humanistic spirit, the Church in Peru from the outset reflected the militant ethos of a state at war. The process of conversion of the natives to Christianity in the Andes, therefore, took on much more of a raw political meaning than missionary, idealistic zeal. It signified the acceptance by the vanquished of the new authority of their conquerors while it provided the latter with a useful rationale and justification for conquest.

The Indians' reception of the missionaries' message of conversion was facilitated not only by the seeming omnipotence of the conquerors' religion, but by the offer of spiritual relief after the brutality of the conquest. Reception, however, did not imply complete abandonment of old beliefs and rituals. On the contrary, while the natives paid superficial allegiance to the new religion as a political act or in genuinely deeper spiritual ways for relief from their suffering, they simultaneously continued to worship their old deities and to practice their traditional rituals without much interference, at least initially, from the Spanish clergy. As Stern put it, "from indigenous vantage points, Christianization implied not the substitution of one religious pantheon or framework by another, but a selective incorporation and redeployment of Christianity within a frame work of indigenous understandings" (*JLAS*, 1992, p. 20). In time the persistence of native religious beliefs and rituals would be viewed by Church authorities, however, as "laxness" in the conversion process, provoking, as you shall see, a concerted campaign at midcentury to stamp out native religious rites and ceremonies.

Several religious orders formed the Church's initial "strategic reserve" in the spiritual conquest of the Andes. They included the Franciscans, who arrived in 1534, followed by the Dominicans, Augustians, Mercedarians, and Jesuits (the last to arrive in the early 1570s). These five holy orders provided the bulk of missionaries who served on the front lines of the spiritual conquest, establishing *doctrinas*, or evangelical units, at the parish level that were designed to proselytize and "civilize" the natives through methods that combined both persuasion and coercion.

Although the church authorities, with the sanction of the state, resorted to coercion, through periodic harsh campaigns mounted to extirpate idolatry, they also devised more benign tactics of persuasion. Thus, a colonial cultural policy emerged that emphasized the propagation of the faith by means of visual representation, through paintings and prints, as well as the catechism. The latter was facilitated, for example, by the publication and diffusion of doctrinal aids and confessionals, such as the *Doctrina Christiana y Catecismo para la Instrucción de los Indios* (1585). As for colonial painting, it was given impetus by the Council of Trent (1545–63), which recommended conversion through the use of the visual arts. This recommendation resulted in the development of such important colonial schools of painting as those of Cuzco, Lima, Chuquisaca, and Quito. Called on to decorate the numerous churches that sprang up in Cuzco, for example, the Spanish painter Iñigo de Loyola arrived in the former Inca capital in 1545 and began training Indian and mestizo artists in the art of producing didactic religious paintings. In time, according to Gisbert (1980, p. 104), 70 percent of the painters of the the School of Cuzco, founded by Diego Quispe Tito (1611–81), were Indians, and the school was producing not only religious iconography for viceregal churches, monastaries, and convents, but scenes of the great public ceremonies and festivals of the viceroyalty and portraits of the Spanish and Indian nobility.

While the initial Andean evangel was less utopian and idealistic than its Mexican counterpart, it did yield a number of individuals who stood out as examples of European humanism in Peru. One was Domingo de Santo Tomás, the Dominican friar who arrived in Peru in 1540 and soon spoke out against the abuses of the *encomienda*. He became a professor of theology, specializing on matters related to the Indians whom he came to know closely in extensive travels to the interior. A correspondent and ally of Bartolomé de las Casas, Santo Tomás worked on a project to allow Indians to purchase their freedom from *encomenderos* and later published the first grammar of the Quechua language in 1560. He also participated in a traveling debate before audiences of Indians and Spaniards with Juan Palo de Ondegardo, a defender of *encomenderos'* rights. The debate centered on the role of the *en-*

comendero in postconquest Andean society, with Santo Tomás advocating a colonial order run by councils of native chiefs in alliance with agents of the crown and Church.

The regular clergy, whose members were devoted mainly to the evangel, soon came to be outnumbered by the secular clergy, who assumed the principal role of ministering to the growing Hispanic population in Peru. As such, they congregated, like their parishioners, in the towns and cities, generally avoiding the heavily Indian rural areas where the evangelical friars were at work saving souls. At the local level, they founded parishes, and in their pastoral activities, they were notably less idealistic and more morally decadent than their missionary counterparts. When they did come into contact with the native population, they became notorious for extracting excessive payments for ecclesiastical services and often colluded with the *encomenderos* and *corregidores* in the exploitation of Indians.

With two distinctly different ecclesiastical entities in Peru, the crown ultimately entrusted the secular clergy with the overall organization and management of the Church in the viceroyalty. At the apex of ecclesiastical organization was the archbishop, who administered the entire Church in the viceroyalty from Lima, which was established as an archbishopric in 1546. Bishops oversaw specific dioceses, or bishoprics, and administered the Holy Office of the Inquisition, which was founded in Lima in 1570 to protect the colonists from the heresies of Protestantism or Judaism or moral corruption like sexual perversion. As for the composition of the clergy, it was overwhelmingly white, with both regulars and seculars drawn from the peninsular, and, in time, creole (the offspring of Spanish parents born in the New World) sectors of the population. Indians were largely excluded from the clergy because of Hispanic ethnocentrism and so were mestizos, until later in the eighteenth century, because of their presumed illegitimate origins.

THE CRISIS OF THE 1560S AND THE TOLEDAN REFORMS

By the 1560s Spain faced a mounting crisis in its Andean colony. Although the civil wars and rebellions had largely ended when Pedro de la Gasca defeated and executed Gonzalo Pizarro in 1548, the extension of royal power and the consolidation of the state were still incomplete. More important, the early economy of plunder, based on the extraction of surplus wealth and labor from the Indian population by the *encomenderos*, had reached its limits and was in decline. *Encomienda* income was down, largely because of the demographic decline, as well as increased crown regulations that limited the amount of tribute that could be collected. Furthermore, Inca gold and loot had been exhausted and distributed, and there were no new *encomiendas* to grant, leaving newly arrived immigrants, who continued to pour into Peru, with few prospects or sources of easy income. Finally, the easy phase of silver production from surface veins at Potosí and elsewhere had come to an end by the 1560s.

What alarmed Madrid most about the economic slowdown was the prospect of falling revenues. Hapsburg Spain now relied heavily on its Andean colony to fund its ambitious geopolitical aims in Western Europe and the Mediterranean, to the point that it had borrowed heavily against future American revenues. As Andrien summarized it, "the pillaging conquest economy established after 1532 had reached its limit, and only a drastic political and economic overhaul of the colonial system could revitalize Spanish rule in the Andes" (1991, p. 124).

Perhaps more ominous, from both an economic and political standpoint, was the fact that the Andean alliance on which the entire colonial enterprise was based was showing signs of unraveling. The Indian population, even those who had initially allied with the invaders against the Incas, were having second thoughts about the arrival of the newcomers whom they originally believed simply represented one more in a long line of Andean contenders for power with whom to ally or accommodate. The continuing violent and rapacious behavior of many Spaniards and the harsh overall effects of the new colonial order caused many natives to alter this assessment. In particular, the gradual ratcheting up of tribute demands, particularly for labor in the silver mines, bore down inexorably on the village economy that was increasingly decimated by the demographic disaster. It was in this general climate that the millenarian religious revival, known as Taki Onqoy, which preached the total rejection of Spanish religion and customs, was discovered by the Spanish authorities in Huamanga in 1564. The uncovering of this nativist, anti-Spanish upheaval alarmed the authorities, particularly the clergy, and illustrated the potential danger of allowing the last Inca holdout at Vitcos in Vilcabamba to persist.

TAKI ONQOY

Taki Onqoy, which literally meant "dancing sickness," reflected the general demoralization and disillusionment that pervaded the Indians of the Huamanga region three decades after the conquest. Converts to the sect expressed their conversion and spiritual rebirth by a sudden seizure in which they would shake and dance uncontrollably, often falling and writhing violently on the ground. The leaders of the Taki Onqoy claimed that they were messengers from the native gods and preached that a pan-Andean alliance of Indian gods would destroy the Christians by unleashing diseases and other natural calamities against them. According to a witness in the official inquiry into the heresy undertaken by the authorities: "When the Marques [Francisco Pizarro] entered this land, [his] God defeated the wak'as [Andean spirits] and the Spaniards defeated the Indians. However, now the world has turned about, and this time God and the Spaniards [will be] defeated and all the Spaniards killed and their cities drowned; and the sea will rise and overwhelm them, so that there will remain no memory of them" (quoted in Spalding, 1984, p. 247).

Out of this cataclysm or *pachacuti*, a new, regenerated, and purified Andean world would emerge, a paradise free of the European oppressors and the diseases and destitution that they had wrought. In preparation for the coming annihilation, they called on the natives to withdraw from contact with the Spanish and renounce all cooperation with the colonial regime. If they did, "there would be no illness or death but health and the increase of their goods." Wachtel believes that the Taki Onqoy's millenarian vision of destruction and re-creation of the world coincided with the cyclical view of history embodied in Andean tradition. It constituted simply another turn in the Andean cycle (the Spanish invasion having been the last) in which the "wak'as would create another new world and other people" (Spalding, 1984, p. 248).

The authorities estimated that out of a total population of 150,000 inhabitants in Huamanga, perhaps 8,000 were active participants in the Taki Onqoy sect. What they feared most was the spread of the "contagion" beyond Huamanga, since the *taquiongos* called on all ethnic groups to unify in their resistance to the Spaniards in a Pan-Andean alliance. The Spanish invasion had been successful precisely because it had taken advantage of the structural divisions of the multiethnic Andean world through a strategy of divide and rule. Now the Taki Onqoy preached the revolutionary idea of Andean unification, which, if combined with the continuing sporadic guerrilla resistance of the neo-Inca state at Vitcos, Vilcabamba, or with the outbreak of the rebellion of the Huancas in 1565, had the potential to bring down the entire colonial order some three decades after Cajamarca.

Like all such mass social movements, given the steadily deteriorating social and economic conditions of the Andean peasants, the message of the Taki Onqoy fell on fertile grounds. Duly alarmed, the Spanish authorities moved quickly and energetically, through a Church-sponsored anti-idolatry campaign, to suppress the heresy before it had a chance to spread and perhaps turn violent. The movement's leaders were seized, beaten, fined, or expelled from their communities in a systematic campaign of repression. While there is disagreement among scholars on the extent of Taki Onqoy (Ramos, 1993), its appearance revealed a deep current of unrest among the Indian population. Indeed, it added one more dimension to the general political and economic crisis confronting the colonial order in the 1560s.

Viceroy Toledo and His Reforms

To meet this crisis and undertake a program of reorganization that would lead to a revival of its Peruvian "treasure house," Madrid dispatched in 1569 one of its ablest administrators and diplomats, the fifty-three-year-old aristocratic Francisco de Toledo, to be the fifth viceroy of Peru. Toledo, later nicknamed the Peruvian Solon, was cut from the mold of sixteenth-century European statesmen whose primary goal was to expand the power and scope of the national state. This was the age of the rise of royal absolutism, and Phillip II's appointment of Toledo to Peru conformed to the notion of "all power to the king." Accordingly Toledo's aims in Peru were to aggrandize Spanish power by consolidating viceregal rule and to revive the flow of Andean silver to the metropolitan treasury. In more specific terms, his charge was to end Indian unrest, bring the *encomenderos* to heel, and reorganize the economy.

To accomplish these ends, Toledo, drawing on a treatise on governing Peru written in 1567 by Spanish jurist Juan de Matienzo, set about to implement a blueprint of reforms that focused on three main changes: (1) concentration of the Indian population into major settlements called *reducciones*, (2) regularization and monetization of the tribute system, and (3) creation of a draft system of forced labor for crucial sectors of the economy, particularly the silver mines. While each of these reforms addressed, as you shall see, a variety of problems, taken together all three sought to resolve what Toledo believed was the main obstacle to the economic development of the colony—the mobilization of labor. In his view, the Indian population still remained firmly ensconced in its preconquest, nonmonetary, subsistence, and barter modes of production and exchange, outside and largely divorced from the rapidly expanding Spanish sector of the economy. Yet it was precisely the development of the Spanish sector of the economy on which the future prosperity and political stability of the colonial enterprise depended. And that sector needed a steady and reliable source of labor to prosper.

On his arrival in Peru, Toledo undertook an extensive and prolonged five-year inspection tour of the colony (*visita general*) from 1570 to 1575, traveling slowly and ceremoniously with a phalanx of seventy jurists, clergy, and retainers. The *visita* was designed not only to assess local conditions, but to impress his authority throughout the kingdom. It did not take him long to perceive, in light of the earlier Taki Onqoy upheaval, the potential threat that the neo-Inca state at Vitcos posed to the colony. He therefore dispatched an expeditionary force against the remote Inca fortress and, after a difficult campaign, succeeded in capturing it, together with the reigning Inca, Túpac Amaru. Forty years after Cajamarca, Toledo finally formally ended the conquest by executing the last Inca in a public ceremony in the main plaza of Cuzco in 1572. "With the execution of Túpac Amaru, Cuzco," in the words of Castro-Klarén, "was decentered and all eyes in the viceroyalty had to turn to Lima as the condensation of a new power game (p. 6).

At the same time, Toledo mounted a concerted campaign to discredit the Inca Empire in the eyes of the natives and thereby further legitimate and solidify Spanish rule. A commission was appointed to investigate the empire with the purpose of exposing the Incas as tyrants and longtime oppressors of the Andean masses. The commission's final report mustered evidence to depict the Incas as usurpers of the land and enslavers of the people. The objective was to justify morally the Spanish invasion by portraying it as the liberation of the Andean masses from Inca oppression and hence from the devil and evil itself.

Furthermore, in the mind of Toledo and others, the Taqui Onqoy heresy revealed the full extent to which the native religions continued to flourish among the Indians. In the context of the general rebellion and uncertainty before Toledo's arrival, the persistence of Andean religious practices constituted a clearly subversive and potentially dangerous challenge to continued European colonial rule. Thus, the new viceroy ordered the authorities, both church and state, to undertake "the extirpation of idolatries and sorceries and the neutralization of the dogmatizers so that the doctrine of the Evangel can be planted in earth prepared to receive it" (quoted in Spalding, 1984, p. 249).

The lion's share of this campaign fell upon the Church bureaucracy, whose front line was composed of the local parish priests, or *doctrineros*, who staffed the some 451 Indian parishes throughout the viceroyalty (excluding Upper Peru) in 1572. In many respects, these *doctrineros*, who were armed with the considerable power of the pulpit, confessional, and sacraments, were the watchdogs of the colonial system. Since they were the crown officials in the closest, regular contact with the native population, the *doctrineros* were uniquely positioned to carry out such campaigns, as well as to ferret out any other potentially subversive activity in the communities, such as the Taqui Onqoy. Spalding likened these campaigns against native beliefs and ceremonies carried out by the *doctineros* in the villages to the Inquisition, describing them as "brutal affairs that were essentially medieval autos-da fe" (1984, p. 265). In effect, the acceptance and practice of Christianity by the native population in the second half of the century came increasingly to constitute a sort of litmus test of loyalty to the colonial regime. Conversely, its rejection in favor of traditional Andean religious beliefs and rituals came to be seen as a sign of disloyalty and subversion. Surrounded as they were by a "sea of Indians," it is not hard to understand why the Spaniards frequently carried out such campaigns over the next century.

To facilitate such policies of social control, as well as the mobilization of labor for the colonial economy, Viceroy Toledo, as the next measure in his reform program, ordered a census to be taken of all the Indians in Peru between the ages of eighteen and fifty. The results, which took some time to compile, showed a male Indian labor force of 1,677,697 belonging to 614 *ayllus*. With this information, Toledo then decreed the resettlement and concentration of Indians from their nucleated and dispersed villages into *reducciones*, or larger towns. The purpose of such a massive, forced resettlement was to establish direct state control and facilitate the Church's Christianization of the native population, while enhancing the collection of the tribute tax and the allocation of labor. In the viceroy's words, "the reduction of the Indians to villages and parishes makes them easier to manage, to be governed and given religious training" (quoted in Spalding, 1984, p. 214).

If the reduction policy to "rationalize" indigenous settlement patterns seemed logical enough to the Spaniards, to the Andeans it seemed quite the opposite and, indeed, extraordinarily destructive. For one thing, it was an assault on the dispersed kin networks and archipelago pattern of Andean settlements that found tiny hamlets "rationally" tucked into every conceivable nook and cranny of the highly vertical and variegated Andean landscape, with its multiple climatic and productive zones. For another, by concentrating the population into relatively large settlements, it exposed them to greater danger from the pandemics that regularly swept down from the north throughout the sixteenth century.

Underlying the congregation plan was the Spanish settlement policy in the Indies of creating two "republics," one of Europeans and the other of Indians. Although ostensibly created to protect the Indian population against exploitation by settlers, the "republic of Indians became a euphemism for a regime of de-tribalization, regimentation, Christianization, tribute and forced labour" (Richard Morse quoted in Bethell, 1984, p. 82). The plan mandated the "reduction" of anywhere from 20 to 100 ethnic groups or villages into two or three new settlements modeled on the grid plan. The overall supervision of these Indian towns was assigned to *corregidores de indios* (Indian agents who were appointed by the crown at the provincial level). The *corregidores* were charged with the general administration of justice, the control of commercial relations between Indians and Spaniards, and the collection of the tribute tax. They were assisted by the *curacas*, members of the native elite whom the Spaniards had chosen, as we have seen, to convert into a hereditary, provincial nobility linked to the state bureaucracy.

The resettlement of the native population into *reducciones* under the rule of the *corregidor*, sounded the death knell of the *encomienda* system, for it effectively transferred control of Indian labor away from the *encomenderos* to the state. At the same time, Toledo moved to phase out the *encomienda* system by co-opting the remaining *encomenderos* into magistracies and other offices. In the words of one historian, "the corregidors served as local political or economic agents of the state who effectively took control of the countryside away from the independent-minded *encomenderos*" (Andrien, 1991, p. 125)

The *corregidores* now used their office in similar fashion to the *encomenderos* whom they replaced to accumulate wealth, establishing alliances of mutual interest with local and regional elites. Working hand and glove with these elites—*curacas*, Indian functionaries, municipal officials, rural priests, landowners, merchants, miners, and others, as well as with their Indian and mestizo subordinates—the *corregidores* stood at the head of a local power group that, with ready access to state officials, institutions, and urban elites, came to dominate rural Andean society. The alliances that were forged among these elites, moreover, were more often than not reinforced by the mutual ties of kinship, friendship, and patron-client relations that were pervasive throughout the Hispanic world.

While the *reducciones* of Toledo's *"repúblicas de Indios"* facilitated the the maximum degreee of control and exploitation of the Indian population by the Spanish regime, these new Indian towns also became principal focal points for the cultural transformation of the indigeneous population. It was in these towns that the Church established its paramount presence and where the evangelizing clergy came into the closest contact with the natives on an everyday basis. Making use of public ceremonies, as well as the sacraments, as tools of legitimation, they, more than anyone else, incorporated the Andean peoples as legitimate subjects of the crown.

Turning to Toledo's second major reform, the viceroy sought to regularize the tribute tax by converting it into a head tax. He established a fixed rate, based upon the ability of a district to pay, which was determined by a regular census of its resources and population every two to five years. On the basis of this census, the tax was then calculated and levied on all able-bodied men aged eighteen to fifty. Even more important, Toledo converted the payment of the tribute tax from goods to silver.

The monetization of the tribute system obliged the Indian peasantry either to sell their products in the marketplace for currency (or deliver them to the corregidor who theoretically set the price according to fair market value) or to seek wage work outside the community in the expanding Spanish sector of the economy, so they could pay their tribute obligations to the state in cash (silver). In this way, Toledo established a key mechanism not only to draw the native population into the Spanish market economy, but to stimulate the circulation of labor between the Indian and the Spanish sectors of the economy. In the case of the latter, it would theoretically ensure an adequate supply of workers for the urban, transportation, mining, manufacturing (*obrajes*) and agrarian (hacienda) sectors.

The precise amount of the tribute tax levied is difficult to estimate, but it has been roughly calculated at somewhere between 4 and 7 pesos per person. Although this seems like a relatively small amount to be derived from each peasant household, in the aggregate it amounted to a substantial transfer of income from the Indian to the European sector of the economy. The distribution of tribute income (only currency receipts) reveals the uses to which the tax was put: salaries of provincial administrators—13–26 percent, salaries of parish priests, or *doctrineros*—20 percent, salaries of *curacas*—4–10 percent, *encomenderos* (before statization)—40–60 percent.

The third major reform instituted by the new viceroy was a continuing, rotating draft of Indian labor from the *reducciones* to work in the silver mines in Peru and Upper Peru (Bolivia). In theory, this forced-labor system, called *mita* in Spanish (and *mit'a* in Quechua, for "turn"), was to comprise up to one-seventh of all the able-bodied male inhabitants every seven years to work up to four months in the mines at a stipulated wage. The Indians were to be drawn from sixteen highland provinces stretching from Cuzco to southern Peru and Bolivia. In practice, the percentage recruited, by agents of the *corregidor*, from the villages was often even higher and the term at the mines longer.

In the minds of the Indians, this new Spanish *mita* recalled the previous Inca practice, designed for the purpose of public works. However, there was a crucial difference. In the Inca system, the *mit'a* was an element of the larger social contract involving reciprocal benefits between the community and the state. The Spanish *mita*, on the other hand, was a purely exploitative colonial mechanism, with no real benefits flowing back to the community from the state.

Although the *mita* was primarily intended to ensure a regular supply of native workers to the mining sector, which had experienced a labor shortfall during the 1560s, it was also directed to other activities that were deemed important to the state. These activities included work on haciendas that produced foodstuffs for the viceregal capital, as well as in enterprises that provisioned services (postal and transport) and luxuries to the elites. For example, the Huarochirí *mita* provided labor for the mines of Nuevo Potosí and the coastal plantations near Lima, for road maintenance and services at *tambos*, or way stations, on the route from Lima to Cuzco to Potosí, and for the cutting and transportation of glacial ice for purposes of refrigeration in Lima.

In monetizing and statizing the tribute system and creating the *mita* draft, managed by the newly appointed *corregidor de indios*, Toledo had gone a long way toward refining the system of expropriation of native surplus on which the colonial system was based. This process of appropriation was further enhanced by a notorious practice that, while technically illegal and certainly not condoned by Toledo, became widely practiced from the sixteenth century on by all members of the colonial elite, particularly the *corregidores*: the *repartimiento de mercancias (reparto)*, or forced sale of goods to the Indian population.

Since the expenses of the office of the *corregidores* far exceeded either their state salaries or ability to use the office for private gain, it became a common practice for the *corregidores* to sell goods to the Indians. In effect, the *corregidores* became merchants who used their administrative powers (judicial and police) to compel the Indians under their jurisdiction to buy European goods at high, fixed prices. These goods ranged from useful items, such as mules, iron tools, and steel knives, to others of questionable value to the indigenous household, such as imported linens, woolens, textiles, and silk stockings.

Although a recent revisionist study (Baskes, 1996) portrayed the *reparto* in Mexico as a more benign and voluntary practice, the weight of the historiographical evidence in the Andes sees it in strongly negative terms. Morse argued that it was a form of extortion—"commerce for control and spoilation" that further enhanced the income of the *corregidores* and other members of the colonial elite who practiced it (local priests, hacendados, miners, and even members of the *curaca* Indian elite). In the larger scheme of the economy of plunder, the *reparto* served the real function of fostering the circulation of goods and currency between the Indian and the European sectors in a limited market economy. Although illegal, its importance to the colonial order was recognized and justified by an eighteenth-century viceroy who wrote that "since it is well known that the provinces cannot maintain themselves without a distribution, nor would there be anyone who would administer justice in them, these [*repartimientos de mercancías*] have come to be tolerated" (quoted in Spalding in Collier et al., 1982, p. 333). By this time, however, the volume of the *reparto*, in terms of both absolute amounts of money extorted and the relative inability of Indians to pay the amounts demanded, had risen radically after the sixteenth century, provoking, as you shall see, sharp political disruption.

Altogether the significance of Toledo's reforms in the colonial order were far reaching both economically and politically. Most important, the monetization of the tribute, the creation of the *mita*, and the practice of *repartimiento de mercancías* substantially increased the capacity of the colonial state and society to appropriate the surplus production and labor of the Indians. In effect, these levies forced Indians to provide a portion of their labor and production to the European sector of the economy. Second, *mita* labor, together with the investment in new technology and infrastructure ordered for Potosí, contributed to a substantial increase in Peru's output of silver. Because of the powerful spread effects of silver mining, that increase, in turn, generated an extensive internal economic expansion in the Spanish sector of the economy that was also made possible by the greater availability of Indian labor.

On another, more political, level, the patrimonial nature of the state was also enhanced by the Toledan reforms. The increased income generated by the tribute tax, together with the royal fifth from the rising silver output, became the financial basis for the exercise of patronage by the crown. This was a traditional method of the Spanish government whereby political offices were distributed to loyal and worthy subjects to ensure effective royal control of the polity.

Economic success in the new colonial order now came to depend as much on politics as on entrepreneurial skills, since the state controlled access to the key factor of colonial production—Indian labor. As Spalding put it, "the power of appointment, together with the authority to assign access to the labor and goods of the Indian population, became a major determinant of social and economic position for members of European society in Peru." Moreover, "by making the state the major source of access to the surplus generated by the Andean population . . . , the colonial system gave to the political sphere an extreme degree of control over the [economic] development of the viceroyalty" (1984, p. 167). For those, such as Hernando de Soto (*The Other Path*, 1989), who contend that Peru's current underdevelopment is due to the enduring legacies of the neomercantilist and patrimonialist state (that is, the state's excessive regulation, intervention, and control of the economy), its origins are to be found here.

Despite the obvious harshness of this new colonial system and the individual hardships it imposed in the Andes, the Indian population did not remain wholly passive and compliant in the face of its introduction. On the contrary, the natives more often than not resisted, adapted to, and survived the new regimen with an admirable Andean tenacity in the face of adversity. They were also aided in their survival by certain favorable trends that lessened the extractive pressures on their resources. For example, the population decline, while sapping the community of its labor power, also lowered internal demands on its own resources and output. For another, it was neither in the interests of the state nor the elite, which systematically siphoned off its surplus wealth and labor, to destroy the essential self-sufficiency and ability of the Indian community to reproduce itself.

As a result, the state, for practical and moral reasons, placed statutory and regulatory limits on colonial expropriation. These laws enabled the natives to appeal to the courts for relief from the exactions that exceeded the population and resources of the community, as well as for the prerogative to challenge attempts by colonists to usurp their lands. Indeed, in a remarkably short time, the natives became adept at resorting to Spanish legal institutions to defend their interests. They also creatively found ways to produce, trade, and generally engage in the new commercial economy, with profits serving to bolster their communities' relative autonomy. For example, profits from renting out community lands went back into the *caja de comunidad* (community strong box), which could be used to pay the tribute or buy out the labor draft, thereby lowering or eliminating burdensome colonial levies. In these and other ways, then, the Indians managed to turn adversity to advantage in order to survive the inexorable and often brutal pressures imposed by their new masters.

Whereas many historians previously portrayed a static, deterministic, one-sided social process of colonial oppression in which the Indians passively and fatalistic accepted and submitted to the invaders, they now see a more complex social dynamic of give-and-take, accommodation and resistance, and adjustment and compromise in Indian-European relations in the Andes. Moreover, they show that when the power networks that emerged at the core of the Andean economy and polity fractionalized into opposing interests, the native population quickly seized the opportunity to press forward their own interests, often with considerable success.

A good example of this process on the macrolevel was the struggle for justice waged by elements of the Church and state on behalf of the Indian population against colonial interests who were intent on enslaving the natives. The outcome of that struggle was the demise of the *encomienda* and the development of extensive social legislation to protect the Andean population from the excesses of colonial exploitation. It was to this legislation that the natives became adept at appealing in the law courts and tribunals of Andean colonial society. "The natives made the most of the opportunity, and entangled the colonials' exploitative practices in labyrinthine adjudications whose final outcomes were often uncertain" (Stern, 1982, p. 115). Thus, conflicts at the local level between elite factions over the treatment and uses of the Indian population gave the natives openings to defend themselves from one abuse or another. In this context, they lined up on one side or the other and, in return, could claim help in their adjudications.

As admirable as the extensive code of Spanish colonial social legislation in defense of the indigenous population is in hindsight, there was a downside to its proclamation. However effective such legislation and the court process was in assuaging the burdens of exploitation, in the end it served to strengthen the colonial system against any overt, radical, revolutionary challenge from the oppressed population. For "the establishment of a working system of justice, which sometimes ruled on behalf of the natives to the detriment of their exploiters, did not vindicate or somehow balance the colonial legacy. Rather, colonial justice played a crucial—perhaps indispensable—part in the subjugation of the natives to an exploitative society that lasted for centuries. Far from vindicating an exploitative experience, 'justice' rooted it into the fabric of colonial Andean society" (Stern, quoted in Collier et al., 1982, p. 293). And the raw and brutal nature of colonial exploitation was nowhere more visible or commonplace than in the great silver mines.

THE SILVER MINES

After the initial spurt in production after their discovery, the output of silver from Potosí declined as the veins near the surface became exhausted. As profits and wages declined, so did the supply of Indian laborers, who found the work of extracting the ore increasingly onerous. Plummeting revenues and reports of labor shortages, among other factors, were a catalyst in prompting the crown to appoint Toledo to reorganize the mines and the economy with an eye toward increasing silver revenues. From Madrid's perspective, "how could the king safeguard Spain's power in Europe, fight the French, repel the Turks, and prepare for war with England, if a primary source of American treasure dried up?" (Larson, 1988, p. 50).

Toledo concluded that part of the problem of declining production at the mines stemmed from inadequate technology. Upon learning of the new patio process and the discovery of the mercury mines at Huancavelica, the new viceroy authorized the construction of refineries, called *ingenios*, in which the amalgamation process of applying mercury to extract the silver chemically from the ore could be carried out. He also approved the development of a water-supply system involving new dams and canals to provide the power to generate the mills whose number increased to seventy-five by the turn of the century. The cost of these investments, some 3.5 million pesos, was to be born by the mine owners, in return for the state's provision of the necessary mercury and labor supply. The crown would collect the royal fifth, a profit on the mercury sold at Potosí, and other tax revenues while the miners retained four-fifths of total production. To ensure control and a steady supply of mercury to Potosí, Toledo expropriated the Huancavelica mines and then let out concessions for its production to private individuals.

The new patio refining process, introduced at Potosí in 1571, converted silver mining into a "big business" by shifting power away from the producers, many of them Indians, to the relatively few owners of the new refineries and mills (75 out of 500 mine owners in 1585) and their merchant backers. The upshot was the creation of a new interlocking elite of refiners and silver merchants that came to dominate silver production in the Andes.

Toledo also realized that without a steady, reliable, cheap source of labor, mining (and the general economy) would not advance sufficiently. As I discussed earlier, in his mind both the free market and the *encomienda* system worked imperfectly to mobilize sufficient Indian labor to accomplish the tasks of urban construction and agricultural expansion, let alone the mining sector. To resolve the labor problem, Toledo installed the *mita* system of draft labor. In effect, the viceroy devised a major subsidy to the miners at Potosí by providing them with a disciplined, regular supply of workers drawn from the communities at about a third of the cost of a *minga*, or free-wage laborer. Moreover, this subsidy did not include the costs of reproducing labor which was entirely born by the community and not "capital," that is, the mine owners.

The first *mita* recruits arrived in Potosí in 1573 from the immediate surrounding areas. Eventually, the recruitment area for the Potosí *mita* was vastly extended to an area over 200,000 square miles, constituting much of southern Peru and present-day Bolivia. It drew about 13,500 *mitayos* per year, or about 4,500 working one week on and two off at any one time. When their families who traveled with them are counted, some 50,000 people moved in and out of Potosí each year. The wages of the *mitayos* in the mines varied, depending on the work, from 2.75 to 3.5 reales a day, but did not include the substantial travel expenses over long distances from the communities to the mines (up to two months and a thousand kilometers). The practice of *mita* provided ample evidence for exponents of the so-called Black Legend of Spanish colonization.

In the first place, *mita* had a particularly deleterious impact on the Indian communities. It drained off able-bodied workers at a time when the communities were experiencing the effects of the demographic collapse. It also caused many Indians to flee their communities to evade the *mita*. By the eighteenth century, it has been estimated that 40–60 percent of the population of the Archbishopric of Cuzco were *forasteros*, or Indian migrants who had left their original communities and were not liable for the *mita* draft. With fewer workers available to work in the fields, subsistence production also fell, malnutrition and famine spread, and the "grim reaper" of disease intensified.

If the impact of the mita on the communities was devastating, its effects on the individual *mitayo* were often equally destructive. Abuses abounded and mortality soared. *Mitayos* were often forced to work beyond their term, for wages below those set by law and under conditions that were generally harsh. According to one historian, "a summons to labor in the mines came to be viewed as a virtual death warrant." The worst conditions prevailed at the mercury mines at Huancavelica, which in the 1620s had 2,200 *mitayos*, or about one-sixth of those at Potosí. There "the discomforts and dangers suffered by all miners—semidarkness and air befouled by sweating bodies and human waste, the smoke of candlewick, and toxic molds and dusts— were compounded by mercury poisoning and its implacable and hideous course." At Potosí "the most killing labor in the mines was that of carrying on one's back a large and heavy basket of ore, climbing up hundreds of feet through narrow, precipitous tunnels, clutching at ropes and finding toeholds in notched logs, struggling, antlike, to reach the mouth of the mine, where one's exhausted, sweating body would be blasted by freezing winds upon emergence" (Padden, 1975, p. xx). Three-quarters of the *mitayos* labored in these conditions, whereas free Indians invariably avoided them. While *mita* labor was utilized throughout colonial society, nowhere did it acquire the notoriety that it did in mining.

It should be pointed out that the *mitayos* were a decided minority of the workforce at Potosí, but because of the truly horrible conditions under which they labored, they tended to draw the most attention of contemporary observers and later historians. Actually, a dual system of labor existed at Potosí, consisting of *mitayos* and free labor. In 1603, for example, only 4,500 of some 11,000–12,000 Potosí miners were *mitayos*, the rest being *minga* free labor, although some of these, according to Bakewell, may have been off-duty *mitayos*.

In sum, Toledo's mining reforms revived the mining industry at Potosí and elsewhere and perfected the cash cow on which the crown came to depend for centuries. With the introduction of the patio amalgamation process, *mita* labor, and other reforms, output once again soared, almost sixfold from 1575 to 1600, during which Potosí produced almost half of all Spanish American silver.

3 Transition and Consolidation of the Colonial Order, 1600–1730

The last quarter of the sixteenth century, then, saw a revival and sixfold expansion in silver production. Toledo's reforms had made the Viceroyalty of Peru the largest silver producer in the colonies, producing almost half the silver in all Spanish America. This extraordinary period of mining renaissance, however, would not last. Beginning in 1600, silver production in the viceroyalty began a long, protracted decline that would endure for more than a century. The impact of this century-long decline on the viceregal economy has been the subject of considerable debate in the colonial historiography.

The traditional interpretation of this economy was that silver production at Potosí shaped an "enclave" economy, with surplus wealth flowing out to the metropolis and little or no ancillary or "spread" effects of capital (or wages and demand for locally produced goods) reinvested back into the local economy to spur internal production. The main economic stimulus from Potosí silver, according to this view, was the transatlantic trade in which silver was exchanged for imported imputs (capital and machinery to run the mines) and luxury items manufactured in Spain and Europe for consumption by the small colonial elite. Peru thus became a classically "dependent" economy, devoid of local production and dependent on the export of raw materials (silver) and the import of manufactured products. Then, with the decline in silver production in the seventeenth century, the transatlantic trade, based on this exchange, likewise went into eclipse and Peru entered a century-long period of depression.

The revisionist view of colonial economic development paints a different picture. Economic historian Carlos Sempat Assadourian argued that considerable capital from the "dominant" silver production was not drained off to the metropolis but, rather, remained in Peru. It stimulated the development of what he called Andean "economic space" devoted to internal production and exchange. Assadourian's thesis was taken a step further by Kenneth Andrien, who contended that rather than experiencing a depression as a result of declining silver production in the seventeenth century, Peru underwent a restructuring away from silver exports and the transatlantic trade toward a more diversified, self-sufficient, and regionalized economy. Both historians de-emphasized the standard "enclave" view of the colony and instead stressed Peru's capacity during the sixteenth and seventeenth centuries for considerable internal production and exchange.

Dynamization of the Internal Economy

By the turn of the seventeenth century, Potosí, at one end of the main colonial "growth pole" that stretched from the mining center to its Lima-Callao terminus, had reached a population of 100,000. Most of the supplies and provisions for this mining population came from surrounding Andean producing regions. Some were relatively nearby. For example, mule trains brought wheat and flour (for bread) and maize (for *chicha* corn beer), worth over 2 million pesos, into the city in 1603. By this time, the Indian population in Potosí alone consumed an estimated 1 million jugs of *chicha* annually. Much of these provisions came from the rich agricultural region of the nearby Cochabamba Valley, which became the main cereal bowl for Upper Peru.

When such areas could no longer meet the growing demand at Potosí because of spatial limitations, the production radius for Potosí expanded to include other, more distant regions, markets, and products. For example, Tucumán and Córdoba in northern Argentina came to specialize in raising and provisioning mules, the main means of transporting goods in and out of Potosí. Similarly, central Chile developed into a major wheat-growing area that exported not only to Potosí, but to Lima and the coast, particularly after the devastating earthquake of 1687. Other Andean products included coca, yerba mate (tea), freeze-dried potatoes, and beef jerky.

Finally, I should mention textile workshops (*obrajes*), which sprang up in Cuzco, Ayacucho, and as far north as Quito. These workshops produced cheap, rough knit clothing made out of course woolens, supplied to the *obrajes* by highland herds, for the burgeoning Potosí labor market. It was in this way that the entire Viceroyalty of Peru, from Ecuador in the north to northern Argentina and central Chile in the south, was articulated or drawn into a single, rationally organized economic space around the main Peruvian "growth pole" of Potosí–Lima.

Assadourian estimated that these and other Andean products absorbed about half the silver produced at Potosí. Put another way, the silver from Potosí that was used to purchase Andean products in the entire viceroyalty amounted to roughly 60–70 percent of the value of the international flow of silver exports and manufactured imports that linked Peru to Europe. For Assadourian, this internal production shows that Andean development cannot be characterized as an enclave economy or relegated to a scant reflection of metropolitan commercial interests. Rather, a robust internal trade and production emerged to satisfy popular demand for foodstuffs and low-cost consumer goods from urbanizing Indians and mestizos working in the Potosí mines. Indeed, Assadourian showed that the value of this popular market was a good deal larger than the elite market for European goods imported to meet the demands of consumers in the much smaller, wealthier Spanish and creole population.

All segments of the colonial population participated in the development of this internal Andean economy, not the least being the Indians. Rather than resist the new commercial forces introduced by the Spaniards and retreat into community autarky in defense of subsistence and corporate integrity, many native Andeans chose increasingly to intervene in local markets. At the elite level, I already discussed the case of Don Diego Caqui, the son of a *curaca*, who became a successful entrepreneur in Tacna. To defend their autonomy and independence, some communities grew cash crops for the market, acquiring the necessary wherewithall to litigate land claims or "rent" laborers to avoid the *mita*. Other villages adopted cattle raising to meet rising urban demand, while still others rented lands out to Spaniards who were eager to produce for the same market.

As a result, some members of Indian society began to accumulate land and income well beyond their subsistence needs and to emerge alongside their European counterparts in the Andean market economy. This situation led Spalding to suggest that as it evolved and matured, "the colonial economy of Peru was not a dual system, but an integrated economic system. In this system the labor power and a great deal of the actual volume of goods that circulated in the viceroyalty was drawn from the Indian communities" (Spalding-Collier et al., 1982, p. 339). Stern, who pioneered research in this area, suspects that the Andean response to the new commercial forces reflected "the genuine ambiguities and ambivalences of colonial life, . . . an attempt to hedge bets, or more precisely, to protect one's well being by developing diverse and sometimes deliberately ambiguous socioeconomic relations that might later be used, as needed, in either a 'traditional Andean' or 'colonial European' direction" (Stern, 1995, p. 84).

Just as some Indians creatively sought to turn the new commercial order to their advantage in some fashion, others resorted to tried-and-true Andean principals to bolster their postconquest position. Thus, the Lupaqa peoples intensified traditional barter-and-trade arrangements with other ethnic groups on the shores of Lake Titacaca to ensure supplies of *chuño* (freeze-dried potato) and quinoa for their own communities. Other communites reconstructed in a similar manner the microeconomies of the "vertical archepelago" to undermine or "defeat" the Toledan *reducción* system.

Indian responses aside, the evident extent of this evolving commercial system calls into question the tradional picture of a Spanish aristocracy parasitically living off the production of the Indian masses and disdaining investment in production and commerce. It is true that colonial elites often displayed their wealth in sumptuous lifestyles of conspicuous consumption. But this seigneurial behavior had a particular, calculated function—to impress upon the various colonial castes and orders the extent of the elites' political and social power. Certainly, there is ample evidence from the sixteenth and seventeenth centuries that some elites simply sought to acquire land, retreat into autarchy, and live off their rents in a seigniorial, medieval economic style, becoming, in effect, a class of rentiers.

However, more often than not, just as miners sought to improve productivity and profits, *encomenderos* and landowners acquired land for commercial and productive purposes, and they did so by a variety of means: occupation of vacated Indian lands, encroachment onto Indian lands or neighboring land, receipt of *mercedes*, or land grants from the crown or local *cabildos*, and regular purchase. Their estates were often carefully constructed as integrated units that were located specifically in rising regional markets around mining and political-administrative centers. So in this sense, the early colonial period gave rise to a European entreprenurial logic that included, in addition to the more stagnant rentier model, an expanding and aggressive investment-accumulation-reinvestment pattern. Can this forming colonial economy be called capitalistic, however? Stern did not think so:

> The colonial market place had rules that mixed outright coercion with mercantile incentive; its hired laborers never developed into an expanding and stable wage-labor proleteriat; its scale, logic, and cycles of growth and decay contrasted sharply with those we associate with modern capitalist economies. Often, the colonial marketplace harnessed noncapitalist relations of production to more modern goals of profit accumulation through investment and market sale. These features distinguish the colonial economy from modern capitalism (and also from classical images of precapitalist economies). (1995, p. 74)

There were other archaic, clearly noncapitalistic, colonial practices. One such practice was the *repartimiento de mercancías*, or forced sale of goods to the Indian population at inflated prices. Equally anachronistic was the failure to develop adequate mechanisms for credit and the circulation of capital that never went much beyond a few successful individuals such as a handful silver miners in Potosí; various merchants in Potosí, Lima, or other provincial cities; or, more important perhaps, the Church.

The Church became a major source of whatever credit was available in the postconquest society, largely because of the considerable wealth it acquired early on from bequests, dowries, and rents. However, much of its considerable accumulating capital that might have been more productively reinvested in developing the economy went into building the lavishly decorated churches that spread out along the main commercial circuits and settlements of the early viceroyalty. Like the extensive expenditure of profits on luxurious lifestyles by *encomenderos*, hacendados, and other wealthy individuals, the Church built its impressive monuments to God to impress upon the Andean masses its power and authority.

Although silver production in Potosí was the mainspring of the developing colonial economic system, Lima was its hub. As the outlet for silver

The City of the Kings, Lima, imagined by Felipe Guamán Poma de Ayala (1615) drawing entitled *Civdad/La Civdad de los Reis de Lima* . . . in his *El primer nueva crónica y buen gobierno*, vol. 3, John V. Murra and Rolena Adorno, Quechua translations by Jorge L. Urioste (Mexico City, 1980), p. 950. Reproduced courtesy of Siglo Veintiuno Editores, Mexico City.

bullion on the Pacific, Lima and its nearby port of Callao also received and distributed the manufactured goods from the metropolis for the growing Spanish settlements along the growth pole. The two-way flow of imports and exports through Lima concentrated both wealth and administration— public and private—in the city. As a result, Lima became the headquarters for many of the largest estate owners and operators; merchants connecting their Andean trading operations with sources of supply in Spain; and all types of service providers, from craftsmen to lawyers who needed access to the system in a central place. Not far behind came the governmental and Church organizations, established to administer the vast viceroyalty. Finally, once population, commerce, and administration reached a critical mass, major cultural institutions, such as a university (1551), printing press (1583), and theater followed suit.

By the end of the century, Lima was already noted for the great volume of its trade and business, as well as the extravagant consumption patterns of its elites. In 1610, its population had grown to 25,000 and was estimated to consume annually some 240,000 *fanegas* of wheat, 25,000 of maize, 3,500 head of cattle, 400 sheep, 6.9 tons of rice, and 200,000 bottles of wine. One contemporary observer, Bernabé Cobo, noted in 1653 that in the city, there were over 200 luxurious carriages, trimmed in silk and gold, worth 3,000 pesos or more each. Furthermore, he calculated that the total worth of the city's stock of jewels and precious metals, excluding finery, tapestries, and articles of worship, amounted to 20 million ducats, with another 12 million ducats invested in the large slave population. Conspicuous consumption pervaded all classes to the extent that it was difficult to distinguish the various social strata by dress alone. Madrid merchants, limited by sumptuary laws in Spain, found a booming market in the sale of silks, brocades, and fine linens in Lima. Yet Cobo's account suggests that as much of this wealth derived from the salaries of ecclesiastics, bureaucrats, and the military—in other words, from the city's administrative and bureaucratic functions—as from its extensive trade, commerce, and production.

The accumulation of wealth in Lima also made possible the development of an active cultural life, much of which reinforced imperial policies of the crown's command and control of colonial society. For one thing, an important courtly life revolved around the viceroy and his administration in which jurists; clergymen; and low-level intellectuals, poets, and plastic artists intermingled in the city with the rising number of lettered mestizo and Indian teachers and musicians, sculptors, and painters. San Marcos University, modeled after its counterpart at Salamanca in Spain, became an important venue for the sons of colonists to receive the necessary education to become eligible for positions in the high bureaucracy. By 1570, it had sixteen academic chairs, including one in Quechua (replaced by mathematics in 1678), and offered courses of study in the arts, theology, medicine, civil law, and cannon law. Access to the university, however, was limited to male Spaniards and creoles, while the *castas* and women were excluded.

The founding of the Jesuit College some time later in Cuzco, was similarly important for the education of the sons of the Inca nobility whom the crown had co-opted and drawn into its imperial colonial project. The assumption was that once assimilated into Spanish ways, these Indian leaders not only would become loyal vassals of the crown, but would impart their knowledge to their communities and ethnic groups among their people. Once operative, these schools began turning out graduates who were fluent in Spanish with an education equivalent to regular university graduates.

School and university life, as well as the cultural life of the colonies, was also enhanced by the arrival of the printing press in Lima in 1583, although at first, it printed mainly preaching manuals and catechisms for missionary work. Books, however, had been imported from the outset, and despite state controls, a surprising number of titles appeared early in the libraries of leading citizens and the religious orders. Even with the establishment of the Inquisition in Lima in 1569, a variety of books continued to find their way into the viceroyalty through such illicit means as smuggling.

Public ceremonies, including lengthy parades and other public events, also became a hallmark of the cultural life of the viceregal capital (and other cities). They occurred at regular intervals during the year, related to either important religious holidays; the departure of the silver fleet; or the arrival of a new viceroy, bishop, or other high-ranking official. "The objective was to construct for the subjects of Colonial America a visible sense of the power of the metropolitan center which, from a great distance, ruled their lives" (Castro-Klarén, "Lima," in Valdés, 2000). In this sense, these public ceremonies were also an extremely effective means of mass communication that were designed to convey and thereby perpetuate to the plebian sectors of colonial society the power and glory of the crown.

Transition from a Mining to a Diversified Economy

Silver mining continued to form the axis of the viceregal economy during the first half of the seventeenth century. While Potosí continued to be far and away the top producer in the viceroyalty, other silver lodes were opened up at Castrovireyna, Cailloma, Chachapoyas, Pasco, and Oruro, to name a few. The combined total production of all these mines far exceeded that of New Spain until late in the century. Nevertheless, production declined steadily as the century progressed. At Potosí the decline in output was precipitous, falling in value from a little over 7 million pesos in 1600 to almost 4.5 million pesos in 1650, and finally to just under 2 million pesos in 1700. Production at the other mines dropped as well, but not quite as sharply.

The causes of the decline in silver production varied. Some were structural, such as flooding that was due to deeper shafts, increased costs for mercury in the refining process, and a decline in the quality of ore. Others may be attributed to the mismanagement of mercury shipments, higher taxes, a growing shortage of *mita* labor, and periodic lawlessness at isolated mine heads. All these problems contributed to rising costs and falling output. Similar problems hobbled the output of mercury at Huancavelica, whose production also declined from a high of over 13,000 quintales in 1582 to a low of 2,000 quintales in 1689.

Silver from the mines continued to be shipped overland to the Pacific port of Arica, where it was loaded onto ships for the ten-day trip to Callao. To control silver exports, Lima had been designated the official administrative center for all imperial trade in South America. From Callao, the silver was picked up in late May by the Royal South Seas Fleet, which transported it by armed convoy to Panama where it was unloaded and packed on mules for the overland trip to Portobello on the Atlantic. In Portobello, the Silver

Cadden mule train rendezvoused with the Atlantic treasure fleet, which unloaded European manufactured goods at the annual Portobello fair on the Colombian coast and took on Peruvian silver for transshipment to Spain. Merchants from Lima then purchased these goods at the fair in exchange for silver specie for distribution and resale throughout the viceroyalty. Since the crown required that all imports and exports be channeled through Lima, the city's merchants acquired a virtual monopoly on all legal commerce and trade in the colony.

With the fall of silver production in the viceroyalty, particularly after 1640, Lima and its merchants also began to experience a decline. Other factors worked to weaken the viceregal capital's economy and loosen its monopolistic grip on colonial commerce. Foreign interlopers increasingly attacked Spanish shipping in the Pacific, driving up costs while the price of goods from Spain purchased by Lima merchants also rose. The latter was a consequence partly of the inflation caused by the large amounts of American silver pouring into the metropolis and partly of the decline of Spanish manufacturing, which forced merchants in Seville to purchase European manufactures. To extract high profits, Lima merchants themselves tried to restrict the supply of goods into the viceroyalty so as to keep prices and margins artificially high. But higher prices and declining silver output sharply reduced the volume of the transatlantic trade; the number of sailings between Panama and Lima fell by fully one-third in the second half of the seventeenth century.

Falling silver production, the faltering transatlantic trade, and the overall decline of Spain itself during the seventeenth century have long been interpreted by historians as causing prolonged depression in the viceroyalties of both Peru and New Spain. For example, in the case of Peru, John TePaske and Herbert Klein showed that revenues flowing into the royal treasury of Lima dropped precipitously in the second half of the century. They concluded from these data that Peru fell into a deep, century-long depression between 1650 and 1750, never really regaining its former grandeur and increasingly becoming overshadowed by Mexico.

Andrien, however, challenged this view. He argued that falling silver production and the declining transatlantic trade did, indeed, disrupt the Peruvian economy and caused a dramatic fall in royal revenues. However, he saw no evidence of a sustained depression or malaise in the viceroyalty as a result of these trends. Rather, he maintained that the Peruvian economy underwent a restructuring toward internal reinvestment, diversification, and more self-sufficient production. Merchants, miners, and producers simply shifted their entrepreneurial activities away from the transatlantic trade and into production for local markets, a phenomenon already visible on a smaller scale by the end of the sixteenth century. The result was a surprising degree of regional diversification that stabilized the viceregal economy and insulated it from the fall in silver output during the seventeenth century. In short, the seventeenth century was marked by a transition from an externally oriented mining economy to an internally more diverse but relatively stable and self-sufficient economy.

The market for such internal production and import substitution continued to be the growing urban centers that became the focus of increasingly vibrant regional economies. These regional economies included not only the Rimac and neighboring valleys of Lima, whose population more than tripled between 1610 and 1680 from 25,000 to 80,000, but places like Zaña, north of the coastal city of Trujillo; Cuzco in the southern highlands; and Cochabamba in Upper Peru, not to mention the more distant outposts of Quito, Guayaquil, and Santiago. They drew on the viceroyalty's rich natural resources and varied climatic zones. According to one contemporary observer who wrote at the beginning of the seventeenth century "all Peru lacks is silk and linens, for they have a surplus of everything else, and do not have the need to beg nor wait for any other kingdom or province in the world" (quoted in Andrien, 1985, p. 18).

As the mines diminished in importance, Peru's rural economy picked up. Along the coast, the Indian population collapsed from 900,000 in 1530 to under 75,000 in 1630, opening up the fertile bottom lands of the river valleys to Spanish immigrants who were eager for land and farming opportunities. The subsequent Europeanization of the coast in terms of population and production was notable and became an enduring feature of Peruvian society. A variety of European crops were raised: sugar and cotton along the north coast; wheat and grains in the central valleys; and grapes, olives, and sugar along the southern coast. Fruits, vegetables, and livestock were also produced in abundance throughout the entire coastal region.

In the highlands, both Spanish and Indian farmers raised a wide array of crops and livestock, depending on the climate and soils. In Arequipa in the south, they raised grapes, sugar, cereals, olives, and peppers. Elsewhere cotton was grown in Huánuco, Cajamarca, and Chachapoyas; tobacco in Cuzco; coca and other indigenous crops in Huánuco, Huamanga, Cuzco, and La Paz, among others; and potatoes and cereals throughout the sierra. The arid *altiplano*, or high plains, less conducive for agriculture, emphasized grazing and livestock production. The mining centers and highland and coastal cities continued to provide a steady demand for both agricultural and livestock production.

More outlying regions, as you have seen, were also linked to the urban markets of Peru. Chile produced olives, grapes, cereals, and livestock and exported the surplus to Peru. Throughout the grazing areas of the Rio de la Plata, meat, skins, wool, and mules were shipped to Peru, along with wine from Mendoza and wheat, corn, and barley from Tucumán and other areas. Even distant Paraguay chipped in with yerba mate tea to Potosí. To the north, Quito produced cereals, coca, potatoes, cotton, sugar, wool, and pack animals, while Guayaquil grew cochineal and cacao.

Land-tenure patterns in these regions were as varied as their production. They usually depended on local conditions and numerous other factors, including consumer demand, the distance and strength of markets, availability of investment capital, climate, and fertility of the land. Small estates, or *chacras*, developed near cities with high demand and prices and supplied a variety of foodstuffs in what today might be called truck farming. For example, small holdings producing wheat and other produce for Potosí predominated in the Cochabamba valley. Cuzco, too, was surrounded by *chacras*, while larger haciendas dotted the Camino Real, the road to Potosí and Lima. Around Arequipa, as both Kendell Brown and Keith Davies have shown, grape-producing *chacras* produced a profitable wine and brandy industry, with sales to Cuzco, the silver mines of Upper Peru, and Lima. After 1650, however, Arequipa declined because of rising competition from Ica, Nazca, and Pisco, which captured the Lima wine and brandy market and made inroads in Upper Peru.

The archetypical landed estate that emerged to meet the demands of urban markets in the late sixteenth and seventeenth centuries was the manorial hacienda. These haciendas were larger than *chacras*, but still relatively modest in size and should not be compared to the great estates that emerged later in the eighteenth century. They relied on a moderate number of servile Indian workers and produced agricultural staples and meat for variously sized, often fluctuating, urban markets. In 1689 Cuzco had some 705 such haciendas, worked on average by fifteen to twenty Indian laborers, with 15 percent owned by women, often widows, and 7 percent owned by the Church or religious orders. Since they were largely diverse, self-sufficient units, these haciendas could adapt easily to changing demand, expanding or contracting their production according to market conditions.

Large plantations also existed in Peru, mainly along the north coast. They were more capitalized landed estates, worked by African slave labor and Amerindian migrants and specializing in high-demand cash commodities, such as sugar and cacao, for urban as well as export markets. The sugar plantations of Lambayeque, north of the city of Trujillo, were the most lucrative Peruvian plantations. Smaller than their Brazilian or Caribbean counterparts, they produced mainly for regional, rather than distant European, markets. Ramirez's careful study of these estates showed that the Lambayeque plantations comprised 100 to 200 acres, employed under fifty slaves and migrant Amerindians, sent most of their production to the Lima market, and flourished between 1650 and 1720.

Another type of landholding was the ranch type *estancia*, a low-capital and labor-intensive enterprise that developed throughout the viceroyalty. In the northern sierra, for example, numerous sheep ranches were carved out of Indian lands and employed Indian laborers. *Estancias* arose, too, in the cold, arid altiplano of Puno in the south, although Indian communities that raised llamas and sheep tended to predominate in that region.

Labor in the agrarian sector was negatively effected by the sharp decline in the Indian population during the sixteenth century and its slow recovery in the seventeenth. Although the shortage of Indian labor was a potential problem for landowners, the increasing willingness of Indians to leave their communities and move from place to place compensated for it. Toledo's concentration (*reducción*) plan of the 1570s had largely failed. The *reducciones* were designed to improve the administration of the native population (Christianization, collection of the tribute, and organization of the *mita*), but were generally poorly located, often on marginal lands, and suffered from a steady loss of population owing to the periodic epidemics that swept across the Andes. For these reasons and to evade the *mita* and tribute, many Indians left the *reducciones* and drifted back to their former homes, went to other communities, or sought work in the Hispanic sector (mines, towns, and estates) for wages that were rising in response to the labor shortage. Wightman estimated that these Indians, known as *forasteros*, represented over half the population of the bishopric of Cuzco by the 1690s, up from around one-third in 1645.

Those who settled on estates became the basis of a perminant labor force, known as *yanaconas*, who received wages and/or usufructs of parcels of land from which they supported their families, while others obtained employment and settled outside the Spanish towns in nearby native residential "anexes." In either case, they sought to abandon the status of "natives," subject to the tribute and *mita*, by transfering to the status of *yanacona* or mestizo. This situation seems to suggest a process of the rupture of the Andean communal order and dissolution of ethnic identities as natives took "flight" from the *reducciones* or their original communities of origin. According to this line of thought, *forasteros* gradually fell into a larger generic category of "Indian," an identity imposed on them by the dominant Spanish order, thus increasingly becoming symbols of dependence and colonial exploitation.

In his work on the southern Andes, Thierry Saignes however, saw a much more complex process of "rupture," followed by "recomposition," in which the migrants succeeded in forging links and establishing an ethnic identity with their new communities or actually retaining ties, through periodic remigrations to their old communities. In the case of the former, migrants entered native residential anexes, located outside the towns where they worked, and through traditional mechanisms, such as *cabildos*, *cofradías*, and *compadrazgo*, they acquired civic and religious responsiblities that legitimated their incorporation into their new places of residence. Likewise, when *forasteros* entered communities, they gained acceptance and integration, legitimacy and identity by hiring out their labor to wealthy Indians, marrying local women, developing kinship ties, and acquiring responsiblities through the festive duties of the *cargo* system.

As for retaining ties with their native communities after they became *forasteros*, Siaignes showed that the Indians followed migratory routes that sometimes circled back to their original communities, only to be sent off by the local cacique to become colonists in a new verticle archipelego, but they still retained their ethnic identities to their old *ayllus*. In the end, what Saignes described was a fluid and intricate process in which native Andeans improvised economic and political stragegies that enable them to offset the pressures of tribute, *mita*, and population decline and to forge new or retain old ethnic identities.

The marketing of Peruvian agricultural products, most of which tended to be large and bulky, was severely hindered by the enormous difficulties of transport and communication in the Andes. Certain products, like sugar and wine, however, were high in value and relatively low in bulk and so found profitable markets in distant places. On the other hand, mining markets tended to be notoriously volatile because of their boom–bust productive cycles, causing the production and profits of surrounding haciendas to fluctuate widely. The major means of communication in the Andes was by mule trains that employed large numbers of mule skinners, or *arrieros*, throughout the viceroyalty, who worked with mules imported from the Andean foothills of northern Argentina.

The seventeenth century also saw the development of manufacturing in the colony, although not nearly to the extent of agrarian enterprises. Textile manufacturing, particularly after the recession of 1620 in Europe slowed the importation of European textiles, flourished to meet popular demand for rough-hewn cotton and woolen garments, as well as blankets, hats, sandals, and ship rigging. The largest *obrajes* were located in the provinces of Quito, Conchucos, Cajamarca, and Cuzco and could employ as many as 400 workers. Owners were sometimes ranchers who could also supply their own raw materials to their factories. Quito was particularly renowned for its public and private *obrajes*, which more than doubled from 55 in 1620 to 117 in 1690. At the peak of the "industry" at the end of the century, they employed over 10,000 workers who produced 1 million to 2 million pesos worth of cloth for sale in Lima and New Granada.

Another important industry that developed in the viceroyalty in the seventeenth century was, as Larry Clayton found, shipbuilding. The industry was stimulated by the western coast's isolation from shipyards in Havana and Europe and the demand for ships to defend the silver fleets moving between Lima and Panama, as well as for the growing intercolonial trade in the Pacific. Guayaquil was particularly well positioned to develop such an industry. It received sufficient wood from interior forests, cloth for sails from highland *obrajes*, rope and fittings from Chile, and pitch and tar from Nicaragua. With these inputs, its shipyards could keep costs well below those in Europe and produce three to four ships a year for the navy and merchant marine.

As in textile manufacturing and shipbuilding, local capital also sustained a vibrant wine industry in Arequipa and along the southern coast. Early attempts by Philip II (1556–98) to proscribe the industry so it would not compete with Spain were soon abandoned as impractical, and Peru became a producer of high-quality wines and brandy. The crown was content to tax the industry that supplied the urban markets of the viceroyalty and exported significant amounts to Chile and Mexico.

Finally, a large number of small-scale artisan industries flourished throughout the viceroyalty, supplying the lower-cost goods that were only sporadically available from Europe during the seventeenth-century depression. These goods included leather goods, glass, arms, furniture, wood products, and work tools whose production in the cities, towns, and estates employed a significant number of Spanish, Amerindian, mestizo, and black craftsmen.

Despite the regionalization of the Peruvian economy during the seventeenth century, Lima remained the commercial hub of the viceroyalty, even if at a slower pace than the previous century. The city's merchants were active in both the Atlantic and developing Pacific trade, receiving many of the goods imported or produced elsewhere in Peru and distributing them throughout the viceroyalty. Clayton pointed out that over sixty merchants had assets of over 100,000 pesos, and several had assets of from 500,000 to 1 million pesos. Organized into a powerful guild, these merchants exercised considerable economic and political power in the viceroyalty that diminished only partially with rising commercial competition late in the century from Buenos Aires and Santiago.

Lima merchants, along with the entire viceregal economy, suffered a major blow, however, with the devastating earthquake that struck the central coast of Peru in 1687. Food production and distribution were severely disrupted along the coast, and the authorities in Lima were forced to control the sale and distribution of bread to forestall hoarding and starvation. Outbreaks of disease followed, causing Amerindians in particular to flee the city, whose population dropped by half within five years, from 80,000 to 40,000.

Agricultural production sagged from, among other things, damage to irrigation works along the arid coastal region. Food imports from the highlands were insufficient to prevent prices in Lima from soaring. Wheat prices, for example, rose from 2 to 4 pesos per bushel to over 20 or 30. As a consequence, merchants began to import large quantities of Chilean wheat, stimulating production in the central valley and enabling Chile to take over as the main supplier for the entire viceroyalty. This change dealt a major blow to Peruvian landowners along the coast who were never able to regain their dominant share of the market.

Another peripheral area of the viceroyalty to gain at Lima's expense during the seventeenth century was Buenos Aires. The development of Buenos Aires had been constrained by the fact that the Straits of Magellan were closed to prevent European access to the Pacific, so that the crown could retain tight control over the export of silver through Lima and Panama. Buenos Aires could import only what was necessary to sustain the colonies in the Rio de la Plata. However, despite these constraints, the city at the mouth of the River Plate had become a major center for contraband trade in the late sixteenth century and saw its population soar from only 1,000 in 1615 to over 7,000 by 1700. Using its strategic location on the Atlantic, Buenos Aires became a conduit for illegal European imports that were destined for the mining markets of Upper Peru in exchange for Peruvian silver, estimated in 1620 at 100,000 pesos. It continued to make inroads into this market after the 1687 earthquake, further eroding Lima's formerly predominant position in this trade.

By the end of the seventeenth century, Lima was in decline. According to Andrien, "the recession in the Atlantic trade, the fall in mining output, the growth of competing regional economic centers and the earthquake of 1687 all worked to undermine the power and influence of the viceregal capital" (1985, p. 28). At the same time, the regional economies of Peru continued to grow more diverse, autonomous, and stable. Andrien attributed the diversification to several specific factors. The first factor was the growth of the European population. Although estimates are risky, by 1650 almost a quarter of a million people seem to have left Europe to settle in the viceroyalty. Much of this population was concentrated in Potosí, whose population peaked in 1650 at around 160,000, and Lima, which may have reached 80,000 at the time of the 1687 earthquake. The second factor was the native population that had become increasingly integrated into the European sector of the economy by the turn of the century. Indeed, the thrust of the Toledan reforms had been to force the Andean population to participate both as producers and consumers in the developing colonial economy.

A third factor was the increasing number of black slaves who were imported from West Africa to work on the sugar, wheat, and grape-producing estates along the coast. Blacks increased from 3,000 in 1550 to over 60,000 by 1650, stemming the labor shortage caused by the demographic collapse of the native population along the coast and adding to the popular consumer market for goods produced in the viceroyalty.

The fourth factor was the availability of investment capital. Much of this capital came from the Church, whose accumulation was, in part, lent as rural credit to estate owners to finance expanded production at 5 percent interest. Moreover, some clerical institutions, like the Society of Jesus, as Cushner's work has shown, invested heavily in agricultural enterprises. The Jesuits ran successful wine, sugar, livestock, yerba mate, wheat, and even textile enterprises, with returns on investments in some cases (sugar) as high as 10 percent. Most sources of credit in the colony, however, came from merchant banking houses, which took greater risks than their more conservative counterparts, but charged higher interest rates on their loans. Although popular among borrowers despite such rates, these banks often had a precarious existence, with many failures and a high rate of turnover.

A final stimulus to internal economic expansion and diversification during the seventeenth century came from governmental spending. Even though governmental receipts fell during the second half of the century as a consequence of the slowdown in mining output and the transatlantic trade (from taxes), a greater proportion of this revenue, as Andrien and others have shown, remained in the viceroyalty, rather than being remitted to

Spain. Although only 36 percent of the revenue collected by the viceregal treasury remained in Peru in the late sixteenth century, this figure rose to 95 percent at the end of the seventeenth century.

The main reason for this dramatic turnaround was defense. Beyond Iberia, European interest in the kingdom of Peru, like the Spaniards', was kindled by reports, both real and exaggerated, of the fabulous wealth that had been discovered there in the sixteenth century. The news was made more concrete when the English adventurer Francis Drake seized 447,000 pesos off the coast of Peru during his voyage of global circumnavigation from 1557 to 1560. Inspired by potential trade and plunder, as well as religious and political antagonisms toward Catholic Spain, foreign interlopers sailed around the tip of South America through the Straits of Magellan and began operating with some frequency during the seventeenth century in the South Sea, as the west coast of the Pacific was called. The English were soon joined by the Dutch, most notably Joris van Speilbergen, who managed to defeat the Peruvian fleet off Cañete in 1617, and Jacques l'Hermite at the head of the Nassau fleet, who managed to blockade Callao for a time in the 1620s.

During the course of the seventeenth century, these and other foreign expeditions managed to disrupt and delay the departure of the silver fleet from Callao and forced the viceregal authorities to take extensive defensive measures. These measures included a sharp increase in funding for arms, shipbuilding, metal foundries, and supplies for new and existing garrisons. Accordingly, the percentage of the Lima treasury's spending on defense rose from 16.5 percent in 1610 to 25 percent in 1650 to 43 percent in 1680, while the remittances to Spain fell from 51 percent to 35 percent to 5 percent for the corresponding years. Most of these expenditures were spent locally on defense-related production and manufacturing, giving a further stimulus to internal development.

If local capital, both private and public, provided a major boost for economic development in the viceroyalty during the seventeenth century, the Atlantic trade, although diminishing, still accounted for a significant amount of the colony's commercial life. One indication of the continuing importance of the trans-Atlantic trade and its tax receipts is that the Lima treasury remitted over 100,000,000 pesos to Spain during the course of the century. Moreover, whatever slack occurred in the transatlantic trade was picked up by the expansion of intracolonial trade in the Pacific, which became increasingly attractive to colonial merchants. Some idea of the scope and range of this trade was provided by Andrien:

> Merchants from Guayaquil sent tropical woods, charcoal, cacao, and cloth to markets in Lima, Central America, and Mexico. Producers in central and southern Peru shipped wine, brandy, sugar, olive oil, wheat, textiles, and silver to Pacific ports from Chile to Acapulco. Soap, sugar, textiles, cotton and tobacco were sent from Quito and northern Peru to markets in Lima and New Granada. Finally, Chile sent wine, wheat, meats, salt, tallow, and

commodities from the Rio de la Plata, such as hides and yerba mate, to Lima (1985, p. 35).

A particularly vibrant trade also developed between Peru and New Spain during the century. Lima merchants sent silver, mercury, wine, and cacao north in exchange for textiles, clothing, jewelry, leather goods, books, and even luxury goods from the orient. Indeed, the latter sometimes amounted to 90 percent of the trade and involved the famous Manila galleons which linked the far east with the port of Acapulco in New Spain. These galleons sent large quantities of American silver east in exchange for silks, porcelains, musk, tapestries, pepper, ivory, jade, damask and other luxuries. Peruvian demand for these luxury items, in fact, eventually came to exceed the carrying capacity of the Manila galleons, so that Peruvian traders inaugurated direct trade between West Coast ports and the Orient.

In macro-economic terms Chinese demand for American silver served to bolster prices in Peru and Mexico and to finance viceregal government and the slave trade. China absorbed about half of the global production of silver, the bulk of it from American mines. In exchange, Peruvian and Mexican silver miners and Manila galleon traders and merchants received the large supply of luxury goods from the Orient, earning large profits. They, in turn, made loans to the royal government for administrative costs and to slave traders who financed their purchases of African slaves for the coastal plantations and elsewhere.

The crown tried, unsuccessfully, to stop the drain of silver to the Orient by placing numerous restrictions on this trade. The trade was so lucrative to American merchants, however, that such restrictions merely increased the level of contraband. One contemporary estimate in 1638 for Lima alone put the value of the oriental contraband trade at 2,000,000 pesos a year. And the oriental contraband trade was only one part of the generalized problem of illegal trade throughout the empire. For example, in 1686 only one-third of the total intracolonial trade was estimated as being within the law, that is, duly registered and taxed by the authorities. By the 1690s, Lima officials were complaining bitterly of the high level of illegal commerce being conducted between Buenos Aires and Potosí. Ironically, even members of the Lima Consulado were implicated in such illicit trade.

To sum up, then, the seventeenth century saw a shift away from the silver mining enclave of the sixteenth century to a more diversified and self-sufficient regional economy. According to Andrien, "the retention of more mineral wealth in the colony, the growth of the Spanish population, the closer integration of the European and Amerindian economies, larger investments by clerical and merchant groups in local enterprises, the development of credit facilities, and the Pacific trade all stimulated the aggregate demand for locally produced goods" (1985, p. 39). Far from entering a period of depression or even an "autonomy of stagnation," as one historian put it, the seventeenth-century Peruvian economy was characterized by regional diversity and overall stability, with no evidence of a sustained downturn or malaise. This does not mean, of course, that the economic cycle was devoid of regional ups and downs.

Royal Government, Fiscal Crisis, and Decline

While the economy of the Peruvian viceroyalty underwent a substantial restructuring during the seventeenth century leading to greater diversification and overall stability, rather than decline, the fiscal condition of the viceregal government severely deteriorated. Geared to receiving revenues from the collection of taxes on silver mining and the transatlantic trade, the colonial treasury in Lima needed to alter its tax structure and find new sources of revenues if it was going to maintain the level of its expenditures and remittances to Spain. To do so, it had to increase taxes on sectors of a now more diversified and regionalized economy, no easy task given the inherent opposition of local creole elites to the imposition of new levies on their operations.

In statistical terms, the problem was that 70 percent of royal revenues came mainly from the silver-mining centers while various port taxes and sales taxes that were collected in Lima-Callao were dependent on the flow of silver through the capital. As the silver output declined and royal revenues fell, the crown resorted to increased borrowing, withheld funds normally sent to Spain, and imposed new taxes, without trying to offset the shortfall by reducing spending. These essentially stopgap measures managed to sustain treasury revenues until the 1660s. However, the royal bureaucracy made no attempt to impose new levies during this period on the various colonial elites, such as the clergy, landowners, and merchants. So when revenues fell off sharply after 1660, they came at a time when the mother country had entered a protracted financial crisis in the face of severe challenges to its continuing political position in Europe.

Andrien did not attribute the problem of colonial revenues to the economy, which, he maintained, did not experience depression during the century. Rather, he blamed institutional and administrative failures on the part of the royal government and bureaucracy. "Somehow the institutions of the viceregal government and the men who staffed them," he wrote, "failed their sovereign by sacrificing the needs of the metropolis and the solvency of the colonial government itself during the imperial crisis of the seventeenth century" (1985, p. 75). Much of the problem derived from the structure of the colonial government and the way it was designed to function ever since its establishment in the sixteenth century.

Because the Indies were regarded as the possession of the Kingdom of Castile, Peru had been governed in accordance with the laws and institutions of Castile. This meant that the major body responsible for policy on the Viceroyalty of Peru was the Council of the Indies, one of several councils established in Castile to govern the realm. The king and his principal ministers, therefore, established policy on Peru after consulting with the Council of the Indies.

Given the vast distance between Madrid and Lima, as well as the broad geographic expanses and difficult terrain of the viceroyalty itself, the crown attempted to retain control over such a far-flung domain and its administrative officials by means of "pen, ink and paper," as the eminent historian of Spain and America John Elliott put it; that is, Madrid erected a bureaucratic system in Peru and America by trying to legislate and thereby regulate virtually every aspect of colonial life. This gave rise in the course of time to an enormous corpus of some 3,500 laws and provisions related to the Indies that were compiled and finally published in four volumes as *Recopilación de las Leyes de Indias* in 1681. The upshot of such a deeply legalistic system was the thorough bureaucratization and routinization of the colonial government in Peru.

While "pen and ink" worked to "chain" Peru's royal officials to Madrid, the diffusion of authority became another essential mechanism of the royal government in the viceroyalty. Madrid had a virtual phobia for the concentration of power in the public sector and therefore elaborated a bureaucratic system that was replete with extensive checks and balances, overlapping jurisdictions, and generally ambiguous lines of authority throughout its colonial administrative hierarchy. This diffusion of authority resulted, on the one hand, in endless frictions and conflicts among royal officials that sapped the efficiency of the system. On the other hand, it ensured a maximum amount of control from Madrid, which could effectively play one official off against another and act as the ultimate arbitrator in all such disputes. At the same time, it allowed a considerable amount of space for royal officials to maneuver and exploit the weaknesses of a system in which power was so widely dispersed. In the end, the structure and function of the royal government in Peru sacrificed administrative efficiency for metropolitan control. Judged by the extraordinarily long period of relatively stable colonial rule in Peru after the civil wars of the 1540s, such a bureaucratic system, at least from the perspective of the metropolis, was more of a success than a failure.

The main administrative unit in this system was the viceroyalty. The first viceroyality was established in New Spain with its capital in Mexico City in 1535, to be followed shortly thereafter by Peru and its capital Lima in 1543. In 1543, the first viceroy, Blasco Núñez de Vela, arrived in Lima to take up his administrative duties as the chief administrative officer of the new kingdom. Colonial viceroys were generally drawn from the ranks of Spain's nobility and were appointed to renewable six-year terms. Of the twenty-five viceroys who were appointed to New Spain between 1535 and 1700, nine moved on to become viceroys in Peru. The viceroy exercised both executive and judicial functions, since he also served as the president of the *audiencia*, or main judicial court.

At first glance, as the king's alter ego in Peru, the viceroy appeared to be an extremely powerful official, indeed, and, in many respects, he was. But like other major royal officials in the New World, he was constricted by the vast number of laws and decrees that poured forth from the distant Council of the Indies in its effort to micromanage and thereby control the colony. It is true that some flexibility for initiative and maneuver was afforded the viceroy through the "obedezco pero no cumplo" (I obey but do not carry out) rule that enabled crown officials to delay the implementation of decrees that seemed clearly to run counter to the real situation or conditions prevailing in the colony. Still, even the viceroy's hands were usually tied by the extensive and often minute instructions he received from Madrid. Then, too, the viceroy and other crown officials were subject to thorough investigations of their administration. These investigations were done either through periodic *visitas* that were conducted by independent judges on specific matters or *residencias* that were carried out at the end of terms. Both devices enabled aggrieved parties to bring charges against royal officials. One such *visita* of a viceroy in Peru generated a mammoth report of almost 50,000 pages.

Another major check on viceregal power was exercised by the *audiencia*, the second most important branch of royal government in America. Six *audiencias* were established in the viceroyalty of Peru during the sixteenth century: Panama (1538), Lima (1543) Santa Fe de Bogotá (1548), Charcas (1559), Quito (1563), and Chile (1563). Each was composed of *oidores*, or judges, who, in addition to their judicial and investigative functions, oversaw the observance of royal laws and administered the viceroyalty between viceregal appointments.

There were numerous other royal offices that stood between the viceroy and *audiencia* judges and the local *cabildo*, or town council. Outlying or frontier jurisdictions, for example, were subject to the rule of governors and captains general with special military functions. The all-important matter of tax collection was organized by an army of treasury officials with main offices (*cajas reales*) in key economic centers. A further important administrative subdivision within the viceroyalty was the *corregimiento*, which was based on an area surrounding a city or town and ruled by a *corregidor* who was appointed by either the crown or the viceroy, depending on its importance.

At the very base of government in Peru, and perhaps its fundamental point of contact with the citizenry, was the city or town, with its ruling municipal council, or *cabildo*. Despite its largely rural character and the rise to importance of the hacienda, or great estate, Hispanic Peru, like most Mediterranean societies, was organized and revolved around urban centers. Even on the outlying estates, the lord was considered a *vecino*, or citizen, of the nearest town and more often than not maintained a residence there. The jurisdiction of the town, in fact, extended well into the surrounding country-side.

Each town was governed by a *cabildo*, composed of the *corregidor*; several *alcaldes*, or lay judicial officials who attended to legal matters; and *regidores*, or town councilors who administered town affairs. The duties of the *cabildo* included levying local taxes and controling the supply and price of wheat and meat and the allotment of building lots. By virtue of their appointive nature or, in the case of elections, restrictive eligibility requirements based on property, the *cabildos* came to be dominated by and instruments of local, creole oligarchies composed of wealthy merchants, miners, and landowners. As such and as the only local institution with channels to the hierarchy of crown officials reaching all the way to the Council of the Indies in Madrid, the *cabildo* was not only the main instrument of local self-government, but a focal point for local family rivalries in the struggle over local resources and power.

The nature of this governmental system, with its diffuse, decentralized, and patrimonial characteristics, was relatively well suited for the purposes of extending royal authority to Peru during the sixteenth century. During this time, the crown was particularly concerned with proscribing the power of the conquistadors and taxing the principal sources of wealth—mining and the transatlantic trade. Power was dispersed and limited, divided among the king; his principal advisory councils; the viceroy, or king's representative in Peru; and the *audiencias* and further subdivided among the various other functionaries who administered the system down to the local level.

The seventeenth-century fiscal crisis, however, demanded a different, more modern, and efficient administrative system, capable of concentrating power and lines of authority to carry out successfully a major shift of the tax burden to recalcitrant local elites. In this endeavor, it would also need a disciplined, meritorious, and professional bureaucracy that would uphold the interests of Madrid and not be undermined or corrupted by local interests. In Weberian terms, this meant the creation of a modern, rational-legal bureaucratic authority, something the crown was only partially able to achieve in the course of the seventeenth century.

To some extent, Madrid had succeeded in creating a professional corps of governmental officials to staff its empire in the sixteenth century. Francisco de Toledo, the dedicated, loyal, and skilled viceroy of Peru from 1569 to 1581, was, in many ways, the embodiment of such a corps and testimony to Madrid's success. However, faced with the pervasive decline in colonial revenues as the seventeenth century unfolded, as well as impending bankruptcy at home and military defeat in Europe, the crown made a fateful and ultimately disastrous decision in 1633. Desperate to raise more revenue throughout the empire, Philip IV's chief minister, the Conde Duque de Olivares, decided, despite serious reservations, to sell many imperial offices in the New World, including all high-ranking treasury appointments.

In hindsight the results were predictable. When offices were sold to the highest bidders, often to compromised, local, wealthy creoles, the quality of office holding in the viceroyalty quickly eroded. Inexperienced, corrupt, and inefficient officials, firmly tied to local interests, succeeded in gaining control of many important offices, including the central treasury office in Lima. Even though substantial revenues were derived from the sale of such offices in the short run, over the longer term, effective administration and decision making were severely compromised in the face of powerful local groups and interests. Viceregal authority sagged badly. Moreover, seen from a modern perspective, the sale of offices in the colonial period may also explain the low level of public morality among civil servants today. The practice doubtless weakened any notion of disinterested public service and infused into the political culture the corrosive idea that office holding was an opportunity for selfish, private gain, rather than for the general public good.

The immediate consequences of the sale of public offices in Peru were severe. First and foremost, the quality of administration declined. Whereas heretofore the viceregal bureaucracy had been staffed almost exclusively by experienced and arguably competent peninsulars, a significant number of creoles, with little training, now took possession of many offices. In one instance, in 1641 a wealthy creole purchased an appointment in the Lima treasury for his fifteen-year-old son who would assume the office at age twenty-five. In such circumstances, standards for promotion were severely disrupted, and the morale among career civil servants plummeted.

As for the treasury and the crucial problem of falling revenues during the second half of the seventeenth century, the sale of offices proved particularly damaging to Madrid. Concerted efforts were made by the crown to broaden the tax base to maintain revenues, but to no avail. Groups allied with local, creole elites and vested interests were able to buy key offices and block any attempts at tax reform, as well as to gain increasing influence over imperial administration. As a result, revenue remittances to Spain dropped precipitously, contributing to the country's military and political decline. Moreover, influence peddling and corruption became pervasive, while the influence and authority of the viceroy waned.

Finally, if the quality and effectiveness of royal government in Lima declined, the primacy of the City of Kings in the viceregal economy was also severely undermined. The financial and political decline of the capital, the diminishing productivity of the mines, the recession in the transatlantic trade, the diversification of the colonial economy and the disastrous consequences of the 1687 earthquake all worked, as I discussed earlier, to undermine the viceregal capital and its elites by the end of the seventeenth century. The city and its place in the viceroyalty was replaced by what Andrien called "a more cantonal viceroyalty . . . made up of regions less dependent on either Lima or Madrid" (1985, p. 206).

While the royal government generally weakened in the seventeenth century, its other arm in governing Peru, the Church, was consolidating its formidable position in colonial society, mainly because the Church continued to accumulate money and property at a steady rate. Settlers' bequests flowed into particular religious houses to be used as chantries to say mass for the departed, as dowries for unmarried daughters, or as other endowments. Money acquired in this fashion was usually lent as credit, or *censos*, while property might be worked directly or leased to renters. In this way, the Church as an institution became a formidable financial and economic power in Peru, although not to the same degree as in New Spain.

Of particular interest because of their business prowess were the Jesuits who, as Macera and Cushner showed, astutely acquired estates and managed them in a productive and entrepreneurial fashion. At the time of their expulsion from Peru in 1767, the Jesuits owned eleven sugar plantations along the northern and central coast, as well as the important sugar estate "Pachachaca" and a large *obraje* in Abancay. Their entire holdings in Peru amounted to 5.7 million pesos. The Jesuits were unique in that they financed their acquisitions, whose production often complemented each other, from profits or outside loans, not simply from bequests. Profits from these enterprises, among other things, financed the Jesuit's extensive educational activities and urban projects throughout the viceroyalty.

Endowments and profits from similar enterprises also financed the large number of monasteries and nunneries that emerged in the viceroyalty during the colonial period. These monastaries and nunneries housed a large number of men and women, not only the orders' friars or nuns and various novices, but students, servants, slaves, and artisans. By 1621, over 1,000 friars in Lima alone belonged to the main monastic orders, and their monasteries were splendid architectual structures, replete with elaborately carved baroque woodwork, paintings of the Cuzco or Lima schools, beautifully tiled patios, extensive orchards, and enormous kitchens, that often occupied more than one or more square city blocks. Many of these orders operated *colegios*, or schools that provided opportunities for mestizos and other *castas* to gain literacy and learning, which were otherwise closed to them at the university level.

As for the secular clergy, they not only acquired landed wealth, but received regular income from tithes levied on the settler population to support their various activities. Depending on the population and wealth of a particular jurisdiction, the tithes, together with regular bequests, might convert a particular bishopric into a major source of credit and investment capital in the region. Indeed, both the secular Church and the religious orders served as the major financial institutions for much of the colonial period.

The Church's preeminent place in colonial society, of course, derived fundamentally from the central role that religion played in colonial society. What accentuated an already intense ritual life were the common dangers, uncertainties, and insecurities of everyday life. Cities and towns lacked even the most rudimentary public health provisions and sanitation, exposing the population, especially on the tropical coast, to disease and epidemics. Regular garbage disposal and sewer systems other than streets as gutters were nonexistent, and popular personal hygiene was largely unknown. Hospitals, given the poor state of medicine, were mainly places of contagion and death, while giving birth was particularly dangerous to women's health. In short, one could be struck down at any moment by some plague or disease and carried off to the Great Beyond.

Other hazzards to life and limb abounded. Attacks by pirates became increasingly common along the lightly defended coast. Natural calamities such as El Niño precipitated climatic changes and led to bad harvests and occasional famines. Earthquakes rocked Lima in 1655, 1687, and 1746, to name the most severe, causing numerous casualties, not the least from the flimsy construction of popular housing. When the more solid Church structures came down as well, they often took a high toll among those who, paradoxically, had sought them out for protection from continuing tremors.

Crime or mayhem were other sources of daily danger. Cities were redoubts of wealth and opportunity for criminals to operate from, particularly on festival, ceremonial, or market days when they were teeming with people, many of whom came in from the nearby countryside. More feared were attacks by bands of brigants, who operated on back roads and hence made travel hazardous and by groups of runaway slaves or Indians. Although such forays might not be frequent, they often became the source of rumor or legend and spread fear in the popular imagination.

Given this perilous state of affairs, it is no wonder that the population sought the spiritual protection and comfort offered by religion (although this of course is not the only explanation), expressed in a variety of ways, from popular religious celebrations and ceremonies and regular Sunday mass to participation in *cofradías* or even the monastic life. Needless to say, from a macropolitical perspective, the large number of such faithful gave the church hierarchy, from the archbishop down to the parish priest, immense authority and power. Such authority, which was regularly exercised from the pulpit and confessional, contributed to the overall social and ideological control of the population. It also helps to explain, as you shall see shortly, the emergence of revered popular religious figures, such as Santa Rosa de Lima (Isabel Flores de Oliva) and her contemporary San Martín de Porras, a mulato barber. These saints' lives of deep devotion to religion and to selfless service to their fellow man were the alleged sources of miracles that led them both eventually to be cannonized by Rome.

The seventeenth century also saw a vigorous and harsh effort by the Church to purge the Indian population of their native religious practices. The causes of what would seem to be a costly and purely vindictive campaign to suppress idolatry lay, in part, in the realm of widespread geopolitical and religious fears in the colonies. By the seventeenth century, Spain was facing a broad array of Protestant enemies, who were intent upon defeating the power of the Catholic Hapsburg dynasty in Europe and annexing its empire, with its fabled silver wealth, in America. The lure of such riches had brought a number of foreign interlopers, buccaneers, and pi-

rates—English, Dutch, and French—into the Caribbean during the late sixteenth century and forced Spain to improve her defenses, especially to protect the silver fleets in route from Mexico and Peru to Seville. The Dutch appearance in the South Seas and attacks on Peruvian shipping and ports in
the early seventeenth century heightened fears of the hated and demonized
Protestants to a fever pitch in Lima and along the Peruvian coast.

Deepening fears of foreign attack or even invasion created a climate of
internal suspicion against "foreigners" whose views or beliefs might run
counter to established orthodoxy. Such had been the case in Spain itself and
was expressed in the intensification of the Inquisition and the expulsion of
the Jews and Moriscos at the turn of the sixteenth century. According to
Pierre Duviols, the same psychology triggered the church's sudden, vicious
campaign to extirpate idolatry, that is, to root out native Andean religious
beliefs and ceremonies. In geopolitical terms, the fear was that a rebellious
or deviant Indian "fifth column" (fully 60 percent of the colonial population) might somehow be mobilized by Spain's enemies to threaten royal
power in Peru. After all, the connection between political loyalty and belief
in orthodox Catholicism had been well established in Spain and America
since the conquest. This was exactly the mentality that informed Francisco
de Ávila, the feared "extirpator of idolatry," who, with the full support of
the archbishop of Lima, spent much of his life relentlessly pursuing native
"disbelievers and heretics."

Campaigns took place in the 1620s, 1640s, and 1660s and periodically
thereafter until 1730, when they appear to have died out. After the first campaign, a priest and participant, Pablo José de Arriaga, published a guide for
future investigators that carefully recorded native beliefs and practices. Using original trial recordings, Spalding described the Inquisition-like tactics
that accompanied one particular campaign against idolatry in the parish of
San Lorenzo Quinti, Huarochirí, in 1660:

> The investigation began with a secret denunciation supplied by an anony-
> mous informant, naming a number of people as idolaters, witches, and
> priests of the traditional ceremonies. These people were brought in for ques-
> tioning and then locked up for the duration of the investigation. . . . [They]
> were threatened and some were even tortured to elicit confessions and full
> descriptions of traditional ceremonial practices. . . . Finally on May 28, sen-
> tence was pronounced on 32 people from Quinti and neighboring villages.
> . . . The sentences ranged from public humiliation to lashings and even ex-
> ile and imprisonment in the House of Santa Cruz, the Lima prison for peo-
> ple regarded as the most unregenerate of the priests of the native beliefs
> discovered by the inquisitors. (1984, pp. 255–256)

The Indians' turn inward toward their old religions and beliefs was in
reaction to the harsh, exploitative colonialism imposed by the Europeans
and forms part of what Burga (1988) detected as the emergence of a collective longing for a new Andean utopia in the seventeenth century. By this

longing for Utopia, he meant an ensemble of attitudes and behavior, expressed in books, rituals, painting, religious syncretism, and even popular festivals, that sought to restore the defeated Andean society. Such manifestations illustrate that in the collective popular imagination, the idea of an Indian restoration was what made it possible to withstand the oppression and exploitation of the colonial order. For Burga, this produced a "revolution in Andean mentalities" because although the Indian peoples may have become outwardly more distant from their divinites and myths, they could not abandon their rituals, their political order, or the basic principles that regulated the functioning of their societies. In the end, the Andean utopia constituted a powerful mechanism for creating a new indigenous identity and sense of ethnic power by preserving, through symbolism and ritual, the Indians' traditional culture as a way of surviving in the hostile world of Hispanic colonialism. Such a restoration, as you shall see, would loom large in the outbreak of widespread Andean unrest and rebellion that rocked the colonial order in the eighteenth century.

A Tripartite Social Order

Peruvian society in the seventeenth century increasingly took on the characteristics of a tripartite society: Indian, mestizo, and Hispanic. Such caste segmentation was the result of the initial Spanish colonial policy of separating the Indians in their communities or *repúblicas de indios* from the *repúblicas de españoles* of Spanish settlers. The official classification of Indians, or "indios," provided the basis for the fiscal demands of both the state and Church, while appearance on the tributary lists legalized the *comuneros'* (Indians' living in native communities) access to community land. But in the real world the crown policy of apartheid was imperfect, since, as has been mentioned, the ties, both commercial and cultural, between the Indian and Spanish worlds a century after the invasion were widespread and numerous.

Contact between the two cultures from the beginning innaugurated, of course, the processes of miscegenation, deracination, and *mestizaje* (acculturation). The impact of conquest and colonization on the Indian community was devastating from a demographic and human rights standpoint and caused a continuing outflow from the communities of natives who sought to escape not only the colonial burdens of *mita* and tribute payments, but the deadly consequences of the epidemics. While many of these emigrants were *forasteros*, or outsiders, who eventually resettled in other native communities, others gravitated toward the growing Hispanic settlements, where they were pulled into various occupations and tasks that were in high demand. Taking up residence in the Spanish towns and cities (or, rather, their Indian *anexos* outside), native Andeans and their children over time swelled the ranks of the increasing mestizo sector of the population, assimilating elements of the language, dress, religion and customs of the dominant Spanish population.

In the racial and religious context of colonial Peru, mestizos and *castas*, however, suffered a twin prejudice in the eyes of the European and creole elites. On the one hand, they were presumed to have been conceived out of wedlock and therefore carried the opprobrium of illegitimacy, considered a carnal sin in the Catholic Church. Indeed, the illegitmacy rate for Lima in the seventeenth century was high for all castes, over 40 percent for whites and mestizos and 70 percent for blacks and mulattos. On the other hand, mestizos lacked the so-called purity of blood—the insistence on the absence of any taint of Judaism or non-Catholicism that was required of good family, lineage, and descent in Hispanic culture. In the case of the mestizos, the suspicion of idolatry lingered from their Indian past. While revealing the persistent and deeply rooted racism in the Hispanic world, many of these prejudices were codified in Spanish and colonial law. For example, proof of purity of blood was required of candidates for public office and postulants for entrance to the university and, in turn, was a requisite for entering the professions, such as the law.

The construction of social categories and divisions over the course of the colonial period was a complex matter, indeed. Over time, it involved multiple Hispanic factors of race, ethnicity, class, estate, occupation, and culture that were imported from the metropolis after 1532, not to mention the diversity of ethnic patterns of the former Inca Empire that fragmented after the collapse of Tawantinsuyo but took a long time to disappear if, indeed, they have. In broad strokes, Spanish officials ignored this Andean ethnic mosaic and, in their fiscal and census records, resorted to classification by phenotype into three broad categories: Indian, mestizo, and mulatto. By the eighteenth century, the elaboration of such a caste system had reached such a seemingly pathological obsession that there were extraordinarily elaborate attempts to categorize the multiferious permutations and combinations of interracial couplings. This classification went hand in hand with the idea that one could ascend the social order through intermarriage with a lighter racial counterpart, producing a "whitening" effect in one's offspring. Cahill (1994) uncovered one such genealogical system of classification in eighteenth-century Cuzco that provided a grand total of twenty-one socioracial categories (español + indio = mestizo real; mestizo + india = cholo; tente en el aire + india = salta atrás and so on; p. 119) This hydralike caste classification system, however, was eventually over taken by the economic notion of class at the time of independence and thereafter.

The privileged sector of the colonial order, of course, was composed of white Spaniards and their creole American counterparts who stood, by virtue of the conquest, in a commanding position above the Indians, *castas*, and Africans—the so-called people of color—in Peruvian society. Although they liked to think of themselves as being of purely Spanish extraction, the considerable postconquest miscegenation more than creeped into the ranks of the creoles. While the *encomenderos* had failed to acquire the status of a feudal nobility in Peru during the sixteenth century, a privileged, increasingly powerful and entrenched creole oligarchy emerged, alongside the peninsular elite, during the seventeenth century, despite the crown's efforts to prevent it. Membership in this ascending elite was based on early settlement in Peru, the acquisition of wealth, and influential connections. A few conquistadors who acquired wealth and *encomiendas* succeeded in surviving the civil wars in Peru and retained their wealth to constitute such an elite. Other settlers who enriched themselves, particularly in mining or high commerce, also gained entrance into this privileged class. Still other creoles gained or enhanced their elite status by making influential connections at court to gain sources of patronage. In addition, marriages were arranged between influential creoles and royal officials or other important peninsulars that also tended to solidify elite status, even though the crown expressly prohibited such unions as contrary to royal interests. The formation and expanding power and influence of local, creole elites was given impetus by the weakening of royal authority in Peru that coincided generally with the decline of Spanish power in the seventeenth century.

The nucleus of the emerging elites in Peru, as among all classes and castes, during the colonial period was the family. The family's main characteristics were solidarity and cohesiveness. Families also tended to be large with numerous children, while households often sheltered a sizable number of relatives of diverse ages and generations. Marriages tended to be arranged, uniting multiple family lines over generations and often bringing in property in the form of dowries. *Mayorazgo* (inheritance by the eldest son) was not typical, so wealth was redistributed to children, male or female, in a relatively equal fashion. Although children tried to fit into family enterprises in a complementary fashion, places could not always be found, so some were led into the priesthood or nunneries.

Leading families and their rivals typically formed alliances or, in Lockhart's words, "clustered" in cities, towns, and regions and placed family members in key political or economic positions. Their business enterprises might be run by different members of the family, but tended to operate strategically in a unified and interlocking manner. Extended family members, including poorer and more distant relatives, were also included in these families. Combined with characteristically Hispanic patron-client relations that reached beyond the immediate family circle, this familial unit formed a tightly knit, hierarchical constellation that was capable of contesting with rival families for the control or domination of a particular locality or jurisdiction.

The role of Spanish women in such a family also mirrored Iberian patterns. By the second half of the sixteenth century, the number of Hispanic women in Peru had more or less reached parity with that of Spanish men. However, parity did not mean equality, and women took on the specific female roles assigned to them in the strongly patriarchal Hispanic culture. By custom and law, men had primacy over women, although legal protection for women was included in Spanish colonial codes. Typical female roles meant to marry by family arrangement (often at the early age of nine to twelve), remain in the home, raise children, and practice the domestic arts. These, of course, were not insignificant social tasks, for they served, as Asuncion Lavrin noted, as the primary mode of transmission "of Hispanic domestic and material culture and of religious and social values" to the New World (*CHLA*, II, 1984, p. 323). Moreover, as was already noted, marriage alliances were crucial for forging through kinship family social networks that might enhance family status and position in the viceregal society.

Such domestic roles, however, did not preclude taking on the business operations of an estate or other enterprise under certain circumstances, such as widowhood. Indeed, recent research has turned up a surprisingly large number of colonial Spanish and creole women who distinguished themselves running family businesses. Under the law, women were not prohibited from inheriting, owning, or disposing of property. At the same time, one does not normally find them in the professions or in institutional hierarchies, save the Church to which they often retreated if unwed.

One response to the dominance of men in colonial society may have been the choice, particularly among upper-class women, of life in a convent. Such orders as the Franciscans, Augustinians, Dominicans, and Carmelites established convents in Lima and other cities during the seventeenth century. In Lima, for example, there were thirteen nunneries that contained up to a fifth of the city's female population. The nunneries were invariably oriented toward the contemplative life and were supported mainly by wealthy benefactors. Well-to-do postulants brought dowries as if they were entering marriage, and many purchased cells in their convents and brought slaves to attend them. For the most part, nunneries attracted women who did not marry, were strongly religious, and sought a degree of independence from normal colonial life. Since they were mainly tied to the elites, these, like other religious orders, accumulated wealth and became economically important institutions in colonial society, as Burns (1999) detailed for Cuzco.

Religiosity also found expression outside the nunneries, whose capacity became increasingly strained in the seventeenth century, among the growing number of women who lacked the necessary dowries to enter convents. These women formed lay religious communities, called *beaterios*, which were more austere than convents and whose extremely pious members, known as *beatas*, undertook various types of social work among the poor. In the strongly religious atmosphere of colonial Peru, *beatas* were highly respected, unmarried women who lived from the charity of alms and gifts from the general public and who devoted their lives to charitable community and religious work. One such *beata* was Isabel Flores de Oliva (1586–1617), the daughter of a modest Spanish family in Lima who became the ideal of creole womanhood, the center of a religious cult, and one of the most revered women in colonial society. Known for her charitable work among the poor and reputed to have performed small miracles, Santa Rosa de Lima, as she came to be known, became the New World's first saint, canonized by Rome in 1671.

Another similarly famous *Limeña* (woman from Lima), if for entirely different reasons, was La Perricholi (Miqueta Micaela Villegas, 1739–1819) who typified the *tapada*, another archetype colonial Peruvian woman. The *tapada* was a woman of dubious morals who coquettishly graced Lima's streets using shawls (*tapadas*) to hide her identity and as a way of gaining the attention and seducing male passersby. La Perricholi was an actress who became the scandal of Lima society in the eighteenth century by, among other things, openly seducing the elderly Viceroy Manuel de Amat y Junient and becoming his mistress. La Perricholi's fame became legendary in Peru and has been the subject of operas, literature, and films down through the ages. Both the *beata* and the *tapada* may have been, like the choice of becoming a nun itself, a manifestation of the defiance of colonial Peruvian women who were constricted in a male-dominated society.

With the rise of the first generation of American-born creoles in the second half of the sixteenth century, the process of differentiation from peninsulars and identification with their native land increasingly began to shape a distinctly creole culture. Almost from the beginning, a sense of separateness and difference from the newly arriving Spaniards developed among the first generation of creoles and mestizos who expressed this difference in a variety of ways, including language. For example, American-born Spaniards began referring to peninsulars as *chapetones*, or tin horns, and to themselves as *Españoles Americanos*, or American Spaniards. This sense of difference was also nourished by the fact that beyond Lima, creoles interacted with the native population in various degrees and therefore inevitably absorbed aspects of their culture.

In time, as Brading and Lavalle showed, a distinct creole consciousness, or nativism—a nascent reflection of autonomy from the peninsular—was expressed not only in an active creole cultural life, but in social life. It was, of course, nourished by the accumulation of wealth in Lima and other urban centers of the viceroyalty. In Lima the lives of the creole elites revolved around the city's main institutions, such as the *cabildo*, *audiencia*, convents or monasteries, and *cofradías* (lay religious brotherhoods), as well as the viceregal court and the various ceremonies and celebrations that occurred regularly in the "city of the kings." Finally, with the patronage of the viceroy and other well-to-do elites, Lima boasted an active, mostly Baroque theater, artistic, and literary life.

However, because of the closed and hierarchical organization of the colonial order, tightly enclosed by official regulation and the censorship imposed by the Inquisition, the literary and intellectual production of the creole and peninsular elite was largely limited and confined to scholasticism and the verbal pyrotechnics and stylistic gymnastics of Gongorismo (the literary style of the Spanish poet Luis de Góngora) and the Baroque. What little room was left for the truly creative and societally critical forms of literary expression found an outlet mainly in satire, such as the biting satirical poetry of the Baroque poet Juan del Valle Caviedes (1650–97). Moreover, if the Baroque spoke to the Eurocentric literary fashions established at the viceregal court in Lima, its counterpart in colonial architecture were the mestizo architectural styles whose building facades and interior spaces were fashioned and decorated by Indian artisans who brought strong pre-Columbian styles, motifs, and techniques to their work.

It is interesting that, as in architecture, what was much more lasting of the literary and intellectual production of the colonial period was not the Baroque or satirical poetry produced in the courtly salons of Lima, but the production of a new class of Andean—mestizo, Indian, and creole—intellectuals. Such were the two towering Andean intellectuals, Garcilaso de la Vega, Inca (1539–1609) and Guamán Poma de Ayala (ca. 1535–1615), both of whom were born in Cuzco and wrote works aimed at recovering the history and culture of the Incas, whom the Spaniards had, starting with Toledo, done their best to erase. Garcilaso was the son of a royal Inca princess and Spanish captain of the conquest who was born in Cuzco and educated at San Marcos, but left Peru for Spain in his early twenties where he wrote his great work *Comentarios reales de los Incas* (Córdoba, 1609). As for Guamán Poma, he wrote *Primer nueva crónica y buen gobierno* (ca. 1615), a long and prolifically illustrated history of Inca and Spanish rule that also incorporated an appeal-plan for "good government" to the Spanish king Philip III. "The fact that neither Garcilaso nor Guamán Poma were residents of Lima speaks of the contested centrality of Lima" (Castro-Klarén, "Lima," in Valdés, 2000).

4 From Imperial Reform to Reluctant Independence, 1730–1824

Peru in the seventeenth century had, in many ways, drifted away from Spain—its creole elites becoming more powerful politically and economically, its economy more diverse and autonomous, and its population increasingly mixed. At the same time, silver production at Potosí had sharply declined, the transatlantic trade had slowed, and tax remittances to Madrid had dropped. During the eighteenth century, Spain would try, under the aegis of a new ruling dynasty, to reverse these trends with an eye toward reviving colonial production and revenues, as well as regaining peninsular and thereby metropolitan domination of the viceregal government. Such a "recolonization" of Peru would be accomplished by a bold effort at reform in the second half of the century. However, although somewhat successful in its immediate goals, Spain's reforms also stirred the discontent of large and important segments of Peru's population, paradoxically opening the way to independence in 1824.

Mining, Population, and Economic Advance

Peru's century-long decline in silver production was reversed, as was the steady fall of its Indian population, during the course of the eighteenth century. In the case of silver, output at Potosí increased modestly but steadily from the 1730s until the 1790s. The recovery was stimulated by a reduction in taxes (in 1735, the royal fifth was reduced to a tenth), improvements in the supply of mercury, increased demand and prices from Europe, and stabilization of the labor supply owing to positive demographic trends and continuation of the *mita* labor system. Despite these changes, the structure of the industry remained precarious and archaic, based on draconian exploitation of the *mita* laborers, low levels of investment and technological innovation, and absentee ownership.

Compared to Potosí's modest recovery, silver mining in Lower Peru, paced by mines at Cerro de Pasco (1630), advanced rather smartly. Cerro became the viceroyalty's second leading producer, with the value of its output increasing from a modest 300,000 pesos during the first quinquennium of the century to a peak of 11.2 million pesos in the last quinquennium. Moreover, new mines were opened up at Cailloma in Arequipa and Hualgayoc in Cajamarca, so that overall production in the viceroyalty rose sevenfold, from a low of 2.3 million pesos in the first decade of the eighteenth century to a peak of 40.6 million pesos, before it dropped off at the end of the century. As a result, stimulated by a revival in silver production, the overall economy of the viceroyalty experienced a gradual, if often regionally uneven, growth from 1730 to 1770.

Demographic trends also played an important role in this advance. Unlike New Spain, Peru's predominantly Indian population had continued to fall steadily during the seventeenth century, reaching its nadir between 1688 and 1721. Recovery was slow and frequently interrupted by other epidemics, as well as the death toll from a number of Indian rebellions. By the 1792 census, the overall population of the viceroyalty had reached a little over 1 million, up from perhaps 600,000 in 1620. This figure, however, excluded Puno (part of the Viceroyalty of Buenos Aires until 1796), so the total population of what would become Peru was actually around 1.2 million, or 8.7 percent of the entire Spanish American colony's 12.58 million inhabitants.

Ethnically the population was now approximately 56 percent (including Puno, 62 percent) Indian, 13 percent Spanish, and 27 percent mestizo or *casta*, the latter the fastest-growing sector in the viceroyalty. Black and mulatto slaves, located mainly on the coast in and around Lima, numbered about 40,000. In fact, the city of Lima in the middle of the seventeenth century was half black, testimony to the pervasiveness of slavery in this quintessentially aristocratic city.

Fertility rates varied according to ethnic categories, but were generally low. For the most part, European women had higher fertility rates than Indian women, a reversal of the pattern in modern industrial societies in which the lower strata tend to have larger families. Also, overall mortality rates began to come down, however hesitantly and sporadically, by the end of the century, possibly affected by efforts to improve public health, particularly in the cities. Foremost among these efforts were vaccination campaigns against smallpox in 1780, 1797–98, and the early 1800s. Still, life expectancy at birth was only about 30 years around 1800. Lima's population remained steady at around 50,000 until the end of the century, down from 80,000 before the earthquakes of 1687 and 1746, whereas Potosí's population had dropped to 30,000 (1750). There were a number of other cities with populations over 10,000, including Cuzco, Arequipa, Trujillo, Cerro de Pasco, and Huamanga.

A slowly rising population and the revived output of silver from the mines, then, constituted the twin ingredients for the gradual, but uneven economic advance that occured in Peru between 1730 and 1770. Agricultural and livestock production expanded accordingly in response to greater consumer demand. However, with the exception of the highly efficient Jesuit wine- and sugar-producing estates, we have little statistical information on prices, productivity, or profits in the agrarian sector. The yield on investment of the typical highland estate was probably fairly meager, not exceeding 5 percent and largely dependent on high prices during crop failures and the ensuing shortage-induced speculation.

What is more clear is that during the last quarter of the eighteenth century, the viceroyalty was greatly influenced, both economically and politically, by the imperial reform program known as the Bourbon reforms. Economically, the reforms had a contradictory impact on Peru, although, on balance, they seemed to have contributed to an economic upturn in the Andes between 1775 and 1810. On the one hand, the reforms applied to the mining sector accelerated the output of silver, and the introduction of free trade within the empire produced a pronounced revival of foreign trade. On the other hand, radical administrative reforms paradoxically contributed to shrinking the size of the viceroyalty through the excision of vast regions on its northern and southern periphery, thereby reorienting commercial flows away from the center and its commercial and administrative capital, Lima. Overall, the late eighteenth-century colonial reform program undertaken by the Bourbons signified a concerted attempt by Spain to restore the once lavish flow of revenues from its Andean treasure house.

The Bourbon Reforms

The change from Hapsburg to Bourbon rule in Spain at the beginning of the eighteenth century set in motion a process that would lead to widespread reforms, first in the peninsula and later in the colonies. It also innaugurated more than a century of enmity between Bourbon Spain and England that lasted until independence in 1824 and, among other things, raised continuing fears in certain circles in Peru of an English invasion. In 1700, the infeebled Charles II died without an heir, creating a dynastic crisis that culminated in the War of Spanish Succession (1700–13) and the ascension of a branch of the ruling French Bourbon family to the Spanish throne. Under the impetus of the Bourbons and new ideas percolating from the French Enlightenment, Spain was reorganized into a more absolutist state with a somewhat more efficient economy; a streamlined ministerial, rather than councilar, bureaucratic structure; and a relatively modern army. The new Bourbon state also initiated a series of reforms to tighten its administrative control over the Church and other ecclesiastical matters. It was not until the assumption of Charles III (1759–88) to the throne, however, that the Spanish reforms were generally extended to America.

From the perspective of Madrid, its empire in America was, by the eighteenth century, threatened both externally and internally. The erosion of Spanish sea power in the New World had reached such a sorry state that foreign buccaneers and interlopers had not only penetrated the Caribbean, but also rounded the cape and become active in the Pacific, threatening west

Map 4. Colonial Latin America: Political Organization. *Source:* Mark A. Burkholder and Lyman L. Johnson, *Colonial Latin America*, 3d ed. (New York, 1998), 257.

coast ports and capturing and sacking Guayaquil in 1690. Furthermore, during the 1680s, the Portuguese had managed to establish a colony at Sacramento on an estuary of the River Plate from which substantial contraband, including quantities of British textiles, penetrated the Spanish trade monopoly in southern South America.

Equally or more damaging to imperial control was the fact that local creole elites had managed, through bribery, intrigue, and the sale of offices, to forge alliances of convenience with crown officials in such a way as to compromise seriously imperial interests. To reverse these adverse external and internal threats to metropolitan interests and revive imperial fortunes, the Bourbons needed to reassert Spain's military power in America and regain control over colonial administration. Once these goals were accomplished, then Spain might hope, by introducing necessary economic reforms, to restore its lagging revenue flow from the colonies.

England's capture of Havana in 1762 during the Seven Years War (1756–63) finally provoked Spain to undertake measures to revive its military position in the New World. Shortly thereafter, Spain moved to strengthen its general defenses and establish local militias in the Caribbean and New Spain. In Peru, Viceroy Amat (1761–76) increased the royalist forces to 100,000, the majority of which were comprised of local militias, led by both peninsular and creole officers. In 1776 a royal expedition expelled the Portuguese and retook Sacramento on the eastern side of the River Plate.

The securing of colonial frontiers was accompanied by the crown's dramatic expulsion of all Jesuits from the New World in 1767. The Jesuits had grown rich and powerful in the two centuries since they had arrived in America and, consequently, were widely resented by varous creoles and peninsulars alike. In Peru some ninety-seven Jesuit enterprises, valued at 5.7 million pesos, were taken over by the state and auctioned off at a fraction of their value to the private sector. The expulsion resulted in a considerable loss of management and entrepreneurial efficiency in Peru, not to mention the important Jesuit educational establishment of teachers, schools, and universities in Lima, Cuzco, and elsewhere.

Even more far reaching than the expulsion of the Jesuits was the major reform and restructuring of colonial administration. The creation of two new viceroyalties out of the former Viceroyalty of Peru, mainly for commercial and defensive purposes, radically altered the geopolitical and economic balance in South America. The first was created on the northern rim of Peru and South America in New Granada in 1717 and made permanent in 1739. The second was created in the Rio de la Plata in 1776, after the expulsion of the Portuguese from Sacramento. Most significant for Peru, the Audiencia of Chuquisaca of Upper Peru (roughly Bolivia today) was detached from the old viceroyalty of Peru, so that silver from and goods to Potosí no longer flowed through Lima on the Pacific, but more logically through Buenos Aires on the Atlantic. With the rupture of the old Lima-Potosí circuit, Lima suffered an inevitable decline in prosperity, much to the shragrin and protest of its mercantile establishment, as did the southern highlands (Cuzco, Arequipa, and Puno).

In addition to these large jurisdictional changes, Spain was particularly bent on reasserting its administrative control over the colonial bureaucracy, which had fallen into decay during the previous century. The *audiencia*, the high court and key advisory council to the viceroy, was a case in point. It had become packed with wealthy creole lawyers who had purchased their way onto the court in increasing numbers during the late seventeenth and early eighteenth centuries. According to the calculations of Burkholder and Chandler, this trend peaked in the 1740s when 36 out of 66 *audiencia* positions in Lima went to creoles, two-thirds through outright purchase.

As part of the reforms, introduced by Minister of the Indies José de Gálvez (1776–1787), who had developed a strong dislike for creoles while *visitador* in Mexico (shared by his peninsular appointees to viceregal government), the crown halted the appointment of all creoles to the *audiencia*. It also subsequently increased the size of the body so that more *peninsulares* could be appointed, often selecting Spaniards of relatively low social status, which further angered the creoles. As a result, the number of creoles was reduced to about a third or quarter of all justices on colonial *audiencias* by 1810. A similar ecclesiastical policy replaced creole superiors with Spaniards in the religious orders throughout the viceroyalty. Inevitably, this exclusionary policy, which included the end of the sale of most high-ranking offices by the 1750s, produced discontent among sectors of the creole class that would deepen dangerously over time.

Another major administrative reform was the intendant system, introduced in Mexico by Gálvez in 1765 and brought to Peru by Visitador Antonio de Areche in 1777. The new intendants were similar to provincial governors (there would eventually be eight intendancies in Peru) who were responsible, with the assistance of subdelegates in charge of each district, for the collection of taxes, promotion of public works, and general stimulation of the economy. Salaried, professional career bureaucrats sent from Spain, they were theoretically to remain independent of the local creole elites whom they were impowered to govern and control.

Other reforms were undertaken to increase the flow of income from Peru, which had fallen to a trickle during the first half of the century. The sales tax, or *alcabala*, was increased from 2 percent to 4 percent to 6 percent; new customs houses, strategically located throughout the viceroyalty to ensure collection, were established; and a host of other levies were introduced, such as one on brandy (*aguardiente*). At the same time, the administration of fiscal affairs was improved. For example, a cadre of salaried treasury and customs officials now collected the taxes that had formerly been farmed out to private individuals or groups contracted by the crown. As a result, it was in the sphere of revenue collection that the Bourbon reformers reaped their greatest harvest, purging some of the worst inefficiencies and corruption from the system through better bureaucratic management and modernization. This reform became readily apparent with the rise of tribute revenues to the royal treasury that far exceeded the demographic increase of Indians in the late eighteenth century. For Peru total receipts in the year 1789 rose to 4.5 million pesos, 1.2 million from silver mining and 920,000 from Indian tribute alone.

The Bourbon reforms, of course, had been greatly influenced by the Enlightenment in Europe, whose ideas, particularly in the scientific realm, spread to America during the eighteenth century. One of the main vehicles of its diffusion to the Viceroyalty of Peru were numerous scientific expeditions from Europe that brought with them the new natural sciences—physics, botany, chemistry, archeology, and history. These expeditions were embraced by creole intellectuals, who were anxious to apply the new knowledge to learn more about themselves, their environment, and society. A French expedition in 1735, for example, measured the geographic limits of Peru and collected a vast array of descriptive data on the viceroyalty. Two Spanish scientists on the expedition, Jorge Juan and Antonio de Ulloa, later published a comprehensive and critical report on the colonial administration. In a similar vein, a Spanish physician, Cosme Bueno, published *Descripciones geográficas del Virreinato del Perú* in a series of Lima almanacs in the 1760s and 1970s.

The stifling grip of scholasticism, moreover, gradually loosened at centers of learning, such as San Marcos University whose expansion of knowledge in the natural sciences was highlighted in 1723 when the medical faculty accepted the explanation of the circulation of blood. Similarly, the Jesuit colleges were teaching the ideas of Descartes, Newton, and Leibnitz long before the order's expulsion in 1767. The new Enlightenment's currents of thought even penetrated intellectual circles in the secular clergy and the other monastic orders. In fact, by the end of the century, enlightenment thought was relatively commonplace in viceregal intellectual circles, and many such ideas circulated openly in the pages of *Mercurio Peruano*, published in the early 1790s.

In general, however, the state of education in the viceroyalty in the eighteenth century remained a luxury of class privilege and was inhibited by an urban populace that "lived around the plaza, the market and the church, not the school house" (Castro-Klarén, "Lima," in Valdés, 2000). According to Macera, by the end of the eighteenth century there were only 5,000 students in primary schools, most of whom belonged to the aristocracy. Education was generally not accessible to the "middle" or plebian sectors of the population, while most books were imported and accumulated mainly in private or ecclesiastical, rather than public, libraries, such as those of the Enlightenment intellectual Hipólito Unánue.

Beyond the intellectual and cultural sphere, the greatest impact of the Bourbon reforms occurred in the economic sphere. During the seventeenth century, the level of contraband trade throughout the Spanish Empire in America had reached overwhelming proportions. Spain's military weakness enabled her European rivals to operate virtually unchallenged in the Americas, thus shredding, as you have seen, the crown's trade monopoly and introducing huge amounts of contraband goods throughout the colonies. Moreover, as a result, during the War of Spanish Succession, Spain's ally France obtained permission to operate merchant fleets and trade freely all along the west coast. From 1701 to 1724, 153 French merchant ships, which regularly rounded Cape Horn from the Atlantic, visited west coast ports, flooding the region with European merchandise.

Such actions rendered increasingly marginal and irrelevant the old fleet system operating between Lima, the Portobello fair, and Seville. Thus, between 1699 and 1713, only one fleet arrived at Portobello, where Lima merchants picked up their usual lot, only to be sharply undercut by French merchandise upon their arrival back in Lima. The arrival of single foreign merchant ships to Callao and other west coast ports continued, with the viceroy's cognizance, for most of the century even after 1713.

By 1778 the old trade monopoly was a virtual shambles, leading the crown to open up the empire to greater free trade. The fleet system was finally ended, and trade within the empire was permitted between all major ports in Spain and the New World. In the succeeding decade alone, the transatlantic trade soared as registered exports tripled, customs revenues more than doubled, and imports reached unprecedented levels. In 1786 alone sixteen ships landed 22 million pesos worth of goods at Callao.

This dramatic increase in foreign trade, the jump in silver output, and rising taxes were soon reflected in revenues received by the royal treasury in Lima. According to TePaske, royal income climbed sharply, from 12 million pesos (1776–80) to 16 million pesos (1781–85) to 18.5 million pesos (1786–90). Moreover, as silver mining expanded, the demand for manufactures at Cerro de Pasco and elsewhere in Lower Peru increased, providing Lima merchants with an alternative market to Potosí for the distribution of goods received from abroad. This market proved all the more important, since the *reparto* system, largely supplied by Lima merchants, was curtailed after the introduction of the intendant system in 1784.

According to John Fisher's estimates, silver output in Lower Peru doubled, from around 250,000 marks in 1776 to over 500,000 marks in 1792 and reached a peak of 637,000 marks in 1799, from which it gradually decreased until 1810. By comparison, the production of the mines at Potosí improved moderately during the same period before it entered a decline beginning in 1796, when ore taillings ran out and mercury supplies from Europe were cut off by war. Fisher thought that it is a myth, largely created by the merchant Consulado of Lima, to consider that Lima was ruined or Peru was thrown into a depression as a result of the administrative reform of 1776, although he acknowledged that some trade was inevitably drawn away from Lima to Buenos Aires. On the contrary, he believed that the revival of the transatlantic trade after 1778, together with increased silver production in Lower Peru, not only contributed to greater prosperity throughout the viceroyalty in the late eighteenth century, but served to cushion Lima from the loss of the Potosí trade.

Although there was some inevitable economic dislocation from the shift, it seems that Lima's commercial elites adjusted to the new policy of free trade. Afterall, the city was already becoming the main force in rearticulating imports and exports, from the south (the former Lima–Potosí axis) to the center/north (Lima–Cerro/Hualgayoc axis), which now became the new pole or core of the viceregal economy in the eighteenth century.

If general economic activity seems to have picked up in the last quarter of the century, some local Peruvian commodities did not fair well. This was particularly true in the case of Andean wool. The production of wool for the *obrajes* that had emerged at the end of the sixteenth century to produce rough woolens for the lower or popular segment of the consumer markets of Potosí and other cities had expanded rapidly in the southern *altiplano*, which was ecologically suited for sheep raising. The wool was then transported to *obrajes* in Huamanga (Ayacucho), Cuzco, and elsewhere or produced on the ranches around Cajamarca and Quito, which also contained *obrajes*, all four cities becoming large textile centers in the Andes.

The increasing influx of large quantities of cheap imported British textiles during the eighteenth century, as well as the abolition in the 1780s of the *reparto*, or forced sale of goods by the *corregidores* to Indians, hurt the formalized commerce in woolens. Foreign competition ultimately forced the Quito industry to shift from producing high-quality cloth for Lima to coarser woolens for the northern market of New Granada. In Huamanga, the primitive *obrajes* studied by Miriam Salas depended almost exclusively on the *reparto* and were forced to try to redirect their output to Lima after the reforms of the 1780s.

The Cuzco *obrajes*, even though they benefitted from being closer to their markets, were also adversely affected by imports. Tandeter and Wachtel's study of commodity prices found a drastic drop in the price of woolen textiles shipped from Cuzco's *obrajes* to Potosí beginning in the early eighteenth century. Prices stabilized between the 1740s and 1781, but then plummeted the following decade because of a huge influx of cheap British textiles that were imported to Potosí through the port of Buenos Aires. With their rudimentary operations, most Andean *obrajes* were simply unable to compete with foreign imported textiles.

The production of at least two other commodities was either less than robust or negative during the second half of the eighteenth century. Jacobsen argued that the demand for livestock in the viceroyalty, aside from the bustling mining districts of Cerro and Hualgayoc, was modest during the period. In the case of sugar production, it had been in a general decline, since it reached its apogee in the late seventeenth and beginning of the eighteenth century. According to Ramirez, the fall in prices was due to several factors: growing international competition from Brazil and the Caribbean; regional competition; the spread of small-scale producers; the elimination of the slave trade, which supplied most of the labor force for the plantations; and the increasing indebtedness of the planters. Still, production figures from 1791 indicate that sugar continued to be an important product, with a large internal market as well as considerable exports to Chile. Furthermore, many plantations shifted production to cheaper derivatives, such as *aguardiente* (brandy), which developed a considerable market in the mining communities.

The production of other coastal agricultural crops shows a mixed picture. Wheat production declined, not as generally believed because of the great earthquake of 1687, but because of increasing imports from Chile that could be exchanged for sugar. According to Flores Galindo (1984), this exchange became profitable to Lima merchants, who controlled shipping and the bread business and who were able, through loans and purchase agreements, to dictate their choice of crops to be cultivated along the coast. The result was the displacement of wheat for sugar and alfalfa, the latter being expansive because of the need to sustain the growing number of mules required for transport between Lima-Callao and the interior. For Flores Galindo, this displacement helps to explain how coastal agriculture became increasingly oriented toward exports (sugar) at the expense of production for an internal market (wheat).

All this adds up to an improved, if uneven, economic picture in the viceroyalty during the last quarter of the eighteenth century. Aggregate economic growth was reflected in increasing silver output, rising foreign and perhaps domestic trade, improving agricultural production, and growing governmental revenues. Silver mining, in particular, with its demand for inputs and supply of specie, was a leading sector. Only textile manufacturing registered a downturn during the 1780s, but rebounded somewhat in the 1790s as a result of international conflicts. At the same time, the center of economic gravity shifted from the south to the center and north, as the Potosí–Lima circuit was replaced by the Cerro de Pasco/Hualgayoc–Lima circuit. Still, the overall integration of the viceregal economy was hindered by the continued vitality of the native subsistence economy and the high transportation and transaction costs of the rugged Andean terrain. Regional specialization remained confined to the north coast sugar zone, which contracted in the second half of the century.

This generally positive economic picture was clouded beginning in the mid-1790s as a result of the outbreak of the Napoleonic wars in Europe, which caused a sharp decline in imperial trade, and a waning of the imperial reforms instituted by Spain. While mining output, according to Fisher, remained relatively strong through the first decade of the nineteenth century, as did Lima-based commerce, other sectors of the economy increasingly stagnated after 1796.

The Age of Andean Insurrection

The eighteenth century is well known in Peru as the age of Andean insurrection. Two and a half centuries after the conquest, a series of popular uprisings rocked the viceroyalty to its very foundations. They threatened not only to overturn the ancien régime, but, in some regions, to replace it by resurrecting the Inca empire, under the rule of descendants of the old Inca kings. O'Phelan estimated that between 1720 and 1790, over a hundred violent insurrections involving large numbers of Andean peasants, sometimes led by dissident *castas* and creoles, occurred against the colonial order.

Two uprisings are particularly notable. One was led by Juan Santos Atahualpa, a messianic *serrano* (highlander) and self-proclaimed descendent of the murdered Inca, who in 1742 rallied disaffected Indians and mestizos in the central montaña (see map in Stern, 1987, p. 41) in a ten-year war against the colonial regime. Another rebellion was headed by a disaffected Indian *curaca*—José Gabriel Condorcanqui—who in the early 1780s mobilized the peasantry of a vast region in the southern highlands.

The central *montaña* (bordering the present-day highland departments of Huánuco, Pasco, Junín, and Ayacucho) during the seventeenth century was the object mainly of missionaries, primarily Franciscans, in search of souls and a few intrepid entrepreneurs hoping to exploit its resources. The latter, probably searching for gold, discovered instead valuable salt deposits in the Gran Pajonal that the native Campas or Ashaninkas had extracted and used as a form of money. Just as their predecessors after the conquest, the missionaries had to overcome the abuses inflicted on the natives by the salt miners to gain the necessary confidence to carry on their evangel. The natives were also suffering from the European diseases against which they were virtually defenseless. By the middle of the eighteenth century, the missionaries had succeeded in organizing, according to Millones (1995), 32 missions of approximately 300 inhabitants each, or a total of 9,000 persons, administered from the Intendency of Tarma. Depite the good intentions of the Franciscans, various native rebellions roiled the region prior to the appearance of Juan Santos.

In addition to the indigenous population, *serranos* (Indians, *castas*, and whites) had also increasingly migrated to the region for economic or political reasons. Some took part in the expanding trade of products from the *selva* (tropical forest) that, in addition to salt, included coca leaf, fruit, wood, cotton, and other valued resources. The missionaries and landowners, moreover, had brought highland servants and laborers, and dissident sierra Indians, blacks, and *castas* had escaped into the more remote areas seeking refuge. In short, a mixed population of natives and *serranos* in the central montaña formed a multiethnic and racial society.

What little we know of King Juan Santos Atahualpa, Apu Inca, Huayna Capac, Christian Indian of the city of Cuzco, as he was described in a missionary account, comes from various documents of the period. He was an Indian or mestizo, probably born in the neighboring sierra and educated at Cuzco, who had possibly traveled to Africa with a Jesuit whom he served. Evidently, his arrival in the Gran Pajonal coincided with a series of earthquakes and tremors whose power he was soon reputed to possess. Claiming to be one of the last Inca kings, he apparently wore the insignia of the

Inca royal family and lived the life of an ascetic, eating little, chewing *coca*, and avoiding contact with women.

In May 1742, Juan Santos declared his intention of expelling all Spaniards and their black slaves from Peru. Proclaiming an end to colonial oppression, he promised to usher in a new era of prosperity for "his children." In addition, he spoke of restoring the empire, one in which the Indians would propagate their own forms of Christianity. Such millenial sentiments were not uncommon at the time among the Andean indigenous peoples.

According to Stern and others, such popular longings and beliefs were a response to the deepening discontent and sense of despair of the Indian population in the missions where life was less than the utopia originally imagined by their founders. For one thing, the Franciscans took a dim view of polygamy, which was a widespread practice among jungle tribes, particularly among their *caciques*, or headmen. More significant was the terror associated with the outbreak of unknown diseases, made more virulent in the confines of these urban enclaves. Equally distasteful was the regimentation of mission life to a people who placed great value on personal liberty. Moreover, although the Franciscans generally treated their charges well, mission Indians and others were often abused by the European salt miners and other Spaniards who were out to enrich themselves on the backs of native labor. Finally, scholars have pointed to the disruptive presence of runaway highland Indians (*retirados*), who had managed to escape from the more expoitative conditions of Spanish rule in the sierra. Their more direct experience with Spanish oppression may also have contributed to the restiveness of the jungle Indian population.

Gathering as many as 2,000 natives of various tribes, an extraordinary number considering that most scattered communities contained at most only a few hundred inhabitants, Juan Santos quickly gained control of the Gran Pajonal. The *selva* had never been an area in which imperial control, either by the Incas or Spaniards, had been much more than nominal, so that when the authorities tried to quell the uprising by sending expeditions from the highlands, they continually met with failure. European troop formations and tactics were hardly effective in the dense Amazonian rain forests.

More vexing to the Spaniards was the threat that the rebellion posed to contiguous areas of the central highlands (the districts of Huanta, Jauja, Tarma, and Huánuco). Indeed, it erupted at a strategic point in the Central Andes/*montaña* where the transit from one area to the other was comparatively easy. It is interesting that the same area would spawn the Comasino guerrillas 130 years later during the War of the Pacific (1879–83), chronicled by Mallon (1983). An area of similar highland/lowland transit is Huanta in Ayacucho, where the the *Rebelión de la Sal*, chronicled by Husson, occured in 1896 and the Shining Path operated in the 1980s and 1990s.

In the case of Juan Santos, the fear among Spanish officials was that the rebellion would reach into the Indian population in the highlands, where it apparently did have some support and therefore would become an even

Túpac Amaru II. Courtesy of Mariella Corvetto and Ward Stavig.

more serious pan-Andean uprising. Indeed, in 1752 Juan Santos's forces did move briefly into the highland community of Andamarca. But this proved to be the last serious encounter between Juan Santos's followers and colonial forces. Thereafter the movement seems to have receded, and its leader inexplicably disappeared, perhaps murdered by one of his own lieutenants.

Unlike the Juan Santos rebellion, we know considerably more about the other great Andean rebellion of 1780, led by José Gabriel Condorcanqui who adopted the name Túpac Amaru (Royal Serpent in Quechua) after the last Inca executed by Toledo in 1572. A moderately wealthy landowner, muleteer, and *curaca*, Túpac Amaru was born in 1738 in the town of Surinama, fifty miles southeast of Cuzco. A physically imposing figure, he stood five feet eight inches in height, taller than most Indians, and wore the dress of a Spanish nobleman, including a black velvet coat, gold waistcoat, beaver dress hat, silk stockings, and shoes with gold buckles. Once the revolt erupted, some contemporaries related that he often wore an Inca insignia around his neck. This insignia was significant, for, like Juan Santos before him, Condorcanqui attempted to tap into popular currents of millenarianism as a way of rallying the Indian population against the colonial regime. A short, but vicious civil war ensued before the forces of Túpac Amaru II were defeated and their leader was captured and executed.

The causes of peasant unrest during this period have been much debated by Andean scholars. Lewin and Fisher saw it as a reaction to colonial oppression—a harbinger of the later outbreak of the wars of independence. O'Phelan emphasized, as you shall see, the crown's tax reform policies initiated by the Bourbons. Szeminski, on the other hand, viewed the rebellion in more traditional Andean terms, that is, as following a deeply rooted Andean logic and worldview. Similarly, Burga attributed it to the resurrection or rebirth of the idea of an Andean utopia (*renacimiento andino*). Finally, Flores Galindo interpreted the rebellion as an anticolonial, protonationalist movement, underlining its emphasis on the unity of all native-born Peruvians, with the goal of expelling the Spanish. Although all these explanations contribute to our understanding of the rebellion, the Bourbon reform stands out, particularly its "tightening of the screw" of colonial exploitation by way of increased fiscal and other demands by the crown in the second half of the eighteenth century.

Fiscal issues, particularly taxation, primarily lay at the root of colonial social unrest. While various sectors of the social order felt the consequences of this process, it was the Indian population that bore the brunt of imperial change and rose up in violent protest. Nowhere was this more apparent than with the crown reforms, which tended to intensify the *reparto de mercancía* (*reparto*), or forced sale of goods to the Indians by the *corregidores*. Beginning in the 1670s, in an effort to expand forcibly stagnant markets and revive revenues, the crown undertook new measures that had the effect of intensifying the *reparto* system. For example, it limited the office of the *corregidor* to five years and put it, along with other offices, up for sale to the highest bidder. Since remuneration for the office had always been dependent upon the *reparto*, the new *corregidor* was now under a specific time constraint to profit from his "investment" and to pay off his merchant creditors for the goods he would now "sell." With the decline in the transatlantic trade, Lima merchants as a logical alternative intensified their links with the *corregidores* to exploit the internal market further through the *reparto*.

Along with the intensification of the *reparto*, the crown later moved to increase the tribute, or head tax, on the Indian population and the *mita* labor draft assigned to the mining (*mita de minero*) and other sectors of the economy. Jacobsen, for example, estimated that the collection of the tribute in Cuzco increased by a factor of 16 between 1750 and 1820. All three of these devices served to intensify the demands on labor to expand productivity, not to mention eroded the legitimacy of the *curacas* who had trouble collecting the taxes and whom the Bourbons would later move to replace. With the lack of capital and new technology, the only way to increase productivity was to intensify the level of exploitation of labor in the mines, estates, and *obrajes*. In the case of the *reparto*, Golte estimated that the quantity of man-hours mobilized to pay off the debts, incurred by Indian workers at the hands of the *corregidores*, more than tripled between 1754 and 1780.

One way to ensure a greater number of workers for mine owners, *obrajeros*, and hacendados was to revise the census on which the tribute and *mita* were calculated. A revision of the census was ordered by Viceroy Castelfuerte in 1719. Castelfuerte believed that local officials, particularly priests and *corregidores*, were not registering the exact number of Indians in their districts so they could divert royal income from tribute and *mita* labor to their own pockets. He also moved to close a loophole whereby Indian peasants tried, through bribery, to exempt themselves from their tribute and *mita* obligations by registering as mestizos. The new census required mestizos, the fastest-growing segment of the population, to produce documentary evidence of their birth. This measure, which might force mestizos into the category of Indian, understandably provoked and outraged this segment of the population. For the crown, it promised more *tributarios*, drawn now from both the Indian and mestizo sectors of the population.

Pressures on Indian peasant communities also intensified in other ways during the eighteenth century. For one thing, the population again began to increase after 1720, leading to deteriorating man–land ratios in the Indian communities. At the same time, agricultural estates, reacting to state incentives to increase production, expanded their borders at the expense of community lands. A shrinking land base and rising population not only made it more difficult for the peasant subsistence sector to feed itself or generate a salable surplus for the outside marketplace, but expelled its labor force into an increasingly exploitative labor market.

The upshot of these trends was a generally deteriorating standard of living for the Andean peasantry in the second half of the eighteenth century. Golte referred to the "pillaging" of Peruvian rural society, while Larson described "the gradual pauperization" of the peasantry. Still another historian pointed out that the system of colonial exploitation now lost whatever measure of paternalism and accommodation that it previously had. In short, Spanish colonialism in the Andes assumed its most naked and ruthlessly oppressive form. Under these circumstances, strategies of Indian resistance changed from covert and passive (surreptitious religious practices, for example) to open and violent confrontation, ushering in the age of Andean insurrection. The obvious target of Indian wrath would be the *corregidores*, who symbolized the worst features of the intensified colonial oppression.

Although the revolts occurred sporadically from the 1720s and remained relatively brief, limited, and local, the great rebellion of Túpac Amaru that erupted in 1780 was an organized, mass movement that engulfed the entire southern Andes from Cuzco to La Paz. Significantly, the movement's epicenter was in the heart of Indian Peru and the production and commercial circuits based on the Potosí mines that were subject to the exactions of tribute and *mita*, but the economies and politics of both Upper and Lower Peru were substantially integrated and highly sensitive to any fiscal and commercial pressure.

That unity was broken in 1776 when Charles III suddenly separated Upper Peru from the Viceroyalty of Peru and incorporated it into the newly created Viceroyalty of the Rio de la Plata. This change was followed in 1778 by the policy of "free trade" within the empire, which opened American ports, including Buenos Aires, to unrestricted commerce with Spain. Among other things, these reforms severely disrupted the traditional trade routes that had united the region economically over the past two centuries. Silver from Potosí was now directed to Buenos Aires, while imported goods moved through the Atlantic port into southern Peru, competing with Cuzco's production of textiles. The resulting stagnation of Cuzco's economy adversely effected the bulk of the population, including Túpac Amaru and many of his supporters, who blaimed the colonial regime.

These important administrative and economic changes were preceded by sharp increases in the *alcabala*, or sales tax, from 2 percent to 4 percent in 1772 and then to 6 percent in 1776, and its more efficient collection through the establishment of a series of customs houses throughout the region. The implementation of these measures was charged to the new Visitador General Antonio de Areche who arrived from Spain in 1777. The visitador general also instructed the *corregidores* to collect the sales tax. This change made the *corregidores* the targets of popular protest not only by peasants who resented the *reparto*, but also by mestizo and creole hacendados and merchants who were adversely affected by the collection of the *alcabala*. Indeed, the tripling of the sales tax during the 1770s affected a much broader segment of the colonial population—hacendados, *obrajeros*, miners, small landholders, retailers, muleteers, and artisans—and especially the middle sectors of small producers and traders on whose modest incomes such a regressive tax weighed disproportionately the heaviest. This fact ensured that the rebellion would not be confined simply to the Indian population in sporadic, spontaneous, and easily repressed local rebellions, as had occurred earlier. Rather, it would make for a multiethnic and socially diverse movement, involving middle- and upper-class mestizo and creole elements who were capable of transforming specific, local revolts into a widespread, regional rebellion.

Some creole participation in the Túpac Amaru revolt may also be laid at the feet of the "anticreole" policy of Charles III's minister of the Indies, José de Gálvez (1776–87). As I noted earlier, Gálvez made a concerted effort during his tenure to curtail creole participation and influence in the colonial government, which, he believed, had become detrimental to Spain's interests. Consequently, a serious rift developed in colonial society between the creoles and the Spanish crown.

The broad current of discontent against the Caroline fiscal reforms erupted in the 1770s in a series of revolts, sixty-six by one count, the most notable occurring in Urubamba, La Paz, Arequipa, and Cuzco. In Arequipa, for example, a popular riot, inspired by the local elite, broke out in 1780 in protest against the sharp increase in the *alcabala*. As a result, the newly built customs house was burned to the ground and its director was forced to flee for his life before the authorities were able to reestablish order.

Although put down in each instance by the crown, these revolts culminated in the mass mobilization of 1780, led by Túpac Amaru. José Gabriel Condorcangui, whose father was a *curaca*, had been educated at the Jesuit College of San Francisco de Borja in Cuzco, the school established to educate the sons of the Indian nobility. When his father died in 1750, he inherited 350 mules, which he used to transport goods to Potosí, as well as land, including coca estates, and some mining interests. Ten years later, José Gabriel married Micaela Bastidas Puyucahua, a mestiza from a nearby community with whom he had three sons and who later occupied a high leadership position in the rebel army.

José Gabriel's position as *curaca*, however, was soon challenged from several quarters, and he became involved in extensive litigation to defend his rights to the office. In 1777 he found it necessary to travel to Lima to defend himself in a lawsuit with a rival who also claimed to be a legitimate descendent of Túpac Amaru I. While pleading his case in the courts, he made several petitions to the authorites. One was to be granted a Spanish title of nobility. Another was made in behalf of the Indians in his district to be exonerated from the Potosí *mita*, noting the horrible conditions in the mines and the scarcity of able-bodied men in his district. In both the court litigation and petitions, José Gabriel became increasingly frustrated and embittered with the colonial administration, for the court case remained undecided and his petitions on the *mita* were apparently rejected by the new Visitador General Areche.

During his stay in Lima, José Gabriel also became aware of new ideas from Europe percolating in intellectual circles, as well as events occuring in the United States. Although books and discussion about the enlightenment were proscribed by the authorities, the new ideas circulated at San Marcos University, which José Gabriel visited, and among acquaintances he encountered. His wife Micaela later commented that José Gabriel's "eyes were opened" at this time, and Walker concluded that "bits and pieces of enlightment thought and the growing dissatifaction with colonialism rubbed off on Túpac Amaru" (Walker, ms. 1997, 19).

A deeper ideological influence on José Gabriel derived from the currents of neo-Inca revivalism and nationalism—what Burga (1988) referred to as the Andean utopia—which were rippling through the Andes in the second half of the eighteenth century. Dating back at least to the 1750s and probably earlier, descendants of the Inca elite attempted to recover and validate Andean cultural traditions, embodied in a nostalgic and romantic reaffirmation of past Inca glories and triumphs. One manifestation of such a revival was the veneration of the Incas and celebration of their heritage by members of the Indian nobility of Cuzco. Indeed, a veritable cult of Inca antiquity flourished in the old Inca capital around the midcentury. In public ceremonies in Cuzco, *curacas* proudly dressed in elaborate Inca garb and exhibited other symbols of Inca primacy including flags, conch shell horns, and the ancient symbol of the sun god and the Incas. According to Rowe (1976), paintings of the Inca kings sought to legitimate further the royal Inca past. It is interesting that even some creoles adopted Inca dress and furnishings.

It appears that the sources of inspiration for such neo-Inca nationalism were accounts of Inca history like Garcilaso de la Vega's *Comentarios Reales de los Incas* (*Royal Commentaries of the Incas*), which was first published in 1609. Its republication in 1722 proved to be incendiary to the Indian gentry, such as the *curacas*, who learned from its pages not only the glory and justice of the Inca past, but the cruelty and treachery of the Spanish conquerors. The *Comentarios'* relevance was made more meaningful in the context of the centralizing reforms of the Bourbons, which, in the case of the *curacas*, was felt in the curtailment of their powers and loss of status that they were experiencing at the hands of the corregidors. By affirming their Inca heritage, the Indian gentry was attempting to reaffirm its corporate rights that were established under the Hapsburgs, but were now being restricted by the Bourbon reformers. A direct link between Garcilaso's work, neo-Inca revivalism, and Túpac Amaru II was noted by the bishop of Cuzco when he wrote in 1781:

> [I]f the *Comentarios* of Garcilaso had not been the reading and instruction of the insurgent José Gabriel Amaru, if his continuous invectives and declamations against the Spaniards had not taken such root in his mind . . . if these and other readings of certain authors of this kingdom had not been accepted by the traitor in all that they uttered about the conquest, Túpac Amaru would not have embarked on the detestable audacity of his rebellion. (quoted in Brading, 1991, p. 491)

The neo-Inca nationalism flourishing among the Indian gentry of Cuzco and elsewhere in the southern Andes was accompanied by the reemergence of widespread millenarian sentiments among the indigenous masses of the region who had long harbored a belief in the miraculous return of the Inca to deliver them from their suffering. Indeed, over the centuries since the conquest, millenarianism had ebbed and flowed among the native Andean peoples. It centered on the myth of Inkarrí, the ancient Inca creator god Viracocha, who would return to restore an alternative Andean utopia of justice and harmony in the lands of the former empire. Accordingly, many Andeans believed that the last Inca's decapitated body had been regenerating underground and that at some preordained moment would reappear to lead a recovery of the mythologized old order. In the Andean belief system, time was cyclical, and the great moments of temporal change, known as *pachacutis*, or cataclysms, were led by representatives of Viracocha, who were seen as having returned to earth to overturn the existing unjust order of things.

If by assuming the name Túpac Amaru II, José Gabriel was trying to assume the mantle of such a redeemer, according to Andean mythology, the alias' revolutionary potential among the increasingly restless Indian peasantry, chaffing under the "tightening colonial screw," could not have been higher. The assumption of the name by José Gabriel came, moreover, when the native Andean masses themselves were viewing the Inca past, according to Flores Galindo, as an idealized egalitarian society, free of the lords and masters of the colonial world. In this sense, identification of the peasantry with the Incas had a decisively subversive ring to it. Furthermore, such a utopian vision of the past merged with the universal experience of colonial bondage, which was symbolized in the term Indian (*indio*) now commonly used by Spaniards to categorize all natives, regardless of their ethnic orgins. This term suggested to Fores Galindo a socioeconomic and racial stigma that served to construct a collective Andean outlook of shared oppression that polarized Andean society on the basis of class and race on the eve of the Great Rebellion.

Frustrated by his inability to move crown officials in Lima to adopt his proposals for reform, Túpac Amaru II returned to his home in Tinta and decided to mount a rebellion ostensibly to force the authorities to undertake a revision of the colonial order. He and his fellow conspirators chose November 4, the feast day of King Charles III, to put their plan for rebellion into action. Like other leaders of premodern popular uprisings, Túpac Amaru II raised the banner of rebellion in the name of the king, summed up in the term *"viva el Rey y muera el mal gobierno"* (Long Live the King and Death to Bad Government). His professed quarrel was with the king's immoral subordinates in the colonies who subverted the monarch's just laws and mercilessly exploited the Indian masses for their own selfish profit. Couching the movement in such a way was the standard and accepted way of negotiating political rights and grievances at the time.

The precipitating event of the uprising was the seizure by Túpac Amaru

II of the widely hated *corregidor* of Tinta, Antonio de Arriaga, whom he accused of exceeding the legal limitations of the *reparto* by selling more goods and collecting higher fees to the Indians than were allowed. In subsequent declarations, the rebels called for the abolition of the *alcabala*, the *reparto* system, and the Potosí *mita* and the reduction of the tribute by 50 percent. Túpac Amaru II also had personal reasons for his dislike of Arriaga, who had been hounding him to pay off the considerable debts he owed not only to the *corregidor* but to the customs authorities. Arriaga was promptly tried and convicted of his "crimes" by the rebels, and on November 10, he was hanged in a public ceremony.

Following the execution, Túpac Amaru II led a rebel force into the province of Quispicanchis, where they devastated a hastily assembled Spanish militia at the battle of Sangarara. One report estimated the dead at 576, including a number of creoles and women, many of whom had sought refuge in a church that was put to the torch by the rebels. News of this alleged atrocity by the rebels led the bishop of Cuzco to denounce Túpac Amaru II and the authorities to present the movement in subsequent propaganda as a caste war of Indians against whites (creoles and Europeans). Such a depiction proved costly to the rebels, since they had hoped to attract creoles and mestizos to the movement. Prior to the battle, the rebel forces had also ransacked two *obrajes* where Túpac Amaru II, acting like an Inca according to traditional Andean norms, seized and distributed quantities of cloth and *coca* to his followers. Significantly, following the battle, Túpac Amaru II and his wife Micaela commissioned a portrait depicting the two as an Inca king and *coya* (queen), rejecting the plumed tricorner hat and mestizo attire of earlier days.

From Quispicanchis province, the rebels, instead of attacking Cuzco, chose to divide their force, one part returning to Tinta to gather reinforcements and the other part, led by Túpac Amaru II, moving south to extend the offensive to the Lake Titicaca area. The delay in taking Cuzco proved to be a major tactical error, however, because it allowed royalist forces time to move up from Lima and fortify the city. As a result, when Túpac Amaru II returned from the south and finally laid siege to Cuzco on December 28 with about 6,000 troops, he encountered stiff resistance, not only from the royalist army sent there to defend it, but from loyalist Indians who were mobilized by the rival Pumacahua clan. This resistance by loyalist Indians reveals the complex ethnic antagonisms and divisions among native Andean communities that would prove one of the main reasons for the defeat of the revolt. Unable to take Cuzco by siege, Túpac Amaru II fell back to his original base in Tinta on January 10.

As it turned out, the siege of Cuzco represented the high point of the rebellion, after which Túpac Amaru II's forces experienced a series of military defeats at the hands of royalist troops and Indian loyalists under Pumacahua. These setbacks culminated in the capture and imprisonment of Túpac Amaru II and his wife Micaela on April 6 by royalists led by Field Marshal

José del Valle, who commanded a force of 15,000 troops. The rebel leaders were then taken to Cuzco and summarily tried and convicted of treason. On May 18, 1781, before a large throng gathered in the central square of Cuzco, Túpac Amaru II was forced to watch the hanging of several family members and the execution of his wife by garroting. The gruesome scene was completed when, after being tortured and then unsuccessfully drawn and quartered (his limbs could not be separated from his body by the horses), the rebel leader was beheaded.

With Túpac Amaru's capture and execution, the Cuzco (or Tupamarista) phase of the Great Rebellion (1780–81) ended, although some of his forces continued to operate under the command of Diego Cristobal in the Lake Titicaca region and Upper Peru. These forces succeeded in briefly joining a similar rebellion, led by the Katari brothers, which had broken out a few years earlier in Upper Peru (present-day Bolivia) and that threatened to take La Paz in 1781. The Katarista insurgency lasted until 1783.

In the aftermath of the Great Rebellion, Gálvez (minister of the Indies) instituted measures to try to "reconquer" the southern Andes to ensure that another such massive Indian uprising in the region would not occur. A reign of terror, for example, was unleashed not only against Túpac Amaru II and his family, but against anyone who had shown the slightest support for the rebellion. The torture and execution of Túpac Amaru and the public display of his amputated limbs throughout the Cuzco region before burial served as one such brutal warning to potential rebels. An even more pointed demonstration was the application of the infamous *quintado* (execution of every fifth able-bodied man) in various Tupamarista villages throughout the region.

Moreover, recognizing that Inca nationalism could serve as a vehicle for rebellion in the person of another pretender like Túpac Amaru II, the authorities moved with dispatch to try to eradicate Inca nationalism. Among other things, the government decreed the abolition of the hereditary position of *curaca* in 1787 and banned the wearing of Inca royal garb; the display of any paintings or likenesses of the former Inca kings; the production of any dramas or spectacles portraying the Incas; the use of any Inca symbols, such as flags or conch shell horns; and even the writings of the Inca Garcilaso de la Vega and others that might encourage the recovery of Inca culture. In short, any vestiges of the Inca past that might serve to revive the general idea of an imagined "golden age" were outlawed by the state in a secular campaign reminiscent of the Church's effort two centuries earlier to extirpate idolatry.

In addition to the stick, the colonial regime employed the carrot to implement its postrebellion strategy of Andean pacification. On the matter of reforming the colonial system of exploitation, which constituted the other dimension of Túpac Amaru II's rebellion, the crown adopted a more conciliatory position. It established a new *audiencia* in Cuzco in 1787 that would ostensibly be more responsive to local needs and concerns, particularly Indian complaints for justice. Furthermore, not only was the *reparto de mer-*

cancías abolished in 1784, but the *corregimiento* was reorganized and replaced by the new intendancy system, so that the popularly hated office of *corregidor* was eliminated. *Corregidores* were replaced by new crown officials called *subdelegados*, who served under the intendent's authority, but who proved as abusive to the Indians as the *corregidores* whom they replaced.

Visitador Areche also tried to abolish the *curacas*, with mixed success because the native *caciques* (headmen) fought a protracted struggle in the courts to retain control of their office. Over time, however, the indigenous aristocracy withered, losing whatever status and position it had held as "intermediaries" in the colonial order. This loss of status, in turn, produced a leveling effect in which all natives increasingly came to be considered "indios," part of the vast Indian underclass whose rights increasingly dwindled and whose privations and humiliations seemed to deepen.

Although these postrebellion administrative reforms changed the face of the colonial system, they did not alter its fundamental purpose: to collect the tribute tax from the indigenous population that was necessary to finance internal security in the wake of the uprising and the interminable wars in which Bourbon Spain was engaged in Europe. In place of the *curaca* system, as Sala i Vila (1996) showed, a flood of creoles, mestizos, and other "outsiders" came to control the collection of the tribute, thus gaining access to community labor and land that they proceeded to exploit and appropriate for themselves. As a result, undercurrents of social and political alienation continued to roil the indigenous population down to the end of the century and beyond, propelling local protests and nascent separatist movements that became a notable feature of late colonial Andean society.

As for internal security in the wake of the revolt, after 1783 the crown deployed regular Spanish troops in several Andean provinces and demobilized the creole militias that it considered suspect. Viceregal defense, reflective of the elite's awareness of the dangers of Indian rebellion, now took on as much an internal function of social control as it did its traditional external role against potential foreign invasion.

Responding to Gálvez's efforts to pacify the native population in the wake of the Great Rebellion, the Indian population undertook to defend itself in a variety of ways. One of the most effective ways, according to Walker (1999), who examined over a thousand trial records dating from 1783 to 1821, was to resort to the courts to defend their community autonomy from the continued abuses of the subdelegates and other officials. Fearful of the renewed possibilty of native unrest and revolt and still heavily dependent on the collection of tribute, the colonial regime, through the courts, often responded favorably to many of these suits. In this way, the colonial pact, in its time-honored way, continued constantly to be renegotiated and remade.

In the end, the Great Rebellion of Túpac Amaru II, if the rebellion in Upper Peru is included as well, cost upward of 100,000 lives out of a total population of 1.2 million, or almost 10 percent of the population, and left a traumatic legacy of Andean race relations in the Peruvian popular consciousness

for a century or more. Indeed, it opened an enormous breach between Indian and Spanish Peru that has still not been closed more than 200 years
later. At the same time, the Great Rebellion unified the ranks of creoles and
Spaniards in a common cause against the threat posed by the indigenous
masses to their privileged positions at the top of the Andean hierarchy. The
outbreak of social revolution graphically illustrated to the creoles the dangers of mobilizing the subaltern classes in behalf of their own developing
grievances and frustrations against the dominant peninsular class and the
royalist regime. In this sense, then, the inherent inability of the rebels to construct a viable creole-Indian alliance, together with the fundamental ethnic
divisions and atomization of the Indian population—effectively exploited
by the royalist regime—doomed the Great Rebellion to failure.

On the other hand, the revolt by Túpac Amaru II revolt did show signs,
in its uses of the Inca past and its multiethnic character, of the emergence
for the first time of a protonationalist, counterhegemonic, and anticolonial
political project for the Andes. Even though it was never able to articulate
any clear vision of what exactly the postcolonial Andean polity would be
like, the indigenous nationalism that it expressed would be reformulated
and rekindled at various times and places in the country's future. At this
moment in the country's evolution, however, the movement's social base—
the weakened *curaca* class and petty middle sectors—was, as Walker observed, simply too weak and too anemic to overturn the accumulated weight
and power of the colonial order.

As for independence, it would remain for a much more narrowly defined and exclusionist, Lima-based creole liberalism, with the crucial assistance of outside forces, finally to defeat the Spaniards and end three centuries of Spanish rule in the Andes. Until then, Peru would remain for
another generation a bastion of Spanish power on the South American continent.

Fall of the Royal Government and
the Coming of Independence: 1780–1824

Historical interpretations of the origins of Peruvian independence have generally fallen into three categories. The traditional, or patriotic, view, pro-
pounded by the oligarchical state prior to 1968, was that Peruvians of all
ethnic and social groups—Indians, mestizos, and creoles—were mobilized
and led by "heroic" creole leaders in a popular uprising against Spanish
rule. This official version was taught in the schools at all levels and fostered
the myth of "creole nationalism" to unify the nation under elite rule.

The nationalist and populist Velasco Revolution of 1968, whose symbol
was Túpac Amaru II and that sought to revindicate and incorporate the indigenous masses through land reform and other changes, articulated an alternative discourse of "indigenous nationalism." In this version, indigenous

leaders, such as Túpac Amaru II were incorporated into the pantheon of the heroes of Peruvian independence, alongside the familiar creole ones, thereby serving in a similar way to unify the nation, but this time in a much more inclusive and popular fashion.

Both the "creole" and "indigenous" versions of nationalism were then challenged by a revisionist Marxist school of historians, headed by Bonilla and Spalding (1972, 1981), that emerged in the early 1970s. Bonilla and Spalding argued that nationalism was absent from Peru in 1820 because creoles were unconvinced of the necessity of independence. For one thing, their economic and financial interests were intimately bound to the old regime. Moreover, in light of the experience of the Túpac Amaru II rebellion, they feared that mobilizing the indigenous masses in behalf of independence might bring about a wider social upheaval that would threaten their vital interests. At the same time, Bonilla and Spalding argued that the Indian population had still not sufficiently recovered from the defeat and subsequent repression of that rebellion, nor were they free of traditional ethnic rivalries and cultural differences to unify effectively in behalf of independence. Finally, they maintained that Indians had no reason to make common cause with the creole class, whom they viewed, along with the peninsulars, as their oppressors.

This view of independence has much to recommend it, particularly as an explanation for the concrete fact that Peruvian independence was more "conceded" than "won." By this term, historians mean that the overthrow of the old regime was the result of the intervention of foreign armies, first the forces of General José de San Martín from the south and then the northern army of General Simón Bolívar, under whose banner the last royalist forces in Peru and South America were defeated at the Battle of Ayacucho in 1824.

Since the 1970s, a new generation of historians, while accepting the advances of the revisionists, have moved to decenter Lima from their study of the overthrow of the old Spanish regime. They have described a much more complex, fragmented, and regional movement in which the rebellion of Túpac Amaru II played a more decisive role, for it expressed a multiethnic, cross-class and protonationalist vision whose themes, as I discuss next, would continue to resonate in various provincial rebellions leading up to independence.

Popular participation in the movement for independence sometimes occurred in behalf of the patriots' cause and sometimes in support of the royalists. This variability gave the struggle the added dimension of a civil war, but a contest involving a wide variety of social strata and ethnic groups on the local level. Popular mobilization might be from above, through recruitment (forced or voluntary), or below, in a more spontaneous manner. In either case, it was often instigated by leaders of peasant communities or local caudillos who were able to activate clientelist networks or by outside military leaders (royalist or insurgent) who elicited local popular support. Given what had happened in the Túpac Amaru II revolt, the dilemma for both patriot and royalist commanders was to ensure sufficient control over such popular forces that they could not threaten their own elite groups or property.

Montoneras, or Indian guerrilla forces, for example, played an important role in rolling back the royalist army in the central sierra, as Rivera Serna (1958) and others have shown. Black slaves also fled south-coast plantations to join the invading army of General San Martín. On the other hand, the royalist army, which managed to avoid defeat until the Battle of Ayacucho, was conscripted largely from peasants in the Cuzco and Lake Titicaca regions of the southern highlands. Moreover, according to the work of Husson (1992) and Méndez (1996), there was considerable royalist support among the Iquichana Indians in the province of Huanta who rose in rebellion after independence (1826–28) for the restoration of Ferdinand VII and viceregal Spanish rule. How the subaltern classes reacted in the conflict over independence, as Manrique observed, depended on the specific correlation of forces in a particular localty. However, generally speaking, the bulk of the Indian peasantry remained passive spectators to the struggle for independence, sensing correctly that the outcome, in the hands of the creole elites, would not bring about any fundamental change in their condition of colonial subordination.

Most historians have found the deep origins of independence in the attempt by Spain under Charles III to regain tight control over the colonies in the second half of the eighteenth century. These measures, as you have seen, incited protest from a wide range of colonial social and ethnic groups. In particular, they tended to alienate creoles who had de facto emerged with considerable political and economic power as a consequence of Spain's decline and separation from the colonies during the previous century. Moreover, in the course of gaining this autonomy, the creoles had acquired more of an identity of their own, which led them increasingly to differentiate themselves as a group from their peninsular rulers. Finally, the Enlightenment provided an intellectual framework of new ideas and a critical spirit that, in certain creole quarters, fueled a reformist and sometimes radical discourse to challenge the old regime.

A severe blow to greater creole autonomy, as I noted earlier, occurred when Minister of the Indies José Gálvez (1776–87) began to replace creole officials with peninsular Spaniards. By 1803 only one *Limeño,* José Baquijano y Carrillo, and one other creole were members of the *audiencia,* whereas between the 1740s and 1770s, Lima's creoles had constituted a majority. This anti-creole policy led the creoles from the 1790s on constantly to demand that the crown appoint at least one-third to one-half of all governmental positions to creoles.

However, if Peru's creoles chaffed at such efforts to exclude them from office and at other reforms that were designed to extract greater revenues through higher taxes, many were well integrated into the mercantilist colonial economy. They were part of a colonial elite that included north-coast landowners, Lima merchants and shippers, and the silver miners of Cerro de Pasco and Potosí. Standing at the center of this elite were the merchant-creditors of Lima who, by virtue of their crucial location at the crossroads of commercial, financial, and political power, occupied a commanding position within the viceregal economy. The merchant-creditors, in turn, dominated the *Tribunal del Consulado,* a powerful mercantile corporation with tight connections to the political apparatus and institutions of royal government, including the *audiencia.* Despite greviances with the existing system, the overwhelming interests of this colonial elite lay in the maintenance of the royal government.

This situation led Flores Galindo (1984) to conclude that the colonial ruling class did not fracture in Peru as it did elsewhere in Latin America, thereby avoiding for a time the revolutionary events unfolding throughout the continent. For him, the essential unity of the elite, together with its fundamental self-interest in maintaining the system, explains why Peru remained largely loyal to the crown until it was finally liberated from the outside by San Martín and Bolívar. Timothy Ana's (1979) analysis of Lima's ruling elite came to a similar conclusion in a somewhat different way. Out of a total population of 63,809 inhabitants in 1813, Ana calculated the size of the elite at about 1,500 persons, only a third of whom were producers of real wealth (Flores Galindo's mercantile elite). The rest, according to him, were dependent on holding office in the royal administrative and ecclesiastical apparatus. Thus, their careers and livelihoods were intricately bound up with the royalist regime, which explains their ambivalent, if mainly loyalist, attitude toward the crown.

Another reason why Lima remained a bastion of royal power down to independence in 1824 lies in the elites' attitudes toward the subaltern classes. Although the Lima elites might be reluctant to jeoporadize their fundamental economic and employment interests by taking up the cause of independence, they also harbored fears that colonial social controls over the popular classes might unravel in such a conflict. Fully a third of Lima's population, for example, was composed of black slaves, while nearby estates relied heavily on slave labor. Although far removed and not readily threatened by the Túpac Amaru II rebellion, which had unleashed the Indian masses and raised the specter of social revolution in the Andes, *Limeños* were concerned about the potential of slave rebellions on the coast. Such concerns proved real in the face of the response of south-coast slaves to San Martín's appeal to join his invading army, as well as the brief rioting by the urban plebes that erupted in Lima when royalist forces evacuated the city on July 5, 1821, four days before San Martín's army occupied it.

If Lima remained understandably a center of reaction and royal domination during the first quarter of the nineteenth century, the situation in the southern highlands was another matter. After all, the Túpac Amaru II rebellion, which began as a reaction against Bourbon absolutism, had engulfed the Andes in a brief but violent, anticolonist upheaval. While the rebellion revealed deep protonationalist sentiments among broad sectors of the sierra population, it also brought out the strong regional antipathy to Lima's political domination of the viceroyalty. Resentment of the exercise of royal dominance by Lima officials in local matters ran deep in provincial elite circles. This resentment not only fueled demands for greater autonomy and even separatist tendencies, but it would inform the postindependence debates on the future form of republican government between conservative forces in favor of centralism and liberals advocating decentralization and federalism.

Although there were no major manifestations against Spanish rule between the end of the Túpac Amaru II revolt in 1783 and the turn of the century, there continued to be doubts in Lima as to the loyalty of Cuzco, which had expressed some sympathy, at least initially, for the revolt. After the suppression of the rebellion, the crown had moved to demobilize the creole militias, whose loyalty to the crown had been in some doubt, and to replace them with garrisons of regular Spanish troops in Cuzco and elsewhere in the southern highlands. Moreover, the newly created *audiencia* of Cuzco, rather than being seen as an instrument to decentralize power in response to opinion in the province, was viewed as another mechanism of *Limeño* domination. Finally, the region's economy continued to suffer from the long-term disruption of Andean trade circuits with Upper Peru caused by the imperial reorganization of 1776, the declining production of silver at Potosí, and the advent of free trade within the empire in 1778.

It was in this context of administrative discontent, economic stagnation, and the continuing attraction of Andean cultural nationalism and utopianism that a conspiracy against the royalist regime was uncovered in 1805 in Cuzco. The protagonists were two *Cusqueño* creoles, the mineralogist Gabriel Aguilar and Juan Manuel Ubalde, a member of the *audiencia*, both of whom were representatives of the provincial middle class, who plotted to seize control of Cuzco, declare an Inca as king, and expel the Spaniards. What is notable about this plot, according to Flores Galindo (1987), was its expression, like the Túpac Amaru II revolt earlier, of a distinctly Andean cultural dimension that seemed to appeal to a diversity of social classes— poor indigenous peasants and rich Indian nobles, restless creoles and impoverished mestizos. The latter now constituted 22 percent of the entire viceregal population in the census of 1795.

In contrast to the southern highlands, where economic stagnation and neo-Inca nationalism continued to provoke anticolonial activities, the discontent with colonial rule in the central highlands was based on economic advance. The eighteenth century had seen, as I noted earlier, a major shift in the economic gravity of Peru, based on silver mining, from Potosí in the south to Cerro de Pasco and Huarochirí in the center. The prosperity and spread effects of mining in the region in the second half of the century, as Mallon (1983) related, spawned an emerging, upwardly mobile bourgeoisie of merchants and miners of relatively modest origins who were blocked from further advancement by the social and political monopoly exercised by the dominant local peninsular elite and their creole allies. For them, the idea of free trade and a more open economic and political system was an attractive alternative to the closed colonial order and worked to loosen their loyalties to the crown. As you shall see, it was precisely these groups that organized the *montoneras*, or Indian guerrilla bands, that would provide a substantial pocket of support for independence.

Shortly after the 1805 Cuzco plot was exposed and quickly suppressed by the authorities, royal power in Peru was jolted by the Napoleonic invasion of Spain in 1808. The capture of Charles IV and his son Ferdinand VII (to whom he had been forced to abdicate), together with the imposition of the French usurper Joseph Bonaparte as king brought into question the legitimacy of continued Spanish rule throughout all Spanish America. In the absence of the legitimate king, did sovereignty revert to the people? This doctrine was picked up in liberal circles from the American Revolution of 1776 and the French Revolution of 1789, but was also founded on older neo-Thomist notions. Answering this constitutional question in the affirmative, dissident creoles in the colonies deposed the peninsular authorities and formed local governing juntas in La Paz, Quito, Caracas, Santiago, and Buenos Aires between April and September 1810.

This overthrow of peninsular authorities did not happen in Peru, but considerable confusion and uncertainty did reign in the viceroyalty between 1809 and 1814. The collapse of the monarchy in Spain led Viceroy José Fernando de Abascal (1806–16) to move to ensure the loyalty of the Lima elite by adopting a policy of *concordancia*, at the same time taking measures to tighten royal political control throughout the interior. Abascal was particularly concerned about converting Peru into a bastion of defense against the main center of rebellion that had broken out in the River Plate Viceroyalty at Buenos Aires and its far reaches in Upper Peru, including La Paz. Toward this end, he appointed Brigadier General José Manuel de Goyeneche y Barreda (1776–1846), a loyal creole and native of Arequipa, as military commander of Cuzco and president of the *audiencia*. Goyeneche raised an army, including Indians from the Pumacahua and Choquehuanca clans, that managed to defeat insurgent forces in La Paz in 1811. This successful royalist effort, however, placed a considerable manpower and financial burden on Cuzco that added to its already considerable list of complaints against the colonial regime.

To complicate matters further, a great deal of confusion between 1809 and 1814 arose around the implementation of the liberal reform program of the Junta Central at Seville and the Cortes or parliament at Cádiz, which had been formed to rule in the name of the imprisoned Ferdinand. Viceroy Abascal, who was an extremely capable administrator but unabashed absolutist, did not look favorably on any attempts from Spain to liberalize colonial rule, that is, to consider shifting some decision-making power to the colonials or, even worse, the abolition of the tribute (passed in 1811) that would have severely compromised viceregal finances and undermined the whole edifice of the colonial order. To the dismay of many *Cuzqueño* liberals, he and the *audiencia* of Cuzco actually tried to obstruct implementation of the reforms that were voted by the Cortes. In addition to declaring Spain a constitutional monarchy, the Cortes also called for the election of delegates by the *cabildos* throughout America to present their grievances against Spanish rule.

Even in Lima, the prospects of colonial liberalization tended momentarily to energize a small group of liberals over the prospects of change. Liberalism had emerged in Peru during the 1780s as the ideas of the Enlightenment filtered into intellectual circles and beyond from abroad. One of its leading advocates and exponents was José Baquijano, whose address welcoming the new viceroy in 1781 had initiated a whole generation of debate over the Spanish colonial system. The Real Convictorio de San Carlos, which housed the humanities faculty of San Marcos University, was a center of Enlightenment thought in which the ideas of Locke, Descartes, and Voltaire circulated among teachers and students. It was in the halls of San Carlos and in the pages of the influential journal *Mercurio Peruano* (1791–95), whose guiding light was the other leading *Limeño* enlightenment intellectual Hipólito Unánue, that the first criticism of the Spanish colonial system emerged, along with a moderate reformist discourse calling for change. Espousing intellectual freedom and rationalism, as well as natural rights and the equality of man, the biweekly *Mercurio* also published numerous scientific articles that deepened knowledge of Peru's natural resources and distinct environment.

Although the generation of Baquijano and the one that followed in 1808 produced an array of brilliant intellects, including Manuel Lorenzo Vidaurre, José Faustino Sánchez Carrión, and the priest Francisco Javier Luna Pizarro, few of these so-called intellectual precursors of independence actually advocated separatism or the cause of independence. Members or aspirants to elite circles and anxious to obtain the sinecures and perquisites of the colonial and ecclesiastical system, most couched their criticisms of the treatment of the Indians or the Spanish monopoly system in measured tones and advocated good government, equality for creoles, and greater autonomy for Peru. They were reformers and constitutionalists, not separatists or revolutionaries.

If liberal hopes for change and greater autonomy were raised by the reforms of the Cortes, articulated in the new Spanish Constition of 1812, they were largely dashed by the conservative reaction that followed the restoration of Ferdinand VII in 1814. In general, there was little conspiratorial activity among the Lima elite during this entire period, ending with San Martín's capture of Lima in 1821. The plots that were hatched in the capital, mainly after the liberation of Chile in 1818, involved a tiny, unrepresentative minority of the population, were poorly organized and conceived, were met with apathy by the public at large, and were quickly suppressed. This was not, however, the case in the rest of Peru, particularly in the southern provinces, where several serious armed uprisings occurred. Lima's creoles, nevertheless, uniformly supported the repression of these revolts by the viceregal regime. This support reflected, among other things, their fear that these provincial uprisings constituted a threat to Lima's historical political dominance over the country. The first major revolt in the provinces against the crown erupted in 1811 in Tacna, a region economically linked to Upper Peru that it supplied with wine, *aguardiente* (brandy), oil, fruits, and rice, as well as some imported manufactures. It was significant on two counts: first, because of the desire that it expressed in southern Peru for reunion with Upper Peru and, second, because it illustrated that provincial creoles were willing to entertain alliances with the Indian masses to overturn Spanish rule. The revolt fizzled when news was received that a rebel army from Buenos Aires, which the Tacna rebels had hoped to link up with, had been defeated by royalist forces under General Goyeneche at La Paz. Other similarly unsuccessful provincial revolts broke out in Huamanga, Huánuco, and Tarma in 1812 and the Intendancy of Arequipa in 1813.

The most serious provincial challenge to Spanish rule in the years leading up to 1821, however, occurred in Cuzco in 1814. For a short time, the rebellion spread to all southern Peru (including La Paz in Upper Peru) and even appeared to threaten Lima itself. Its leadership, the three Angulo brothers and José Gabriel Béjar, came from the creole and mestizo middle class that was educated, articulate, and ambitious for power. The Angulo family were local *hacendados* who were also active in mining and commerce, having educated their sons at the University of San Antonio Abad in Cuzco, a center of dissident ideas. Beginning as essentially an urban movement, the revolt was supported by a cross section of Cuzco society, including members of the lower clergy and the bishop of Cuzco. Later it expanded into the countryside, gaining the allegiance of several Indian leaders, including the powerful Mateo García Pumacahua, who had been instrumental in the defeat of Túpac Amaru II in 1781 and whose clan represented one of the "sacred *ayllus*" of Cuzco. Now over seventy years old, the old Indian *cacique* (headman) was apparently resentful at having been replaced by the viceroy as president of the *audiencia*.

The causes of the revolt were both political and economic. They derived, in part, from the conflict between those who welcomed the liberal reforms of 1812, but were frustrated by the *audiencia*'s failure to implement them. Then, liberal hopes for reform were completely dashed in late 1814 with the restoration of Ferdinand VII to the Spanish throne, the abolition of the liberal constitution of 1812, and the reimposition of an absolutist regime. These developments coincided with the continuing economic stagnation of the region and the drain of manpower and resources committed by Viceroy Abascal to the supression of the revolts for independence in La Paz.

Again there were manifestations of Indian nationalism while the revolt's leaders emphasized the multiethnic dimensions of the movement. The leaders also declared their intention of creating an independent empire spanning the continent, with its capital not in Lima, but Cuzco. Flores Galindo (1987) believes that this was another instance, like that of Túpac Amaru II, of Andean rebels using the Incas to construct an alternative, counterhegemonic, anticolonial movement in the southern highlands. Certainly, the work of Arequipan poet Mariano Melgar (1790–1815), who was executed for his participation in the 1814 rebellion, lends credence to this view. It expressed strong nationalist sentiments, together with a progressive radicalism, and, anticipating *indigenismo*, concern for the oppressed Indian masses. Melgar's poem "Marcha Patriótica," for example, celebrated Pumacahua's triumphal entry into Arequipa in 1814, while others innovatively integrated the *yaravi*—popular, pre-Hispanic love songs played on the guitar.

Had the Cuzco rebels been successful, Basadre (1973) believes, outside intervention would have been unnecessary and the new Peruvian nation would have had a much more popular multiethnic base than the narrow, creole republic conceived by the propertied and intellectual classes after 1821. In the end, both the racial composition and separatist intentions of the rebels and the excesses of some of the Indian guerrillas against all "exploiters," were enough once again to turn *Limeño* creoles against the Cuzco rebellion. Had the creoles lent their support, the movement would almost certainly have succeeded in overturning Spanish rule in Peru. However, the movement was finally dispersed by a royalist army sent from Lima, and its leaders were rounded up, summarily tried, and executed for treason in 1816.

In the years following the defeat of the Cuzco revolt, the center of revolutionary activity would shift from the southern highlands to Lima and the coast. For the moment, however, there was a hiatus of activity that coincided elsewhere on the continent with the concerted royalist offensive that reconquered former rebel territories in Venezuela and Colombia and stymied the insurgency in the River Plate. This royalist resurgence essentially ended the first phase of the independence struggle and, with the restoration of the absolutist Ferdinand VII in Spain, the possibilty of reforming the colonial pact in favor of more autonomy for America, including Peru. Henceforth, the options would either be some form of monarchy (constitutional or absolute) or independence.

Abascal now took the opportunity of retiring to Spain in 1816, handing over power to a new viceroy, Joaquín de la Pezuela, who inherited a formidable royalist army that numbered some 70,000, although the majority were members of the militias that had been restored in the wake of 1808. However, Pezuela was left a mounting fiscal crisis, with a nearly empty treasury, sharply declining silver output, falling coastal agricultural production, and increasing military costs. The main culprit was the declining economy, precipitated by a sudden, sharp drop in silver production after 1812, particularly at Cerro de Pasco, which now accounted for 60–70 percent of the total viceregal output. The fall in silver production, together with the political uncertainties related to the wars for independence elsewhere on the continent, worked to slow down general economic activity and hence capital investment throughout the viceroyalty. Moreover, when San Martín's army in the River Plate unexpectedly marched over the Andes and successfully captured Chile in 1818, Peru's lucrative exchange of sugar for wheat was suddenly ended, severely damaging coastal agricultural and Lima mercantile interests.

With the fall of Chile, viceregal defense became even more imperative. It was funded by higher taxes and increased contributions from wealthy *Limeño* elites that absorbed what little surplus was available for reinvestment to sustain the faltering economy. An estimated 5 million pesos apparently had gone to fund Spanish military campaigns in Europe between 1777 and 1814 while thereafter these "contributions" went to finance royalist armies in Peru and elsewhere on the continent. One index of the economic crisis shows that the country's total production of around 8.7 million pesos was much too low to sustain annual imports of approximately 5 million pesos and additional governmental expenditures, including defense, of 4 million–5 million pesos a year. The result was growing deficit spending by the viceregal government, so that the internal debt grew from 8 million pesos at the beginning of the wars for independence to 11 million in 1816 to a minimum of 16 million–20 million pesos in 1819.

Although Peruvians continued to chaff under the burden of increased taxes and forced contributions levied to maintain royalist forces, the cause of independence drew few outward manifestations until the naval landing of San Martín's 4,000-man expeditionary force of Argentines and Chileans at Pisco, 200 kilometers south of Lima, in 1820. Promising freedom for south-coast slaves, San Martín managed to entice a large number of blacks to abandon their plantations for his army. Shortly after he moved his force by sea to the port of Huacho in the north, a number of northern coastal cities declared for independence. The most important city was Trujillo, where the intendant, the Marquis de Torre Tagle, had a long record of personal grievances related to frustrated expectations for appointment to higher office.

Torre Tagle's declaration of independence was accompanied by outbreaks of guerrilla activity against royalist forces in the central highlands. In the central highlands, the mountanous terrain, the proximity to Lima, and the large number of muleteers who were connected to the silver mines and peasants who were involved in the market economy made conditions ideal for the organization of *montoneras* by a dissident bourgeoisie of miners and merchants in support of independence. San Martín's position had been further enhanced earlier when Ferdinand VII in 1820 was forced to restore the liberal constitution of 1812 and seemed more inclined to negotiate a settlement of the colonial conflict, since Spain was in no position to send further troop reinforcements to America.

In this atmosphere, the ever-cautious San Martín adopted a wait-and-see approach, hoping that his mere presence would rally Peruvians to the rebel cause and show royalist authorities the futility of any military resistance. He even entered into brief discussions with the viceregal regime in which he expressed his preference for a new independent but monarchical government under a prince from the royal Spanish family. Nothing came of these talks, although in their midst Viceroy Pezuela was replaced in a military coup by General José de la Serna.

Sizing up the military situation, De la Serna concluded that he was unable to defend the capital and evacuated his forces momentarily to the Callao fortress of San Felipe and then to Huancayo in the central sierra. This evacuation caught San Martín by surprise and left Lima suddenly defenseless and without authority for four days, leading to the outbreak of popular disturbances in which mobs attacked the commercial establishments of peninsular merchants. Upon entering the city unopposed on July 10, 1821, San Martín quickly restored order.

Almost three weeks later, on July 28, San Martín declared independence, assumed the position of provisional ruler, or protector, and called for the election of a congress. A month later, he issued a series of liberal-nationalist postcolonial decrees, including freedom for all children born of slaves, abolition of the Indian tribute (unaware that it had actually been renamed *contribución* a decade earlier) and forced labor, and the transcendental declaration that hereafter all Indians were to be called Peruvians (in theory making all Peruvians equal). He also ordered peninsulars to be expelled from the country and their property, along with that of their royalist creole allies, to be confiscated. Of the 10,000 Spaniards in Lima, only 1,000 remained after the expulsion was carried out. Already severely weakened from continual loans and donations to defend royal power in America, the old colonial ruling class was effectively destroyed by these confiscatory measures.

Initial enthusiasm for San Martín and his new republican government was quickly sullied, however, by, among other things, growing economic paralysis. The confiscation of proroyalist haciendas and recruitment of slaves into the liberation army disrupted food production on the coast and resulted in severe shortages and price inflation for comestibles in the capital. Silver production all but ceased, resulting in a severe shortage of both bullion to purchase foreign goods and metal coins as circulating specie for internal commerce. As the economy ground to a halt, tax revenues, mainly from customs and mining, dried up, and the government resorted to further forced contributions and the wholesale printing of money. Ultimately, these deteriorating conditions fanned the fires of public discontent and resentment against the new republican government and "foreign" rule. Indeed, most of San Martín's advisers and appointees were Argentines who were universally disliked as outsiders, particularly the autocratic and arbitrary minister of war Bernardo Monteagudo.

When the navy went unpaid, Admiral Thomas Cochrane, a mercenary who commanded the Chilean fleet, added insult to injury by deserting and returning to Chile with the government's entire bullion reserve. Ironically, most of the Chilean fleet was now composed of Peru's merchant marine, which shippers had turned over to the viceroy for the defense of Lima-

Callao, but which had been captured by the Chileans. The loss of these ships dealt another blow to Lima merchants and traders, whose previous dominance of the Pacific trade was now assumed by the ports of Valparaiso and, to a lesser extent, Guayaquil.

By mid-1822, only a year after San Martín triumphantly entered Lima and proclaimed Peruvian independence, his government was in disarray, and his prospects for liberating the interior were dim. He was further hampered by the deterioration of his health, having suffered since childhood from tuberculosis and now increasingly from opium addiction, used in ever larger amounts as a painkiller. Ill and unable to mobilize his army to move up into the sierra to challenge the still-formidable royalist forces under de la Serna, San Martín decided to travel to Guayaquil in July to meet with General Simón Bolívar, whose northern forces were gradually closing the remaining pincer on Peru.

This historic meeting between the two great liberators of South America lasted four days and seemed to reach no specific agreement or timetable on how to liberate Peru. Since no written record was kept of the meeting, what transpired is not altogether clear, although Bolívar appears to have offered to send troops to Peru. We do know that upon his return to Lima, a sick San Martín, perhaps realizing that Peru was not big enough for both liberators and sensing the waning of his political influence as yet another outsider ruling the country, decided to step down as protector. In September 1822, he submitted his resignation to the newly convened Congress and immediately sailed for home.

The fifty-one-delegate congress, composed mainly of lawyers, physicians, churchmen, and military officers, now assumed power, first appointing a junta that ruled ineffectively for only a few months. Then, under pressure from the army for stronger leadership in what Basadre called Peru's first military coup, it appointed the Lima aristocrat José de la Riva Agüero, a longtime proponent of independence, as the first president of the republic. Riva Agüero spent much of his four-month tenure feuding with Congress and presiding over a 1.2 million-pound foreign loan from England. When royalist attacks compelled the evacuation of the government from Lima to Callao, Congress then deposed Riva Agüero, named Torre Tagle president, and invited Bolívar to enter Peru. However, Riva Agüero refused to relinquish power or recognize the new regime and moved his government to Trujillo, where he entered negotiations with the royalists. When Bolívar landed in Callao on September 1, 1823, he found that Peru now had two presidents and was virtually bankrupt. Under pressure from the army to end the political chaos, Congress, despite the suspicion of many that Bolívar was a Napoleon-like usurper, made him military dictator and commander of the armed forces.

For a time, not even the genius of Bolívar could reverse the plummeting fortunes of Peruvian independence and the pestilential political anarchy of Lima. Eventually, Bolívar determined that Lima could not be held and withdrew to Trujillo in the north to secure a more viable base from which to mount an attack on royalist forces in the sierra. Lima was again reoccupied by a loyalist army from February until December 1824 and witnessed the extraordinary defection of President Torre Tagle and almost the entire patriot leadership back to the royalist side. By March 1824, all but the north was once again under Spanish control, and the patriot cause seemed lost.

Bolívar nonetheless persevered and began to rebuild his forces in Trujillo. Turning over the administration of the government to the able and patriotic Sánchez Carrión, the liberator patiently gathered an army of over 10,000, composed of Colombians and what was left of the patriot forces. Strategically, he decided to ignore the coast and Lima to concentrate his force against the royalist army in the central sierra. In June 1824, he moved his army into the sierra, where he received aid from the guerrilla *montoneras* that had never ceased operating in behalf of independence. After winning a brief battle at Junín on August 6, Bolívar divided his force, sending his lieutenant Antonio José de Sucre in pursuit of de la Serna, who had retreated farther into the high *altiplano* of Ayacucho and returning himself to the coast to retake Lima.

In the first few days of December, Bolívar achieved his goal of reoccupying Lima, while Sucre followed shortly thereafter on December 9 by capturing the entire 7,000-man royalist army under de la Serna, effectively ending almost three centuries of Spanish control. (Some scattered royalist resistance was snuffed out by Sucre in Upper Peru in April 1825, securing the independence of Bolivia, while a small detachment of royalists who were holding out in the San Felipe fortress in Callao finally surrendered after a long and brutal siege on January 23, 1826.) After a generation of vacillation and intermittent struggle, the deed was finally done: Peru was at last free. But its people and their leaders now faced the daunting challenge of constructing a viable new government, based on untried republican principles and capable of exerting a measure of national unity over a vast, but still largely undefined territory.

5 Republican Utopia and Postindependence Instability, 1824–40

Postcolonial, republican Peru was confronted at the outset of independence by a number of complex problems. Perhaps the most severe was the fundamental contradiction underlying the imagined new nation of the creole founding fathers and expressed in the country's new constitutions. The Bolivarian elites who had brought about the separation from Spain had based their successful challenge to Spain and the colonial pact on the "revolutionary" ideas of popular sovereignty derived from the eighteenth-century European Enlightenment. Peru's independent republic, therefore, was founded on the liberal principles of democracy, citizenship, private property, and individual rights and protections, which, even if occasionally modified to fit local circumstances, in one way or another were written into the various constitutions from 1824 on. Although this notion of popular sovereignty, which theoretically made all *Peruanos* equal, had been effectively applied by creole dissidents to challenge the power of the peninsular ruling class, it in no way corresponded to the sociopolitical reality of three centuries of Spanish colonial rule that Nugent called "aristocratic sovereignty."

Colonial Peru, on the contrary, was a highly stratified, hierarchical, and wholly unequal society that was based upon the fundamental differences among its peoples. "Distinctions based predominantly on race (Indian, mestizo, white), gender (female and male), ancestry (Spanish or not), and land ownership segregated the population into what were (in theory) fixed and inherited social categories that did much to prescribe the life possiblities of the people who occupied them" (Nugent, 1997, p. 15). The rulers of this sociopolitical order were drawn invariably from the white, male elite of Spanish descent, who, in turn, garnered the lion's share of the benefits of that order. In such a patriarchical, patrician, and paternalistic order, the ruling classes were charged with protecting the vast majority of the population (Indians, mestizos, and women) whom they considered essentially "minors"—social inferiors who were incapable of looking after themeselves. Consequently, at its birth and subsequently throughout most of its republican history, the state was weakened by the unresolved conflict between two opposing notions of sociopolitical legitimacy.

Map 5. Peru circa 1830. *Source:* Paul Gootenberg, *Between Silver and Guano: Commercial Policy and the State in Postindependence Peru* (Princeton, NJ, 1989), 2.

The circumstance of the vast Indian majority was typical of this conflict. The native Andeans had been relegated in colonial times to the so-called Indian Republics or towns, where they had been subject to the missionizing and civilizing projects of the Catholic kings and their successors. Resettled or "reduced" to these Christianized Indian *pueblos*, which were granted limited self-government but overseen by royal officials, the indigenous population would hypothetically acquire the virtues of Christian civility and good government. They were also protected by crown laws from the encroachment of members of the Spanish Republics or towns, their counterpoint in the organization of colonial society. However, just as the crown had invented two separate republics (or nations) in their configuration of colonial society, the creole framers of independence, under the influence of the Enlightenment, proceeded to invent or superimpose the idea of a single Peruvian nation. In reality, this was a fiction from which native Andeans continued to be excluded. As Thurner put it, after 1824 "the national community imagined by Peruvian creoles neatly elided the Indian majority" (1995, p. 292).

Indians did not accept this new state of affairs passively, however, and began shortly after independence in certain places to "contest" this creole conception of nation by demanding that the new postcolonial republican state uphold their traditional "Indian rights," based on the old *repúblicas*. These demands quickly became the basis of a negotiation on the local level between the *caudillos*, who emerged as the new political actors and arbiters of the postindependence order.

The *caudillos* were the result of another postcolonial problem. With the collapse of the colonial state in 1824, the centrifugal political tendencies inherent in Peru, but normally held in check by the center (Lima), reemerged with a vengence. On the one hand, power dispersed to the countryside, where a loosely connected and often conflictive network of seignorial landowners (*gamonales*), in association with larger landowners (*latifundistas*), asserted their authority. These rural elites wielded de facto political control over vast areas, frequently held public office, and remained largely free from the restraints of a weak republican central state in Lima. The cornerstone of their power was their control of the land and dominion over a servile labor force, composed of Indian peasants whose labor and services they appropriated. In short, Peru at the beginning of the republican era was a mosaic of regional agrarian societies resembling a feudal order.

In this contradictory and fractured postcolonial environment, a series of atavistic strongmen, or *caudillos*—the ubiquitous military leaders who ruled Spanish America in the nineteenth century—emerged after 1824 to contest for political power. Most were military figures, having established their reputations in the wars for independence and their power base in the army. Having lasted for a prolonged period, the wars had legitimated the use of force in the resolution of political disputes, while the army, along with the Church, emerged as one of the few relatively coherent institutions in postindependence society. However, this coherence did not mean that the military was unified. On the contrary, it was shot through with personal rivalries and factionalism that further contributed to the chaotic nature of politics after 1825.

By skillfully manipulating Hispanic personalism and clientelism, these ubiquitous Andean *caudillos* mobilized supporters and held out the largess of the national treasury and appointments to offices as rewards for loyalty. They also established alliances with various landed elites and Indian communities, used force or the threat of force to defeat their rivals, and negotiated support from civil society to gain power at the local, regional, and national levels. The result was that early Andean republican society, in the context of unchecked class and regional conflicts and the relentless rivalries of officers and elites, was perpetually pulled apart and destablized. Replete with an assortment of elections, annulments, plots, conspiracies, coups, putches, and rebellions, Peru experienced no less than twenty-four changes of regimes, averaging one per year, between 1821 and 1845, and the Constitution was rewritten a total of six times.

Nevertheless, although it appears that the decades following independence were utterly chaotic and a seemingly meaningless personalistic scramble for spoils and power, Andean *caudillos* did espouse, as Gootenberg (1989) and others have demonstrated, recognizable programs and represented discernable regional or social blocs. Put another way, "behind the chaos and bald power struggles lay important disagreements about the relationship between state and society" (Walker, 1999, p. 158). Thus, Andean *caudillos* also generally cleaved to one or the other side of the liberal-conservative divide that also characterized Latin American politics in the nineteenth century, although it did not prevent them from opportunistically switching sides or blurring positions or ignoring constitutions for personal advantage, which they often did.

In general, conservatives advocated a strong, centralized state; protectionist trade policies; and the continuation of the corporatist configuration of society. They were also antiforeign, often lapsing into xenophobia while they chastized the liberal penchant for importing foreign ideas and ideologies. Liberals, on the other hand, favored a less centralized, often federalist, state; reduced powers of the presidency; free trade; and the curtailment of corporate rights and were occasionally anticlerical. Neither side, moreover, proposed drastic changes for postindependent Latin America, sharing as they did the idea of "aristocratic sovereignty" that embodied their essentially hierarchical, racist, and elitist view of social organization.

In all the turmoil of the 1820s and 1830s, politically two *caudillos* stand out: the conservative General Agustín Gamarra from Cuzco and his boyhood friend and later arch-rival General Andrés Santa Cruz. Gamarra served as president from 1829 to 1833 and again from 1839 to 1841. Santa Cruz was president briefly in the early 1820s and then became the architect of the short-lived Peru-Bolivian Confederation and its president from 1836 to 1839 (he was president of Bolivia from 1829 to 1839). Both had fought under Bolívar in the wars for independence and were involved in the inumerable intrigues that characterized the politics of the early republic.

Administratively, Peru adhered to many of the jurisdictions of the colonial regime, although the names were changed. For example, the essential division of the country into intendencies was retained, but the name was changed to departments, which were governed by prefects and were further subdivided into provinces, ruled by subprefects. Both the departments and their capitals were important regional centers of authority that exercised a considerable amount of power, since the national government depended on their revenues, mainly the collection of the Indian tribute tax (now *contribución indígena*), periodic military support, and the ability to maintain some degree of order in the interior. The subprefects in the provinces were important because at the local level, they oversaw the collection of taxes; gathered and disseminated information; and, in times of war, recruited soldiers and provided supplies. They, in turn, worked with local tax collectors—agents of the Indian community authorities (*alcaldes*) and a group of petty *misti* (Quechua for "white") officals—who now assumed the role of mediators between the new republican state and Indian society that was formerly held by the defunct *curaca* aristocracy. Like the latter, these petty state officials developed webs of clientage and modes of coercion that penetrated deep into postindependence Indian society. Despite the constant civil wars and disturbances that marked the early republic, the central state continued to collect taxes and operate, much as it had in the colonial period. Finally, Peru's borders, largely adhering to the outlines of the Bourbon colonial viceroyalty, were unsettled and fluid, the focal point of foreign interventions and wars.

One of the few institutions, as I mentioned, to survive relatively intact from the struggle for independence was the Church. In 1792 the Viceroyalty of Peru had 1,818 secular and 1,891 regular clergy, mainly creoles, to serve a population of a little over 1 million inhabitants. In Lima there were 67 churches and chapels, 19 monastaries, and 14 convents. Despite the expulsion of the Jesuits and the confiscation of their enterprises by the state in 1767, the Church was amply supported financially by various endowments, incomes, and fees, including the profits, in the case of the orders, of a great number of haciendas and agrarian properties. In general, the Bourbon reform in its statist and centralist thrust, had succeeded in subordinating the Church, although it still fared well under the "enlightened despotism" and paternalism of the crown.

At the same time, according to Klaiber (1992), contrary to opinion, the Church was not "oscurantist," but was actually fairly liberal, having received the ideas of the Enlightenment, some of which became the focal point of the independence movement. Indeed, the secular clergy, which was predominantly creole, identified with the independence movement, while the regular clergy, comprised mostly of peninsulars, remained loyal to the old regime. However, the disorders of independence and its aftermath negatively affected the Church. Economically, for example, the Church lost much of its wealth as a result of the wars and, in contrast with the colonial period, steadily lost ground fiscally throughout much of the century.

One of the main issues to confront the Church in the postindependence period was the effort by the nascent republican state to retain control of the institution by means of the traditional right of patronage (formerly royal, now national). Consequently, in the wake of independence, the government forced all bishops to abandon their dioceses, and Bolívar moved unilaterally to name new ones. The papacy in Rome rejected this effort to establish a national patronage, however, and not until the mid-1830s was a compromise reached giving Rome the right to approve the acceptability of all appointees.

In this way Rome protected itself against the possible anticlericalism of liberal governments and gradually imposed its more conservative ideological influence or "romanization" of the national church in Peru. As a result, the first bishops who were confirmed in Peru in the 1830s and 1840s, who would be responsible for reorganizing and shaping the institution for the foreseeable future (including the seminaries and therefore the production of the new priesthood), were both ultramontanist and conservative. This fact led Klaiber to assert that "the pluralism that had characterized the church during and after independence (there were royalists, liberals, and moderates among the clergy) was extinguished and replaced by an intellectual uniformity with respect to religion, politics and society" (1992, p. 47).

Beyond the conflict between church and state after 1824, the one issue that stands out during this period was the division over whether to follow a free or protectionist policy on trade. On the side of free trade stood generals Orbegoso, Vivanco, Santa Cruz, and others—liberal *caudillos* who represented the free-trade aspirations of southern regionalism. They were largely defeated, however, by a group of better-organized conservative nationalists, composed of planter aristocrats, *consulado* monopolists, and sierran producers who were centered in Lima and the north. Led by generals Gamarra, La Fuente, Salaverry, and others, these conservative nationalists were able to install a series of protectionist regimes in Lima that generally held sway until the early 1850s.

Economic Decline and Revival

There is no disputing the fact that Peru entered the postindependence era in economic crisis. Peru was geographically isolated, politically unstable, and economically prostrate, and its future appeared dim, indeed. This state of affairs was captured in the memoirs of Hipólito Unánue, the country's first minister of finance, who wrote in 1822:

> [T]he treasury was empty. Agricultural lands within thirty leagues of the capital were but one vast expanse of desolation. The mines were occupied

by the enemy. Callao was in enemy hands, hindering all trade. The economic resources of the people had been drained as a result of the many taxes, and they had been reduced to famine because of the total siege which they had suffered. One saw nothing but misery and desolation wherever one looked." (quoted in Bonilla, *CHLA*, III, 543)

Perhaps the biggest blow was to silver mining, the mainspring of the Peruvian economy, which suffered a dramatic decline during the 1820s when flooding and then the ravages of war crippled production, particularly at Cerro de Pasco. Moreover, the central sierra, which had experienced the main clash between patriot and royalist forces in the early 1820s, was economically devastated. There the rich agricultural bounty of the Mantaro Valley, for example, had been severely depleted to sustain the two largest armies on the continent, not to mention the general destruction they caused, as they maneuvered toward their showdown in Junín.

In the southern sierra, the traditional colonial economy, based on what remained of the Lima–Potosí commercial axis, also collapsed. This collapse led to regional fragmentation that, together with the disintegration of the central government, favored the rise of local elites who nevertheless remained relatively weak until after 1850. In general terms, these groups consolidated their power over the Indian population by propagating an ideology based on their presumed racial, that is, biological superiority over the indigenous masses. At the same time, Indian political power in the communities deteriorated with the disappearance of the *curaca* class, who had served as ethnic lords since pre-Hispanic days.

Agricultural production along the central and northern coasts was in an equally sorry state. The rural economy of this region had been experiencing a long-term decline, dating from the late colonial period, owing to natural disasters, shifting trade patterns, the expulsion of the Jesuits, and the effects of various Bourbon reforms. The wars for independence inflicted more damage on producers of sugar, cotton, wine, and foodstuffs, from Cañete south of Lima to Lambayeque in the north. Not the least was the disruption in the labor supply caused by the recruitment of slaves and peasants into the opposing armies that were contesting independence. Recovery was delayed after 1824 by continuing political upheaval, the general flight and scarcity of capital, and the unwillingness of foreigners to risk investing in such an unsettled political and economic environment.

In these circumstances, coastal landowners looked inward to urban markets and interregional Pacific markets for the possibilities of reviving production and exchange. Herein would lie the essentially protectionist outlook of Lima and the coast, where producers sought to prevent foreign imported foodstuffs, particularly from intrepid Yankee traders and speculators who were attracted to the Pacific coast by the urban food shortages caused by the war. Indeed, by 1825, these traders were supplying almost $2 million annually in flour, cooking fats, tobacco, rum, coarse cottons, and other items to hard-pressed Peruvian consumers.

Planters, on the other hand, looked to reactivate their heavily damaged estates with an eye toward their former market in Chile, where they had sent sugar and tobacco in return for wheat that was milled into flour for Lima bread bakers. This lucrative trade, which was transported by Peru's merchant marine and amounted to over $1 million in 1791, was completely destroyed in the wars of independence. Its collapse opened the way for the decline of Lima-Callao's formerly dominant position in Pacific and international trade and the rise of the neighboring ports of Valparaiso and Guayaquil. The latter became the preferred entry points for European manufactured goods to the west coast, transported around the tip of South America, rather than across the more costly overland Isthmian route. In the face of this competition, Lima and northern elite groups—planters, millers, and merchants—undertook a concerted campaign to try to reestablish trade with Chile.

An entirely different and rival economic formation and outlook emerged in the south. There agriculturalists, generally small producers from Moquegua to Ica with its commercial center in Arequipa, had historically oriented their production of wines, brandy, and foodstuffs toward the mining markets of Potosí and Upper Peru. These items, as well as imported manufactured goods were transported and sold by legions of muleteers and traders who had plied this lucrative trade circuit since the second half of the sixteenth century, although the trade was disrupted by Buenos Aires after it became the seat of a viceroyalty in 1776. As a result, southern agriculturalists, exporters, and merchants saw their salvation after independence in developing the region's trading ties with newly independent Bolivia through a policy of free trade.

They would be joined in the mid-1830s by producers and exporters of wool (first sheep, then alpaca and, to a lesser extent, vicuña and llama), who found a growing overseas market in the British textile industry. Moreover, both groups shared a long-held antipathy to the monopoly that Lima merchants, not to mention politicians, had exercised over the region. The upshot was a growing secessionist sentiment that found expression in the short-lived Peru-Bolivian Confederation (1836–39). So, for more than a generation, the commercial interests of the south, oriented toward Bolivia (and Great Britain), and those of Lima and the north, oriented toward Chile, sharply vied for control of the state, contributing in the process to its fundamental disunity and weakness.

The third major region, constituting the bulk of the country's economy, was the central highlands, where mining and agriculture held sway. The Cerro de Pasco silver mines, which had replaced Potosí as the major producer and exporter of metals in the eighteenth century, did not experience the collapse during the nineteeth century that historians previously believed. Production did reach a nadir in the period 1814–1818 of 837,716 marks (down from 1,472,543 marks from 1804 to 1808), which was followed, over the next two decades, by a general expansion, interrupted by periods of ups and downs, to reach a high of 1,690,328 marks from 1839 to 1843. The dips occurred with the costs of repairing and draining some of the larger mines after damages incurred during the wars. Together with Huarochirí, Cerro de Pasco produced about 65 percent of Peruvian silver (up from 40 percent) during the first two decades of the postindependence period. Most mines were small- to medium-scale operations, scattered over a broad territory, with only rudimentary technology and relatively few Indian laborers.

Silver production, then, provided the economic stimulus to a single region that stretched from Cerro de Pasco west to the fertile Mantaro Valley and east into the jungle toward the department of Huánuco. The most dynamic agricultural producing area in this region was the Mantaro Valley, whose land tenure system was and still is characterized by small landholders, rather than seignorial haciendas, as in the south. Espinoza Soriano attributed this unusual land tenure to a special dispensation from King Philip II to the Huáncas that had barred the hacienda system from the valley as a reward for their alliance with Pizarro against the *Cuzqueño* faction during the conquest. As a result, the indigenous communities of the Mantaro Valley remained free of domination by haciendas, unlike the seignorial south, while its peasantry became a dynamic, independent, and commercially vibrant force in the region. Typical of their energy and initiative, according to Contreras (1987), was the fact that a third of the labor force at Cerro came from seasonally migrating peasants from the Mantaro Valley, who reinvested their earnings back into their community plots.

The advance of silver mining during the 1830s was one of the few national economic bright spots, with exports of bullion and coin amounting to 82 percent to 90 percent of exports, but draining the country of silver to pay for an initial burst of foreign imports during the first half of the 1820s under a short-lived liberal regime. Before it experienced a postwar economic contraction after 1825, Peru was flooded with cheap foreign imports, valued at $4–$5 million annually, principally from Great Britain ($1.5 million) but also from France ($800,000) and the United States ($1.2–$2 million). Although they benefited consumers, these cheap foreign goods, particularly textiles, which composed 90 percent of British imports, severely injured the native artisan class, as well as what remained of the highland textile industry (*obrajes*) after the late colonial liberalization of trade via Buenos Aires. As a result, protectionist sentiment was strong in places like Cuzco.

The fortunes of the mining industry and its spread effects shaped the contours of agricultural production and trade circuits in the highlands. Mining's progress or the lack of it translated roughly to a period of self-sufficiency for haciendas and Indian communities during the more recessionary 1820s while their mining markets were depressed, followed by a revival of production and economic activity during the recovery of the 1830s. There was a discernable decline in the population and importance of urban areas (deurbanization) in the decade or so after independence that tended to reinforce indigenous patterns of production and exchange. Among other things, this decline led Langer and others to suggest that the early nineteenth century represented a period of revival of the Andean ethnic economies of Indian communities that had not been seen since the middle of the sixteenth century.

One indication of such an indigenous economic florescence was the growing importance of Andean fairs, which served not only to facilitate intra-Andean trade through traditional Andean bartering mechanisms, but to link the Indian sector with the nascent wool-export economy. This was the case, for example, with the Vilque fair on the *atliplano* outside Puno in southern Peru, which, by 1840, was thriving as a place where Indians sold primarily camelid fibers (alpaca, llama, vicuña) and purchased goods from outside merchants. Indeed, international demand for various highland wool fibers grew steadily during the 1830s, with bulk exports to Great Britain valued at $650,000 by 1839. This demand stimulated a substantial expansion of animal herds mainly on Indian lands from Cuzco to Puno, with their products collected at fairs like Vilque and delivered to British trading houses located in Arequipa. The economy of the south also benefited from the export of nitrates ($300,000 in 1839), as well as quantities of bark, copper, and cotton.

The generally dismal picture of the macro-Peruvian economy immediately after independence is reflected in what little we know about the trend of prices. Thanks to a pioneering study on prices by Gootenberg (1990), we know that Peru experienced general price deflation until the midcentury. Disruptions of supplies from blockades, urban shortages, military exactions on the civilian population, severe agricultural destruction in the Chancay and Mantaro valley breadbaskets and the flight of plantation slaves, all contributed to a period of sharp, war-induced inflation between 1815 and 1824. Prices rose as much as 40 percent by 1822, which may have caused the political pressures behind the decision to declare free trade in 1821. Thereafter, the prices of manufactured imports plummeted, off-setting a steep rise in the price of domestic foodstuffs.

Prices then underwent a remarkable stabilization and deflation from 1825 to 1846. Two major *caudillo* wars (1833, 1836–39) disrupted this trend, so that combined with the independence wars of 1815–24, the overall secular trend in prices from 1800 to 1846 was down. Prices during this period sank on average about 1 percent annually. Production on coastal estates seems to have recovered quickly after independence, but because of the disruption in the traditional export market (sugar and tobacco), the estates shifted to foodstuffs for the beleaguered domestic urban market whose population and demand nevertheless continued to be depressed. Moreover, the prices of imported textiles fell by 50 percent owing to a sharp drop in Atlantic shipping costs and the gradual dismantling of Peruvian tariffs. Prices were also depressed by the shortage of specie, as large amounts of silver coins were exported abroad (estimated at 27 million pesos between 1819 and 1825).

The same study suggested that this period of prolonged deflation had a generally "democratizing effect" on the population, closing the social distance between the elites and popular classes. Hardest hit were the urban mercantile elites, whose incomes plummeted while the real income of day laborers and subsistence farmers actually rose. At the same time, pressures on community and subsistence holdings by large landed estates waned as prices fell, markets evaporated, and the value of land collapsed. This situation led Gootenberg to conclude that "there were many loosening social hierarchies during the post-independence era: between landlords and peasants, artisans and apprentices, masters and slaves."

The condition of state finances during the depressed postindependence years was also dismal. At the time of independence, the country was already saddled with a considerable debt from the previous regime, as well as from the heavy military expenditures levied to pay off Bolívar's Colombian soldiers. Initial foreign loans totaling 1,816,000 pounds sterling were contracted during the first half of the 1820s from British bondholders. However, the investors and speculators on the London money markets grossly miscalculated the country's prospects and shortly saw their capital vanish into default. By the late 1820s, the foreign debt was five times the government's annual revenues, and by 1848, it had grown to an estimated 4,380,530 pounds sterling. The internal debt likewise grew to an estimated 6,646,344 pesos by 1845.

Governmental revenues during this period are difficult to calculate because no formal state budget was drawn up until the 1840s. Estimates of revenues range from 1,500,000 to 3,000,000 pesos between 1826 and 1840 to 4,500,000 to about 6,000,000 between 1824 and 1849. Data from 1840 show that the sources of governmental revenues varied, half coming from customs duties, about 1,200,000 pesos from a head tax on Indians (*contribución indígena*) and another on mestizos (*castas*), with smaller amounts from various other taxes, rents, and fees. A penurious state continued to raise funds from time to time by selling off state assets, such as public lands or slaves, and by exacting forced loans and contributions from wealthy merchants.

All these sources of revenue, however, were not enough to meet state expenditures during this period, so budget deficits were chronic, amounting to roughly 30 percent during the *caudillo* era. Because of the frequent wars and rebellions during the postindependence period, military expenditures represented the largest share of the budget, amounting to an estimated 48 percent in 1827, 59 percent in 1831, and as much as 70 percent in other years. Substantial revenues were also absorbed by the governmental bureaucracy whose budget, along with the military, proved difficult to control or reduce because of the unrest that it might cause. Thus, instances of state bankruptcy or failure to meet bureaucratic or military salaries, perpetuated a vicious cycle of renewed unrest and warfare, economic destruction and confiscation, fiscal collapse, and more *caudillo* uprisings.

It was previously thought that chronically bankrupt regimes during the postindependence period inclined governments to follow a liberal trade policy. Low tariffs, it was argued, accelerated free trade and hence imports, which provided a steady stream of customs duties into the national treasury. It now appears that exactly the opposite occurred between 1828 and 1841, that is, fiscal breakdown led to protectionism, not free trade. The reason was that the *caudillos* sought emergency financing in the form of loans and tax bonds from the merchant elite to cover immediate deficits. Between 1821 and 1845, these merchant loans amounted to a minimum of 2.7 million pesos to the Lima treasury. Since Lima merchants and monopolists were strongly opposed to opening the economy to foreigner traders, a strong lobby for a protectionist, rather than a liberal, political economy was created. Indeed, such a system of ready credit to the state was institutionalized in 1834 by the creation of an autonomous, quasi-state merchant loan bank (*Ramo de Arbitrios*), run by the still-powerful merchant *consulado*. This credit ensured a military-merchant symbiosis on behalf of a nationalist-protectionism policy that carried the day from the late 1820s to the 1840s and was relatively impervious to liberal challenge. The state was, in effect, completely captured by Peru's dominant conservative merchant elite and their planter allies.

Population and Society: Social Change and Continuity

Attempting to assess the size and distribution of Peru's postindependence population is akin to entering a demographic no-man's-land. The general weakness and disarray of the fledgling republican state precluded not only any serious budget or record keeping, but a concerted official effort to enumerate the population. In the absence of an effective state census, the Church, with a truly national reach, was a major statistical source. Carefully keeping records of births, deaths, and marriages, the Church guarded its statistical monopoly tenaciously, without which the collection of the *contribución indígena* (Indian tribute tax) or the enrollment of the Indian labor force for the army or public works would have been impossible. Holding a monopoly over the keeping of vital statistics simply added to the power of the Church during the nineteenth century.

His discovery (1991) of an official 1827 census led Gootenberg to place the postindependence population at 1,516,693. On the basis of a 1836 census, Basadre calculated a slightly lower number: 1,313,736 inhabitants. These figures may be compared to the previous colonial count of 1,076,000 in 1791, which excluded Puno (about 200,000), and the only other relatively accurate census of the nineteenth century, carried out in 1876, of 2,699,000. On the basis of the 1827 count, annual compound growth rates amounted to 0.56 between 1791 and 1827 and 1.18 between 1791 and 1876. These rates of growth fall within the typical range for what Gootenberg called buoyant preindustrial societies. If one allows for the half-century lag in Peru's belated mid-eighteenth-century recuperation from the Indian biological holocaust, the rates also coincide with the general pattern of demographic growth experienced throughout Colonial Latin America after 1700. Indeed, well into the nineteenth century, Peru, as elsewhere, experienced high rural fertility and low life expectancy.

The regional distribution of Peru's postindependence population reveals a continuing colonial pattern, again suggesting continuity, rather than change. Thus, in 1791 the Indian south predominated with over half (52.6 percent) the population followed by the mestizo, commercial, and mining center, with 28.3 percent, and the agrarian north, with 19.1 percent. This pattern held relatively constant until the 1860s, when the guano boom began to draw an increasing number of migrants toward the coast. Still, during the period 1791 and 1876, the key regional division in the country between coast and sierra (including the *montaña*) remained relatively constant at about 25 percent and 75 percent, respectively. Urbanization during that period remained remarkably low, further reflecting the predominantly rural character of the country.

One important finding from the demographic studies of the nineteenth century by Kubler (1952) and Gootenberg (1991) is the apparent stabilization of the Indian population at around 62 percent. This stabilization reinforces the notion that the transition to independence was one of general continuity, rather than social change, for it implies the reversal not only of several hundred years of biological decline, but of European encroachment on and assimilation of Indian communities. It was not until after the War of the Pacific (1879–83) that the process of social and cultural change and its attendant *mestizaje* began to erode the Indian population, so that the 1940 census recorded that only 46 percent of the population was ethnically Indian.

Continuity, rather than change, also seems to have been the rule in other areas of postindependence society. It is true that the liberal decrees of the 1820s, particularly the abolition of caste distinctions, such as the tribute tax on Indians (1821) and Bolívar's decree declaring *comuneros* private owners of their parcels (1824), represented potentially important social changes. The purpose of the "privatization" of communal lands, according to prevailing liberal doctrines, was to create a class of prosperous independent farmers as a social foundation for a republican government, while abolition of the Indian head tax confirmed the new ideas of equality. However, the penurious republican state quickly rescinded these liberal decrees and reinstituted the tribute tax (then called the *contribución indígena*) in 1826. The *contribución* constituted fully 40 percent of the government's revenues that it could ill afford to lose. As for Bolívar's "privatization" decree, it was followed by a massive land grab by *mistis* (non-Indians), so that Congress passed a new law in 1828 that greatly curtailed the sale of such lands.

Continuity, rather than change, can be seen in other ways, too. Natives continued to perform the *mita* (renamed *servicio a la república*) for involuntary, unpaid work on public works, such as roads. Although San Martín decreed the law of free birth, slavery still existed until its abolition at the midcentury, and the ruling elites remained largely the same, save for the replacement of the peninsulars by the creoles (Bonilla, Spalding, 1972, 1981). Colonial institutions, such as the church and the military, persisted as pillars of the new order, while the collapse of the colonial bureaucracy deprived the natives of the nominal protection of institutions like the *audiencia* to which they could appeal in behalf of their rights. Moreover, with the disappearance of the indigenous aristocracy (*curacas* and other native nobility) whose position and legitimacy had been systematically eroded by the state after the Túpac Amaru II rebellion, all Indians were lumped together, in the eyes of the creoles, as a monolithic, ethnic underclass.

Finally, in restoring the *contribución*, the state tacitly retained the old colonial land-for-tribute compact—that is, in return for acceptance of the head tax, it allowed the natives to retain control of their "corporate" lands and to exercise political authority in their communities. Such a "pax Republicana" also reaffirmed the old colonial social division along the lines of caste and race, which ran directly against the republican notion of equality but had the "virtue" of reconfirming the domination of the privileged creole elites who now controlled the country. Thus, the colonial division of Indian and non-Indian society, as I noted earlier, persisted after independence.

In this regard, creole claims to power over this underclass continued to be based on a profoundly racist attitude that essentially viewed Indians and other *"castas"* as "the other" and constituted an official ideology. Thus, the first constitution, written in 1823, virtually denied Indians citizenship in the new republic, for they were prohibited from learning how to read and write, from owning their own land, and from exercising a profession with a title. As Méndez put it, "with the dissolution of the colonial state, Indians stopped being subjects of the king, but did not become Peruvian citizens" (quoted in Urbano, 1992, p. 20). Given the weight of such postindependence sociopolitical continuity, based on de facto segregation and domination, some historians have argued that the traditional chronological dividing line between colony and republic is artificial.

If this return to the status quo ante under republicanism seems outwardly to have been deleterious to Indians, broad economic and political conditions worked in other ways to favor them, both individually and as a group. For one thing, the generally depressed economy discouraged outsiders from usurping their land. Indeed, the hacienda, reflective of the general economy, was not expansive, but in decline in places like Cuzco where the number of estates, according to Mörner (1978), fell from 647 in 1785 to only 360 in 1845. Conversely, demographically the Indian population was growing while most, at least in Cuzco, remained in their communities (84 percent) as opposed to outmigrating to escape hardship or seeking refuge on haciendas (16 percent). Moreover, the general disruption of communications and markets as a result of the wars, together with a reduced Hispanic sector, allowed the native population to operate more on their own terms and worked to reinvigorate traditional intraethnic trade circuits. In the Colca

Valley in the southern highlands, for example, the traditional *misti* society of *haciendados*, miners, and merchants seems to have virtually disappeared after independence, and Indian herders delivered their wool directly to Arequipa.

At the same time, a weak state that was dependent on the head tax for a large part of its revenues was not in a position to exploit the peasantry or allow the alienation of its land. Therefore, Indian communities had greater room to manuever and negotiate with local officials who, less able to rely on the national or regional government to enforce tax collection, were more flexible and open to cultivating good relations with the natives. In addition, the Indians vigorously defended their rights when challenged in the courts and other venues, as they had done throughout much of the colonial period. The fact that the Indian population paid their head tax without protest led Walker (1999) to conclude that they did not retreat into self-sufficiency and fared generally better than previous historians have believed under the new republican regime.

Generally speaking, not until the revival of the state and the onset of capitalist expansion later in the century would outside pressures (enclosure) once again be exerted on Indian society that would, over time, threaten its existence and viability. Until then, the postindependence economic and political disintegration served to enhance Indian circuits and autonomy and generally revive Andean ways.

Slavery and Emancipation

If the communal Indian sector of Peru experienced a measure of stabilization and revival as a result of independence, the slave population also made progress toward the goal of emancipation, at least on an individual level, if not collectively. Although a total of 9 million slaves had been forcibly brought to the Americas between the sixteenth and nineteenth centuries, only 1.5 million (17 percent) were brought into Spanish America (the bulk going to the British colonies in North America and the Caribbean and to Portuguese South America). Of this total, slightly less than half (700,000) went to Cuba while the remainder was distributed to the rest of Spanish America.

The Viceroyalty of Peru received about 100,000 slaves during this period, of whom about 40 percent were settled in or found their way to the capital of Lima. In the cities, particularly the viceregal capital, slaves performed most of the essential, everyday workload, serving as artisans, water carriers, muleteers, and house servants. In the coastal countryside, slaves predominated on the sugar plantations of the north coast, where they labored as field hands, mill workers, and house servants. They were also heavily used in truck-farming estates on the outskirts of the major coastal cities.

Despite the intensification of the slave trade between 1790 and 1802 throughout Spanish America, the number of slaves in the viceroyalty declined in the quarter century or so before independence. Thus, in 1812 there were 89,241 slaves in the viceroyalty, of whom 35,696 (still 40 percent) lived in the province and city of Lima. A little over a decade later, this number had fallen to 50,400, which constituted only 3.8 percent of the total estimated population of 1,325,000 in the viceroyalty, but appreciably higher on the coast where they were concentrated. By the time their emancipation was decreed in 1854, slaves numbered only 25,505 in Peru. There were, however, a significant and growing number of free blacks (*libertos*), estimated at around 40,000 after independence.

Throughout the coast, slaves were a significant portion of the labor force. In the cities, they predominated in such occupations as food vending, water carrying, and wet nursing and filled the ranks of artisans and skilled laborers. In Lima, for example, slaves worked as shoemakers, bricklayers, porters, painters, bakers, and watchmen, receiving a wage, part of which they turned over to their masters, and part of which they sometimes saved and accumulated to purchase their freedom.

Slaves were also commonly found as household servants in both urban and rural areas. Thus, they were heavily involved in such tasks as cooking; cleaning; laundering; and, where there were infants, child care. Well-liveried male slaves drove the carriages and formed the retinues of the well-to-do on their daily rounds and to evening social affairs like the theater. Their female counterparts attended to their mistresses' daily needs and were often seen carrying little rugs to churches that lacked pews or seats. The English traveler Clements Markham reported that slaves were ubiquitous in the houses he visited in the countryside around the midcentury, attending to meals and waving fans to cool the diners and keep the flies at bay.

The condition of slaves in the countryside depended, to a great extent, on the size of the estates in a country in which there was great diversity in the units of production from place to place. On the extensive sugar and winery estates of the north and south coasts, for example, there were large concentrations of slaves, a few with 600 or more. On these enormous plantations, the slaves' conditions varied, but in general relations between owner and slave were more impersonal and less direct than on smaller units of production. Whippings and other harsh treatment were common, always ordered explicitly by the owners and carried out in public as an example to others. Slaves who escaped were brought back and forced to work in chains for the number of days they had been absent from the plantation.

To encourage marriage, out-of-wedlock children born to slave couples were sold. Married women, however, who bore children were given less rigorous work assignments and better food and quarters. The slaves' workday began at 7 A.M. and lasted until 4 P.M., with a two-hour dinner break at midday. After work (and on Sundays), the slaves could work on their subsistence plots, but at the end of the day, they were locked up in the plantation *barracones*, or slave quarters.

Conditions were somewhat different on medium and small estates. Of the approximately 200 estates in the province of Lima in the 1820s, 47 percent were no larger than 145 hectares, and 16 percent were 73 hectares or smaller. These estates contained roughly twenty to fifty slaves each. From her research on slavery, Hünefeldt determined that the average estate in the province of Lima around 1813 contained about forty-five slaves. The twenty-one men and thirteen women of her fictional, prototypical hacienda Pando were managed by a *mayordomo* (overseer) and his wife, since the owner lived in Lima. Married slaves on Pando had access to small subsistence plots, where they could grow various staples and thus could shoulder part of the cost of reproducing themselves. The surplus from these plots, which they sold in nearby markets, also enabled them to save for their manumission or that of their children.

The condition and circumstance of slavery underwent change as a result of the struggle for independence. The issue of independence, as I mentioned earlier, divided the creole class, whose ambivalent attitudes prolonged the struggle and delayed the ultimate outcome. One of the creoles' major apprehensions centered on the question of slavery and fears that rebellions by Indians and blacks would inevitably occur with the loosening of authority and social bonds in the wake of independence. The memory of the Túpac Amaru II rebellion of 1780 was still fresh in the minds of creoles, while *Limeños* had, during most of the colonial period, harbored, according to Hünefeldt, the fanciful notion that some day an African tribal chief would arrive from the sea to lead his people in rebellion.

At the same time, the movement for independence raised pressures and expectations among the slave population for abolition. Early in the century, Spanish authorities, under pressure from the British, had pressed for the abolition of the slave trade, so that the last slaves arrived in Peru in 1812. The liberator San Martín, whose Argentine expeditionary army of 4,500 to Chile had contained a majority of slaves and to which Peru's slaves flocked on its appearance on the south coast, took some steps to improve the condition of slaves. For example, probably hoping to gain more recruits, he declared the law of the free womb in 1821. However, the political power and social conservatism of the planter-mercantile elite, as well as San Martín's own skepticism about the wisdom of manumission, substantially slowed any momentum toward abolition during the early 1820s. Even the more liberal-minded Bolívar took little action toward manumission, perhaps because he was unable or unwilling to counter the powerful planter class that masked its self-interest in the view that emancipation would do further economic damage to the country and impede its recovery.

Nevertheless, numerous slaves, recruited into the armies of both contending forces, did receive their freedom as a reward for military service. Others, unwilling to join either patriot or royalist armies, took advantage of the chaos of war and its general tendency to loosen social ties to run away, frequently joining the growing bands of maroons (fugitive black slaves), guerrillas, and highwaymen who infested the roadways and countryside outside the major coastal towns and cities before, during, and after independence. Operating on the fringes of society, these bands, according to Aguirre and Walker (1990), attacked haciendas, *tambos* (roadside inns), and villages and were the subject of constant complaints from the general citizenry and authorities. Occasionally, these bands attained enough cohesiveness and organization to be incorporated into the patriot forces, as reported by General Miller in the south. Overall, however, they may be considered an expression of the general social malaise that accompanied the economic deterioration and political decomposition that marked the collapse of the colonial order and the onset of independence.

If creoles generally shared the planters' opposition to the abolition of slavery, this did not stop their ambitious and quarreling leaders from recruiting black slaves into their informal armies during the *caudillo* wars with the promise of manumission, just as their counterparts on both sides had done during the wars for independence. And just as before, once victorious, the *caudillos* invariably reneged on their pledges, causing widespread disillusionment among the black population. When emancipation finally came after 1854, it was not the result of any intense campaign for abolition or strong liberal sentiment among the creoles, both of which tended to be weak and vacillating in the postindependence years.

Rather, emancipation came as much from inertia, the decline in the number of slaves, and the persistent individual insistence of black slaves themselves through self-purchase as from creoles' altruistic sentiments pricked by international pressure or self-interested calculation, such as the presumed benefits of free wage labor by progressive planters. Moreover, when it did come after 1854, emancipation was made possible by the ability of the state to compensate slaveholders for their loss, as well as by plans to replace the slaves' labor with imported indentured Chinese coolies—factors that also proved critical in the ending of slavery in other parts of Spanish America.

Over the three decades after independence until the final emancipation of the slaves decreed by President Ramón Castilla in 1854, the main argument for maintaining slavery came from the slave owners, who argued that agricultural progress depended on a dwindling, but still crucial, slave labor force, in view of the difficulties of attracting native workers to work on plantations. The problem was that the Indians were located in the wrong part of the country (the sierra), were difficult to recruit, and were not entirely reliable since they were free to leave the estates and return to their communities at planting, harvesting, or festival time. Furthermore, the slave owners believed that slaves were cheaper than other forms of labor, a belief apparently grounded in fact, according to Macera's comparative study of the relative costs of wage labor, Chinese coolie indentures, and slaves during the postindependence period.

The price of slaves had been depreciating since the beginning of the century, possibly because of an aging population. For example, in 1800 Haitin put the average price of a male slave at 465 pesos and that of a female slave at 494 pesos. Between 1824 and 1854, the top price for a slave in Lima, according to Blanchard, ranged between 300 and 400 pesos. However, in the decade or so before emancipation (1840–54) both Aguirre and Blanchard calculated the average price of male slaves had dropped to 289 pesos and of female slaves to 267 pesos. The fact that slaves could be rented out for wages and therefore earn a return for their owners, in addition to their market value, meant that the slave owners had a strong vested financial interest in opposing emancipation. Moreover, with few ready sources of revenue, the *caudillo* strongmen who ruled after 1824 were not about to alienate such a powerful and wealthy interest group, who were more than willing to contribute funds to one *caudillo* or another to protect their investment.

Despite the persistence of slavery, the number of slaves in postindependence Peru continued to fall. For example, in the city of Lima, which had the highest concentration of urban slaves, the slave population, according to Hünefeldt, declined in both absolute and percentage terms from 13,482 in 1792 (25.6 percent) to 8,589 in 1818 (15.8 percent), to 5,791 in 1836 (10.5 percent) to 4,500 in 1845 (6.9 percent). In general, this long-term decline in slaves in the city and the viceroyalty may be attributed to the abolition of the Atlantic slave trade in 1808 and the social loosening and unrest, along with the economic and political turmoil accompanying the wars for independence and the increasing incidence of individual manumission by self-purchase among the slave population itself.

Indeed, self-purchase had been an important avenue to manumission ever since colonial times, although it was much more common on the smaller, more diversified estates around the cities than on the large, specialized sugar and winery haciendas. It was a factor, as Hünefeldt showed in her study of Lima, in why rural slaves invariably tried to be transferred to the capital. Estate owners often acquiesced in such transfers because agricultural productivity had been falling since the beginning of the nineteenth century. Thus, the best way to profit from their investment was to allow some slaves to leave for the city and hire themselves out as apprentice artisans. In this way, the slave owners would receive a portion of the slaves' wages and hence another source of income.

Many of the first and most successful slaves to leave the estates around Lima were women who, with their mercantile and domestic skills, could most easily make their way in the city's marketplace or homes of the well-to-do. Whether men as apprentices or women in the markets, slaves found a way of accumulating through earnings and wages the wherewithall to purchase their freedom. Over the long term, Hünefeldt argued this persistent trend of hiring out and self-purchase by individual slaves eroded the basis of slave holding, as the number of slaves continually declined, both in real terms and in relation to the free black population. Indeed, Hünefeldt and Aguirre showed that individual agency—that is, the slaves' own action—was a powerful impetus in undermining slavery. For example, slaves elaborated a wide range of individual strategies to gain their freedom, which in-

Afro-Peruvian water carrier in Lima circa 1830, unsigned water color in the style of Pancho Fierro. Courtesy of the Peruvian Embassy. Photographed by Wendy Walker.

cluded resorting to the civil and ecclesiastical courts, various moral appeals often upheld by the Church, and astute negotiations with owners. These actions led Hünefelt to conclude that slaves "learned how to use the internal contradictions of an exploitative system to their advantage and to appropriate the tools of oppression and transform them into instruments of liberation" (1994, p. 6).

Still, in considering the possibilities of self-purchase in Lima in the late colonial period, one must keep in mind that there were relatively few occupational and economic opportunities, for slaves or others. The manufacturing infrastructure of the city, according to Haitin, was relatively small—a few flour and chocolate mills; several textile mills; and some factories producing ceramics, woolen hats, and soap. The state-owned tobacco factory was closed in 1791. As a result, 76.9 percent of the economically active population was employed in service-related jobs. Artisans made up another

16.9 percent. Slaves were represented in both sectors, but they were not officially counted and therefore not included in these figures.

Despite this bleak picture, the city was still the main hope for mobility for slaves, and the steady transfers of slaves to the city explains the increase of the urban black population, both slave and free, during the first half of the nineteenth century and the concomitant decrease in the number of rural slaves. Once in the city, slaves strategically sought out ties in the black community, often through membership in black *cofradías* (lay religious brotherhoods), and constructed family ties through marriage. Both served as anchors and support for their pursuit of freedom. The Lima black community was varied and diverse, composed of slaves and freed slaves—maroons, mulatoes, blacks, and *zambos* (half Indian and half black). This racial diversity, as well as differences in social status, explains, according to Hünefeldt, the general absence of slave revolts, at least in the city of Lima.

The number of free blacks continued to grow in the decades after independence, mainly through self-purchase, but also from the generous acts of their masters. In fact, in her study of Lima, Hünefeldt found that the proportion of slaves who purchased their freedom was similar to that of the rest of Latin America—about 40–60 percent. Of the rest, about a third were freed by their masters. Finally, in terms of gender, about two-thirds of those manumitted were women.

Although slaves and free blacks made up a substantial portion of the artisans and skilled workers in Lima-Callao, the majority of this important socioeconomic sector of the capital were actually ethnically mestizo. Lima artisans, who numbered between 3,000 and 5,000 in the 1820s, had been employed ever since colonial times in producing finished, luxury goods for the capital's elites. These goods included fine furniture; leathergoods; tailored clothing; buttons; tin; silver and gold trinkets; and such exotic, locally customed luxuries as Lima's famous *saya y manta* cape worn by the city's fashionable ladies. Organized into some 400 small workshops and a variety of guilds, Lima's artisans, strategically concentrated in the capital, became a potent political force in favor of protectionism and against free trade after 1824. Indeed, they were quick to react to the flood of foreign crafts and mass-produced goods that poured into local markets in the mid-1820s. Joining their natural allies, the city's merchant elites, Lima's artisans constituted the popular base for the pro-tariff, nationalistic, protectionist coalition that succeeded in raising tariff levels from 50 percent to 90 percent between 1828 to 1840.

Politics in the Age of the *Caudillo*, 1824–1845

Although our knowledge of Peruvian politics in the first two decades after independence is analogous to a scholarly black hole, some recent works have begun to illuminate the subject. The major fault line in the politics of this period lay, as I have said, on a north–south axis. Conservatives were centered in Lima and the north coast, where they raised a protectionist-statist banner and sought to maintain corporate interests, revive colonial monopolies, and establish strict social controls over the common people. They were intensely authoritarian, even if their social base rested on the darker-skinned *Limeño* popular classes, or *castas*, such as artisans and the more marginal peddlers, vagrants, and migrant Indians of the city.

The conservatives were particularly incensed at Bolívar's liberal plan to open the country to foreign traders and constantly resorted to a patriotic rhetoric that decried the role of foreigners or foreign ideas in Peruvian affairs while they purported to defend the new nation's sovereignty. Their main *caudillo* leader was the *Cuzqueño* General Agustín Gamarra, who actually managed the herculean feat of occupying the presidency twice (1829–33 and 1839–41) and completing a four-year term during what was essentially an era of "the revolving presidential door." The conservatives' success in gaining and holding power during much of this period was due to their strategic base in and around the capital, the historic nerve center of national politics, administration, and finance.

The main opposition to the conservatives came from the liberal bastion of the southern Andes, with its center in Arequipa. These liberals were joined by a small band of "neo-Bolivarian," cosmopolitan intellectuals and bureaucrats in the capital who espoused a visionary "internationalism" of free trade, but who lacked any tangible political base. Together, they sought to dismantle the protectionist, corporatist, and centralist Lima-centered state and to open the country to increased foreign trade. Their main political problem was their diversity and hence inability to unify, their lack of a social base in the popular classes, and their distance (Arequipa) from the main levers of power in Lima. Even when the liberals were momentarily able to gain power in Lima, as under the caudillo generals José La Mar (1827–29) and Luis de Orbegoso (1833–34), they were too cut off from their southern power base to hold power for any length of time and thus be able to impose their free-trade agenda on the country. In the end, much of their energies were dissipated trying to promote separatist movements in the south that invariably ended in failure.

A case in point was the Peru-Bolivian Confederation (1836–39), which was engineered by General Andrés Santa Cruz, a Bolivian who was president of Bolivia from 1829 to 1839. Santa Cruz had briefly headed Peru's fledgling government after Bolívar's withdrawal to Colombia in 1826 in the chaotic days after independence. A decade later, he saw the opportunity to fulfill the Bolívarian dream of uniting the two countries by taking advantage of the constant civil strife that had weakened the Peruvian state. He was strongly supported by liberals in the southern Andes who had long hoped to reconstitute historic commercial ties with La Paz. Invading Peru and opportunistically siding with one or another faction, Santa Cruz succeeded in capturing Lima and uniting the two countries in a confederation in 1836.

While there was an essential logic to reconstituting the geographic, cultural, and economic boundaries of the old viceroyalty (Upper and Lower Peru), the confederation was probably doomed from the start by an array of national and international interests who were against it. Foremost were the Lima conservatives who railed against the attempt to impose the south's free-trade agenda on the country. Moreover, even if Lima remained the capital, many Peruvians chafed at accepting a Bolivian as their president. Perhaps more significant, the unification of the two Andean countries threatened to upset the geopolitical balance of power on the west coast against Argentina and Chile. Chile, in particular, viewed the confederation not only as a military threat, but as a challenge to its postindependence commercial hegemony of the Pacific trade. As a result, Chile and Argentina (Rosas was antiliberal) declared war on the confederation in 1836–37. A failed initial invasion in 1837 by Chile was followed by another in 1838, supported by a large contingent of Peruvian exiles, including conservative General Agustín Gamarra, as well as some liberals who opposed the autocratic style of Santa Cruz. In January 1839, Santa Cruz's army was crushed at the Battle of Yungay, putting an end to the confederation.

With the collapse of the confederation, the conservative Gamarra regained the presidency (1839–41) and imposed yet another centralist and antiforeign constitution (the sixth since independence). However, he was killed in battle while invading Bolivia in 1841, provoking the outbreak of another civil war and the political disintegration of the country between 1841 and 1845. In 1844 no fewer than four *caudillos* from various parts of the country claimed the presidency.

While politics seemed to be the exclusive preserve of elites during the postindependence period, the popular classes also played a role in the civil struggles. Walker (1999) showed how the political debates between liberals and conservatives in Cuzco were followed by the lower classes in the press, since newspapers were posted in public places and read aloud there and in taverns to assembled, illiterate listeners who were anxious for information. On another level, the guerrilla *montoneras* around Lima, who had participated in the struggle against Spain during the wars for independence and did not immediately demobilize after 1824, tended to attack and loot conservative-owned haciendas and plantations. Aguirre and Walker (1990) suggested that they also apparently collaborated with liberal political factions that helped prevent a conservative political consolidation during the *caudillo* era. On the other hand, conservatives were able regularly to mobilize Lima's mestizo artisans and even *casta* marginals on behalf of their causes, such as protectionism, and used a patriotic political discourse in defense of national sovereignty.

If coastal politics is relatively clear in the postindependence period, the same cannot be said for the politics of the Andes. We do know that the Mantaro Valley in the central Andes, which had supported the cause of independence, seemed to support the liberal faction in the civil wars, perhaps because the landholding structure, like that of Arequipa in the south, was more divided and less *latifundista* than elsewhere in the Andes. Also the valley was a major food supplier to Lima, which would incline its inhabitants against conservative trade policies to exchange Chilean wheat for northern sugar.

In the province of Huanta in the department of Ayacucho, which had been a bastion of royalist support from the time of the Túpac Amaru II rebellion down through independence, a serious popular revolt against the new republican regime erupted in 1825. Hardly a vague anachronistic throwback to the old order, according to Méndez (1996), its causes lay not only in the harsh sanctions imposed by Bolívar in 1825 on the population in the form of taxes for its militancy in the royalist armies during the wars of independence, but in the precipitous decline in the local commerce of coca that Huanta supplied to consumers in Huancayo, but that had shifted in recent years in favor of a rival center of production in Huánuco.

The revolt, which brought together a group of former royal officials, Spanish and mestizo merchants, and the Iquicha Indians, was led by an illiterate Indian muleteer named Antonio Navala Huachaca. Seeing no particular advantage in adhering to a republican order that denied citizenship to Indians, the rebels apparently sought a return to the ancien régime in which their status and position was at least recognized and, to a certain degree, protected by the state. Although the rebellion was ultimately quelled in 1828 by republican forces, the leaders of the revolt escaped capture in the *punas* of Huanta, where they successfully organized a "parallel government" that resisted the new order over the next twenty years. Méndez argued that this separatist regime was more than simply a "resistance" to the new political authority; rather, it constituted a legitimate political demand by the natives to be recognized as an integral part of the new republican order. The Iquichanos also threw their support to the liberal general Santa Cruz, whose Indian features and background were palpable, and fought under his banner for a united Peru-Bolivian confederation.

Walker also found considerable popular support for Santa Cruz's confederation in Cuzco. On the other hand, the conservative native son Gamarra, a former prefect, defended what remained of the textile *obrajes* through policies of protectionism and state contracts for uniforming the army. He was also successful in attracting the support of the urban plebe through a discourse that not only emphasized "Cuzco First," but was peppered with allusions to the Incas and the city's "glorious past." However, in the countryside, the Indian peasantry generally remained detatched from the *caudillo* wars, and no military leader was able to recruit a mass indigenous following in the decades after independence. To the extent that peasants participated on one side or the other, local conditions and relationships, as during the wars for independence, probably dictated their decision.

6 From Rags to Riches: The Age of Guano, 1840–79

Peru's opportunity to overcome its precipitous postindependence political and economic decline came from the most unlikely source—the mountains of dried dung dropped by seabirds on a few small islands off the central coast. For millennia, these birds had subsisted on the billions of tiny fish spawned in the fertile depths of the Pacific's Humboldt Current and had deposited their excrement on the Chincha Islands. Used by the Incas as a natural fertilizer for agriculture, guano had been virtually forgotten, like much of the valuable Inca knowledge of the Andes, in the frenzied destruction of the conquest. It was not until the agricultural revolution in Europe in the nineteenth century that the nitrate-rich fertilizing properties of guano were rediscovered, and the application of guano to the fields of the northern hemisphere proved to be a bonanza to Peru. Over the course of four decades, from 1840 to 1880, some 11 million tons of guano were "mined," transported, and sold to European and North American markets for an estimated $750 million. Laboriously dug up, carted, and shoveled down chutes to awaiting ships by a relatively small army of about 1,000 imported Chinese indentured coolies, guano, in the words of Gootenberg, became a national "rags-to-riches story: high-style living for [the] elites, bloated budgets, millions in fancy imports, a purchased political peace and unlimited doors to foreign credit" (1993, p. 2). It became the classic Latin American boom-to-bust story, however, when finite guano reserves were finally depleted in the 1870s, causing a default on a massive foreign debt in the wake of financial and economic collapse. More important, it doomed Peru's midcentury bid for sustained growth and development and left a legacy of underdevelopment that would last well into the next century.

Guano's impact and legacy in Peru has been hotly debated by historians. One interpretation, suggested by Jonathan Levin (1960), was that guano produced the classic "enclave" economy with few backward or forward linkages to stimulate national production. There was, accordingly, little, if any, lasting developmental effect on the country. In this version, the wealth from guano was isolated from the rest of the country; financed and exploited by foreigners; and worked by a relatively small, servile labor force with virtually no purchasing power. Profits were remitted abroad, squandered by state corruption and mismanagement, and consumed by a small elite in an orgy of luxury imports.

Hunt (1985, 1973) challenged the "enclave" thesis by arguing that guano produced a typical "rentier" economy similar to the colonial experience with silver. Such an economy was capable of earning massive amounts of foreign exchange from the export of a natural resource. Profits from the guano trade were not dispersed abroad, as Levin's enclave model would have it, but were actually retained at home from some 71 percent of the net sales receipts controlled by the state or national contractors who distributed the benefits in an arguably rational fashion. The real problem, according to this interpretation, was the grandiose, ill-conceived state investment projects (railroads and the like) that failed to diversify the economy or create a new class of national entrepreneurs.

At the same time, the artisan industry, and hence entrepreneurial potential, was destroyed by massive imports from abroad, induced by policies of radical free trade and the lavish spending habits of the elite. Perhaps the most pernicious effect of the rentier economy of guano, however, was psychological. Since such an economy allegedly produced wealth not through individual effort, but only from the simple fact of ownership and exploitation of resources by a captive labor force, entrepreneurial skills were not developed and remained stunted. Thus, the example of colonial silver and Indian labor was repeated in the nineteenth century with guano and Chinese indentured coolies.

Other historians have chipped in with their views. Mathews (1968) found that the main problem was with foreign firms who tried to open the country to an "imperialism of free trade," even if Peruvians managed to drive some hard bargains. Other historians pointed to evidence of diversification and development brought about by guano in the rise of cotton and sugar estates along the coast (Burga, 1976), in market development and modernization in the central highlands (Manrique, 1987; Mallon, 1983), and in the organization of a functioning state bureaucracy and system of finance (Trazegnies, 1980).

Perhaps the most widely accepted interpretation of the guano era came from several dependency and neo-Marxist Peruvian historians. These historians argued that Peru's lost guano development can be placed squarely on the shoulders of the aspiring civilist ruling class that failed to formulate a "hegemonic national project" for the country. In their view, Peru failed to produce a national bourgeoisie that was capable of putting the country on the road to national, capitalist development. Rather, the "guano" elite became a *"comprador"* (purchaser) class that mediated British capital and the guano trade through a regime of liberal free trade in an overarching system of imperialism.

These interpretations not withstanding, it is clear that the guano boom presented Peru with an enormous opportunity for development. Equally important, according to Gootenberg, it brought about a major shift in economic policy, with transcendental long-term implications. Beginning in the mid-1840s, Peru began to move away from the decidedly nationalist-protectionist regime that had held sway since independence to a decidedly more open and liberal political economy. What precipitated this historic policy shift was the growing realization by the military *caudillos* and the powerful Lima merchant elite that liberalism now better suited their basic political and economic interests in the evolving guano era than did continued protectionism.

For their part, the military *caudillos* immediately saw in guano an alternative means of emergency state financing. The relative isolation of guano as a source of income for the state meant that it was immune from the chronic politico-military conflicts of the *caudillo* era. This realization led the state immediately to declare guano a state monopoly in 1841 and to establish a "consignment" system for its commercialization. Under this system, guano would be auctioned off to private merchants in return for loans or advances on future profits to the state. As it turned out, consignment tended to favor foreign over domestic merchants, since they were in the best position to develop markets for guano in Europe and the United States and had ample capital to make loans to the government. Moreover, the fact that foreign merchants could facilitate the state's interests in the exploitation of guano led the military *caudillos* to look more favorably on the liberal policy demands of this sector for free trade and a more open economy. Therefore, they gradually began to move away from their former protectionist stance, although it took several years and the development of a more stable political system before they fully embraced the idea of a liberal regime.

As for the powerful Lima merchant elite, its shift toward economic liberalism was precipitated by the increasingly predatory behavior of the *caudillos* in the early 1840s, before guano revenues came on line in sufficient amounts to stabilize the state. At that time, the country once again fell into a new series of fratricidal civil and international wars that lasted four tumultuous years, from 1841 to 1845. Desperate to finance their individual efforts to consolidate power, the warring *caudillos* proceeded to "cannibalize" the remaining financial resources of the dominant merchant elite. This process was aptly symbolized in the "looting" by various *caudillos* of the Ramo de Arbitrios, the institution that had been established before the discovery of guano to "regularize" the process of forced loans that financed the *caudillo* state. The arbitrary destruction of the Ramo, which bankrupted a number of prominent *Limeño* merchants and financiers, proved to be the last straw in the mercantile elite's support of the prevailing system of *caudillo-*military rule and its nationalist-protectionist orientation. It marked the beginnings of the politico-ideological transformation of this class from a position of obdurate protectionism to a new free-trade liberalism. The Ramo's destruction also led the merchant elite to contemplate the advantages of a civilian regime, although this idea would take more time to germinate, particularly with the arrival of an imposed order under General Ramón Castilla in 1845. Only in the 1860s, with the realization that they could extract greater profits from the guano trade for themselves individually and collectively as a class, would civilian rule become a major political project of the country's elites.

There were both winners and losers in the historic realignment from national to international markets. The foreign trading houses, whose numbers increased during the 1830s and 1840s, not only became major players in the international guano trade, but they gained access to the Peruvian market for their imports, mostly luxury items for the upper end of the domestic market—the upscale middle- and upper classes who were enriched by the guano bonanza. As for the Peruvian merchant elites, they prospered as intermediaries for their new foreign allies, providing the retail outlets for luxury imports and facilitating local political and financial channels for the commercialization of guano.

The losers from this economic opening turned out to be the former allies and clients of the mercantile elites—the petty merchants and artisans who were now no longer useful and therefore expendable. Both groups had formed the popular base for the nationalist-protectionist policies of the merchant elite, but were severely affected by the avalanche of foreign imports that followed in the wake of the guano bonanza and the progressive lowering of tariffs after 1845. In the case of the artisan class, their upscale market was virtually eliminated by the doubling of luxury imports in the late 1840s. Similarly, the petty retail distribution networks were now bypassed by the combined forces of the *consulado*-foreign retailing establishments. According to Gootenberg, "a thriving and nationalist 'middle sector' that had once dominated Lima was largely pushed aside during the 1840s as its commercial economy rapidly internationalized" (1989, 115).

The sociopolitical implications of the internationalization of trade during the guano era were also substantial. The "declasse" artisan/retailer middle sectors denounced the "oppressive" free-trade policies of the "guano-eating" mercantile aristocracy. They came to constitute the "social problem" of the 1850s and took to the streets on more than one occasion, as in the protectionist riots of December 1858, to protest their decline and increasing pauperization. By then, their political marginalization by the ascendent liberal elites, however, was complete, their guilds and former influence in full political retreat.

Castilla and the Pax Andina

The first *caudillo* to tap into and benefit from the guano boom was General Ramón Castilla, who also proved to be one of the most adept soldier-politicians in the country's history. A first-generation mestizo from a merchant family from Tarapacá in the south, Castilla rose to become a dominant force in Peruvian politics between 1845 and his death in 1868. During this period, he twice served as president, from 1845 to 1851 and again from 1854 to 1862.

Castilla began his rise in politics as a military officer who was loyal to the conservative general and president Agustín Gamarra and was able to establish a regional power base in Arequipa, where he married into one of the city's wealthiest families. Drawing on the increasing financial bounty from guano, as well his formidable political skills that combined a pragmatic, if liberal, bent with an inclination to build consensus, Castilla moved skillfully during his first term to consolidate the power of the presidency and of the central state. As a result, for the first time since independence, a stable political order, or pax Andina, began to emerge in a country that had known nothing but political revolution and economic disruption for a generation since independence.

Rapidly rising guano revenues enabled Castilla to forge his pax Andina during his two presidential terms. State revenues from guano exports rose from 250,000 pesos in 1846–47 to 5 million pesos in the mid-1850s to 18.5 million pesos in the early 1860s. The rising importance of guano revenue can be seen by the fact that it represented only 5 percent of government income in 1846–47, but 80 percent in 1869 and 1875. At the same time, guano-induced imports doubled between 1847 and 1851 to nearly $10 million, yielding an additional 3 million pesos in customs duties to the treasury in 1851–52.

This fiscal largesse enabled Castilla and his successors to forge the beginnings of a national state, with working congresses; legal codes and statutes; expanded governmental agencies and ministries; and, for the first time, a national budget. Castilla was also able to exercise an increasingly formidable power of patronage that he used to consolidate political power on the basis of expanded employment and public works. At the same time, he enlarged and modernized the military, thereby enhancing the power of the central state by improving its ability to put down the endemic political revolutions mounted by regional and local *caudillos* who were contending for power.

Finally, the enhanced power of the state, through greater fiscal strength, enabled Castilla to curtail the power of the Church. An earlier generation of liberals had succeeded in establishing the principal of national patronage (*patronato nacional*), nationalizing the wealth of monasteries (1833) and abolishing special eccesiastical courts (1856) that had long provided immunity for churchmen from civil prosecution. Then in May 1859, Castilla abolished the tithes, which had been the principal source of Church income since colonial times. Although he softened the blow by committing the state in the future to pay the salaries of all church officials and to help support the seminaries and Church-run hospitals, in reality from this point forward, the level of this support progressively diminished for the remainder of the century. The upshot was the gradual impoverishment of the Church, which together with the increasing secularization of society, severely undermined the Church's ability to attract and train competant new members to the priesthood as the century wore on.

In addition to consolidating the state, Castilla achieved lasting fame for abolishing the *contribución indígena* and freeing the country's slaves in 1854.

Both measures considerably broadened his social base as he began his second presidential term and earned him the enduring title of "liberator" in Peruvian history. The abolition of the *contribución indígena* significantly narrowed the revenue base of the state, making it precariously dependent in the long term on guano, a finite and increasingly depleted natural resource. Furthermore, it also significantly lessened the presence of the guano-era state in the highlands, thereby widening the gap between Indian society and the government in Lima. Moreover, since the "land for *contribución* compact" no longer applied, local *gamonales* (strongmen), according to Thurner (1995, pp. 306–07), were no longer restrained in their relations with the communities by agents of the central state. This led them to appropriate illegally the *contribución* that formerly went to Lima and to commit other abuses and aggressions (land enclosures, for example) that intensified social conflict in the sierra during the second half of the century, particularly during and after the War of the Pacific.

As for the abolition of slavery, it also proved problematic in some ways. Manumission affected some 25,505 black Africans, located mainly on the coast. Slaveholders were compensated some 300 pesos per slave, at a total cost to the state of 7,651,500 pesos. Some of this capital, as you shall see, was reinvested by planters to increase the productive capacity of sugar and cotton in order to take advantage of rising international demand and prices. Less positive, from a human rights perspective, was the fact that plantation owners, unable to secure an alternate supply of labor from highland Indian peasants, began to traffic in another form of slavery. Between 1849 and 1874, some 100,000 Chinese coolies were shipped to Peru as indentured servants, mainly from southern China through the port of Macao. The conditions in the trans-Pacific passage were such that the mortality rate among coolies arriving in Callao ranged from 10 percent to 30 percent. Those who survived were immediately deployed to replace slaves on the coastal sugar and cotton plantations; to labor on the guano islands, along with a small number of Polynesians and convicts; and later to build the railroads that became the developmental panacea of the governing elites.

The treatment of coolie labor paralleled that of black slaves earlier, even though they came on indentured contracts of up to seven years, after which they could technically go free. Even then, endebtedness to their employers for payment of their passage or other expenses incurred on the plantations or guano digs compelled many to remain in what Rodríguez Pastor (1989) called "semi-slavery." Also like their African predecessors, they endured harsh working and living conditions, including frequent whippings, lockdowns after dark in plantation barracks (*galpones*), and general exploitation. Without female companionship (few women were imported as coolies), homosexuality was widespread, and the consumption of opium, often trafficked in by the plantation owners, became habitual. Under such appalling conditions, it is not surprising that various forms of resistance developed on the plantations, including flight, crime, riot, and rebellion.

After completing their contracts, many Chinese eventually chose to leave their work sites for towns and cities along the coast, including Lima, to engage in petty commerce and trade. Cut off from the dominant culture by language and customs, they tended to congregate in their own ethnic barrios, where they became the targets, during hard times such as the War of the Pacific (1879–83), of discrimination and pogroms. In 1874, the coolie trade, which had enriched a group of traffickers known as "*Chineros*," was terminated by the government after strong and persistent protests by the Chinese government and the international community.

The state could not have undertaken most of these measures without a general reform and stabilization of the fiscal regime, along with the increasing flow of guano revenues, mostly from emergency loans from the consignees. The problem was not only the inevitable pressures from various interests exerted on the state to increase expenditures, but the limits imposed on governmental borrowing by the enormous internal and external debt. This debt derived from loan defaults, as well as claims for damages dating back to the wars for independence and subsequent civil wars. It amounted to an estimated $40 million, and until it was seriously addressed by the government so as to open access to credit markets, spending would continue to outrun revenues, resulting in persistent budget deficits. For example, while guano revenues in the form of loans and advances rose to $5.5 million between 1841 and 1849, they covered only one-tenth of the governmental expenditures during this period. In 1847 and 1851, the budget shortfall amounted to 20 percent and 25 percent, respectively.

To resolve this fiscal problem, Castilla began the task of consolidating the national debt, a process that took several years and was completed only during the term of his successor, José Rufino Echenique (1852–54). Debt consolidation was a complex process of recognizing, restructuring, and reimbursing the internal and external debts over the period 1846 to 1853. On the one hand, historians agree that the recognition and restructuring of the foreign debt served to restore Peru's credit in London money markets that had remained closed to the country since the defaults of the mid-1820s. A final agreement with British bondholders was concluded in 1849 by which repayment of the consolidated debt would begin in 1856. At that time, the British trading house Anthony Gibbs and Company, the major consignee since the early 1840s, would deposit half the revenue from guano sales in the Bank of England.

On the other hand, there is disagreement over the outcome of the consolidation of the internal debt, which transferred upward of $25 million dollars to those who claimed reimbursement for damages or unpaid loans from the state going back to independence in 1821. The standard interpretation views debt consolidation as a massive fraud that served to reconstitute Peru's traditional ruling class. These claims rose from a modest $1 million in 1845 to $4 million in 1849 to more than $23 million by 1853. A revisionist interpretation by Quiroz (1987), however, questioned the view of debt consolidation as unrestrained class greed. Rather, Quiroz saw it in terms of a massive speculation by both national and foreign interests that, in effect, deprived the traditional landed families of their share of the spoils of consolidation. During the 1840s, these interests shrewdly bought up the worthless, defaulted bonds in anticipation that the state, enriched by guano revenue, would restore their original value. The main beneficiaries among the 2,000 bondholders, the vast majority of whom resided on the coast, were the 100 who held 62.3 percent of the total value of the bonds.

There were two important, long-term consequences of debt consolidation. First, a new elite centered in Lima, consisting of governmental functionaries, urban rentiers, retired *caudillos*, coastal planters, and especially the *consulado* merchants, was capitalized by the transfer of funds from the state treasury and emerged in the 1850s as a powerful, new plutocracy. This elite had already begun to form during the previous decade from the numerous opportunities to profit from the developing guano boom and expansion of the state. For example, its members gained valuable governmental sinecures, import licenses, and public contracts and made profitable loans to the government against the projected income from guano. Needless to say, in these and other lucrative enterprises, they benefited from the expanded opportunities for graft and peculation in a society whose public morality had always equated public office as an opportunity for profit.

The formation of the guano-era plutocracy and the state's financial bonanza also served to revive and reinforce the economic and political power of Lima and the coast. In this sense, the midcentury guano boom led to a deepening, long-term division between the modernizing coast and the economically lagging sierra that has been much noted by scholars over the years. Remote from the guano boom, the sierra was little affected, other than an increased demand from Lima for foodstuffs. This demand for foodstuffs, along with a moderate demand from the mining sector, stimulated some expansion of cattle estates in the central highlands (Manrique, 1978) and commercial development in the Mantaro Valley (Mallon, 1983; Manrique, 1987). Less positive, as Deustua (1986) showed, was the fact that surplus capital generated from the region's silver mines flowed into guano, benefiting the coast, rather than the interior. At the same time, production in the sierra, aside from wool in the south, remained largely moribund during the guano age. By contrast, guano acted as a powerful stimulus to the growth and "development" of the coast.

This stimulus can be seen in the dramatic recovery and expansion of the coastal haciendas in the 1860s, which had been in a prolonged decline since the 1790s that was exacerbated by the dislocations of independence. The advent of transoceanic steamship transport and the California gold rush of the 1850s revived agricultural production all along the west coast of South America at the midcentury (Gilbert, 1977; Engelsen, 1977). Another factor was rising international demand and prices for sugar and cotton, the latter as a result of disruptions in production related to the coming of the American Civil

War. A final impetus toward the expansion, modernization, and specialization of the sugar and cotton estates was spurred by a wave of anticlerical legislation that compelled the Church to give up much of its prime agricultural lands along the north coast. The beneficiaries were the brash parvenus of the guano boom, whom the old families disparagingly dubbed with the sobrique *"salido del guano"* (having come out of guano), a double allusion to the origins of their fortunes and their social backgrounds.

Thus, investment in this process came from the profits from guano, state indemnities to planters for freeing their slaves, and increasing credit from banks and commercial establishments, also capitalized by guano. The presence of later president José Balta (1868–72), railroad builder Henry Meiggs, and guano consignor and international financier Auguste Dreyfus as major new estate owners in the coastal province of Jequetepeque shows concretely how guano capital was transferred into export agriculture (Burga, 1976). Sugar production centered in the fertile river valleys between Trujillo and Chiclayo on the north coast, where it came to account for 68 percent of the sugar exports by 1878. Production rose from 610 tons in 1860 to 83,497 tons in 1879 when it constituted 32 percent of the total exports. As for cotton, production rose from 291 tons in 1860 to 3,609 tons in 1879 and likewise tended to concentrate in certain coastal departments; Piura (14 percent of the exports), Lima (38 percent), and Ica (42 percent) (Hunt, 1985, 267). The development of both commodities also derived from their proximity to Lima for access to credit, as well as local port facilities for easy transoceanic shipment to foreign markets.

Other than specialization in sugar and cotton, however, coastal agriculture remained largely stagnant. The value of sugar and cotton production was 47 percent and 5.5 percent, respectively, at the end of the 1870s, whereas rice accounted for 4 percent, wines and other liquors for 28 percent, and other food crops for 15.5 percent. Even with the surge in the demand for food brought about by railroad construction in the 1860s and 1870s, coastal haciendas paid little attention to the production of staples, leaving this new market to be filled largely by Chilean imports or from the Mantaro Valley breadbasket in the central sierra.

Unlike either sugar or cotton on the coast, the wool trade of southern Peru owed its steady evolution during this period not to the guano boom, but to the increasing demand from British textile factories and the evolving free-trade policies of the state. Among the products of the sierra, only wool had sufficient value per unit weight to overcome the high cost of transportation to coastal ports for exporting. The value of exports grew fourfold from £/122,000 in 1845–49 to a peak of £/489,000 in 1870–74. While hacendados produced a substantial share of sheep wool on their estates, much of the finer alpaca was produced in the Indian communities. At first, the wool was collected by autonomous large Peruvian merchants, some of whom exported it themselves. From the 1870s and 1880s, however, collections were made by sales agents (*rescatistas*) from foreign merchant firms in Arequipa who crisscrossed the *altiplano* from Cuzco to Puno, haggling and coercing the campesinos to obtain the lowest prices. They got their biggest cache of raw wool, however, at the annual fairs, such as the one that brought 10,000–12,000 peasants to Vilque in the *altiplano* of Puno.

The second major long-term impact of debt consolidation was the creation of a sociopolitical base—the new guano oligarchy that was allied with foreign interests—that enabled the liberal state finally to triumph. Indeed, debt consolidation in Peru can be seen as the equivalent of the midcentury liberal land reforms elsewhere in Latin America. These reforms "privatized" the corporate landholdings of the Church and Indian communities, thereby consolidating new elites under the aegis of the emerging liberal, capitalist state. In effect, the revalued bonds of debt consolidation were Peru's counterpart of "land reform" as the catalyst for the formation of Latin American capitalism and liberalism at the midcentury.

While the consolidation of the national debt opened the path to liberalism, its final emergence depended on other important measures undertaken by the government. In 1850, the Anthony Gibbs and Company won a long-term extension of its guano contract with the government, despite a concerted effort by a group of national merchants, the so-called *hijos del país* (native sons), to win the concession. In effect, the government could not have proceeded with debt consolidation without the formidable financial reserves of Anthony Gibbs and company to dispense to its claimants, clients, and creditors. Driving a hard bargain with Gibbs, the state was able to raise its share of profits from guano from around one-third in the late 1840s to almost two-thirds in the following decade. At the same time, the portion of guano revenues that covered governmental expenditures jumped from 6 percent of the $5 million budget in 1847 to over 50 percent of the $10 million budget in 1855 (it would subsequently rise to 80 percent in 1869 and 1875). For the entire guano era between 1840 and 1880, it has been estimated that the Peruvian state captured 60 percent to 70 percent of the income derived from guano.

Further steps were taken to consolidate a liberal regime in the early 1850s. A series of commercial treaties were signed with Britain, France, and the United States that put Peru's external commerce on an orderly and reciprocal basis. Moreover, for the first time since independence, elections for the presidency brought about a peaceful transition of power to Castilla's successor General José Echenique (1852–54) in 1852. This orderly presidential succession was welcomed by the international commercial and financial community as another example of the growing stability and reliability of the Peruvian state in the guano era. Finally, after a bitter legislative struggle, free-trade liberals succeeded in 1851 in defeating the remaining protectionist lobby of artisans and industrialists and lowering tariffs to 15–25 percent. With these measures and the victory of Echenique, who campaigned vigorously for free trade, the triumph of liberalism was complete. From this point to the end of the century, liberal economic norms and policies, supported by a powerful new oligarchy, would shape the country's political economy and dominate its politics.

Peru's brand of liberalism, it should be noted, was hardly an orthodox version of its Western ideological counterpart, however. Indeed, it was severely distorted in two important ways. First, following the colonial penchant for mercantilism and statism, guano was made a state monopoly, thereby violating the liberal principal of laissez faire. Thus, Peru's newfound commercial and fiscal liberalism was diluted by a heavily statist institution that tried to set prices, maximized profits (over 70 percent), and expanded state expenditures by a factor of eight to ten times over the period 1850–70. To critics abroad, such a heavy dose of statism, not to mention the later "nationalizing" of the trade from foreign to Peruvian merchants, brought into serious question Peru's commitment to liberalism. This view was further reinforced by the nature of the debt consolidation, which served not only to enrich a small group of plutocrats and speculators, but to open the state to an orgy of graft, corruption, and peculation. As Gootenberg colorfully put it, "Peru's elitist free trade, like protection before, hinged largely around a symbiotic relationship between capital elites and the central treasury, now transformed into a *menage a trois* with their welcome seduction of foreign financiers."

Although much curbed, regionalism and political instability did not totally disappear, even as the new oligarchy and liberal state took shape from the early 1850s. Castilla's successor, General Echenique, proved to be an inept and corrupt leader whose mismanagement of the final stage of debt consolidation—marked by a massive increase in claims, many of them fraudulent—led to increasing political discontent and turmoil. Castilla, who realized that Echenique was undoing many of the gains that he had made in stabilizing the country and putting it on a more solid financial and developmental course, took advantage of the turmoil to return to power. He staged a successful provincial revolt, with support from Arequipa, Ayacucho, and Huancayo, and overthrew Echenique in 1854.

It was during his second term (1854–62) that Castilla gained the mantel of liberator by freeing the slaves and abolishing the old colonial tribute tax on Indians (both in 1854). On the other hand, the liberator personally led his crack cavalry in a brutal repression of the three-day protectionist riots by artisans and small shopkeepers that broke out in Lima in December 1858. While Castilla sided with the newly ascendent liberals on these and other matters, he was not happy with their passage in Congress of a new liberal constitution in 1856. He managed to replace that constitution in 1860 with a more conservative charter that restored many of the powers and prerogatives of a strong chief executive and central state—the political foundation for his pax Andina.

The Apogee of Guano

During the decade of the 1850s and early 1860s, under the aegis of a triumphant export liberalism and Castilla's strong hand, Peru reached the apex of its guano-induced rise from rags to riches. Guano exports leaped from $4.3 million to $12.5 million annually between 1852 and 1857 before they leveled off at around $20 million in the early 1860s. The state managed to recover upward of 70 percent of the profits on these exports, which enabled it to triple its budgetary outlays (profits plus advances on future deliveries) to $20 million by 1860. From this *"afluencia fiscal,"* as Basadre labeled it, sprang the edifice of a modern state bureaucracy. However, such outward signs of fiscal prosperity masked the fact that the government was consistently running large budgetary deficits that, in turn, were financed by huge, guano-secured loans from abroad.

The guano boom also acted as a demographic magnate for Lima, swelling its population from a low of 55,000 after independence to 94,195 in 1857 and transforming it physically into a fashionable, if overcrowded, "Europeanized" metropolis. Lima's grand boulevards were lined with ornate mansions, graceful parks, and imposing new public buildings. Family fortunes soared, and the ranks of the plutocracy grew apace, not only from profits by merchants that rose nearly three times after 1845, but from the $25 million state "consolidation" giveaway. Affluent *Limeños*, culturally oriented to Europe, sported the latest continental fashions and consumed vintage French wines, among the wide array of available imported goods, valued at upward of $15 million by 1860. Like all elites, this largesse of wealth led to occasional orgies of public display and conspicuous consumption. Such was the case with the celebrated ball that was held in Lima in 1873 in which the fine dresses and jewels of each lady had been especially imported from Europe at a cost of 10,000 to 50,000 *soles* each. On a more sober note, greater prosperity also helped move political conflict from the battlefields of the *caudillo* wars to the halls of Congress, where representatives of the elites now discussed and debated the nation's future.

The attraction of Peru's guano boom also acted as a magnate for foreign immigration to Peru. By 1857 the population of Lima was 23 percent (21,557) European. If one includes the number of Latin American migrants and Chinese immigrants, 25 percent and 3 percent, respectively, over half the population of the capital was composed of foreigners. As for the country as a whole, some 45,000 foreigners, many attracted to work on constructing the railroad, resided in Peru in the same year.

One of the most successful immigrants was William Russell Grace, who, along with a handful of other Irish escaping the potato famine, arrived in Peru in 1851. Finding a job with a local ship chandler in the bustling harbor of Callao, Grace eventually became a partner and then the sole owner of the firm that ultimately became W. R. Grace & Company. Although William moved in 1862 to New York, where he later became the city's first Irish-born mayor, his younger brother Michael remained in charge of the Peruvian operations. In time, as Clayton (1985) demonstrated, the firm expanded into railroad building; silver mining; sugar; rubber; nitrates; and, above all, shipping.

Despite such success stories, there was a decidedly darker side to the guano era in the City of the Kings. The gap between the rich and the poor grew increasingly wider. Inflation soared some 70 percent between 1855 and 1865, even higher in foodstuffs and basic staples. Over the same period, the wages of urban workers dropped approximately 25 percent. Small retailers and services were edged out of business by the hundred or so larger firms that came to dominate the city's businesses, half of which were foreign owned. Likewise the number of workshops stagnated, and the income of local craftsmen plunged to 1830 levels. Both groups were the victims of the torrent of luxury imports that flooded the capital from abroad. By 1857 the rate of permanent unemployment in the city had reached more than 17 percent of all male workers, an astonishing rate considering that the guano boom was reaching its peak.

With popular hardship increasing amid such regal affluence, severe outbreaks of social unrest erupted. As early as 1851, Ludite workers destroyed the markers for Lima's first railroad line. Then, in the aftermath of the liberal revolt that deposed Echenique in 1855, mobs sacked the homes and businesses of the richest and most prominent guano traders and merchants. Foreigners, too, increasingly became the targets of popular wrath after each change of regime.

The most serious outbreak of social unrest, however, occurred in 1858. Shortly before Christmas, a peaceful march on Congress protesting lower import duties by a ragtag group of craftsmen, unemployed laborers, vagrants, and political radicals turned violent. Three days of rioting ensued that resulted in the sacking of several upscale French shops and the burning of the train to Chorillos, an elite symbol of progress. Order was finally restored by the army, but not before the riot had claimed a dozen casualties.

If the fortunes of the city's artisans and downtrodden now reached a low point, not so those of the plutocracy, which a few years later made a successful bid to wrench control of the country's guano concession from the longtime concessionaire Anthony Gibbs and Company. The Peruvian challenge came from the Sociedad Consignataria del Guano, composed of the most powerful Lima merchants, who had been active in a modest way in the trade since 1850. Capitalized by the massive transfer of funds from the state's recent debt consolidation, the sociedad replaced Gibbs in 1862 to become the sole consignor to Britain, the principal European guano market.

As the group's guano profits and capital accumulation soared, it branched out into a variety of other enterprises, including insurance, railway, gas, immigration, and later nitrate companies. Perhaps the most important of these enterprises were the country's first banks, which reaped large speculative profits, sometimes as high as 35 percent, from short-term public loans. Thus, the Banco del Peru was founded in 1863 with assets of 10 million pesos. Many of its shareholders were also principals in the National Guano Company (Companía Nacional del Guano), formerly the sociedad.

Scholars of the dependency school have argued that little in the way of productive investment or economic diversification took place during the guano era except in the expanding sugar and cotton estates along the coast. This view, however, overlooks some important economic repercussions from the guano boom. For example, the country's first banks, capitalized by guano profits, served to facilitate and modernize commercial transactions. These banks issued notes that circulated as money, even if they were not at first regulated or controlled by the state. Heretofore commercial activities had been hindered by a chronic shortage of currency, mainly silver coins, that had been heavily exported to cover the chronic trade imbalances of the postindependence period. This currency shortage had become so severe in the 1830s and 1840s that large amounts of debased national and Bolivian coins found their way into circulation. To bypass such a chaotic monetary system, Lima merchants had introduced commercial bills to transact their businesses. This archaic system was rendered obsolete by the issuance of bank notes after 1860.

Equally important was the credit function of the new banks. The banks granted commercial loans collateralized by the stock and financial assets of a variety of companies worth some 42 million *soles* (S/) in Lima capital markets in 1874. They also helped mobilize capital in the export sector and were instrumental, as were new mortgage banks, in revitalizing coastal agriculture. The latter, for example, made credit available to commercial agriculture at rates of interest well below those of the merchant houses that had traditionally lent money to hacendados in return for a guaranteed portion of their crops (known as consignment contracts). Thus, the Banco de Crédito Hipotecario, founded in 1866, extended approximately S/12 million to cotton and sugar estates from 1867 to 1881 (Quiroz, 1993, pp. 29–32). The fact that the lack of bank regulation resulted in widespread abuses, including the notorious favoritism and dishonesty of some managers and directors, does not negate banking's contributions to growth and development during the guano era.

As might be expected, the growing economic and financial power of the guano-era plutocracy of merchants, financiers, and planters also translated into increasing social and political influence. During the early 1860s, for example, several exclusive social clubs were founded in Lima that served to differentiate this new elite and to promote its cohesion and solidarity as an aspiring ruling class. At the same time, the new elite's reformist and developmentalist ideas began to appear in one of Lima's most influential journals, the *Revista de Lima*. The *Revista* was founded in 1860 by banker-politicians Manuel Pardo y Lavalle and Luis Benjamín Cisneros, both antimilitarists and strong advocates of political democratization and economic liberalism. Pardo became the main ideologue and architect of the Civilista (Civilist) Party, the country's first civilian-based political party to challenge the long reign of military rule in the country. In effect, *Civilismo* became the political expression of the new oligarchy. Pardo went on to become the party's first successful presidential candidate in 1872, thus breaking the hammerlock that the military had exercised on political power for almost five decades.

The Rise of Civilismo

Born into an aristocratic family in 1834, Pardo was Peru's best-known, self-made capitalist millionaire during the apogee of the guano age. Educated at Lima's San Carlos Academy and then at the College du France, where he studied political economy, he became a leading guano trader, importer, and financier. In 1862 he founded the Banco del Perú and was president of the National Guano Company when it took over the concession from Gibbs in the same year. By the middle of the decade, he had turned his business acumen in a political direction. Over the next dozen years, he became the country's most dominant political figure, minister of finance in 1866–67, mayor of Lima from 1869 to 1872, the country's first civilian president from 1872 to 1876, and acknowledged leader of Congress until his assassination in 1878.

Writing in the *Revista* in the early 1860s, Pardo was particularly concerned about how to channel the immense state revenues from guano into a more diversified, sustainable development. He was well aware that guano was a finite resource that was rapidly being depleted. He also knew that the state was squandering a large portion of its bonanza on unproductive and needless expenditures. Indeed, we now have a more precise idea of how governmental revenues were spent during the guano era. Over half was spent on expanding the civilian bureaucracy (29 percent) and the military (24.5 percent). Other expenditures included railroad construction (20 percent), payments for national and foreign debt consolidation (11.5 percent and 8 percent, respectively), and reduction of tax burdens on the poor (7 percent). Finally, Pardo was troubled by the elite's propensity to overconsume costly foreign imports that had led to a severe balance-of-payments problem. According to him, Peru was consuming from abroad three times what it produced, a condition that "cannot be eternal."

Pardo's solution was "to turn guano into railroads" to stimulate national production and productivity. By this term, he meant deploying state guano income, along with foreign loans, into a major program for building railroads across the Andes to open up the interior for development. He wrote that "without railroads, there can be no real material progress today; and even though it may seem an exaggeration, without material progress there can be no moral progress in our masses because material progress gives the population wellbeing, and removes them from brutalization and misery. We

Manuel Pardo, founder of the Civilista Party and first Civilian president, 1872–76. Reproduced with permission of the General Secretariat of the Organization of American States.

can conclude therefore, that without railroads civilization will travel very slowly" (quoted in Kristal, 1987, p. 61).

This was not an altogether novel idea, for the railroad had become the harbinger of industrial development and a developmental panacea throughout the Western world. A surge in railroad building followed in several Latin American countries in the 1850s, including Peru, where the first operative line in South America actually opened in Lima-Callao in 1851. The success of that line and the particular promise that it held for the Andes led to numerous proposals and reports on the railroad's potential for Peruvian development. Pardo's plan was significant not only because it was espoused by the influential leader of the Civilista liberal elite, but because of its uniquely "developmentalist" thesis.

The predominant dependency interpretation of this plan was that Pardo sought to apply the Western model of railroad expansion as a means of modernizing and strengthening Peru's neocolonial economy. Rather than integrate the country and open up an internal market for national production, as occurred in the West, this railway system, according to the *dependentistas*, simply served the narrow class interests of the new export oligarchy and tied Peru's neocolonial economy to foreign markets in an increasingly dependent relationship.

It now seems, upon careful examination of Pardo's writings, that his railroad project was not a blueprint for "outward oriented export development" afterall. Rather, it was a call to develop the productive potential of the internal, domestic market, that is, a latter-day program for import substitution industrialization. A railway network into the interior would lower transport and transaction costs, which, together with the "natural protection" afforded by Peru's highlands, would work to dynamize internal production and manufacturing aimed at the popular consumer market. Thus, in his famous treatise in *La Revista* on the province of Jauja (later published as *Estudios sobre la provincia de Jauja*, 1862), he wrote that with its

> cheaper wages and foodstuffs, primary materials, ready coals and even better, powerful waterfalls, why can't Peru establish factories for coarse cloth, rough cottons, and linens, or those for ordinary pottery, for leathergoods, and a host of potassium and chemical products. On the contrary, these are the industries within reach of the secondary classes, and those that best advance the welfare and progress of the nation. (quoted in Gootenberg, 1993, 84)

If Pardo's railroad-development project made eminently good sense in terms of creating a more integrated national economy, less dependent on exports and based on small-scale, popular production, its wider appeal to the dominant elites at the midcentury was based on other, more predictable, liberal attitudes and biases. For example, the plan catered to prevailing notions of liberal paternalism by holding out the prospect that railroads and the ensuing development would serve to uplift the morals of and civilize Peru's downtrodden and lethargic Indian masses. Perhaps more important, it also promised to end, once and for all, the endemic *caudillo* revolts that perpetually festered in the provinces regularly to threaten the aspiring hegemony of the Lima-based central state. Thus, Pardo's program of national communications and national development based on railroads embodied the long-term civilist political mission of establishing orderly civil rule throughout the country. Whatever the appeal, Congress reacted to Pardo's plan by quickly authorizing the building of the country's first major trunk line to Jauja in 1861.

While railroad building as development gained momentum, Castilla was replaced as president in 1862 by General Miguel San Román. In April 1863, San Román died in office and was succeeded by another general, Vice President Juan Antonio Pezet (1863–65). Pezet was immediately confronted with an international crisis when Spain, using as a pretext the death of two Spanish citizens on a northern estate, attempted to seize the guano-rich Chincha islands as indemnity. Peruvians, including Castilla, were naturally outraged by this affront to their national sovereignty, but Pezet chose to capitulate to the Spanish demands under the threat of the bombardment of Callao in 1865 by a Spanish fleet that had been sent to the Pacific.

This capitulation led Colonel Mariano Ignacio Prado (1865–68), a liberal, to oust Pezet and seize power later that year. Prado proceeded to organize an effective defense against Spanish aggression by reinforcing the gun batteries at Callao and forging a defensive alliance with Chile, Ecuador, and Bolivia. After bombarding Valparaiso, the Spanish fleet was repelled in an artillery barrage when it attacked Callao, leading Spain to withdraw from the Pacific, but not before it carried off a substantial cache of guano from the islands. The whole episode proved to be enormously expensive and a further drain on Peru's already strained treasury, forcing the government to borrow even more money abroad, secured by ever depleting guano reserves.

Another significant event during the Prado administration was the outbreak in 1867 of a serious Indian rebellion in the province of Huancané in the department of Puno. This rebellion marked the beginning of a proliferation of Indian rebellions in the late nineteenth century, after a quiescence of more than three-quarters of a century following the suppression of the Túpac Amaru II rebellion in 1782. This period of quiescence may have been due to the inability of the weak republican state and society after independence to match the level of extraction from the peasantry reached by the much more efficient late colonial regime. As I previously noted, the dissolution of the colonial regime seemed to have brought about a florescence of the Indian sector and greater autonomy of the Indian community, which may also explain the absence of rebellions in the postindependence period.

Forces, however, were at work in southern Peru to alter this situation. Indian lands, which accounted for much of the flourishing wool trade, were under increasing pressure from landowners who wanted to gain greater access to this lucrative trade. Thus, a process of land consolidation, which saw the transfer of land from smallholders to hacendados and a corresponding increase in the number of tenants on large estates, took place in the region in the second half of the century. Increasingly forced out of the wool trade, the Indian peasants found it difficult to meet their tax obligations to the state at a time when guano revenues were flagging and the government began to reinstitute, if in disguised and altered forms, the previously abolished *Contribución Indígenas*.

The rebellion in Huancané was led by Colonel Juan Bustamante, a well-known liberal politician, merchant, and defender of Indian causes in Puno. It was directed at the increase in taxes on the peasantry, particularly the imposition of the *Contribución Personal*, a labor tax imposed by Prado to help repair roads and bridges. This and other taxes occurred at a time when the price of wool was falling, squeezing the income of smallholders who were hard pressed to pay these levies. Bustamante's political ambitions also played a role in the uprising, since he was a staunch defender of the liberal Prado government that was coming under increasing pressure from conservatives. According to Gonzales (1987), the rebellion remained localized, however, and was eventually repressed by forces that were trying to overthrow Prado after considerable bloodshed and the death of Bustamante in 1868.

In the meantime, Prado faced a deepening civil war over a new liberal constitution voted by Congress in 1867. The new constitution provoked the opposition of General Pedro Diez Canseco in Arequipa and Colonel José Balta in Lambayeque who led a successful revolt to depose Prado and restore the 1860 conservative charter. The victorious provincial forces then named Balta president (1868–72).

Balta was a conservative army officer who served an undistinguished four-year term characterized by inefficiency and corruption that was, nevertheless, significant from a number of perspectives. First, his ascendancy in 1868 marked the last presidential contender to come to power by way of a provincial revolt and thus represented the end of the vulnerability of the central government to regional or provincial challenge. Money and the massive railroad-building program he carried out, it seemed, would finally consolidate Lima's control over the country during the guano age.

Second, Balta's enormous and expensive railroad-building program led to a massive increase in foreign borrowing that would eventually threaten the country's financial viability. Moreover, in an effort to raise governmental income from guano, Balta's finance minister, Nicolás de Piérola, rescinded the guano contract held by the oligarchy and turned it over to foreign capitalists in exchange for partial cancellation of the foreign debt. Third, reacting to this attack on its economic base, the Civilista oligarchy mobilized politically to dislodge Balta from power, capitalizing on public disenchantment with the notorious corruption of the regime. This campaign opened the way for the antimilitary reaction that led to the popular election of Civilist Party candidate, Manuel Pardo, to the presidency in 1872. For the first time since independence, a civilian, not a military figure, would exercise political power in the country.

Finally, during the Balta administration, a serious rebellion of Chinese coolies, the principal plantation labor force on the coast, occurred in Pativilca in 1870. Known as "the rebellion of the painted faces" (Rodríguez Pastor, 1979, 1989), it involved some 1,200–1,500 Chinese who went on a brief, but bloody rampage—looting, burning, and destroying property in an orgy of spontaneous violence, directed against the harsh working and living conditions prevailing on the plantations. Order was quickly restored by the army, but not before some 300 Chinese were killed.

To construct Peru's railway system in 1868, Balta turned to the North American Henry Meiggs, who had just completed over 200 miles of track in Chile. Meiggs, dubbed "The Yankee Pizarro" by his major biographer, had come to South America in 1855 "on the run" from the law in California, where he had overspeculated in real estate and sold forged railroad stock. During the next decade in Peru, Meiggs landed contracts totaling over $130 million for the construction of 990 miles of track, 700 of which were completed before his death. In the process, he made a fortune, much of it from bribes, swindles, and kickbacks, which he spent lavishly on high living and charitable donations. He died poor and heavily indebted in 1877, the victim of Peru's financial collapse of the 1870s. His legacy, however, was one of the most spectacular railroad systems in the world, having sent locomotives higher than they had ever gone before.

To build his colossal lines, Meiggs recruited an army of over 25,000 Peruvian and Bolivian Indians, Chilean *rotos* (urban workers), and Chinese laborers. Although these workers were relatively well paid and treated for the times, thousands died from the hazards of altitude, climate, and disease. In addition to foreign workers, Meiggs had to import virtually everything that he used in constructing his railroads: blasting powder, medicines, workers' clothing, rolling stock, tools, machinery, construction materials, and lumber, mostly from the United States. The prototypical early capitalist promoter, Meiggs combined modest engineering ability with a flamboyant personality and extraordinary financial and entrepreneurial talents. Such was his reputation that his funeral in Lima was attended by 20,000 to 30,000 people, the vast majority of whom were the poor peons on whose backs his Andean system had been erected.

To finance the building of Meiggs's railroads, as well as other extravagant projects, Balta turned to his finance minister Nicolás de Piérola, who engineered a major reorganization of the guano contract system. A Catholic and Hispanophile traditionalist who had been educated in a seminary, Piérola defended the interests not only of the Church against the anticlericalism of the Civilistas, but the more traditional, rural landholding elites against the new export plutocracy. He had no use for Pardo and the Civilistas whom he and other critics on the Right attacked in *El Proceso Católico* and *La Patria*—conservative journals that responded with disdain to the progressive ideas voiced by the Civilistas in *La Revista de Lima*.

Although the conflict between the old landed elites and the new agricultural exporters was as much cultural as political, the two groups divided over such fundamental issues as control of labor and the role of the state. The old hacendado class depended on control of the land and absolute domination of the Indian labor force, whereas the new planters and growers argued in favor of the efficiencies of a free labor market. For the latter, prosperity depended, in part, on attracting wage labor away from the traditional sector. As for the state, the new export elite required a more activist state that would be able to exact higher taxes and revenues to build the infrastructure necessary to serve an export economy. In this way, the new Civilista plutocracy threatened the traditional economic and political hegemony of the traditional hacendado class.

Piérola, who became, in the words of Quiroz (1993, p. 36), "the civilian heir to the *caudillo* tradition" in Peruvian politics, planned to finance Balta's railroad expansion by greater borrowing abroad. He did so by shifting the guano contract in 1869 from the national contractors, whom Piérola and his conservative supporters saw as a spendthrift clique bent on personal aggrandizement at the expense of the national interest, to a French firm headed by the international financier Auguste Dreyfus. The Civilistas countered by labeling the move a sellout to international finance and wraping themselves in the flag of national sovereignty. Whoever was right, such a drastic move against the plutocracy's fundamental economic interests was bound to stir up the lasting enmity of the Civilistas.

The upshot was a massive increase in Peru's foreign debt and a predictably bitter reaction from the displaced Civilista elite. The foreign debt, which in 1865 stood at only S/9 million prior to the War with Spain, now soared from S/90 million in 1869 to S/185 million in 1872. Debt service alone in 1872 consumed S/13.5 million out of the total guano income of S/15 million. To make matters worse, Dreyfus, who was intent on monopolizing the world guano market, proved to be considerably less prudent than Gibbs had been in guaranteeing adequate guano reserves to back the government's increased borrowing. Finally, the sudden massive inflow of foreign funds ignited a severe inflationary spiral, as well as a short-lived, speculative banking boom between 1869 and 1872. The number of banks, for example, rose from four in 1868 to sixteen in 1873, far exceeding the capacity of the national economy. This situation set the stage for a severe financial crisis in 1873 when the world economy plunged into a depression.

Meanwhile, the political reaction to the faltering economy and the corruption and failed policies of the Balta regime was intense. Led by Manuel Pardo, who had become the popular mayor of Lima in 1869, the Civilistas mounted a strong campaign to end military rule and establish a civilian government based on respect for the law, republican institutions, and civil liberties. The key, as Pardo and his fellow Civilistas saw it, was to reduce sharply the bloated armed forces. As Pardo put it, "Peru wants public works instead of fifteen thousand soldiers" (quoted in Kristal, 1987, p. 66). Under their plan, the military would be restructured into a much smaller professional army, augmented by a national guard that could be mobilized in times of national emergency.

Pardo and the Civilistas also put forward a developmental agenda. It included the construction of public works (railroads, roads, irrigation) to facilitate production, commerce, and exports; the encouragement of foreign immigration, which would bring progressive skills and values from Europe while "improving"—that is, "whitening"—the racial composition of the nation. It also called for the promotion of a work ethic and an end to governmental corruption and sinecures and the encouragement of investments in productive industry, rather than the squandering of wealth through consuming luxury goods. By this time, the spending proclivities of some *Limeño* families had reached such outlandish proportions that these families were even importing the doors and windows of their homes. Much of the Civilista program was directed against the conservative opposition and what the progressives considered the decadent ethos of the old landholding class. Altogether, Civilismo stood in opposition to the old seignorial order that it hoped to eliminate and expressed the new capitalistic spirit and "democratizing" ethos of the new export bourgeoisie. Indeed, the program sounded much like a latter-day clarion call for modernization.

Pardo won a resounding victory at the polls in the elections of 1871–72, but was prevented from assuming office by a military coup against Balta, led by Balta's minister of war, General Tomás Gutiérrez and his brothers Marceliano and Silvestre. What was notable about the affair was not the rather predictable response from elements of the military, but the fact that the attempted coup aimed at the popular Pardo provoked an orgy of rioting from the Lima populace. In short order, Balta was arrested and then murdered by his guards; Pardo was rescued by the warship *Huascar*, commanded by a widely respected naval officer named Miguel Grau; and Tomás Gutiérrez was seized and killed by an enraged mob of citizens who proceeded to mutilate his body. Not content to end it there, the mob hung the naked bodies of Tomás and Silvestre from the twin bell towers of the National Cathedral. Then, after decapitating them, the rioters burned the fallen bodies, together with that of Marceliano, in a large urn in front of the cathedral.

The savagery of the rioting and its gruesome ending has been interpreted in various ways. Civilista commentators romantically saw it as a spontaneous and heroic popular uprising in defense of civilian rule and electoral democracy. In fact, Giesecke (1978) mustered considerable evidence that it was a more organized and directed movement, composed of elements of the dispossessed artisan class that had been ruined by two decades of radical free trade. In the end, the failed coup further disgraced the military and legitimated Pardo's fledgling Civilista government.

Economic Crisis and Descent into the Abyss

Pardo's popularity would be sorely tested, however, by the onset of an economic crisis that would plunge Peru into bankruptcy and eventually lead to a catastrophic war with Chile by the end of the decade. No sooner had Pardo assumed office than the new president was confronted with the impact on Peru of the world depression of 1873 that caused a sharp decline in the country's exports. By 1878, for example, cotton production had dropped to one-third of its 1872 level. This economic decline could not have occurred at a more unfavorable time for Peru's grossly overextended financial system. Meanwhile, income from guano, whose reserves were now nearing exhaustion, plummeted 35 percent from £4 million in 1869 to only £2.6 million in 1875. Consequently, Peru struggled to refinance its external debt while unemployment skyrocketed and salaries to governmental employees, whose numbers had unjustifiably soared during previous regimes, went unpaid.

Pardo met the crisis with an austerity program that nevertheless spared his pet railroad-development project. The bureaucracy was paired, the armed forces were reduced by three-quarters, and new taxes were introduced to raise revenues. Pardo also tried to replace the dwindling guano income with nitrates, a fertilizer now competing with guano on the international market. A number of Peruvian, Chilean, and other foreign firms were just beginning to produce nitrates in the province of Tarapacá in southern Peru. In 1873 Pardo moved to establish a state nitrate monopoly, and two years later, he expropriated these firms in return for nitrate certificates issued by the government. Nitrate sales proved to be disappointing, however, and the government soon fell into arrears on the certificates. Pardo's actions caused the former owners, who had moved to Chile, which also produced nitrates in the Atacama desert near the Peruvian border, to help stir up growing popular antipathy toward Peru and her ally Bolivia.

The impact of the government's austerity measures and the deepening economic decline quickly dissipated Pardo's original popularity. His policies also alienated the powerful institutions of the Church and the military. The former objected to his efforts to promote the expansion and secularization of education, which, along with railroad construction, were crucial to his development program. Pardo believed that economic and political development hinged on extending education to the popular classes, particularly the unintegrated Indian masses, and in making higher education less philosophical and theoretical and more practical and utilitarian. As for the military, it could not tolerate the drastic reductions in its budget and personnel. As a result, Pardo was forced to quell several military revolts during his term, several instigated by his longtime rival Piérola, who denounced, among other things, the president's anticlericalism.

By the final year of his term, Pardo faced the prospects of a banking and fiscal collapse. When efforts to refinance the foreign debt failed in January

1876, Peru was forced into bankruptcy, paralyzing public works (all railroad construction had already been suspended in August 1875) and causing the value of her bonds to plunge from 77.5 percent in 1875 to 17.15 percent in 1876. The banking system also tottered on the verge of collapse until the government intervened to guarantee the banks' monetary issue. With civil and military unrest on the rise, Pardo paradoxically saw no alternative but to persuade the Civilista Party to turn to a military leader, former president-dictator General Mariano Ignacio Prado (1876–79) as its candidate in the 1876 elections.

Under Prado, the country somehow managed to avoid temporarily total financial collapse, at least until the outbreak of the War of the Pacific in 1879. The new president was able to renegotiate the foreign debt in 1876 with the Council of Foreign Bondholders in London. The agreement, known as the Rafael contract, set up a foreign creditor company, the Peruvian Guano Company, that would administer the guano income to service the defaulted debt. Moreover, rising income from sugar exports eased the foreign exchange crisis, which had accompanied the banking crisis and debt default of 1876. Still, Prado was unable to quell the deepening political antagonism between Piérola and the Civilistas, particularly after the assassination in 1878 of Pardo, whose followers suspected was the work of the Pierolistas.

The outbreak of the War of the Pacific in 1879, however, ended all prospects for economic recovery. In the middle of the war, which pitted Peru and Bolivia against their stronger southern neighbor Chile, the Peruvian Guano Company and its London bondholders reached a settlement with Chile that deprived Peru of its guano income. At the same time, the banking system collapsed when the government issued a worthless new currency, the *Inca*, that was totally unbacked by reserves. Peru thus came to the end of the guano era virtually penniless, having squandered a treasure almost as bountiful as the mother lode in silver discovered at Potosí more than three centuries earlier.

Historians still debate the reasons for Peru's failure to take advantage of this golden opportunity. Certainly, in a hypothetical sense, the idea of converting the bonanza into state spending on worthwhile development projects represented a rational program for progress. The problem was that railroads, because of the extreme and unique geographic obstacles to be overcome, were an extraordinarily expensive device by which to bring about economic progress. They also turned out to be less integrative than export oriented, so that once they were finished after the war, they would foster an externally oriented pattern of development

Still, over the long term, the railroads did stimulate some commercial development and a degree of capitalist modernization, as, for example, in Junín, in the years following the debacle of the Chilean war. However, even this eventual, partial payback in investment was negated by the fact that the railroads fell into foreign hands (in the so-called Grace Contract of 1886) as a result of the bankruptcy produced by Peru's defeat in the war. Thus, Peru lost the one concrete legacy of the guano era, a national communication system, to foreign owners who would eventually acquire substantial mining holdings (now linked by railroad to the coast) and thus further profit from the railroads' construction. It is little wonder, then, that Peruvian historians have been less than generous to the guano-era elites who they, in many ways accurately, have accused of gross corruption, ineptitude, and extravagance in managing the guano bonanza.

Hunt argued that the failure to marshal the formidable guano accumulation for the purposes of industrializing the country, as Pardo had proposed, was due more to the absence of a bourgeois mentality among the new, largely *"rentista"*-minded plutocracy. Manrique (1995) agreed, but added that the limits of the internal market in a country in which more than 60 percent of the population was Indian, a large portion of whom were living at the level of subsistence, proscribed any concerted investment in industrialization. In this sense, the oligarchy's profoundly racist views toward the indigenous population precluded efforts to integrate the country in a way that would have served as the basis of industrialization. Manrique correctly concluded that the elite's persistent attachment to Spain and the Hispanic past and concommittant refusal to utilize, as Mexico did, the idea of a great pre-Columbian past to forge the idea of nationhood, largely doomed the country to perpetual underdevelopment.

Another view attributes Peru's developmental debacle to the misguided interventionist policies of the state that prevented the private sector from taking firmer control of the national economy. For example, the banking system was continually undermined by the damaging monetary and other policies followed by the state. More important, as Quiroz (1993) persuasively argued, the state's propensity for establishing monopolies first over guano and later over nitrates, while consistent with traditional mercantilistic practices dating back to the colonial and postindependence periods, exacerbated the problem of the debt by facilitating nonproductive expenditures on a bloated military and governmental bureaucracy, not to mention the opportunities created for massive corruption.

Whatever the merits of these interpretations, it may be said with certainty that wider forces, such as the impact of the worldwide depression of 1873, combined with the exhaustion of the guano deposits and the debacle of the onset of the War of the Pacific, ended whatever prospects Peru had for a great developmental leap forward in the middle of the nineteenth century.

7 War of the Pacific and Reconstruction, 1879–95

The origins of the War of the Pacific lie in the barren, but mineral-rich Atacama Desert, a great, empty, arid expanse stretching some 600 miles along the Pacific. When nitrate deposits were discovered there, the region became the focal point for conflicting territorial claims by Peru, Bolivia, and Chile. Peru claimed a 235-mile strip of the desert that included the coastal provinces of Tacna, Arica, and Tarapacá. Bolivia claimed the next 240 miles, comprising the province of Antofagasta from the Loa River south to the twenty-fifth parallel. Chile, however, disputed these claims, proclaiming sovereignty northward to the twenty-third parallel. All three countries viewed the desert's nitrate deposits, at a time of general financial strain in the 1870s, as a potential source of important revenues.

This was particularly true for Peru, which had seen its guano production and income evaporate at the same time that the world economy was plunging into the depression of 1873. Two years later, the country declared bankruptcy. For the Pardo government, nitrates constituted an alternative source of income to guano and a potential solution to its financial difficulties. Therefore, it formed a governmental monopoly in 1873 to purchase nitrates from local producers for resale in the European market. This plan proved impractical, however, because of the falling prices, since the government could not guarantee adequate returns to producers. Hoping to regulate production and income better, Pardo nationalized the industry in 1875. This action antagonized the nitrate producers, many of whom were Chilean or European capitalists who subsequently began to lobby for the removal of the province of Tarapacá from the Peruvian monopoly and ominously to help Chile build up its military forces.

Peru's armed forces at the time were in a state of decline. They were so partly because of the government's financial problems that necessitated budget cuts, but also because of Pardo's Civilista philosophy of curtailing the armed forces' long-standing power in the political affairs of the nation. Consequently, the army's manpower had been reduced from 12,000 in 1870 to only 4,500 in 1875. To offset this decline, Pardo reestablished the national guard and created both a military college and naval school to improve professional and technical training. More damaging than the cut in army per-

Map 6. Guide Map to Chilean Expansion. Key: A. Original Chile-Bolivian boundary; B. Claimed by Chile in 1842; a. Established by treaty in 1866, but in A–B nitrate revenues were divided equally; C. Original Peru-Bolivian boundary; D. Boundary of Chile as a result of the War of the Pacific, 1883, with D–E to be occupied by Chile ten years; d. Chile-Peruvian boundary by settlement of 1929. *Source:* William Jefferson Dennis, *Tacna and Arica* (New Haven, 1931).

sonnel, Pardo canceled contracts for new warships that might have ensured the naval superiority in the Pacific that Peru had enjoyed since the 1850s. He did so when Chile was refurbishing and purchasing new vessels for its fleet.

At the same time that Pardo was contemplating ways of extracting more revenue from southern nitrates, he was negotiating a defensive alliance with Bolivia. He was fearful that the Bolivians might decide to form an alliance with Chile that would not only imperil Peru's nitrate fields, but tip the delicate balance of power in the region to its longtime Pacific rival. The treaty was signed on February 6, 1873, with each country agreeing to come to the mutual assistance of the other if its territorial sovereignty was violated by a third party. Peru unsuccessfully tried to make Argentina, which had its own lingering border dispute with Chile in Patagonia, a party to the agreement. This attempt led Chile to suspect that the 1873 treaty was not only aimed against it, but was offensive in design, not defensive as was claimed. Such an interpretation of the treaty by Chile seems hollow, however, given the woeful state of military preparations of both Peru and Bolivia and their seeming inability to carry out any aggressive actions against their better-organized Pacific neighbor. So in addition to nitrate wealth in the disputed territory, the conflict was fueled by deep geopolitical and commercial rivalries. The former involved a fledgling regional balance of power in southern South America dating from the breakup of the old colonial regime and the emergence of several new, competing nation-states in the postindependence period. As for the latter, commercial competition between Callao and Valparaiso over control of trade along the west coast went back even further into the colonial period and had been one of the sources of war between the two countries in 1836.

The precipitating event of the War of the Pacific was a 10-centavo tax per hundred weight levied by the Bolivian government on all nitrates exported by the Anglo-Chilean-owned Antofagasta Nitrate Company in 1878. Without sufficient capital or a bourgeoisie to develop its own nitrate deposits, Bolivia had granted concessions to the company and other Chilean entrepreneurs and their British associates to exploit the deposits. The Antofagasta company had been aggressively pouring capital, managerial and technical skill, and labor into the Atacama to develop its holdings for some time. Indeed, by the end of the 1870s, it and other European firms had come to control almost half the nitrate-producing capacity of Tarapacá, of which they were deprived by Pardo's nationalization. This expansion of Anglo-Chilean capital and expertise along the Bolivian littoral had also opened the way for foreign funding to modernize the Bolivian silver mining industry, further linking the interests of international capital and Bolivian mining interests.

The 10-centavo tax increase levied on the Chilean nitrate companies, although small, violated the terms of two previous treaties between Bolivia and Chile in 1872 and 1874. The latter treaty had recognized the boundary between the two countries at the twenty-fourth parallel and prohibited any tax increases on Chilean commercial interests or exports from the region for twenty-five years. When the Antofagasta company refused to pay the tax, Bolivia placed an embargo on its exports and arrested its manager, provoking Chile to send warships into the Bay of Antofagasta and, shortly thereafter, on February 14, 1879, militarily to occupy the lightly fortified Bolivian port whose population, because of the development of the nitrate industry, was by then 80 percent Chilean. Bolivia responded by declaring war on March 14 and by invoking the treaty of mutual alliance with Peru that obligated Peru to enter the war on its side.

Peru was hardly prepared for war. Most of its fleet languished in dry dock for repairs, and its army units were scattered throughout the country. For a while, it tried to stall for time while negotiating with Chile. However, these talks, headed by historian and diplomat José Antonio de Lavalle, quickly reached an impasse because Chile demanded that Peru renounce its treaty with Bolivia and declare its neutrality. Peru feared that its ally Bolivia might reverse course and settle with Chile with the object of stripping Peru of its nitrate-rich province of Tarapacá. Mariano Ignacio Prado, the former president and hero of the War of 1866 with Spain, now occupied the presidency. Prado refused to disavow the 1873 treaty, leaving Chile no choice but to declare war on both Peru and Bolivia on April 6, 1879. In the end, Peru had a strong interest in protecting its substantial nitrate industry, on which the government had pinned its financial hopes and the country's future development.

At the outset, the war's outcome, as St John (1992, p. 109) pointed out, could not have been easily predicted, for both sides hypothetically possessed certain advantages and disadvantages. The allies' advantage in total population over smaller Chile, for example, was balanced by the latter's more homogeneous and better educated and motivated citizenry. Still, compared to its neighbors, Chile was a much more stable political entity, possessing a strong, institutionalized state and constitutional order that had seen the orderly presidential transfer of power six times between 1831 and 1879. Nevertheless, at least in the beginning, it is clear that the Chilean public was certainly not all that united in pursuing the war and was hampered, as was Peru, by severe political strife throughout the contest. Chile was also supported by Great Britain, which had developed strong political and economic ties with Chile ever since independence. Those ties were, no doubt, reinforced by the nitrate holdings that Peru had nationalized in Tarapacá. They were also strengthened by influential British financiers who held defunct Peruvian bonds caused by the 1875 declaration of bankruptcy and who held out the prospect that the bonds might conceivably be redeemed from reparation payments in the case of a Chilean victory. Finally, in comparison to its opponents, Chile's army was exceedingly well organized and equipped with modern Krupp artillery and French-made rifles.

In the final analysis, it was probably Chile's superior armed forces, particularly naval strength, and overall strategy at the outset of the war that sealed the allies' fate. The Chilean army, for example, was relatively combat ready, having been actively engaged for the past couple of decades in campaigns against the Mapuche Indians. Moreover, in the early 1870s, Chile had set out to build up its naval forces to control the Pacific, so that at the outset of the hostilities, its ships and sailors had a three-to-one advantage over Peru. This advantage proved crucial, for on May 21, 1879, even though the Peruvian fleet had succeeded in sinking the Chilean corvette *Esmeralda* in the first major naval engagement of the war, the Peruvian ironclad *Independencia* ran aground on a reef off the port of Iquique during the battle. The loss of the *Independencia* left Peru with only the much smaller ironclad *Huáscar* to challenge its more powerful Chilean counterparts the *Blanco Encalada* and the *Almirante Cochrane*. In spite of this disadvantage, the *Huáscar*, commanded by Vice Admiral Miguel Grau, managed to keep the Chilean fleet off balance with a series of brilliant naval maneuvers over the next five months. These maneuvers succeeded in buying time for the deployment and concentration in the south of Peru's army units, which were now in a position to defend Iquique and link up with Bolivian detachments in Tacna.

However, the allied cause at sea was dealt a second and decisive blow on October 8 at the Battle of Angamos. In that battle, the *Huáscar* was ambushed and captured by the two Chilean ironclads, and most of its officers, including the legendary Grau, were killed. Grau's heroic resistance against heavy odds made him one of the few authentic Peruvian heroes to emerge from the general debacle of the war, and his memory is still revered by the Peruvian public. Nevertheless, Chile now completely controlled the vital Pacific sea lanes off Peru, so it could concentrate its forces for attack and resupply anywhere it chose along the coast. Naval supremacy also enabled Chile to impose an embargo designed to shut down Peru's exports in an effort to cripple financially Peru's ability to prosecute the war. For the allies, after the loss of the *Huáscar*, the end seemed only a matter of time.

Nevertheless, Peru managed to stave off defeat far longer than most observers anticipated. With its back to the wall, the country summoned up a spirit of resistance that stymied Chile's desire for a quick, successful conclusion to the war. For the moment, Chile slowly followed up its naval victories with a land invasion of 10,000 troops on the south coast at Pisagua on October 28, after which its army marched north, where it won a tactical victory over the allied forces at Tarapacá in November. From that point, Chile occupied the entire province of Tarapacá, whose revenues from nitrate production now allowed Chile to finance its war effort, as well as pay off 50 percent of Peru's debt to British creditors. By June 1880, Chile had routed the allied forces in the south, taken the provinces of Tacna and Arica, and forced Bolivia to abandon the war. Only the heroic sacrifice of a Peruvian detachment, commanded by Colonel Francisco Bolognesi, defending the port of Arica provided some solace for the country's military reverses and yielded yet another martyr to a losing cause.

In September 1880, a 3,000-man Chilean expeditionary force, commanded by General Patricio Lynch, landed on the north coast to plunder

Peruvian soldier and wife circa 1880. Courtesy of the Library of Congress and Deborah Poole.

the rich sugar plantations there. The aim was to raise revenues, deprive the country of foreign exchange, and force the Peruvians to sue for peace. In the event, Lynch's expedition, which was particularly merciless in leaving a trail of death and destruction, had the opposite effect of stiffening Peruvian resistance to the invaders.

Meanwhile earlier, as Peru began to experience this string of military reverses and a mounting political crisis, President Prado took the inexplicable act of secretly abandoning the country on December 18, 1879, to travel to Europe ostensibly in search of loans to purchase additional ironclads. Four days later, Nicolás de Piérola, his main political rival, overthrew the government and declared a dictatorship to save the country. Piérola, however, inherited a country weakened by increasing political factionalism and an economy that was collapsing. Commerce was stagnant; creditors were unwilling to lend money to the government; and, even worse, the guano islands, still a main source for the country's foreign exchange, had been seized by the Chileans. Together with General Lynch's ravishing of the sugar industry, the loss of the guano islands crippled Peru's vital export capacity and ability to generate foreign exchange and thus its ability to prosecute the war.

In addition to these economic and financial difficulties, increasing political conflict between Piérola and the deposed Civilistas undermined the effort to defend Lima from another advancing Chilean expeditionary force that had landed in Pisco in December 1880. Forced to defend the capital with a hastily organized local militia and remnants of the defeated army in the south, Piérola failed to draw on the expertise of many returning officers whose political loyalties he suspected. Instead, he reinforced the Lima militia with ill-prepared Quechua- and Aymara-speaking Indian recruits who were sent and led by his provincial landowning allies whose own military expertise proved minimal. In the end, Peru's poorly led and equipped 19,000-man improvised militia, deployed in two long, ill-conceived defensive lines outside the capital by Piérola, stood little chance against Chile's better led and equipped 25,500-man invasion force, supported by modern artillery. Both sides suffered heavy casualties in the decisive battles of San Juan and Miraflores, but Lima fell on January 15, 1881.

With the capital now in enemy hands and suffering, as you shall see, from the depredations of both the invading army and angry mobs, Piérola abandoned the city for the central sierra to try to rally Peruvian resistance. Piérola's abandonment of Lima, however, left no government with which to negotiate a peace, so the Chileans constructed a rump government headed by Francisco García Calderón, a prominent Civilista, who convened remnants of the 1879 Congress in the Lima suburb of La Magdalena. This Congress ratified García Calderón as interim president, but hamstrung his ability to negotiate a peace settlement by prohibiting the ceding of any national territory. This nationalistic position, which coincided with the mercantile elite's reluctance to relinquish control over the valuable province of Tarapacá, drew support away from Piérola in the interior and in favor of García Calderón's government. With the country's elites now increasingly divided over how to prosecute or conclude the war, García Calderón tried to get the United States, which had generally been favorable to Peru's position in the conflict, to intervene to bring about a peace settlement. Chile reacted by abolishing the Magdalena government and exiling García Calderón to Santiago in September 1881.

Meanwhile, the situation in the interior had become increasingly confused. Revolts against Piérola, who had so far refrained from attacking the invaders, broke out in Arequipa, Puno, and Ayacucho. This encouraged Vice Admiral Lizardo Montero, whom García Calderón had designated as his successor, to declare himself president. Piérola, seeing his popular support evaporate, then dissolved his government and left the country for Europe. This left General Andrés Avelino Cáceres as the main organizer of the resistance in the central highlands, where he had been appointed guerrilla commander by Piérola.

Cáceres was one of Peru's more able officers, having distinguished himself earlier in extracting a large force of Peruvian troops that had been surrounded and threatened with annihilation by the enemy near Arica. His reputation had grown at the Battle of Miraflores, where his troops had fought heroically and where he was wounded in action. After eluding the enemy forces occupying the capital, he recuperated from his wounds and had joined Piérola at Jauja in April 1881.

Placed in charge of the resistance in the central sierra, Cáceres adroitly channeled the peasants' anger over the depredations committed by the invading Chilean army that had moved up from the coast to occupy the agriculturally rich Mantaro Valley near Huancayo. With the bounty of their communities threatened by the occupying army and themselves the target of racist epithets from Chilean soldiers, the Indian peasants readily responded to Cáceres's nationalistic call to organize *montoneras* to defend their cherished lands and drive out the invaders. Within a few months, the Quechua-speaking, former landowner who knew intimately the idiosyncrasies of his men, had forged a guerrilla army, based on a multiclass, multiethnic coalition and led by local notables, which included some 5,000 mostly Indian peasants. This force proceeded to harass and stifle the enemy over the next few years, inflicting a major defeat on the Chileans in the Mantaro Valley in July 1882.

While Caceres was acquiring his reputation as El Brujo de Los Andes (Wizard of the Andes), in what came to be known as La Campaña de la Breña (Campaign of the Craggy Ground), in the northern highlands General Miguel Iglesias, a landowner from Cajamarca who had served as Piérola's minister of war and fought heroically in the defense of Lima, assumed command of the Northern Army of Resistance headquartered in Cajamarca city. However, Iglesias's defense of the north against the Chilean invasion of Cajamarca in mid-1882 turned out to be rather lukewarm, and he soon issued his famous Manifesto de Montán, which called for a negotiated peace with Chile without any territorial preconditions, contrary to the earlier mandate of the Magdalena Congress. In reaction to this "collaborationist" position and again revealing the extent of intra-elite disagreement over how best to deal with the Chilean occupation, two separate resistance movements, led by hacendados Manuel José Becerra and José Mercedes Puga, emerged in different parts of Cajamarca. Nevertheless, in December 1882, Iglesias convened an Assembly of the North, composed largely of family members, friends, and allies, which "elected" him president and authorized him to seek a peace settlement. This authorization came in the wake of failed negotiations, mediated by the United States, between President Montero and García Calderón (from his exile in Santiago) and Chilean officials.

With this impasse, Chile turned away from the Montero government and increasingly supported Iglesias, who was now opposed by Cáceres, leader of the resistance. Iglesias's "peace party" was supported by landowners who opposed the continuation of the war in the highlands that they saw as a direct threat to their estates and the social control that they exerted over the peasantry. Unlike the Lima mercantile elites, the landowners had no interest, other than a certain sentimental attachment, to the possible loss of

Tarapacá, which they were perfectly willing to sacrifice in behalf of their survival as a ruling class in the sierra (Manrique, 1995, p. 177). In the event, Chilean forces supporting Iglesias managed to defeat Cáceres at the Battle of Huamachuco on October 18, 1883, and proceeded to recognize General Iglesias as president. Two days later, the two countries agreed to the Treaty of Ancón, which ended the war.

The agreement ceded the province of Tarapacá to Chile and stipulated that a plebiscite would be held in the provinces of Tacna and Arica after ten years to determine their destiny. The winner was to pay an indemnity to the loser of 10 million Chilean pesos or their equivalent. Most of the other provisions of the treaty dealt with issues pertaining to guano and nitrates, over which the war had fundamentally been fought. For example, the guano islands were returned to Peru, but not before 1 million tons were sold and divided between the Chilean government and Peru's creditors. Although there was considerable opposition to the treaty in Peru, where its terms were viewed as too favorable to Chile, it was ratified on March 10, 1884, by a Constituent Assembly convened by Iglesias.

Civil War, Socioeconomic Turmoil, and Reconstruction

At the end of the war, Peru's economy lay in ruins. Everywhere the invading Chilean forces passed, the toll in death and destruction was substantial. After the Battle of Miraflores, Lima—the Pearl of the Pacific of the guano age—was sacked and looted by the victorious Chilean soldiers. The victors, moreover, added insult to injury by carrying off to Santiago virtually the entire 58,000 volumes of the National Library. Likewise, the machinery of the Escuela de Artes y Oficios, set up by the government to retrain displaced artisans during the guano era, was shipped to Chile. In the north, the punitive Lynch expedition razed the sugar plantations of owners who refused to pay stiff tributes and shipped home their valuable machinery as the prizes of war. Sugar production, which had boomed during the late guano years, plummeted by two-thirds. Damage to the communications system, particularly the half-finished railway system, was also extensive.

Production and income plunged all across the economic spectrum. One indicator was the state, whose revenues fell from around 35 million *soles* in 1879 to just over 1 million in 1883. Nitrate and guano income all but disappeared, while income from sugar, wool, silver, and other exports dropped to a quarter of the prewar levels. With the decline in exports, imports fell to 1840 levels. The country's financial infrastructure also quickly withered. Of the country's twenty largest banks in 1877, only the native-owned Banco de Callao and foreign Banco de Londres, México y Sudamérica survived the debacle. Virulent war-induced inflation and devaluation, reaching 800 percent, ravaged the currency, while silver poured out of the country to pay creditors and for imports. Individual citizens, of course, suffered the brunt of the economic and financial collapse. A rough quantification of the impact on the social classes by a contemporary observer estimated that the ranks of millionaires had dropped from 18 to 0, the rich from 11,500 to 1,725, and the middle class from 22,148 to 2,000. The number of beggars who roamed the country skyrocketed to half a million.

Social conflict under such conditions was inevitably exacerbated. The prevailing system of authority and social control, fragile during normal times, unraveled with sometimes bloody consequences in the face of the invading armies or in the chaotic aftermath of defeat. Along the north coast sugar belt, for example, plantation coolies reacted to the approach of Chilean forces by hailing them as "liberators" and sacking the estates of their masters. A similar response earlier had seen a thousand or so indentured Chinese coolies rise up in rebellion and abandon the cotton estates near Pisco to join the invaders whom they also viewed as "liberators." After Lima fell to the invaders, mobs attacked the Chinese quarter and Chinese shops scattered around the city in a spasm of racism and violence. Similar pogroms scapegoating the Asian population occurred as well in several towns along the coast. The same Lima mobs also vented their wrath against the city's wealthy, who fled for their lives to the British Embassy while their properties were sacked and looted before they were set on fire.

Similar outbreaks of social conflict, associated with the mobilization of Cáceres's *montoneras*, had accompanied the spread of the war into the central and northern highlands. In addition to attacking the invading Chilean army, the peasants also turned on sectors of the landholding class and seized their estates and cattle as war booty, accusing them of collaborating with the enemy to save their property. Historians Favre (1975) and Bonilla (1980) interpreted these actions, together with the uprisings of the Chinese coolie workers on the coastal sugar and cotton estates, as expressions of incipient class war. For them, the war undermined the traditional elite's social control and authority, unleashing the long-repressed resentments of the popular classes against their masters in a society that was deeply divided by class conflict. Moreover, Favre and Bonilla contended that the peasants had no concept of the nation-state, failed to understand who the invading enemy was (misunderstood as "General Chile"), and therefore in their confusion could not express a patriotic or nationalist outlook.

The latter view, however, was challenged by revisionist historians Manrique and Mallon, who pointed to the actions of Cáceres's peasant *montoneras* against the Chilean invaders who threatened their land as well as against the "collaborationist" landlords. They stressed that in some areas, these same peasant guerrillas continued to occupy many of the latters' estates and retain their cattle after the war ended, considering them legitimate booty of war, and that some of their leaders even articulated a larger political vision of democratic reform that aimed to alter the traditional power monopoly of the sierra elite. For Mallon (1995, p. 213) this represented the genesis, or embryo, of a multiclass, nationalist, popular reform movement with important reformist implications. In support of their case, both historians noted that the Mantaro Valley was ethnically heterogeneous and commercially advanced, with a population of market-oriented small farmers and merchants—just such a socioeconomic configuration that was conducive to the formation of an alternative popular project for reform.

The hope that Cáceres might support these local subaltern efforts to redefine the nature of citizenship and political power faded under the realities of elite-dominated, postwar politics. Now Cáceres, ambitious for the presidency, needed the political support of the powerful landowning class for his campaign to unseat Iglesias as president and leader of the postwar reconstruction. Toward this end, he disavowed the peasant wartime occupations of *gamonal* estates in Junín and called for a return to the prewar land-tenure system and elite's balance of power over the peasantry. Although he was able to negotiate a compromise between the communities and landowners over disputed property in some areas, Cáceres and his representatives were forced to take a harder line in others. For example, in Comas, Cáceres abandoned his former *montonera* allies and moved to repress those peasants who refused his order for the restitution of land and cattle that they had expropriated as war booty. Still, enforcement of the order proved difficult because the peasants, aided by the local terrain, were able to resist for some time efforts by the army to remove them from the lands of former owners. Sadly, once viewed as valiant citizen-soldiers in the war against the Chilean invaders, the Comasino peasants were now portrayed in official postwar discourse as backward, ignorant, and barbaric Indians.

Despite such isolated popular resistance, Cáceres's strategy of guaranteeing the preexisting land-tenure system consolidated the elite's support for his struggle against Iglesias. Moreover, once the Chilean invaders withdrew from the country in August 1884, Iglesias lost the main instrument for maintaining his control of the government. Likewise, he suffered politically for being seen in popular eyes as having collaborated with the enemy during the war and given away the national patrimony in the unpopular Treaty of Ancón, a view effectively propagandized by Cáceres's supporters. In contrast, Cáceres succeeded in capitalizing on his professional military skills and heroic popular image as the leader of the anti-Chilean resistance during the war.

Cáceres's main vehicle in bringing down the presidency of Iglesias, however, would be his loyal *montoneras*, who had proved so effective against the Chileans. After initially being held at bay during 1884 by the army, they finally succeeded, with considerable popular support in the streets of Lima, in taking the capital and forcing Iglesias to resign and go into exile in December 1885. Cáceres became provisional president for a year, during which he founded the Constitutionalist Party (Partido Constitucional) under whose banner he would run and easily win the ensuing election for president. Meanwhile, the Civilistas, who had allied with Cáceres against Iglesias, had regrouped around the leadership of Aurelio Denegri, a wealthy merchant and miner, and Piérola and his Democratic Party (Partido Demócrata) abstained from voting. With his election, Cáceres became the dominant political figure in the country for the next decade, a period of national reconstruction that historians have dubbed the "second militarism," (after the first following independence in 1824).

Cáceres, National Reconstruction, and the Era of the Second "Militarism," 1885–1895

While Cáceres was contesting Iglesias for power, the civil war also took on a social dimension in early 1885 in the Callejón de Huaylas, a 150-mile-long corridor between two mountain ranges in the northern department of Ancash. The department was still under the control of Iglesias when the Iglesista prefect, Colonel Francisco Noriega, announced the reimposition of the poll or head tax of two gold *soles* on the Indian peasantry in February. Coming as it did on top of the economic devastation of the war, the tax fell hard on the population of this predominantly agricultural region.

The Indian village leaders of the region, led by Pedro Pablo Atusparia, resorting to the normal process of redress and grievance, petitioned the prefect, stating their inability to comply and asking for a reduction and delay in paying the tax. Although there is no record that Atusparia had taken part in Cáceres's guerrilla forces that had resisted the Chilean invasion, some of his kinsmen had. Noriega denied the petition, claiming, among other things, that it contained disrespectful language and a veiled threat against the established order. Atusparia was then arrested, along with twenty-four of his associates, and tortured to reveal the name of the petition's alleged author, since the *varayoc*, or village *alcalde*, himself was illiterate and had relied on a lawyer to draft the document. Part of the torture consisted of chopping off his and his compatriots' long braids, indigenous status symbols and therefore a particularly humiliating form of punishment.

The following day, a large crowd of Indians gathered in the main plaza of Huaraz to protest the arrest of their leaders, only to be fired on by panicky soldiers. This act ignited the mobilization of the Indian peasantry, probably abetted by *misti* (non-Indian) supporters of Cáceres. The next day, 4,000 to 5,000 Indians attacked and seized the city, releasing Atusparia and his fellow chiefs from jail and burning the homes of Iglesias's sympathizers. In a matter of days, the main towns of the valley were similarly attacked, and Iglesias's supporters were targeted.

For their part, the Iglesistas tried to turn the tide against their attackers by resorting to a favorite creole discursive device—accusing Atusparia's "*Indiada*" (Indian mob) of unleashing a race war against all whites. This was precisely the tactic used by the colonial authorities to rally public opinion against Túpac Amaru II a hundred years earlier, and it had the same de-

sired effect in alarming Lima, where Provisional President Iglesias, still cling-
ing to power, quickly dispatched forces to repress the movement. In Ancash
the tactic, according to Stein (1988), had a similar affect, as local supporters
of Cáceres closed ranks with Iglesista alarmists and distanced themselves
from Atusparia's movement, turning the conflict from a strictly civil one to
a social or race war from below.

Actually, the objective of the Indian rising was hardly racially motivated,
nor was it, according to Thurner (1997), an antifiscal movement, that is,
against the payment of taxes, as Kapsoli (1977) and Stein (1988) concluded.
Rather, Indian opposition to the poll tax was based on its illegitimacy, since
the emergency wartime conditions under which it had been levied by Piérola
in 1879 no longer applied. As Thurner put it, "the poll tax was hastily imposed in a moment of severe economic duress by an illegitimate, collaborationist regime installed by the Chileans and opposed by most of the highland Peruvian population" (1997, p. 422). In addition, to be legitimate in the
eyes of the indigenous peasantry in the postwar years, any such tax had to
carry the state's implicit protection of their lands, just as the old *contribución
indígenas* had done before its abolition in 1854 (or, indeed, the tribute tax
during the colonial period). This protection was considered crucial, since
landlords had taken advantage in the intervening decades by enclosing the
Indians' lands. Finally, Atusparia's forces were incensed over Noriega's arbitrary vitiation of the customary negotiation process by repressing the attempts of the Indian *alcaldes* to mediate the dispute.

In the end, the Northern Pacification Force sent from Lima, under the
command of Colonel José Iraola, managed to defeat the rebels in battle and
force Atusparia to surrender. However, some of Atusparia's more radical
lieutenants, led by the miner Pedro "Uchcu" Cochachín, who did, in fact,
advocate the extermination of all whites, continued to resist, only to fall victim to a massive wave of repression in which entire Indian villages were
wiped out at the hands of Iraola's army. The final death toll was in the thousands, but Atusparia, who had tried unsuccessfully to control the radicals,
was ultimately spared and later absolved of charges. Two days before the
inauguration of Cáceres as president of the republic, Atusparia met with the
president-elect in Lima, and his son was later granted a government scholarship to attend school. More important, Cáceres promised schools, relief
from the poll tax, and state protections of community lands, promises he
later failed to keep.

Upon taking office on June 3, 1885, Cáceres had to face the imposing task
of reconstructing the wartorn country whose foreign debt alone amounted
to the enormous sum of £40–50 million. Commercial transactions were obstructed by a badly depreciated paper currency and a severely reduced
"banking system" (only two private banks survived the war) that was incapable of financing the reactivization of trade and commerce. Thus, the surviving sugar and cotton planters were at the mercy of obtaining credit from
the few foreign merchant houses, such as Gibbs & Sons, W. R. Grace & Co.,

and Graham Rowe, which remained strong enough to conduct business after the war. Their properties severely damaged by the war and hobbled by heavy mortgages contracted during the late guano era, many planters were unable to survive the crisis and lost their estates to foreign creditors in a wave of postwar foreign takeovers. For example, W. R. Grace & Co. foreclosed on the Peruvian-owned Cartavio estate in 1882 and proceeded to invest substantial sums in its expansion and modernization. Other planters simply sold their estates to their financially stronger, more efficient competitors. This wave of postwar concentration and foreign penetration of the sugar industry would, as you shall see, have important political repercussions in the twentieth century.

The postwar restructuring of the financial system hinged largely on the shift by the government and the surviving banks to a new silver-backed currency. This shift was politically difficult to carry out, however, since a hard currency was advantageous to creditors, but detrimental to the numerous debtors, such as the agroexporters who sought to pay their debts in depreciated currency. Moreover, the public at large could lose substantially on the value of the paper currency that it held should merchants refuse to accept it, as they began to do in late 1887. This refusal led to public disturbances like the one at the plantation town of Laredo in the province of La Libertad, where a mob attacked Chinese merchants who refused to accept the paper currency paid out as wages to the sugar workers. The government finally moved to stabilize the value of the currency during 1887–88 by calling in all paper money in circulation and exchanging it for a new, more adequately backed, currency. So worthless had the old currency become that shortly after the government's recall, bonfires could be seen around Lima fueled by piles of the old bills. Eradication of the old currency brought about a more stable financial system, but not without adverse repercussions on both debtors and consumers.

In an effort to aid reconstruction on the local and regional levels, Cáceres gradually reimposed the Indian head tax (*contribución personal*), which had been suspended during the war. Revenues from the tax were turned over to departmental boards (*juntas departamentales*), under the newly passed Law of Fiscal Decentralization, to be distributed for local projects and ends. Both measures can be seen as favorable to the *gamonal* class upon whom Cáceres depended for his rise to the presidency and on which the weak central government relied to maintain law and order in the hinterland (Manrique, 1995, p. 182). At the same time, the availability of significant local funding led to intense struggles between various factions of landowners and their clients for the control and dispersement of these funds that often erupted into violence and bloodshed. Such disputes, together with the persistence of banditry as the social consequence of widespread popular impoverishment, made the pacification of the country difficult during Cáceres's ten-year rule.

The most serious obstacle to economic recovery, however, was the foreign debt, which had festered since the country declared a unilateral moratorium on payment in 1876. Without an agreement with foreign creditors to restructure the debt, Peru's impending export-led recovery would stall for lack of access to both foreign credit and investment. As a result, shortly after he assumed the presidency, Cáceres entered into extended negotiations with the main group of foreign bondholders, represented by Michael A. Grace, who arrived from London in late 1886. The final deal that was cut three years later between the government and the bondholders, known as the Grace Contract, was highly controversial, but probably the best that Peru could get under the circumstances. In return for the cancellation of the debt, Peru agreed to turn over control of its railway system for sixty-six years, deliver its remaining guano exports, and grant free navigation rights on Lake Titicaca to the Peruvian Corporation, the company formed to implement the agreement. Peru also agreed to pay £80,000 a year for thirty-three years and to grant 2 million hectares of land in the central jungle to the corporation.

What the country gained in return for these concessions was a restored credit rating in international money markets and the restoration and completion of its badly damaged railroad system. Both proved beneficial to the country over the short run, since the penurious government could once again borrow abroad, and the repair and extension of the railway line into the central highlands in the early 1890s finally opened up the extraordinarily rich and varied mining deposits in the area to intensive exploitation. The opening up of the mining deposits proved particularly important in facilitating a revival in silver production, which led the initial stages of the economic recovery under Cáceres, with a total value of almost $33 million between 1886 and 1895. But as critics of the Grace Contract were quick to point out, Peru's long-run recovery and development would once again become heavily dependent on foreign investment and markets. Consequently, nationalists strongly attacked the contract and fought hard, but unsuccessfully, to defeat it in Congress. It was passed in early 1889.

The Grace Contract quickly had its intended effect as foreign investment, particularly from Great Britain under the leadership of the same Michael Grace, began to flow into railroad construction, the oil industry, mining, cotton textile manufacturing, and sugar production. This investment boomlet between 1890 and 1892, however, was short lived. It was punctured by the outbreak of the Baring Crisis, which triggered the international depression of 1893, and the sudden plunge in the price of silver, the latter severely affecting countries like Peru that were on the silver standard. British capital investment largely dried up, leaving the field open, for the moment, to native capitalists and financiers and, toward the end of the century, to North American investors.

Along with efforts to reconstitute the liberal export economy, Peru experienced an important postwar boost from import substituting industrialization (ISI). ISI occurred in response to a weak currency, the revived demand by war-ravaged consumers for necessities, and the unintended protectionist impact of the tariff of 1886, which was passed mainly to raise revenues. As the recovery deepened, the number of manufacturing and artisan workshops in Lima alone would rise impressively, numbering around 150 by 1899 and employing perhaps 6,000 workers.

As Peru struggled to recover economically, its politicians and intellectuals, reflecting the somber public postwar mood of criticism and introspection, sought to explain the causes of the country's military debacle. In formulating such a national critique, they also debated the remedies and proper course for national reconstruction and development. Cáceres found the explanation for defeat in the social and political disunity of the country. This lack of unity had allowed "opportunists and collaborators," which he associated with the pernicious greed of bureaucrats and capitalists, to undermine the country's chances for victory. In negotiating the Grace Contract, Cáceres, like Balta in the Dreyfus affair, seemed to be spurning local capitalists in favor of foreign firms in the quest for national reconstruction.

Others like the writer Ricardo Palma, whose political sympathies lay with Piérola, the Church, and the traditional landed oligarchy, blamed the loss on the Civilista export elite and the backwardness of the Indian population. From the ranks of the Civilistas, on the other hand, came a varied and learned response from a new generation of intellectuals who emerged from the cloisters of the venerable San Marcos University. Informed by the tenets of positivism, this "generation of 1900," as it came to be known, would reinvigorate the ranks of Civilismo, just as the party's orientation shifted away from the interests of the older prewar plutocracy to a new export elite born out of the postwar economic recovery.

The nucleus of the generation of 1900 was comprised of Javier Prado, philosopher and son of the former president; sociologist Mariano H. Cornejo; law professor Manuel Vicente Villarán; and lawyer and progressive legislator José Matías Manzanilla. These men were imbued with the rationalist and materialist doctrines of Comtian positivism, which extolled science, rationalism, and practical knowledge as opposed to scholasticism and the importance of hard work and diligence as the path to development. As for the war and the country's past debacles, they blamed the oppressive and backward legacies of the Hispanic past, including the Church, whose traditional values and practices in their view had hindered progress. Although they rejected the Spanish past, they were optimistic about the future, which they envisioned would be led by a progressive, enlightened elite. On the Indian population, they believed that the lack of assimilation had contributed to national disunity and defeat, and they argued that through education and material progress, the Indians could, in time, be integrated into the mainstream of the nation.

A more radical critique and alternative discourse emerged from the acerbic pen and oratory of the iconoclastic Manuel González Prada (1848–1918). Born into an aristocratic *Limeño* family of Spanish origins and educated at the renowned San Toribio Seminary, González Prada had felt a profound humiliation in Peru's resounding military defeat. After the war, he organized *El Círculo Literario*, whose members not only discussed literary themes,

Manuel González Prada (1848–1918), essayist, writer and political radical who exerted great influence on the reform generation of 1919. Reproduced with permission
of the General Secretariat of the Organization of American States.

but debated political and economic topics related to national reconstruction
and unification, to which they were dedicated.

Later in 1891, shortly before he departed for Europe, González Prada
turned *El Círculo* into a political party that he called *La Unión Nacional*. Originally, the party espoused a number of Civilista ideas (González Prada had

actually been associated with the Civilistas before and immediately after the war), such as the need to promote European immigration as a means of "improving the races." However, after he assimilated such diverse ideologies as positivism, romanticism, socialism, and anarchism while he was in Europe from 1891 to 1898, the party came to express an alternative, radical, antioligarchical, and populist discourse that was to influence greatly future Peruvian reformers, such as Guillermo Billinghurst, José Carlos Mariátegui, and Víctor Raúl Haya de la Torre.

González Prada attributed Peru's defeat to the fact that the majority of the Indian population remained indifferent to the war. Because of their isolation and lack of education, the Indians felt no obligation to fight for the nation, a concept, he argued, they did not understand. Thus, he wrote that "the hands of Chile mangled our skin and crushed our bones, but the real winners, the weapons of the enemy, were our ignorance and our spirit of servitude" (quoted in Kristal, 1987, pp. 112–13). González Prada attributed this spirit of servitude to the Spanish colonial past, as well as to the backwardness and ignorance of the landed aristocracy. It was this autocratic and idle aristocracy and its corrupt collaborators—the local judges, governors, and priests—who formed what he called "the trinity of brutalization" that had exploited and victimized the Indians for centuries. The reference to the priests also highlighted González Prada's staunch anticlericalism and the fact that he held the Church, if not Catholicism itself, responsible for the backward state of the Indians, indeed the country. While González Prada was at first confident that the condition of the Indians could be uplifted through material progress, improved transportation, and education, his optimism soon faded and turned to pessimism. After he returned to Peru from Europe in 1898, he began to espouse anarchist views and to urge the Indian population to resort to violence to break their chains of oppression. Curiously, despite his focus on the need for the redemption of the Indian peoples, González Prada never actually visited the sierra to observe their conditions firsthand.

González Prada's attention to the Indians, however, helped revive *indigenismo*, an urban-based, liberal literary and cultural movement that called for the moral and material uplifting of the Indian that dated back to the 1840s. The movement was also spurred by the publication of the novels of the *Cuzqueña* writer Clorinda Matto de Turner (1854–1909), particularly her famous novel *Aves sin nido* (1889), and later the foundation of the *Asociación Pro-Indígena*. The sudden revival of *indigenismo* in Lima and elsewhere was also a response to the renewed surge of postwar peasant uprisings, such as the bloody Atusparia revolt in 1885, and the continuing ferment of peasant nationalism in Junín dating back to the war itself.

Meanwhile, Cáceres's politico-military hold over the country more or less continued unabated. Constitutionally prevented from "reelection" in 1890, Cáceres chose as his successor a loyal lieutenant, Colonel Remigio Morales Bermúdez. In return, he expected the favor to be returned four years later. Morales, however, proved to be an indecisive leader and died unexpectedly in April 1894. Dissatisfied with the elevation of a civilian first vice president to the office, Cáceres carried out a coup in favor of the more pliable second vice president, another military officer who agreed to engineer Cáceres's "reelection" in 1895. This move did not stop the main civilian political parties from jockeying for position for the upcoming presidential succession. While Cáceres, with the support of his presidential ally, prepared to carry out his own "reelection," the Civilistas and Democrats, whose mutual enmity had endured since Piérola's engineering of the Dreyfus Contract in 1869, agreed to a historic rapprochement. The ensuing coalition set the stage for Piérola's return from exile in Chile to rally a broad-based popular movement against Cáceres's planned fraudulent reelection, known as the "Revolution of 1895."

The "Democratic *Caudillo*," as he came to be called, now entered the most productive phase of his long and controversial career. Born in 1839 in Arequipa, the son of a Spanish colonial official and socially prominent and devoutly religious, creole mother, Piérola received the best education available at the time. At the age of fourteen, he entered San Toribio Seminary in Lima, where his father hoped he would prepare for the priesthood. After the death of his parents in 1857, however, the handsome, energetic, if impetuous, young man was drawn into the fast-paced commercial world of Lima during the guano boom. Soon he was also attracted to conservative politics, supporting such politicians as Vivanco, Pezet, Echenique, and Balta. In 1869 he became Balta's finance minister and engineered the celebrated Dreyfus Contract, earning him the opprobrium of the liberal, Civilista plutocracy.

Piérola's conservatism was shaped by the Catholicism and Hispanic traditions that permeated the old colonial city of Arequipa, his early family years and life in the seminary. He believed that Catholicism and a firm authoritarian hand at the head of a centralist state were the key political ingredients necessary to hold together a geographically disparate, heterogeneous and highly class based society. If a popular caudillo was the embodiment of such a political vision, Piérola himself possessed the requisite attributes—an elegant and aristocratic bearing, intense religious devotion, boundless ambition and energy, an unshakable belief in his own personal destiny and a charismatic personality that attracted the masses.

The conditions for Piérola's popular assault on power in 1895 lay in the economic slump of 1893–94, part of the world-wide depression which, among other things, triggered the collapse of the international price of silver, Peru's main engine of post-war recovery. This caused the value of the Peruvian *sol* to drop from 31 to 24 pence, a 35-percent devaluation. The ensuing popular distress, particularly among urban workers and artisans, fueled Piérola's call to arms against the increasingly unpopular Cáceres. It also persuaded the Civilists to withdraw their former support for Cáceres and agree to form a coalition with Piérola and the Democrats to end the decade long military rule of the "hero of La Breña." In a brief but bloody attack on Lima under cover of heavy fog, Piérola's irregulars managed, despite heavy casualties on both sides, to defeat Cáceres in house-to-house fighting and take the national palace. The old war hero, who had remained too long in power, was granted safe passage through the body-strewn streets of the capital on his way into permanent exile.

8 The Aristocratic Republic, 1895–1919

Peru now entered a unique period in its modern history, marked by rare political consensus; widespread political stability; and, at least initially, autonomous growth and development. Generally known in Peruvian historiography as the "Aristocratic Republic," it was to last, with short interruptions, from 1895 until after the end of World War I in 1919. The consensus derived, in part, from the pact between the Civilista and Demócrata parties that had major advantages for both sides, not the least being the joining of forces to overturn Cáceres's oppressive rule. For his part, Piérola understood that without the backing of the emerging Civilista oligarchy, it would be impossible to rule. As for the Civilistas, Nicolás Piérola became their "man on horseback"—the quintessential charismatic Andean *caudillo* who was capable of rallying broad popular support and pacifying the country.

In the long run, however, the Civilistas were the main political beneficiaries of this political alliance. After Piérola's four-year term came to an end in 1899, they cleverly outmaneuvered their Demócrata rivals by gaining control of key governmental positions, particularly the electoral apparatus, that enabled them to capture the presidency in 1900. Thereafter, through electoral manipulation and other tactics, they were largely able to retain control of the presidency, except for a brief respite before the outbreak of World War I, until 1919.

Under Piérola's rule, the country underwent an impressive degree of modernization, economic diversification, and expansion brought about by an unusually favorable conjuncture of factors. First, the new political consensus not only involved the two main political parties, but embraced a wide array of economic interests. These interests included the coastal sugar planters, emerging industrialists, and merchants, as well as the commercial and landowning elites in different regions of the highlands. All agreed on the need to create a propitious climate for investment and mechanisms for social control over the masses.

Second, the slowdown in foreign investment after 1892 forced a turn toward the accumulation of domestic capital to sustain the economic recovery. International demand for a diverse spectrum of Peruvian raw materials picked up as the West recovered from the depression of 1893–94 and entered a period of industrial expansion. Peruvian exporters, aided by a favorable exchange rate after the 1892 devaluation of the *sol*, were able to expand the production and sales of such agricultural products as sugar, wool, cotton, and coffee, as well as industrial minerals like copper, zinc, and lead. Profits were then plowed back, as is normally the case, into modernization to increase efficiency and production.

In this instance, however, profits were also reinvested in local manufacturing as entrepreneurs discerned a growing internal market as a result of the rising demand for local goods by wage laborers and capital goods, both in the export sector. For example, by the mid-1890s, there were 24,000 sugar workers and 66,600 mine workers whose wages fueled the popular consumer demand that was increasingly met by local manufacturers. Likewise, the capital goods for the construction of sugar mills and smelters for silver and copper were produced in local foundries, as was equipment for extending the railways into the mining zones.

Many leading sugar planters, miners, and export merchants were in the forefront of this manufacturing trend. For example, the sugar planter José Pardo, who, like his father before him, was shortly to become president, established and managed the Lima textile factory La Victoria from 1897. In the central highlands, businessman Eulogio Fernandini developed one of the largest smelters in the region from machinery laboriously hauled by mule train into his hacienda Huaraucaca in the same year. Pardo was also involved in the establishment of a series of banks and insurance companies that mobilized and directed capital into manufacturing and whose boards of directors included many leading exporters.

This powerful, if relatively brief, surge in import substituting industrialization during the closing years of the century can be quantified in several ways. The number of urban firms manufacturing such mass consumer items as beer, candles, soap, cigarettes, shoes, shirts, furniture, wines, and textiles rose 60 percent between 1890 and 1902. Many of these enterprises were relatively small-scale artisan firms started by foreign immigrants, particularly Italian-Peruvians, whose forebearers had immigrated to Lima between 1840 and 1870 before the War of the Pacific in 1879. Along similar lines, the share of imported consumer goods fell from 58 percent in 1891–92 to 49 percent in 1900 to 39 percent in 1907. The drop was particularly striking in textiles—over 50 percent—between 1897 and 1907. It was the result of the establishment of five new cotton textile mills in the decade from 1892 to 1902, financed and run by native industrialists, such as Pardo. Local production of textiles rose from less than 5 percent in 1890 to 42 percent in 1906. The output was comprised mainly of the cheaper or popular-grade fabrics, indicating the popular nature of local demand. Overall, there were perhaps 150 modern factories employing some 6,000 workers by 1899, and the industrialists, at the behest of Piérola, had organized their own interest group, the Sociedad Nacional de Industrias a few years earlier.

An expanded financial network of banks and other credit institutions facilitated the mobilization and flow of capital to both the export and manufacturing sectors. Bank capital quadrupled in a decade, and a stock exchange was established in 1896. So successful was the new financial system that the government was able to finance its entire budget deficit by issuing new bonds in 1898.

Piérola's fiscal and economic program enhanced the trend toward autonomous growth and development, as well as the centralization and streamlining of the state. For example, Piérola raised tariffs to protect infant industries and incentivized road building in the interior as a spur to commerce and trade by authorizing the mobilization of construction crews from local Indian communities. In addition, the tax system was completely reorganized, with the scrapping of the old Indian head tax and the establishment of a new state collection agency to replace the old practice of tax farming. The abolition of the *contribución personal* was aimed at undermining the revenue base for Cáceres's decentralized Juntas Departmentales. In its place, Piérola substituted a new tax on salt in 1896, a regressive levy that hit peasant households equally hard as the old head tax, but whose revenues would now go directly into the national treasury. The new tax created a storm of popular protest and resistance, particularly in places like the provinces of Huanta and La Mar, where violent peasant protests were brutally repressed by the authorities (Manrique, 1988; Husson, 1992).

Piérola also created a ministry of development (*Fomento*), which immediately undertook to revise the anachronistic laws governing commerce and mining, some of which dated back more than a century to the Bourbon reforms of the late eighteenth century. Anxious to foster close cooperation between the state and civil society, Piérola encouraged exporters and miners to follow the industrialists in organizing their own Sociedad Nacional Agraria and Sociedad Nacional de Minería. Ironically, in economic policy, he now appeared as much a modernizing, Civilista capitalist as a Catholic, Hispanophile traditionalist.

Finally, Piérola undertook to restructure the armed forces, an institution that had cast a long shadow over the political course of the country since independence. Indeed, as one of the few relatively coherent institutions during the nineteenth century, it was, as Sinesio López (1978, p. 1000) put it, the state. The war and Cáceres's dictatorship had the effect of swelling the ranks of the military and, after the brief interlude of the first civilismo in the 1870s, returning it to its preeminent role as arbiter of the nation's politics. As only the second civilian during the century to occupy the presidency, Piérola was well aware of the need to bring this Andean leviathan under control, if only for his own political survival. As a result, the new president cut the size of the regular army and imported a French military mission to reorganize and professionalize the institution. One important outcome of this effort was the establishment of a new military academy at Chorillos, on the outskirts of Lima, to train the officer corps in the latest methods and techniques of modern warfare.

If Peru experienced a period of economic progress and political stability during the Piérola administration, the country continued to be ruled in a largely autocratic, paternalistic, and undemocratic manner. For example, the 1890 constitutional amendment requiring men to be literate in order to vote was reaffirmed by the Congress in 1895, on the premise that "the man who does not know how to read or write is not, nor can he be, a citizen in modern society" (quoted in Mallon, 1995, p. 275). Expressed another way, the original Senate Commission wrote that "it is not in the interest of the Nation that many participate in elections, but rather that those who participate do so well," a perfect prescription for the emergence of oligarchical rule that would be the hallmark of the "aristocratic republic."

Basadre is no doubt correct in his belief that the popular and charismatic Piérola lost an excellent opportunity to integrate the lower classes into the nation's political process. More than likely, he did so because he, like the lords of colonial Peru, paternalistically viewed himself as the father of his people, often boasting that "when the people are in danger, they come to me." More recently, Mallon (1995) showed how both Cáceres and Piérola consolidated the new modern state by openly allying themselves with sectors of the hacendado class in various regions of the country and reconstructing the hierarchical, patron-client relations of authority that had frayed during the external and civil wars of the 1880s. Where that strategy failed, repression and exclusion, rather than negotiation and incorporation, became the modus vivendi of the state, cloaked as it invariably was in an official discourse that "othered" the subaltern classes and their aspirations for justice and greater political participation.

Despite its increased authority and reach, the central government nevertheless continued to rely on the regional power of the *gamonales* to keep order in the provinces. With peasant unrest momentarily quelled after the wars, powerful sierra landlord clans mobilized their "clients" and contested for local power. The winners not only succeeded in controlling local offices, but were "elected" to Congress, where they supported the national government in return for a virtual blank check to rule as they pleased in their particular localities or fiefdoms. Such a quid pro quo between the central state and local landowner factions was a defining feature of the Andean *gamonal* system.

To some extent, at least initially, the economy of the sierra shared in the postwar recovery of the nation, which was led by expanding silver mining in the center during the 1890s. Silver mining managed to revive quickly after the war, and new deposits were discovered and developed by native entrepreneurs in the 1880s at Casapalca and in the 1890s at Morococha. By 1890, silver production had recovered its prewar levels, but the collapse of silver prices in 1892 and Piérola's suspension of silver coinage in 1897 adversely affected profits in the industry. By the turn of the century, however, silver exports entered a period of steady decline.

Just as silver exports began to drop, international demand for copper exploded as a consequence of the second Industrial Revolution in the West. Like silver, copper mining in Peru was initially at least locally controlled.

But this situation was to change dramatically shortly after the turn of the century, for once the central railway was completed to Oroya in 1893, the rich copper lodes at Morococha and Cerro de Pasco and a smelter at Casapalca became accessible for large-scale development.

These developments set the stage in 1901 for the sudden appearance of a powerful U.S. syndicate, capitalized by the fortunes of the likes of the Vanderbilts, Hearsts, and Morgans, which dwarfed the size of local capital and even rivaled the financial capacity of the Peruvian government itself. In a short time, the new U.S. corporation bought up most of the locally owned mines at Cerro and Morococha and then acquired the main smelter at Casapalca at the end of World War I. The takeover and rapid expansion of the heretofore locally controlled Peruvian copper industry by the Cerro de Pasco Copper Corporation marked the beginning of a wave of North American penetration into the mining industry over the first quarter of the twentieth century. Thus, by the end of World War I, the rich Cerro Verde copper mines in the south had been acquired by Anaconda, and various copper, silver, and gold deposits in the north were bought by the American Smelting and Refining Company.

According to economic historians Thorp and Bertram (1978, p. 85), it does not appear that native miners were forced to sell out to foreign capital because of either economic crisis or the inability to develop their holdings, as is commonly believed. Rather, the decision to sell seems to have been dictated solely by price and the different assessments by local and U.S. mining interests of the future prospects of the industry. Moreover, the native mining entrepreneurs who chose to sell out accrued large financial windfalls from the buyouts.

Whether the foreign takeovers in mining were good or bad for the country in economic terms over the long run is a complex question. Copper mining probably expanded faster with the heavy input of foreign capital and technology, but profit repatriation stunted local development. In the case of Cerro de Pasco, the returned value for the period 1916–37 amounted to between 50–60 percent of the profits, a surprisingly high figure in comparison to other foreign-owned companies in the extractive sector in Latin America. (In Chile, the figure for the three main copper companies was only 30–40 percent.) Nevertheless, the domination of mining by foreign companies like Cerro inhibited the development of local expertise and management and increased, particularly in the absence of governmental regulations, the level of general economic dependence.

With this said, it cannot be denied that, at least initially when local control predominated, there were some important spread effects from the expansion of silver and copper mining regionally. Indeed, the expansion stimulated a degree of local agrarian production and commerce in the central highlands, as it did coffee growing along the Eyebrow of the Jungle (*Ceja de Selva*) on the eastern slopes of the Andes. Also incentivized by strong international demand, coffee exports quadrupled between the end of the War of the Pacific and 1902. While some profits from these three exports inevitably flowed out of the region toward Lima and abroad, enough remained to generate local production and commerce, keyed to the urban sector, and generally to energize the regional economy. As a result, a new regional elite began to take shape in the center, composed of both miners, progressive landowners, and merchants and *arriviste* outsiders from the coast.

As market forces accelerated in the central sierra, progressive-minded landowners and entrepreneurs sought to expand their holdings under cultivation and/or to introduce capitalist relations of production to increase output and maximize profits. This economic growth and market demand led to the expansion of the haciendas and the concomitant process of enclosure of peasants' and communities' landholdings. Manrique argued that peasant communities, in both the center and the south, were vulnerable to this process because the conflict with Chile had seen their manpower and much of their agricultural output drawn off for the war effort (1995, p. 197). As a result, many communities were left vulnerable to land encroachment by *latifundista* competitors during the postwar recovery, which was led by sharply rising wool exports.

The volume of alpaca and sheep wool, for example, rose from a postwar decade-low average of 2,624 metric tons to a peak of 5,286 metric tons in the second decade of the new century. Because it straddled both the modern and traditional sectors of the economy, the mode of production of the southern wool trade was unique. The bulk of production, primarily high-quality alpaca and sheep wool, came from peasant herdsmen in the traditional sector in the *altiplano* and was articulated by Arequipa-based merchant firms that exported the product through the modern sector mainly to British importers. Large-scale haciendas in the modern sector also produced significant amounts generally of low-grade sheep wool, completing what was essentially a triangular structure of production and exchange that included peasants, merchants, and *hacendados*. The latter two made up the core economic elite of the south and had few connections with the regional elites developing in the center and north.

With international prices for wool exports rising steadily after the war, the value of grazing lands followed suit. This situation touched off a process of land concentration and consolidation as both the number and size of haciendas increased at the expense of Indian communal and smallholdings. In their zeal for profits, *hacendados* resorted to the foreclosure of debts, as well as purchase, to increase the size of their estates. Indeed, the process of endebtedness and enclosure was so widespread from the end of the War of the Pacific to the outbreak of World War I that there was a truly dramatic expansion in the number of haciendas in the *altiplanos* of the departments of Cuzco and Arequipa. Manrique (1986) recorded the number of haciendas in Puno, for example, as increasing from 705 to 3,219 from 1876 to 1915. Similarly, Jacobsen found that in the province of Azángaro, the number of haciendas increased from 110 in the 1820s to 250 to 300 by 1920, mostly during the postwar period of civil unrest and economic dislocation of the 1880s.

Moreover, not only did large numbers of Indian peasants lose access to their land, whether in communities or on smallholdings. The traditional patron-client loyalties between landlords and peasants were strained as well by the high-handed actions of the former in their unscrupulous pursuit of profits. Both actions in the aggregate contributed, as you shall see, to the outbreak of a wave of violent peasant revolts that swept through the southern highlands during the second decade of the twentieth century.

Despite the postwar recovery and the expansion of exports like silver, copper, coffee, cocaine, and wool and their residual impact on the regional economies of the highlands, the overall economic development of the sierra paled in comparison with the growth of coastal exports, which soared during the first two decades of the twentieth century. By the end of World War I, the bulk of total exports in Peru were concentrated on the coast in sugar (42 percent) cotton (30 percent), and petroleum (5 percent). At the same time, foreign capital began to predominate over local capital, as copper, silver, and oil production fell under foreign control, while sugar, cotton, and wool remained in the hands of the nationals. This trend was particularly unfavorable after 1920, since the volume of and profits from exports in the foreign-dominated mining sectors tended to rise sharply, while the expansion of and profits from exports slowed in sugar, cotton, and wool.

The upshot of these trends was that by the 1920s, Peru, in comparison with its neighbors, had a much more highly diversified export sector comprising five or six important products. This situation made Peru relatively more resilient to sectoral downturns in the international marketplace. In effect, while the demand for some exports might fall, others might rise, exerting a "cushioning effect" on the overall economy. The downside of this export structure was the extent of foreign control and the concomitant repatriation, rather than the reinvestment of profits in the country.

The leading export crop on the coast was sugar, which had expanded dramatically during the 1860s, but was crippled, as you have seen, by the impact of the War of the Pacific during the early 1880s. As the industry struggled to recover after the war, a period of consolidation and concentration occurred. Some planters went bankrupt and were bought out or taken over by creditors, surviving planters or new immigrant families (the Italian Larco and German Gildemeister families, for example) with access to foreign sources of capital, as occurred in the Chicama Valley near the city of Trujillo on the north coast.

Production mainly for export soared during the mid-1890s (up 83 percent in the decade) and again after the outbreak of World War I (up 77 percent), so that sugar became the country's leading export commodity. At the same time, the industry tended to concentrate on the north coast, reaching 75 percent of the total production by the early 1920s. The lack of seasonality owing to the extremely favorable climatic conditions on the north coast also enabled planters to institute economies of scale, which, in turn, contributed to the process of land concentration.

Moreover, initially at least, the industry developed linkages with the wider economy through technological advances and capital formation. These linkages occurred, however, only in the short run, since increasing mechanization after 1900 held the labor force steady over the next couple of decades and tax payments to the government remained small. In addition, capital formation from high profits, particularly during World War I, were increasingly reinvested to expand export capacity in the mistaken anticipation that the wartime boom in foreign demand would continue. Substantial sugar capital was also held in foreign savings banks during the war. As a result, during World War I, the proportion of returned value in sugar fell, but during the 1920s, the worldwide oversupply and falling prices caused profits and capital formation to dwindle.

Another important export crop on the coast, with greater demand linkages than sugar, was cotton. The structure of the cotton industry differed from the structure of the sugar industry in that it was a seasonal industry that relied on sharecropping, known as *yanaconaje* (Peloso, 1999). Cotton growers provided land for these tenant cultivators in return for half of each crop and hired seasonal migrant laborers to work their best, most fertile lands. Although small, independent peasant cultivators also grew cotton, the industry was dominated by large landowners, since irrigation was crucial to cultivation. Merchants, particularly British houses such as Duncan Fox and Graham Rowe, came to control the commercialization of cotton, providing the necessary loans through a system known as *habilitación*.

Cotton growing and exports expanded rapidly along the coast after the War of the Pacific. The period of the greatest growth was between 1905 and 1920, when it averaged 10 percent a year. Unlike sugar, production for internal consumption was also important after the rise of the cotton textile industry in Lima. For example, production destined for the Lima mills rose from 17 percent in 1901 to 24 percent in 1904. Cotton growing tended to concentrate in Cañete and Ica along the south coast, where it displaced sugar and wine vineyards as the preferred cash crop. The industry was given a considerable boost when Fermín Tangüis, a grower, bred a disease-resistant plant especially well suited to the ecological conditions of the central and south coasts between 1908 and 1912. As a result of the introduction of the Tangüis variety, as well as the declining price of sugar after the war, the area devoted to cotton growing continued to expand, especially in the department of Lima, where it displaced sugar as a cash crop.

The returned value in cotton proved to be significant, since the lion's share of profits was accrued by the producers, including the large number of peasant or tenant cultivators. Moreover, a growing number of migrant workers came down from the highlands during the slack season between planting and harvesting and earned extra income in the cotton harvest. The number of migrant workers in cotton had risen to 21,000 by 1916 and grew to 41,000 in 1923. When these workers returned to their highland communities after the harvest, they brought back earnings that they reinvested in their own plots and spent on community activities, such as religious festivals. As for the larger growers, they provided not only raw materials for the domestic textile industry, but other cotton by-products that were processed into cottonseed oil, soap, and candles. While many growers were active in developing these nascent industries, their entrepreneurial activities in the wider economy and their political clout at the national level did not match their counterparts in Big Sugar. In sum, cotton earnings provided significant stimulation to the development of both internal manufacturing and a domestic market.

Another predominantly regional export, but one of relatively short duration, was rubber from the eastern Amazonian rain forest (Stanfield, 1998). The rubber trade was characterized by a boom–bust cycle related to international demand and production and produced scant internal linkages to the larger domestic economy. It was triggered by a boom in the demand for rubber in the industrializing West in the second half of the nineteenth century. In the 1880s, rubber began to be systematically gathered in the Brazilian and Peruvian Amazon. The industry, such as it developed, was extremely primitive, based not on the organization of plantations, but on the collection by Indian labor from rubber trees scattered throughout the region. Great fortunes were made, as Peruvian production rose to 3,200 tons annually by 1912, representing about 30 percent of the total exports. Reflecting this booming trade, the settlement of Iquitos expanded from a tiny fishing village of 200 in 1851 to a small city of 20,000 by World War I.

During World War I, however, international prices began to plunge, as more efficient plantations in the Far East took over the bulk of production, and the worldwide supply quickly outran the demand. As a result, the regional Amazonian economy, which had seen most of the profits from the trade expended on luxury imports to sustain the ostentatious lifestyles of the rubber barons (Carlos Fitzcarrald, Julio Arana, and the immigrants Kahn and Victor Israel), collapsed and sank into stagnation. The greatest losers, however, turned out to be the thousands of Indian laborers who were ruthlessly harnessed to production and died from overwork, malnutrition, and disease. The extent of the exploitation of labor in the region was such that it produced an international scandal over the treatment of local Indians along the Putumayo River by the Peruvian Amazon Company between 1908 and 1912. In the end, the Amazonian rubber boom, which was over by 1920, had produced little of lasting economic consequences. It did, however, help to perpetuate the myth of an Amazonian *El Dorado* of hidden potential wealth and resources that might somehow in the future work to pull Peru out of its chronic underdevelopment.

Another sector of Peru's commodity-rich economy that was energized by sudden foreign demand and rising value was the oil industry. To an even greater extent than the copper industry, the oil industry fell heavily under the yoke of foreign domination. Confined to the extreme northwestern part of the country, the oil industry dated from the 1860s, but began to develop at the end of the century. Negritos was by far the largest and most productive field, increasing from 59 percent of the total output in the 1890s to 80 percent in the 1920s. Overall, oil production expanded in fits and starts during the 1890s and early 1900s, but only really took off in 1904, owing to the rapidly rising international and internal demand. Prices rose prior to World War I, but then stagnated during the war because of disruptions in shipping. Refineries at Talara (Negritos) and Zorritos dated from the 1890s.

The industry quickly took on many of the characteristics of a foreign enclave. Fields were located on the coast in an isolated desert region 600 miles from Lima. Shortly before World War I, Standard Oil of New Jersey began to buy up Peruvian oil fields, the most important being the British-owned Negritos, and consolidated its holdings under the control of the International Petroleum Company (IPC), a Canadian subsidiary of Jersey Standard.

IPC's profits over the next several decades were extremely high, and the returned value was concomitantly low. Between 1916 and 1934, for example, Thorp and Bertram estimated that IPC's foreign exchange contribution to the local economy was zero. Over the same period, profits amounted to 70 percent, with labor costs of 8 percent, payments to the government only 6 percent, and imported inputs of 15 percent. Not only were taxes outrageously low, but there was no governmental regulation. Because of its high profits, IPC could allocate large funds to buy the friendship of governments and influence legislation with impunity.

Emergence of the Oligarchy

A large body of literature dating from the 1960s attributed Peru's chronic twentieth-century underdevelopment to the formation of a tightly knit network of wealthy individuals, with similar interests and ideological orientations, who came to exercise political and economic domination over the country after the War of the Pacific. This closed, paternalistic elite (also referred to as a "bourgeoisie" or "plutocracy"), formed through the intermarriage of a small circle of prominent families, purportedly not only gained control of the state and its resources during the Aristocratic Republic, but used them to enhance their own individual and class interests. Furthermore, the indictment suggests that this elite lacked a "national project" for development; opted for policies to foment exports, rather than industrialization; operated "irrationally" in an aristocratic, rent-seeking (or "rentier") manner; and allied with sierra landlords (*gamonales*) and foreign capitalists to ensure its control over the country and to promote its own narrow, selfish, class interests. The result, according to this "dependency" view, was overspecialization in elite-controlled commodity production for export and overreliance on foreign capital and markets that created a dangerous economic dependence and put the country at risk.

There seems little doubt that an oligarchy, composed of exporters and Lima businessmen linked to the developing export economy, emerged in Peru at the end of the nineteenth century. Made up of some thirty to forty prominent families with large interests on the coast, this group and its political expression—the reconstituted Civilista Party—was described by Basadre as being

> composed of large urban property holders, the great sugar and cotton planters, prosperous businessmen, lawyers with the most famous practices, doctors who had the best clientele and university professors; in short, the most successful people in the country. The party's directorate was made up of urbane gentlemen, some connected to the countryside, in something like a Creole adaptation of the English country squire. They had an intense club life, resided in houses furnished in the colonial style with rugs and curtains at a time when fresh air was shunned. They dressed in black frock coats and the most fashionable trousers, made by French tailors in the capital, and lived in a happy world, interconnected by marriages within their group. (1968–69, XI, p. 127)

At the core of this elite, according to Gilbert (1977), an informal group, known as the Twenty-Four Friends, met regularly at the exclusive Club Nacional to discuss the management of national affairs. It included two men who occupied the presidency for a total of twenty-four years (José Pardo and Augusto B. Leguía), at least eight Cabinet ministers, including five treasury ministers, three presidents of the Senate, and the publishers of Lima's two major newspapers. Presidents were also drawn from the remnants of the old regional elites (Piérola and Eduardo López de Romaña from the south), as well as from the prewar guano and nitrate oligarchs (Manuel Candamo and Guillermo Billinghurst, respectively). Moreover, two of the oligarchy's most powerful families displayed a diversity of economic interests; the Aspíllagas in sugar, cotton, mining, banking, insurance, and shipbuilding and the Pardos in sugar, banking, insurance, real estate, and manufacturing, but most were based in one particular economic activity. In social terms, the oligarchy formed a closed, close-knit, and cohesive group—a virtual closed caste—bound together by ties of family and kinship.

Culturally and intellectually, the oligarchy had other defining characteristics that derived squarely from the influence of turn-of-the-century Belle Epoque Europe. Paris was the mecca for Peru's elite, a fact illustrated in the literary career of one of its most illustrious intellectuals and spokesmen, the young aristocrat Francisco García Calderón. Son of the former president during the Chilean occupation, García Calderón spent most of his adult life in France, where he wrote what amounted to the political manifesto of his class. Written not surprisingly in French, not Spanish, *Le Perou contemporaine* (1907) expressed a wholly elitist perspective on government and politics that disdained the masses who would be controlled by what he called "Democratic Caesarism"—that is, the rule of an autocratic, if paternalistic, natural elite.

This ruling class, happily ensconced in comfortable splendor in Lima, was thoroughly Eurocentric and Frenchified, but it hardly knew the rest of the country, except for occasional visits to their country estates (mostly on the coast). Accordingly, their social distance from the masses and inherently racist view of Indians and other *castas* was increased by their utter ignorance of the interior, which few of them knew from firsthand experience. Many, like the wife of González Prada (who himself never visited the sierra), were shocked when, during the war with Chile, thousands of Indian recruits "invaded" Lima at the behest of their patrons in a last-ditch effort to defend the city from the enemy. The vast Peruvian interior and its downtrodden Indian peasantry were, for them, an imagined "barbarism," coinciding perfectly with D. F. Sarmiento's famous characterization of Argentina. Similarly, Lima represented "civilization," where, according to the nineteenth-century British traveler Squier, if three of its better-off inhabitants knew Cuzco firsthand, another thirty had graced the streets of London.

What may be questioned about this early twentieth-century oligarchical formation is not its existence, but the range of its reach and the extent of its political dominance. The political history of Peru between 1895 and 1919, as you shall see, does not suggest such omnipotence. Rather, it was a period rent with political conflict, factionalism, and party splits, even within the dominant Civilista Party that gained the presidency in 1904 and held it, with some interruption, until 1919. This conflict was due, in part, to the personalism and intense individual and clan rivalries that characterized Peruvian politics. Víctor Andrés Belaúnde, one of the country's leading conservative intellectuals of the early twentieth century, called attention to this fact when he stated that "the political parties ought not to be taken seriously into account; even less so what is attributed to them by way of program or characteristics. Our parties are . . . abstract nouns, inconsistent and ephemeral personal groupings" (quoted in Miller, 1982, p. 105). Three of Peru's early political parties were entirely based on personal loyalties to an individual *caudillo*—Cáceres (Constitutionalist), Piérola (Demócrata), and Durand (Liberal). Even in the more institutionalized Civilista Party, several distinct factions surrounding a particular individual can be readily discerned—those attached to Augusto Leguía, Rafael Villanueva, and the Pardos, to name just a few.

Similar political manifestations could be found in Congress, where presidents Piérola, Leguía, and Pardo all found it convenient to place their brothers in key positions. Such a penchant for personalism and clientelism was roundly satirized by González Prada, who characterized José Pardo's first administration (1904–08) in the following way: "José Pardo in the presidency, Enrique de la Riva Agüero as chief of the cabinet, a Felipe de Osma y Pardo in the supreme court, a Pedro de Osma y Pardo in the post of the mayor of the municipality, a José Antonio de Lavalle y Pardo in a fiscal's post, a Felipe Pardo y Barreda in the legation in the United States, a Juan Pardo y Barreda in Congress" (quoted in Miller, 1984, p. 106). For the sardonic González Prada, this was a retroactive dynasty, the intelligence of its members decreasing from generation to generation even as its vanity and pride increased.

Beyond González Prada's evident dislike for the Pardos, his remarks highlight the driving force of the political system—the penchant to exercise control over the spoils of state power for one's personal, family, or clan interest. As another contemporary put it, "public administration is a chain of compadres" in which, again alluding to the Pardos, "for them government is like an hacienda, with a patron, empleados and peones" (quoted in Miller, 1984, p. 113). The struggle to create and control such a web of patronage was intense from the president down to the Congress and opened the way for strong personal rivalries that could severely undermine oligarchical cohesion.

In addition to personal rivalries, oligarchical divisions also occurred along economic or regional lines. Burga and Flores Galindo (1979), for example, argued that three distinct groups in the oligarchy could be observed—one based on sugar on the coast, another on miners and *latifundistas* in the central sierra, and still another on the wool trade in the south. Others see the oligarchy as composed predominantly of coastal growers, exporters, businessmen, and bankers, all coalescing in Lima around the state and with links to foreign capital (Flores Galindo et al., 1978). Economic power and proximity to the government facilitated the oligarchy's penetration and control at the center, while alliances with sierra *gamonales* ensured control over the outlying provinces where the reach of the central government remained weak and tentative.

Still another historian, Gorman (1979), contended that the oligarchy represented a multiplicity of different sectoral interests in an extremely nonintegrated and heterogeneous national economy. The existing political parties, however, were unable to intermediate these disparate interests at the level of state policy. The evidence for the latter argument is ample enough when one considers the divisions just among the agricultural interests. For example, sugar and cotton growers disagreed vehemently over specific issues, such as who should pay taxes. What was crucial for both groups was sufficient access to the state to ensure control over local officials whose police, judicial, and water distribution powers were central to the planters' interests. Of course, on the larger questions of the role of the state in society or the need to control the popular classes, the oligarchy did share a common mentality and outlook.

If the sources of disagreement and discord within the oligarchy were manifold during this period, they seem to have been clearly evident in the Congress. Between 1886 and 1919, the number of presidential ministers who were overturned was remarkably high—by one count 57 ministers of justice, 64 ministers of war, 65 ministers of finance, and 70 ministers of government. Moreover, the legislature also rejected the budgets sent for approval by the president in 1901, 1903, 1911, 1914, and 1917 and defeated a number of other important presidential initiatives. This discord was due largely to the fact that the coastal elite and the president had to share power in the legislature with a disproportionate number of representatives from the landholding *gamonal* class in the interior. Although this sharing of power led to a certain interdependence between the coastal elites and the sierra *gamonales* on matters concerning social control, it also explains the divisions over numerous specific issues that affected the oligarchy and the export economy, ranging from the gold standard and banking and monetary laws to export duties and concessions to foreigners.

If the oligarchy was less than omnipotent, it was also more modern and entrepreneurial than has heretofore been represented. The dependency view was that it was a regressive social class with a rentier mentality that inhibited development and was unable to promote modernization. In a revisionist view, Quiroz (1993) argued that, on the contrary, it was a dynamic, entrepreneurial class that acted in largely rational, capitalistic ways and diversified its traditional economic activities from trade and agriculture to finance, manufacturing, and urban development. The fact that Peru's economy faltered during the 1920s and exhibited serious structural problems, including dependence, was due not to the presumed anachronistic, seignorial behavior of the oligarchy, but to other causes.

Moreover, this progressive oligarchy did not lack a capitalistic development project for Peru, as was often alleged by the *dependentistas*. Believing that the country possessed a natural environment that was particularly conducive to agricultural and mining development, its policy prescriptions for growth and modernization emphasized the liberalization of state patrimonial prerogatives; attraction of foreign capital; mechanization of agrarian and mining production; development of the infrastructure, such as railways, roads, and urbanization works; construction of large irrigation projects; and attraction of European immigration, preferably Anglo-Saxons. Also important was the assimilation of corporate properties belonging to the Church and Indian communities, as well as the "feudal" *latifundistas* into the modern sector of the economy and the integration of the Indian population into a modern, wage labor force that would be capable of fostering capitalist production and growth.

In view of this developmental program and the uses of the state to implement it, one may question the elites' presumed liberal, evolutionist interpretation of the relationship between the state and society. That view, as expressed by one scholar who has studied elite economic thought, suggests that the oligarchy firmly believed that "the destiny of society is fundamentally decided on the level of the individual, and the state is only an orienting factor which has neither the means nor the responsibilities to predetermine, much less realize, a particular type of society" (Gonzalo Portocarrero, quoted in Love and Jacobsen, 1988, p. 145). Such an ideal type of classical, laissez faire liberalism, however, was, in fact, much more complex and complicated. Indeed, Jacobsen (1988, p. 146, 1993) persuasively argued that a more multifaceted mix of liberal and interventionist approaches to economic and social issues characterized elite rule during the Aristocratic Republic. This view would certainly square with the patrimonial and interventionist traditions of the Peruvian state, as well as the personalistic and clientelistic patterns of elite political behavior mentioned earlier. Both Jacobsen (1993) and Trazegnies (1980) emphasized these contradictory strains (liberal and traditional) of the oligarchy and suggested that in Peru, it sought to carry out a traditionalist type of modernization.

Much of the driving force for the elites' program of liberal, capitalist development derived from their reaction to the disastrous consequences of the War of the Pacific. They had seen not only their national patrimony seized, but their longstanding absolute control over the country momentarily evaporate in the face of a foreign invader and a widespread popular uprising. To avoid the repetition of such a calamity in the future, they thought, Peru had to foster sound liberal and fiscal policies designed to develop new sources of wealth to replace the disastrous overspecialization and spendthrift habits of the guano age.

This new attitude was summed up by Finance Minister Augusto B. Leguía (1903–08), a leading spokesman for the progressive, Civilista elite, when he stated that "that prosperous and comfortable [prewar, guano age] situation just had the appearance of being so; we were deceived, remained deceived and thus we succumbed. Today we do not live with largesse, but we have honesty. Our budgets are balanced." Another member of the elite, Manuel Vicente Villarán, a progressive Civilista and positivistically inclined law professor at San Marcos University, expressed the new capitalistic spirit of the times when he stated that "it is no longer cannons that attain triumph but trusts, cartels and *comptoirs*" and that "for us today wealth is a matter of dignity, honour, perhaps independence, more than a matter of comfort and culture" (quoted in Quiroz, 1984, p. 54). Such a view, of course, inevitably led the oligarchy to forge links or alliances with foreign capital, virtually the only source of investment available to develop the diverse, natural resource-rich Peruvian economy.

Even as liberal capitalism was justified as a means for modernizing Peru and fortifying the ruling classes, serious political fissures in the oligarchy manifested themselves early in the Aristocratic Republic. The rapprochement between the rival Demócratas and Civilistas, which had enabled Piérola to triumph in the "revolution of '95," soon began to crumble as the Civilistas, under their astute leader Manuel Candamo, maneuvered to gain the upper hand in the governmental coalition. In 1899, both parties were able to compromise on a candidate to succeed Piérola—the southern planter and Demócrata Eduardo López de Romaña (1899–1903). However, during López de Romaña's administration, the Civilistas gained control of most important political offices, including the crucial electoral apparatus of the Junta

Electoral Nacional. This control enabled party leader Manuel Candamo to win the presidency in 1903. From then until 1919, the political history of Peru was essentially dominated by the Civilista Party.

The domination of the Civilista Party, however, did not mean an end to oligarchical divisions or political factionalism, for the party itself had divided into major factions. The split was largely along generational and personal, rather than ideological or programmatic, lines. The older generation, led by party leader Isaac Alzamora, struggled to control the party against the challenge of a younger generation, led by José Pardo—son of the first Civilista president Manuel Pardo. Candamo had been able to keep the peace between the two warring factions, but his sudden death in early 1904 set off a fierce struggle over the selection of a successor. Pardo won the contest in 1904 and momentarily pacified the factions during his four-year term.

Pardo then chose businessman and Civilista "young turk" Augusto B. Leguía, his minister of finance and top political adviser, as the party candidate for president in 1908. The more conservative and aristocratic members of the old guard resented Leguía, whom they viewed as a middle-class upstart without the necessary connections to the old families. For his part, Leguía, although a loyal party man, resented this snubbing by the old guard, and after his election, he arbitrarily proceeded to marginalize it from leadership positions in his new government. This, as well as Leguía's attempt to bring some prominent Demócratas into his government, led to a deepening party split that culminated in a fierce struggle by both factions to control Congress.

When the president tried to rig the congressional elections of 1911, his Civilista opponents formed the "Bloque" with members of the opposing parties. Then, after an armed clash between the two sides outside the Congress building on July 13, the anti-Leguía wing bolted from the party to form the Partido Civil Independiente. Leguía's arbitrary attempts to rule independently of the party hierarchy, rather than any ideological, economic, or social differences within the party, resulted in the substantial weakening of civilismo as a political force. According to González Prada, "thanks to Leguía, Civilismo stopped being the strong wood of construction, becoming converted instead into a weak and worm-eaten stick only good for throwing into the fire" (quoted in Stein, 1980, p. 32).

At the same time that the ruling party began to unravel, the country's social order was undergoing some fundamental changes. Peru's population had grown slowly in the last quarter of the nineteenth century, from 2.7 million, according to the official census of 1876, to an estimated 3.7 million in 1900—an average annual rate of increase of about 1 percent. A decade later in 1910, the number of inhabitants had risen to 4.2 million, and a decade after that to 4.8 million in 1920, with the average annual rate of increase rising to 1.2 percent and 1.5 percent, respectively (Webb and Fernández Baca, 1990, p. 97). The gradual trend upward in the average annual rate of growth coincided with the economic recovery and expansion from the 1890s.

As for the population of Lima, it remained virtually stationary—100,000 in 1876 and 104,000 in 1891—reflecting the impact of the war and civil turmoil of the 1880s. However, with the quickening pace of the economy, it rose 35.5 percent to 141,000 by 1908 and 59 percent to 224,000 in 1920. The nearby port of Callao, the major transshipment point for the burgeoning export economy, had over 34,000 inhabitants by 1905. In contrast to Lima, the country's other main urban centers—Arequipa, Cuzco, and Trujillo—contained only 35,000, 18,500, and 10,000, respectively in 1908. Much of Lima's population growth during these years reflected a rising stream of migration from the interior to the economically active center. This internal migration, which would increase dramatically at times throughout the century, can be seen in the growing percentage of Lima's population who were born outside the capital. It stood at 37 percent in 1858, 58.5 percent in 1908, and 63.5 percent in 1920.

Another factor in Lima's, if not the country's, population growth from the 1890s on was the general improvement in public health after the turn of the century. With urbanization and modernization came better sanitation facilities and medical treatment that helped to reduce the incidence of such lethal diseases as malaria, typhoid fever, and smallpox. After 1895, the mortality rate began to fall, signaling the onset of "demographic modernization"—that is, steadily rising fertility rates and population. The final completion of the central and southern railroads connecting the coast with the sierra also facilitated the greater movement of people from the interior, even if their main purpose was to open the way for the exploitation of the interior's abundant natural resources. The Central Railway was completed from Lima to La Oroya in 1893 and then extended to the important sierra market town of Huancayo in 1909. The Southern Railway was finished in 1908 and joined the port of Mollendo to Cuzco via Arequipa and Puno on Lake Titicaca.

Formation of the Working Class

As Peru's population gradually expanded and urbanized and its export economy diversified and grew during the Aristocratic Republic, so did its labor force. In the modern sector of the economy, sizable concentrations of workers could be found on the sugar (30,000) and cotton plantations (35,000) of the coast, in the sierra mines (silver, gold, copper—20,000–25,000), in the oil fields of the far north coast, and in the workshops of the newly completed railway system. The estimated 30,000 rubber and wool workers were more dispersed and isolated. Including the latter workers, this amounted to perhaps 80,000 to 120,000 workers, or 5–8 percent of the total estimated labor force of 1.53 million in the 1890s.

Despite the growing numbers of workers, however, several factors slowed their organization in these enclaves into labor unions or syndicates.

These factors included isolation and distance from the more dynamic urban sectors of labor, particularly in the capital, and strong control by employers, enhanced by the support not only of local authorities but of the central government. Labor activities and disturbances did occur as early as 1910 among the sugar workers on the plantations outside Trujillo on the north coast, but were quickly put down by the authorities.

The story was different, however, in Lima, where workers were to be found in factories, mills, shops, and construction sites, as well as on the docks of the nearby port of Callao. If one also includes the category of artisans, the number of "workers" in Lima grew from around 9,500 (9.5 percent of the population) in 1876 to almost 24,000 (16.9 percent) in 1908 and over 44,000 (19.8 percent) in 1920. The figures for Callao are over 4,000 in 1905 and 8,400 in 1920. Since they were concentrated in the capital, the Lima-Callao working class was more dynamic than its rural-provincial counterparts. In Lima-Callao, as Blanchard (1982) pointed out, the working class had access to national political leaders and institutions, foreigners and foreign ideas, and the intelligentsia of journalists and intellectuals—all of whom could be counted on to react to labor's collective demands and agitation.

The mobilization of workers went back to the late 1850s during the guano era, when the first mutual aid societies were formed and labor agitation erupted in Lima and spread to some provincial cities. Like the guilds of the colonial period, mutualism emerged to protect the interests of artisans from the threats of incipient manufacturing and rising imports. From the collection of dues, the societies also provided financial aid to their members who became sick, disabled, or unemployed and to cover funeral costs.

More militant labor agitation in the form of riots and strikes also occasionally occurred during this early period of labor history. However, it was not until after 1895 that industrial actions or strikes began to occur frequently in Lima among textile workers, bakers, railway workers, stevedores, and factory workers, but were confined to each individual sector and generally involved demands for higher wages and improved working conditions. Because of their strategic position in the export economy, railroad and port workers in nearby Callao were generally more successful than other workers in pressing their demands. The government feared any disruption in the flow of products to and from abroad that might disrupt the economy and reduce revenues in both the public and private sectors.

Labor's progress was relatively slow, however, until World War I. A law of professional risk, which provided worker's compensation for accidents and injury on the job, was introduced in Congress in 1904, but did not become law until 1911 because of conservative opposition. (It was still the first law of its kind in Latin America and second in the hemisphere behind Canada). By that year, there were sixty-two mutual aid societies, averaging about two hundred members each, grouped in one of the two main labor confederations in Lima. In general, labor favored a moderate policy of conciliation with the government, rather than confrontation.

Not long into the new century, however, anarcho-sindicalism emerged to challenge the conservative, nonconfrontational approach of mutualism. Anarchism was a militant, anti-status quo ideology that spread throughout Latin America during the late nineteenth and early twentieth centuries. It was brought to Peru by none other than Manuel González Prada, that inveterate rebel and defender of the downtrodden Andean Indians and worker masses. González Prada returned to Peru in 1898 from a seven-year sojourn in Europe, where he had become, among other things, a confirmed anarchist. Europe during the 1890s was percolating with new movements challenging the moral, political, and artistic conventions of the times. One of the more extreme movements was anarchism, which advocated social justice and total individual freedom in a stateless society with limited private property.

If Europe, with its rapid industrial advance and growing urban proletariat, exposed to the vicissitudes and exploitation of early laissez faire capitalism, proved a fertile breeding ground for such radical ideologies, so did Peru's neocolonial, export-oriented version. Indeed, anarchism proved appealing to both sectors of Peru's heterogeneous working class. Artisans, who valued individual enterprise, saw it as a protection against the dislocations threatened by the inexorable advance of mechanization and the factory system. For the nascent proletariat, which was the product of these very forces, it promised the means to challenge the low wages, periodic unemployment, and dismal conditions under which they lived and labored.

Urban living and working conditions were generally bad. Factory housing at the textile mills of Vitarte and La Victoria, for example,

> continued to be small, dark, damp, [and] airless, without running water and toilets, and now increasingly expensive. They were situated in the most unsanitary parts of the city where diseases like typhoid, intestinal disorders, tuberculosis, plague, and malaria were endemic: on the edge of the Rimac River, near the hospital and the camp for incurables, and close to the lazaretto where those suffering from plague were isolated. Dung heaps were a common sight in these areas, adding to the health risks. (Blanchard, 1982, p. 51)

Working conditions were equally bleak. The workday at Vitarte was $13^{1}/_{2}$ hours, while at San Jacinto it lasted from 7 A.M. to 10 P.M.

In this socioeconomic milieu, anarcho-sindicalism thrived. Anarchist newspapers from Spain and books by Proudhon, Bakunin, Malatesta, and others were readily available in Lima and even in provincial cities like Trjuillo and Arequipa. Soon a number of home grown anarchist newspapers made their appearance, beginning with *Los Parias*, founded by González Prada in 1904, and followed by others with names designed to appeal exclusively to workers, such as *El Hambriento* and *El Oprimido*. At first, anarchism's main contribution was the promotion of a distinct working-class culture. Various theater, musical, and literary groups sprang up with working-class participants developing distinctly proletarian themes and causes. Cultural circles were also organized to discuss the latest ideas of Bakunin or Kropotkin, while at the Vitarte textile factory, workers created a special day of worker celebration called the *Fiesta de la Planta*. These new educational and cultural activities, and the profusion of newspapers that promoted them, suggests the predominantly artisan composition and leadership of Lima's incipient labor movement, with its relatively high level of cultural and educational attainment.

The first major strike under anarcho-sindicalist influence occurred in 1904 among dock workers in Callao. Although ultimately unsuccessful, it produced the movement's first martyr, whose public funeral provided a platform for its leaders to proselytize the city's workforce, as did a large May Day celebration the following year keynoted by González Prada. Thereafter, both events were regularly celebrated by anarchists and mutualists alike, with a parade to the martyr's tomb, speeches, and evening entertainment, with workers given the day off by their employers. Although no doubt a popular outlet for a holiday fiesta, the May Day celebrations, according to Blanchard, also forged a sense of unity and class consciousness among Peru's fledgling working class.

It was not until 1911, however, that the growing influence of the more militant anarcho-syndicalism made itself fully felt in the labor movement. In that year, a new anarchist newspaper *La Protesta*, appeared, edited by Delfin Lévano, the son of one of the movement's early leaders. The year 1911 also witnessed the first general strike in Lima. The strike was led by textile workers at Vitarte who demanded higher wages, a ten-hour day, and the elimination of night work. When the strike committee was arrested, various other groups, including bakers, coach drivers, and anarchists, joined to proclaim a general strike in sympathy and solidarity. The next day the city was virtually paralyzed by a general work stoppage, and the government was forced to capitulate to the workers' original demands. The strike proved a huge success and revealed the revived strength of the labor movement on the eve of the 1912 election of Guillermo Billinghurst, arguably the first populist president in the country's history.

In some ways, Guillermo Billinghurst was an unlikely champion of Lima's new working classes. Born in 1851 in the southern province of Arica, he was the son of a wealthy businessman who had made a fortune in the nitrate trade of Tarapacá. The family's British origins derived from his grandfather who, like a number of his compatriots, participated in the early nineteenth-century Wars for Independence. Since the Billinghurst fortune came from nitrates, rather than from land and the family had closer business ties to Santiago than Lima, it stood at the margins of the thirty or forty families who ruled the Aristocratic Republic.

No lover of the Civilista power elite, Billinghurst supported the Demócrata Piérola in the "revolution of '95" and was rewarded by being appointed first vice president. His aspiration to succeed to the presidency was dashed, however, by Piérola's own future political ambitions. Hoping to position himself for a later return to office, Piérola continued his alliance with the Civilistas by choosing as his successor the noncontroversial southern sugar planter Eduardo López de Romaña, who was acceptable to his allies.

This choice ended Billinghurst's friendship with Piérola and momentarily drove him to the political sidelines and back to his business interests. However, sensing the political possibilities of the emerging working class, he soon returned to politics and won the mayoralty of Lima in 1909. During his two-year term as mayor, Billinghurst undertook a number of popular reforms that benefited labor. These reforms included price supports for meat sold in poor neighborhoods; the prosecution of illegal price gouging by vendors; the destruction of some urban slums, including the Chinese ghetto; the construction of low-cost housing for workers; improvement of the city's water supply; and intervention in strikes on behalf of labor. By the end of his two-year term, Billinghurst was a popular figure in the capital among the laboring classes as the presidential elections of 1912 approached.

The Civilista choice to succeed Leguía in office was the northern sugar planter Antero Aspíllaga. However, Aspíllaga's prospects were uncertain, given the divisions in the party that had led to the formation a year earlier of the anti-Leguía Partido Civil Independiente. When the Independent Civilistas failed to come up with a suitable candidate of their own, a large number of working-class clubs put forth Billinghurst's candidacy a month before the election. Flushed by their own newfound power in the successful general strike a year earlier, workers rallied on behalf of the popular ex-mayor, and on the last Sunday before the election, Billinghurst's electoral strength was revealed by a huge demonstration in the capital that drew over 20,000 supporters, in contrast to Aspíllaga's 2,000. When a few of Billinghurst's supporters unfurled a banner contrasting the future cost of bread between the two candidates—the smaller loaf at 20 centavos if Aspíllaga won and the larger loaf at 5 centavos if Billinghurst won—the former nitrate trader was dubbed "Pan Grande" in the popular press and urged to declare his candidacy formally.

The problem was that Billinghurst had little time to organize his campaign, and Leguía refused his last-minute request to postpone the election. With the government's electoral apparatus firmly on the side of Aspíllaga's candidacy and limited suffrage (literacy and property qualifications) restricting popular participation, Leguía's denial aroused the workers to call another successful general strike on the day of the election. This strike had the intended effect of so disrupting the election that the necessary one-third votes on election day were not cast. As a result, the election was thrown into Congress, where Billinghurst and Leguía struck a deal. In return for selecting the president's brother as first vice president, Leguía, who held a congressional majority, ordered his supporters on August 9 to vote for Billinghurst. For the moment, the dubious oligarchy acquiesced, not only because they were divided, but because they were convinced that however much he was a reformer, Billinghurst was one of them and would not jeopardize the fundamental interests of his class.

As president, Billinghurst was immediately faced with a series of strikes, now that the workers believed that for the first time, they had a real advocate in the presidential palace. Billinghurst responded with several favorable interventions on the side of labor, which further consolidated his position as labor's patron. Not only did he believe in their cause and want to pay back his electoral debt, but without a political party of his own or the support of one, he was precariously dependent on the support of labor in a hostile, conservative Congress. As an outsider in the Aristocratic Republic, his only real political asset, as the election had shown, was his ability to mobilize the workers in the streets to exert pressure on Congress and the establishment for reform. In the end, however, this dangerous tactic would prove politically fatal by provoking the oligarchy to bring Billinghurst down by force after only eighteen months in office.

The impending political showdown was not long in coming and revolved around the constitutional question of whether the new president could by-pass Congress in implementing his new budget. With little support in the Congress, the new president opted to negotiate a loan of £500,000 from the British Peruvian Corporation and to issue his new budget by presidential decree. One significant provision of the budget was a 9-percent reduction in the allocation to the armed forces. Nationalists in the army and elsewhere were also roiled by rumors that Billinghurst was about to sell the contested provinces of Tacna and Arica to Chile. When additional rumors of a conspiracy to overthrow the regime surfaced, Billinghurst responded by mobilizing worker demonstrations, which occurred not only in Lima, but in Arequipa, Trujillo, and Cuzco, the latter amounting to over 10,000 people. The editors of the English-language newspaper *West Coast Leader* seemed to have it right when they commented that Billinghurst was bent on "a social revolution" in which "the concentration of power in the hands of the few, the elimination of the great mass of the people as anything but a passive factor in the government of the nation [was being] undermined and overthrown" (quoted in Blanchard, 1977, p. 268).

Such direct participation by the masses in the traditionally closed, elitist political system, however, was an unacceptable challenge to the oligarchy. The rumored conspiracy against Billinghurst ominously involved important members of the political parties, the business community, and the army. After Billinghurst began to distribute arms to his supporters on the afternoon of February 3, 1914, and they took to the streets firing their weapons in the air, the conspirators, led by Colonel Oscar R. Benavides, commander of the Lima garrison, arrested the president at dawn the next day and sent him into exile in Chile. The "undiscipline" of the masses and the prospect of arming the workers could not, in the end, be countenanced by the officer corps. As for the oligarchy, the sugar planter Ramón Aspíllaga put it best in a letter to his brother and presidential candidate Antero two days later, when he referred to "the insolence of the masses" and their February 3 demonstration as the principal cause of the coup.

The *golpe* (military overthrow of the government) led by Benavides was significant, among other things, in that it foreshadowed the future role of the armed forces in national politics. At the same time, it was a consequence of the professionalization of the military begun in 1896 by Piérola. The latter was paradoxical, for Piérola had sought not only to redress the country's past military failure, but to subordinate a reformed military to civilian authority. Toward that end, the Francophile Piérola had imported a French military mission to do for Peru what the Prussian General Emil Körner was doing for Chile, namely, to reorganize, restructure, and generally modernize the armed forces.

The chief of the newly appointed French mission, Colonel Paul Clement, had undertaken his task with enthusiasm, to the point that he adopted Peruvian citizenship and later became army chief of staff. Under his direction, the Escuela Militar de Chorillos was established in 1898, and a new military code of justice, modeled after the French equivalent, was adopted. A military draft for men aged twenty-one to twenty-five was also adopted, and the top-heavy officer corps was substantially reduced.

Benavides, a member of one of Peru's most influential families, was the product of this professionalization of the armed forces. He graduated first in his class in 1906 from the Escuela Superior de Guerra—the general staff school also founded on the French model in 1904. He later studied in France and served on missions in Germany and Austria before he returned home to participate with distinction in a brief border clash with Colombia in 1911. Two years later, he was elevated to army chief of staff. Within six months of the coup, the general, now provisional president, confronted the most serious national crisis since the end of the War of the Pacific. In August 1914, World War I erupted in Europe, an event that would initially plunge the export-dependent Peruvian economy, like the rest of Latin America, into a tailspin.

World War I and Its Impact

The outbreak of the war in Europe cut off lucrative export markets, pushed up freight rates and the price of manufactured imports, and interrupted the flow of loans and credit from European banks and money markets. These disruptions, in turn, caused factories in the Peruvian periphery to close and unemployment to rise. As commodities destined for export piled up in ports and warehouses, production was halted and workers were dismissed. For example, in the sugar estates and towns of La Libertad, 75 percent of the workforce was thrown out of work. In Lima the textile mill El Inca cut wages by 55 percent between August and November 1914. To make matters worse, some 1,500 unemployed Peruvian nitrate workers arrived in the capital by ship following the suspension of production in the Chilean nitrate fields.

Financial problems mounted as the sharp decline in European imports caused a massive decline in governmental duties, which fell from £616,491 in the first half of 1914 to £568,351 in the following twelve months. Since Peru was unable to meet payments on its relatively small foreign debt, its credit abroad was further compromised. To make matters worse, the banking system faltered as deposits fell, loans were cut back, and profits were reduced.

These unrelenting financial pressures served to deepen Benavides's desire to withdraw as soon as possible from the presidency, an office he felt uncomfortable holding as a professional army officer. Therefore, he suggested in 1915 that a "Convención de Partidos" (general convention) of all the political parties should be convoked to select a civilian president. The convention, the first of its kind in history, met in August, and selected former President José Pardo y Barreda president on the third ballot. Although still seriously divided, the traditional elites of the Aristocratic Republic, harboring a nostalgia for the "better days" of the first Pardo presidency, decided to put their trust in a known political quantity, rather than seek new leadership or direction.

Once in office Pardo immediately attacked the government's financial problems by increasing taxes and revenues. The most important measure was an export tax on agricultural and mineral products which, although unpopular with elite producers, went a long way to stabilizing the country's finances. The tax fortuitously coincided after 1916 with a general recovery and then boom in Peruvian exports to the European belligerents who were now facing critical shortages of essential commodities because of the war. This enabled the Peruvian *sol* to stabilize and then appreciate in value, so that by July 1918 it was being exchanged for the British pound sterling at a substantial premium. Higher tax revenues enabled the government to resume servicing the debt which in turn improved the credit worthiness of the state.

Sugar exports, for several reasons, led the export bonanza. First, a year before the war the Panama Canal opened, reducing the distance to Liverpool by half and cutting the trip to New York by two-thirds. Transportation costs dropped accordingly. Thereafter, the United States replaced Britain as the main importer of Peruvian sugar. Second, the industry had made substantial investments to increase production capacity between 1908 and 1914. So when foreign demand resumed after the initial war-induced trade disruptions and prices began to climb, Peruvian producers were in a position to increase rapidly their production. Exports soared between 1914 and 1920, except for a bad harvest in 1917, land under cultivation increased sharply and profits skyrocketed.

Some idea of the windfall to sugar planters can be seen in the balance sheets of the Aspíllaga brothers' plantation Cayaltí in the Department of Lambayeque which between 1911 and 1913 earned £70,285, but in 1914 alone earned £71,713, a figure that grew to £222,243 in 1919. This led Antero As-píllaga to state that " . . . as many other sugar producers and industrialists we give thanks to the Germans for the bonanza that has come to us . . . " (quoted in Albert, 1988, p. 109). This windfall, as you will see, was not shared by the sugar workers whose numbers increased sharply, but whose relative wages actually declined during the same period.

Cotton production, on the other hand, experienced a much sharper ini-tial dislocation from the war than sugar, but exports rebounded by mid-1915. Both in volume and earnings cotton exports hit record levels in 1916 and climbed steadily thereafter, except in the drought year 1917. As a re-sult, land devoted to cotton production increased an estimated 75 percent to 100 percent during the war while food staples were conversely taken out of production. This had a serious impact on urban food supplies and prices, contributing, as you will see, to the upward spiral of inflation and con-comitant social unrest in Lima during the last years of the war.

Like cotton and sugar, wool exports, the engine of growth for the re-gional economy of Southern Peru whose entrepot was Arequipa, also expe-rienced a short, initial downturn and then an ensuing boom as the war in Europe unfolded. While export volumes rose modestly in response to for-eign demand, soaring prices resulted in a quadrupling in the value as well as the earnings of wool exports from the quinquenniums 1910 to 1914 and 1915 to 1919. This bonanza too had serious social consequences, as it deep-ened peasant unrest in the region leading to the Rumi Maqui Rebellion of 1915–16 to which we shall turn shortly.

The outbreak of World War I had a similar impact on the mining in-dustry, but with somewhat different economic, if not social consequences. Unlike sugar and cotton, in which Peruvian or immigrant ownership pre-dominated (only 25 percent of sugar production was owned by foreign firms), mining by World War I was largely foreign dominated. For exam-ple, 90 percent of Peru's copper production was produced by two compa-nies, Cerro de Pasco and Backus and Johnson. Initially the war forced a 50-percent cut in production, but from 1915 prices and production rose rapidly in response to international demand until 1917. Windfall profits for the mine owners were substantial, and another round of foreign takeovers occurred after 1916. Thus, the war accelerated and deepened the process of de-nationalization and monopoly control in mining, inhibiting national devel-opment through profit remission and the limitations on native entrepre-neurial activity.

The petroleum industry was also under foreign control by this time and followed a similar course during the war. The International Petroleum Com-pany exercised a virtual monopoly in the industry, enabling it successfully to challenge the government on a number of issues. The most serious was IPC's decision not to pay the new mining tax instituted by the Pardo gov-ernment, thereby provoking nationalists to attack the government for "sell-ing out" to the imperialism of international oil interests.

The war had another important impact on the economy. It marked the increasing commercial presence of the United States in the economy. This was true not only in the area of investments and capital flows, as in mining, but in the overall amount of trade between the two countries. Already in 1913, 30 percent of Peru's imports and 33 percent of her exports were accounted for by the United States. Much of this trade was dominated by the W. R. Grace & Co., which was not only the largest trading company in Peru, but owned the Cartavio sugar company; controlled almost half the textile industry by 1918; and was active in banking, insurance, and other businesses as well. The growing U.S. commercial presence was due partly to the opening of the Panama Canal in 1913 and partly to the adverse impact of the war on British and German commercial relations with Peru and the rest of South America.

A commonplace in the literature is that the disruption in imports to Latin America during World War I stimulated a process of import substituting industrialization (ISI) in the region. However, this thesis was challenged by Albert (1988), who persuasively showed that ISI in Peru was largely negligible between 1914 and 1918. Rather, imports resumed 12 to 18 months after the outbreak of the war as the ensuing export bonanza enriched mainly the elites, enabling them to resume their lavish spending on consumer goods from abroad. Foreign buyouts in the mining industry likewise increased the elites' wealth and spending on imports. At the same time, as the wartime export bonanza deepened, the elites had little inclination to question either the trend toward denationalization in mining or to replace the liberal model of export-led growth with a policy of ISI. Indeed, if anything, the boom in sugar and cotton exports persuaded the planters, unwisely as it turned out, to make large investments to increase their export capacity in the erroneous belief that foreign demand and prices would continue to soar even after the war ended.

Although there were several reasons for the relative weakness of manufacturing growth during the war, in the main it appears that the elites had either withdrawn from or downgraded their interest in manufacturing since the period of robust ISI growth between 1897 and 1907. Profiting as a class from the export boom, the oligarchy's vision of development reemphasized export-led growth. Indeed, they could argue that as long as exports and profits continued to rise while imports stayed relatively constant, the country's balance of payments and general financial condition would remain favorable. Such a view, however, myopically ignored the deteriorating living conditions of the workers and set the scene for the increase of social unrest as the war approached its end in 1917.

The first signs of serious social unrest as a result of the economic disruptions of World War I occurred in the Southern Andes with the outbreak of the Rumi Maqui Rebellion of 1915–16. The rebellion began when several hundred Indian peasants attacked the haciendas of two prominent landowners in the remote province of Azángaro in the department of Puno on December 1, 1915. Driven off by heavily armed estate employees with losses estimated between 10 and 132, the attack's leader José María Turpo was hunted down, brutally tortured, and executed six weeks later.

Turpo, it turned out, had been organizing peasants along with Teodomiro Gutiérrez Cuevas, an outsider who had originally came to Azángaro as Billinghurst's appointed representative to investigate peasant unrest in the area in 1913. Gutiérrez was a midlevel army officer who had held several governmental positions in Puno since the turn of the century and who believed that the lot of the Indian population could be improved by certain educational and legal reforms. After fleeing to Chile after the overthrow of Billinghurst, Gutiérrez, who also apparently harbored anarchist inclinations, assumed a more militant position, and in September 1915, returned clandestinely to Puno, where he joined Turpo and other peasants in their organizational efforts.

From the few surviving documents of the movement, we know that Gutiérrez assumed the name "Rumi Maqui" (Hand of Stone) and, conjuring up the beneficent image of the Incas, appointed himself "General and Supreme Director of the indigenous pueblos and armed forces of the Federal State of Tahuantinsuyo" [Jacobsen, 1993, p. 340]. He proceeded to appoint a number of officials in outlying districts to this new federal state, most of whom were not drawn from the ranks of the established community authorities.

The uprising was directed against land-grabbing landlords and abusive local authorities who sought to monopolize the production and commercialization of wool at the expense of peasant communities. What was particularly significant about the rebellion was the combination of socioeconomic goals with a political agenda that emphasized greater autonomy and a millenarian discourse that stressed "Indianness." The latter appeal, according to Jacobsen (1993, pp. 239–42), however, was no romantic, atavistic throwback to Inca times, as is sometimes suggested. Rather, it was a device to fortify the community against the efforts of a new *gamonal* elite to depict Indians in racist terms as "barbarians" in order to justify their own attempts to impose a new, harshly exploitative neocolonial domination over native Andeans in the context of the commercial bonanza of the wool trade.

Meanwhile, unrest began to stir in Lima and elsewhere, partly inspired by international events. Workers' uprisings in Russia were leading to the Revolution of 1917 and subsequent seizure of power by the Bolsheviks in the name of the proletariat. These events were publicized around the world in the media and captured the imagination of workers, intellectuals, and the public, not the least in Peru where working-class newspapers, such as *La Protesta*, trumpeted the dawn of a new proletarian world order. At the same time, the rising cost of living and stagnation in wages brought on by the European war provided a similarly explosive social context in which the revolutionary events, ideas, and ideologies circulating from Russia and Europe could find resonance.

Although real wages did not decline in the sugar industry, according to Kammann (1990), the cost of living rose sharply, eroding the workers' standard of living in an industry that had experienced windfall profits during the war. Much of the cause for this deterioration can be attributed to soaring food prices, brought on by the massive conversion of acreage from foodstuffs to cash crops precisely to profit from the export boom. Various administrations tried to address this problem by requiring plantations to set aside a fixed portion of their land for the cultivation of staples, but to little avail.

Despite the deteriorating conditions of rural workers during the war, there were significant obstacles to their effective organization and mobilization. On the one hand, the considerable numerical size and concentration of rural workers in the strategic export sector on which the economy depended for growth and the state depended for the bulk of its revenues gave them a certain strategic leverage over capital. On the other hand, it was in the vital interest of both governmental authorities and employers to collaborate closely to maintain control over rural workers in the export sector. Such a degree of unity was not possible, however, for the socially heterogeneous and geographically fragmented workforce that labored in this sector. Not only were enclaves of workers on the coastal plantations, sierra mines, and northern oil fields separated geographically from each other, they were also ethnically and racially differentiated, as well as divided according to category of work performed, that is, whether they were permanent, short-term, contracted workers or sharecroppers. All this meant that rural workers might have different interests and outlooks that hindered their organization of an effective, unified labor movement.

Take the example of the most common form of rural worker on plantations, the category of contract, or *enganche*, labor. Its ranks were composed of Indian peasants from the highlands who were given advance payments to work for a specified, temporary term, originally in the mining sector. This system of cheap, migratory labor became more common after the War of the Pacific because of the ruinous condition of the postwar sugar industry and the acute scarcity of labor on the coastal plantations once the trade in Chinese coolies was ended in the 1870s. Indeed, *enganche* became a profitable business for *enganchadores* (labor contractors)—local merchants, landlords, and even governmental officials—who sprang up after the war in the highlands to organize the system. *Enganchadores* often had the unsavory reputation of taking advantage of their mostly illiterate and often vulnerable recruits with questionable recruitment practices. However, with the need for plenty of cash to pay off debts, cover expenses for religious festivals, or carry out their own farming activities, peasants found ample reason to sign up for such work in ever larger numbers. In time, the labor contractors' exploitation and manipulation of these *enganchados* contributed to a rising tide of rural protest during the second decade of the century, and numerous calls for increased governmental regulation of contract labor were made by urban social reformers. On the other hand, the fact that they were transitory and moved back and forth from their small plots to these temporary jobs made the task of organizing what one historian called "proto-proletarians" into the labor movement extremely difficult.

As for ethnic and racial divisions, Asian indentured servants continued to constitute a portion of the rural labor force on the coast, even after the Chinese coolie trade was officially ended in 1874. Because of the labor shortage after the War of the Pacific, the flow of contract labor from both China and Japan resumed in 1899, although it was much more regulated by the government than before. By 1923, when the trade was suspended, some 11,764 Japanese laborers had arrived in Peru, a figure that was mirrored by the 15,000 immigrant workers who arrived from China in roughly the same period. The fact that Asian workers often enjoyed relatively better wages and living conditions, because as immigrants they fell into a more regulated category of labor than their Peruvian counterparts, caused resentments and divisions between the two groups that occasionally erupted in violence. Indeed, native rural workers, like their urban counterparts who had rioted in the past against the Chinese in Lima and elsewhere, harbored similar attitudes of prejudice against Asian workers.

In spite of these and other formidable divisions and obstacles to labor organization, strikes in rural areas became more widespread and intense than in the capital during World War I. The most serious disturbance occurred in the coastal Huaura Valley in 1916 among sugar and port workers who demanded, among other things, a 50 percent raise in wages, together with shorter working hours. Violence ensued before the authorities were able to restore order and decree a modest 10 percent wage increase. Similarly, violent labor outbreaks occurred the following year in the copper mines of Cerro de Pasco and the sugar estates of La Libertad. The oligarchy placed the blame for these disturbances on "outside," anarchist agitators who, while quite active in stirring up workers' discontent, in truth simply found a fertile soil for their militant activities in the workers' deteriorating living and working conditions during the war years.

Labor, especially rural labor, was not the only victim of accelerating inflation and falling living standards during the war. The middle sectors were also suffering. These sectors had experienced substantial growth during the first two decades of the century, partly because of accelerating urbanization, which saw a steady rise in the population of Lima from 172,927 in 1908 to 223,807 in 1920 (a 30 percent increase). Employment in import-export commerce, traditionally the city's most active sector, amounted to an estimated 15 percent of Lima's male population, more than twice the proportion of factory workers. As the economy advanced, so did the number of banks (from 4 in 1897 to 12 in 1928), insurance companies (from 2 in 1899 to 13 in 1928) and factories. When combined with the expanding infrastructure of transportation and government to serve a more complex economy, the number of white-collar workers and professionals grew accordingly. These white-collar workers and professionals included office workers, petty bureaucrats, retail clerks, bookkeepers, lawyers, physicians, engineers, storekeepers, teachers, and university students.

By the turn of the century, the number of white-collar workers was sufficient to warrant the founding of the Sociedad Empleados de Comercio (SEC) in 1903. From its inception, the SEC not only undertook the kind of mutualist role of covering the medical and funeral expenses of some of its members, but lobbied the government in behalf of white-collar workers. With the onset of the war and the concomitant inflationary spiral, the membership rolls of the SEC expanded, and the organization, like labor, became more militant in pressing employers and the government for reforms.

The growth of the middle class can also be seen in the expansion of the educational system and the growing literacy of the population. For example, enrollments of university students, including those of San Marcos University, rose 82.5 percent in the decade prior to 1917. There was a corresponding percentage increase in the number of normal schools that graduated most of Peru's teachers during this period. Finally, the number of primary and secondary schools also rose from 220 in 1915 to 327 in 1919, a 48 percent increase.

These rising educational indices also suggest an increasing mass of readers who consumed the growing number of magazines and newspapers (from 167 in 1918 to 197 in 1920 to 473 in 1928) in circulation by the end of World War I. During the war, Lima's two major daily newspapers, *La Prensa* (Demócrata-liberal) and *El Comercio* (Civilista-independiente), which represented different oligarchical interests, were joined by *El Tiempo*, which catered to the emerging middle class, and the anarchist *Los Parias* and *La Protesta*, which were read by the workers.

All this points to the fact that there was not only a significant material expansion during the Aristocratic Republic, but a cultural one as well. This cultural effervescence was led by a new generation of intellectuals, the so-called generation of 1919, which now came to the fore. The biographical profile of this generation stood in marked contrast to its predecessor, the generation of 1900. The latter, led by such bright lights as José de la Riva Agüero y Osma, Víctor Andrés Belaúnde, and Francisco García Calderón, all came from social backgrounds in the creole aristocracy that had taken over the political reigns of the country at the beginning of the Aristocratic Republic. Born in the 1880s, they had all grown up and been shaped by the national calamity of the War of the Pacific, which led them to wrestle with the problem of what had gone wrong. Several had been influenced by the ideas of European positivism, from which they extracted the "scientific" precepts that would form the intellectual and philosophical underpinnings for the rationalization of state and society during the Aristocratic Republic.

In contrast, the new generation of 1919, whose leading figures were José Carlos Mariátegui and Víctor Raúl Haya de la Torre, were born in the 1890s. With some exceptions, they were of mestizo and middle-class origins. These class and ethnic differences set them distinctly apart from the aristocratic generation of 1900, which, in the words of Luis Alberto Sánchez, "had everything in its favor: newspapers, money, social position, official favor, a coincidence of values with the governing class, inoffensive theories, vapid idealism, their own university" (quoted in Chavarria, 1979, p. 56). Many of the generation of 1919 also came from the provinces, part of the growing migration of people from the interior to the capital as the economic center of gravity shifted toward the littoral. Their provincial origins tended to give them a more national outlook, which coincided with one of their major intellectual preoccupations—the creation of a truly national, as opposed to Lima centered, culture. The members of the generation of 1919, unlike their earlier counterparts, were also, by and large, strong political activists—more "pragmatic" in Sánchez's words. Finally, they were much more interested in plumbing Peru's history and culture for clues to finding answers to contemporary problems.

The two leading figures of the generation of 1919 both had provincial, mestizo, and middle-class roots. Víctor Raúl Haya de la Torre was born in 1895 in Trujillo in the heart of the sugar-growing country of the north coast. Although he had aristocratic ties on his mother's side to the old planter class that went back to the independence period, Víctor Raúl's father, Raúl Haya, stood, by family and profession, squarely in the ranks of the provincial middle class. Born into a family of schoolteachers in Cajabamba in the adjoining department of Cajamarca, Raúl Haya moved to Trujillo, where he made a good marriage and career in business, journalism, and politics.

During Víctor Raúl's youth, Trujillo, a seignorial city and cradle of independence, and its fertile agrarian hinterland, were undergoing the wrenching shift to a modern, industrialized sugar monoculture. The resulting class conflict pitted an emergent, rural proletariat, composed of dislocated small farmers and migrant workers from the adjacent highlands, against a new, modernizing corporate elite who were bent on converting the traditional, patrimonial-style plantations into more efficient, factory-like operations. Chaffing under the more disciplined, regimented, impersonalized, and exploitative plantation system, the sugar workers soon began to organize and protest.

So the youthful Víctor Raúl watched and reacted as this formerly placid provincial capital began to seethe with labor unrest. As a teenager, he took to hanging out at the local labor hall down the street from his house, where he mingled with the new breed of labor organizers, some of them sent up from Lima, who propagandized their radical, anarchist ideas. These ideas would be reinforced by the newspapers, broadsides, and other radical literature that constituted the makeshift "library" of the hall where Víctor Raúl would sit transfixed reading for hours on end. Víctor Raúl also formed part of a bohemian group of young local writers, artists, and intellectuals that included the great Peruvian poet César Vallejo. Later, he would attend the University of Trujillo and then, in 1917, would move to Lima and San Mar-

Víctor Raúl Haya de la Torre (1895–1979), founder and head of the APRA Party for more than half a century. Photograph in the Alfred Metraux collection, courtesy of Daniel Metraux. Photographed by Wendy Walker.

cos University to pursue a degree in law and plunge into radical student politics.

José Carlos Mariátegui, on the other hand, was born in 1894 in Moquegua on the south coast. His mother was a mestiza from a small town in Chancay, not far from Lima, who married into the *Limeño* creole upper class. However, José Carlos's father abandoned the family shortly after his birth, and he grew up fatherless and in modest economic circumstances, supported by his seamstress mother while suffering from frail health from an early age. When he hurt his knee in a school-yard accident in 1902, his mother brought him to Lima, where he was operated on unsuccessfully, leaving him crippled for the rest of his life. Perhaps the sedentary life of a long recuperation led to a passion for reading, and by age eleven, he was already devouring works by Anatole France, Manuel Beingolea, and Francisco and Ventura García Calderón.

Eventually José Carlos was physically rehabilitated sufficiently so that he was able to go to work as a copyboy for *La Prensa* in 1909. By dint of fourteen-hour workdays and an acute intelligence, the precocious, if frail, young Mariátegui, who stood about five feet two inches and weighed barely over one hundred pounds, worked himself up to reporter in 1911 and soon gained a readership for his witty coverage of the Lima social scene. However, as the capital became engulfed in labor strife and the economic dislocations of World War I, the intense young journalist increasingly turned his attention to political and social concerns. Meanwhile, as Haya and Mariátegui came of political age, the high hopes harbored by the Civilistas that the electoral return of José Pardo to the presidency in 1915 would stabilize the Aristocratic Republic from the political and economic turmoil of the war proved illusory. As president, Pardo resorted to the kind of arbitrary and personalistic rule that had roiled the party a decade earlier under Leguía. Initial measures to stabilize the economy, moreover, proved only momentarily successful, as exports recovered, but then took off, triggering a severe inflationary spiral.

The political and economic deterioration of the Aristocratic Republic now entered its denouement. As Pardo approached the end of his term in 1919, he led a weakened civilismo that was seriously vulnerable to challenge. Yet who would the new political contenders be? Certainly not candidates from the traditional parties, which, like the Civilistas, appeared weak and divided. The Demócratas, who had been increasingly marginalized by Civilista control of the electoral apparatus since 1903, had virtually collapsed with the death of their leader Piérola in 1913. The other parties were similarly dependent on aging, personalistic leaders—the Constitutionalists under Cáceres and the Liberals under the *caudillo* Augusto Durán. The Liberal Party derived from a faction that had broken off from the Demócratas in 1899, but at best had never become more than a minority party in congressional coalitions in the ensuing years. The main problem was that none of these parties had developed a new generation of leaders who were capable of meeting the challenges of the postwar years. So, on the eve of the elections of 1919, the elite parties were in a virtual state of collapse. As Stein (1980, p. 38) so aptly put it, they were "imposing colonial houses still owned by many of their most prominent members; impressive facades that hid aging structures beset by internal decay."

The Great Strikes of 1918–19

Onto this rickety political superstructure of the Aristocratic Republic burst a watershed event—the massive strike for the eight-hour day in January 1919. The underlying cause of the strike lay in the deteriorating living conditions of the Lima-Callao working class whose wages continued to stagnate in the face of spiraling postwar inflation. Faced with growing labor unrest, Pardo belatedly pressed Congress to pass a series of labor laws, many of which had been proposed by José Matías Manzanilla more than a decade earlier. Perhaps the most important was a law signed on November 25, 1918, that was designed to protect women and children in the workplace. Paradoxically, this new law became the main catalyst for the strike.

Over a thousand women worked in the textile mills; garment centers; soap; candle, and biscuit factories; the post office; and the telephone exchange of Lima-Callao. Their wages, however, were far less than their male counterparts, so they began to press for change. In fact, they had showed surprising militancy earlier when they formed the Sociedad Labor Feminista (Feminist Labor Society) and the Sociedad Progreso Feminista (Feminist Progress Society), the latter in 1916. The Feminist Progress Society was composed mainly of seamstresses, but claimed to speak for all working women. When the law was finally passed at Pardo's behest in 1918, it established several protections, including the eight-hour day for both women and children aged fourteen to eighteen.

Rather than quieting the workers, implementation of the law had the opposite effect; it led male textile workers as well to strike for the eight-hour day at existing or higher wages. The mill owners reacted negatively to these demands because the market for textile products had dropped sharply with the end of the war. They saw the strike as a "blessing in disguise"—an opportunity to reduce production—and they immediately began to shut down the mills and furlough their workers.

The textile workers were shortly joined by the city's bakers, tanners, and sawmill workers, all of whom likewise demanded the eight-hour day. Soon a general strike committee (Comité Pro-Paro General) was formed as militant anarchists, such as Nicolás Gutarra, Héctor Merel, and Julio Portocarerro, moved quickly to widen the workers' participation in the strike. The anarchists were particularly strong in the textile and baking industries and had long advocated the eight-hour day. The spreading mobilization was given added impetus with the outbreak of strikes in January at the Zorritos petroleum works in Piura and the Casapalca copper foundry in Cerro de Pasco, the former for the eight-hour day and the latter for increased wages and lower food prices. These strikes, which were accompanied by sporadic violence and the loss of life, gave the impression that the movement was spreading outside Lima and led organizers in the capital to announce a forty-eight-hour general strike on January 12.

Lima's workers generally reacted to this call, and by noon the capital and port city were virtually paralyzed, with markets, factories, and the tram system closed down. At this point, university students joined the movement. The Federation of Peruvian Students (Federación de Estudiantes del Perú) appointed three representatives, including Haya de la Torre, to assist the strikers. However, at this moment, they represented just one more group to support the strike, and their participation, which later became more significant, was relatively minor.

As the strike intensified, the Pardo government now confronted a serious dilemma. It was particularly fearful that the longer the strike continued, the greater potential it would have to replicate the so-called Tragic Week (La Semana Trágica) in Buenos Aires that had ended a few days earlier in a bloody confrontation between striking workers and the army. Moreover, the government realized that the longer the strike went on, the more damage they would inflict on the precarious postwar economy and that repression would serve little purpose, given the workers' massive response to the strike. All these concerns weighed particularly heavily on the country's elite, whose general level of anxiety and apprehension over possible popular unrest had heightened ever since the outbreak and turmoil of the Russian Revolution of 1917. On January 15, therefore, Pardo gave in to the strikers' demands and decreed the eight-hour day at existing wage levels. The jubilant strikers responded shortly thereafter by calling an end to the strike.

The strike's outcome was obviously a huge victory for the strikers and has long been interpreted as the founding moment, the coming of age of the Peruvian labor movement. A revisionist view by Parker (1995, p. 417) acknowledged that labor won an important tactical victory, but questioned labor's assertion that the government had totally capitulated to the strikers and that a new era of labor militancy had dawned. It is true that momentarily, at least, the strike's outcome had the effect of intensifying the workers' unity and militancy. Union membership promptly increased, and new unions were formed, including the Federation of Textile Workers of Peru (Federación de Trabajadores en Tejidos del Perú) that brought together textile workers from around the country into a single national confederation. Significantly, the student leader Haya de la Torre, who had developed friendships with a number of the strike's anarchist leaders, chaired the workers' committee that organized the new confederation. This friendly relationship between Haya and the textile workers would provide a critical source of support for the aspiring young politician and reformer in the years ahead. In addition, Haya would be prominently associated in the popular mind with the successful struggle for the eight-hour day, one of the first such labor triumphs to occur in all Latin America.

Perhaps buoyed by their recent success but misinterpreting the Pardo government's response as a capitulation, the strike's leaders tried to press their advantage by seizing on another burning popular issue of the day. In April the Committee in Favor of Lowering the Cost of Living (Comité Pro-Abaratamiento de las Subsistencias), which had originally appeared without much success in 1916, was now reconstituted. Almost overnight, it brought together a wide range of labor and popular organizations representing some 30,000 workers in Lima-Callao. The main reason for its success lay in the intensifying postwar inflationary spiral that had seen the prices of some basic foodstuffs double between December and March.

The leader of the new committee was the fiery anarcho-syndicalist orator and organizer Nicolás Gutarra, who had played a prominent role in the successful January strike. Receiving no response from the Pardo government to a series of proposals to lower the cost of living, which included a freeze on the prices of basic food staples, rents, and freight rates, and measures to force farmers to grow more food crops, the committee called for another general strike on May 27. The strike was timed to take advantage of the political uncertainty resulting from the May 18–19 presidential elections to determine Pardo's successor. In the elections, the Civilista and official candidate Antenor Aspíllaga appeared to have lost to his challenger, ex-Civilista, former president, and political maverick Augusto B. Leguía (1908–12). Aspíllaga appealed for a recount to the Supreme Court, claiming that irregularities in balloting had occurred in the countryside, where he was considered to have much of his electoral strength.

Unlike the previous strike, this time there was widespread violence and looting that provoked Pardo to call out the army and impose martial law. When the government also arrested and imprisoned the principal organizers, the steam seemed to go out of the strike, and the committee declared it over on June 2, after which martial law was suspended and the government assumed a more conciliatory stance. The press later reported that the strike had cost over 100 lives and over 2 million *soles* in property damages. Over 200 small shops, owned mostly by Asians, had been destroyed when frustrated looters turned once more on this highly visible minority.

No sooner had calm seemingly returned to the capital than the focal point of protest shifted to venerable San Marcos University, where reform had been gestating for some time. Even though the remote origins of the movement went back to the turn of the century, it was given new life by events in Europe at the close of World War I. For one thing, the widespread death and destruction caused by the European war produced a deep disillusionment with the capitalist order in the West, particularly among young people and intellectuals. At the same time, the outbreak of the Russian Revolution of 1917 and the rise of socialism and communism raised hopes that a new, more humane and just order was about to dawn.

These sentiments spread quickly to the universities in Latin America, producing their first concrete results at the University of Córdoba in Argentina in 1918. There, students declared the need for society to cleanse itself of the sordid materialism and capitalist excesses that they believed had brought on the conflagration of the war. This new ideological current merged into the already powerful stream of anti-imperialist sentiments against U.S. intervention and dollar diplomacy in the Caribbean dating from the Spanish-American War of 1898. At San Marcos, the rising generation of 1919, increasingly sensitized to the social struggles of the workers at the end of the war, now began to vilify the established professorate as agents of a local plutocracy, allied with Yankee businessmen. In their minds, these professors were guilty of "corrupting" Latin America's youths with the false doctrines of materialism and unrestrained capitalism that they identified with the tenets of positivism that had been steadily promoted by the previous generation of 1900. The time had come to put an end to the monopoly exerted by this generation of professors over the university administration and curriculum and to institute sweeping reforms.

The catalyst for the outbreak of university reform in Peru was the arrival in Lima of the Argentine socialist Alfredo Palacios in May. A powerful orator, Palacios appeared before a large crowd at San Marcos University to explain the Córdoba movement. The speech had the immediate effect of galvanizing the students into action and was widely covered in a new, progressive newspaper called *La Razón*, founded by Mariátegui shortly after he left *El Tiempo* in a dispute with his editor. Indeed, it was at the offices of *La Razón* that several San Marcos students and workers had met earlier to coordinate strategy in the second workers' general strike. Already at San Marcos, the students were demanding a series of reforms that would eventually include the removal of several professors and the introduction of student *co-gobierno*—that is, the right to participate in university administration, including the selection of faculty. Student support for these demands now intensified with Palacios's appearance at San Marcos. Among the reforms' chief advocates were future historians Raúl Porras Barrenechea and Jorge Basadre and the later founder of the Alianza Revolucionaria Popular Americana (APRA), Haya de la Torre, and his compatriots Luis Alberto Sánchez and Manuel Seoane.

In the midst of these tumultuous events, another political thunderbolt erupted. On July 4, Leguía executed a preemptive coup against the Pardo government after a series of Supreme Court decisions had been promulgated in favor of his opponent Aspíllaga over the alleged voting irregularities in the May elections. Leguía calculated that his victory was now threatened by his enemies, who were reported to be maneuvering to have the disputed election decided in Congress where he had few supporters. Four days after he carried out his coup, Leguía ordered the release of the leaders of the general strike, who proceeded to organize a huge demonstration in favor of the new president. Appearing on the balcony of the presidential palace, Leguía addressed the popular throng in an emotional speech in which he thoroughly identified himself and his new administration with the workers' cause.

Leguía, of course, was no newcomer to Peruvian politics. He had served as finance minister in Pardo's first presidency and then as president from 1908 to 1912. However, his return to the presidency in 1919, after a long period in the "political wilderness" as an outcast from his former party, revealed the virtual bankruptcy of civilismo and the weakness of the traditional parties of the Aristocractic Republic. It also demonstrated Leguía's uncanny ability to harness to his own political ambitions the strong currents of social and political change that were buffeting the country.

9 Populist Challenge, 1919–45

Augusto B. Leguía was the quintessential turn-of-the-century, self-made capitalist, whose entrepreneurial genius had catapulted him into elite business circles. He came from a modest but well-connected, middle-class family from Lambayeque on the north coast. Educated at a British commercial school in Valparaiso, Chile, Leguía had first made his mark in the business world as an agent and manager of the New York Life Insurance Company. From this early connection with British and American economic interests, he was to acquire a lifelong belief in what one historian called "the foreign demonstration effect." Thus, he strongly believed that Peru's path to development lay in its ability to attract capital, technology, markets, and business know-how from the advanced countries of the West, a "modernizing outlook" that would inform his political career.

Leguía married into the family of an important British sugar grower named Henry Swayne, whose estates on the north coast the young Leguía eventually took over and transformed, with the help of credit from merchant-bankers in Liverpool, into the profitable British Sugar Company. He later diversified this sugar exporting business into insurance, finance, railway building, and rubber extraction. Through the marriage of his daughters to the prominent Chopitea, Ayulo Laos, and Larrañaga families, moreover, Leguía cemented ties to a powerful financial group backed by large-scale credit from British and American sources.

Leguía's first term as president had ended badly, with a severely divided Civilista party. He subsequently broke from the party and was later forced by Pardo into exile in London and New York, where he renewed his business and financial links with an eye toward reconstructing Peru's battered postwar economy. Sensing the political vacuum of the postwar Aristocratic Republic, as well as the possibilities presented by the social unrest that was threatening to topple that order, Leguía returned to Peru in early 1919 to become an independent candidate for the presidency.

His Civilista opponent was the old planter Ramón Aspíllaga Barreda, whose conservative and aristocratic background offered little appeal to a public that was demanding change. Leguía now cashed in on his anti-Civilista reputation and went on the attack against his former compatriots, whom he characterized as anachronistic and politically bankrupt in the face of the formidable economic and social challenges facing Peru in the postwar years. He adroitly directed his appeal to the disenchanted middle- and working classes, promising to draw on his background as a successful businessman and ties to international finance to embark on a new program of national modernization and reform. This program was designed to create what he called *La Patria Nueva* (the new fatherland) and included a stronger, interventionist state capable of renewing rapid economic growth, especially in the export sector. Export-led growth would be stimulated by large infusions of foreign loans and investments and facilitated by a massive road-building project to improve the transportation infrastructure. In short, Leguía promised to lead Peru's inflation-weary popular classes into a new era of prosperity and sustained economic growth.

Once installed in the presidency, Leguía moved quickly to consolidate his control by attacking his political enemies in the Civilista Party. Mindful that they had tried to block his election, the new president unleashed a systematic campaign of repression to dismantle the party and force its leaders into exile. This proved to be another nail in the Civilista coffin.

With the traditional Civilista power base crippled and isolated, Leguía moved during his first term to root his regime in a countervailing social group, the new middle class. Perhaps the best measure of this political shift was the expansion of the public bureaucracy, which experienced a fivefold increase during Leguía's eleven-year rule, known as the *Oncenio*. Thus, the number of public administrators rose from a scant 898 in 1920 to 5,313 in 1931, leading one opponent of the regime, the respected Víctor Andrés Belaúnde, to label the Leguía government, not inaccurately, as "bureaucratic Caesarism."

The dramatic growth in public-sector employment was also mirrored, to various degrees, in the general rise in middle-sector occupational groups (physicians, lawyers, businessmen, engineers and technicians, civil servants, accountants, journalists, and students) in Lima during the same period. Leguía catered to these groups in many ways. For example, he pushed Congress to pass the Ley del Empleado in 1924, which addressed many long-standing white-collar grievances. Likewise, during his eleven-year rule, Leguía also addressed middle-class desires for greater educational opportunity by reorganizing, expanding, and modernizing the educational system, with the advice and assistance of imported North American educators. During the *Oncenio*, the number of students in the country rose by 62 percent from 195,000 in 1920 to 313,000 in 1930.

The expansion and incorporation of the urban middle classes, of course, would not have been possible without the resumption of economic growth after the dislocations of World War I. To accomplish this goal, Leguía energetically sought foreign investment and loans, particularly from the United States, whose trade and investments to South America, as was indicated earlier, had shot up dramatically after the opening of the Panama Canal in 1913. The increase came at the expense of British and European interests, which were quickly eclipsed by those of the U.S. Thus, the North American share of direct investment in Peru, which, according to Stallings (1987, p. 247), stood at 10 percent in 1900, rose to 40 percent in 1914, 69 percent in 1919, and to a high-water mark of 74 percent in 1924. The United State's share of Peru's imports and exports showed similar increases, reaching highs of 62 percent and 46 percent, respectively, in 1919.

During Leguía's *Oncenio*, U.S. and British direct investments in Peru rose from $161 million to $209 million. By 1930, the U.S. share of this investment was $143 million, 80 percent of which was in mining and petroleum. Over roughly the same period (1919–31) Peru's public external debt soared even more dramatically from $12 million to $124 million, mostly from New York banks. In short, Leguía's "New Fatherland" would be based on a model of "debt-led development." Foreign capital and loans would provide the impetus not only to resume economic growth, but to "modernize" the country, that is, to promote capitalism, which Leguía strongly advocated.

If Leguía held out the prospects of modernization by way of American capital and business, exactly what this meant in terms of national development is not altogether clear. Historians Thorp and Bertram, as well as Drake, argued that his intention was simply to borrow abroad and make favorable concessions to foreign capital, to stimulate growth, finance the expansion of the bureaucracy, and open up opportunities for graft and corruption to the new plutocratic elite that came to be favored by and supported his regime. It is in this light that Leguía's vast road-building and public works projects, as well as the dramatic expansion of the foreign-owned export sector (copper and petroleum), are seen. According to this view, moreover, from a national developmental standpoint, Leguía's economic policies resulted in the stagnation or decline of both the native-owned export sector (sugar, cotton, and mining) and the domestic manufacturing sector. The only real winners from Leguía's modernization program were U.S. corporations (Foundation, Cerro, Standard Oil, and Frederick Ley & Company).

On the other hand, historians Caravedo (1977), Burga and Flores Galindo (1980), and Quiroz (1993) contended that Leguía sought to industrialize the country and thereby favored the formation of a national industrial bourgeoisie. From this perspective, Leguía's road-building and public works programs promoted the expansion of the internal market by improving transportation and access to markets and by generating greater wage employment (and governmental salary rolls), consumer demand, and spending power. The same can be said for the high rates of migration to Lima from the provinces and the rise of the middle class during the *Oncenio*, which led to an observable increase in small savings accounts in local banks. If the number of manufacturing concerns declined during the 1920s compared to the decade from 1895 to 1908, they were offset by the rise of heavily capitalized concerns in the construction sector (roads, ports, railroads, sanitation, irrigation, and refrigeration facilities, among others) in which domestic groups participated jointly with foreign capital. Finally, according to this view, tariff and credit policies during the latter half of the *Oncenio* were favorable to local manufacturers.

These two interpretations of Leguía's economic policies are not necessarily incompatible. The spread of capitalism was facilitated by foreign investments, and, given Peru's chronic export-dependent economy, both foreign and domestic investments naturally gravitated toward that sector. Leguía saw the state as facilitating this process by expanding the infrastructure and services that enhanced exports and hence export-led growth. Still this did not mean that development of home manufacturing and the internal market was not also an important economic goal. In public speeches Leguía expounded on the importance of industrialization and the role of foreign capital. "To the economic world Peru is a producer of primary resources," he declared. "It is about time that we transform those primary resources into modern artifacts. It is a duty, therefore to channel the energies of the nation towards industry" (quoted in Kristal, 1987, p. 189). On other occasions, Leguía liked to say that "we are tribute payers to foreign capital, still indispensable to construct our railroads, to sanitize our cities, to irrigate our arid coasts; but this corresponds to a transitory stage of our progress which leads necessarily to future independence" (quoted in Drake, 1989, p. 221). The problem was that national capital alone could not carry out "the urgent imperative to create industries" (quoted in Kristal, 1987, p. 190).

Leguía entered into negotiations with several New York banks for his first major foreign loan, a $15 million refunding loan, in 1921. The eventual terms of the loan, which was made by Guarantee Trust, are indicative of the extent to which Leguía would become subservient to foreign, especially U.S., interests. The banks insisted on a number of extraordinary guarantees. The first was the appointment of an American financial adviser to Leguía's inner circle who would be consulted in advance of any new governmental economic policy and who would administer the national customs service and any other newly created financial agency. Leguía acceded to these demands, and William Cumberland, a State Department foreign trade official, was appointed to the positions. Cumberland had been a student of Princeton economics professor Edwin Walter Kemmerer, who would recommend and help carry out major reforms of the monetary, banking, and fiscal systems in several South American countries from 1923 to 1931. He later revealingly reported to the State Department that Leguía was not so much interested in such reforms than having someone who could facilitate a line of credit from New York banks.

After further investigating the financial situation in Peru, Guarantee Trust made a number of additional demands, including the creation of a central bank and an exclusive option on any future loans backed by customs revenues. At this point, Leguía resisted turning over complete control of Peruvian finances to a foreign bank, but he did create the Central Reserve Bank and appointed Cumberland to its board of directors. With the State Department's prodding, Guarantee Trust finally made a $2.5 million loan in 1922 guaranteed by petroleum revenues, considerably less than the $15 million originally sought. Leguía then promptly spent the loan within a month.

Indigenismo and Indian Rebellion

If Leguía's program was directed politically, at least initially, toward the middle- and working classes, it also reached out for the moment to the Indian peasantry and its defenders. As in the case of his favorable response to workers' demands in 1919, the new president responded positively to spreading Indian unrest in the southern Andes and its resonance among urban intellectuals in the *Indigenista*, or pro-Indian, movement. As you have seen, the prices of wool plummeted after 1917 following an unprecedented boom before and during the war. For example, prices paid for top-grade Peruvian sheep wool fell from 50.5 pence per pound in 1918 to 39.5 pence in 1920 and to 11.5 pence in 1921. This drop in prices had a deleterious impact on the incomes of peasants and landlords in the south, where wool production and exports constituted the main engine of economic growth.

In response, landlords and wool traders tried to recoup profits by squeezing peasant producers in numerous ways that led to increasing land and other disputes. The peasantry responded to this "overexploitation" by defending their rights and demanding redress from the authorities, often resorting to local demonstrations, confrontations, and small-scale actions— what James C. Scott labeled "passive resistance." For their part, the landlords denounced such actions, which they exaggerated to justify their increasing "repression" and classic landgrab. They portrayed such passive resistance to the government and the public as an incipient peasant revolution aimed at abolishing all property rights and exterminating whites. As the Indian peasantry organized to resist this economic squeeze by the *gamonales* and their agents, they sought out and gained allies among sympathetic sectors of the provincial, urban middle class who took up their defense, often as lawyers and journalists. It was in this context that the *Indigenista* movement was revived and became a powerful urban force in defense of the Indian cause.

The "modern" roots of the *indigenismo* go back to the aftermath of the War of the Pacific in 1884, when the Indians came to be viewed as objects of political and social reform. At this time, various writers, scholars, and political activists formed the *indigenista* school, which evolved from a literary form of nineteenth-century romantic liberalism into a powerful and militant movement for social and political reform in the early twentieth century. During this period, *indigenismo* linked the radical postwar social and political critique of González Prada in Lima with the provinces, where the downtrodden Indian masses resided. In doing so, it also opened the eyes of the Lima intelligentsia and general public to the plight of the Indians, which had heretofore been almost completely ignored. Jorge Basadre called this rediscovery of the Indians the single-most-important event in twentieth-century Peruvian history.

Perhaps the central work that ignited *indigenismo* was the novel *Aves sin nido* by Clorinda Matto de Turner, published in 1889. In this early Peruvian novel, the authoress exposed the systematic exploitation and oppression of Indians in a small Andean town by a triumvirate that included the governor, the local priest, and the justice of the peace. Indeed, it was the latter's secretary, the infamous *tinterillo* (petty lawyer) who used his power and knowledge to defraud the illiterate and ignorant Indians of their land. The novel was a sensation in Lima and acted as a catalyst for the ensuing search to rediscover Indian Peru and improve its condition.

A milestone in this effort was the establishment of the Association Pro-Indígena (Pro-Indian Society) in 1909 by Pedro Zulen, a young student at San Marcos University. The society aimed to educate the public about the abysmal conditions of the Indians to stimulate reforms. Toward this end, it published the *Deber Pro-Indígena* in Lima from 1912 to 1917. During this time, numerous scientific and scholarly studies, influenced by the criticism of González Prada and the ideas of social positivism then circulating in the universities, appeared on various Indian subjects, ranging from the Inca Empire to Indian customs and ways to reform their condition. Even liberal members of the aristocracy addressed the problem, arguing that only through education, improved hygiene, and religion could it be solved. This liberal discourse contrasted with González Prada's more radical pronouncements that the problem was fundamentally economic and social in nature.

After World War I, both socialism and nationalism infused *indigenismo* with a new political consciousness. Young *indigenistas* turned away from the older generation's inclination to study the Indian toward more militant and revolutionary objectives. Some saw the Indian as the agent of a socialist-agrarian revolution, while others emphasized a new revolutionary nationalism based upon what they saw as a glorious Indian past long ignored.

Other than Lima, Cuzco was the other center of this burgeoning *indigenismo*. In Cuzco, the city's elite had cultivated the Inca tradition throughout the nineteenth century, and many proudly proclaimed their lineage to the Inca nobility well into the twentieth century. More recently, the generation of 1909 dedicated itself to restoring the city's former preeminence in Peruvian life. In 1911 the Yale archeologist Hiram Bingham rediscovered the long-lost Inca city of Machu Pichu, causing a renewed interest in history and archeology among *Cuzqueño* students. By the 1920s, a new *indigenista* school of thought, called the Grupo Resurgimiento, had emerged in the former Inca capital that was composed of Luis Valcárcel, author of *Tempestad en los Andes*; José Uriel García, author of *El nuevo Indio*; Dora Mayer de Zulen; and the painter José Sabogal. From 1927 to 1930, they published *La Sierra*, which pursued a nonideological, nationalist line, although most of the group were sympathetic to socialism.

The other main *indigenista* school was formed in Lima around Mariátegui and his avowedly Marxist journal *Amauta*, which appeared from 1926 to 1930 and openly identified *indigenismo* with socialism. For Mariátegui and Haya de la Torre, writing in *Amauta*, the fundamental obstacle to the Indians' progress was the *latifundia* system, and the solution was radical land reform.

Indigenismo was expressed in a variety of ways and forms. In novels they ranged from the works of Matto de Turner to regionalist fiction, such as *Cuentos Andinos* and *Matalache* by Enrique López Albújar, which colorfully captured the presence of the Indians in provincial settings. In the other arts, it appeared in the paintings of Sabogal, the music of Daniel Alomia Robles (whose opera *El condor pasa* debuted in 1913), Julio C. Tello's pioneering preInca archaeological work at Paracas and Chavín, and the social essays of Hildebrando Castro Pozo, to name only a few of the best known. Since much of the cultural and political effervescence of *indigenismo* was centered in the capital, it was, of course, far removed from its subject and therefore largely an imagined abstraction. In the provinces, on the other hand, *indigenismo* embodied strong anticentralist and regionalist tendencies and revindications of the traditional preponderance of Lima.

At first, Leguía was sensitive and politically responsive to the new currents of *indigenismo*, as well as to the upsurge in peasants' protests that was rippling through the southern highlands. For both political and economic reasons, the new president found it expedient to take measures against the object of Indian protests—the *gamonal* class that had been longtime allies of his Civilista opponents. As a proponent of modernizing capitalism and a progressive member of the elite, he also viewed the *gamonales* generally as "feudal" relics and obstacles to progress. At the same time, since *indigenismo* had penetrated large sectors of the mestizo, urban middle- and working classes, Leguía saw political advantages in embracing the movement, which meant siding with the Indian peasantry against the *gamonales*. As a result, the president attempted to forge an alliance with elements of the provincial middle class, sectors of which had taken up the cause of the peasantry.

The goal of this alliance was to try to bring about a fundamental shift in the correlation of landlord-peasant power on the local level, thereby fostering the spread of capitalist modernization. This would be no easy task, given the fact that the historically weak Peruvian state had traditionally relied on a quid pro quo with provincial landlords that allowed them free reign over local affairs in return for exerting control over the peasantry. To modify this arrangement, Leguía moved to expand the power and range of the central state, establishing a network of new political authorities on the local level whose task was to challenge traditional *gamonal* hegemony.

Coincidently, as the "Indian problem" emerged as a key issue in the developing debate about Peru's national identity, Leguía proclaimed a policy of "official *indigenismo*." For example, he created an Office for Indigenous Affairs in 1920, headed by the distinguished sociologist Castro Pozo, and established a national holiday to celebrate El Dia del Indio. Both actions signaled the government's intention of institutionally assimilating the Indian into the mainstream life of the nation. So did the official recognition of Indian communities in the new Constitution of 1920, the first such recognition in the history of the republic.

The government now moved to become the intermediary in property disputes between landlords and peasants. This move not only enabled the government to protect and exercise control over the peasantry, but provided it with a key mechanism for integrating the peasantry into the developing capitalist economy. It also had the effect of curtailing the power of the *gamonales* who had heretofore maintained the upper hand in disputes with the *comunidades* and the peasantry.

Second, in mid-1920 Leguía established a governmental commission to investigate the causes and to propose remedies for the upsurge in peasant unrest in the south. That unrest had produced over 7,000 formal complaints to the authorities from disgruntled peasants in the region since 1917, over 6,000 of which were related to land disputes. When the commissioners arrived in the province of Azángaro in Puno, they were met by "8,000 Indians in military formation and carrying sticks and a few guns," ready to present their grievances (Jacobsen, 1993, p. 345). Encouraged by the government's response to their struggles, which raised their expectations for concrete change, the peasants began to organize politically to promote their cause. In June 1920, migrants from the highlands founded the Comité Central Pro-Derecho Indígena "Tahuantinsuyo" in Lima, with branches in the *altiplano*, which was immediately given official recognition by the government. Over the next two years, national congresses called by the Comité Central met and passed a series of reform proposals: the establishment of schools and medical services in communities and haciendas, the return of community lands, improved wages and working conditions for *colonos* (tenant farmers) on haciendas, the separation of Church and state, new local authorities chosen by the communities, and the abolition of compulsory labor for the construction of roads (recently introduced by Leguía). According to Jacobsen (1993, p. 346), "this reformist program was packaged in redemptionist discourse containing both millenarian and anarcho-syndicalist elements." It was then disseminated to the communities by delegates who returned from the congresses with *indigenista* literature that was read aloud at community meetings.

The prevailing view among historians of this cycle of protest and rebellion in the southern highlands between 1915 and 1924 is that they were essentially spontaneous, uncoordinated millenarian movements, with vague, impractical, and largely unattainable goals (Burga and Flores Galindo). However, the revisionist view stated by Jacobsen (1993) seems more persuasive, namely, that the peasants were often highly organized, established tactical "outside" alliances, and promoted a practical political agenda that they cloaked in the unifying millenarian language of "the reestablishment of Tahuantinsuyo." Indeed, the peasants' program largely coincided with that of their middle-class *indigenista* allies. For example, the ability of the Comité Central to organize at the national level reflected similar efforts at the local level by the peasants to organize politically to defend their interests. Thus, the Indians of Toccroyoc, in the province of Espinar in Cuzco, which purportedly had the largest Indian population in the entire Andean area, organized intensely in 1920–21 under the leadership of

Domingo Huarca. Their aim was to break free from the commercial wool monopoly established by merchants and the authorities in the provincial capital Yauri, as well as to defend themselves against the abuses of the *gamonales*.

Soon the Leguía government became alarmed over signs of spreading peasant mobilization and militancy of the peasants, which in some cases were beginning to degenerate into acts of violence. These incidents included the sacking and setting on fire of various haciendas, in which estate *colonos* also took part. As a result, fearing that the movement was becoming more threatening to the established order, the president began to retreat from his pro-Indian policies and anti-*gamonal* actions.

The climax of the peasant movement occurred in late 1923 in the community of Huancho in the province of Huancané in Puno. In an effort to break free from the prevailing *gamonal*-controlled patterns of wool commercialization, the *comuneros* of Huancho tried to boycott the urban market in Huancané and to establish their own market. This idea caught on in other communities in both Huancané and Azángaro provinces, where peasant producers moved to set up their own "autonomous" markets. Confrontations with the authorities escalated until the peasants finally organized an attack on the town of Huancané, the capital of the province. The attack was repelled by the town's inhabitants and was then followed by ruthless repression organized by the authorities and the army. In the end, perhaps 2,000 community peasants died in the two provinces.

The repression at Huancané had the effect, along with improving economic conditions brought about by the recovery of wool prices after 1923, of quieting the peasants' militancy throughout the *altiplano*. Even though banditry and cattle rustling became endemic forms of social protest in the region for some time to come, the peasantry remained largely quiescent in the face of the resurgence of *gamonal* power. They did so even when Leguía fell from power in 1930 and populist forces, led by the APRA Party, challenged oligarchical power in the early 1930s. After Huancané, Leguía's "official *indigenismo*" degenerated into hollow rhetoric, and the status quo ante of law, order, and social control generally returned to the Andean countryside for at least another generation until the 1960s. In the meantime, the Leguía administration pressed ahead with its program to modernize the country. Opening Peru's economy in an unprecedented way to American capital, loans, and technical know-how, Leguía not only provided highly favorable facilities for American companies, but lavished praise on North American institutions and life.

In addition to hiring U.S. financial experts, Leguía brought North American specialists to Peru to revamp the educational system, reorganize the navy, reform the tax bureau, establish a school of aviation, improve urban hygiene and sanitation, manage automobile traffic in Lima, administer the Agricultural Bank, reform the secret service, and plan large-scale irrigation works. He declared that "my hope is to put an American in charge of every branch of our government's activities" (quoted in Drake, 1989, p. 217). Such was the extent of Leguía's Yankeephilia that he ordered a portrait of President James Madison hung in the presidential palace and actually declared July fourth, a national holiday in honor of the United States.

With the advice of this legion of American advisers, Leguía instituted a plethora of new laws that were designed to streamline public administration and the economy. New codes were written to modernize commerce, mining, and agricultural activities, accompanied by new banking, budgetary, tax, and customs legislation. The Central Reserve Bank, the first such institution of its kind in South America, was created in 1922 and was modeled after the U.S. Federal Reserve system.

In addition to streamlining public administration, Leguía sought to modernize and rationalize Lima, which had become, since the turn of the century, a thriving commercial, bureaucratic, and industrial city. The fact that the centennial of the country's independence (1821) and anniversary of the Battle of Ayacucho (1824) would occur during his administration, spurred Leguía's program of urban modernization. The Foundation Company, a North American construction concern, was contracted to widen and pave the city's main streets and avenues. The new traffic grid accommodated the increasing number of automobiles in the city and led to the development of the first outlying suburbs, where the construction of middle- and upper-class housing boomed. At the same time, the city's old center was cleaned up, and many dilapidated buildings, both public and private, were torn down and replaced by new ones. As a result, Lima was transformed during the *Oncenio* into a beautiful, modern city, one of the most impressive in all of South America, with wide boulevards, spacious parks, and elegant shops and hotels. It became a showplace not only to celebrate the centennial of independence, but to attract the foreign investors and entrepreneurs on whom the administration was counting for an economic boost. At the same time, the boom in urban construction and employment spurred the local economy. Big contracts were let out to Leguía's friends and cronies, and construction jobs opened up to a large number of migrants from the provinces who were attracted to the capital by the prospects of higher wages and living standards.

The transformation of Lima was accompanied by a concerted effort to improve the country's chronically limited transportation system. In 1920 the administration passed a law, known as the *Conscripción Vial*, which required all men aged eighteen to sixty to work six to twelve days each year on the national road system. As a result of this and other measures, the number of kilometers of roads built during the *Oncenio* almost doubled, from 10,643 in 1926 to 19,465 in 1930. Improved communications to the interior not only helped the central government expand its reach into remote areas and extend its authority as never before, but accelerated the pace of trade and commerce in the interior. Some progressive *hacendados* took advantage of the rising demand for and better access to markets by expanding their borders at the expense of neighboring communities to bring more land under production and by taking steps to modernize and rationalize their operations. Their actions often resulted in the dislocation and proletarization of their *colonos*, who lost their traditional pregrogatives in the old paternalistic regimen.

Indian communities were not immune to these changes. Increasing commercial opportunities, along with growing population pressures, accelerated the process of economic and social differentiation inside the communities. The upshot was greater social stratification, polarization, and class conflict. Rich traders and market-oriented peasants emerged alongside poor, landless laborers and worker peasants who were pushed or pulled into the wider labor market (mines, estates, towns, road and rail construction and the like).

The expansion and modernization of estates, with such attendant social dislocation, had actually been under way in the central highlands since before World War I. There the Lima-based Olavegoya group, for example, purchased estates that they consolidated and rationalized into large-scale production to meet the growing demand for sheep and cattle products in Lima and the mining centers. The Olavegoya group, whose *sociedades ganaderas* were among the most successful joint-stock companies on the Lima Stock Exchange between 1910 and 1930, was an example of the developing capitalism and entrepreneurship that Leguía encouraged at both the regional and national levels.

A similar process of modernization was carried out by the powerful Fernandini family and the Ganadera de Cerro de Pasco, the latter a division of the American copper mining company that sought to provision its growing workforce. The Ganadera acquired some thirty haciendas, covering 270,000 hectares (1,057 square miles) in the region. Indeed, the growth and concentration of mining operations opened up a large potential market for provisioning by nearby estates and propelled the development of capitalism in the interior.

As might be expected with the expansion of the transportation system and the dislocations occuring in rural society, an increasing number of people were on the move during the *Oncenio*—to the mines and coastal plantations, but most of all to the dynamic and glittering capital. Some 65,000 *provincianos* moved to Lima between 1919 and 1931, amounting to 19 percent of the city's inhabitants. The migrants came from all social strata, including the middle- and lower middle classes, their transition and adjustment often facilitated by family and kinship ties with those already established in Lima. Many regional associations, composed of *provincianos* from the same town or province and numbering forty-four in 1928, received the newcomers and provided a new set of social relations to replace the complex network of relations that they had left behind in the countryside.

The flow of migrants from the interior poured into a city that was already undergoing an intense process of "massification," that is, the emergence of the popular classes into the life and public spaces of the city, heretofore dominated and monopolized by the elites. Since the masses had already burst onto the political scene during the previous decade, their emergence during the 1920s took on more of a cultural aspect. One particularly salient example was the transformation and popularization of sports, specifically soccer (football), from a predominantly elite leisure pastime at the turn of the century to one taken over by *Limeño* subalterns by the end of World War I.

Soccer had been introduced into the port of Callao by English sailors in the 1880s. From a sport played mostly by the small British colony in Lima, it, like most things European, was quickly assimilated by the elites whose sporting clubs began fielding organized soccer teams, along with those for polo, cricket, and the like. It was not long, however, before workers took up the game, first, in Callao among steveadors and sailors, and then in the various working-class *barrios* and factories of Lima. Moreover, an increasing number of soccer clubs sprang up over the next couple of decades, not only spontaneously in the workplace and neighborhoods as expressions of working-class culture that, among other things, fostered solidarity and cohesion, but also sponsored and organized by factory owners and managers as elite mechanisms of social control. In this sense, "football constituted a true barometer of Lima society which was in all aspects in full process of massification" (quoted in Stein, 1986, vol. I, p. 141).

By the 1920s, the sport's popularity had grown immensely and was becoming increasingly professionalized, as indicated by the opening of the recently constructed National Stadium, the extraordinary expansion of coverage in the press, and the appearance of an intense rivalry between Alianza Lima and Universitario de Deportes. Alianza was composed of players from the black, working-class *barrio* of La Victoria, while Universitario, as the name suggests, included mainly university students from middle- and upper-class backgrounds. The ensuing titanic competition between the two teams, consumed avidly by inhabitants of the city, can be interpreted as a symbolic playing out on the soccer pitch of the class conflicts that were increasingly dividing Peruvian society.

At the same time, the huge acceptance of Alianza by the *Limeño* public in the 1920s occurred in the context of the adoption of the Afro-Peruvian *marinera* as the national dance, the popularity of the *décima* rhymes of popular black poets, and even the flourishing of the annual popular religious procession of El Señor de los Milagros. While the latter had pre-Columbian antecedents that went back to Pachacamac, as Rostworowski (1992) showed, it was also promoted as a religious celebration by black Catholic brotherhoods (*cofradías*) among the polyglot working classes. In any case, all may be seen as a valorization of blackness and the unique cultural contributions of the black community, up from slavery. Likewise, they were still another example, along with *indigenismo* and the celebration of El Señor de los Milagros itself, of the increasing assertiveness of popular culture into a public space no longer the exclusive reserve of the *Limeño* elites.

Although Leguía's reformist program and economic growth had opened the way to considerable social change during his first term, the president did little to revise the country's political institutions and mode of governance. Behind a reformist veneer, the president operated like a traditional *caudillo*, organizing his own clientelist political networks and handing out political favors and concessions to the new plutocracy that benefited from his policies. Still, for a time, cloaked in a reformist mantle that gradually disipated, Leguía managed to retain a measure of popularity. This situation abruptly changed with the popular protest stirred by the announcement by Archbishop Emilio Lissón on April 25, 1923, of the administation's plans to consecrate Peru to the Sacred Heart of Jesus in a public ceremony presided over by the president as "Patron of the Church."

Ever since independence and the advent of the republic, the Church had been exposed to periodic attacks from civil society. Its hierarchical, authoritarian, corporatist, and paternalistic structure mirrored the old colonial order that had now formally collapsed and was in the process of slow disintegration. At the same time, as the forces of modern capitalism intensified, driven by the midcentury guano boom, the Church found itself more and more at odds with the growing secularization of society.

One manifestation of this trend was the steady decline in the number of Peruvians who entered the priesthood as the century wore on. Long seen as a desirable haven that provided a comfortable and respectable life to members of the middle and upper classes, the clerical vocation was increasingly avoided by young people, who found greater opportunities in the expanding capitalist sector of society. As a result, by the turn of the twentieth century, the Church faced a growing shortfall of qualified Peruvian priests, illustrated by the fact that 17 percent of the priests in 1900 were foreign born.

In the political realm, the liberal reforms of the first half of the nineteenth century had culminated in the republican state's successful assumption of the *patronato real* (now *patronato nacional*), which reestablished its control over the Church. As it became increasingly subservient to the state *and* the forces of secularization advanced, the Church more and more adopted a defensive and conservative posture. This tendency grew stronger under the anticlerical onslaught of González Prada after the War of the Pacific, while among the positivist civilist intellectuals and elites, antireligiosity (and racism) became broadly fashionable. To combat these secular forces that were arrayed against it, the Church evinced, beginning in the 1860s and lasting down through the *Oncenio*, a growing spirit of militancy in which it tried to mobilize its forces—clerical and lay—to defend and protect its position in society (Klaiber, 1992).

It was in this context that Archbishop Lissón, an outspoken conservative, a promoter of Catholic Action (militant pro-Catholic lay groups), and a strong defender of the Church orchestrated the dedication ceremony to the Sacred Heart. The ceremony was timed to be followed by the order's annual public procession, which had become the offical expression of the Church militant. However, to many, Lissón's proposal seemed to be a blatant political attempt by the regime to influence the Catholic vote in behalf of Leguía's unconstitutional bid for reelection to a second term. It also stirred longstanding anticlerical sentiments in liberal and progressive circles. A massive protest of the archbishop's announcement was quickly organized by Haya de la Torre, the veteran leader of the 1918–19 worker-student mobilization for the eight-hour day and university reform movement.

Profiting politically from his leadership roles in these movements, Haya de la Torre had managed to win the presidency of the Federación Estudiantil Peruano in October 1919. One of his first acts was to organize a national congress that met in Cuzco in early 1920 and passed a series of progressive resolutions, the most notable of which was the proposal to create so-called *universidades populares* (UPs), whose purpose was fundamentally to consolidate the worker-student alliance of 1918–19. These student-run popular universities would provide various educational and social services to the workers, aimed at raising their overall level of culture and thus realize the anarchist ideal of true freedom and emancipation of the proletariat. The first UPs were inaugurated by Haya in January 1921 in Lima and the nearby textile manufacturing town of Vitarte.

The UPs became enormously successful, attracting as many as 1,000 working men and women at one event alone in Lima in 1923. By that time, numerous UPs had also sprung up in several provincial cities. In addition to a wide variety of night classes taught by students, numerous cultural events were organized to raise the workers' civic and national consciousness, including literary-musical homages to the Incas, various temperance campaigns, and student-worker "friendship" picnics in the woods around Vitarte. A year after they were founded, the UPs were renamed in honor of González Prada (now called UPGPs), something the founders had avoided initially for fear of unduly rankling the authorities. For although the expressed purposes of the UPGPs were cultural and educational, with many student-teachers harboring left-wing political orientations, a political dimension was hardly absent.

After Archbishop Lissón's announcement of the forthcoming Sacred Heart ceremony, Haya and the UPGPs immediately sprang into action and became the focal point of opposition to the event. After drawing up a "declaration of principles" at a public meeting at San Marcos, which focused mainly on anticlerical demands for ecclesiastical reform, the movement's leaders led several thousand demonstrators on May 23 in a march to the Plaza de Armas. There they were confronted by mounted police, and a clash ensued in which two protesters and three policemen were killed. This march was followed two days later by a funeral procession for the two "martyred" demonstrators at which Haya delivered an electrifying funeral oration. Fearing that the protest demonstrations would galvanize wider opposition to Leguía's reelection, Lissón decided to suspend the proposed ceremony, declaring that the projected consecration of the nation to the Sacred Heart of Jesus had been "turned into an arm against the legitimately established government and social institutions" (quoted in Klaiber, 1977, p. 133). Haya, whose popular reputation had soared as a result of the protests, now went into hiding. He was finally arrested in October and sent into exile, clearing the way for Leguía to "arrange" his reelection a year later.

Mariátegui, Haya, and the New Left

With the exile of the activist Haya in 1923, the leadership of the Peruvian Left and its intellectual center of gravity shifted to the figure of José Carlos Mariátegui, who had only recently returned from a four-year exile in Europe. In 1919 Mariátegui had accepted a government stipend to go abroad, a move ostensibly undertaken by Leguía to remove one of the most prominent critics of his new government. Mariátegui's first stop was Paris, where he became intoxicated with his initial contact with contemporary European culture and politics.

From Paris Mariátegui journeyed to Italy, where he was to remain for most of his exile, partly because its benign climate was beneficial to his delicate health. In Rome he met and married Anna Chiappa and became an acute observer of Italian politics, as reflected in his "Cartas de Italia," which relates the rise of fascism, the splintering of the Italian Left, and the founding of the Communist Party of Italy. At the same time, he was reading, among others, Benedetto Crose, Karl Marx, and Georges Sorel. Meeting in Genoa with three fellow Peruvians in 1922, Mariátegui and his compatriots determined to form the first Peruvian Communist cell.

The brilliant, young, autodidactic journalist was now set on his life's mission to develop the worker movement in Peru and to form a Marxist party, for it was in Europe that Mariátegui profoundly deepened his political commitment to socialism and revolutionary Marxism. Moreover, his entire European experience served to broaden his vision of the world, bringing him into contact with the major intellectual and political currents of the times. At the same time, Europe provided the young Marxist with a unique perspective from which to view the problems of Peru and Latin America. As he put it, "we discovered, in the end, our own tragedy, that of Peru. The European itinerary has been for us the best, the most tremendous discovery of America" (quoted in Vanden, 1986, p. 120). Finally, as Basadre noted, as a result of his European sojourn, Mariátegui made the transformation from journalist to theorist and *pensador* (public intellectual).

Back in Peru in November 1923, Mariátegui's house on Washington Street, dubbed the *"rincón rojo,"* or red corner, in downtown Lima immediately became a discursive beehive for the country's leading students, labor activists, politicians, and intellectuals. Here Mariátegui's penchant for initiating communal dialogue and polemical debate emerged, something that would later characterize his remarkable journal *Amauta*, founded in 1926. In addition to bringing this intellectual effervescence to his classes at the UPGPs, Mariátegui plunged back into journalism.

About a year after his return to Peru, however, he fell ill once again, apparently suffering a recurrence of his childhood form of tuberculosis, which necessitated the amputation of his right leg. Now relegated permanently to a wheelchair, Mariátegui rebounded from temporary depression to devote himself passionately to writing, reading, and studying. His first book, entitled *La escena contemporanea*, was published in 1925 to highly favorable reviews, and a year later he embarked on the publishing enterprise that would bring him lasting fame, as editor of *Amauta* which means Inca wise man or teacher in Quechua.

Amauta was a journal of political and literary commentary that contained a broad diversity of themes, all oriented to the editor's socialist perspective. Contributors included not only the progressive stars of the generation of 1919, but such world figures as Henri Barbusse, Miguel de Unamuno, and Diego Rivera. The fame of *Amauta* became continental in scope and even reached across the Atlantic to Europe. The journal was to become, in Mariátegui's words, "the voice of a movement and of a generation" (quoted in Walker, 1986, p. 84).

Walker identifies three major themes in the pages of *Amauta* and in Mariátegui's other writings that have been collected and translated in his *Seven Interpretive Essays on Peruvian Reality* (1971). They were *indigenismo*, Marxism, and nationalism. *Indigenismo* incorporated a diverse and heterogeneous content that ranged from a defense of Indian culture and society—both past and present—to integration of the Indians into the nation to the underlying causes of the exploitation and discrimination of Indians. Having blossomed in the provinces (Cuzco, Puno, Trujillo and Arequipa), as well as in Lima, its impact in the capital was reinforced, as I said, by the large influx of migrants from the interior during the *Oncenio*.

As literary historian Antonio Cornejo Polar has shown, the major portion of the *indigenista* literary and artistic production in Lima was carried out by members of the provincial lower middle class residing in the capital, many of whom had family ties in the interior. In this view, *indigenismo* represented a serious critique of Peruvian society by young provincial intellectuals who denounced the arrogant and exploitative *gamonal* class that dominated their hometowns and regions. These provincial intellectuals not only brought a new sympathetic outlook on the Indians to the capital, but their radicalism was intensified by the hostile, discriminatory reception that they received at the hands of the city's traditional Europeanized elites.

Mariátegui proposed an Andean version of socialism as a prescription for Peru's problems. He wrote:

> Socialism orders and defines the revindication of the masses, of the working class. And in Peru the masses—the working class—is four-fifths Indian. Our socialism will not be, then, Peruvian or even socialism if it does not primarily identify (*solidarizarse*) with indigenous revindications. (Mariátegui, quoted in Walker, 1986, p. 83).

For Mariátegui, Peru was an underdeveloped, primarily agrarian country with a majority of its population located in the rural Andean interior and with a small and relatively weak industrial sector and working class. Thus, in the pages of *Amauta*, Mariátegui featured a broad range of indigenous themes—the Inca past, Indian conditions, and their current struggles. According to Flores Galindo, "without the expression of *indigenista* poets and essayists and without the peasant uprisings in the South, Mariátegui's Marxism would have lacked an essential characteristic—its challenge to progress, that is its rejection of a lineal and Eurocentric view of history" (quoted in Walker, 1986, p. 83).

The final theme in Mariátegui's work, the defining preoccupation of the generation of 1919, was how Peru, a geographically fragmented, ethnically diverse, and class-divided country, could consolidate itself as a nation. This debate over the "national question" during the 1920s, which can be readily followed in the pages of *Amauta*, was soon joined by the Right in the person of Víctor Andrés Belaúnde (1883–1966), who challenged a number of Mariátegui's assertions in *Siete Ensayos*.

Born in Arequipa of middle-class background at the end of the War of the Pacific, Belaúnde was strongly influenced by the White City's more socially fluid, democratic, and regionalist ethos that stood in marked contrast to the oligarchy of the north coast or seignorial southern highlands. He was also a devoted Catholic, having been steeped in the Catholic traditions of his family, the city, and his religiously grounded education. After graduating from San Marcos University in 1901, where he was influenced by positivism, he went on to have a distinguished career in teaching and diplomacy. In 1914 he received acclaim from a public lecture he gave at San Marcos entitled the "Present Crisis." In this lecture and his writings, he envisioned the regeneration of the country by the middle class, decried the exploitation of the Indians, and called for their protection by the state. An outspoken critic of Leguía, he was exiled in 1921.

Belaúnde's rejoinder to Mariátegui appeared in *La realidad nacional*, which he published in 1930 as a Christian counterpoint to the Marxist exegesis in *Siete ensayos*. Belaúnde agreed with Mariátegui's analysis in a number of areas, such as the pernicious influence of Lima and the northern oligarchy in the country's development, the need for political and economic decentralization, and the importance of religion in Peruvian life. On the other hand, he criticized the author of *Siete ensayos* for polarizing the country's Spanish and Indian heritage, extolling the Indian over the mestizo, and reducing the problem of the Indian exclusively to land and its solution via collectivization. Peru's problems were founded not just on class, he contended, but on culture and race, and Catholic religious practices among the natives were not simply superficial, counterproductive, and expendable, but a deep spiritually grounded faith.

In contrast, Belaúnde energetically defended the Church and its historical project of converting and protecting the Indians, as well as the country's Catholic, Spanish heritage. At the same time, the synthesis produced from the fusion of the two races formed the basis, in his view, for unifying the country, particularly in psychological and spiritual terms. The Indian problem, moreover, could be solved by education, limited land reform (expropriation of unproductive estates), and perhaps cooperativization, which was closer to Andean communal traditions. Overall, Peru needed to achieve a blending of the best of Western culture and politics with that of Catholic medieval, corporative traditions. In short, Belaúnde advocated a kind of social democracy and corporatism for Peru, not Soviet collectivism or oligarchical capitalism.

Meanwhile, Leguía continued his version of nation building by centralizing the power of the state; expanding its reach through an ambitious road-building program; and encouraging the flow of foreign, particularly North American, trade, capital, expertise, and culture. From 1924 to 1928, for example, Peru received over $130 million in loans, more than ten times that of the previous five years.

While earlier in his administration Leguía had struggled to persuade international lenders to open their pockets to Peru, New York banks, now flush with capital during the Roaring Twenties, began to compete furiously to float loans throughout Latin America. Funds poured into finance new railroad construction; irrigation; sanitation; and, most controversially, the questionable practice of canceling the internal debt (by substituting foreign debt) whose servicing alone required substantial foreign exchange, thereby creating future problems. Spurred by favorable assessments of Peru's economic stability and encouraged by the State Department, two of the largest banks in the U.S., J. and W. Seligman and National City Bank, collaborated in floating $100 million in loans to Peru in 1927 and 1928. Ignoring warnings from, among others, the president of Peru's Central Reserve Bank, the banks threw caution to the winds in a veritable "dance of the millions."

This torrent of foreign loans coincided with an influx of foreign imports and an increase in consumption by the emerging and increasingly prosperous urban middle classes, who also adopted foreign values and culture. In Lima, for example, exotic cafés, horse racing and gambling, and the exclusive sport of golf all proliferated, as did numerous bilingual high schools, such as the Anglo-Peruano where the children of the well-off and newly rich learned English and American or British values. The outcome of this orgy of foreign consumption was an inevitable nationalist, often anti-American, backlash that gathered momentum as the decade wore on.

Finally, Leguía's determined efforts to resolve a series of longstanding and sensitive border disputes contributed to a growing nationalist criticism of his regime. For example, the Solomón-Lozano Treaty of 1922, which established the Putumayo River as the northern boundary with Colombia, seemed to favor that country and was extremely unpopular in Peru. Equally contentious was the festering dispute over the ultimate disposition of the provinces of Tacna and Arica, which Chile had seized from Peru in the War of the Pacific. When an agreement between the two nations to hold a plebescite in the disputed provinces to decide their fate was announced in 1925, such was the nationalist reaction that it provoked a general strike, a student riot, and a mob attack on the U.S. Embassy in protest against American mediation of the dispute. Even though the plebescite was never carried out, a chance meeting of diplomats from the two countries on board a ship traveling to an inter-American conference resulted in renewed negotiations and an unexpected final agreement. According to the Treaty of Lima in 1929, the disputed provinces were divided between the two countries, Tacna going to Peru and Arica to Chile, along with $6 million and port facilities for Peru in the Bay of Arica. Again the Leguía regime's compromise resolution of the Tacna-Arica dispute angered nationalists, including Mariátegui, who expressed his outrage in the pages of *Amauta*.

While Mariátegui infused the pages of *Amauta* with the progressive nationalist, indigenista, and Marxist themes of the period, he also used the journal as a forum for organizing the working class. Perhaps because he did or because he published an issue of *Amauta* devoted to the theme of imperialism, *Amauta* was closed and Mariátegui was arrested in June 1927 by the authorities on the trumpted-up charge of conspiring in an alleged plot to overthrow the Leguía government. An international outcry by prominent intellectuals, however, forced his release from jail after six months, and *Amauta* was allowed to resume publication in early 1928.

That same year marked an important split between Mariátegui and Haya de la Torre—both of whom sought in their own ways to adapt and shape Marxism to Peruvian reality. Haya had been sent into exile after he had led the fight against the dictator's attempt in 1923 to have the Church consecrate Peru (and, by implication, his regime) to the Sacred Heart of Jesus. After stopping briefly in Panama and Cuba, where he made strong anti-Leguía and antiimperialist declarations, Haya arrived in Mexico, where he lived for a while on a stipend from the Ministry of Education, headed by the sympathetic José Vasconcelos.

The following year, Haya proclaimed the formation of the Alianza Popular Revolucionaria Americana (APRA), a continent-wide youth movement directed against the expansion of North American imperialism. Before an assembly of the National Federation of Students in Mexico City on May 7, 1924, the twenty-nine-year-old Haya unfurled the red flag of APRA, imprinted with the golden map of Latin America or Indo-America, as he referred to it. The latter expressed Haya's strong *indigenista* sentiment, shaped by his growing up near the fabled pre-Columbian ruins of Chan-Chan and a 1917 eye-opening trip to Cuzco, in a country where *indigenismo*, under Vasconcelos's aegis, had become the official governing policy after the revolution of 1910. In announcing the formation of APRA in Mexico, Haya was also implicitly identifying his fledgling movement with the ideals of the Mexican Revolution.

Two years after the formation of APRA in Mexico, Haya published the official program of the movement in an article in the *Labour Monthly* (1926), entitled "What Is the APRA?" In it, he outlined what became the celebrated five points of APRA: action against Yankee imperialism, political unity of Latin America, nationalization of lands and industry, internationalization of the Panama Canal, and solidarity of all oppressed peoples and classes of the world.

In the meantime, the young Peruvian had traveled to England, where he addressed students at Oxford University and then to the Soviet Union, where he attended the World Congress of Communist Youth, which was being held in conjunction with the Fifth World Congress of the Third International. His travels at this time, as throughout his exile, were financially supported by an American benefactress named Ana Melina Graves, whom Haya had befriended while working as a teacher at the Colegio Anglo-Peruano in Lima. In Russia, Haya learned much that would be useful in developing his political ideas and tactics. He was impressed with the towering figure of Leon Trotsky not only as an intellectual but as a man of action, as well as with the fervor with which Russian youths had embraced communism, almost as a religious faith with strong mystical and moral strains. Later Haya would similarly seek to harness the religious energies of Peruvians, expressed through the Church and in certain popular religious forms, for his own political ends and those of his APRA Party.

In the end, although borrowing liberally from Marxism-Leninism, Haya chose to remain independent of international communism and to control his own Indo-American movement. The break with the Third International came in 1927 at the Anti-Imperialist Congress at Brussels. There he refused to sign a declaration condemning all imperialism, based on his belief that imperialism was the first, rather than the last, stage of capitalism. This inversion of Marxist-Leninist doctrine was necessary, according to Haya, because underdeveloped countries needed to acquire the investment, skills, and technology that would enable them to progress to the next stage of capitalism, which would then open the way for the great socialist transformation. Such ideological heresy proved anathema to Moscow and led the following year to a break with Mariátegui over the "correct" revolutionary course for Peru.

The rupture was precipitated by Haya's announcement in January 1928 in Mexico, on his way back home, of his candidacy for the presidency of Peru as the head of a new party called the Partido Nacionalista Libertador, supposedly already operating in Peru. Adopting the old anarchist slogan of land and liberty (*tierra y libertad*) the new party called for the union of all working peoples—that is, a cross-class alliance of workers, peasants, intellectuals, and the middle classes. It also espoused a radical, antioligarchical program that included land for those who worked it, abolition of laws favoring *gamonalismo* (rule by local bosses and oligarchs), anti-imperialism, and economic independence.

When news of the new party arrived in Lima, it was roundly condemned by Mariátegui, who saw it as an opportunistic ploy to promote Haya's political ambitions by a handful of intellectuals, with no roots or grounding in the masses. Indeed, Mariátegui likened it to the kind of old conspiratorial creole politics (*política criolla*) associated with the old regime that he and the

Left condemned and hoped to do away with. But Mariátegui's criticism of Haya's tactics did not stop there; it went on to reveal deep ideological discrepancies.

Haya's conception of Peru had emerged in a collection entitled *Por la emancipación de la América Latina: Artículos, mensajes, discursos, 1923–1927*, published in Buenos Aires in 1927. Haya saw Peru as essentially a feudal country, dominated by the landed *gamonal* class, with a weak industrial base so that neither a national bourgeoisie nor a proletariat had sufficiently formed. Capitalism was not developing internally, but, rather, was brought to Peru through the worldwide expansion of imperialism. Consequently, the main problem in Peru was "national," rather than class, in nature. That is, foreign imperialism oppressed a wide array of classes, particularly the middle sectors that were just now beginning to redefine the nation. Thus, for Haya, nationalism, not class conflict, was the crucial variable in any future revolutionary transformation, as he believed it had been in the Mexican Revolution and in the formation of the Kuomintang of Chiang Kai-shek in China.

For Haya, socialism was not immediately possible in Peru. Rather, imperialism, the first stage of capitalism in Peru, which brought needed capital and investment, must be encouraged, but its oppressive, negative impact could be ameliorated by what Haya called the anti-imperialist state. Such a state would be capable of negotiating the terms of capitalist expansion in Peru, so that the necessary factors of production advanced, but not at the expense of the popular classes. Drawing on his experience in Trujillo, Haya saw the middle classes as particularly vulnerable to the dislocative and absorptive impact of foreign corporations (sugar, mining, and petroleum), unlike the workers in these industries, who generally made the highest wages in Peru.

Alongside a strong state sector, Haya advocated the "cooperativization" of agroindustries, such as sugar, and a private sector led by national industry and commerce. The political base of support for Haya's anti-imperialist state would be a popular front, or cross-class alliance of peasants, workers, intellectuals, and the middle classes. Haya envisioned that the leadership of this alliance would be drawn from the middle classes, not only because they were more numerous and better educated, but because the working class was still minuscule and culturally backward.

Mariátegui, on the other hand, saw Peru in a fundamentally different way than did Haya. He believed that capitalism had been slowly developing in Peru since the guano age. Imperialism in its monopoly stage was not only contributing to this advance, but was the fundamental cause of what he called Peru's semicolonial condition. The only way to defeat colonialism and imperialism was not through the construction of some anti-imperialist state, as Haya envisioned, but by adopting socialism.

More important, Mariátegui rejected the idea that Peru's transformation could be led by the petit bourgeoisie, a role that only the working class, he believed, could assume. Here, according to Meseguer, Mariátegui drew on his experience in Europe, where he had seen the revolutionary posture of the middle classes degenerate into the political base for the rise of fascism.

As for the expansion of the middle sectors in Peru during the *Oncenio*, Mariátegui saw them as fundamentally avid consumers of imperialism, both materially and culturally, hardly the stuff on which to build or lead a national liberation movement. Finally, he believed that they were too heterogeneous to form the necessary class solidarity to carry out a truly socialist revolution. Only the working class, broadly defined as workers and peasants, authentically rooted in the national culture and organized in its own socialist party could, in his view, develop the unity and consciousness to carry out such a grand transformation. In Peru, the vague outlines of such a worker-peasant vanguard was already to be found in the mining sector, where peasant migrants were drawn to work in the mines for wages and many were eventually proletarized into a permanent workforce.

Haya and other Apristas (members of APRA), trying to stake out an authentically nationalist position on the Peruvian Left, attacked Mariátegui's ideas as excessively "theoretical" and "Europeanist." However, in reality Maríategui was hardly dogmatic in his embrace of Marxism and communism, as Burga and Flores Galindo (1978, p. 192) pointed out. For him, the task was to wed Marxism to the unique historical conditions of the Andes by integrating the ideas of *indigenismo*, and drawing on the experience of collectivism implicit in Peru's Incaic past (the *ayllu*, for example), as well as on the struggle for the eight-hour day and the Indian peasant uprisings of Atusparia and Rumi Maqui. This creative melding of the Andean experience and Marxism brought Mariátegui into conflict with the strict Communist orthodoxy of the Third International.

The final break between Haya and Mariátegui came in 1928. It was precipitated by an editorial by Mariátegui in the September issue of *Amauta* in which he outlined his differences with Haya and took the opportunity to redefine *Amauta*'s aims and goals in an avowedly class-based and socialist organ. This shift coincided with his founding in 1928 of the new Socialist Party of Peru, which adhered to the Third International (his previous conflicts with the organization having been ameliorated) and sought to solidify its ties to the labor movement. Under the leadership of Mariátegui, the new party undertook to unite labor in a truly national labor union, the Confederación General de Trabajadores del Perú (General Confederation of Peruvian Workers). Mariátegui's increasing activism, however, put an added strain on his precarious health, which began to deteriorate rapidly as the decade of the 1920s drew to a close. He died on April 16, 1930, at the age of thirty-five, apparently from a staphylococcic infection while being treated in the hospital.

Economic Weakness and the Onset of the Depression

Mariátegui's death came almost four months before the military overthrew Leguía in August 1930. The main cause of the dictator's demise lay in the highly precarious and vulnerable state of the Peruvian economy in 1929 when the American stock market crashed, ushering in the worldwide depression. Having borrowed heavily from abroad to fund his Patria Nueva, Peru's "dance of the millions" now came to an abrupt end.

A sectoral examination of the economy during the *Oncenio* further reveals the artificial nature of the country's seeming prosperity at that time. The agroexport sector, which had been the key to growth since 1900, slowed after World War I. At the same time, the mining sector, although advancing, was almost completely taken over by foreign companies, with the result that profits were remitted abroad, and returned value and therefore capital reinvestment and accumulation remained low. As for agroexports, such as sugar, cotton, and wool—the mainstays of the export-led growth from 1900 to 1920—they stagnated during the 1920s and provided little reinvestment to sustain internal demand.

In the case of sugar, the war-induced bonanza of the 1910s had led producers erroneously to reinvest their profits to double the capacity in anticipation of a continuing boom in demand and prices abroad for their product. In the event, the exact opposite occurred, and world capacity soon produced an oversupply that caused prices to enter a decade-long slump. The ensuing squeeze on profits in Peru caused the industry to consolidate further and concentrate along the north coast. At the same time, capital accumulation and reinvestment remained weak, and the planters' influence on national politics waned. All this had a particularly negative impact on the regional economy of the north coast and led to the rise, as you shall see, of the radical APRA Party.

As sugar declined, many planters in the center and south switched to cotton which in the early 1920s experienced an export bonanza, because of the boll-weevil plague that struck American production in 1920. This switch to cotton coincided with the introduction of the new high-quality, disease-resistant variety of cotton pioneered by Pisco grower Fermin Tangüis and of pima cotton from the U.S. by a local Piura merchant named Emilio Hilbck in 1918. Exports to the U.S. boomed until 1925, when the U.S. boll-weevil plague abated, and severe flooding along the coast in 1926, caused by the climatic effects of El Niño, wiped out the Peruvian cotton crop and otherwise adversely effected coastal agricultural productivity. Cotton now entered the same conundrum that sugar had encountered in 1920, although its returned value owing to local ownership and the rising employment of workers (from 21,000 in 1916 to 41,000 in 1923) remained substantial. However, in both industries, the decline in profits was quickly passed on to the worker who suffered, in the case of cotton, a 30 percent decline in real wages between 1916 and 1930.

The collapse of the postwar international wool market, in a similar fashion to sugar, plunged the south of Peru, where wool accounted for 73 percent of exports, into a regional recession, further constraining Peruvian exports during the 1920s. The collapse of the market for wool is illustrated by the per capita earnings of wool exports during the decade that plunged from $362 in 1920 ($139 in the south) to $176 in 1930 ($59 in the south). It is significant that the coup that was to bring down Leguía was mounted from Arequipa in the south, the entrepot of the recessive wool industry. Although less important nationally, the collapse of the rubber industry in the Peruvian Amazon, whose decline began in 1912, was completed in the 1920s. The ensuing depression in the region provoked political unrest, several unsuccessful military revolts against Leguía in Iquitos, and strong support for the new APRA Party in the elections of 1931.

In general terms, the decade of the 1920s, then, saw a move away from cotton, sugar, wool, and rubber production whose values as a percentage of total exports declined. This was a significant shift in the relative composition of exports, since these four cash crops had dominated the value of exports during the first two decades of the century. At the same time, the value of oil and copper exports as a percentage of total exports rose sharply over the same period.

Copper production was greatly enhanced by the construction of a huge new smelter and refinery at La Oroya in the central highlands by the Cerro de Pasco Corporation. After the refinery opened in 1922, the overall level of metal production in the country leaped more than 50 percent. Smaller independent plants were unable to compete, so that Cerro gained complete control over the smelting and refining of all minerals in the region. In addition, Cerro took over the Northern Peru Mining and Smelting Company in the highlands of the department of La Libertad. By 1929, according to Dore (1988, p. 103), these two companies, together with a third U.S. firm, accounted for more than 97 percent of Peru's mineral exports.

Soon after the Oroya refinery's opening, polluting particle emissions from the plant's smokestacks began to damage crops and livestock within a twenty-mile radius. As a result, thirty peasant communities and twenty-eight hacienda owners sued Cerro for damages. This prompted the company, as part of the ensuing settlement, not only to install pollution control devices on its smoke stacks, but to buy up more than 200,000 hectares of land in the region, presumably at bargain prices. Together with its other agricultural holdings, Cerro now became the largest landowner in Peru, and its separate Ranching Division now comprised 325,000 hectares.

By the 1920s, "la Companía," as the Cerro de Pasco Copper Corporation was widely known, had come to dominate virtually every aspect of life in a large portion of the central highlands. Its original extension of the central railroad to its main holdings and subsequent growth and demand for provisioning had opened up the agriculturally rich Mantaro Valley to commercialization and capitalization. At the same time, the company's demand for land and labor had served to proletarianize large sectors of the peasant population. It was not only the largest landowner, but the largest employer in the country. As Dore put it (1988, p. 121), "la Companía" owned virtually everything in its vicinity, from roads, water, and electric power to schools, hospitals, politicians, and priests. Indeed, it even printed and circulated its own script money that it paid to its workers to spend in company stores.

The petroleum industry also experienced sharply increased production during the 1920s, rising tenfold from 3,000 barrels annually in 1920 to 30,000 barrels in 1929. However, although the returned value from profits of the Cerro de Pasco Copper Corporation between 1916 and 1937 were around 50 percent on average, the returned value from oil profits was only only 16 percent of income from 1916 to 1934, or only $1.4 million. The International Petroleum Company (IPC), whose major concession was under a legal cloud on the matter of tax payments for subsoil rights going all the way back to 1824, protected its lucrative position and interests by making payments to various governments, often at times of fiscal crisis. This was the case with Pardo in 1915 and again with Leguía in 1922 when IPC gave him $1 million. In return, the government promulgated a new petroleum law that, among other things, capped royalties at 10 percent on the output of crude oil, acknowledged the long-disputed IPC ownership claims, and exempted IPC from royalty payments on production while freezing its export tax liability for fifty years. This sweetheart agreement produced an understandable outcry from nationalists.

As for the domestic industrial sector of the economy, it continued its long-term decline, begun in 1908. Import substituting industrialization was weak during World War I, and the sector entered a period of stagnation during the 1920s because of the weakening internal demand for domestically produced goods, as opposed to foreign imports that were generally favored by urban consumers. For example, new manufacturing firms between 1918 and 1933 numbered only forty-two, or an increase of 13 percent in fifteen years, and overall employment generally remained flat and actually decreased in textiles. The culprits were a stable exchange rate, declining tariffs, rising domestic inflation, and falling international freight rates, all of which favored imported goods. Moreover, there was, as I noted, little domestic surplus available for investment in manufacturing, either from the weak agroexport sector or the largely foreign-dominated mining sector.

The wage-and-income picture for the 1920s was likewise cloudy. Overall, average wages for the first two decades of the century rose steadily, then sharply during World War I, and reached a peak in 1920, from whence they declined and then stabilized at the middecade. Real wages, however, contracted sharply during the war owing to the initial economic slowdown and then the soaring inflation of the late 1910s. During the 1920s real wages and salaries grew slowly overall, while employment in the export sector decreased. The wartime decline in real incomes had been so great, however, that several occupational groups failed to return to their prewar living standards until the end of the 1920s. Likewise, income inequalities widened during the same period, since only a few persons or groups garnered the lion's share of the expansion of cotton production or were favored by the regime's peculation in governmental spending. This was particularly true in the area of urban improvements. Two foreign firms, the Foundation Co. and Frederick Ley & Co., were the main beneficiaries of the construction boom in Lima, which saw real estate values double in the city between 1921 and 1925 and increase by a factor of five in outlying areas. Political favoritism, corruption, rampant speculation, imports of luxury goods, the flight of capital were the hallmarks of an economy awash in foreign loans and governmental spending. One contemporary observed that these loans

> fictitiously and considerably increased the purchasing power of Peruvians. . . . Every individual who, honestly, or not, but with relative facility, obtained some share of this money, became a larger consumer of what are called the "good things of life" such as jewels, autos, wines, dresses, materials for the construction of their chalets, etc. (quoted in Thorp, 1984, p. 87)

Although Leguía's successful pursuit of foreign loans served to prop up the generally weak economy during much of the decade, it could only succeed for the short term and made Peru extremely vulnerable to any external "shock." The beginning of the end came in late 1928, when American bankers restricted further loans to Peru, finally concluding after numerous warnings that their investments were now jeopardized by excessive governmental spending, waste, and corruption. This assessment coincided with a general shift in investment funds in the United States from foreign bonds to stock equities during the orgy of speculation that led to the October 1929 Wall Street crash, further drying up capital available to Peru and other Latin American countries.

On the matter of governmental corruption and misuse of loan funds, bankers estimated that no more than 30 percent of these funds actually went into public works projects. The rest was consumed by governmental fraud and corruption. Examples abound, many exposed to public light by investigations after Leguía's fall from power. The irrigation project of Olmos was a case in point; enormous governmental sums were expended on land expropriations that advantaged political favorites, including the president's son. Indeed, Juan Leguía was a notorious figure in the administration who used his position to shake down countless foreign companies that were doing business in the country. According to one foreign banker, he tried "to rub up against every foreigner who comes to Peru and tries to do business there, with a view to horning in on any commission or transaction he might get" (quoted in Stallings, 1987, p. 259). One particular payoff amounted to more than $400,000.

When midnight finally struck and the "dance of the millions" finally came to an abrupt end, Leguía and his successors were forced to cut governmental spending dramatically—50 percent between 1929 and 1932—after it had quadrupled in the previous ten years. Without the continuation of foreign loans and the earnings on custom receipts on exports, the government was on the verge of bankruptcy. This situation, in turn, threatened the solvency of the country's banks, which like their foreign counterparts, had engaged in heavy lending to the government. At the same time, the prices of Peru's principal exports, which had actually begun to fall as early as 1926, plummeted after Black Tuesday, causing the dollar value of exports to fall 72 percent from 1929 to 1932 (copper, 69 percent; wool, 50 percent; cotton, 42 percent; and, sugar, 22 percent). Imports also dropped by 50 percent during this period, as consumer purchasing power collapsed because of the devaluation of the national currency, restrictions on credit, and wage cuts and layoffs of workers.

The workers in Lima were particularly hard hit. By November 1931, 25 percent of the city's labor force was unemployed. The heaviest attrition was in construction, which bore the full brunt of the shutdown of public works projects, and whose unemployment rate reached a staggering 70 percent. This heavy attrition tended to have the greatest impact on the city's large number of rural migrants, who were relatively unskilled and employed as laborers in the construction industry. In response, the government urged many of the rural migrants to return to their homes in the interior. By contrast, the more highly skilled workers in the textiles industry experienced only 12 percent unemployment. Layoffs of workers were also dramatic in the previously prosperous mining sector, where employment dropped precipitously from 32,000 miners in 1929 to 14,000 in 1932.

The onset of the depression did not dislocate only the working classes as export products piled up on the docks and internal consumption and production collapsed. The distress of the middle classes was also intense. The income of lawyers, physicians, and other professionals fell sharply, the government bureaucracy went unpaid, the universities were shuttered, and schoolteachers went without pay.

Leguía, like many of his counterparts throughout Latin America, was unable to ride out the political storm that followed in the wake of this economic and social collapse. Seemingly oblivious to the precariousness of his regime, he was seized, on the afternoon of August 25, 1930, by a group of army officers upon his return to the government palace from his customary twice-weekly visits to the race track. The coup was organized by Lieutenant Colonel Luis M. Sánchez Cerro, the commander of the Arequipa garrison. Arriving in Lima four days later, the young army commander was greeted as a "liberator" by crowds estimated at 100,000, the largest, spontaneous mass demonstration in Peruvian history. One Lima commentator described the event as "a sort of resurrection of the romantic *caudillismo* that characterized the first years of the republic" (Víctor Andrés Belaúnde, quoted in Stein, 1980, p. 85). Having brought down the longstanding dictatorship, the audacious, dark-complexioned Sánchez Cerro would go on to establish close ties as a popular hero with large sectors of the Lima populace that would later catapult him to victory in the presidential election of 1931.

Born in 1889 into modest circumstances in the northern city of Piura, Sánchez Cerro was the son of a notary public who could scarcely afford to send his son to public school. After graduating from high school at age sixteen, he chose an army career, entering the national military school at Chorillos outside Lima. Several years later, when he was promoted from lieutenant to captain, he had the highest examination score of all the candidates.

It was not long before the young officer's ambition for power surfaced, when he mutilated a finger in an attempted coup against the Benavides government (from which he gained the sobriquet "El Mocho"). During the *Oncenio*, he took part in two unsuccessful coups against Leguía, for which the dictator exiled him to Europe. Seemingly unrepentant, he purportedly declared, in a conversation at the home of Mariátegui upon his return the second time in 1929, that he would overthrow the tyrant and become president. True to his word, his third conspiracy from Arequipa was successful. The coup's *Manifesto de Arequipa* denounced the dictator and promised to "moralize" government and liberate the country from the domination of foreign creditors.

In coming to power, Sánchez Cerro had accurately calculated Leguía's weakening base of support in the military and elites. Pro-Leguía sentiment among the junior officer corps, for example, had shifted over the dictator's controversial 1929 settlement with Chile over the Tacna-Arica dispute and by the precipitous decline in their salaries as a result of the depression and ensuing devaluation of the currency. Decentralists in Arequipa, long a hotbed of regionalist sentiment, opposed Leguía's centralism in administrative and fiscal affairs and began forming the Decentralist Party, which was founded shortly after the coup in 1931. Composed mainly of elements from the middle sectors, the Decentralist Party sought greater provincial autonomy from Lima and a larger emphasis on regional development. Exporters had already turned away from Leguía in 1928, when the president turned a deaf ear to their pleas for governmental aid in response to the sharp decline in international sugar and commodity prices and their profits. The onset of the depression only widened the rift with the oligarchy, which quickly moved to embrace Sánchez Cerro as a strongman capable of controlling the restless masses and of resurrecting the elites' economic and political fortunes.

Sánchez Cerro governed Peru for six months, from September 1930 through February 1931, as the head of a military junta. During that time, he undertook a number of measures that consolidated his popularity among the masses, particularly in Lima. Deriving his immediate legitimacy from strong anti-Leguía sentiment, he imprisoned the dictator and orchestrated a campaign of prosecution and persecution against many of Leguía's followers, who were charged with public corruption and malfeasance. His popularity was also bolstered by his abolition of the hated *conscripción vial*, the establishment of civil marriage and divorce, and particularly by the distribution of food rations at local police stations to the growing legions of unemployed people in Lima. Indeed, together with the mayor of Lima, Luis

Antonio Eguiguren, the president implemented a series of popular social measures and charitable deeds to alleviate the plight of the poor. At the same time, Sánchez Cerro manifested an essentially conservative populism, surrounding himself with advisers who were drawn from the Civilista elites of the former Aristocratic Republic. In this sense, he represented the return to power of the old Civilista oligarchy, which had been politically marginalized by Leguía during the *Oncenio*. In the forefront of his supporters were the sugar and cotton planters, who prevailed on him to intervene in their behalf with governmental aid to their respective industries. They also convinced him to invite Princeton economist Edwin Kemmerer, who had advised a number of recent Andean governments on fiscal and financial reforms, to come on a mission to Lima for the same purpose.

Opposition to the government surfaced, however, over Sánchez Cerro's maneuvering to arrange his "election" to the presidency. He was increasingly attacked in the press. In addition, opposition to him emerged in the armed forces among senior officers, who resented the rule of a subordinate in the presidential palace, and among some junior officers who had taken part in the Arequipa revolt, but had not been sufficiently rewarded with promised promotions. As a result, a series of military revolts broke out throughout the country that also included elements of the former Leguía regime. Unable to control the situation, the president suddenly resigned from the junta on March 1 and announced that he would go into voluntary exile. This announcement threw the government into turmoil as to who would govern. A few days later minister of war Colonel Gustavo Jiménez, a rival of Sánchez Cerro and a proponent of the fledgling Aprista Party, engineered the installation of a new junta, headed by the veteran Cuzco politician and old Pierolista David Samanez Ocampo. Meanwhile, Sánchez Cerro was escorted to a ship in Callao harbor by an adoring crowd, which showed that the popular mystique of the "hero of Arequipa" was still very much alive.

One important measure undertaken by the new junta headed by Samanez Ocampo was a revised electoral law decreed in May 1931. The law removed property qualifications on voting and instituted the secret ballot, so that now all literate men over age twenty-one could take part in forthcoming elections. As a result, the size of the electorate rose 59 percent, from 203,882 in 1919 to 323,623 in 1931. This increase in eligible voters served as the basis for the organization of mass-based political parties for the first time in Peruvian history.

The Samanez Ocampo junta also hosted the arrival of the Kemmerer mission in March 1931. Within a month, the mission had devised an adjustment-and-reform program for the country's ailing financial and fiscal system. The plan recommended credit and monetary stringency, high reserves in the Central Bank, and liquidation of several large banks. Other recommendations for reform concerned banking, budgeting, abandonment of the gold standard, the tax code (to include income and property taxes), the customs code, and the debt. Hoping that the recommendations would restore confidence in the economy, the junta quickly adopted the plan in principle, but implementation proved extremely spotty. For one thing, the regime refused to implement the recommendations aimed at the agroexport sector that strongly supported the government.

Kemmerer's banking reforms, for example, which included the reorganization and strengthening of the Central Bank (which became the Central Reserve Bank), through such measures as higher reserve requirements and greater powers for the superintendent of banks, helped to modernize financial transactions and to save the remaining banks from going bankrupt during the depression. The same could not be said for his fiscal reforms aimed at curtailing the soaring budget deficit owing to plummeting governmental revenues. While the post-Leguía administrations cut public works sharply during 1930–31, they were unable or unwilling to reduce the governmental bureaucracy, whose number had increased 20 percent and whose salaries had risen 33 percent since 1926. The main problem was how to overcome strong opposition from public employees, labor unions, and members

Railroad workers in Cuzco, 1928. Photograph by Martín Chambi, reproduced with the permission of Teo Allain Chambi.

of the armed forces, particularly since the value of the *sol* and, therefore, of their salaries, had plunged 50 percent since 1930. Meanwhile, labor unrest was growing, first in the central Andean mining districts of Malpaso, near Oroya, and elsewhere. It was followed by an unprecedented wave of strikes among textile, sugar, and oil workers, as well as among chauffeurs and telephone operators in Lima. At Malpaso, workers' actions were precipitated by the Communist-led unions that had organized the mine workers in September and October 1930 and declared a general strike against the Cerro de Pasco Copper Corporation. This confrontational strategy of direct action had been adopted after Mariátegui's death by Eudocio Ravines, the new head of the Communist Party (CP), in the belief that it would trigger a general workers' uprising throughout country. The underlying assumption was that the Wall Street Crash of 1929 and the onset of the world depression signaled the final collapse, as predicted by Marx and Lenin, of the international capitalist system.

However, the CP's new confrontational strategy in the mines proved to be a colossal failure. The government vowed to crush the Communists, and the ensuing state repression at Malpaso and elsewhere left the CP isolated and ineffective. This repression of the CP, in turn, opened the way for the new nationalist-populist APRA party, led by the charismatic Haya de la Torre, as the only viable political alternative on the Left. As you shall see, APRA would take full advantage of the CP's tactical error, at the very moment that the Peruvian masses were surging into the political arena for the first time in history.

As for Kemmerer's request for Peru to enter negotiations with the international banking community over payment of the external debt, the government took a firm nationalistic position. It did not deviate from Sánchez Cerro's earlier position, when he had purportedly declared in private to Kemmerer that "all bankers are crooks" and that "Peru could not pay . . . one cent of her foreign debt. To ask her to do so would be like asking a starving man to give up food necessary for his life" (quoted in Drake, 1989, p. 240). So on the same day that Kemmerer issued his final report, the government officially suspended most payments on the foreign debt. Peru thus became the second South American country after Bolivia to default on its debt, although it did continue to recognize its obligation and to maintain service on at least a small portion of it. It was not until 1952 that the government resumed full payment on the suspended debt. Kemmerer finally left Peru at the end of 1931, his work generally praised by the bankers and the country's elites, but heavily criticized by the Left, which denounced him as a tool of American "imperialism" and "financial domination."

Meanwhile, the election campaign had heated up in July 1931 with Sánchez Cerro's return from a four-month exile to run in the October elections for the presidency. The political vehicles for his campaign were the newly organized Partido Unión Revolucionario (UR) and the daily newspaper *La Opinión*. Sánchez Cerro also gained the support of Eguiguren, the popular mayor of Lima, and the important daily *El Comercio*, edited by the intensely anti-Aprista Antonio Miró-Quesada. According to Stein (1980, p. 114), much of Sánchez Cerro's popular appeal came from the unskilled workers and lumpen proletariat of Lima—humble street and market vendors, construction workers, street sweepers, and laborers in small artisan industries. Many were recent migrants, and as a group, were characterized by a high degree of poverty and unemployment, as well as the lack of union representation. They identified with the candidate's mestizo appearance, declaring that "he's *cholo* [brown skinned] like us," in a widely heard refrain at public meetings. The urban plebes also responded to the candidate's charisma, stirring oratory, and image as a *caudillo* strongman who had brought down the hated dictator. Remarkably, a network of 100 to 150 loosely organized Sanchezcerrista neighborhood clubs spontaneously sprang up in Lima's lower-class barrios, such as Rímac, La Víctoria, and Barrios Altos, perhaps numbering 20,000 members at the height of the electoral campaign.

Support at the upper strata came from members of the old Civilista oligarchy, who had been out of power since 1919 and who, although disdainful of Sánchez Cerro's modest social origins, nevertheless embraced his conservative program and *caudillo* style as conducive to their own political and economic agenda. In particular, they saw in Sánchez Cerro the proverbial "man on horseback" who could reestablish social control over the masses, now unleashed into the streets by the economic debacle. The core of his movement, however, came from a group of upper-middle-class, right-wing nationalists with fascist political leanings and former ties to the Aristocratic Republic. These nationalists were particularly critical of what they considered Leguía's "sellout" over the Tacna-Arica dispute and held strong revanchist sentiments toward Chile.

The candidate's program was essentially conservative and corporatist in tone while populist in style. Sánchez Cerro promised to restore order along traditional social and economic lines after the disastrous Leguía dictatorship, rather than embark on any radical new restructuring of the country. To blue- and white-collar workers alike, he offered social security measures, and to the Indians, he offered full citizenship and communal protection. Land reform was espoused, but couched in terms of opening new lands for colonization, rather than redistribution. Orthodox, deflationary economic policies were proposed to cope with the depression. At the same time, Sánchez Cerro attacked the opposition APRA candidate Haya de la Torre as anti-Catholic, antimilitary, and antinationalist.

In the meantime, Haya de la Torre had returned to Peru in August after seven years in exile to organize his fledgling APRA Party and to oppose Sánchez Cerro with his own bid for the presidency. He brought with him the influences of both European fascism and communism as he set out to build a mass party, based on the idea of a "popular front," or populist cross-class alliance between the middle sectors and the organized working classes.

These ideological influences were particularly manifested in the rigidly hierarchical structure of the party, which had constructed a chain of command that resembled a civilian army, with rigid discipline imposed on the rank and file from above.

The APRA Party's program was more progressive than Sánchez Cerro's UR, but by no means called for a radical, "revolutionary" restructuring of society. In fact, Bertram (1991) called the programs of the two parties remarkably similar, their differences a matter of degree. Moreover, while Haya sounded somewhat radical in campaign speeches, in private he was reassuring the American ambassador in Lima that he represented no threat to foreign capital. The APRA program itself advocated an end to governmental corruption; the creation of an efficient, technocratically oriented public administration; future nationalization of mining and petroleum operations; the separation of church and state; the adoption of universal sufrage, including women, eighteen year olds, and illiterates; and the establishment of a national social security system. To carry out this program, Haya envisioned the creation of a strong, interventionist state (*el estado anti-imperialista*), run efficiently by a cadre of highly educated technocrats. These technocrats would organize the state along corporatist lines in a "functional democracy," designed to arbitrate among the various contending interest groups and sectors of society. In the end, the best of capitalist and socialist solutions, Haya declared, would be applied to resolve Peru's fundamental problem of underdevelopment.

Haya directed his appeal particularly to organized labor, the rural sugar proletariat of his native north coast, small and medium-sized landowners and businessmen, the professional classes, white-collar workers, and governmental bureaucrats. In many respects, these were the same social strata that had earlier supported Leguía and now naturally gravitated to Haya. They posed a delicate problem, however, for Haya, who wanted the vote of ex-Leguiistas, but in the highly charged political atmosphere of anti-Leguiismo could not make any overt appeals to the fallen dictator's supporters.

The campaign itself, reflecting the political polarization brought on by the economic crisis, was one of the bitterest of the century. Charges and countercharges were exchanged by the two candidates and their followers, who often resorted to the most personal invective imaginable. Sánchez Cerro was depicted by Apristas as a tool of the oligarchy and characterized personally as a madman and even a gorilla. Sanchezcerristas responded by ridiculing Haya and his associates as "little rich kids" and the APRA as anti-Catholic, on the basis of Haya's leadership of the 1923 Sacred Heart protest. They also charged that APRA was antipatriotic, on the basis of the fact that the party had its own flag and anthem, and that Haya was a crypto Communist, on the basis of references in his speeches and writings to Marx, Engels, and Lenin. Apristas were condemned as Leguiistas, and Sanchezcerristas were condemned as Civilistas.

In many ways, APRA's appeal, as Vega-Centeno (1991) has shown, went beyond ideology and program. It took on the attributes of a moral crusade, with its followers exhorted to become examples of the Aprista "new man"— morally pure, self-disciplined, and physically fit. The movement also displayed distinctly religious overtones and symbolism, a "brand of political Catholicism" in the words of Stein (1980, p. 175). Haya was likened in party propaganda to Christ, surrounded by his acolytes, who were depicted as loyal apostles and disciples. Slogans, such as "only Aprismo will save Peru" (*sólo el Aprismo salvará el Perú*), not only reflected the polarized state of the electorate, but represented a call for salvation and redemption through adhesion to the party. In some ways, such an absolutist, "salvationist" discourse—characteristic of many Latin American populist parties—proved antithetical and contradictory to the democratic ideology espoused by the party, since it eschewed dialogue and consensus with the opposition, which was depicted as the heinous enemy. At the same time, Haya assumed the mantle of the charismatic *caudillo*, a paternalistic father figure and teacher who would instruct and protect his "children" (the Peruvian masses) from the economic storm engulfing them. In short, these unique characteristics enabled APRA to forge a close, enduring relationship with a substantial minority of the electorate who would follow Haya for more than half a century, despite his numerous ideological and programmatic zigzags and embrace of his former persecutors in the oligarchy (*convivencia*, 1953) and the armed forces (1979).

In what Basadre called one of the fairest elections in history, Sánchez Cerro defeated Haya for president by a margin of 152,062 (50.7 percent) to 106,007 (35.4 percent) in the October 1931 elections. Nationwide, Sánchez Cerro won in his home department of Piura in the north; in the south, where he had launched his "revolution" against Leguía; and in the center, including populous Lima-Callao. Haya had a majority in his native north-coast region and in the Amazonian department of Loreto, where he capitalized on discontent from the cession of part of the department to Colombia in August 1930.

Sánchez Cerro was innaugurated president on December 8. His subsequent sixteen-month presidency was marked by civil insurrection, economic hardship, and foreign war. Barely a month passed without some sort of violent disturbance or military uprising. The polarized atmosphere was intensified when Haya returned to his bastion Trujillo after the election and declared that while Sánchez Cerro might occupy the presidential palace, in point of fact he, Haya, was the "Moral President of Peru."

At about the same time, the newly elected Constituent Assembly convened in Lima to draw up a new constitution. Over the next month or so, it would be the scene of heated debates between the Right and Left over a number of issues, not the least those related to the old problem of church-state relations. The surge in anticlericalism was led by the Apristas, although almost immediately after he assumed power, Sánchez Cerro had decreed obligatory civil marriage and the right to divorce. These proposals, along with others involving lay education and the right of women to vote, prompted the Church into a vigorous defense of its traditional prerogatives, led by conservative intellectuals Víctor Andrés Belaúnde and José Luis Riva Agüero.

On extending the suffrage to women, liberals feared that the clergy would manipulate women to vote in a conservative way. Ultimately, the Assembly, which formally became the Congress after promulgating the new constitution in 1933, would approve Sánchez Cerro's decrees on civil marriage and divorse, making them law in 1934. The Assembly also confirmed once again that only literate male citizens aged twenty-one or older (and not serving in the armed forces) could vote and reaffirmed the sacred union of Church and state.

During the debates on these and other important issues, such as decentralization, state intervention in the economy, a presidential or parliamentary system, protection of Indian communities and others (Balbi and Madalengoitia, 1980), the Apristas assumed an extremely obstructionist position. Sánchez Cerro reacted in February 1931 by expelling and then deporting the twenty-one-member Aprista delegation elected to the Assembly, along with Coronel Jiménez whose pro-Aprista sympathies and conspiratorial activities were well known. Already the president had involked martial law (Ley de Emergencia) in response to a number of violent incidents around the country that he attributed to APRA and the CP.

Rapidly the country plunged toward the abyss of civil war. In March, the president was severely wounded in an assassination attempt by a group of Apristas while attending Sunday mass. In May, Haya was arrested on charges of subverting the public order, and in the midst of his trial, an Aprista inspired naval mutiny was suppressed in Callao harbor. Then in July, with Haya in prison and the main party leaders in exile, local Apristas organized a mass uprising in Trujillo.

The revolt was led by militant sugar workers whose anarchist traditions inclined them to take direct action. They succeeded in capturing the local army barracks and seizing control of the city, before army reinforcements were able to arrive from Lima to retake it. In the meantime, the insurgents executed dozens of captured army and *Guardia Civil* personnel who were being held in the Trujillo prison.

This violent act triggered a bloody reprisal by the government after the army regained control of the city. Thousands of suspected rebels were rounded up and shot amid the pre-Columbian ruins of Chan Chan. This reprisal innaugurated a severe repression and persecution against the party that lasted for years and led it to develop a collective psychology of martyrdom that helped it survive. At the same time, the execution of the officers by the rebels spawned an intense feud between the armed forces and the party that would endure for more than half a century and effectively bar Haya from elected office until 1979. Ever since the founding of APRA, the hierarchy of the armed forces had been suspicious of the party and its founder, whose views were seen as revolutionary, antimilitary and un-Peruvian.

While struggling to restore order and political stability, Sánchez Cerro could do little to stem the economic decline of the depression. His response was simply to undertake more deficit spending. The purpose was not to engage in constructive Keynesian pump priming but, rather, to meet the public payroll (government and military) and hence forestall any political threats to his regime. Thus, the administration drew down the Central Reserve Bank's gold reserves by 48 percent, thereby forcing the country to abandon the gold standard in May 1932, which caused another sharp fall in the value of the *sol*, this time from 28 to 16 cents. At the same time, the money supply, or currency in circulation, as well as available credit contracted sharply, severely curtailing commerce and trade. By early 1933, the economy had reached rock bottom.

Perhaps to divert public opinion, Sánchez Cerro seized on a border incident with Colombia to mobilize the armed forces. The crisis was precipitated in September 1932, when an armed band of Peruvians, organized by rubber and sugar interests who had lost land in Leguía's settlement over Leticia (the Salomón-Lozano Treaty of 1922), illegally retook the land and were subsequently backed by Peruvian army units in the area. Colombia succeeded in expelling the invaders in early 1933, compelling Sánchez Cerro to recall from Europe former president General Oscar Benavides, a longtime supporter and hero of the 1911 conflict with Colombia, to assume command of the Peruvian forces. He also ordered the draft of all 21–25-year-old men into the army.

Several weeks later, Sánchez Cerro fell victim to an assassin's bullets as he was being driven from a ceremony reviewing troops that were being sent to the front. The perpetrator, who was immediately killed by the enraged crowd, turned out to be a seventeen-year-old member of the Aprista Party named Abelardo Mendoza Leyva. Among other things, the slaying of the president had the effect of confirming right-wing opinion that APRA was indeed a violent, subversive organization that must be suppressed to preserve the public order. It also catapulted the generally respected Benavides into the presidency, since the Constituent Assembly immediately selected him to fill out the remainder of Sánchez Cerro's term in office (to 1936).

Elite Divisions, World War II, and the Realignment of APRA

From the perspective of the ruling elites, the new president brought just the right credentials and skills to the presidency, at precisely the moment when the depressed economy finally began to revive. For one thing, he was the hero of the 1911 war against Colombia in the Putumaya rubber districts, the

Former two-time president and retired general and Mrs. Oscar R. Benavides, member of Peru's elite "forty families," 1940. Reproduced with the permission of the General Secretariat of the Organization of American States.

same disputed area as the 1932–33 Leticia conflict. Two years later, in 1913, Benavides was made army chief of staff at the age of thirty-seven. He then successfully engineered the ouster of the populist government of Guillermo Billinghurst (1912–14) and went on to serve as provisional president (1914–15) during the stormy early years of World War I before he turned the country back to Civilista rule. Stepping in to replace the fallen Sánchez Cerro, he faced a situation not unlike his previously successful stint in office.

In the event, Benavides was able to establish a viable, moderately conservative government between the political extremes of the Right and Left. His slogan "peace, order and work" was well suited to the public mood, which was weary of the political partisanship, violence, and economic hardship of the past few years. Quickly taking advantage of his military and nationalist credentials, the new president successfully negotiated a peace settlement with Colombia (concluded in 1934) over the Leticia conflict, which he believed Peru was ill prepared to settle militarily.

With peace assured, Benavides tried to reduce domestic political tensions by ending martial law and declaring a general political amnesty for all political prisoners, including the imprisoned Haya de la Torre. However, fears that APRA might win the 1934 congressional elections prompted their cancelation by the government. APRA reacted by hatching a number of conspiracies to overthow Benavides. The result was a renewed cycle of plots and insurrections from both the Right and the Left, punctuated by military revolts, the exile of several Aprista leaders, and the assassination by party militant Carlos Steer of Antonio Miró-Quesada, the virulently anti-Aprista editor of *El Comercio*.

Amid these developments, the economy began a vigorous export-led recovery. In comparative terms, Peru was one of the Latin American countries that was least affected by the depression and recovered faster, beginning in 1933, than its counterparts elsewhere, except for Mexico and Chile. Two reasons for this situation were that foreign firms, which accounted for over 50 percent of the exports, suffered the brunt of the initial decline, and cotton, which had a high return value and significant spread effects, led the recovery of exports. In addition, Peru's default on the debt in 1932 served to double its import capacity overnight, which had the salutary effect of immediately stabilizing the exchange rate.

In policy terms, Peru essentially reacted to the crisis in predictable ways, rather than try a radical new direction. After "adjusting" by defaulting on its debt, the government simply waited for the international market—that is, demand and prices—for its main commodities to go up again. When that happened beginning for silver, gold, and copper in 1932 and for cotton and sugar in 1933, Peru simply resumed its traditional export-led growth model. Unlike most Latin American governments, it did not resort to import substituting industrialization policies. Thorp and Bertram attribute this decision to the fact that Peru lacked a national bourgeoisie that was capable of pushing forward such an industrial agenda. Tariffs during the 1930s remained essentially unchanged, rising nominally from 19 percent in 1927 to 20 percent in 1936. Consequently, the manufacturing sector experienced only slow growth (aided by currency devaluations that made imports more expensive, but hindered by unemployment and wage reductions that depressed local consumption).

Over the intermediate term, this export-led recovery was enhanced by an overall rise in return value as foreign domination diminished and local control correspondingly rose. For example, foreign-dominated copper, silver, and oil as a percentage of total exports dropped from over 50 percent in 1930 to 23 percent in 1950, while lead, zinc, and gold exports expanded under a new generation of local ownership. At the same time, locally controlled sugar and cotton returned to a dominant position in exports, from 29 percent in 1930 to 53 percent in 1945, while the former export mainstays coffee and wool also increased their shares. In sum, total agromineral exports produced by foreign companies dropped from 60 percent of total exports in 1930 to 30 percent in 1950, opening the way for greater local control, return value, and spread effects.

The improving economy, in turn, allowed Benavides to increase taxes and governmental expenditures for paternalistic social welfare measures. Between 1933 and 1936, for example, laws were passed providing for a minimum wage, workers' compensation and pensions, and social security benefits. To administer the latter, a new Welfare Ministry was created, funded by contributions from corporations, workers, and the government. In addition, Benavides attacked unemployment with a public works program that employed 30,000 to 40,000 workers by the end of the decade. Such measures, together with continued police repression—a carrot-and-stick approach, if you will—served to control a wave of labor strikes, led by the Confederación de Trabajadores Peruanos, founded by APRA in 1934.

The improving economy and social climate also enabled Benavides to proceed with national elections that were scheduled at the end of his completion of Sánchez Cerro's term in 1936. However, the elites were divided on how to deal with the APRA, which persisted in its conspiratorial strategy of attempting to subvert the armed forces and police against the regime. A right-wing faction, headed by the Miró-Quesada family and cotton oligarch Pedro Beltrán, advocated the iron-fist approach, whereas the moderates, led by the Prado family and Benavides himself, believed in a more conciliatory policy.

Fissures in the oligarchy were further revealed by the fact that the Right could not agree on a single candidate. On the far Right was Luis M. Flores, head of the *Unión Revolucionaria*, Sánchez Cerro's old party. A former interior minister, Flores was a self-styled fascist who had organized a 6,000-strong paramilitary force of black-shirted party militants to attack APRA and the CP on the Left. Another right-wing candidate was Dr. Manuel Vicente Villarán, a former Civilista, who was supported by Beltrán, ultra conservative intellectual José de la Riva Agüero and several leading sierra and coastal landowners.

Riva Agüero was the most articulate voice of the Catholic Right in the 1930s. Along with Belaúnde, he had helped turn the Catholic University, founded in 1917, into an important center of the political Right, as well as for the intellectual rebirth of the Church. At the same time, Riva Agüero became an enthusiastic apologist for Mussolini and, like other members of the oligarchy and traditional sectors of the middle classes, saw in fascism an effective prophylaxis against the contagion of bolshevism. Although they were ultimately unsuccessful in gaining power, Peruvian fascists nevertheless remained a potent force during the 1930s and became strong advocates for Franco and the Falangists in the Spanish Civil War.

In opposition to the extreme Right, moderate conservatives in the oligarchy supported the *Frente Nacional*, which was created by Benavides in an effort to occupy the political center-right. It was a conglomeration of centrist parties headed by oligarch, Benavides ally, and former prime minister Jorge Prado y Ugarteche. Mention should also be made of the Church's increasing activities in politics at this time, mainly through the organization of a number of Catholic lay groups that the hierarchy had been encouraging since the 1920s. One such group was the Unión Popular (UP), which was inspired by the social teachings of the Church in *Rerum Novarum* (published in 1931), which advocated reforms along the lines of social democracy governed by a corporative state. Another was Catholic Action, which had begun as early as 1929 at the parish level in Lima, but spread to the provinces thereafter and became a national organization in 1935. Although these groups were active in the electoral process in behalf of one or another candidate, they were, of course, not political parties, but would intellectually and otherwise prepare the way for the rise of the Christian Democratic Movement after World War II (Klaiber, 1992).

In the elections of 1936, APRA put forward Haya de la Torre as its candidate, but with grave doubts as to whether the Benavides government would conduct fair elections. Therefore, it hedged its bets by hatching yet another plot, this time involving David Toro, the president of Bolivia. In return for arms and support for an uprising, APRA promised to back landlocked Bolivia's aspirations for access to a Pacific port that it had lost in the War of the Pacific. The Benavides government, however, discovered the plot and used it as an excuse to disqualify Haya's candidacy. With APRA out of the running, Eguiguren withdrew from the *Frente Nacional* and became a candidate himself in the belief that Apristas would now vote for him as the more progressive candidate. When Eguiguren took an early lead in the October voting, Benavides suspended the count and replaced his cabinet with an all-military one. Under pressure from the president, Congress, on the pretext that Apristas had indeed voted for Eguiguren, annulled the election and extended Benavides's term to December 8, 1939. Benavides then disbanded the Congress and assumed full dictatorial powers for the next three years.

Benavides continued to benefit during the remainder of his term from the improving economy. National income rose 61 percent from 1935 to 1939, largely because of strong export performances in cotton, oil, and other minerals. This higher income enabled the president to increase social outlays, expand public works projects (housing, roads, and irrigation) and raise taxes on the wealthy, but still balance the budget. At the same time, Benavides kept the military budget at about 14 percent of total expenditures, much of it going to purchase new weapons and equipment. Thus, thanks to the economic recovery, Benavides was able to more than double public expenditures, from a low of 91 million *soles* in 1932 to 221 million in 1938. When his term ended in 1939, he then maneuvered in behalf of Manuel Prado y Ugarteche, who headed a moderate electoral alliance called the *Concentración Nacional* (a replica of Benavides's earlier *Frente Nacional*).

Manuel Prado belonged to one of the wealthiest and most prominent families in Peru and was a leading member of the moderate-conservative faction of the oligarchy. His father was General Mariano Ignacio Prado, who had served as president in the years leading up to the War of the Pacific (1876–79), but whose reputation had been forever sullied by his abandonment of the country on the eve of the war ostensibly to seek arms in Europe. His sons Jorge and Manuel, along with Benavides, had engineered the overthrow of Billinghurst in 1914 and then opposed the administration of Leguía in the 1920s. Jorge Prado was Benavides's choice for president in the ill-fated elections of 1936, while Manuel served in Benavides's cabinet in 1939. Prior to running for the presidency, Manuel presided over Peru's most important bank—the Banco Popular—and had extensive holdings in the insurance industry, textile manufacturing, and cattle ranching in the central sierra.

The election, coming on the eve of the outbreak of World War II, revolved around the issue of fascism. Prado's *Concentración Nacional* consisted of nonfascist and antifascist sectors that included industrialists and moderate sectors of the oligarchy, who advocated greater state expenditures, capital investment in industry, and political liberalization. The right wing was represented by the ticket of José Quesada Larrea and Luis Flores and was backed once again by the intensely anti-APRA daily *El Comercio*. It included the oligarchical Right, led by cotton planter Pedro Beltrán, which advocated traditional liberal, free-market economic policies and an authoritarian state. As for APRA, it remained officially proscribed and underground, but inclined toward Prado, whose moderation and strong antifascism were considered more advantageous to the party than was his hard-line opponent. With the government counting the votes and many Apristas voting for him as the "lesser of two evils," Prado easily won the election with 187,000 out of the 339,000 (55%) ballots cast. To ensure the allegiance of the armed forces, many of whose officers were not in favor of Prado's election, Benavides took the precaution of decreeing an 18 percent salary increase shortly before the balloting.

Prado was a "conservative modernizer" who moved Peru in a more democratic direction, after a decade of dictatorship, by establishing a climate of greater tolerance toward APRA and the Left. The new president recognized that his election was largely the result of Aprista votes. He also believed, as had Benavides, that the best way to neutralize the party's radical and conspiratorial nature was through co-optation, rather than confrontation. As a result, Prado established a tacit alliance with APRA, pursuing a more expansionary fiscal policy that was designed to buy off the party's sizable middle-class base. Overall, this meant that Peru under Prado (1939–45) and his successor José Luis Bustamante y Rivero (1945–48) continued Benavides's modest movement toward a more expansive state and political economy. Consequently, during the 1940s, Peru became one the leading Latin American exponents of fiscal expansion, increasing governmental spending more than four and a half times from 1939 to 1948.

The outbreak of World War II had a major influence on the Prado presidency. Initially, it clouded the economic prospects for a country that was dependent on exports and foreign markets. With European markets in question, Prado recognized that the continuing prosperity of the country depended on improving relations with the U.S. as a buyer for Peruvian commodities. For its part, the U.S. was desirous of shoring up hemispheric relations and defense, which, among other things, meant gaining access to badly needed Peruvian raw materials. These raw materials included rubber, quinine, and sugar and certain minerals, such as copper, vanadium, and molybdenum, as well as petroleum for its war industries.

A policy of wartime rapprochement between the two countries was further consolidated when APRA began to soften its anticapitalist and anti-American rhetoric. For example, at the outset of the war in 1940, Haya declared that the "twenty isolated and divided Indoamerican countries only subsist[ed] because the U.S. guaranteé their existence and sovereignty " and then called for "a democratic interamericanism purged of imperialism," (quoted in Drake in Rock, 1994, p. 123). Such moderation marked the beginning of an overall shift to the right by the party as it sought to realign itself with the new international correlation of forces (democratic versus fascist) and to exploit its opening with the more amenable Prado to gain legalization and legitimation in the political system. The latter was no doubt impelled by the brutal repression that the party had been subjected to during the previous decade. Moderation toward the U.S. was further influenced by the New Deal's Good Neighbor, anti-interventionist policy in Latin America, as well as radical reformism at home, all of which meshed well with Aprista doctrine. Thus, APRA not only dropped its strident campaign against Yankee imperialism, but urged cooperation with and capital investment from the U.S. Socialism would come, Haya now reasoned, only when Peru became more capitalist, and capitalism could occur only with the infusion of American investment.

During the war, Peru received a series of missions from the U.S. dealing with economic, cultural, medical, and military matters. On the economic

and military side, for example, bilateral trade and lend-lease agreements—
the latter amounting to $18 million—were signed. The Prado government
also allowed the U.S. to install a military base at Talara. Perhaps more important, Peru agreed to the imposition of wartime price controls on raw materials, which aided the American war effort, but reduced Peruvian profits
on minerals and other commodities. Therefore, Peru's foreign exchange reserves were held down compared to other Latin American countries, as was
its progress toward greater economic self-sufficiency. The country did, however, receive a greater inflow of U.S. investments, which served to assuage
economic uncertainty and stimulate growth.

Diplomatically, Prado responded to the outbreak of the war by moving
from a position of declared neutrality in 1939 to a break in relations with
the Axis powers in 1942 and finally to a full declaration of war in 1945. After Pearl Harbor, he also ordered the deportation of 1,800 Japanese residents
for internment in the U.S. and the confiscation of Japanese (but not German)
property, which he distributed to his political friends and allies. This act was
the culmination of strong popular and elite pressures against Japanese commercial and business interests, inflamed by a virulent anti-Nipon propaganda campaign by the UR party during the 1930s. APRA and Haya also
joined in the general anti-Japanese bashing, hoping to curry favor with the
U.S. for its campaign for legality.

Another important effect of the war and improved relations with the
Left could be seen in labor relations. Indeed, during the Prado administration, the first tentative steps toward the incorporation of the labor movement, which had been severely repressed and marginalized during the 1920s
and 1930s, were taken by the government. First, because of the war, both
APRA and Communist labor leaders refrained from labor agitation, which
redounded to the benefit of the economy and the administration and calmed
right-wing discontent. Coincidently, APRA also stopped plotting with sectors of the military against the government, again as part of its strategy to
gain formal access to the political system. The Communists, on the other
hand, were willing to collaborate with the pro-American administration because the Soviet Union had formed an alliance with the Allies after Hitler's
attack on the Soviet Union in 1941.

Prado responded to these conciliatory gestures by lowering the general
level of repression, releasing many imprisoned Aprista leaders, and permitting the party to resume organizational activities, even though it continued to be officially proscribed. This climate of greater political toleration was
extended to organized labor, with the number of labor unions recognized
by the government rising from 33 during the Benavides administration to
118 during the war.

APRA's influence on the Prado administration showed up in other areas, too. For example, at the party's insistence, Prado adopted a more nationalistic stance in one area, the foreign-controlled oil industry, by refusing
to grant exploration rights to foreign companies in either the Amazon or the

sierra. This refusal was significant because by 1938, production from the IPC's north-coast La Brea y Pariñas fields, which had risen sharply during the 1930s and provided the Benavides government with 12 percent of government income, began to fall precipitously. As a result, oil production dropped from a peak of 15 million barrels in 1936 to a low of 10 million in 1940, a figure that held steady during the rest of the decade.

The imposition of governmental controls was another area suggestive of Prado's tacit alliance with APRA. After the outbreak of hostilities, shortages in food supplies and rising prices threatened the politically sensitive block of urban consumers in the country. Inflation, for example, rose from 8.2 percent in 1941 to 14.3 percent in 1944. The government reacted by instituting controls on food prices in 1943 and raising subsidies on staples the following year. It also raised the minimum percentage of land allocated to the production of staples on the export-oriented coast. Finally, the marketing of rice, whose growing had increased dramatically on the north coast during the previous decade, was taken over by the state. These interventionist measures, although they protected urban consumers and forestalled popular protests, disincentivized producers and aggravated the adverse trend, noticeable since the 1930s, in the internal terms of trade.

In a similar vein, Prado established local market quotas on sugar to ensure that supplies would be adequate to meet local consumption and, at the same time, increased taxes on sugar exports. The industry's fortunes had improved from the depressed situation of oversupply during the 1930s to market shortages and rising profitability during the war years. By squeezing the industry for tax revenues and restricting acreage for exports, however, Prado and his successor Bustamante incurred the wrath of the still-powerful sugar elite.

The administration also increased taxes on cotton exports, which had led the economic recovery during the 1930s, but had declined after the outbreak of World War II. World cotton prices had recovered quickly after 1932, so that Peru's share of world production doubled, from 1.5 percent in 1932 to 3.0 percent in 1939. During this period, acreage devoted to cotton production increased from 130,000 hectares in 1933 to over 190,000 hectares, or nearly half the cultivated land on the coast in 1938. Thereafter, however, cotton acreage dropped back to 125,000 hectares in 1943 as a result of a sharp decline in demand from the combatants who had built up large stocks of cotton in anticipation of war. Still the cotton sector benefited from a substantial purchase agreement with the U.S.

As for the manufacturing sector of the economy, the onset of the war and ensuing shortages produced a short-term growth spurt of around 10 percent a year between 1938 and 1942. The previous decade had seen some dynamism in local industries during the early years of the depression, particularly in the production of textiles, shoes, soap, pharmaceutical, hats, and paint. Growth rates in the early 1930s, however, were considerably below those of Argentina and Brazil, which saw manufacturing grow at 7 percent and 8 percent, respectively, during that period. Industrial growth then slowed during the second half of the decade, only to pick up at the end of the decade and then fade and stagnate again from 1943 to 1947.

An important milestone of the Prado government was the 1940 national census, the first in three-quarters of a century. The census revealed that the country's population had almost tripled since the 1876 census, from 2.6 million to 6.2 million inhabitants. Of this total, 2.2 million were urban while 4.0 were rural, confirming the still predominantly agrarian character of the country.

On the basis of these figures, the growth rate of the population averaged 1.3 percent between 1876 and 1940, but varied on the regional level, from 1.6 percent for the coast and *selva* to 1.15 percent for the sierra. These average figures, however, conceal the fact that the rate of population growth steadily increased during this period. Urban growth was even more rapid, with Lima increasing 4 percent a year from 1920 to 1940 and other cities also accelerating. In regional terms, the coastal population grew in excess of 2.0 percent a year, and cities grew more than 3.0 percent a year from 1920 to 1940.

If the census of 1940 revealed the increasing urbanizing tendency of a still predominantly rural country, it also signaled what Manrique (1995, p. 266) called a revolution in thinking about the racial composition of Peru's population. The 1940 census, the last one to classify the population by race, registered 52.89 percent of the population as white and mestizo, 45.86 percent as Indian, 0.47 percent black, and 0.68 percent as oriental. These figures illustrated that Peru was primarily a mestizo country, no longer the overwhelmingly Indian one postulated by the *indigenistas* of the 1920s.

Perhaps the most important event to occur during the Prado years was the outbreak of a border war with Ecuador in 1941. A series of border incidents in disputed territory on the Pacific and in a much larger area in the eastern Amazon, led to the eruption of full-scale military hostilities between the two countries in July 1941. Neither Prado, who was sensitive to his father's sullied reputation in the War of the Pacific, nor the Peruvian military, which had suffered serious defeats not only in that war, but with Colombia over Leticia a decade earlier, were prepared for any outcome other than outright victory.

Prado preferred to pursue a diplomatic solution. However, the army, under the command of the highly competent General Eloy G. Ureta, spoiled for a fight, calculating its chances against a considerably smaller foe whose armed forces and population were outnumbered more than three to one. After renewed border clashes, Ureta issued an ultimatum to the government in June 1941 either to sanction an attack in the Tumbez region or be overthrown by the military. Ureta then exceeded his orders with a full-scale advance, paralleled by coordinated operations by the army in the Oriente and the navy along the Pacific coast.

The coordinated Peruvian campaign was highly effective, and Ecuadorian resistance evaporated in less than three months. Anxious to shore up continental unity in the face of the war in Europe, the U.S. pressed for a quick settlement of the conflict at the meeting of hemispheric foreign ministers in Rio de Janeiro in January 1942. In the subsequent Rio Protocol, Ecuador agreed to cede some 13,500 square kilometers to Peru in the Oriente, although twenty years later, in 1962, it disclaimed the agreement, reopening the dispute to future conflict. The favorable outcome of the war boosted public support for the Prado administration, but also made a hero and potential political rival out of General Ureta. A young officer and future president Manuel Odría also made a reputation for himself in the war.

Temporarily unified during the war, the armed forces experienced renewed factionalism at its conclusion, accentuated by the presidential aspirations of both Ureta, the war hero, and former president Benavides, who remained popular within the institution. The blatant politics of promotions and intense jockeying for support among the two presidential aspirants prompted disgust among reform-minded junior officers, led by Major Víctor Villanueva, who clandestinely organized the Committee of Revolutionary Army Officers (Comité Revolucionario de Oficiales del Ejército—CROE). Their discontent was, in one sense, a generational reaction against the intense political partisanship that had characterized civil-military relations during their rise in the ranks in the tumultuous 1930s. Contemptuous of their superiors, whom they accused of "playing politics" and grossly "unprofessional" behavior, the CROE called for fundamental civilian and military reforms, particularly in the area of promotions, training, and military justice (Masterson, 1991).

Meanwhile, in the larger political arena, when it became increasingly clear that the Allies were going to emerge victorious from the world war, a new democratic spirit, encouraged by the U.S., swept over Latin America as Prado's term drew to a close in 1944. This spirit had the effect of deepening the tendencies toward the incorporation of APRA and organized labor into the Peruvian body politic, both increasingly advocated by the U.S. Similarly, the head of the Mexican labor movement and leader of the Confederation of Latin American Workers (Confederación de Trabajadores de América Latina—CTAL), Vicente Lombardo Toledano, visited Lima and urged Prado to allow the formation of a new labor confederation. This visit led Prado in 1944 to permit APRA and the CP to organize the Confederation of Peruvian Workers (Confederación de Trabajadores del Perú—CTP), which became affiliated with the CTAL.

The founding of the CTP coincided with a pickup in labor activity, as the militancy of workers increased, along with the growth in wartime production and rising inflation (83 percent between 1939 to 1945). In late 1944 APRA called a successful general strike that, among other things, helped it gain control of the CTP from the Communists the following year. However, with the approach of elections, the party then urged greater restraint on labor militancy as its own prospects in the elections brightened.

As the elections, scheduled for July 1945, drew closer, political maneuvering over the presidential succession intensified. Marshall Benavides returned to Peru to test the electoral waters, but became instead a broker in search of a consensus civilian candidate who would be acceptable to the military. At the same time, General Ureta stepped forward with the backing of the Miró-Quesada clan, elements of the old UR party, and right-wing sectors of the armed forces. To counter the right, a reformist, cross-class alliance—the *Frente Democrático Nacional* (FDN)—representing new industrial and middle-sector groups that had emerged during the war years, was formed in Arequipa. It selected José Luis Bustamante y Rivero, a distinguished legal scholar and diplomat of middle-class origins, as its presidential candidate. A progressive Catholic of high principles but little political experience, Bustamante boldly sought to end the pattern of alternating oligarchic-military rule in the country by allying with APRA to carry out a program of democratization and social reform. As a condition of his candidacy, he insisted on APRA's legalization and incorporation into the FDN coalition.

Benavides, recognizing the strong political winds in favor of democratization and against a military candidate, retired from the race, but not before he declared in favor of the FDN and APRA's desire for legalization. Benavides hoped to block his rival Ureta from election, as well as to avoid a further split in the military among rival factions. APRA, however, was still wary of Prado's commitment to completely open and free elections and so revived its conspiratorial tactics by working surreptitiously with CROE leader Major Villanueva, who was planning a civilian-military uprising.

The uprising, scheduled to occur in early 1945 at the Ancón air base, was discovered and foiled by the government, but not before Haya de la Torre had withdrawn APRA support for it, in the wake of a formal pact with Bustamante for party support for his candidacy in return for legalization. Shortly thereafter, Prado followed suit and legalized the party. After thirteen years of almost continuous official persecution and clandestine operation from 1932 to 1945, APRA (now renamed the Partido Aprista Peruano, PAP, to avoid the constitutional ban on "international" parties) finally emerged from the "catacombs" and presented a slate of candidates for Congress in the elections. The extent to which Haya and APRA had shifted to the right is illustrated in a high-profile speech he made on May 20, 1945, only a few doors and within earshot of the oligarchical Club Nacional. In the speech, he declared that "it [was] not necessary to seize the wealth of those who possess it but rather new wealth should be created for those who do not have it" (quoted in Masterson, 1991, p. 82).

The ensuing campaign between the FDN's Bustamante and Ureta, the candidate of the *Unión Nacional Democrática* (UND), was relatively uneventful. The FDN, which included both the PAP and the CP (now the Socialist Vanguard), put forward a mainly Aprista program that included autonomy for trade unions, the promotion of more "just" relations between labor and capital, moderate land reform, protection of civil liberties, political and economic "decentralization," tax and fiscal reform, industrial and export promotion, and expansion of public education. Ureta and the UND confined themselves to making more general appeals for the protection of family and the Church and the forging of national unity. The results of this relatively open and fair election gave Bustamante and the FDN an overwhelming two to one margin of victory (305,590 to 150,720). Also elected under the FDN umbrella were 18 Aprista senators and 46 deputies out of a total of 46 senators and 101 deputies in the Chamber of Deputies. Although it did not constitute a majority, PAP was the largest voting bloc in the new Congress. The outcome of the election immediately increased the influence of Haya de la Torre in the new government, a political reality that prompted a dinner in his honor at the home of Pedro de Osma Gildemeister, scion of one of Peru's forty families. APRA had moved almost 180 degrees from its original position of attacking the oligarchy to embracing its old adversary.

10 Democracy and Dictatorship, 1945–63

Reform Frustrated: The "Trienio" of Bustamante y Rivero, 1945–48

With the election of reformer José Luis Bustamante y Rivero, the first freely elected president since 1931, Peru entered the postwar, "democratic springtime" with high hopes. Not only was a new era of political freedom and democratization at hand, but the possibilities for economic restructuring and reform had never been better. Yet, within three years, the democratic-reformist promise of 1945 was dashed by a military coup and the onset of a dictatorship in October 1948. A similar opportunity would not recur for another generation until the early 1960s.

President Bustamante's goals at the outset of his regime were to democratize the country, carry out social reform, and integrate APRA into the political system. His primary hope was to replace the oligarchical-military rule of the past two decades with a genuinely democratic government, based on social justice, and in this way to forestall what he saw as the possibility of a violent revolutionary upheaval. This latter goal was possible now that APRA appeared to have "revised" its anti-imperialism, its penchant for violence, and its socialist agenda. Although still suspicious of the party's early revolutionary and authoritarian tendencies, Bustamante believed he could guide APRA along a moderating path, drawing on the positive, rather than the destructive, elements of its reform program.

In retrospect, this does not seem to have been a realistic calculation. For one thing, Bustamante had little practical political experience to match that of his erstwhile allies, particularly the astute and wily Haya de la Torre, whose party had managed to survive a generation in the catacombs against successive waves of severe state repression. Moreover, unlike the unity and cohesiveness of APRA, Bustamante was a political independent without a party. He led a fragile, loose-knit array of parties and groupings—the Frente Democrático Nacional (FDN)—that were united only in their opposition to continued military-oligarchical rule and the need for change. So while Bustamante's FDN had a clear majority (55 percent) in Congress, APRA dominated the alliance with 74 of its 108 delegates (69 percent). (APRA held 28 of the 35 FDN seats in the Senate's total of 46 seats and 46 of the 73 FDN seats in the Chamber of Deputies' total of 101). In short, APRA would dominate the new Congress and not be subject to easy manipulation by a president whose own political base was tenuous at best.

To be sure, for the moment Bustamante counted on the tacit approval of the oligarchy, which was now ready to accept a more moderate APRA into the political game. But any moves toward reform that might threaten the agroexport's economic hegemony would trigger immediate oligarchical opposition. Finally, in such a highly political atmosphere, which called for precisely the kinds of skills that Haya possessed, Bustamante had declared that he was not a "politician." However popular such a declaration of antipolitics was during the electoral campaign, it augured poorly for a president who needed practical negotiating skills to hold his coalition together in the face of a highly disciplined, politicized, and expectant APRA.

Whatever chances Bustamante had for achieving his goals, they were dimmed at the outset when the two leaders held their first meeting after the election. Already their different personalities—the gregarious Haya versus the reserved Bustamante—had seemed to cool their earlier contacts. But personal chemistry aside, when Bustamante offered APRA only two of the eight cabinet posts in the new government, the offer was categorically rejected by Haya, who had also expected to be named prime minister. Considering the weight of Aprista votes in Bustamante's election, Haya apparently considered the offer a personal affront and refused any further discussion. The new administration had begun on a highly discordant note.

Once in office, Bustamante faced an assortment of problems. The end of the war had brought on economic difficulties, such as a weakening balance of payments and inflationary pressures from pent-up demand caused by wartime controls. Freed from past restraints, the labor movement also unleashed a series of strikes aimed at restoring wages that had lost much of their purchasing power, that were again due to wartime controls. Flush from his popular electoral victory, Bustamante could do little to reign in the new militancy of organized labor. After all, organized labor had been heavily repressed for two decades, was now largely controlled by APRA, and harbored high expectations for change.

Politically rebuffed by the president's cabinet appointments, APRA proceeded to assert its power in Congress by engineering a change from two-thirds to a majority vote necessary to override presidential vetoes. With APRA holding 50 percent of the congressional seats, Haya ensured party discipline by requiring all Aprista representatives to deliver to him undated letters of resignation. The party then introduced its own legislative program and blocked the government's austerity proposals that were designed to reduce spending and raise taxes. Unable to counter APRA's control of Congress, Bustamante finally relented after six months and agreed, in early 1946, to bring three Apristas into what thereafter came to be known as the "Aprista cabinet." This move opened the way for legislation addressing the economic problems, which, together with rising export demand and low imports owing to worldwide manufacturing shortages, momentarily buoyed the economy in early 1946.

Having skillfully outmaneuvered the new president on the political front, APRA might have been expected to push forward a significant reform program, considering its longstanding populist inclinations and recently demonstrated electoral clout. However, APRA was constrained from doing so because of its preelectoral agreement with Bustamante and the oligarchy to refrain from carrying out its original radical program in return for political legitimacy. This tactic was confirmed shortly after the election by sugar baron Augusto Gildemeister in a letter to cotton magnate Pedro Beltrán when he reported that APRA was telling "our workmen . . . that everything would remain as it was, no partition of the land nor other properties or money, but creation of new wealth for the whole country through them all. It is really very funny" (quoted in Portocarrero M., 1983, p. 88). While Gildemeister was amused at APRA's turnabout, the new stance posed an important dilemma for the party leadership: how to rationalize the sharp departure from its philosophical and programmatic origins to the party faithful. This dilemma may explain, at least in part, the ambiguous leadership exercised by Haya in subsequent years, as well as the intensification of the internal division and conflict in the party between militants and moderates.

In any event, APRA and Peru lost a significant opportunity for reform. The government, with APRA now dominant in both Congress and the Cabinet, proceeded along a decidedly moderate course. For example, economic nationalism was eschewed when a new oil exploration agreement was signed with IPC, the very symbol of foreign imperialism in Peru. Likewise, no agrarian reform law was proposed, although a law regulating coastal tenancy contracts (*Ley de Yanaconaje*) was passed in 1947. Fiscal and monetary policy, consisting of controls on exchange rates and prices, particularly on food, remained largely the same as during the Prado years. Perhaps what is most revealing is that no efforts were made by the populist APRA to expand suffrage.

On the other hand, APRA managed cleverly to reinterpret the meaning of "creating rather than redistributing wealth" and thereby to reaffirm its populist, if not its "revolutionary," credentials. A redistributionist policy would come not through land reform or the nationalization of industry, but through the expansion of the state; for example, the government would increase the wages, salaries, and benefits of workers. In education, teachers' salaries would rise 60 percent, and universal education through high school would be instituted. The government also expanded its public works program, particularly in the areas of the construction of schools and public health facilities. Finally, the government continued to subsidize the basic food consumption of urban consumers, although at the expense of rural, often small-scale, producers.

A major recipient of the state's new redistributionist policies under the APRA/Bustamante cogovernment (*co-gobierno*) was labor. For example, according to the Colliers (1991, p. 324), the rate of official recognition of new unions rose from a meager annual rate of 10 under Benavides and 20 under Prado to 90 during the period 1945–47. A total of 264 unions received official recognition from 1945 to 1947. An even more important issue for labor was the rising postwar cost of living, which more than doubled between 1944 and 1948. Labor negotiators were successful in matching and even slightly exceeding this rate of increase for workers' wages, at least through 1947, after which they began to lose ground once again. Working conditions likewise improved substantially as a result of the implementation of state-initiated collective bargaining agreements. As a result of all of these policies, labor was incorporated for the first time into the political and economic fabric of society. On a purely political level, this incorporation was symbolized by the sharp increase in working-class representation in Congress during the APRA/Bustamante *trienio* (6 APRA worker deputies, 4 CP worker deputies, and 1 APRA worker senator).

Labor was not the only recipient of APRA-directed state largesse emanating from APRA's control of Congress. The party made a conscious effort as well to "incorporate" the urban middle sectors to solidify the other component of its political base. Toward this end, generous salary increments were decreed to *empleados* (employees), particularly in the public sector. In addition, as the state expanded, the party made sure that it inserted "loyalists" into the administration. The aim was twofold: to distribute patronage to its political clientele and to "infiltrate" the public sector with Apristas who formed party "cells" that were loyal to Haya and the APRA directorate. In the same way, APRA penetrated the unions, secondary schools, and universities, which then came under partisan party control. Accordingly, "this led to the accusation that APRA was 'hegemonic,' and 'totalitarian' and inclined to surreptitiously gain control of the government and thereby incapacitate the Chief Executive" (quoted in Cotler, 1978, p. 267).

Overall, APRA's relatively moderate policy agenda, however, was well received in Washington, which had noted with pleasure the party's turn away from its strident prewar anti-imperialist and nationalist stance. Perhaps even more important, as the outbreak of the Cold War loomed on the horizon, the United States was encouraged by Haya's outspoken anticommunism. Indeed, the party had used its postwar access to state power and resources to great advantage in its rivalry with the Communist Party for control of the labor movement. By 1947 the American ambassador in Lima was reporting to the State Department that "I am of the opinion that Haya deserves our moral support in an appropriate fight against Communism" (quoted in Haworth, 1992, p. 184).

Although APRA's main political thrust centered in the urban areas, the party was not inactive in the countryside. There rural workers were also growing restless in anticipation of change under the new reformist government. On the sugar estates, union activity, largely inactive since the early 1930s, increased, and strikes and work stoppages in behalf of higher wages and better working conditions multiplied. Likewise, sharecroppers, known as *yanaconas* on the south coast (Ica) and far north (Piura) cotton estates organized to press their demands for greater security and written contracts. Landlords in the cotton sector had long relied on *yanaconaje* to expand production in a system in which capital and credit were in relatively short supply.

Efforts to improve the conditions of *yanaconas* began in the early 1930s, when the Partido Socialista, founded in Piura in 1930, had worked to organize the Federación General de Yanaconas y Campesinos del Perú. Likewise, a large part of APRA's 1931 agrarian program was aimed at improving the circumstances of *yanaconas* and other tenants on commercial farms. As a consequence of the increasing pressures from their tenants, landlords, not only on the coast but on commercial estates in the highlands, began to evict *yanaconas* and *colonos* and replace them with wage laborers. *Yanaconas* were sharecroppers on coastal commercial estates whereas *colonas* were hacienda workers in the highlands who received usufruct to small garden plots in return for various nonwage tasks on the estate.

Tenants resisted these efforts and fought not only to secure their rights, but to obtain a greater degree of independence from the landlords' control. In the election of 1945, APRA had made extravagant promises to tenants to gain their votes, such as the elimination of rent payments and even the distribution of estate lands to them. Under pressure to fulfill these promises after the election, APRA sponsored the *Ley de Yanaconaje*, which passed Congress and was signed by Bustamante in 1947. The law prohibited the eviction of tenants, required written contracts, and established improved conditions. But as it turned out, landlords often managed to evade the law, so the process of evictions continued.

The mobilization of rural labor and APRA agitation were also not limited to the coast. In the highlands, particularly where the web of commercial activities continued to expand during the 1930s and 1940s, tenants (*colonos*) and modernizing landlords increasingly came into conflict. As local markets opened up and land became more valuable, *colonos* and their landlords each tried to maximize their commercial opportunities. For landlords, this often meant restricting or even evicting *colonos* from their plots to reorganize labor on a more profitable wage-labor basis. *Colonos*, on the other hand, organized, with the help of APRA, to resist their eviction and proletarization.

Conflict over tenancy arrangements involved not only access to parcels on agricultural estates, but to grazing rights on cattle and sheep ranches. With beef and lamb in growing demand in the cities, plantations, and mining enclaves, ranchers sought to rationalize their operations by trying to eliminate traditional pasturing and other arrangements and to convert to wage labor. These attempts provoked ranch workers and shepherds (*huacchilleros*), like *colonos*, to organize and resist.

For both *colonos* and *huacchilleros*, the balance of power in the contest often tipped in favor of landlords because of demographic trends. Accelerating population growth altered the highland labor market from one of relative scarcity to increasing oversupply. For example, the rate of population growth rose from 1.9 percent annually in 1940 to 2.2 percent in 1950 to 2.7 percent by 1961. (Burga and Flores Galindo, 1980, p. 66, showed the trend a little more sharply; e.g., 1.5 percent in 1910 to 3.0 percent in 1960.) According to census data, the rural population stood at 1.6 million in 1876, rose to almost 4 million in 1940, and grew to 5.2 million in 1961. This increase was partly due to the sharp decline in the mortality rate after World War II, which dropped from 27 per thousand in 1940 to 15 per thousand in 1961. During the war, many new medicines were developed, including penicillin, streptomycin, sulfa, and cortisone, and they became increasingly available after the war in the Third World. At the same time, public health programs and facilities multiplied in the cities and then spread into rural areas as governments and private foundations earmarked funds to eradicate diseases that were now treatable with these new "wonder" drugs.

With a proliferating labor supply, it was in the landlords' interest to terminate tenancy arrangements and resort to the growing "reserve army" of workers who were willing to accept relatively low wages to work on their lands. Still, advantaged as they were by these favorable trends, modernizing landowners did not always prevail in the struggle over tenancy arrangements and, as often as not, were fought to a standstill by strong resistance from *colonos* and *huacchilleros*.

The same demographic trends affected sierra Indian communities, sharpening the perpetual struggle between landlords and the communities for access to land, water, and labor. Conflict was inevitable, given the rising population of peasants on a relatively fixed base of arable land—in other words, a deteriorating man–land ratio. This situation was aggravated in places like the central highlands, where the spread of commerce was causing land values to rise. Under conditions of growing scarcity, peasants increasingly invaded disputed lands after 1945 as communities tried to take back lands usurped by contiguous estates.

Internal conflicts over access to resources also occurred within communities, as Mallon (1983) showed, where social differentiation was deepening under the same twin pressures of population growth (deteriorating man–land ratios) and commercialization (the emergence of a strata of rich peasants). With diminishing access to land, many *comuneros* were forced to leave their homes and migrate to the mines, plantations, and cities in search of work. According to census data, the proportion of migrants in the population increased sharply, from 9.5 percent in 1940 to 23.2 percent in 1961 and to 26.4 percent in 1972.

In this context of demographic change, rural conflict, and rising mobilization, Aprista organizers and lawyers, many of whom had only recently been released from jail, were active on the local level among the peasantry after 1945. However, on the national level, the party was unwilling to jeop-

Matrimonial couple, Sicuani, 1934. Photograph by Martín Chambi, reproduced with the permission of Teo Allain Chambi.

ardize its hard-won legality to mount a full-scale challenge to the Andean seignorial system. Indeed, such a challenge would have constituted an attack on the sierra landholding (*gamonal*) class, which still maintained a disproportionate representation in Congress and inordinate power on the local level (part of its long-standing quid pro quo with the state). Furthermore, the political benefits of undertaking such an assault were limited, given the political potential of peasants who were largely atomized, dominated, and lacked the right to vote. As was mentioned earlier, even with control of Congress, the party did not move to expand suffrage.

To the party leaders, it made more sense to address the problems of the modern, coastal, urban society, where the bulk of APRA's worker–middle-class political base resided, than those of rural areas. Thus, compared to other Latin American countries at the time, APRA represented a classic urban-oriented populist political phenomenon. Still, this stance did not preclude the possibility of Apristas at the local level collaborating with peasant groups to press for change.

To many, the party's relative inattention to the rural question was only one more example of the ideological and programatic "revisionism" that it had pursued since the beginning of World War II. As a result, the internal divisions in APRA became more accentuated and contentious during the triennium. With all its vaunted unity and solidarity, the party had, from its earliest days, been divided between a moderate faction that was committed to reform and democratization and a more militant, revolutionary wing. During the repressive 1930s, this division had been submerged by the larger imperative of maintaining internal discipline through a hierarchical, semimilitary organizational structure in order to survive. When the party emerged from time to time from underground during political "openings," internal divisions developed, often with a vengeance, as they did after the 1945 election.

Perhaps to contend with this factionalism or as a result of it, Haya had developed an ambiguous style of leadership that promised, in effect, "all things to all men" (Davies, 1971). Such a style of leadership was not necessarily detrimental while the party was confined to the catacombs, with the enemy and the objective of survival clearly defined. However, when the party gained a share of power in the mid-1940s, such an ambiguous, indeed vacillating and indecisive, style of leadership became more of a liability. In practice, it meant that Haya developed a tendency, indeed a pattern, to encourage the militant wing, then pull back and actually side with the moderates. This tendency was particularly evident when Haya consistently withheld support at the last minute for revolutionary conspiracies, that were often originally encouraged by Haya and spearheaded by the militant faction.

Frustrated by such actions, as well as by the regime's general moderation, party militants took the offensive in early 1946. In April, they unleashed several attacks against the established, habitually anti-Aprista, press. Shortly thereafter, Bustamante, according to Haworth, (1992, p. 182), candidly admitted to the American ambassador that when he assumed the presidency, he should have immediately organized an anti-APRA police force and that it had certainly been a mistake to curtail the activities of the secret police. The wave of APRA violence culminated in the bombing of the house of the minister of government in December 1946 and the assassination of Francisco Graña Garland, the aristocratic editor of *La Prensa*, in January 1947.

Bustamante responded by forcing the resignation of the "Aprista Cabinet" and replacing it with a largely military one, and appointing General Manuel A. Odría, a hero in the 1941 war with Ecuador and staunch anti-Aprista, as minister of government and police. However, these actions were not enough to assuage the outrage of the agroexport elite, which was already rankled by the government's statist economic policies, including controls on foreign exchange and prices, pro-labor policies, and increased taxes on exports—all of which curtailed its profits.

With sharply increased social spending, the only way the government could balance its budget and avoid a deficit was to increase taxes, particularly on exports. Since postwar international demand and prices for sugar and cotton were soaring, windfall profits on producers became an obvious target for new governmental revenues. Consequently, from 1945 to 1948, taxes as a percentage of exports rose, according to Portocarrero (1983, p. 123), from 7.5 percent to 31.7 percent on sugar and 8.4 percent to 21.5 percent on cotton. Seen another way, fully 60 percent of the 40 percent increase in the government's 1946 budget came from increased tax revenues on sugar exports.

The elites' rising discontent with the regime during 1947 must also be seen in the overall context of the deteriorating economic situation. As the European combatants gradually recovered after the war, Peruvian exports, after experiencing a 12 percent increase in 1946, fell in the next two years 18 percent and 21 percent, respectively, as did the prices received by exporters. At the same time, imports rose 23 percent in 1946, 36 percent in 1947, and 11.7 percent in 1948 while prices to consumers steadily climbed. Coming as it did with state-mandated wage increases, the overall expansion of the state budget, and rising consumer prices, the deteriorating balance of trade and payments led to an inevitable surge in inflation. For example, the cost of living increased 60 percent between 1944 and 1947, in spite of continuing governmental controls.

The upshot was rising shortages of basic consumer commodities in the marketplace, the emergence of a black market, and the government's institution of a form of rationing. Rationing, in turn, inflamed public opinion, since people now had to endure not only shortages and high prices, but long lines and a rationing system that favored members of the "ruling" APRA party. In short, governmental mismanagement, together with adverse international trends, had, by mid-1947, raised the specter of economic chaos. Such economic fears, combined with increasing APRA violence, inflamed the oligarchy and gave it the opening to attack and ultimately bring the government down.

The main leader and spokesman for the Right at this time was Pedro Beltrán. A wealthy cotton planter from Cañete who had received a large dose of economic liberalism from the London School of Economics, Beltrán returned to Peru and, together with Gildemeister and other oligarchs, purchased *La Prensa*, which, under his editorship, became a vociferous critic of APRA and the government. As economic conditions worsened and APRA violence increased, Beltrán also formed the Alianza Nacional, a coalition of parties drawn together to oppose the government.

The ascendancy of the Right and its concerted political counterattack on the APRA/Bustamante cogovernment culminated in mid-1947 with a boycott of Congress by conservative and leftist legislators. The walkout prevented a quorum and effectively paralyzed the government. Paradoxically, it was a tactic similar to the one used by APRA during the first six months to stymie the Bustamante government and force the appointment of the "Aprista Cabinet."

The closing down of Congress immediately heightened political tensions that resonated in the military, which had always been a pluralistic institution with major cleavages not only between the army and navy but between junior and midgrade officers and senior officers. At the same time, severe cleavages existed between enlisted men and officers in all the armed services, on the basis of class, ethnicity, language, and education. Often this cleavage had resulted in the brutalization of the enlisted men and, in general, had worked to undermine the morale and unity of the armed forces.

With the government effectively halted by the political stalemate between Congress and the Executive and the economy in a shambles, the country entered a downward spiral of political polarization, military conspiracy, and violence. APRA responded to the congressional boycott by calling a general strike that, in turn, caused Bustamante to suspend constitutional guarantees for thirty days. At the same time, APRA conspired to bring the government down forcibly when militants hatched a military plot, including the navy, designed to trigger a popular revolt in February 1948.

Of all the branches of the armed forces, the navy harbored the sharpest division between officers and enlisted men, and APRA hoped to exploit this schism. Officers, who were trained at the Escuela Naval (Naval Academy), were typically admitted as much on their upper-class family backgrounds and connections as on academic merit. Rank-and-file draftees, on the other hand, were ill educated and had little opportunity to gain the training and expertise that were necessary for promotion, which contributed to generally low morale within the ranks. APRA had previously exploited this discontent when it inspired an unsuccessful uprising of noncommissioned officers on two cruisers in May 1932. Eight sailors who were killed in that unsuccessful revolt were subsequently enshrined as martyrs by the party to the Aprista cause.

This time, the APRA plot centered on naval units in Callao, but the authorities, supported by air force and army units, uncovered and quickly suppressed it in February 1948. In its aftermath, right-wing civilian and military elements, including Minister of Government Odría, urged Bustamante once again to outlaw the APRA. However, the president refused. He apparently hoped to play a centrist, moderating, and mediating role between the political extremes of what he now called the "sect" (APRA) and the "clan" (Beltrán, Gildemeister, and the oligarchical Right), but with little political or popular support. The president's refusal led Odría to resign from the Cabinet and to begin plotting against the government himself. By mid-1948, Bustamante was completely isolated between the two groups, and it was now only a matter of time before his government would be overthrown.

The first attempt to bring him down came from the Right, apparently engineered by Odría, but it was foiled by the government in July. Then in the early morning hours of October 3, a major naval revolt erupted at Callao, involving 500 sailors and 100 civilians and organized by militant elements of APRA under the former head of CROE, Major Víctor Villanueva. The organizers apparently went ahead with the revolt without orders from Haya de la Torre, whom they feared, would pull back at the last moment in favor of a coup being organized by more senior, pro-APRA officers in the army. However, without the full support of the party leadership, the rebel cause was doomed. For the revolt to have succeeded, Apristas would have had to have taken to the streets in large numbers to show broad popular support for it. This support did not materialize, and the army high command rallied to suppress the revolt, but not without heavy fighting and the death of 60 combatants and 175 civilians, which, according to Masterson (1991), made it the most serious insurrection since the 1932 Trujillo revolt.

Bustamante responded by authorizing a wholesale crackdown on those who were suspected of involvement in the Callao revolt and, belatedly, issuing a decree outlawing the APRA. Over a thousand civilians, along with 800 naval personnel (or 17 percent of the 4,800 officers and enlisted men) were arrested and interrogated in the revolt's aftermath. Overall sentiment among the officer corps now swung heavily against the APRA.

Against a backdrop of worsening inflation and food shortages, as well as student disorders in Lima, Odría and the armed forces high command carried out a successful coup against the government on October 29. The following day, Bustamante was sent packing into exile in Buenos Aires, and Odría, who had organized the coup from Arequipa, arrived in Lima to assume the provisional presidency. The entire affair had been carried out without the conspirators firing a single shot.

The Reaction: Odría's Dictatorship, 1948–56

Odría's coup followed closely the pattern of earlier military takeovers in the century. Like the coups of both Benavides in 1914 and Sánchez Cerro in 1930, Odría's "Restoration Movement" was an effort to curtail the forces of insurgent populism, notably those of Billinghurst (1912–14) and then the APRA. Once again, the armed forces had embraced its historic role as guardian of the elites' interests in the face of populist challenge. In this role, Odría also fit the traditional personalistic, *caudillo* style that was characteristic of his military predecessors.

One of the most vehemently anti-Aprista officers in the army, Odría was born in 1897 to a prosperous family in Tarma, a city in the central Andes. His grandfather was a career army officer who had distinguished himself in the defense of Peru against the Spanish invasion of 1866. As a young man, Odría followed his grandfather into the army, graduating first in his class in 1915 from the Chorillos Military Academy. His career progressed uneventfully until he commanded the First Light Division in the 1941 border war with Ecuador, from which he emerged as a hero. When he was appointed to Bustamante's cabinet in 1947, Odría, according to Masterson (1991, p. 99), was known as a shrewd, politically tough general who was an excellent judge of people.

Having seized the reigns of power, Odría cracked down hard on APRA and the Left (CP), which were both proscribed. Over a thousand Apristas were arrested, including party leaders Ramiro Prialé and Armando Villanueva, although Haya de la Torre eluded capture. Unions linked to APRA were closed or taken over by leaders who were sympathetic to the regime. Within the military, Odría pursued the pro-APRA faction, many of whom, like Major Villanueva, were jailed or exiled. Finally, in January 1949, Haya came out of hiding and sought diplomatic asylum in the Colombian Embassy, where he would remain for the next five years because the government refused to grant him safe passage out of the country. Haya's prolonged confinement not only became a cause celebre outside the country, but deprived the now-clandestine APRA of his leadership, which was assumed by his close lieutenants Manuel Seoane and Luis Alberto Sánchez.

At first, Odría's rule was marked by his embrace of the oligarchical Right, represented by the Miró-Quesadas, Pedro Beltrán, and Ramón Aspíllaga. Several members of the "clan" had, according to Masterson, allegedly financed the October coup with a sum of 8 million soles. So for the moment, at least, Odría pursued the "clan's" economic liberalism by moving quickly away from the controls imposed by the previous Prado and Bustamante governments back to "orthodox," pro-export economic measures. Beltrán was appointed head of the Central Bank, and the country resumed service on its foreign debt for the first time since Leguía defaulted in 1930. This action opened the way for an influx of foreign investments, which reached $800 million by 1956, including $300 million alone from the United States between 1950 and 1955.

At the same time, realizing the need for popular support while he consolidated his power, Odría signed a decree that greatly expanded social security coverage for workers. He also ordered pay raises, ranging from 15 percent to 25 percent for army officers and the police and the construction of a modern military hospital in Lima. Indeed, overall, Odría increased the military budget during his first year by 45 percent. These moves foreshadowed the clientelism and paternalism that would mark the Odría regime and temper the economic liberalism so dear to the heart of his supporters on the Right.

Having promised elections, Odría nevertheless had no intention of stepping down in favor of another candidate. He also was not about to become a prisoner of the Right, dependent on the clan for his political future. Moreover, the rise to power of fellow army officer Juan Perón in neighboring Argentina on the basis of populist support had not gone unnoticed by Odría. For all these reasons, the Peruvian general found it politically expedient to increase sharply public works and later to patronize the growth of squatter settlements that were springing up around Lima in response to increased migration from the sierra.

The means to finance these popular, but expensive, social policies fortuitously coincided with the outbreak of the Korean War in 1950. During the war, prices and the demand for Peruvian metal exports, particularly copper, suddenly boomed, providing the treasury with windfall revenues to cover the costs of various state-sponsored construction projects. Exporters, however, chaffed at the continuation of tight monetary (credit) controls that were designed to hold up the free-market exchange rate, leading Beltrán to resign from the Central Bank in March 1950. To the conservatives, such controls smacked of the same costly "statist" policies pursued by Bustamante in 1948 to placate urban labor and the middle class.

Odría also decreed a comprehensive Internal Security Law in July 1949, which gave the government sweeping search-and-seizure powers and suspended the right of habeas corpus for suspected political crimes. Although the law was aimed at APRA, it could be used against any potential political opponent. This was a particularly ominous move, considering that Odría had promised to hold free elections.

In early January 1950, Odría announced that elections for president and Congress would be held in July. The government, however, invalidated the opposition candidate, and Odría easily won reelection. Once "elected," Odría embarked upon a program of military populism that was modeled after his counterpart's in Buenos Aires. Like Perón, Odría's political target was the urban poor who, over the past decade, had migrated to the capital in search of work and a better life. Indeed, from 1940 to 1961 the number of inhabitants of metropolitan Lima exploded from almost 600,000 to nearly 2 million, an average of just over 5 percent a year. A large portion of these inhabitants were migrants from the countryside, mainly from the departments of Ancash, Ayacucho, and Junín, who settled in *barriadas* (squatter settlements) that increasingly ringed the city on three sides.

These settlements were an entirely new phenomenon in Lima, and by 1961, they contained over 300,000 inhabitants (75 percent of whom were migrants), or 20 percent of the metropolitan population. They also constituted part of what Hernando de Soto (1989) would later call the informal economy, since both their housing and their work fell outside "normal," that is, legal, property and employment relations with the state. By constructing a paternalistic relationship with these populous, new communities, Odría hoped to avoid a more dangerous situation: an attempt by APRA or the Left to mobilize the squatters to make radical, perhaps violent, demands on the state, thereby threatening the status quo. To forestall this possibility, Odría chose to channel assistance and favors, as Collier (1976) showed, to these settlements in order to incorporate them into the state and to forge a loyal political clientele for his increasingly authoritarian rule.

This assistance included access to land, services, and charitable activities, as well as public works aimed at employing the newcomers. Although there was some cost to the state for this assistance, a good portion of it did not add to the national budget. A notable example was the establishment of the María Delgado de Odría Center of Social Assistance, organized by the president's wife, who fashioned her role after Eva Perón. The center channeled private charity to the *barriadas* in various high-visibility activities that received widespread publicity in the media.

Another example was the president's use of his office to promote the formation of individual squatter settlements. In this case, Odría would personally intervene at a particular moment or stage in the invasion process (takeover of vacant lands) to ensure its success and thereby legitimate the occupation. Similarly, the establishment of settler associations that were loyal to Odría served to channel support in the form of political demonstrations or other manifestations in favor of the regime. At the same time, APRA's or the CP's efforts to organize and mobilize squatters were suppressed.

One important, unintended side effect of Odría's support for the formation of squatter settlements was to encourage further migration from the countryside and thus urbanization. Public works projects, which stimulated employment and a construction boom in Lima during his term as president, had the same effect. Such policies also served, whether consciously or not, to diffuse tensions and conflict between landlords and peasants in the rural sector. Thus, rural out-migration served as a "safety valve" to popular pressures that were building up against the traditional *latifundia* and thereby delayed the eventual collapse of the *gamonal* class and the traditional rural order until the late 1960s.

Another similarity with Perón was Odría's paternalistic attitude toward organized labor. It is true that he ruthlessly tried to root out Aprista influence in the unions and replaced many union leaders with persons who were loyal to him. But that did not necessarily mean that he was antiworker, just anti-Aprista. On the contrary, the president decreed seven across-the-board pay increases during his term in office, and many believed that he did more to advance the condition of workers than anyone in Peruvian history. Be that as it may, one of Odría's main goals was to undermine labor's relationship with APRA and to gain control of the movement.

Economically, Odría's rise to power represented an important shift back to export promotion. Indeed, beginning in 1950, Peru experienced a great wave of export expansion that would last until the mid-1960s. During this period, the volume of exports rose three and a half times, doubling in the 1950s alone. Taking a slightly longer perspective, from 1942 to 1970, export earnings grew at the remarkable rate of about 10 percent a year, the highest, in the country's history.

In the agroexport sector, Odría revived Leguía's idea of large-scale, government-financed irrigation works and encouraged private projects as well. As a result, the total irrigated land area along the coast increased 19 percent from 1952 to 1962. The increase was absorbed completely by Peru's two principal export crops—sugar (42 percent) and cotton (45 percent)—which enabled the production of these two crops to increase by 63 percent and 59 percent, respectively. Since domestic sugar consumption had been rising since the 1930s, however, this increase in production served only to keep export levels constant in absolute numbers. Thus, the proportion of sugar that was exported dropped from 87 percent in the 1930s to less than 50 percent in the early 1970s.

During the 1950s sugar exports went mostly to Chile and Japan. A decade later, Peru was sending the bulk of its exports to the United States, which turned away from its traditional supplier, Cuba, after the Castro revolution of 1959. Most of the increase in sugar production during this period came from increased investments, particularly in mechanization, which had the effect of displacing labor. With the demand for sugar workers declining and migration from the sierra increasing, a surplus labor market developed for the first time on the coast. This development led planters finally to abandon the *enganche* labor-recruiting system, which disappeared completely from coastal valleys by the 1950s.

As for cotton, foreign demand rose during the 1950s, stimulated by the Korean War, which enabled cotton to reassume the lead in total exports. The number of hectares devoted to cotton production rose sharply, from a low point of 120,000 in 1947 to a peak of 230,000 in 1956, enabling output to expand 75 percent. The expansiveness of both the cotton and sugar sectors had a favorable overall impact on the economy during this period. Because of its labor-intensive and income-distributive characteristics, cotton production contributed to a stimulus in consumer demand (from tenants and laborers). At the same time, sugar, with its capital-intensiveness and high return value (estimated, on average, at around 80 percent), provided important investment funds and linkages to the local economy. For example, by the late 1950s, sugar giant W. R. Grace & Co. was producing substantial amounts of paper from cane residue, as well as chemicals from complexes integrated with its sugar mills at Cartavio and Paramonga.

During Odría's government, the fishing industry began what would become a spectacular expansion over the ensuing two decades. Actually, the industry dated back to the immediate postwar period. The production of canned fish, which stood at under 6,000 metric tons in 1945–49, more than tripled during the 1950s to a high of 21,000 in 1955–59. The industry was pioneered by a new group of middle-class entrepreneurs, who included future fishmeal baron Luis Banchero Rossi.

Although the agroexport sector (including fishing and livestock) constituted the bulk of total Peruvian exports during the 1940s and 1950s, its percentage of total exports dropped steadily from 65 percent in 1945 to 48 percent in 1960. Coincidently, mineral exports as a percentage of total exports rose from 33 percent to 50 percent over the same period, mainly from copper, lead, zinc, and iron. Oil, however, continued its long-term decline from the 1930s to the 1960s.

Important stimuli to the upturn in mining production and exports were favorable prices on the world market and a new mining law passed under Odría in 1950 that liberalized the tax system. Local entrepreneurship, which had experienced a resurgence since the withdrawal of foreign firms beginning in the depression, reached its zenith during the early 1950s and then began to recede. However, foreign capital began to move back into mining at this time. The most notable example was the formation in 1952 of the Southern Peruvian Copper Corporation, which invested $200 million to develop the vast Toquepala deposits near Tacna. The Cerro de Pasco Copper Corporation also began to develop its lead-zinc deposits at Cerro de Pasco and Casapalca, as did Marcona its iron deposits. As a result, foreign, as opposed to local, control of mining reversed its decline and rose from a low of 49 percent in 1950 to 73 percent in 1960. The spread effects of this overall surge in the mining sector were significant, particularly in domestically produced capital goods and local purchases of supplies. The Odría administration also tried to stimulate oil production by encouraging foreign investment in exploration, but with little success in discovering new deposits. Consequently, oil production continued to decline, reaching only 1 percent of exports in 1964, while imports rose to over 4 million barrels a year by 1960 to cover the rising domestic demand.

Having staked his regime's economic future on a resumption of export-led growth, Odría did little to encourage import substituting industrialization. No effort was made to raise tariffs while imports rose as controls were lifted and credit from the Banco Industrial declined. Industrial growth managed to increase 8 percent a year, but most of it was related to export processing and supplies to small and medium-scale mining operations, not to the production of consumer goods. Only when an export recession interrupted growth at the end of the Korean War in 1953–54 did Odría take a more positive attitude toward the manufacturing sector.

U.S. firms, however, began to increase their investments in the manufacturing sector during the 1950s. A good example was W. R. Grace & Co., whose sugar operations actually became secondary to the manufacture of a range of products, such as paper, chemicals, biscuits, machinery, textiles, and paint. This situation led Goodsell (1974, p. 52) to observe that "there is hardly a Peruvian participating in the money economy who does not eat, wear or use something processed, manufactured, or imported by Casa Grace."

While agroexports expanded briskly during the 1950s, domestic food production barely managed to keep pace with increasing demand caused by urbanization and rising living standards. Traditionally, food production had been relegated to the sierra, while the coast specialized in exports. However, historically, agricultural production tended to lag in the highlands, where land was less productive, resources were less available, and governmental policy was more discriminatory. During the 1950s, the rate of agricultural output in the sierra, according to one admittedly sketchy estimate, amounted to a little more than 1 percent a year. But production in some areas, such as the Mantaro Valley that supplied Lima, was quite robust.

The coast was also a source of food production, but mostly when the demand for exports was slack. However, because of the export boom of the 1950s, foreign exchange was available to import foodstuffs to meet the rising demand. The proportion of food imports to total imports during the 1950s rose moderately from 13.6 percent in 1951 to 15.7 percent in 1955, falling back to 14.4 percent in 1960. Overall, then, food supplies roughly matched demand during the 1950s, despite a strong growth in the gross national product (GNP), low inflation (on average, 7–8 percent per year, with food slightly higher), and modest imports. This supply and demand equilibrium was probably because per capita income growth and, hence consumption, remained low, if not largely stagnant, during this period.

The state continually overlooked the needs of agriculture for credit, technical assistance, public investment, and the like. For example, small farmers, who represented 80 percent of the agricultural workforce, received only 24 percent of the credit dispensed by the Banco de Fomento Agropecuario from 1948 to 1953. Conversely, large-scale export agriculture on the coast (principally sugar, cotton, and rice) received the bulk of both state and commercial bank credit. Overall, the effect was to disincentivize investment in nonexport agriculture relative to other more profitable sectors of the economy.

Although the export boom engendered by the Korean War served to consolidate Odría's power in the early 1950s, opposition nevertheless developed in both the armed forces and on the oligarchical Right. Within the army, Odría's increasing authoritarianism, paternalism, and manipulation of promotions rankled those officers who were strong advocates of professionalization and reform. Some saw the need to modernize the mission of the armed forces beyond the traditional concept of defense and internal order. In their view, both were intimately linked to broader societal problems, such as underdevelopment and the nonintegration of the Indian population, on which the army depended for most of its recruits.

Several officers, including General José Del Carmen Marín, one of the leading intellectuals and theoreticians in the army, pressed for the creation of a specialized training and studies center to prepare officers better for command. Such training, they envisioned, would not be confined strictly to military matters, but would include the study of other societally related issues. After several years of lobbying, the Centro de Altos Estudios Militares (CAEM), or Center for High Military Studies, was founded in 1950. It was modeled on the National War College in Washington, established three years earlier, and similar centers in other countries, such as France. At first, Odría tried to undermine the importance of CAEM by having only officers who were approaching retirement assigned to the center's first classes. However, with the persistence of General Carmen Marín, who was appointed the center's first director, many of the most promising young officers entered and graduated from the CAEM, and its importance and prestige grew.

At the same time, discussions at the CAEM deepened over the country's national security doctrine, and a consensus was developing that the role of national defense needed to be redefined to include social and economic development. Such thinking reflected the belief that threats to internal security, deriving from the country's social problems, were as serious as the traditional threat of cross-border invasions. National security depended as much on finding ways to alleviate the problems of underdevelopment and to close the great divide that separated and marginalized the Indian population, as to increasing the armed forces' technological modernization and combat readiness to confront a potential foreign enemy. This line of thinking actually went back to French theories of colonial pacification in the early 1920s that were derived from that country's earlier role in professionalizing the Peruvian military in the first decades of the century.

While the CAEM was taking root as a progressive new center of training and study for the military's best and brightest, Odría was moving to shore up the military's traditional combat role. Having displayed a strong commitment to anticommunism, Odría was able to develop cordial ties with the Eisenhower administration during the early years of the Cold War. These ties led to the signing of an important military assistance pact with the United States in 1952 that formalized the latter's increasing involvement with the Peruvian military since World War II. Under the agreement, according to Masterson, the United States increased its military assistance to Peru from a mere $100,000 that year to $9.1 million by the end of Odría's term in 1956.

Opposition to Odría intensified when the export boom suddenly turned into a recession at the close of the Korean War in 1953–54. Confronted by a mounting trade deficit that would reach $70 million in 1953 and the ensuing depreciation of the *sol*, which led to the outbreak of serious labor unrest, the president cracked down on civil liberties and forcibly broke up several strikes. He was also compelled to curtail public works expenditures and reduce the military budget, always a risky proposition even for a soldier-president. Close on the heals of these developments, Odría, now increasingly cozy with the more moderate sector of the oligarchy led by Prado, decided to allow Haya de la Torre to leave the country to go into exile. This move further enraged the Right, both civilian and military, but was aimed at alleviating opposition from APRA-dominated organized labor.

Haya now emerged from the Colombian Embassy, where he had spent the past five years reading and reflecting on APRA's future course, more convinced than ever to continue down the path of rapprochement with capitalism, the oligarchy, and the United States. He also continued to lobby U.S. officials to pressure Odría to restore civil liberties and legalize the party.

Fortunately for Odría, the economy pulled out of the recession and resumed its export-led growth in 1954, even as the dictator thwarted a series of attempted coups by rivals in the armed forces. Confounding his critics, who accused him of planning to remain in power at the end of his term in 1956, Odría announced that national elections would be held in June 1956 and that he would not be a candidate. Three presidential candidates emerged to contest the election, with APRA again playing the determining role. Odría backed the lackluster candidacy of Hernando de Lavalle, a lawyer and banker, who immediately sought APRA's endorsement.

A more formidable candidate was forty-four-year-old architect and university professor Fernando Belaúnde Terry, who had been elected to Congress in 1945 as a member of the FDN. Belaúnde was supported by forward-looking sectors of a new middle class that had emerged since World War II, principally students, professionals, and technicians. Many had backed the ideas of Bustamante and were attracted to Belaúnde's charismatic style and oratorical brilliance. Belaúnde's popularity was given a sharp boost when Odría tried unsuccessfully to have the Junta Nacional Electoral annul his candidacy. Youthful, handsome, and debonair, Belaunde also appealed to women, who had finally won the right to vote a year earlier in 1955, thanks to the efforts María Delgado de Odría.

The third candidate was sixty-seven-year-old, former president Manuel Prado, who returned unexpectedly from Paris to enter the campaign. Although APRA was unable to present its own slate of candidates, it opened negotiations with each candidate to secure a pledge of legality in return for the party's endorsement. Haya de la Torre immediately found the candidacy of Belaúnde distasteful, partly because of his personal dislike of the candidate and partly because his youthful, upstart opponent's moderate, reformist ideas represented a serious, competitive challenge to APRA.

In the end, a few days before the elections, the experienced Prado struck a deal with APRA in the so-called Pact of Monterrico. In return for APRA's support, Prado agreed to legalize the party and to allow Haya to run for president in 1962. Odría accepted the pact, knowing that his candidate Lavalle had no chance to win and because Prado gave assurances not to investigate charges of corruption against his regime. Known as the policy of *convivencia* (coexistence), the agreement gave Prado the necessary support to win the election with 586,000 votes (45 percent), as opposed to Belaúnde's surprisingly large 457,000 (36 percent) and Lavalle's 222,000. Significantly, the size of the electorate had tripled since 1950 to 1.25 million voters (with the addition of women, although illiterates, and therefore more than than two-thirds of the total voting-age population were still excluded).

Prado, the "Convivencia," and the Agrarian Crisis, 1956–62

The inauguration of Prado as president in 1956 represented the final apogee of direct oligarchical rule in the twentieth century. Prado's term was characterized by relative stability and, after eight years of dictatorship, a return to democratic government. The president faced little military opposition, and only one botched coup attempt occurred in early 1958. Although there was an international recession within a year of his taking office, export-led growth resumed in 1959 and advanced strongly until the end of his term. Unemployment increased in 1957–58, as did labor unrest, but APRA's tight control of the union movement enabled Prado to weather it. Finally, although land invasions and landlord-peasant tensions intensified in the highlands, various proposals for land reform were cleverly obstructed by elite maneuvers in a Congress controlled by the president. In short, Prado represented a stand-pat approach to the problems facing the country, even as it became increasingly obvious that fundamental reforms needed to be made.

Economically, the long wave of export-led growth, which stretched from 1948 to 1968, now entered its mature phase. The growth of export volumes accelerated, from 10 percent a year during the 1950s to a remarkable 21 percent from 1959 to 1962, before dropping back to 5 percent during the mid-1960s. The real GNP grew accordingly, from 4.7 percent a year from 1950 to 1959 to 8.8 percent from 1960 to 1962, before it fell thereafter to 3.9 percent until 1968. Per capita GNP growth over the same period registered 2.4 percent, 5.9 percent, and 1.3 percent, respectively.

Peru's complete integration into the international market during this period was accompanied by continued large inflows of foreign capital. Not only was the country's orthodox, free-market economy attractive to foreign companies, but the repatriation of profits was virtually unrestricted. During the 1950s and early 1960s, Peru became one of the most propitious countries in South America in which to invest and increasingly came to be dominated by foreign capital.

Despite the favorable overall trend of the economy, Prado encountered problems during the first half of his term as a result of the effects of the international recession of 1957. In particular, the United States raised tariffs on mineral products and began to dump surplus cotton stocks onto the world market. Consequently, Peru's export-led advance in these commodities was momentarily halted, which had wider sociopolitical repercussions. Prado responded with deflationary policies that brought him into conflict with organized labor. At the same time, the oligarchy chaffed at their declining profits that they could not offset with significant wage cuts because of APRA's defense of the unions. With the balance of payments worsening and capital flight accelerating, Congress voted no confidence in the government in 1959, bringing down the Cabinet.

Prado reacted by shifting to the Right and appointing Pedro Beltrán once again as prime minister. Beltrán applied a monetarist stabilization program to try to bolster the flagging economy. Although this program caused a momentary wave of strikes in the mining, oil, construction, factory, and bank sectors, APRA played an important role in the government's mediating of labor's grievances. More significantly, three components of Peru's diversified export economy provided the impetus for an economic turnaround in the second half of Prado's term. Fishmeal output took off; production at the giant, new Toquepala copper mines came on line; and sugar exports to the United States surged in the wake of the Cuban Revolution of 1959.

The boom in fishmeal production came about because of market opportunities and technological innovation. Fishmeal production soared in Peru beginning in the mid-1950s. The number of fishmeal factories, for example, went from 17 in 1954 to 69 in 1959 to 154 in 1963. Coincidently, production increased by a factor of 20 from 1954 to 1959 and then tripled again by 1963.

While local elites and foreign companies participated in a small way in its meteoric rise, the fishmeal industry was mainly the creation of a new group of middle-class entrepreneurs. Of both native and immigrant origins, they included the Banchero, Elguera, Madueño, and Del Rio families. At the initiative of Banchero, they formed a successful cartel in 1960 that comprised 90 percent of the country's producers and was able to counteract falling prices in the early 1960s by reducing production. As for the established elites, for the most part they left the risk taking to the newcomers and chose instead to participate in the boom indirectly through their control of financing.

The bonanza in fishmeal production and exports gave the overall economy a huge boost. For one thing, its return value was extremely high, around 90 percent, and the multiplier effects of its backward linkages to the capital-goods sector and to internal consumption (from its wage bill) were powerful. Indeed, the fishmeal boom created as well a large, well-paid labor force, comprised mostly of unskilled sierra migrants to the coast. Centered in the port of Chimbote on the northern coast, which grew explosively during the 1950s and 1960s, the industry diverted the migrant population away from overcrowded Lima.

While fishmeal production gave the Peruvian economy a substantial lift out of the recession of 1958, assistance also came from developments in copper and sugar. When the huge Toquepala copper mines finally began production in 1960, after more than a decade of development, their output shortly came to comprise more than a third of the total copper production in the country. As for sugar, Peru gained a large share of the Cuban sugar quota in the lucrative U.S. market in 1961 after the 1959 revolution soured relations between Cuba and the United States. Production was quickly increased to capacity, since domestic demand also had to be met.

The second half of Prado's six-year term, then, was characterized by renewed growth, led by a strong surge in exports (21 percent per year in volume, 1959–62). Although the principal beneficiary of this renewal of the long wave of export-led growth (1948–68) were the urban, coastal, and modern sectors of the economy, certain hinterland regions of the sierra, particularly with market access to the coast, experienced a "commercial awakening" of their own. By an "awakening" Web (1977, p. 27) referred to "a rapid increase in the movement of money, goods and people," over the course of the 1950s and 1960s. The impact of this "awakening," however, was not geographically or socially uniform; it was confined mostly to the sierra regions with easy access to Lima and the central coast and to a rural bourgeoisie made up of merchants, artisans, bureaucrats, small- to medium-sized landowners, and other inhabitants of small towns and provincial cities.

One such notable hinterland to the coast, principally Lima, was the Mantaro Valley, in the central highlands of the department of Junín. With its bustling market town and capital Huancayo and its relatively divided land-holding structure, it became the breadbasket of Lima, provisioning the capital with a large portion of its food and labor needs. Huancayo itself had grown from 27,000 in 1940 to 64,000 in 1961, or about 4.2 percent annually. It had developed since the 1920s as an organizing center for the mining economy, which had established important linkages to the wider economy of Junín. It had also developed, according to Long and Roberts (1984, p. 66), into the third-largest manufacturing center outside Lima and Arequipa, led by textiles, tanneries, and breweries.

As a result of the city's economic dynamism, Huancayo attracted a large portion of migrants, both from the villages of the valleys, to work in the textile mills, and from Lima, often foreign born, to work in commerce and business. Overall average wages in Junín rose 47 percent, or 2.3 percent a year, between 1950 and 1967, twice as high as other sierra departments and three times higher than the heavily indigenous southern highlands (Ayacucho, Apurimac, Cuzco, Huancavelica, and Puno). Another hinterland area of dynamic growth was the Santa Valley in the department of Ancash, which ranked just after Junín, but well above other sierra departments, in wage levels.

Although less studied, the northern departments of La Libertad, Cajamarca, and Piura also showed similar signs of rural modernization during the 1950s and 1960s. In particular, the demands for labor and foodstuffs on the sugar, cotton, and rice plantations of the north coast dynamized production in the adjacent towns, villages, and countryside of the nearby highlands. In the province of Cajamarca, the archaic hacienda system was transformed into profitable dairy enterprises, spurred by state policies that deincentivized traditional food production and incentivized multinational capital and modernizing landowners. According to Deere (1990, p. 179), by the mid-1950s, forty-four major dairy farms had been carved out of older rented or purchased food-producing estates. The traditional hacienda workforce was also reorganized and reduced to coincide with a less labor-intensive industry. In the process, many estate tenants were evicted from their plots.

At the same time, small peasant producers took advantage of the developing and highly profitable market in milk to shift their output away from subsistence or foodstuffs to dairy cattle. The incomes of peasant households increasingly became monetized from milk production (79 percent by 1973, according to Deere), while "imported" products from the coast, such as rice, noodles, and beer, showed up, accordingly, on the shelves of the small village stores. With the spread of capitalist relations throughout the province, land was increasingly bought and sold and wage labor was expanded, which led to greater social differentiation among the region's peasantry.

If some of these hinterland sierra regions showed signs of rising commercialism and incomes, so did some towns in the more remote regions of the Andes. For example, Paucartambo, the district capital of Pasco, grew rapidly after the completion of a road in the 1950s that connected with the central highway. The larger town of Sicuani, the capital of Canchis province in Cuzco, grew 3.2 percent a year (to 10,664) from 1940 to 1961, whereas the province as a whole grew only 0.4 percent. Juliaca, a city located in an extremely poor area in the southern department of Puno, doubled in population over the same period. Other larger sierra cities grew at various annual rates between 1950 and 1966: Cuzco, 3.5 percent; Ayacucho, 1.7 percent; Cajamarca, 2.4 percent; Puno, 2.4 percent; Jauja, 2.0 percent; and La Oroya, 3.0 percent.

If it seems clear that the bourgeoisie in small sierra towns, cities, and "back-door" provinces of the coast garnered the lion's share of benefits from the commercial "awakening" of the 1950s and 1960s, what can be said of the peasant population who lived outside this area in the region at large? It comprised about two-thirds of the total peasant population of the sierra, 40 percent of whom were concentrated in the five southern poorest departments of the southern highlands.

Overall sierra agricultural output per capita grew only 0.8 percent a year from 1950 to 1966, which, according to Webb, probably approximated the per capita income as well. This figure suggests that the great majority of peasants, mainly in the more backward and Indian south, remained mired in subsistence and stagnation, if not outright decline, far removed from these more prosperous and modernizing sierra hinterlands where the peasantry was better off. Their outmoted and rudimentary techniques of production and isolation from markets, whether on haciendas or in communities, stood no chance of competing with the cheap imports and subsidized food policies of the state (not to mention the rising costs of inputs, such as tools, fertilizers, and the like) that had caused the generally deepening adverse terms of trade between city and country since the 1940s. Moreover, natural disasters, such as the 1957 drought and ensuing famine in the southern highlands, particularly Puno, caused a sharp decline in output and per capita income and an upsurge of peasants' migration to the cities.

Put in macroeconomic and sociological terms, the growing inequality and social differentiation that characterized the highland peasant population as capitalism and the internal market advanced in its customarily variegated and uneven way, set the stage for the upsurge in rural unrest and peasant mobilization that suddenly erupted during the late 1950s and that would peak in the middle of next decade. Both the losers, whose incomes declined and who either remained or chose to migrate to the cities, and the winners, who were incorporated into and benefited from the expanding internal market, increasingly saw little use for continuing the traditional *latifundia* (*gamonal*) system and began to agitate for its change.

At the same time, the long-standing quid pro quo between the state and the *gamonal* class to maintain order in the interior was undermined by the ever-expanding reach of the government by means of new roads and agents sent into the remote corners of the country. The improved means of communication (not to mention the revolutionary but little studied impact of the radio) and the increasing corpus of rural migrants in the cities, moreover, would provide the means for the spread of agrarian protest, not just in isolated corners of the sierra, as in the past, but all across the Andean heartland. The recently urbanized rural migrants were now exposed to new ideas and forms of political organizing in the cities that many, in the back-and-forth flow of migration, took back to their communities of origin and disseminated in a variety of ways.

The first major outbreak of peasant strife occurred in the department of Pasco, home of the Cerro de Pasco Copper Corporation, in late 1959. The sierra's smallest department, Pasco contained 138,000 inhabitants in 1960, but, according to Handelman (1975) and others, its peasantry was the most advanced in the sierra. Although predominantly Quechua speaking (60 percent), 90 percent of the population also spoke Spanish, in contrast to only 30–35 percent in the southern sierra. Its literacy rate stood at 52 percent, as opposed to only 23 percent in Apurimac.

Agriculturally, because of its altitude Pasco was mainly a ranching economy that produced wool from llama and sheep raising. In 1960 seventeen families and corporations, including Cerro, owned 93 percent of all arable and pastoral land in the department. These *latifundia* were highly capitalized and efficient, with a salaried workforce, in contrast to their more "feudal" counterparts in Cuzco and the south. Tensions and conflict over access to pasture land had long existed between the Indian communities and corporate ranches in Pasco, and Cerro had attracted a large number of *comuneros* into alternative employment through seasonal migration to the mines.

This "safety valve" for *comunero* employment began to disappear, however, with the advent of the depression of the early 1930s, when the Cerro Corporation moved to cut its workforce and further mechanize its operations so as to reduce costs. From 1940 to 1960, the population of Pasco increased 40 percent, but the labor force at Cerro's mines and Oroya refineries rose only 3–4 percent. *Comuneros* also migrated in increasing numbers to other sierra cities, such as Cuzco and Huancayo, in search of work, swelling the population of these cities from 80 percent to 140 percent over the same period. Exposed to modernity and the idea of progress, they kept their ties with their communities, where they became agents of change.

In 1958 the United States reduced its copper quota, triggering large-scale layoffs at Cerro, which were followed by a series of violent strikes and protests. A leading spokesman for the miners was a local schoolteacher named Genaro Ledesma Izquieta, who had recently migrated to Cerro from the coast. In negotiations with the company and then directly with the Prado administration, Ledesma tied the grievances of the miners with those of *comuneros* who were seeking the distribution of company ranch lands. When the dispute went unresolved, the *comuneros* began to invade hacienda lands. These individual actions involved groups of men, women, and children who ceremoniously announced their occupation by marching onto hacienda lands, sounding horns, waving Peruvian flags, and brandishing pitchforks. In the meantime, Ledesma, who was an Aprista, had been appointed mayor of Cerro de Pasco by Prado at the insistence of APRA. His appointment created a more favorable climate for the peasants' land actions, as did Ledesma's assistance in founding the Pasco Federation of Communities.

When the land invasions spread, however, Prado had Ledesma removed from office and jailed. But despite this and other police actions, the number of invasions over the next two years continued to grow in the department. They culminated in 1962, when a massacre occurred at the Hacienda Pocayán in which the police killed 10–15 *comuneros* and wounded 50. A wave of popular protest immediately followed in several cities, including Lima and Cerro de Pasco, where miners had always maintained close ties with the villages where the invasions were occurring.

Peasant unrest was also developing at this time in the valley of La Convención, located ninety miles northwest of Cuzco in the *montaña* (high jungle region) of the eastern slopes of the Andes. Beginning in the 1940s, a large influx of *comuneros* from neighboring departments in the southern Andes had migrated to La Convención, whose native population was relatively sparse. They were recruited by landlords who were opening the valley to cocoa, sugar, coffee, and tea cultivation. Attracted by the promise of land in exchange for labor and the hope of becoming independent farmers, the newcomers swelled the population of the valley from 28,000 in 1940 to 62,000 in 1960.

Because of their education, as well as their ambitions, the *comunero* migrants from such places as Cuzco did not share the "feudal" mentalities of many of their counterparts from elsewhere who had experienced hacienda peonage. Hardly passive and resigned, they had high expectations for advancement that were frustrated by the subsequent actions of their new landlords. As the price of coffee soared 1,200 percent after World War II, from 1.2 *soles* in 1945 to 14.8 in 1954, many converted their plots entirely to the cash crop. Meanwhile, as output in the valley tripled, landlords sought to increase their bonanza by reneging on their original contracts, evicting their tenants (*colonos*) and converting their operations entirely to wage labor. For their part, the *colonos* resisted these illegal actions and hired new migrants, called *subalegados* (subtenants), to substitute for their work obligations on the estates, so they could devote full attention to coffee raising on their own plots.

As early as 1952, the *colonos* formed a *sindicato* (union) to defend their interests, but it did not progress much until 1958, when several hacienda unions formed the provincial Peasant Federation of La Convención and Lares (Federación de Trabajadores Campesinos—FTC). Composed of both *colonos* and *alegados* (labor tenants), the new federation received the assistance of radical lawyers in Cuzco and established ties to the Communist-controlled Cuzco Labor Federation. By 1960, the FTC comprised 130 unions with a total membership of 11,000 campesinos.

The same year, the FTC made a series of demands to the landlords. They included reduced labor obligations, cash rent payments, direct sale of their coffee to the market without the landlords' interference, and long term (six to eight years) leases on their plots. Upon hearing the news of the land invasions in Pasco, the union also called a strike and asked its members to stop paying rent on their plots. This move coincided with the arrival in La Convención of Hugo Blanco, a Cuzco agronomist and Trotskyite whose father-in-law had helped form the FTC several years earlier and who was fluent in Quechua. Renting a small plot as a hacienda *alegado*, Blanco hoped to politicize and radicalize the movement as the spearhead of a wider peasant revolt that he envisioned spreading throughout the highlands.

Under Blanco's leadership, the strike expanded to include the entire valley, and the peasants took de facto control of their plots. By late 1962, the peasants had even succeeded in seizing 40 of the 380 haciendas in the region, before Blanco was forced to flee into the jungle to evade arrest by the authorities. Blanco's flight, together with the government's repression of the land seizures in Pasco, effectively ended what was the first phase of peasant mobilization in the sierra which had developed during the second half of Prado's term, from 1959 to 1962.

By this time, the Cuban Revolution under Fidel Castro and the Chinese Revolution under Mao Tse-tung had reoriented the thinking of many on the Left, including young urban radicals like Blanco, about the potential of an Andean peasant revolution. Although Mariátegui and other Marxists, as well as the APRA, had conceived of mobilizing the Indian peasantry in the cause of revolution a generation earlier, they had concentrated their organizing efforts mainly on radicalizing workers or segments of the middle sectors in the cities and enclaves. Blanco was the first actually to attempt such a peasant movement in the cause of revolution (Hildebrando Castro Pozo had attempted to organize peasants in the sierra of Piura for the Socialist Party in the 1930s), even though it did not take place exactly in the highlands. In addition, according to Handelman, it is clear that Blanco's charisma inspired students, many of whom had peasant backgrounds, in Andean cities like Cuzco, Ayacucho, and Huancayo to return to the countryside to organize and promote an agrarian revolution.

The Prado administration's response to the rising tide of peasant unrest was twofold. First, it forcibly tried to repress the movement, concentrating its efforts mainly in the strategically located Pasco area, where the Cerro de Pasco Copper Corporation wielded enormous political and economic power. La Convención was simply too remote and isolated and composed of landowners, who had little political or economic clout beyond the valley, to warrant similar attention. This policy succeeded in the short run in halting the spread of the movement, but the second response—that of land reform—raised the possibility of a longer-term solution. Prado had actually established a commission to study the question of agrarian reform at the outset of his administration in 1956, well before the outbreak of rural unrest. In addition to a possible way of improving the productivity and therefore efficiency and output of agriculture, land reform was seen as the means of reversing the flood of migrants to the cities, where they constituted a potential threat to the established order.

Headed by Prime Minister Beltrán, who was strongly opposed to redistribution as a means of resolving these problems, the commission languished for four years. Then in the midst of the upsurge in peasant mobilization in Pasco and La Convención, it was suddenly revived and issued a report in 1959. The report acknowledged that the government might need to undertake some limited land reform, but only with adequate remuneration to the owners. Although it constituted the first recognition in official circles of the possibility of land reform, the report made few concrete proposals and was never acted upon by the Congress.

Meanwhile, as rural unrest was growing during the last half of Prado's term, new currents of change were stirring within the armed forces. With the relative absence of civil-military tensions, the armed forces were able to concentrate on issues of professionalization and modernization that had been percolating for some time. Foremost among these issues was the changing mission of the military, from a purely defensive posture to one promoting security through national development or "nation building."

Under the developing influence of the CAEM, which graduated an increasing number of officers during the Prado administration, sentiment in favor of such a revised mission grew rapidly. By 1962, 70 percent of the generals in the army had graduated from the CAEM, where the students, according to Masterson, studied under civilian instructors such diverse subjects as sociology, agricultural development, banking, climatology, statistics, and development theory. In this way, officers were trained to approach the question of national security from the wider social scientific perspective of national development and nation building.

The upsurge in Andean peasant unrest after 1958, as well as the successful guerrilla war waged by Castro in Cuba, drove home the urgency of such a "developmental" approach. Indeed, it did not go unnoticed among the officer corps that Castro proceeded to destroy the regular Cuban armed forces once he achieved power. Institutional self-preservation would become a powerful argument in forging a broad consensus on altering the military's historic mission of self-defense to include the new concepts of civic action and counterinsurgency.

The evolution of closer ties with the United States during the Prado administration was another factor in reaching such a consensus. Over $70 million in military aid was received by Peru from the United States from 1956 to 1962, one of the highest figures in Latin America. This amount did not only include technical and logistical assistance and the delivery of military equipment and hardware, including several naval vessels. It also provided aid for civic action programs, such as road-building and development projects, which the United States increasingly promoted after 1960 as a response to Castro. In addition, a large number of Peruvian officers began to receive regular training in counterinsurgency warfare at command and staff schools in the United States, such as the one at Fort Leavenworth, Kansas.

The other traditional pillar of conservative rule in Peru, the Church, was also beginning to stir with change during the late 1950s, when it became more open to international ideological currents and more socially concerned. Although no single factor explains this transformation, several people and events contributed to it. For example, the Partido Democrático Cristiano (PDC) (Christian Democratic Party) was founded in 1956. Under the leadership of Héctor Cornejo Chávez, a former secretary to Bustamante, the PDC came to exercise an important progressive intellectual influence well beyond its relatively small membership of middle-class professionals with a strong sense of social awareness.

Also extremely influential in the changing direction of the Church was the towering ecclesiastical figure of Juan Landázuri Ricketts, who was born in Arequipa in 1913. Landázuri was named archbishop of Lima in 1955 and became the virtual patriarch of the Church until he vacated the position in 1990. An extraordinarily gifted "diplomat" and leader, he not only modernized and reorganized the Church's bureaucratic apparatus, but guided it into a more active social role. This role was evident beginning in 1957 when he announced a plan to meet the pastoral challenges of ministering to the fast-growing Lima squatter settlements that had burgeoned to 120,000 inhabitants. Landázuri also played a key role in the bishop's Pastoral Letter of 1958, which called on Christians to change society in a positive way and criticized "the accumulation of wealth in the hands of a few" as a major contributor to a developing social crisis in the country (Klaiber, 1992, p. 256).

As Prado's term approached its end, the Peruvian people turned in 1962 to the selection of a successor. In many ways, the country was now vastly different from the one that had elected Prado to his first term two decades earlier. The total population had grown 43 percent, from a little more than 7 million in 1940 to almost 10 million in 1960. At the same time, the rate of population increase accelerated more than one full percentage point, from 1.7 percent to 2.8 percent a year.

This overall increase, however, masked the 3.7 percent rate of growth of the urban population, as opposed to the 1.2 percent rate of the rural population. Indeed, the urban population increased three times that of the rural population between 1940 and 1961. This accelerating urbanization is also reflected in the rise in the proportion of cities with populations above 5,000, from 21 percent to 38 percent, a trend that would continue right down to the end of the century. Lima had more than doubled, from a population of 645,172 in 1940 to 1,652,000 in 1961. Since 1940 Peru had also seen a great demographic shift from the sierra interior to the coast. By 1961 the percentage of the population in the sierra had dropped from 60 percent to 51 percent, while the population of the coast had increased from 34 percent to 39 percent.

One major long-term implication of this increasing trend toward urbanization was rising pressure on the state to foster industrialization to create sufficient employment opportunites to absorb the mass of newcomers to the cities, particularly Lima. Another was the increasing governmental imperative to stablize food supplies and costs to forestall potential urban unrest from rising prices and scarcity. This imperative would lead to growing food imports from abroad, as well as increasing governmental subsidies for basic staples to stablize prices, both of which undermined national agricultural production. In this manner, an urban bias was introduced into governmental policy regardless of which political party or group succeeded in gaining power.

Increasingly, urbanization was also transforming the post–World War II cultural landscape of the country. Many intellectuals came to Lima from the provinces in the successive migratory waves that were changing the capital from its mythical viceregal and Hispanic character to one of increasing "cholification." This demographic revolution, with its deep social, economic, and political consequences, had a similar cultural impact.

One of the most important cultural events was the appearance of the novels of José María Arguedas, whose masterwork *Deep Rivers* appeared in 1958 and densely described the complex rural Indian society of the south from which he sprang. In this and other novels, the bilingual Arguedas mounted a serious critique of *indigenista* writers, most of whom, like Jorge Icaza, the Bolivian author who wrote the novel *Huasipungo* (1934), he felt, had written as outsiders to the Indian world. As such, they falsely portrayed the Indians, depicting them as hopelessly victimized and deprived of their agency, their lives simplified and caricatured by urban middle-class writers who, however well intentioned, were remote from and ignorant of the world of real Indians.

While Peru's population increasingly shifted from the countryside to the cities, the country was exhibiting signs of becoming more organized than ever before. By 1960 peasants were invading hacienda lands in the sierra and organizing *sindicatos* to demand agrarian reform, credit, and more state services. Migrants to Lima and other coastal cities had also joined together to make their own land invasions and to form self-help associations, often based on their common regional origins. They demanded elementary governmental services for their new makeshift homes, including potable water, electricity, paved streets, and transportation, as well as more health, educational, and job opportunities.

An expanded working class, too, became better organized into unions, which proliferated at a rapid rate and made increasing demands on the government. The middle classes had grown as well as a result of steady economic growth and were calling for expanded educational opportunities and employment in the public sector. Finally, emerging industrialists pressed the government for higher protective tariffs and credits to expand the manufacturing sector. In short, a variety of important groups organized as never before to press their demands for a greater voice in running the country and for an expanded state that would fulfill their growing needs and aspirations.

By 1960 these rising pressures for greater political participation and action put the traditional oligarchical state more on the defensive than at any time since 1930 or 1945. The ruling elites, for example, continued to be divided about how to respond to popular demands, a division reflected in the country's two major daily newspapers. On the one hand, *La Prensa* articulated the economic interests of the agroexport elite, which advocated an open market economy and a limited, laissez faire state, coupled with a hard line on popular dissent. On the other hand, *El Comercio* pressed a reformist and nationalist agenda, more in keeping with a rising industrial bourgeoisie and elements of the new middle classes and the armed forces. It also kept up a steady barrage of opposition to APRA.

Finally, the winds of change were intensifying in the armed forces in the early 1960s. The implications of the new, broader concept of national security were profound. Chronic underdevelopment not only opened the door to popular rebellion, but weakened the nation's ability to confront its more developed, better-organized traditional rival Chile. It also opened the way for "international communism" to infiltrate the country under the guise of guerrilla movements that, modeled on Castro's successful *foco* (rural guerrilla strategy) in Cuba, took up the cause of the oppressed and downtrodden. Therefore, effective and comprehensive national defense seemed to call for a concerted attack on the causes of Peru's historic underdevelopment, as well as national planning to bring about development. In short, sentiment for what might be called "co-optive" reform, although it was still advocated by a minority of officers, was beginning to percolate within the ranks of the military.

These accelerating forces for change collided with those of the established order in the elections of 1962. Having adhered to the *convivencia* with APRA during his administration, Prado more than lived up to his part of the bargain by throwing his official support behind the candidacy of Haya. For his part, Haya gave reassurances to the elites that APRA was still fully committed to a conservative program emphasizing anti-communism and pro-capitalism. Moreover, the fact that there had been only one isolated, unsuccessful coup attempt during Prado's administration demonstrated to the oligarchy that the party had finally turned away from the conspiratorial road to power. The steady movement of APRA to the right, however, created a vacuum on the left that was quickly filled by several new political contenders.

For example, the *convivencia* had already cost APRA its extreme left-wing faction when a splinter group, called APRA Rebelde, was formed in 1959. This group, which changed its name in 1962 to the Movimiento de Izquierda Revolucionaria, or Movement of the Revolutionary Left (MIR), was led by ex-Aprista Luis de la Puente Uceda. It linked its origins to the failed popular uprising at Callao in 1948 and restated its intention of pursuing the armed road to revolution. In late 1962, the MIR established contact with Hugo Blanco and began preparing for a guerrilla campaign in the sierra that it would eventually launch in 1965. The nonviolent Left was also reinforced by the appearance of several other small parties, including the Movimiento Social Progresista (Social Progressive Movement), which was more influential in the formulation of doctrine than in the actual political arena itself.

The strongest contender to Haya and APRA came from the dynamic Belaúnde Terry. Ever since his strong showing in 1956, the young architect had been preparing for the next presidential election. Within the year, he had founded Acción Popular and begun to travel extensively throughout the country. He sought not only to get to know the "reality" of Peru, but to present his nationalistic and technocratic views for change and development to the public. In this vein, the former university professor also published *La conquista del Perú por los Peruanos* in 1959 (*The Conquest of Peru by Peruvians,* 1965).

The book, whose title made an obvious appeal to nationalism, laid out Belaúnde's ideas for developing the country. They included a promise of agrarian reform; the creation of local, self-help programs called *Co-operación Popular* (Popular Cooperation); a more activist government; civic action programs for the military; greater autonomy and funding for local governments; and a favorable settlement of the long-standing dispute with the International Petroleum Company. The underlying appeal to nationalism also included an idealized image of the Inca Empire, together with praise for Peru's unique multiethnic mix of cultures and races.

The one presidential challenger on the Right turned out to be former president Manuel Odría, who formed the Unión Nacional Odriísta to promote his candidacy. Calling himself a "socialist of the Right," the former general crafted a populist appeal to the shantytowns which he had extensively patronized as president. However, Odría elicited little support within the increasingly professionalized military, which viewed his former regime as an anachronistic throwback to *caudillismo*. He was also an anathema to Pedro Beltrán, who had been one of his leading critics and who unsuccessfully tried to mount a candidacy of his own before throwing his support to Haya de la Torre.

Given the large popular following of the three major candidates, the election turned out to be one of the most intensely contested and significant in years. For the first time in a long time, it gave expression to the rising reformist and nationalist sentiment in the country and a clear choice against the normally victorious oligarchical bloc, now represented by APRA. It was revealing that all the candidates tried to express the spirit of reform and change in the political air.

Nevertheless, there were serious doubts that the military would accept the electoral results if Haya and APRA won. Reflecting the prevailing anti-Aprista sentiment in the armed forces, the minister of the navy warned the

American ambassador that certain parties "which originally drank at communist fountains" had changed their political programs in a cynical play for power (quoted in Masterson, 1991, p. 170). Another high-ranking officer referred to Haya's alleged homosexuality and the long-standing vendetta against the party among a generation of officers who had been heavily indoctrinated as recruits against APRA.

The overwhelming preference in the military was for Belaúnde, whom many, particularly in the army, saw as the type of civilian technocrat who could do the job of modernization that they believed the country urgently needed. For his part, Belaúnde encouraged this sentiment while he played up his candidacy as the alternative to the unacceptable Haya.

As the votes were tabulated after the election on June 10, Belaúnde took a narrow lead, but he was overtaken in unofficial returns as the count continued. The final official results gave Haya 558,237 votes (32.98 percent); Belaúnde, 543,828 (32.13 percent); and Odría, 481,404 (28.44 percent). Since Haya's percentage was slightly less than the constitutionally mandated 33.33 percent necessary for victory, the selection process was turned over to Congress. That 40 percent of the congressional seats were held by APRA seemed to preclude any chance for Belaúnde or Odría, both of whom immediately opened negotiations with Haya. Haya rejected Belaúnde's overtures, but reached an accord with Odría on July 17 in which the former dictator would assume the presidency and Aprista leader Manuel Seoane would become first vice president, with APRA taking control of Congress. This *superconvivencia* proved too much for the armed forces, which removed Prado from office the next day, ten days before the end of his term, and announced the formation of a new Junta de Gobierno.

The Institutional Rule of the Armed Forces, 1962–63

Unlike the previous personalistic coups of Sánchez Cerro in 1931 and Odría in 1948, this time an "institutional" military government was installed, with each branch of the armed forces represented on the junta. Led by General Ricardo Pérez Godoy, chairman of the joint command of the armed forces, the new junta declared the June 10 elections annulled. It also suspended constitutional guarantees for thirty days and declared a one-year limit on its rule, after which it would hold new elections and return to the barracks. Public reaction to the coup was largely apathetic, and the political parties remained quiescent.

The 1962 coup represented the first expression of what Stepan (1978) called the "new professionalism" in the armed forces, which linked internal security with national development. It also expressed the strong antipathy within the military for Haya and APRA, which were poised to assume control of the government as a result of the elections. It is interesting that the military's rationale for its anti-Aprismo stance had shifted 180 degrees in recent years. The traditional fear of APRA radicalism by the conservative military establishment had given way to concerns by reformist officers that a now overtly conservative party (e.g., the *superconvivencia* with the Right) would block the reforms needed to bring about the effective national development that was necessary to bolster internal security. Therefore, the new military government would cautiously proceed to initiate a modest series of reforms that were designed to address the growing social problems that the country faced at the beginning of the 1960s.

Initially, the United States, which had supported the candidacy of Haya, exhibited its dissatisfaction with the end of democratic rule by breaking diplomatic relations and suspending all aid, other than humanitarian assistance. However, unwilling to jeopardize U.S. investments amounting to $850 million, the Kennedy administration relented and recognized the junta on August 17 in return for the restoration of civil liberties and the scheduling of free elections the following June.

During its year in power, the new military government exhibited what some analysts have called "Nasserite" tendencies, alluding to its reformist inclinations to address the problems of poverty and underdevelopment. Others have pointed out the relatively mild forms of repression instituted by the junta, which they described as a *"dictablanda,"* or soft dictatorship, as opposed to a more traditional *"dictadura,"* or hard-line military dictatorship. One of the junta's first reforms, based on a broad consensus in the military, was the establishment of the Instituto Nacional de Planificación, a mechanism for planning national development. The junta also announced a new housing program to alleviate the depressed living conditions of the urban poor in Lima.

Perhaps more significant, the government undertook for the first time an agrarian reform program, however modest it proved to be, in La Convención (Cuzco). It announced a three-year pilot project in which 14,000 *colonos* would receive ownership titles in return for various long-term forms of payments. Twenty-three haciendas would also be expropriated or acquired by the government and redistributed with compensation to their owners. By the time the military left power the following year, however, only one hacienda had actually been expropriated and a small number of *colonos* had received titles.

Although the situation in La Convención eased, bloody riots by workers erupted in December at the Oroya copper refineries and on a sugar plantation on the north coast near Chiclayo. These riots were quickly repressed by the police, but not before several deaths and millions of dollars in damages to equipment, facilities, and crops had occurred. The junta blamed the outbreak on "Communist elements" and ordered a mass arrest of over 800 alleged "leftists" (including Apristas) on the night of January 4. However, little evidence was ever produced by the junta to support its actions, and most of the prisoners were released within a few months.

Shortly after this crackdown, a further indication of the military's general sensitivity to the threat from the Left, the government took an abrupt rightward turn. In the early morning hours of March 3, Pérez Godoy, the head of the junta, was forcibly ousted from the Presidential Palace on the pretext of *caudillismo*. He was replaced by General Nicolás Lindley López, a more conservative member of the junta. The "coup within a coup" demonstrated once again the deep ideological fissures in the armed forces that not only mirrored the society at large, but continued to undermine institutional unity.

The country now prepared for the upcoming June elections that shaped up as a replay of 1962, with Haya, Odría, and Belaúnde once again the major candidates. What had changed in the intervening year of military rule was a growing perception that the time for agrarian reform had finally arrived. For one thing, the threat of the Cuban Revolution had convinced many progressive sectors of the landed elite that reform might forestall revolution. This was the prescription advocated by the Alliance for Progress, the hemispheric reform program designed by the Kennedy administration in 1961, which the United States was heavily promoting throughout Latin America. It was significant that all the major presidential candidates advocated some kind of agrarian reform.

For Belaúnde, the issue had particular political appeal. Recognizing the necessity of broadening his voter support beyond the new middle sectors and cognizant that a new political constituency was emerging from the peasant sector in the highlands, Belaúnde oriented his campaign toward the countryside. He visited hundreds of communities in the highlands, showing attention, for the first time ever by a presidential candidate, to this new voting bloc and promising residents agrarian reform, schools, and other community-based development assistance. The young architect also bolstered his chances by forming a strategic alliance with the small but influential Partido Democrático Cristiano (PDC). A strong advocate for agrarian reform, the PDC agreed to refrain from running its own candidate and instead to support Belaúnde. In return, Belaúnde promised that a member of the party would head the Ministry of Agriculture and the Agrarian Reform Agency in his new administration.

Belaúnde also benefited from support from the Left, much of whose leadership was in jail and therefore able to field only one lackluster candidate. As for the military, it saw Belaúnde as before—an alternative to Haya and APRA and a safe surrogate for their program of gradual, civilian-led reform. With over 100,000 new votes from the PDC, the Left, and peasant strongholds in the south, Belaúnde won a narrow victory, gaining 36.2 percent of the vote, as opposed to 34.4 percent for Haya and 25.5 percent for Odría. His party Acción Popular, however, failed to gain a majority in Congress, which opened the way for an alliance between APRA and Odría's Unión Nacional Odriísta, with the ominous potential for blocking the new president's reforms and frustrating popular expectations for change.

11 From Reform to "Revolution from Above," 1963–75

Fernando Belaúnde Terry inherited the reigns of a country that had undergone an unprecedented period of growth and change, but one that still confronted enormous inequalities and social problems. During the 1950s and early 1960s, Peru's population had grown by 75 percent to 9.9 million, the gross national product (GNP) rose 180 percent, exports had quadrupled, and the national debt had increased by a factor of ten. Nevertheless, despite a relatively stable government, a low but accelerating rate of inflation, and a substantial inflow of foreign investments (second only to Mexico in Latin America), the export boom of the past two decades had reached its peak in 1962 and thereafter began to wane. And although the manufacturing sector was showing signs of picking up, a decade of stagnation, if not decline, in domestic agricultural output was forcing the country to import millions of dollars annually in foodstuffs, not to mention contributing to the torrent of out-migration from the countryside to Lima and other cities. Over the long term, expenditures on food imports had risen from $40 million in 1940 to $134 million in 1965.

Sociopolitically, Peru, at the beginning of the 1960s, had arguably the worst concentration of wealth and income of any country in South America. For example, the top 5 percent of the population received 48 percent of the national income. Even more striking, 19 percent of the national income went to only 1 percent of the population. By contrast, the bottom two deciles received only 2.5 percent.

This duality of wealth and income was reflected geographically. In 1961, the average per capita income was $280 per year in the southern highlands but $870 ($1,230 if one includes property) in Lima, with great variation within each region. The former figure, however, contained an urban bias, which, if factored out, would show that the poorest quartile in the sierra, mostly small subsistence farmers (80 percent), earned between $40 to $120 per year. These farmers were mostly Quechua- or Aymara-speaking Indian peasants who were 70 percent illiterate and who, on average, earned their main livelihood from 0.9 hectares, three head of cattle, and a few other livestock, supplemented by seasonal labor.

This mass of rural poor, falsely portrayed by the statistics as unified and cohesive, was, on the contrary, highly fragmented. It was scattered about the countryside, living on haciendas, villages, and communities or independently as subsistence farmers. One can envision this rural poor as embedded in a society that consisted of a "myriad of small and independent social pyramids, each with a different mix of the relatively rich and poor" (Webb, 1977, p. 13). What kept them fragmented and atomized over time was a process of social domination, based on a series of vertical, hierarchical relationships to local landlords (*gamonales*) who exerted their influence, power, and authority mostly by the traditional means of paternalism and clientelism.

For example, hacienda peons were bound to their owners through clientelism, with each competing independently for favors, as well as protection, from the patron. Landlords offered their "protection" in a number of ways, mostly from the state, which levied taxes (*contribución a la república*), imposed work levies (*ley vial*), or arbitrarily drafted peasants into military service. In this way, the *gamonal* class, which also controlled local governments, exerted a tight social control over its rural workforce.

The landed elite, of course, had much to protect, since its control over the land tenure system was the most extensive of fifty-four countries surveyed in 1961, according to the Gini index of land distribution. By one estimate, 700 hacendados owned approximately one-third of the country's productive land. At the other end of the social scale, a quarter of a million families, 20 percent of all rural families, labored on the modern coastal plantations. Another 22 percent (275,000) were small farmers whose incomes ran the gamut from relatively rich to poor. About 40 percent of the population resided in communities that had less than one quarter of the country's productive land. The income levels of all these rural families varied greatly. Those on the rich coastal plantations earned fully twice as much as their counterparts in the highland communities. As a result, many of the latter, perhaps 250,000, sought seasonal, temporary labor (*eventuales*) on the plantations.

For the vast majority of peasants, of course, land was an extremely scarce resource. McClintock (1998, p. 168) estimated that prior to the agrarian reform, upward of 30 percent of the country's farm families were landless (day laborers, sharecroppers, and migrant workers). The man–land ratio in Peru in 1960 was about .21 hectares of land or pasture per peasant, half as low as that of neighboring Bolivia, Chile, and Ecuador and one of the lowest in the world. Since agriculture accounted for 23 percent of the country's GNP and employed 58 percent of its economically active population, it stands to reason that the lion's share of income went to the 700 or so major hacendados. Many of these hacendados earned 100 times the incomes of their employees.

If such huge rural inequalities posed enormous challenges to reform by the new Belaúnde administration, so, too, did the concentration of wealth and power in the modern sector on the coast, epitomized by Lima. Between 1954 and 1959, per capita income on the coast, for example, grew 4 percent, while that of the sierra fell 7 percent. The capital, Lima, now contained 1.8

Llama herders in the southern altiplano. Reproduced with the permission of the General Secretariat of the Organization of American States.

million inhabitants, about one-fifth of the total population of the country, and accounted for about 40 percent of the GNP. It was also the home of a growing middle class, which constituted perhaps 15–25 percent of the total population and who, as Parker (1998) showed, largely defined or identified themselves in this social category. The ranks of the middle class swelled since World War II because of urbanization, expansion of the state, and the continuing rise in exports and overall received, according to Webb, about 11.4 percent of the national income.

In general, the middle class had similar characteristics of race, degree of education, residential location, income, occupation, lifestyles, and patterns of consumption. There was also a good deal of mobility up (and down) among the classes, owing to the general advance of the economy, with a relatively large number of immigrants (judging from foreign surnames among the elite) reaching the top. Below the upper and middle rungs of the social scale stood a sizable, organized working class, together with the ever-expanding mass of recent migrants who populated the *barriadas* (squatter settlements) that ringed the city.

By virtue of his election, Belaúnde now slipped into the presidential chair on top of this highly problematic sociopolitical hierarchy. Immediately he was confronted with a second wave of land invasions by peasants, who believed that the moment for land reform had arrived. After all, had not the new president campaigned heavily in the sierra on the promise of agrarian reform? So as soon as the new president was inaugurated, many peasants automatically assumed that they were justified in acting to "occupy" contested land. Often brandishing colonial titles, they marched onto disputed hacienda lands in groups, varying from a handful to several thousand, and planted Peruvian flags to indicate that they were taking back lands that were rightfully theirs. The use of flags served to rally support and lent an aura of legitimacy and nationalism to such occupations.

Significantly, the *comuneros* were assisted in their efforts by the rural syndicates and peasant federations that would now proliferate across the highlands during this second wave of land seizures. Indeed, broader contact with urban students, lawyers, trade unions, and other groups enabled the peasantry to articulate their movement better and provided channels into the political system through formal, existing structures. One such federation was the Aprista controlled National Peasant Federation on Peru (Federación Nacional de Campesinos Peruanos—FENCAP) which had begun in the 1930s on the coast organizing sugar workers and small farmers, many of whom had migrated from the sierra. Seeking to capitalize on the sierra peasant mobilization, FENCAP expanded its activities into the highlands in the early 1960s.

The new peasant unions also directed their activities at the *colono* (tenant) population isolated and locked into the hacienda system. Like the *comuneros*, the *colonos'* objective was land, either the recovery of plots usurped by estates in the process of proletarization or the outright distribution of hacienda land. In addition, the *colono* syndicates demanded the elimination of the servile tributes and service required of peasants by their landlords. In place of these "feudal relics," they called for the substitution of regular wages and hours of work, as well as the installation of schools, medical facilities, and other services. In other words, the normal union and labor demands made in the industrial sector were now put forth in the countryside. To force these changes, *colonos* and their leaders resorted to the equally novel use of strikes, a tool that Hugo Blanco had effectively pioneered in La Convención a couple of years earlier, but was heretofore virtually unknown in the highlands.

Neither the *comunero* nor *colono* movements, however, succeeded in uniting into one concerted effort or organization, despite the efforts of the Confederación de Campesinos del Perú, founded in 1947. The fundamental problem was that the two groups had contending interests in that they both made claims on the same hacienda lands. Thus, *comuneros* claimed prior ownership of disputed or usurped areas, while *colonos*, as hacienda workers, claimed rights to the same lands.

Geographically and chronologically, it is possible to divide the second wave of peasant mobilizations into two parts, the first in the northern and central sierra, particularly Pasco and Junín, then in Cuzco and the south. Belaúnde's response to the new outbreak of peasant unrest was at first sympathetic and conciliatory. In September, he introduced a new agrarian reform law to the Congress. A long and complicated bill, it contained 240 separate articles designed to satisfy the peasants' demands for land, as well as to maintain agricultural production. The proposal's principal features included expropriation with compensation (long-term bonds), the formation of cooperatives, and technical and financial assistance from the government. Significantly, the law only marginally affected the large coastal sugar plantations whose efficiency and relatively better paid workforce were considered, especially by APRA, essential to the well-being of the economy.

The proposed land reform was not well received by the Congress, dominated by APRA and the Unión Nacional Odriista. La Coalición countered with its own heavily watered-down bill, which included cash compensation, no restrictions on the size of hacienda holdings, emphasis on colonization projects, and the total exclusion of the APRA-controlled sugar plantations. Over the next eight months, the Congress wrangled over the course of the reform. When a final compromise version, which exempted the big coastal plantations, was ultimately enacted the following May, Prime Minister Oscar Trelles declared it "still born" because of its watered-down nature, bureaucratic red tape, and severe paucity of funding. In the course of the prolonged and heated debate over the reform, the Partido Democrático Cristiano (PDC) accused the government of abandoning its commitments to the reform and broke its alliance with Acción Popular (AP). This act had even greater political ramifications for the administration.

In the meantime, while the bill was stalled in Congress, Belaúnde was forced by the pressure of events in the highlands to issue decrees expropriating 100,000 hectares of hacienda land in Pasco and Junín. For the first time, the government also entered into negotiations with peasant groups, whose voting power and ability to disrupt the system effectively forced the administration to the bargaining table. This marked a historic turning point for the peasants in which the government actually recognized their bargaining power.

When the land invasions and strikes spread to Cuzco and the south, however, the new government took a more hard-line stance. With his reform program still mired in Congress, Belaúnde dispatched special Guardia Civil assault troops to the region to quell the movement. Several bloody clashes ensued, one at the village of Ongoy in Apurimac in October and another at Sicuani in Cuzco in February 1964. By the time the watered-down agrarian reform law was finally passed and the invasions-strikes began to subside, over 300 peasants had been killed in the south.

The final outcome of Peru's first comprehensive agrarian reform law in history was disappointing. According to the Belaúnde administration, 873,000 acres of land were expropriated over the next four years benefiting

12,000 families, while the subsequent Velasco regime put the figure at 783,000 acres benefiting 7,224 families (Masterson, 1991, p. 209; fn. 26, p. 236). In either case, the totals represented only 3 percent of the expropriable land and a few thousand families in a peasant population of at least 1 million. Paradoxically, the beneficiaries of the law turned out to be those peasants who had tenaciously managed to hold on to the lands they had occupied during the first couple of years of Belaúnde's term.

While official efforts at land reform were largely stymied by opposition from oligarchical circles in league with the APRA (La Coalición), a "private," or de facto, version of land distribution began to occur in parts of the sierra. Pressured by the peasant mobilization and unable or unwilling to resist, individual landholders increasingly chose to put their estates up for sale, either in toto or through parcelization into individual lots. In the wake of this private "land reform," formerly rented land became the personal property of peasant purchasers and, consequently, the number and percentage of *minifundistas* in the sierra began to rise substantially.

Moreover, this form of private land distribution had a special impact on the Church and the various religious orders that had traditionally been the biggest landowners in the country. Seeking to avoid a confrontation with peasants and influenced by a deepening spirit of reform, the Archdiocese of Cuzco, for example, issued a Pastoral Letter in 1963 ordering the parcelization of estates held by the Church on terms favorable to the local peasantry. According to Burga and Flores Galindo (1980, pp. 92–94) this ecclesiastical "land reform" not only ended the Church's traditional power as a landlord, but served to sever its historic alliance with the *gamonal* class to control the highland peasantry.

Despite these efforts, overall the issue of land reform bogged down, with the recently enacted reform law ensnared in a welter of bureaucratic red tape and other obstacles. Meanwhile, the problem continued to fester in the midst of governmental repression. It was in this context that a guerrilla movement erupted suddenly in 1965. The origins of the movement also went back to the turmoil produced in the Peruvian Left as a result of the Cuban Revolution of 1959, the Sino-Soviet schism of 1960, and the emergence of a new generation of radicalized students.

In the case of the latter, the rapid expansion of higher education from the mid-1950s had produced a large cohort of students at all levels. Particularly astonishing was the growth of higher education. For example, there were only six universities in the country in 1955, but the number rose dramatically to thirty by the end of the Belaúnde administration in 1968. Between 1956 and 1962, the number of university students doubled from a little over 20,000 to almost 41,000 and then doubled again to 94,000 in 1968. By the end of Belaúnde's term, educational expenditures had reached nearly 5 percent of the GNP and 25 percent of the national budget. This level of spending catapulted Peru to the top ranks of Latin American countries for the period 1960–68.

The social extraction of university students, as might have been expected, broadened considerably. According to the former rector of San Marcos University in 1966, "compared with twenty years ago, when 95 percent of students came from middle and upper middle class homes, the majority of San Marcos students, over 65 percent, are of lower middle and working classes." Many San Marcos students also came from the provinces and, like others, faced limited career prospects upon graduation, as well as the strong cultural and ethnic prejudices prevalent among the *Limeño* elites.

As the student population exploded in the 1960s and the students' frustrations grew, the sudden and unexpected success of the Cuban Revolution, as well as the splintering of international communism, quickly captured their attention and imagination. These events also ruptured the old Left, which began to splinter into a plethora of new revolutionary parties exposing a variety of ideologies and programs, from Maoism to Fidelismo. For example, after the Sino-Soviet split, the Peruvian Communist Party (PCP), divided, and most of its youth wing abandoned Moscow's aegis to form the Maoist-oriented PCP Bandera Roja. The Bandera Roja then split again, with the bulk of its members forming the PCP Patria Roja, while those who remained allied with the Albanian Communists. Finally, a third group, located in Ayacucho, formed the PCP Sendero Luminoso (Shining Path), which espoused a fundamentalist version of Maoism.

Meanwhile, APRA's Left wing, frustrated by Haya's turn to the Right and inspired by the Cuban Revolution, broke from the party in 1960 to form APRA Rebelde, which later became the Movimiento de la Izquierda Revolucionaria (MIR). Its leader was Luis de la Puente Uceda, the son of a Trujillo landowner and distant relative of Haya de la Torre, who had become a militant and dynamic member of the Aprista youth movement. Shortly after Castro came to power in Cuba in 1959, de la Puente traveled to Havana to attend a conference, where, according to Manrique (1995, p. 305), he met Hilda Gadea, a former Aprista youth leader who had married Che Guevara. Upon his return to Peru, he graduated with a degree in law from the University of Trujillo with a thesis entitled *La Reforma del Agro Peruano* (1966).

Soon he and his comrades in MIR were ready to embark on a rural guerrilla movement to test the insurrectionary *foco* theory, modeled on Castro's experience in the Sierra Maestra. Expounded in 1960 by Che Guevara, this theory contradicted long-held Communist orthodoxy, stating that "it is not always necessary to wait until all conditions for revolution exist; the insurrectionary *foco* can create them" (quoted in Gott, 1971, p. 381); that is, a small vanguard of guerrillas could gain the support of peasants in an isolated area and from there, initiate a successful revolutionary war.

Setting up headquarters in 1965 on the Mesa Pelada plateau in the eastern range of the Andes near Cuzco and not far from La Convención, de la Puente's MIR was joined by guerrilla leaders to plan joint operations from two other guerrilla groups, the Ejército de Liberación Nacional (ELN), founded by Héctor Béjar and with ties to the PCP, and Túpac Amaru, a faction of MIR led by Guillermo Lobatón. Two years earlier, the ELN had sent a small group of young intellectuals returning from Cuba to assist Hugo Blanco in La Convención. The band included Javier Heraud, a twenty-one-year-old, award-winning poet from an upper-class *Limeño* family. Crossing the border from Bolivia, the handful of would-be revolutionaries arrived at Puerto Maldonado in Madre de Dios on May 15, but were quickly spotted by the authorities and arrested. Heraud and a companion managed to flee, but they were hunted down and killed by a posse of police and local landowners the following day.

Unfortunately for the Peruvian *focistas* at Mesa Pelada, the Peruvian armed forces were more than prepared to meet the impending guerrilla challenge. Counterinsurgency tactics were nothing new to the army and went back to the influence of the pre–World War II French training missions in Peru that instructed officers in their own colonial experiences. The armed forces drew on that instruction when they reacted quickly to Castro's guerrilla victory in Cuba after 1959. In addition to antisubversive training at the Escuela Superior de Guerra and the Centro de Altos Estudios Militares (CAEM), officers were sent for training to the U.S. School of the Americas in the Panama Canal Zone, as well as to the U.S. Army Special Warfare Center and School at Fort Bragg, North Carolina. Indeed, between 1949 and 1964, 805 Peruvian officers had trained at the School of the Americas, which, after 1960, was increasingly oriented toward counterinsurgency tactics. By the early 1960s, according to Masterson (1991, p. 212) a counterinsurgency unit within the army was fully equipped and combat ready to respond to the guerrilla outbreak led by de la Puente.

Thus, when the guerrillas inaugurated their first action in June 1965, the armed forces reacted quickly and effectively to the challenge. Within six months, the three guerrilla *focos* had been routed in a massive campaign that cost the lives not only of de la Puente and Lobatón, but upward of 8,000 Indian peasants who were victims. The defeat of the insurgency, however, had as much to do with the severe weaknesses of the guerrillas as to the counterinsurgency skills of the armed forces.

For one thing, the MIR and ELN had never seen eye-to-eye on ideological or tactical issues, and the Moscow-oriented PCP, having been heavily repressed by the military government of 1962–63, had never committed its resources to the enterprises. Without much urban support outside of a few bombings and bank robberies, the guerrillas, who were mainly composed of middle-class youths from the cities, also suffered from a linguistic and cultural gap that separated them from the mass of Quechua-speaking peasants whom they were trying to instigate. Lack of support from the peasants may also be explained by the peasants' lingering hope for the long-awaited governmental agrarian reform that still held out the possibility of peaceful, rather than violent, change. Other tactical errors, such as the establishment of a fixed command center at Mesa Pelada, further doomed the enterprise from the beginning.

The immediate effects on agricultural production of spreading social unrest during the 1960s were, of course, highly negative. For one thing, the expectation that some sort of land reform, either legal or de facto, was inevitable caused the landowners to begin curtailing their investments and operations. The reaction of one Cajamarca landowner in 1963 was typical:

> The Agrarian Reform Law will soon be approved and will certainly affect (the hacienda) Udima. Therefore we should plan to dedicate all our attention in the years in which the firm can still do so, to extracting the maximum possible surplus from the *colonaje* and from the hacienda's cattle. . . . We should eliminate the stables and the cheese factory, the alfalfa fields, land reclamation projects, etc., the purchase of feed concentrates and all the activities which force the hacienda to spend money which is never transformed into profits. (quoted in Thorp and Bertram, 1978, p. 283)

As a result of such reasoning, agriculture entered a period of sharp decline during the 1960s because of falling investments, decapitalization, and the transfer of assets to other more profitable sectors of the economy, such as manufacturing, construction, and finance. The per capita output of food crops largely stagnated during the decade, rising on an index of 100 in 1961 to only 103 in 1967 and then falling to a low of 99 in 1969, when the sweeping military-mandated agrarian reform took place. The fact that, in the long run, agrarian reform would make agriculture more efficient did little to alleviate this disinvestment in the short run.

While the agricultural sector suffered during the 1960s, the process of industrialization accelerated. In Latin America industrialization can be traced to the 1950s and even earlier, when many Latin American governments began to institute Import Substituting Industrialization (ISI) policies as a way of increasing both domestic employment, particularly in the rapidly growing cities, and economic growth while preventing social unrest. Peru resisted ISI policies until later, preferring to stick with its time-worn export-led strategy for economic growth. However, the 1958 recession, decreasing opportunities for investment in exports (other than fishmeal), and currency devaluation (de facto tariff protection) the same year all served to encourage a policy shift to ISI.

The following year, Congress finally passed Prado's proposed Industrial Promotion Law (introduced in 1956), which gave generous tariff and tax incentives to industrial enterprises. Once the economy recovered and internal consumption began to rise, both domestic and foreign investors shifted their attention to the manufacturing sector. Further tariff protection was forthcoming from the developmentalist Belaúnde administration, which decreed large rate hikes in 1964 and 1967.

These measures helped to stimulate industrial expansion and diversify the economy during the 1960s. However, for a variety of reasons, this industrial expansion was not integrative or self-sustaining; was highly dependent on foreign capital and know-how; and, most important, failed to attract enough domestic capital and hense advance the postion of an "industrial bourgeoise." The greatest beneficiaries turned out to be foreign companies, whose investment in manufacturing tripled between 1960 and 1966.

Although industrial development and agrarian reform were important elements in Belaúnde's developmental strategy, the centerpiece of his program was the construction of a major north–south highway along the eastern slope of the Andes. The purpose of the road was to open up the Amazonian region to colonization and development, a long and cherished dream of Peruvians since independence and before. As conceived, the highway would traverse a thousand miles of terrain along the *Ceja de la Selva* (literally, the Eyebrow of the Jungle) and would spawn feeder roads east down the slopes into the vast Amazonian rain forest and west to the highlands and coast.

As an architect, Belaúnde found the plan captivating and, over the years, extending into his second term in the 1980s, it became something of an obsession with him. Visitors to the National Palace (the author included) would invariably be ushered into a parlor where a model of the project, color coded for the various stages of completion, was elaborately laid out. The architect-president, classroom pointer in hand, would then launch into an animated lecture on the merits, problems, and progress of the highway.

For Belaúnde, the highway project took precedence over all other parts of his program, including agrarian reform, which it would facilitate. Indeed, opening up access to new land in the Amazon was politically much easier than wresting land away from the entrenched, if weakening, *gamonal* class. Politically, *La Marginal* had other advantages, such as a stimulus for employment and a magnate for international financing from aid agencies. The project was also an "easy sell" to the public, which, as it unfolded, would presumably reap considerable political dividends to the architect-president. Finally, it fit nicely with the military's embrace of civic action and developmentalism as part of its new national security doctrine.

The very scale and cost of the *La Marginal*, whose completion was estimated to take over twenty-five years, also suggested the inauguration of a period of government fiscal expansion unprecedented since the Leguía era of the 1920s. In the event, the Belaúnde administration dramatically increased governmental spending, not only on public works, but on social programs, such as education, public health, and housing. The result, according to Cotler (1991, p. 461), was an increase in spending from 11.5 percent of the gross domestic product (GDP), one of the lowest figures in Latin America at the time, to 16 percent of the GDP in 1968, one of the highest in the region. And since La Coalición successfully blocked efforts to increase taxes to pay for such spending, the government resorted to deficit spending, which increased 95 percent a year between 1965 and 1967.

This expansion of government was a considerable turn about for a country that had one of the smallest state sectors in Latin America in the 1940s and 1950s and even before. Prior to this time, the oligarchical state had concentrated spending mainly on national defense and the maintenance of internal order (the police). State redistributive spending, on the other hand, was relatively insignificant until the early 1940s, and even then, in the combined area of health and education, amounted to an extremely modest 3.8 percent of the GNP by 1958. This was a good deal lower than the average of 5.5 percent for many comparably poor countries that was reported the same year.

Education was a case in point. In 1950 spending for education amounted to only 1.6 percent of the GNP and 14 percent of the budget. A decade later, the percentages had risen modestly to 2.6 and 18.3, respectively, with expenditures focused mainly, as you have seen, on expanding enrollments at the secondary and university levels during the Prado administration. Illiteracy rates among the population over age fifteen also dropped from 53 to 39 percent. By 1960, postwar economic growth, the concomitant expansion of the middle classes, and increased pressure from other groups (peasants, migrants, and unions) had generated a strong and growing public demand for education at all levels. Spending for education thus became one of the fastest-growing budget categories of the Belaúnde administration.

Politics aside, the technocratically and developmentally inclined president, backed by his reformist allies in the military and the progressive political parties, believed that an expanded educational system was the key to progress. The universities would provide the skilled human capital necessary to foment development, keep the economy growing, and generally improve the capacity of the government. On the other hand, no one seemed to foresee that the economy might not expand fast enough to provide sufficient employment for the swelling pool of graduates. This situation, in fact, occurred as the economy stagnated in the 1960s, contributing to dashed expectations, the radicalization of students, and the Leftward shift of the body politic over the next two decades.

These trends, together with the deepening social and political crisis of the country, shaped a new generation of artists, writers, and scholars who were also marked by the Cuban Revolution and the Cold War. Known as the generation of 1950, it increasingly came to the fore during the 1960s and 1970s in a remarkable cultural florescence: an extraordinary generation of poets, according to Higgins (1987), unmatched anywhere in Latin America; social scientists who advanced the various disciplines, such as archeology (Luis Lumbreras), sociology (Julio Cotler and Aníbal Quijano), history (Pablo Macera), and ethnohistory (Luis Millones, Manuel Burga, and Tito Flores Galindo); musicians, playrights, and painters (Fernando de Szyszlo and Armando Villegas); and most noticeably writers (Mario Vargas Llosa, Alfredo Bryce Echenique, and Manuel Scorza) whose works of fiction reached a large international audience for the first time.

While Belaúnde seemed to have his way with Congress over the matter of educational spending, he was unsuccessful in most of his other legislative initiatives. Co-operación Popular, the president's sensible self-help, rural development program modeled partly on the Alliance for Progress, was consistently underfunded by Congress on the grounds that it incited the peasants to seize land. I have already discussed how Congress gutted the agrarian reform program, so that little land was ever redistributed to the peasantry. Although willing to appropriate money for its own partisan programs, La Coalición dominated Congress (61 percent of the seats in the Chamber of Deputies and 56 percent of those in the Senate) consistently refused to raise taxes to cover the expanding costs of the government. It also continually voted "no confidence" in governmental ministers, leading to the censure and replacement of ninety-four ministers during Belaúnde's five-year term. If one adds to this picture of congressional obstruction the still-considerable power of the oligarchy to influence the press, control access to credit, and wield power through associations like the National Agrarian Society (SNA), it is no wonder that the forces of reform that were building during the 1960s were increasingly frustrated and discontented.

Held virtual prisoner by what Haya referred to as the "first power" of Congress, Belaúnde resorted to a carrot-and-stick governing policy that relied on some selective, if relatively mild, repression while liberally increasing social spending. Subsidies favoring import substitution and food consumption, increased spending on public works like *Marginal*, and new housing projects for the urban middle class, however, pushed the budget into the red at the same time that the volume of exports, which had been rising since 1950, stagnated and American investment began to decline. Coincidentally, imports rose, which were financed by increasing the external debt from $235 million in 1963 (8 percent of the GNP) to $680 million by 1968 (18 percent of the GNP). The opposition-controlled Congress, meanwhile, refused to approve a governmental initiative to reform the tax system so as to increase revenues. All this contributed to rising inflation, which averaged 14 percent from 1964 to 1967 and was even higher in the politically sensitive food sector, which reached 70 percent during the same period. By September 1967, the deteriorating economic situation forced the president to devalue the *sol* by 44 percent, after he had repeatedly stated his intention not do so.

Equally or perhaps more damaging to the now rapidly declining fortunes of the government was Belaúnde's failure to resolve the long-festering dispute with the International Petroleum Company. The IPC virtually controlled the country's oil industry, a vital component of the national economy and defense. It extracted 85 percent of Peru's oil from its La Brea y Pariñas and Lobitos fields while refining 60 percent of the country's output in its Talara facilities. Belaúnde had campaigned expressly on the promise that he would reach a quick, negotiated settlement with the IPC over claims of ownership and back taxes. However, four years later, the dispute remained unresolved, damaging the president's personal prestige, roiling nationalist sentiment, undermining relations with the United States, and producing animosity in the armed forces.

In a move that resembled Mexico's nationalization of the petroleum industry in 1938, Belaúnde claimed subsoil rights of IPC's oil fields and substantial reparations (variously estimated at $200 million or $600 million, according to Cotler, 1991, VIII p. 464) from unpaid taxes, but that were considered free under the original contract. However, the IPC's legal position was bolstered by the 1922 agreement with the Leguía government (see chapter 9), which said nothing about subsoil Rights. Nationalist opposition to the company was led by the Miró-Quesada family, whose newspaper *El Comercio* had relentlessly attacked the Prado administration for allowing the company to make major price increases. Opinion in the military was divided over the issue, but a CAEM commission, headed by Colonel Francisco Morales Bermúdez, concluded in 1964 that IPC should be taken over by the Empresa Petroleros Fiscales (EPF), the state-owned petroleum company established in 1946 by the Bustamante government.

In his protracted negotiations with IPC, Belaúnde was caught between the strident demands for the company's nationalization, led by *El Comercio*, and the U.S. State Department, which defended the company and exerted its pressure by freezing AID funds designated for Peru. Moreover, the president's bargaining position was seriously weakened by his own deteriorating popularity after 1965, together with growing opposition from Congress and within his own party in favor of nationalization. As for the military, General Morales Bermúdez, who was now Belaúnde's minister of finance and lead negotiator for the government, now took a more conciliatory position toward IPC than in his earlier CAEM report.

General Juan Velasco Alvarado, who was appointed army chief of staff in March 1968, represented the hard-line faction in favor of nationalization. Velasco had no love for IPC, having been born in Piura, near the company's Talara facilities, where IPC wielded enormous power and influence over local affairs. As an infantry captain during the war with Ecuador, Velasco became further incensed when, according to Masterson (1991, p. 226), the company momentarily refused to allow him to commandeer its vehicles at the refinery to move his troops to the front.

Despite these pressures, Belaúnde announced a settlement with IPC that initially appeared to be quite favorable to his government and the country. According to the so-called Acta de Talara of August 13, 1968, the company agreed to renounce its subsoil rights, turn over the La Brea y Pariñas fields to the government, and drop its insistence on any future contract. In return, the government agreed to cancel all debt claims against the company and to sell the oil extracted from the fields to IPC for refining and marketing by its Talara facilities. However, immediately after the agreement was concluded, the former head of the EPF charged on television that page 11 ("página once") of the agreement, which contained the price of the sale, was mysteriously missing. The ensuing scandal, trumpeted in the opposition press, deprived Belaúnde of public and Congressional support. It also led to the expulsion from the party of AP presidential candidate, Vice President

Edgardo Seoane, culminating a long struggle between warring factions for control of the party.

As the IPC controversy ground to a conclusion, amid a faltering economy and increasing political turmoil, fears of a coup from disenchanted elements of the military developed. Politically, Belaúnde was widely seen as increasingly irrelevant, unable to control even his own party, let alone carry out the reforms he had promised for the country. When a series of contraband scandals, involving high-level governmental officials, rocked the administration, public opinion of the regime soured even further.

In this atmosphere of political stalemate, public scandal, and reformist frustration, Leftist parties began to gain adherents, bolstered by disaffections from APRA, AP, and other reform parties. This tendency was particularly evident in university politics, where APRA lost its traditional hegemony to the emerging revolutionary Left. On campuses throughout the country, radical ideologies, energized by the Cuban Revolution, penetrated both the student body and the professorate. The same incipient radicalization occurred among workers' groups and the union movement. For example, the formation of the independent General Confederation of Workers in 1967 by the Left challenged APRA's traditional leadership of the labor movement.

With the military showing signs of increasing impatience and the Left gaining support, Haya determined that the danger of a coup had become so great that APRA would have to come to the rescue of the floundering Belaúnde government. In effect, the obstructionist policies of La Coalición had succeeded too well, in discrediting not only the president in the eyes of the public, but the fragile democratic system itself. As a result, the weak Belaúnde government appointed yet another Cabinet, endorsed by APRA and led by conservative Finance Minister Manuel Ulloa. Ulloa was able to implement a strong structural adjustment policy, along with other reforms that momentarily succeeded in stabilizing the economy and stimulating the growth of exports.

However, the sudden eruption of the IPC "página once" scandal stripped the regime of its remaining legitimacy, opening the way for a military coup. In the early morning hours of October 3, 1968, the presidential palace was surrounded by tanks, and the president was unceremoniously escorted to the airport, where he was placed on a flight bound for Buenos Aires and exile. The Revolutionary Government of the Armed Forces (Gobierno Revolucionario de las Fuerzos Armadas—GRFA), as the small group of high-ranking officers called their movement, now embarked on a radical experiment of military-led "change from above."

The Military "Revolution" of 1968

Why the military chose to seize power at this time is an intriguing question. Certainly, the armed forces had exhibited open hostility toward the populist ambitions of the often-violent APRA Party and its chief Haya de la Torre since the 1930s. This opposition coincided with the oligarchy's anathema toward the APRA, which had formed the basis for the alliance between it and the military. Since then, the predominantly conservative officer corps had regularly vetoed APRA's concerted efforts to gain power. More than three decades later, however, a more liberal officer corps, reflecting its social origins in the rising middle and lower-middle sectors, as opposed to the elites, had reversed its reasons for opposing Haya and APRA, which itself had undergone an ideological and political metamorphosis. APRA was now allied, beginning with the *convivencia* in 1956, with the old oligarchy, as well as with foreign capital.

Consequently, APRA was seen by many progressive, young officers as the major obstacle blocking the structural reforms that they thought were necessary to modernize the country and halt the dangerous advance of the radical Left. So, beginning in the 1960s the army, along with many middle-class professionals, sectors of the Church, and others, supported the rising political star of the self-proclaimed reformer Belaúnde, whose appeal to nationalism and technocratic vision for modernization was shared by many officers. When Belaúnde not only failed to deliver his promised reforms but was tainted with scandal, the officer corps—increasingly confident that they had the will, the civic responsibility, and the expertise to carry out the transformation of the country—intervened to overthrow his regime and institute radical change.

Moreover, with AP divided and discredited and the PDC too small to win, APRA and Haya stood poised to win the presidential elections scheduled for early 1969. Even though Haya was now an aging and increasingly conservative politician, he still led the best-organized and disciplined party in the country. So once again, the military veto, this time for different reasons, was exercised against its historic enemy. In this context, the IPC fiasco not only raised authentic nationalist concerns, but represented simply the necessary pretext that the GRFA needed to justify its seizure of power.

More fundamentally, dissatisfaction with Belaúnde and the possible ascension of Haya and APRA to power in 1969 does not explain the basic reorientation of the armed forces and its growing inclination for reform. From the 1930s to the 1960s, as I have noted, the military went from being a conservative organization, whose officers were drawn mainly from the upper classes and whose real goal was to preserve oligarchical power, to a more "progressive" institution, socially grounded in the middle- and lower-middle classes and increasingly advocating fundamental societal reform. This institutional transformation, reflected by the mid-1960s in the country's leading military journals, explains the emergence of what Stepan (1978) called a "new professionalism" in the armed forces that saw national security in developmental, rather than in strictly geopolitical and military, terms. As early as the mid-1950s, and then accelerating with the radicalizing impact of the Cuban Revolution in the early 1960s, the armed forces were frustrated by what they saw as the persistent failure of civilian governments to make more progress in the direction of national development.

The first major expression of this frustration and the new orientation of the military occurred in 1962–63, when the armed forces annulled the outcome of the national elections, seized power, and embarked on a series of moderate reforms. The junta also laid the groundwork for the election the following year of its preferred presidential candidate Belaúnde over its pariah Haya. However, the outbreak of the guerrilla movement in 1965 deeply influenced the officer corps, who were called by the president to suppress the movement and who saw firsthand the grinding poverty and oppression of the sierra peasantry. This experience deepened the armed forces' belief in the crucial interrelationship between national security and national development. In time, moreover, its leadership became increasingly frustrated with the civilian Belaúnde administration's failed effort at reform and to achieve such national development. As a result, some elements of the army, particularly the Intelligence Service, which had been deeply involved in the campaign to suppress the guerrillas, became increasingly distressed over the problems of agrarian reform, the conflict between labor and management, and the IPC's perceived threat to national sovereignty.

The leader of the coup, which had been several months in gestation, was General Juan Velasco Alvarado, Chief of Staff of the army and the joint command of the armed forces. Velasco was born in 1910 in Castilla, the lowerclass suburb of Piura, fictionalized in Vargas Llosa's novel *La Casa Verde* (*The Green House*), as the site of the main brothal for the city of Piura. It was precisely this sort of disrespect and typecasting by provincial elites that so riled Velasco in his childhood and youth.

He was one of eleven children born to the the son of a medical assistant and grew up in what he called "dignified poverty," allegedly walking to school barefoot. According to one of Velasco's close friends, "from the time that he was very young he had a keen eye for the small things of right and wrong, and for the social effects of low birth—though he never complained about that. But he experienced physically how it feels to be poor and without rights. I think that from childhood on he knew about hopelessness and about injustice" (quoted in Kruijt, 1994, p. 62). Of average height and rough manner, Velasco would later remind some of former President Sánchez Cerro, also a military officer and native son of Piura. During his army and political career, the general would affectionately come to be known as "El Chino," in reference to his mestizo features.

In 1929 Velasco stowed away on a Chilean ship bound for Lima, lied about his age, and enlisted in the army as a private. (He mistakenly got into the wrong enlistment line, since his aim was to become an officer.) Later he was accepted for officer training at the Escuela Militar de Chorrillos after he finished first in the entrance exams. Graduating in four years, at the head of his class and with high honors, Velasco steadily, if unspectacularly, advanced through the ranks. His forte seems to have been a keen ability to size

General Juan Velasco Alvarado (1910–75) addressing the nation shortly after seizing power in 1968. Reproduced with the permission of the General Secretariat of the Organization of American States.

up the talent; political inclinations; and, above all, potential loyalty of his fellow officers. Not having demonstrated any particular intellectual gifts, however, he was not selected to attend the prestigious, progressive oriented CAEM and therefore made his mark as a troop commander, rather than as a staff officer.

Although his political views were not easily categorized, several colleagues also noted a strong sense of social justice in the rising officer. The U.S. military attaché in Lima during Belaúnde's presidency, according to Kruijt, mentioned Velasco's often expressed dislike of the country's landed oligarchy and the need for effective agrarian reform. Velasco apparently admired General De Gaulle, whom he met while an attaché in Paris, not so much as a military hero, but as a soldier-politician whose strength of leadership stabilized a shaky French government. While in Paris, he also knew Haya de la Torre, but, in line with army views, never showed much sympathy for the APRA, which he viewed at the time as essentially a right-wing party.

On the other hand, Velasco was attracted to the PDC and Movimento Social Progresista (MSP) parties, whose leaders espoused a Christian humanism compatible with his own philosophical outlook. Indeed, Klaiber (1992) asserted that the principal concepts of the military reformers were borrowed from Christian Democracy, particularly the idea of a "third way" between capitalism and communism. Also as was perhaps characteristic of the military mind, neither socialism nor communism held out any interest to Velasco, but he did harbor strong nationalist views, which led him to embrace antiimperialist and anti-oligarchical positions. Like most educated Peruvians, he had read Mariátegui, along with other great Peruvian writers, and was strongly influenced by the *indigenista* anthropologist Hildebrando Castro Pozo who had been his teacher.

Perhaps above all, Velasco deeply believed in the military virtues of authority and respect for law and order, without which no society, he thought, could expect to progress. Indeed, he would rule the country, like he had his troop command and later the army, by decree. This is how one of his closest army associates during his presidency described the general's views:

> Society was to be organized in terms of the recognized need for authority; this was one clear principle of his: there can be no twilight government, no anarchism. "Command will never cease," he said. This was his principle. He looked for firm government, the formula for a strong state. Toward the masses it had to be a paternalistic government. . . . He was convinced that the masses needed him as leader, that new organisms had to be created for them, that they are not free to speak their mind or to do what they want to do. That is to say: at heart he was no democrat. . . . What he wanted was strong authority, a strong government, in the manner of the military: authoritarian, though for the sake of the people, to meet their basic human needs. This was what made him tick, this was his basic idea and his program of government—devoid of party-politics. (quoted in Kruijt, 1994, p. 70)

Finally, it should be said that Velasco was impeccably honest and a fervent family man who brooked absolutely no intrusions into his private life, but did enjoy the exercise of power and the perquisites of office.

Although Velasco led the coup, it was largely conceived by his associates, several of whom were connected to the army's Intelligence Service. The *Plan Inca*, as it was called, began as a contingency plan, the kind often drawn up by army staff on national politics. (It was published only in 1974, rewritten in much greater detail to counter charges of the improvisational nature of the reforms.) The *Plan Inca* took on increasing importance among the conspirators as the political situation deteriorated, particularly after corruption charges were leveled in Congress against the Belaúnde administration in April 1968. In general it called for major structural reforms to be carried out in the areas of industry, land tenure, taxes, banking, and government. Initially four colonels worked on the plan, but the group ultimately included Velasco and four other generals who worked in the utmost secrecy. In the final days of the conspiracy, the intellectual and technical plans for the coup were coordinated at the military academy in Chorillos, headed by General Edgardo Mercado Jarrín.

Unlike the 1962 coup, whose planners were careful to involve all the branches of the armed forces in what was a relatively unified, "institutional" movement, the conspiracy was hatched exclusively within the army, without the participation of the navy or air force. Later Velasco would distribute positions in the junta and his Cabinet equally among the three branches, so that the coup took on the appearance of an institutional regime with a measure of unity. But this appearance belied the existence of serious dissent between the old and new guard in the armed forces, between the navy and air force, and between the right- and left-wing factions of the army.

The aims of the coup were not altogether clear in the first manifesto issued by the new government. Moreover, the still-secret *Plan Inca* was necessarily general and short on specifics. Indeed, one major participant in the coup remarked shortly afterward, "[L]isten, our revolution in reality is not born with a program. It is a group of individuals with good faith and good intentions, with set points that signal a transformation . . . but whose practical application has to be studied" (quoted in Graham, 1992, p. 41).

In retrospect, the GRFA viewed the fundamental problems of the country as its disunity and underdevelopment whose causes were "external dependence" to foreign capital and "internal domination" by a powerful oligarchy. This was a long-standing nationalist and anti-oligarchical critique espoused by progressive sectors of the middle class as far back as the founding of the APRA in the 1930s and increasingly articulated by the new reform parties (e.g., AP and PDC) that had emerged in the 1960s, along with sectors of the Church and armed forces itself. The solution, according to the GRFA, was the eradication of the "enclaves of foreign imperialism" and the shift to an autonomous, rather than export-led, economic model of growth and development.

According to the Five-Year Economic Plan established later for 1971–75, this anti-imperialist–oligarchical strategy was designed to gain national control over the economic surplus and redirect it to a broad stratum of formerly marginalized local entrepreneurs. The authors of this plan believed that Peru had suffered since the early 1960s from the unwillingness of foreigners and the oligarchy to reinvest sufficiently in the economy to achieve adequate growth and development. Hence the breakup of monopoly capital (they used the analogy of opening a dam that had blocked reinvestment in the economy) would serve to bring about a surge of reinvestment that would restore the economy's dynamism and vitality. A restructured and expanded state, of course, would be the mechanism for bringing about this economic revitalization.

To achieve these fundamentally populist developmental goals, the new military government called for the establishment of social solidarity and class harmony under the tutelage of the state. Such a corporatist design was underpinned by the Catholic thought of Thomas Aquinas, Thomas More, Francisco Súarez, and Pope Leo XIII, which envisioned the function of the state, in addition to maintaining order, as actively seeking to promote the common good. It also included references to papal encyclicals, such as *Populorum Progressio* (1967), which addressed Third World problems of hunger, poverty, and economic dependence and further reinforced the government's agenda for radical social reform. A Catholic-corporatist approach of "reform from above" also served to deflect the conservative opposition's charges of "communistic" tendencies in the GRFA and to forestall the possible outbreak of popular disorders that normally accompanied revolutionary transformations. Although populist and coporatist in nature, the GRFA reform plan also incorporated the new national security concerns of the armed forces that were designed to defuse potential class conflict by promoting national development. In this way, a unified, socially cohesive Peru could meet the twin challenges of a potential foreign aggressor outside its borders and revolutionary guerrilla movements inside the country.

As for the age-old problem of the oppression of the indigenous population, it was deemed to be mainly socioeconomic, rather than cultural, in nature. While Túpac Amaru II became the symbol of the revolution, the term *Indian* was largely replaced in governmental decrees and laws by the word *campesino* (peasant). This did not mean, however, that the new military regime ignored the Indians, since its cultural and educational policies embraced the indigenous and *lo Andino*. For example, the glorious Inca past continued to be extolled in offical literature and pronouncements, and Quechua was proclaimed the second national language of the country. Although in highland schools Indians were ordered to learn Spanish, they were also to be instructed in their native language.

To carry out this plan, the government, during what came to be known as the First, or Velasco, Phase (1968–75) of the military's twelve-year rule (*Docenio*), undertook two fundamental reforms. It instituted a sweeping land-reform program that eliminated the age-old hacienda and landowning elite, including foreign companies, from the agrarian system of the country. Although, as you shall see, the reform was seriously flawed, it affected nearly 60 percent of the country's agricultural lands, actually distributing more land than either the Mexican or Bolivian revolutions. When it was finally completed, half of all arable land had been transferred to an estimated 375,00 families (one-quarter of the rural population), mainly to estate workers and tenants (*colonos*). However, all these families by no means benefited equally from the reform. In general, peasants on the more prosperous coastal estates, perhaps 10 percent of all peasants, benefited substantially, while their counterparts in the less-developed and more backward highlands (*comuneros* and *colonos*) gained little or nothing from the reform. It was among the latter that support developed for the Shining Path guerrilla movement of the 1980s. Moreover, the reform totally left out an estimated 1 million *eventuales* (seasonal workers).

The second fundamental change was the dramatic expansion of the state, which assumed a major role in the economy and development process for the first time. Its target was mainly the foreign-dominated sector, which, during the 1960s had attained a significant position in the economy, accounting for 33 percent of the output of the corporate sector. For example, at the end of the Belaúnde government in 1968, three-quarters of mining, one-half of manufacturing, two-thirds of the commercial banking system, and one-third of the fishing industry were under direct foreign control. By contrast, the state controlled only 16 percent of the GDP in 1968.

The Velasco government reversed this pattern, doubling the state sector's share of the GDP to 31 percent. New state enterprises emerged in mining (Mineroperú), fishing (Pescaperú), steel (Siderperú), Petroleum (Petroperú), and industry (Moraveco). By 1975 these enterprises accounted for more than half the mining output, two-thirds of the banking system, a fifth of industrial production, and half the total investment in the economy.

The essential thrust of the Velasco development program was to shift from a laissez faire to a "mixed" economy and to replace the export-led development strategy with import-substituting industrialization. In the words of Velasco, the construction of what amounted to a form of state capitalism was to be "neither capitalist nor communist." At the same time, the state implemented a series of populist social measures that were designed to protect workers and to redistribute income to expand the domestic market. The net effect of the expansion of the state was the creation of 150 new public enterprises and the employment of about 670,000 state employees, more than double the number (300,000) in 1970. Public spending and investment also rose dramatically.

The expansion of the state apparatus was characterized by the rise of a technocratic elite of planners and advisers and the militarization of key personnel. As for the former, a number of important civilian advisers were linked to the Presidential Advisory Committee (Comité de Asesoramiento de la Presidencia—COAP), established almost immediately by Velasco after the October 3 coup. The COAP was initially composed of six trusted army colonels and two additional colonels assigned from the other two services, but soon came to include civilians, such as the sociologist Carlos Delgado; PDC head Héctor Cornejo Cháves; and Ruiz Eldredge, founder of the small, but influential Movimiento Social Progresista (MSP). Ideologically, unlike the more conservative, if nationalistic, junta and initial Cabinet ministers, the members of the COAP were the most radical representatives of the GRFA. From its initial role in advising the president, the COAP operated as "political guardians of the revolutionary process." Indeed, in time its chairman evolved into a kind of "superminister" charged with seeing that the various ministers and ministries carried out the president's revolutionary decrees.

The militarization of the state apparatus began as an effort to "moralize" what the GRFA asserted was not only an inefficient and sluggish governmental bureaucracy, but one that was riddled with corruption and dishonesty. It was somehow assumed that the ethical standards of the armed forces, charged with the larger mission of national defense and imbued with a professional espirit d' corps, were inherently higher than those of the civilian politicians who were viewed as incapable of putting the national interest above selfish, petty, personal ambitions. Moreover, once the nationalizations began to multiply, military officers, both active and retired, became an obvious source of qualified and reliable (that is, trusted) manpower to manage the new state-run enterprises. By the end of the *Docenio*, it was estimated that 40 to 50 percent of the senior officers were political and administrative executives in the government.

To address further the twin problems of dependence and underdevelopment, the new military government also embraced the concept of "Third Worldism." Peru would become a driving force in the creation of an Andean Pact in 1969, designed to help lessen geopolitical and military tensions and to establish a common market with coordinated trade and investment policies that would ostensibly open the path of Peruvian manufactures to its neighbors. It would also become a leader in the "group of 77," the so-called movement of nonaligned countries of the Third World. Furthermore, in a concerted effort to end its perceived economic and political dependence on the United States, the Velasco government would diversify its foreign relations by making trade and aid (economic and military) pacts with the Soviet Union and Eastern European countries, as well as with Japan and Western European nations. In addition, it would establish relations with China (before President Nixon's visit) and refused to stand with the United States in its trade blockade against Cuba. Finally, Peru would enforce a 200-nautical mile territorial limit in the Pacific Ocean, a claim first put forth by the Bustamante government after World War II. The issue of the nationalization of U.S. companies set the two countries immediately at logger heads.

A few days after the 1968 coup, Peru expropriated the IPC and refused compensation on the grounds that the initial contract between the company and the government was invalid. The government then proceeded to reorganize the old state oil company EPF into Petroperú, which took control of the IPC oil facilities in the north. It also began to explore for new deposits in the jungle, partly in joint ventures with foreign oil companies. In response to the expropriation, the United States threatened to apply the Hickenlooper Amendment, which called for the cutoff of all credit and aid from the United States and affiliated international agencies like the World Bank to countries that nationalized U.S. property without compensation. In 1974, after extended negotiations, the two countries did reach agreement on appropriate levels of compensation.

Until 1974, however, relations continued to be roiled by Peru's attempts to diversify its arms purchases away from the United States and its insistence on enforcing its 200-mile territorial limit in the Pacific. In the case of the former, Peruvian officers had been nettled by the refusal of the United

States, as early as the mid-1960s, to allow napalm to be sold to Peru for use by the air force against the guerrillas in the highlands. Then in 1967, the United States refused to sell new jet aircraft to the air force. This policy stirred up resentment in military circles at Peru's "dependence" on weapons from the United States, the argument being that in case of an external war, Peru's armed forces would be at the mercy of the United States. At that time, the Belaúnde government responded by purchasing Mirage jets from the French, which, of course, did not sit well with the United States.

It was this resentment at U.S. military-assistance policies that led Velasco to recognize the Soviet bloc countries and to turn to the Soviet Union for commercial and military assistance. Diplomatic ties were established with the Soviet Union in late 1968, and thereafter a number of trade and weapons-purchase agreements were concluded that led to an increase in trade, from $23 million in 1968 to $283 million in 1975. Indeed, the purchase of Soviet weapons during this period ranked Peru second only to Cuba in this category in the hemisphere.

These agreements brought a hundred or so Soviet technical advisers to Peru during the 1970s, while more than 800 army and air force personnel went to Moscow for training. Only the more conservative navy remained aloof from these arrangements and purchased their ships and equipment from Italy and West Germany. Closer ties with the Soviet Union were facilitated by that country's rapid humanitarian response to the massive earthquake that struck the Callejón de Huaylas in the northern highlands on May 31, 1970, killing 70,000 people and leaving 500,000 homeless.

As for the 200-mile territorial limit, Peru's navy vigorously enforced the limit by seizing U.S. tuna boats fishing in "its waters." These incidents provoked the so-called Tuna War in February 1969, when the United States responded to a particularly controversial seizure by suspending military aid to Peru, which, in response, expelled the U.S. military mission from the country. As a result, a half century of cooperation between the two countries' armed forces was ended, diplomatic relations cooled, and Peru intensified its turn to the Soviet Union and elsewhere for military and other assistance.

On the other hand, the announcement by Velasco six days after the coup of the expropriation of the IPC's holdings conferred widespread immediate popularity on the new military regime and Velasco, in particular. Henceforth commemorated as the official Day of National Dignity, the nationalization, in effect, countered the initial public apathy to the October 3 coup. Over the next few years, the government would announce significant state takeovers in other sectors of the economy, including mining, electricity, transportation, fishing, and foreign trade.

The case of mining was instructive of the new nationalistic course set by the government. When the foreign-owned copper companies, reacting to the IPC takeover, balked at proceeding with plans to develop huge new copper deposits in the south, their concessions were canceled. A new state mining company, Mineroperú, was formed to market all minerals and to develop new deposits. Moreover, the list of expropriated foreign companies multiplied during the First Phase and included ITT (1969), Chase Manhattan Bank (1970), the Peruvian Corporation and Conchán oil refinery (1972) and Marcona Mining (1975). As a result of these takeovers, the level of foreign capital in the economy was reduced, according to Fitzgerald (1979), 40 percent from the Belaúnde period.

In the meantime, within six months of seizing power, Velasco decreed a radical agrarian reform law that became the cornerstone of his revolution. Quoting Túpac Amaru II's cry two centuries earlier, "Peasant, the landlord will no longer eat from your poverty," the president announced decree law 17716 eliminating the hacienda on June 24, 1969. Ideologically, the sweeping land-reform decree drew upon such diverse influences as Christian Democratic cooperativism, Marxist collectivism, and traditional Andean communalism (the *ayllu*). The goals of the ambitious reform were threefold: to eliminate the traditional landed aristocracy (coastal planters and sierra *gamonales*); to remove the potential for peasants' discontent and insurgency (the military's new national security doctrine) by redistributing income; and to improve the productive efficiency of agriculture, which had been eroding since the 1960s at a time of exploding population growth. General Velasco suggested that another reason was to generate additional surplus capital from agriculture for reinvestment in urban industrialization.

The reform was first applied to the expropriation of the sugar plantations of the north coast. But it was done in a way that was designed not to endanger the performance of these modern, capital-intensive, and profitable enterprises. Hence, the subsequent "cooperativization" of these plantations retained efficiencies of scale while they distributed income more equitably. The creation of the sugar cooperatives also had an important political, as well as economic, purpose: to eliminate the political power of the long-reigning planter oligarchy and to undermine the army's old nemesis—the APRA party, whose political base in the north (*"el sólido norte aprista"*) rested on the organized plantation workforce.

In addition to the sugar plantations, the agrarian reform law decreed the expropriation of all haciendas of any size and significance and their transformation into self-managing cooperatives. Although the owners of expropriated estates were compensated with 20–30-year government bonds, the actual amount they received was sharply reduced over time by accelerating inflation. Two major types of cooperatives were created: Agrarian Production Cooperatives (Cooperativas Agrarias de Producción—CAPs), mostly large profitable coastal estates, and Agrarian Social Interest Societies (Sociedades Agrícolas de Interés Social—SAIS), comprising the best sierra holdings. Together, the CAPs and SAISs constituted 76 percent of the expropriated properties; the remainder was distributed in individual plots to peasant "groups," cooperatives, or communities.

The members of the CAPs and SAISs were the former permanent workers, or peasants, of the estates, who now became simultaneously the workers, managers, and shareholders of the enterprise. The *eventuales*, or temporary workers, on the coast and nontenant laborers in the highlands were excluded from membership and thus remained unaffected by the reform. The peasants were given a voice in the administration of the cooperatives through various assemblies and councils, but day-to-day management and policy implementation were charged to technocrats, usually agronomists, who were appointed by the Ministry of Agriculture. The government was the only source of external credit and investment funds for the cooperatives, and after 1976 it had the power to intervene directly in the operation of any cooperative.

The highland SAIS organizations, which constituted about one-sixth of all reform beneficiaries, proved to be the most problematic of the reform program. They were designed to link ex-haciendas with nearby peasant communities, retaining modern improvements on some of the former while providing benefits to the latter. Serious conflicts, however, erupted over the adjudication of "disputed" land between peasants in the communities who pushed for their return and those on haciendas whose interest, like their former masters, was to retain them. Tensions also developed between members of the cooperatives and the state-appointed managers, the former having the power to fire the latter any time they wanted to.

The results of the agrarian reform were mixed. By 1979 the hacienda, which had been a hallmark of Peru's seignorial land tenure system for centuries, no longer existed. Some 8.5 million hectares, representing 60 percent of the country's agricultural income, had been adjudicated to 375,000 families, or 25 percent of all farm families. The clear winners in this reform were the 140,000 ex-hacienda workers on the highly capitalized and profitable coastal estates, who represented only about 10 percent of all agricultural families. They became members of cooperatives whose average share of the property, according to McClintock (1998, p. 174), amounted to $1,900 and whose standard of living during the first decade of the reform improved considerably. Even before the reform, their income was already four times that of the average family living in the most impoverished areas of the highlands.

On the other hand, the overwhelming portion of peasants in the highlands, about 40 percent of the total peasantry, received far less from the reform. For example, one-sixth of all beneficiaries were peasants on poorly capitalized and backward haciendas in the highlands who formed "groups" and chose to receive and work their land individually. The value of the land they received averaged $350, or one-sixth of the value received by their counterparts on the coastal cooperatives. Similarly, peasants in some highland communities, perhaps one-third of the total beneficiaries, received some pasture lands from contiguous haciendas valued at only $50 or less. Finally, most of the peasants in the poorest, most disadvantaged, southern highlands received no benefit at all from the reform. For example, McClintock calculated that in 1975 this was the case for 87 percent of the peasants, mostly *co-*

muneros, in Ayacucho; 82 percent in Apurimac; and 54 percent in Huancavelica.

Equally problematic, the nonresident farm population (*eventuales*) was largely excluded from the reform and, as nonmembers of cooperatives, they continued to be disadvantaged, as under the old system, by the members of the cooperatives. Indeed, the income disparity between the two groups—that is, between the permanent estate workers and temporary workers—significantly widened as a result of the reform and, by the end of the 1970s, was estimated by McClintock to be about two to one.

Moreover, these disparities and inequities in the agrarian reform were not closed by more equitable governmental credit, investment, or pricing policies all of which tended to favor the modern, coastal sector. For example, while government loans doubled in real terms between 1970 and 1976, 40–50 percent went to the main export crops in the modern sector. As for public investment in agriculture, it grew substantially during the 1970s, but the lion's share (64 percent in 1978–79) went to the construction of large-scale irrigation projects, such as at Chira-Piura, Májes, and Tinajones. Finally, food prices between 1969 and 1974 were held to the general rate of inflation by the government to aid the urban poor. But the price of potatoes, the most important crop for peasants, increased less than that of other foods and well below the rise allowed for commodities, such as sugar, meat, and milk produced by well-capitalized enterprises.

At the end of the reform period, only a quarter of the rural population had gained access to the land, which still, according to Masterson (1991, p. 253), ranked Peru, along with India, as having the worst man–land ratio in the world (only 0.18 hectares of crop land per person). Moreover, the reform did little to alter the poverty of peasants in the poorest parts of the country, such as in Ayacucho, where the Shining Path insurgency would emerge a decade later. This fact suggests that the main aim of the agrarian reform—to diffuse the potential for rural insurgency—was largely a failure, probably because of dashed expectations for improvement by peasants in places like Ayacucho. But in a larger sense, the agrarian reform's failures were also due to the inherent flaws in its design and the haste and lack of planning with which it was conceived and implemented.

The economic legacy of the agrarian reform is more difficult to assess. On the one hand, overall agricultural production seems to have risen slightly during the 1970s as compared to the 1960s. Output rose from 12.6 billion *soles* in 1960 to 15.8 in 1978 (measured in 1963 prices). But this increase was not nearly enough to keep pace with Peru's rapid population increase of 3 percent annually or demand for food of 4 percent annually during the same period. In addition, food production lagged behind that of livestock and commodity outputs, so that between 1972 and 1974, the country's food imports grew from 15 percent to 25 percent of the total output. This shortfall was exacerbated between 1978 and 1980 by the worst drought of the century, which caused overall agricultural production to drop 4.7 and 5.3 percent in 1979 and 1980, respectively. Particularly hard hit were such water-dependent crops as sugar and rice, whose output fell as much as 30 percent in 1980.

Once the agrarian reform began to be implemented and the peasants saw the results of the land transfers, they started to form largely spontaneous, grassroots organizations to defend or extend their gains. In time, the government came to realize that without such organized, popular, grassroots support or, indeed, the formation of an official political party, Velasco's overall program of radical transformation and restructuration would flounder. According to one prominent general, "at the beginning of the revolutionary process, no one thought of such things. The participation of the people in the process was talked about, but nothing was done" (quoted in Mauceri, 1996, p. 18). To some extent, the regime's tactical alliance with the Peruvian Communist Party, similar to Odría's in the 1950s and the Pérez Godoy junta's in the early 1960s, served this function, but was not enough. The problem was later put this way by one of the generals:

> Who was going to play stoker to the locomotive of transformation? . . . The revolution had to keep moving, the wheels had to keep turning. How do you do that without a political party? How can you get the masses in motion without a party? (quoted in Kruijt, 1994, p. 116).

Velasco and others were wary of any association with the existing parties, whose excessive clientelism and opportunism he held responsible for the coup in the first place. Nor did he support the idea of the creation of a new party linked personally to a military figure, which he saw as potentially divisive, negative, and corrupting. Consequently, the government chose another option, a "bureaucratic sponsored organization" (Stepan, 1978) called the *Sistema Nacional de Movilización Social* (SINAMOS—literally "without masters" in Spanish), which became the popular arm of the revolution in July 1971.

The main aim of SINAMOS was "to achieve conscious and active participation of the national population in the tasks demanded by economic and social development." In other words, its role was to mobilize controlled popular support to make the revolution a reality. With this mandate, SINAMOS quickly grew into the most powerful official organization in the revolutionary government, with an elaborate pyramidal structure, composed of 7,000–8,000 *técnicos* who were inspired with the necessary dedication and discipline to mobilize and channel popular support for the revolution. Headed by a series of generals, SINAMOS's elaborate bureaucratic structure reached down to the community level, where it operated mainly in the agrarian cooperatives; the Industrial Communities; and, most importantly, the squatter settlements (previously called *barriados* but renamed *pueblos jóvenes* by the Velasco government to improve their unsavory public image) around Lima.

Other than certain instances in the *pueblos jóvenes*, SINAMOS was largely a failure and encountered strong opposition from a number of quarters. Governmental technocrats objected to the "politics" it injected into the planning process, communities rejected its outside manipulation, and the political parties and labor unions opposed its encroachment into their local domain. Moreover, as it turned out, SINAMOS was unable to control many of the mass-based groups that it organized. The creation of SINAMOS revealed the military's technocratic orientation, as well as its strong distrust of traditional politics, politicians, and unions.

Where SINAMOS was most effective, as I just noted, was in the squatter settlements that had grown enormously as internal migration of the rural poor accelerated during the 1950s and 1960s. Although this migratory stream swelled such interior cities as Piura, Huancayo, and Arequipa with peasants who were "pushed and pulled" from adjacent hinterlands, Lima received the greatest cohort of internal migrants. Indeed, by 1970, about one-third of the capital's 3.5 million inhabitants resided in *pueblos jóvenes*. These shanty towns were urbanizations in the process of development, whose origins were almost always illegal and whose locations were generally on the periphery of the city. They also were the result of massive land invasions, such as the one that occupied Comas, a new district in Lima, in 1958. The Comas occupation was carried out by some 10,000 people within a period of forty-eight hours, the largest organized land invasion in Lima's history. By 1972 the district's population had exploded into a satellite "city" of 173,000 inhabitants.

Demographically, these new shantytowns were microcosms of the racial, ethnic, linguistic, and regional diversity of the country. In 1970, four out of five shantytown residents were born outside Lima, and more than half were under forty years old. Many were bilingual speakers of Quechua or Aymara and Spanish. A survey of one *pueblo joven* revealed that a quarter of its inhabitants spoke some Quechua. In this sense, one can speak of the increasing "Andeanization" of Lima and other cities as the inhabitants of the interior arrived, along with their culture, in ever greater numbers to the shantytowns. Ethnically, the vast majority of shantytown inhabitants were and are classified as *cholos*, a slightly contemptuous and condescending, urban term for a recent migrant or "citified" Indian (Dietz, 1998, p. 107). Perhaps the hallmark of *cholo* culture in Lima was their music, known as *chicha*, a combination of the Andean *huayno*, or folk dance, music and the Colombian *cumbia*. With radio as the medium, the production and consumption of *chicha* music, along with Andean waltzes, *huaynos*, and *yaraví*, as well as creole music, such as the *marinera*, have proliferated, as have the attendant number of composers, musicians, singers, and dancers.

In response to the explosion of shantytowns in Lima and elsewhere during the 1970s, the Velasco regime, in addition to changing their names from *barriadas* to *pueblos jóvenes* (young towns), established a new state agency to bring about better conditions and coordinate developmental efforts in them. However, to discourage new invasions on private property, the military government took a hard line against future land occupations. Nevertheless, popular expectations could not be contained for long, and in May 1971 thousands of poor *Limeños* mounted an invasion of the Pamplona district, only to be confronted violently by the police. In a compromise agreement worked out between the government and the Church, the invaders agreed to move to a site prepared by the government, called Villa El Salvador, which had over 100,000 residents within a year. The government also launched a drive to create community development centers in Lima's *pueblos jóvenes,* and within two years, more than 1,000 such centers had been opened in the capital and other major cities, providing a broad range of social services.

The results of the creation of these new community centers by the government were contradictory. On the one hand, they reproduced and fostered the kind of clientelism that was common under the oligarchical regimes of Odría and Prado. On the other hand, they provolked a revolutionary transformation by unintentionally sparking "an uncontrolled popular movement, one that [in time] would help bring down the military regime itself" (Stokes, 1995, pp. 36–37). This movement was brought about not only by the spontaneous emergence of participatory, self-contained community organizations of shantytown dwellers, but by the work of SINAMOS, which organized highly effective neighborhood self-help committees linked to the state.

Once SINAMOS and the regime collapsed after 1975, however, these settlement associations took on lives of their own. In the 1980s, they would evolve, as you shall see, into genuine autonomous grassroots organizations, capable of confronting what would be the greatest economic and social crisis of the century. At the same time, many would be taken over or replicated by cadres from various political, particularly Marxist, parties or progressive representatives of the Catholic Church, often advocates of liberation theology.

Indeed, from the beginning, the Church, as one might imagine, had established an important presence in the squatter settlements. At the outset, ecclesiastical work there was conceived as "missionary," while the majority of priests and religious personnel who engaged in this task were foreign born and financed. Every district had a specific religious group in charge, such as the Maryknoll Fathers in Ciudad de Dios or the Jesuits in El Agustino. Each parish also provided a range of services in the *pueblos jóvenes,* including a medical post, soup kitchen, vocational training center, and children's education center. The latter was particularly important, since the Andean migrants had chosen to emigrate to the city not only to find work, but to obtain educational opportunities for their children.

In 1968, the same year that Velasco came to power, the Church appointed the progressive auxiliary bishop of Lima, Luis Bambaren, as its principal representative to the *Pueblos Jóvenes.* Given the developmental overlap between the Church and the government in the young towns, as well as the fact that the district parishes often became the focal point of the community, it is not surprising that tensions occasionally arose between the two entities.

One early example, was the brief arrest of Bishop Bambaren after he expressed solidarity by saying mass for the invaders at Pamplona in 1971.

In general, however, the relations between the Church and the military reformers were cordial. Indeed, the military reforms were supported by the Church during the early years of the Velasco government, while the same reforms reinforced the progressive tendencies that were transforming the institution. These changes in the Church during the 1960s and 1970s, as elsewhere on the continent, had been spurred by the social encyclicals of popes John XXIII and Paul VI, the reforms of Vatican II in 1959, the widespread revolution of rising expectations, the arrival of progressive foreign missionaries, the demographic explosion of the squatter settlements, and the spread of liberation theology. The latter, in fact, was the creation of a Peruvian priest, Gustavo Gutiérrez Merino, who was an adviser at the Latin American Bishops Council held at Medellin, Colombia, in 1968 and who was influential in developing its social message to Latin American Catholics on the issues of social injustice, human rights, and economic dependence.

Gutiérrez was born in 1928 into a lower-middle-class *Limeño* family and was educated at San Marcos University, where he studied medicine and participated in Catholic Action, a lay group that promoted social development. In 1950 he entered the seminary in Santiago and later got a scholarship to study at the University of Louvain in Belgium, where one of his fellow students was the Colombian priest Camilo Torres, who would later be killed in 1966 as a leftist guerrilla. Ordained as a priest in Lima in 1959, Gutiérrez joined the faculty at the Catholic University and became involved with a progressive group of priests and laity who, in 1968, began to advocate many of his ideas on liberation theology and the progressive renovation of the Peruvian Church. Three years later he published his celebrated work entitled *Liberation Theology* (1971). The book was particularly significant because, in its emphasis on social justice for the poor as the principle mission of the Latin American Church, it represented a sort of declaration of independence of the Church from its historical dependence on Europe.

One area in which the Church was increasingly critical of the Velasco government was its authoritarian tendencies, which came to the fore especially on matters related to the press. For the first few years, the government allowed a relative freedom of the press, permitting some criticism of the regime, but only within certain limits. However, relations between the government and the country's major newspapers began to deteriorate as the pace of reform accelerated. They deteriorated largely because the newspapers were owned by the leading oligarchical families who, as Gilbert (1979) showed, had traditionally operated their newspapers as vehicles to defend and promote their economic interests, rather than as enterprises to make money and report the news fairly and objectively. Gradually, the government began to decree measures that were designed to control the press, which led to the expropriations of *Expreso* and *Extra* in 1970.

Then in 1974 the government expropriated the five remaining national dailies and "sectorized" their editorial functions, that is, turned them over to different organized sectors of the society. In general, the newspapers were handed over to representatives of various socioeconomic groups, such as peasants, industrial workers, miners, slum dwellers, teachers, and intellectuals. Thus, *El Comercio*, previously owned by the Miró-Quesada family, became the peasants' paper, while workers in the industrial communities assumed control of Pedro Beltrán's *La Prensa*. But only those popular organizations that were officially recognized by the government were selected.

These corporatist-style reforms in the political arena were mirrored in the reorganization of the state as it expanded by way of the nationalization process into the industrial sector. Thus, each sector of society was overseen by a plethora of new or reorganized ministries, headed by generals. These ministries included Agriculture, Education, Fishery, Foods, Industry and Trade, Energy and Mining, and Transport and Communication. In effect, the economy and society were "sectorized," with each sector overseen by a governmental ministry. SINAMOS, for example, managed the Confederación Nacional Agraria (CNA), which grew explosively to over a million members, comprising over 2,000 peasant communities and 500 cooperatives by 1977. This situation led Stepan (1978) to describe the process of the military revolution as the reorganization of the organized and the organization of the hardly organized.

Just as property relations were reorganized in agriculture, industry experienced a parallel restructurization. In a series of decrees designed to increase production and harmonize labor-capital relations, so-called industrial communities (Comunidades Industriales—CIs) were formed in both the nationalized, or state, sector and the private sector. In the private sector, for example, companies with more than six workers or $250,000 in gross income had to reinvest profits (in stock) progressively in the name of their workers up to 50 percent of the ownership. They also had to provide for a commensurate level of workers' participation in management and distribute 10 percent of the profits outright to their workers. Finally, it became difficult, indeed almost impossible, under the provisions of the new General Law of Industries for companies, or *estabilidad laboral*, to fire or lay off their workers.

With the implementation of the industrial reform law, workers gained an important share in company ownership, as well as a significant voice in management. However, the hoped-for expansion in production and moderation of labor-capital conflict failed to materialize, and the number and intensity of strikes actually increased. Furthermore, the number of workers who were included in the new CIs, which numbered 3,500 by 1973, turned out to be a privileged minority of the total potential workforce. In the private sector, for example, the always large under- and unemployed population, including the growing informal or underground sector, remained outside the CIs. As for the state sector, where workers received bonds, rather than stocks in the enterprises, only 200,000 workers, or 4.3 percent of the economically active population, belonged to CIs in 1975.

What was not clear, however, was how labor unions would relate to these new industrial communities of workers who now had a share of ownership and management. Shortly after the organization of the CNA in the agricultural sector, the government announced the formation of the *Movimiento Laboral Revolucionario* (MLR), a co-opted trade union federation that superseded the existing labor organizations in the country. Similar coopted "parallel organizations," loyal to the revolutionary government, were also organized among governmental workers, teachers, and other sectors. The aim of the government again was to exercise control over such important mass organizations of workers and peasants and thereby orchestrate popular support for the reforms.

A number of scholars have described the overriding expansion of the state during the *Docenio* as "state capitalism" (Bollinger, 1977; Fitzgerald, 1976; Quijano, 1971). In addition to the economic reforms just described, the state assumed a significant position in the industrial, financial, and commercial sectors of the economy. The purpose was not to displace private or foreign investment, but to bolster "strategic" areas that were deemed important for the advance of industrialization and the development of the domestic market.

For the most part, the economic expansion of the state was aimed at foreign companies and was designed both to rationalize the economy and to reduce its supposed dependence. At no time was it the government's intention to create a centralized, command economy, and the government remained throughout committed to a "pluralistic" mixed economy with various types of public enterprises created by the state. The government also assumed a dominant position in both international and domestic marketing through state monopolies of mineral exports and food wholesaling. Likewise, it gained control of the banking industry, through the purchase of stock, so as to be able to direct the allocation of credit. The allocation of credit was deemed critical to the regime's development plan, which, it was thought, could not be left purely to market forces.

Although the government's intention was for the state to supplement private investment in the economy, its actions had the opposite effect, frightening off the private and foreign sectors from their investment plans. As a result, the percentage of state investment in the economy rose from 29.8 in 1968 to 44 in 1973. Moreover, the government hoped that income from primary exports (principally oil, copper, and fishmeal) would serve to finance state investments in industry. For a time, high prices for sugar, copper, and other exports and substantial borrowing from abroad in anticipation of major oil revenues from new investments in exploration buoyed the regime financially through an initial "honeymoon" period.

Thus, Peru's foreign debt increased from $945 million in 1970 to $2,170 million in 1974 to $4,127 million in 1976. This increase was partly due to the greater availability of loans from foreign banks that were eager to recycle their petro-dollars to the Third World after the world oil embargo of 1973. Foreign loans, in effect, financed the Velasco revolution (along with export revenues) while serving to counteract the cutoff of credit and aid from the United States after the nationalization of the IPC. Only after Peru agreed in the so-called Greene Agreement in 1974 to pay $150 million to settle all pending claims by IPC and other U.S. companies, did U.S. loans again become available to Peru. These loans were particularly critical for the completion of the stalled export development of the Cuajone copper mines formerly owned by the Southern Peru Copper Corporation.

Another major reform in property relations, other than the cooperatives, industrial communities, and state enterprises, was in the area called social property, decreed in April 1974. It was to consist, at least at first, of only new firms, social property enterprises, financed by the state, but subject to self-management, profit sharing, and democratic governance by all workers, temporary and permanent. Strong opposition, the growing scarcity of public investment funds, and demands that the law be applied to existing enterprises, rather than new ones, effectively led to the abandonment of implementation of social property enterprises after Velasco was removed from power in 1975.

The momentum of the reform movement was suddenly jolted in February 1973 when Velasco became severely ill from an abdominal aneurism that required the amputation of his Right leg. Although he returned to work in April, concern for his health raised the question of succession, unsettling relations with his Cabinet as some members began maneuvering for advantage. At the same time, as hopes for a complete recovery waned, the president gradually began to lose touch—first, with his ministers and advisers, then with middle-ranking and junior officers in the army—his main power base—and, finally, with the public at large. Moreover, as his health continued to deteriorate, particularly toward the end of 1974, Velasco's behavior became increasingly erratic and his rule more personalistic and arbitrary.

Then in early 1974 an international recession, touched off by the 1973 worldwide OPEC oil embargo, adversely affected Peruvian export earnings on which the financing of the Velasco revolution was heavily dependent. For example, there were sharp declines in the world prices of sugar and copper, combined with poor yields in the once-booming fishmeal industry. Consequently, international creditors now began to demand that the government implement an austerity program at a time when the pace of reforms demanded greater public expenditures and public expectations for change accelerated. The financial situation was exacerbated by a number of other economic problems, including heavy food and industrial imports, large expenditures for Soviet arms, the reluctance to undertake tax reforms, and inconsistent manufacturing policies.

As the economy deteriorated, labor unrest increased, reversing a period of relative peace that had prevailed since 1968. During the first four years of the Velasco regime, real wages had increased 26 percent, and the regime's conciliatory approach to labor had kept it quiescent. Nearly 2,000 unions were officially recognized by the government between 1968 and 1975, as many as during the previous thirty years. Moreover, the 1970 law of *estabilidad laboral* had given workers a measure of security by prohibiting the dismissal of workers after three months of employment. However, with the economy declining between 1973 and 1975, real wages fell back to 1968 levels, while the number of strikes in the country exploded to unprecedented numbers (779 in 1975).

As labor unrest dramatically increased and the economy deteriorated, along with Velasco's health and leadership, conservative civilian and military opposition to the regime intensified. This opposition coincided with manifestations of popular protests against the regime in the streets for the first time. They culminated in February 1975, when an unprecedented strike by the *Guardia Civil* left the capital virtually unprotected. When the army responded with a tank assault on police headquarters to break the strike, riots, accompanied by widespread arson and looting, erupted throughout the city. Some of the violence, such as at the offices of pro-government newspapers, the headquarters of SINAMOS, and a military club, was directed against the regime. By the time the army suppressed the rioting, civilian and police casualties amounted to 86 dead and 155 wounded. As a result of these events, public confidence in the government declined sharply.

Given Velasco's poor health and the shock of the riots, talk of a successor, already discussed in high government circles, began to intensify. Velasco's finance minister and premier, Francisco Morales Bermúdez, seemed to be the logical choice. A cautious and frugal man, Morales was generally well regarded by his military colleagues of all political stripes. At first, it was generally agreed in the Cabinet that Velasco would formally step down on October 3 and transfer the presidency to Morales, although there was some talk of an earlier date. Morales, however, was not content to wait and staged a "precipitate coup" on August 29 in Tacna, where he had gone to commemorate the anniversary of the province's return to Peru by Chile in 1929. Returning to Lima the next day, he was formally sworn in as president before a reconstituted junta. This marked the beginning of the so-called Second Phase of the 1968 revolution (1975–80), based on Morales's pledge "to deepen and consolidate the revolutionary process."

With the end of the seven-year Velasco period, how may we assess the first phase of the revolution? Certainly, it might be criticized for its authoritarian and antidemocratic character, bordering, as some of its critics argued, on the totalitarian. However, these tendencies might be overlooked if its ambitious redistributory and developmental goals had been reached. Had the massive restructuring of the state and society worked? The answer, a quarter century or so after the event, seems to be no.

For example, on the matter of the redistribution of wealth and income, the historic gap between the traditional and modern sectors—the coast and the sierra—which characterized the dual structure of Peru, was not closed in any appreciable manner. Indeed, outside of the agrarian reform, the thrust of the Velasquista revolution was in the modern, rather than the traditional, sector. Redistribution occurred in the former mainly in the CIs, where workers received monetary and other benefits. However, the number of workers in the CIs constituted only 8 percent of the national labor force, but they were in the top quartile of national income. Perhaps 2 percent of the national income was transferred to this "elite" group of workers, while the vast majority of labor remained outside the CIs and thus was unaffected by the reforms.

As for the agrarian reform, its redistributory impact went a little further, but implied, as in the modern sector, a dualistic outcome of winners and losers. Only those workers who were reorganized into cooperatives, mostly those on the more profitable coastal plantations, rather than on the archaic highland haciendas, gained. A sizable portion of independent peasants and temporary workers were also left out. Thus, the reform, which redistributed about a third of the country's arable land, benefited a quarter to a third of the rural labor force, but excluded the remainder. Moreover, since the agrarian reform constituted only a reform *within* the agricultural sector, which was characterized by its low productivity, rather than a transfer of resources *into* this sector from the modern sector, its overall impact was limited—probably less than 1 percent of the total national income.

On the growth side of the ledger, Velasco's reforms also proved disappointing. By concentrating on the modern sector and transferring surplus capital from the foreign sector and its domestic allies to foment ISI, the government had hoped both to lessen dependence and to generate industrial growth. However, this hope was not realized. Industrial growth, in general, and manufacturing, in particular, remained, according to McClintock (in Gorman, 1982, p. 15), about the same for the period 1971–75 as it had for 1961–70. One reason was the drying up of private and foreign investments, which had been declining as a percentage of the GNP since the 1950s and were now scared off by the government's nationalization program.

In the absence of such investments, the government became the principal investor. By 1972 the state had so expanded its role in the economy that it accounted for more than half the total investments in the economy. Rather than a mixed economy, Peru moved rapidly toward state capitalism. Having largely taken over the foreign sector, the new state-run enterprises failed to generate profits, partly because they had always lost money, had been severely decapitalized in anticipation of nationalization, or because of corruption and mismanagement. Moreover, the government's wage bill increased sharply because of the rising expectations and demands by workers in these enterprises.

To finance its huge public investment, the government resorted to international money markets, quadrupling its foreign indebtedness, from $945 million in 1970 to $4,127 million in 1976, and thus creating a new form of "debt dependency." This option came to an end in 1975, when international banks reversed their easy lending policies and demanded austerity from a government and economy that had slipped into crisis. Inevitably, it seems that Peru, despite the reforms, was still largely dependent for growth on the expansion of the export sector. During the first few years of the Velasco regime, export prices and hence earnings moved cyclically higher, masking the continuing stagnation in production. When prices and earnings then fell, the country could not pay for its increased import bill of foodstuffs and capital goods, expanded defense spending and increasingly unmanageable debt burden from interest on the skyrocketing foreign debt.

To extricate itself from this developing crisis, the government pinned its hopes on a break through in two mineral exports, oil and copper. High hopes for making significant oil strikes similar to those made by neighboring Ecuador in the early 1970s were dashed when only two new, relatively modest wells were located. In copper the pay off on the potential of the Cuajone and Cerro Verde mines was more long term and could not be accomplished in time to offset the crisis of 1975. This left the government no alternative other than to abandon its ambitious and costly reforms and to shift to a second phase of austerity and retrenchment for which Velasco's illness and political troubles simply opened the way.

12 Return to Orthodoxy, Redemocratization, and Populism Redeux, 1975–90

Morales Bermúdez and the Second Phase, 1975–80

The putsch carried out by General Morales Bermúdez deposing Velasco in August 1975, although it was not immediately apparent, signaled the onset of a more conservative phase of military rule. While one prominent progressive general would later call it a "counterrevolution," it can also be seen as the equivalent of a major change in regime, now referred to as the Second Phase to distinguish it from the First Phase under Velasco. Declaring at the outset his intention to keep the revolution on track, without "deviations or personalism," Morales nevertheless tried to steer a middle course between the Velasquista progressives on the Left and right-wing generals who displayed authoritarian tendencies corresponding to the military regimes in neighboring Bolivia (Bánzer) and Chile (Pinochet). The new head of state also sought, in counterpoint to Velasco, to enhance the decision making role of the junta while downplaying his own position to increase interservice consultation and harmonize contending viewpoints within the armed forces.

In economic policy, Morales, the fiscally conservative, former finance minister, pressured by the United States and the International Monetary Fund (IMF), began to institute measures toward liberalization, that is, to reduce the role of the state and correspondingly enhance that of the market economy. Doing so entailed initial efforts to make public enterprises more profitable and austerity measures to reduce the growing budget deficit, to meet the problem of servicing the now $4 billion foreign debt, and to encourage greater foreign and private investments. Workers and the public in general were asked by the new government to accept sacrifices, such as reductions in state subsidies and social expenditures, made necessary, it was argued, by the onset of a global recession. Morales also argued that greater austerity was necessary to "consolidate the revolution."

Liberalization was likewise cautiously extended to the political realm, a reaching out to the traditional parties that Velasco had shunned. Morales took a significant step in this direction on a trip to Trujillo in April–May 1976. Putting aside the fact that his father had been killed by Apristas in

1939, Morales reached across the great, historic divide between the armed forces and APRA and offered APRA the olive branch of rapprochement. Haya de la Torre's price for opening such a dialogue with the government, however, was to insist that it call elections and return the country to democratic, constitutional rule.

Haya could afford to hold out for such terms because, despite the general belt-tightening of the regime, the country's economic situation and hence public support for the regime continued to deteriorate. Under renewed pressure from the IMF and private international banks to take more effective measures to reduce inflation by cutting back public expenditures, Morales announced a drastic austerity "package" in June. It included a 44 percent devaluation of the *sol*, elimination of subsidies on gasoline and food staples, and a 13 percent reduction in the national budget. Although the government tried to cushion the shock effect of the package by decreeing increases in wages, the increases were not nearly enough to match the overall rise in the cost of living. The president later justified his policies by arguing that they were necessary to restore fiscal responsibility so as to encourage greater private-sector investment and reopen the economy to international markets.

Public reaction to this "shock therapy" was swift and violent. Responding to the dramatic increase in the price of gasoline, Lima transportation workers went on a strike that quickly deteriorated into three days of rioting that was quelled only by the declaration of a state of emergency and army intervention. As a result, popular support for the military government virtually collapsed, and rebellions from both the Right and from the Left in the army erupted in quick succession. Although rapidly supressed, the attempted coups gave Morales the pretext to exile a number of pro-Velasco civilians and Leftists and to purge nearly 300 officers and the remaining progressives in his cabinet, replacing them with more conservative members.

The government then moved swiftly to dismantle the reforms of the Velasco period. Significantly, the term *socialism* was dropped from official governmental rhetoric, the Social Property Program was quietly terminated, and agrarian reform was officially declared at an end. SINAMOS, the agency that was charged with Velasco's mobilization project, was closed and the regime's alliance with the Communist Party (CP), the Confederación General de Trabajadores Peruanos (CGTP) and other Leftist groups was severed. Finally, Morales significantly changed the law of *estabilidad laboral* by giving employers the right to dismiss workers for reasons of profitability or behavior.

As the costs of the austerity program were increasingly shifted to the working classes and the social goals and programs of the Velasco era were jettisoned, the New Left and popular sector organizations began to proliferate and mobilize against the government. The origins of the New Left went back to the 1950s with the formation of APRA Rebelde, which became the Movimiento de Izquierda Revolucionarie (MIR), and the Ejército de Liberación Nacional (ELN), a split from the Moscow controlled CP. At the same time, various Maoist groups also broke away from the CP in 1964 in the wake of the tumultuous Sino-Soviet split of the Communist world. The following year, ex-militants from Acción Popular (AP) and various Trotskyites and Marxists from the universities formed Vanguardia Revolucionaria (VR). What all these groups had in common was their sharp criticism of the Moscow-controlled CP, which they viewed as "frozen" in old dogma and tactics (Adrianzen et al., 1990). However, in the 1960s and 1970s, they were not able to unite around a single leader or ideological line.

By the late 1970s, the New Left was composed of a myriad of these and other groups, perhaps as many as twenty, espousing a broad spectrum of radical ideas, from Maoism and dependency theory to liberation theology and the social Christianism still roiling the Church, not to mention Velasquismo, the ideological underpinnings of the reforms of the First Phase. Many groups operated clandestinely and sought to recruit students and subalterns to their particular cause.

As for the emergent new grassroots organizations, one example was the Confederación Campesina del Perú (CCP), which had emerged as the largest peasant federation in the country in the 1970s. With 200,000 members in 1977, the CCP adopted labor's tactics of strikes and land invasions to press the land claims of peasants who had been excluded from the agrarian reform. Finally, there was a revival of activity among the long-quiescent traditional political parties that, with the lifting of press censorship and the revival of an independent press, agitated for elections and the return to a democratic order.

By early 1977, the Morales regime was isolated and politically besieged on a number of fronts: rising public opposition manifested in protests, strikes, and demonstrations; the IMF, which insisted on even more draconian austerity measures; and right-wing generals, who sought to follow the repressive examples of Pinochet in Chile or the Argentine generals who had seized power in Buenos Aires. Moreover, additional evidence of widespread corruption since the advent of the military revolution was surfacing, with charges of kickbacks on weapons purchases and the maladministration of state enterprises. Morales, always the pragmatic realist and concerned with preserving the institutional unity of the armed forces in the face of increasing division and factionalization, was now convinced that he had to get the military out of the trenches of political conflict and back to the business of defending the nation. In effect, this meant that he had to lead the armed forces out of the government and back to the barracks and orchestrate a return to civilian rule.

The matter of national defense had, in fact, become increasingly important ever since the breakdown in 1976 of negotiations among Peru, Bolivia, and Chile over landlocked Bolivia's historic quest for access to the sea. The Morales regime's intent to shift military policy back to the traditional emphasis on military preparedness and national sovereignty coincided with the adoption of an increasingly hard-line position toward the country's traditional Pacific antagonist Chile, to the point that the government conjured up a war scare in mid-1976, with allegations that an invasion from Chile was imminent. Such manipulation of public opinion helped the regime divert attention from its economic and political woes.

In February 1977, the government announced its Plan Túpac Amaru, which, in addition to outlining the regime's more conservative economic goals, called for the election of a Constitutional Assembly. Ostensibly, the purpose was to incorporate the Velasco-era reforms into a new charter, but in reality, the intention was to pave the way for a transition to democratic rule. Before the elections were carried out, however, the country was rocked by a massive general strike in July, organized by the resurgent Left and popular organizations in response to yet another IMF-style austerity package by the government.

To meet the demands of its foreign creditors for a stricter policy of economic reform and readjustment and to confront the deepening economic crisis, the government had issued an economic emergency plan in June 1977 that eliminated basic food subsidies, froze wages, and drastically cut state spending. In response to this draconian measure, the New Left issued a call for a one-day general strike. The result was a massive national strike, the largest of its kind since 1919 almost half a century earlier, which effectively closed the country down for twenty-four hours. In addition to breathing new life into the opposition, the success of the strike forced the government to accelerate its timetable for holding elections and transferring power to civilian rule.

Negotiations were quickly undertaken with the political parties over the timing and terms of the previously announced elections for the Constitutional Assembly. Both APRA and the rightist Partido Popular Cristiano (PPC), which represented the business community, took part in these negotiations, but Belaúnde, still titular head of AP even while he was in exile in the United States, balked. Belaúnde insisted on the immediate calling of general elections, and his abstention proved to be a shrewd maneuver that projected his and AP's image as the main opposition to the military and its revolution. The New Left also abstained from the negotiations, but concentrated on organizing opposition at the grassroots level among the urban poor in the shantytowns, neighborhood organizations, and the workplace. It criticized not only the declining standard of living, but the widely unpopular governmental policy of "disciplining" labor, which had led to the dismissal of thousands of union and other activists from their jobs. The New Left's defiant attitude gained broad sympathy not only among workers, but the urban poor in the *pueblos jóvenes*.

In May 1978, shortly before the elections scheduled for June, another austerity package provoked a second nationwide general strike. Protesting the new measures and calling for the release of jailed labor leaders, labor called for a forty-eight-hour strike that proved as successful as it predecessor. Unfortunately, it, too, was marred by even more street violence. Although the increasing social conflict experienced during the Second Phase was an immediate result of the continuing series of governmental austerity packages, it must also be seen in the context of the persistent economic decline of the country since 1973. By 1977 and again in 1978, the GNP had dropped into negative territory, with the impact falling hardest on the popular classes. Official unemployment had risen from 4.2 percent in 1973, before the oil embargo-induced international recession, to 7.0 in 1978, and underemployment had reached 50 percent. At the same time, according to Mauceri (1996, p. 50), real wages had fallen by one half and the cost of living had quintupled between 1973 and 1979.

Given the dimensions of the economic decline and levels of social conflict, the June elections could not have come at a worse time for the Morales government. And the results were surprising. APRA received 35 percent of the vote; the PPC, benefiting from the absence of AP, 24 percent; and the New Left, in its multiple groupings, a substantial 36 percent. Aside from demonstrating the persistent organizational strength of APRA, the biggest surprise was the substantial shift of the electorate to the Left. Indeed, the New Left won 34 of the 100 seats in the Constitutional Assembly, although its share was divided among six different parties (consolidated from twenty parties prior to the election). In contrast, APRA won 37 seats in the center of the political spectrum. The remaining 29 seats were divided among five parties grouped on the Right. Significantly, the New Left had now emerged as a major force in the new political alignment of the country.

APRA's strong showing enabled Haya, with the tacit approval of the military, to be elected president of the Constitutional Assembly. This marked a historic milestone—the culmination of the eighty-three-year-old leader's long struggle for power. The rapproachment was based on Haya's acceptance of the conditions laid down by the government for the transfer of power: restriction of debate in the new assembly to the codification of the reforms of the First Phase and no discussion of the government's current social and economic policies. For its part, the military, because of the resurgence of the Left, paradoxically now viewed APRA in favorable terms. APRA was the one party capable of exerting some control over the masses in an era of economic austerity and was no longer considered a potential revolutionary threat to the established order, as it had been in the past.

The Constitutional Assembly proved to be a triumph for Haya. His conciliatory and statesmanlike skills were finally, after all these years, fully displayed, ironically as the old *político*, afflicted with cancer, approached the end of his life. Striking a balance between the extremes of the Right and the Left, Haya managed to produce a document that incorporated the major reforms of the First Phase, granted universal suffrage to all citizens aged eighteen years or older, reduced the presidential term from six to five years with no provision for another term, and narrowed the scope of the military in the affairs of the nation. The latter provision was perhaps the most significant, since it limited the role of the armed forces "to guarantee[ing] the independence, sovereignty, and territorial integrity of the Republic." The Constitution of 1933 had charged the military "to guarantee the Constitution and laws of the Republic and to maintain public order," which had served as the legal basis for the military interventions of 1948, 1962, and 1968 (Masterson, 1991, p. 266). In a scene full of drama, Haya signed the charter on his deathbed on July 12, 1979. As for the promised general elections, they were postponed until July 1980 amid the continuing decline in living standards, growing labor militancy, and the unprecedented political advance of the Left.

Given APRA's and Haya's prominence in the successful Constitutional Assembly, the party seemed a logical favorite before the elections. However, the death of its maximum leader severely debilitated APRA and its future chances of capturing the presidency. As one historian put it, "owing to the vertical structure of the party and the cult around Haya's personality, the remaining Aprista leaders were no more than 'satellites' who orbited around the star, illuminated by his light and strength." (Cotler, in *CHLA*, 1991, VIII p. 484).

In the ensuing leadership vacuum, Armando Villanueva del Campo, head of APRA's administrative machine, was able to rally the radical Aprista youths to his cause and to defeat his more conservative opponent, parliamentarian Andrés Townsend Ezcurra. Both men were representative of the party's dominant old guard, which continued in ascendancy largely because Haya had made only a belated effort to bring younger leaders, like his personal secretary Alan García Pérez, to the fore.

On the other hand, the resurgent Left showed promise of a strong showing, empowered by growing labor militancy and the popular grassroots mobilization of unorganized workers in the capital's teeming shantytowns. Indeed, the trade unions, having orchestrated several successful general strikes during the Second Phase, had played a prominent role in forcing the military to return to the barracks. However, its potential in the presidential campaign was severely compromised by its chronic tendency to fractionalize, and in the event, it failed to unite around a single candidate or slate.

Given this situation, only two right-of-center parties—the PPC, headed by Luis Bedoya Reyes, and Belaúnde Terry's AP—were left. The former had done well in the elections for the Constitutional Assembly in 1978, garnering 24 percent of the vote. However, it could not expect to match that figure, since it was inflated by crossover votes from AP, which had abstained from participation. Belaúnde, on the other hand, whom many had counted out as a realistic possibility, made a surprisingly successful return to Peruvian politics after a dozen years in exile teaching in the United States.

The campaign was largely a three-cornered race among Villanueva (APRA), Bedoya (PPC), and Belaúnde (AP), with the Left divided into five different slates. In contrast to Villanueva's efforts to downplay his public image as longtime leader of the "*búfalos,*" the party's infamous shock troops, and his perceived intolerance and inflexibility, Belaúnde sought to emphasize his nondoctrinaire, pragmatic, yet democratic and pluralist approach to governing. Campaigning mostly in the interior, Belaúnde emphasized his past public works and promised policies, left purposely vague, to initiate an economic expansion that would create 1 million new jobs and benefit primarily the provinces. In the end, the former president came off as a benevolent father figure, with a charismatic and gentlemanly manner and vague yet soothing program that appealed to a population buffeted by years of revolutionary upheaval and economic crisis.

The results of the elections, in which illiterates voted for the first time, increasing the electorate by 17 percent, were astonishing in many ways. Belaúnde won a substantial plurality of 45 percent, while APRA experienced a sharp drop to 27 percent from its 1978 high of 35 percent. APRA's fall was matched by that of the PPC, which declined from 24 percent in 1978 to 15 percent, and that of the divided Left, which plummeted to 14 percent, less than half its 1978 total. The results could be explained by the death of Haya and the failure of Villanueva to transcend his heavy-handed, sectarian image and the inability of the Left to unite, leaving little option other than the more moderate Belaúnde over the conservative, pro-business Bedoya.

The Second Belaúnde Administration and the Rise of the Shining Path, 1980–1985

Belaúnde returned to the presidency in 1980 to govern a country that had changed dramatically from the one that had first elected him in 1963. In demographic terms, Peru had exploded during the 1960s and 1970s, its population nearly doubling from 9.9 million in 1960 to 17.3 million in 1980. The increase in Lima-Callao was even more remarkable, from 1.8 million in 1961 to 4.6 million in 1981. Fully one third of the nation's inhabitants now resided in the greater Lima metropolitan area, and over half were under age twenty.

The flow of migration from the provinces to the capital continued its seemingly inexorable course, stimulated by the dislocations of the agrarian reform and the search for economic opportunity. A visible manifestation of this increase was the huge, sprawling squatter settlements that ringed the capital on three sides. Nationally, whereas 47 percent of the population lived in cities in 1961, by 1981, 65 percent of the country's population did so. Logically, this increase in the urban population implied a process of *decampesinization*, or shrinkage of the peasant population, particularly among the servile, floating, and communal peasantry who had been largely left out of the Velasco reforms.

The sweeping reforms of the *Docenio* and their economic repercussions, moreover, had left Peru's burgeoning population in an increasingly unsettled state. For one thing, state-led industrialization had succeeded in expanding the manufacturing sector, but the military's reform efforts to harmonize labor-management relations had largely failed. This failure had opened the way to greater union militancy and the wave of strikes that had accelerated Morales's withdrawal of the military from power. Consequently, if Belaúnde could not reverse the declining living standards, he could expect labor unrest to undermine his new administration.

More ominously, even if the privileged sectors of labor and the peasantry had benefited in relative terms from the industrial and agrarian reforms of the past decade, a far larger portion of the population had been left behind. This portion remained mired in poverty, even though their expectations had been raised by the rhetoric and promises of the revolutionary regime. Furthermore, while the power of the traditional landed and mining oligarchy had been broken, a powerful new class of capitalists, associated with the state and foreign interests, had emerged in its place. Finally, the overall disfunctioning of the state-dominated economic system was propelling, as you shall see, the explosive growth of the informal sector.

All these changes had occurred in the context of rising popular expectations in the early 1970s. These expectations were then abruptly dashed later in the decade, when during the Second Phase of military rule, the Morales government, responding to the international recession and falling commodity prices, made a 180-degree turn to embrace severe austerity measures that sharply depressed real wages. Coinciding with the opening of the political system related to the transition to democracy, this "whip-saw" of expectations triggered widespread popular discontent, politicization, and mobilization, led by the New Left. Belaúnde had managed to ride this wave of distress into office by projecting a fatherly, paternalistic image that conveyed a sense of optimism and hope, as well as the promise of more jobs and a better economy.

Calculating a different response to Peruvians' discontent was Abimael Guzmán Reynoso, an obscure philosophy professor in the remote university town of Ayacucho. Born out of wedlock in 1934 in Arequipa (Mollendo), Guzmán was raised by uncles until the age of twelve, after his mother had died and his father took up with another woman. He was later reunited with his father, a middle-class merchant, with whom he is believed to have had a tense relationship. According to McClintock (1998), this tense relationship was perhaps due to his perceived secondary position in a household with other legitimate siblings. The introverted Guzmán attended a local Jesuit high school in Arequipa, where he excelled academically. According to his own account, the Callao Revolt of 1948 and the Arequipa uprising of 1950 against the dictator Odría pricked his social conscience.

After graduating from high school, Guzmán went on to study philosophy at the University of San Agustín in Arequipa. There he came under the twin influences of an eccentric, but uncompromisingly rigorous Kantian scholar and a social-realist painter and undiluted Stalinist. According to Gorriti (1990, pp. 16–17), Guzmán acquired both a strict methodology and asceticism from the one and a devotion to orthodox communism, as developed in China, from the other. After receiving his degree from San Agustín

Abimael Guzmán, as he appeared in a party pamphlet from the late 1980s. Courtesy of Orin Starn.

in 1961, with a thesis on Kant's theory of space, and a degree in law later that year with a thesis on "The Bourgeois-Democratic State," Guzmán joined the faculty of the Universidad Nacional San Cristóbal de Huamanga in Ayacucho in 1962. He was recruited personally by the president of the university, Efraín Morote Best, along with a number of other promising young foreign and urban intellectuals.

Founded in 1677, the University of Huamanga, or Ayacucho, had recently reopened in 1959 for the first time in three-quarters of a century since the end of the War of the Pacific. Guzmán's recruitment coincided with the government's efforts to reactivate the university and make it a springboard for the development of this remote, impoverished region. Money was pumped in to expand the student body and to develop a strong vocational orientation, including rural extension and development projects. Students were drawn from a wide social spectrum, including a large number from humble, rural backgrounds. The reopening of the university served to awaken a desire for education among Ayacucho's mainly peasant population, to the extent that when Velasco tried to cut back the university's budget in 1969, it triggered a violent public reaction. Indeed, popular expectations for educational advance had become so intense during the 1960s that the most important social movement in the city and region was not for land, but in defense of free education.

Upon arriving in Ayacucho to take up his teaching duties, Guzmán, already a fervent Marxist, began to preach his beliefs in classes and to organize a radical challenge to the local CP. At the time, the CP was "a sleepy group made up of people who listened to Moscow radio over the short wave and would get together on weekends to drink and to praise the latest reported increase in the Soviet Union's pig iron output" (Gorriti, 1990, p. 17). The CP did not prove much of a match for the charismatic and organizing genius of Guzmán, who proceeded to use the university to recruit, educate, organize, and subsidize the creation of a new Communist vanguard.

A spellbinding teacher, Guzmán instantly attracted a devoted coterie of students who were receptive to his message of revolutionary Marxist transformation. Most were members of the first generation of Indian peasants from the surrounding countryside to attend the university. Many hoped to graduate as teachers, aspiring to surpass the social and economic conditions of their parents. Guzmán saw them as the ideal vehicle to forge a revolutionary relationship between town and countryside.

The opportunity to create an alternative CP occurred as a result of the historic Sino-Soviet split of 1960 that resonated throughout Latin America, including Peru and even remote Ayacucho. In 1964 a pro-Chinese faction broke away from the Moscow-oriented CP, headed by its founder and longtime leader Jorge del Prado. Guzmán emerged as the local organizer and leader of the Peking-oriented Bandera Roja (Red Flag) faction, and on campus, he adopted the nom de guerre of Álvaro perhaps after one of Peru's legendary *conquistadores*. Thin, long haired, and invariably dressed in a rumpled jacket without a tie, Guzmán had an intense, earnest, intellectual bearing. He was often seen striding about campus, books tucked under his arms, followed eagerly by a flock of students who hung on his every word. One unimpressed colleague unflatteringly described him as "dry, disagreeable . . . always surrounded by his acolytes—a bunch of *cholitos adefesieros* (stinky little *cholos*)—to whom he would talk about Camus, Schopenhauer. *Reader's Digest* philosophy" (Gorriti, 1990, p. 18). Known as a fierce political infighter and superb political organizer, Guzmán was also something of a lady's man who felt particularly comfortable in the company of women.

In 1964 the 29-year-old professor married 18-year-old Augusta La Torre, the daughter of a downwardly mobile, landowning father who was also a local Communist leader. Augusta was to play a major role in Guzmán's organization, along with a number of other middle-class, mainly Caucasian recruits drawn from the university. These recruits included Osmán Morote, a student of Guzmán whose father had recruited the young *Arequipeño* and who went on to become a professor at the university. Guzmán developed a close relationship with the Morotes, an old and respected family in Ayacucho. Antonio Díaz Martínez, another top leader, was a professor of agronomy at the university who had grown up in prosperous circumstances in Cajamarca but was educated in Lima. The only top leader not recruited in Ayacucho was Julio César Mezzich, who was from an upper-class *Limeño* family of Czech origins.

With the outbreak of the guerrilla movements in the Peruvian Andes in 1964–65, Guzmán was forced to adhere to Peking's policy of noninvolvement. He consequently lost some of his student followers who, eager for action, headed off to the mountains to join one of the Cuban-style *focos*. Subsidized by Peking, Guzmán took the opportunity to travel to Mao's China in 1964, returning again in 1967 when China was in the throes of the Cultural Revolution. At that time, he attended a cadre school in the capital, where he was instructed in the doctrines of "People's War" and learned subversive tactics, taught by a veteran of the underground against the Kuomintang. He later wrote about his classroom experiences with explosives: "we caught our pens, and they blew up. We then sat astounded, and our seats also blew up. It was fireworks all around us. It was carefully measured, just to let us know that you can blow up anything if you have enough ingenuity"—a lesson Guzmán took to heart (Gorriti, 1990 p. 18).

Returning to Peru in 1967 when the last of the Andean guerrilla *focos* was being snuffed out by the military, Guzmán declared the Cuban approach a "petit bourgeois, militaristic deviation," in line with Peking's critique. Likewise when Che Guevara was killed trying to organize a *foco* in Bolivia, Guzmán disdainfully labeled him an exhibitionist. A year later, Guzmán was rehired as a professor at the university and proceeded to reorganize his movement according to his experience in China. Shortly thereafter, however, he was expelled from Bandera Roja.

The expulsion was the result of a heated debate in the late 1960s among the revolutionary parties of the Left. It centered on the desirability, in the context of the Velasco reforms and the Peruvian CP's and Moscow's support of the regime, of rejecting violent revolution in favor of collaborating with the reform effort. Indeed, many former Leftist revolutionaries, including Héctor Béjar and Hugo Blanco, had already joined the Velasco government. Guzmán stood alone in rejecting this position.

After his expulsion, the would-be revolutionary spent the next eighteen months (1970–71) reflecting on his experiences in China and intensively studying the writings of Marx, Mao, and Mariátegui. In February 1970, he formed the Partido Comunista del Perú en el Sendero Luminoso (Shining Path) de Mariátegui, the name that he had given his student group at the university in the late 1960s. From the writings of both Mariátegui and Mao, Guzmán was persuaded of the primacy of the peasantry in the revolutionary process. He now criticized the Velasco regime as "bureaucratic capitalism" in a country that was still essentially "semifeudal" and "semicolonial." Mao had described prerevolutionary China in exactly the same way. To many, that concept hardly seemed to square with the fact that the majority of Peru's population now lived in cities and that industry now accounted for a larger percentage of the GNP than did agriculture. Even in the Andean countryside, most communities had developed commercial ties to local markets. Still, the description did have a ring of truth to it in Guzmán's prospective base and field of reference in Ayacucho and the southern sierra.

The department's economy was largely agrarian, composed mostly of subsistence agriculture, backward estates, and small-scale mining. However, the old *gamonal* class had been significantly weakened by the exodus of *hacendados*, who had incorrectly anticipated the application of the agrarian reform in the 1970s, which, in fact, did not happen. Without a significant industrial or commercial base and with a weak rural landlord class, the department lacked a strong economic elite. Indeed, its only real "industry" was education, with students at the university making up some 10,000 of the city's 70,000 inhabitants. In this sense, the university was to Ayacucho what mining was to Cerro de Pasco and sugar was to La Libertad and Lambayeque. Such economic dependence also explained the strong wave of popular protests organized by Guzmán and others in the late 1960s against the government's efforts to cut the university budget.

At the same time, Ayacucho, disdainfully referred to by *Limeños* as part of *"La Mancha India,"* or Indian stain, consistently received a negligible share of governmental spending. In fact, it regularly ranked at the departmental bottom of public sector investment. This neglect spawned a strong resentment against the capital and the economically more dynamic coast, a resentment that would translate, like the government's cuts in the university budget, into popular sympathy for the Shining Path and its leader. It also contributed to making Ayacucho one of the most backward and poverty-stricken departments in the country. Illiteracy stood at 68.5 percent; the infant mortality rate was 12.8 percent, the highest in the world; and average life expectancy was only 51 years, among the lowest.

Guzmán's students and followers at the university, of course, came out of this environment. Yet as aspiring teachers, most of mestizo or Indian background, they had chosen a profession that was poorly paid and often dependent on uncertain budgets and prospects. Their susceptibility to Guzmán's revolutionary message was not only due to the fact that they eagerly sought to acquire knowledge of the modern world, which they expected would open the way to a better life, beyond the village. They were also hungry to understand the reasons for their historically oppressed condition in the seignorial society that, in the absence of the former *misti* gamonal class, was now subject to a new group of oppressors—the petty mestizo entrepreneurs who had emerged to fill the vacuum left by the departure of the landlords.

In search of the "truth," they found Guzmán's simplified version of Marxist-Leninist doctrines, communicated with the religious fervor of a true believer, utterly convincing. If education was to be the vehicle to free them from their past poverty and a ticket to the modern world, it would also serve to liberate them from their traditional domination and supremely inferior position in the *La Mancha India* underclass. Psychologically, these young followers of Guzmán may, as McClintock has suggested (1998), fit the phenomenon of the "ideal-hungry" followers of revolutionary movements in search of a leader to fill their own needs.

At the same time, it is not surprising, the rigidly hierarchical social structure and authoritarian political culture that characterized the southern Andes would be, as Degregori (in Palmer, 1992) observed, replicated in the relationship between the leader and followers in the Shining Path Party. Organized into tightly compact cadres or cells, the members followed orders that were dictated, from the top down, in a rigid chain of command, by Guzmán, who cultivated a Maoist-like cult of personality. On the other hand, the party offered a strong source of identity and belonging to its youthful members. As a fundamentalist, quasi-religious cult of like-minded and goal-oriented individuals, it held out the opportunity of membership in a tightly knit family of true believers whose lives acquired purpose, meaning, and hope in an otherwise uncertain future.

For a brief time in the early 1970s, the Shining Path succeeded in taking over the university. By this time, Guzmán was known as Dr. Shampoo for his ability to brainwash potential recruits to his movement. Suffering from a serious blood disorder, however, he was unable to remain in the highlands for any extended time. By mid-1975, it was becoming apparent that the military reforms generated by the First Phase had begun to take an economic toll on the country. But the Shining Path had now lost control of the university to an alliance of left-wing parties.

In response, Guzmán, having resigned from his teaching position, ordered his cadres into the countryside to intensify political work in preparation for an armed insurgency. The larger strategy, according to Smith (in Palmer, 1992), eventually was to move operations beyond Ayacucho, establishing an axis of control or influence from south to north, along the main spine of the Andes. In this way, the Shining Path aimed to "liberate" territory and population gradually from the tenuous and increasingly ineffective control of the Peruvian state. In time, this strategy would pave the way for a repetition of Mao's strategy of encircling and eventually conquering the main cities and the state itself.

Temporarily stung by the death of Mao in 1976 and the subsequent emergence of a more conservative Deng Xiaoping in China, the party reacted by reviling Deng and his colleagues as "the dogs who betrayed the Cultural Revolution." It also began referring to other Communist parties around the world, including the Soviet Union, as "rotten revisionists." By dismissing its Communist rivals, the Shining Path was preparing the ground for eventually declaring that it and it only would henceforth become the center of world revolution. In party propaganda, Guzmán would later be loudly proclaimed as the fourth sword of communism after Marx, Lenin, and Mao. Meanwhile, as the country went to the polls in its first presidential election since 1963, the Shining Path would announce its world revolutionary intentions more modestly, burning the ballot boxes in the small Andean market town of Chushi on May 17, 1980. Shortly thereafter, *Limeños* awoke to the strange spectacle of dead dogs hanging from lampposts with the slogan "Death to the Revisionists."

While the Shining Path was going public for the first time, the newly elected Belaúnde was putting together the new government that would implement his program to liberalize and revive the economy. It was a task that the well-meaning, but ideologically antiquated, former president was hardly up to in a country that had simply changed too rapidly and profoundly for him to comprehend. During the past two decades, *un desborde popular* (Matos Mar, 1984), or great overflowing of the masses, had engulfed Lima and other cities, overwhelming their public services and economic infrastructure. This situation had created a widening gap between the state and society that Belaúnde and his new government was now expected by the electorate to close. Unfortunately, the new president, in the view of one analyst, increasingly "projected an image of detachment and, unintentionally, of grandiose and irrelevant vision in the face of deepening social and economic crisis" (Graham, 1992, p. 76).

One of the most visible and problematic manifestations of the *desborde popular* was the explosion in the mid-1970s of a parallel "informal," or black market, economy outside the bounds of normal, legal business activities. This informal economy was the creation of Peruvians who, individually or in small family units, innovatively confronted the limits, barriers, and disfunctionalism of the regular economy and government. They did so by "contriving" their own production, employment opportunities and even community services to cope with and survive the increasingly recessive national economy. Comprising various sorts of "make-work," self-employment, the informal sector ranged from street vending to small and even some large-scale "informal" factories or workshops that manufactured cheap products and components. It was also facilitated by increasing amounts of contraband goods that flowed across lightly controlled border points and were hawked on every street corner in Lima and other cities by an army of peddlers. Since the informal sector fell beyond the scope of government, *"informales"* neither paid taxes nor were regulated by the state.

The idea of the informal economy, together with a prescription on how to harness its populist energies, was popularized in an influential, if controversial, book by economist Hernando de Soto entitled *The Other Path: The Invisible Revolution in the Third World* (1990). The book also comprised a powerful neo-liberal critique and attack on the statist model that Peru had embraced under the Velasco regime. Soto estimated that half Lima's citizens lived in informal housing and 80 percent went to work on informal mass transit, while fully half the country's population was employed in the informal sector. He further observed that informal or voluntary organizations were building the infrastructure of roads, sewage systems and marketplaces of the country's ubiquitous urban shantytowns. This explosive growth of the informal sector had occurred, he argued, because the state, through its maze of bureaucratic red tape, had systematically blocked the initiative and enterprise of individuals who wanted to produce. To prove his assertion, he showed how it had taken a group of his researchers 289 workdays to receive a permit to open a small clothing factory. Thus, for Soto, the state itself was a principal cause of poverty and the informal sector by blocking the potential of small producers.

In a more controversial, but plausible vein, Soto also argued that the informal sector was a popular response to the elites' efforts to keep the peasants from the cities. "Quite simply," he wrote, "Peru's legal institutions had been developed over the years to meet the needs and bolster the privileges of certain dominant groups in the cities and to isolate the peasants geographically in rural areas." Indeed, the elites made it next to impossible for newcomers legally to build a home, get a job, or start a business. There had even been a proposal, according to Soto, in the national legislature during the 1940s to require visitors from the countryside to obtain passports before entering Lima.

Certainly, there is little doubt that a large portion of the *informales* were composed of economically disenfranchised Indians and mestizos who had migrated to the cities over the past quarter century. Yet it was precisely this sector that Velasco had ostensibly tried to assist through his populist reforms and statist policies, including consumer subsidies and import restrictions, agrarian reform (to slow and reverse the rural-to-urban migration), and efforts to forge a more inclusive national identity (Quechua was recognized as an official language). Nevertheless, by the 1980s the informal economy in Peru had grown to one of the largest and most impoverished of any country in Latin America. To Soto and other neoliberals, this phenomenon suggested that the state, which had quadrupled in size during the past decade, continued to be the source of, rather than the solution to, Peru's problems and needed to be radically scaled back.

Philosophically sympathetic to Soto's ideas and now back in power with a working majority in Congress (AP/PPC had 32 of 60 senators and 108 of 180 deputies), Belaúnde began to tackle these and other pressing problems. The problems included establishing future relations with the armed forces, reigniting economic growth, dealing with the demands of a mobilized popular sector, and recognizing and devising a strategy to confront the Shining Path. Given the fact that Belaúnde had been deposed by the military, the former seemed the most immediately pressing and delicate problem. An agreement was shortly reached that left the command structures of the armed forces largely intact in return for the appointment of retired commanders who had been loyal to Belaúnde prior to 1968 to head the institution's three main branches. This agreement meant that civil-military relations were at least back to their pre-1968 state. Thus, the military maintained autonomy over its budget and arms transfers and continued to meddle in certain policy areas, particularly those concerning internal and external security.

As for economic policy, the president reversed his campaign promise to pursue economic expansion immediately in order to create 1 million new jobs. Instead, he appointed as prime minister his former minister of economy Manuel Ulloa, who installed a team of his "Chicago Boys," steeped in the neoliberal, free-market doctrines of Milton Freedom at the University of Chicago, where most of them had been trained. Their policy prescription was designed to enhance the market by reducing the economic preponderance of the state, removing tariff protection from industry, and encouraging private foreign investments. Toward this end, the new administration decided to continue the conservative stabilization policies of the previous Morales Bermúdez regime so as to reduce inflation and gain the confidence of investors. In effect, Peru returned to the traditional, pre-1968 model of economic liberalism based on laissez-faire, export-oriented growth.

Ulloa calculated that a continued recovery of exports, which had been ongoing since 1978, would set the stage in a year or so for the resumption of growth and job creation. His optimism was based on an unexpected 78 percent increase in the export price index between 1978 and 1980 that had stimulated exports and improved the terms of trade. Much of this improvement, however, was due to the completion of Velasco-era projects in copper (Cuajone) and oil (northern pipeline) that increased production at a time of rising prices. This brief export boomlet was also enhanced by illicit coca production, stimulated by the fast-growing demand from the United States. It did not show up in the government's export index, but reached an estimated $700 million to $800 million by 1982 and was the largest single export item for that year. Still, even with these seemingly favorable trends, the rate of economic growth declined from 4.5 percent in 1980 to less than 1 percent in 1982.

Momentarily at least, the government had a brief window of opportunity to reign in the deficit and set the fiscal basis for the resumption of longer-term growth. Initial confidence in the liberalization program and the improving balance of payments enabled Ulloa to secure an infusion of loans from international agencies and banks to fund Belaúnde's proclivity toward large public works programs and weapons procurement to keep the military happy. Ulloa also moved to lower consumer subsidies further and to proceed with a series of currency devaluations, further stimulating exports.

At the same time, the administration's majority in Congress voted the president special powers to roll back the reforms of the *Docenio*. However, since the agrarian reform and *estabilidad laboral* had been made part of the new Constitution, Belaúnde was only able to tighten regulations governing the agricultural cooperatives. In addition, some small state-controlled companies were sold, but the larger ones remained intact, mainly for a lack of buyers. More successful was the president's effort, following those of Morales, to reduce the number of governmental employees, so that in some ministries up to 70 percent of the workforce was let go. On the other hand, althought it aided the government's general budget-reduction policies, the loss of expertise represented by such employees, as Mauceri (1996) showed, contributed significantly, over time, to a severe weakening of the capacity of the state to carry out its functions.

By the end of 1982, Ulloa's liberalization plan had failed to produce the desired effect. The GDP had risen only 1.8 percent and was actually negative on a per capita basis. Agriculture continued to register a poor performance; mining stagnated; and industry; after an initial 5 percent spurt in 1980, declined as a result of an influx of imports (tariffs had been cut in half, from 66 percent to 32 percent), led by textiles. Moreover, exports fell as international demand and prices, particularly minerals, weakened while imports surged. The decrease in exports and increase in imports led to a sharp, adverse swing in the terms of trade, from +21 percent in 1980 to −17 percent in 1981, and a resumption of the trade deficit and balance-of-payment problems. Finally, inflation began to accelerate and international loans dried up in the second half of 1982 in the wake of Mexico's August default on its debt and the onset of the Latin American debt crisis.

With these poor results and confidence ebbing, Ulloa resigned in December 1982 and was replaced by Carlos Rodríguez Pastor, a Wells Fargo banker. The new economy minister saw no other alternative than to accept an IMF–World Bank-mandated structural adjustment program in return for $500 million in immediate standby loans. Yet even as this stabilization plan took shape, it was undermined by Belaúnde's patrimonial style and grandiose public works projects. Following the time-honored practices of clientelism and patronage, the president continued to swell public payrolls with followers and friends as rewards for loyalty and support. At the same time, he pushed forward with expensive, but questionable, public works projects, such as his pet Marginal Highway (*La Marginal*), which had been discontinued during the *Docenio*.

The new stabilization program was dealt still another setback by mother nature. Just as public spending was slashed and credit tightened, a series of natural disasters struck Peru in early 1983. The disappearance of El Niño currents off the coast altered normal weather patterns, producing severe flooding in the north and a prolonged mid-year drought in the south. This weather crippled agricultural output and forced the government into costly imports and disaster relief. Combined with reduced consumer subsidies as part of the austerity program, these natural disasters caused the prices of basic staples to soar. Finally, the absence of El Niño caused the anchovy to disappear from the Pacific and fishmeal exports to plummet. Losses in the fishmeal industry amounted to $10 million, while those in the sugar and cotton industries totaled $42 million.

By the second half of 1983, nature's wrath, the impact of the adjustment plan, and the onset of global recession, which caused a sharp drop in exports, all combined to drive the Peruvian economy into a depression. Over the next two years, export earnings fell to 50 percent of the 1979 levels, and the GDP dropped 12 percent. More specifically, industrial production fell 21 percent, private investment fell 34 percent, and real wages fell 31 percent, and per capita income reached the 1960 levels. At the same time, inflation doubled to an annual rate of 111 percent, and unemployment soared to an official and probably understated 18 percent. As for the informal sector, one index—underemployment—exploded to an estimated 64 percent.

The hardest hit by the deepening economic crisis, which one prominent historian declared to be the worst since the end of the War of the Pacific a hundred years earlier, were low-income groups, particularly the urban poor and the peasantry in the southern highlands. According to one survey, the incomes of 57 percent of the households in the countryside were classified as below the poverty line, while 32 percent were ranked below the extreme poverty level. At the same time, wealth at the top, after having undergone a measure of leveling during the Velasco years, was now once again reconcentrating into a few hands. As a result, Peru continued to rank among the countries in Latin America with the most unequal distribution of income. Moreover, a poverty map of the country, drawn by the Central Bank, revealed the continuing gap in per capita GDP between the modern coastal sector and the more backward sierra. Indeed, per capita income levels in the latter correlated almost exactly with the highest levels of illiteracy, infant mortality, and lowest rates of life expectancy.

Belaúnde's efforts to address these disparities and the deepening distress of the poor were largely inadequate. Continuing austerity meant cuts in social welfare and consumer subsidies that worsened, rather than improved, the widening circle of poverty. The drying up of international loans had all but halted the president's public works program, crippling the construction industry and laying off thousands of workers. At the same time, his emphasis on education increased school enrollments by 1 million between 1980 and 1983. This increase continued a trend in which secondary school and university enrollments in Peru were rising rapidly, well above comparative figures for other, more prosperous, Latin American countries. But this trend only served to raise the potential for radicalization and political mobilization at a time when the economy was contracting sharply and jobs and opportunities were rapidly disappearing. Even Belaúnde's policy of raising agricultural incomes by allowing prices to rise according to the market backfired when low-cost food imports were permitted to undermine the production and prices of traditional Peruvian crops—even the native Andean potato.

As conditions worsened, social unrest increased and several national strikes erupted in the cities and the countryside. Moreover, street crime and social and political violence grew apace. The number of reported crimes, for example, rose from 123,230 in 1980 to 152,561 in 1985. Terrorist acts, such as political assassinations by the Shining Path and the kidnapping of businessmen and other rich people, a hallmark of a new group called the Movimiento Revolucionario Tupac Amaru (MRTA), became more frequent.

MRTA took its name from the eighteenth-century rebel who led a massive Indian uprising against the Spanish crown and was drawn and quartered in Cuzco in 1782. Unlike the Maoist the Shining Path, MRTA, which began operations in mid-1984, was inspired by the Cuban Revolution of 1959, particularly Che Guevara's *foco* strategy. Its origins lay in small, splinter groups of the Left that had not been absorbed into the Izquierda Unida (IU, United Left), organized in the early 1980s, as is discussed later, and that had remote links to APRA Rebelde in the 1960s and the Velasquista Partido Socialista Revolucionaria (PSR) in the 1970s.

Although it received training and support from Cuba, MRTA was nevertheless primarily nationalist; identified the enemy, particularly the United States, more traditionally as imperialism; and drew its leadership from the urban middle class, mainly students. Its underlying strategic assumption was that the democratic government under the floundering Belaúnde would be short lived and that a military coup would force IU into armed opposition and thus into MRTA's arms. MRTA's initial bombing targets in the capital included the American Embassy, Citibank and Kentucky Fried Chicken fast-food outlets. At its peak in the mid-1980s, the movement is estimated to have had about 3,000 guerrillas in the field.

As social and economic conditions deteriorated, a political backlash against the president and his policies was inevitable. It came in the municipal elections of 1983 when Alfonso Barrantes, the head of the newly created IU, was elected the first Marxist mayor of Lima. The origins of IU went back to the transition to democracy in 1980, when the country's traditional Marxist parties decided to embrace the electoral road to power. Paradoxically, this decision had opened the revolutionary path for the more fundamentalist and extreme Shining Path which was one of the few groups that was still committed to the armed struggle. To be able to compete effectively in the electoral arena, however, it became increasingly clear that the plethora of leftist parties and factions would have to form some sort of united front. This goal was accomplished in 1981 by Barrantes, a former Aprista, who established IU and succeeded in knitting together an array of Muscovites, Maoists, Guevarists, and socially progressive Christians.

In his election as mayor two years later, Barrantes received a large vote from Lima's shantytowns and working-class districts that now accounted for half the vote in the capital. IU also won most of the mayoral races in the central and southern highlands. As for APRA, nationwide it made a strong comeback from its dismal showing in the 1980 presidential elections, garnering 34 percent of the popular vote, followed by IU with 30 percent. By contrast, AP received only 12 percent in Lima and 15 percent nationally. Together APRA and IU won an overwhelming 63 percent of the vote against 32 percent for the governing coalition of AP and the PPC.

Both parties had gained heavily by attacking the government's "foreign-oriented" economic policy and its lack of "social sensitivity" to the poor and unemployed. They had also declared their opposition to payment of the external debt and urged a policy of immediate "economic reactivization."

However, the Left's reversal in electoral fortunes from its 1980 debacle was due not only to the economic crisis, but to its successful effort to unite the various parties and factions into IU with a single list of candidates. APRA's turnaround can also be attributed to the emergence of a new generation of leaders, headed by party secretary Alan García Pérez, who opened up the party to new sectors and regions. Making a moderately progressive appeal for change, the new APRA, under García, successfully sought to appeal to sectors of the middle class that were disillusioned with Belaúnde and wanted social change but feared the rise of the Marxist Left.

Belaúnde also experienced growing internal dissent within his own government and party. This dissent came mainly from AP provincial representatives who resented the dominance of the "Chicago Boys" and the "internationalist wing" of the party over the economy. This policy, they argued, favored the interests of big business centered in Lima but ignored the problems of regional development that Belaúnde had talked so much about promoting in his 1980 campaign.

With the government unable or disinterested in providing greater social services in the face of the deteriorating economic and social conditions, the activities of popular grassroots, self-help organizations intensified in the marginal districts of the capital. You have already seen how these organizations originated in the 1970s in the squatter settlements (*pueblos jóvenes*), an outgrowth of the organizations that were carrying out the land invasions and the efforts of both the Church and the state to provide services to these demographically exploding satellite cities. After Velasco fell from power and the military reforms came to an end, state efforts on behalf of the residents of these young towns declined precipitously.

With democratization, however, the political parties, particularly APRA and the Left, and nongovernmental organizations (NGOs) moved to fill the vaccum. Obviously, the former saw a ready-made political opportunity to organize and recruit supporters by replacing, however partially, the state presence in the young towns. Moreover, the ranks of organized labor were already beginning to dwindle as a result of the inability of its leaders to prevent the massive layoffs of workers that would become progressively worse as the economic crisis of the 1980s deepened. By moving into the squatter settlements, the left and labor sought to replenish its declining political base through efforts to assist and recruit in the growing informal sector of the economy located in the young towns.

One highly successful example was the Glass of Milk Program, initiated by the leftist-controlled municipality of Lima under IU Mayor Barrantes in 1984. It guaranteed one glass of milk a day for each child and involved the community in a widespread distribution network anchored by local Comités de Vaso de Leche (CVLs) established at the district level. By 1988 there were 7,458 CVLs in Lima alone.

At the same time, there were also plenty of examples of the spontaneous response of the inhabitants to the deteriorating economic and social conditions in the squatter settlements. Had not Peruvians, when confronted with a crisis, creatively embraced the informal sector as a way to survive the decline of work in the formal sector? In a similar way, the residents of the young towns, often led by women, responded by establishing cooperative neighborhood self-help organizations to confront the current economic crisis. For example, "popular kitchens," organized by women's groups and run by women who purchased food in quantity and cooked low-cost meals communally for members of the community, proliferated in the *barrios* (neighborhoods) of the young towns in the early 1980s. Often assisted by the NGOs, the Church, and international aid agencies, but not the government, the popular kitchens proliferated in Lima and around the country, so that by 1988 there were 643 in the capital alone. At the same time, a small group of women in the young towns, such as Esther Moreno, who served as mayor of *Independencia* from 1983 to 1989, were emerging as political leaders.

This trend was a reflection of the fact that women were becoming increasingly vocal and active not only at the microlevel of *Independencia* and other young towns, but at various levels throughout Peruvian society during the 1970s and 1980s. Indeed, at this time a woman's movement emerged which included women political party activists; women from the barrios; and middle-class feminists, many of whom were the product of the expansion of the university system in the 1950s and 1960s. The latter had become a focal point for new forms of expression and activism by female students promoting, among other things, equality for and greater participation of women in society. This middle-class component of the emergent women's movement could trace its roots back earlier in the century and even further.

For example, Denegri (1996) and others have highlighted a group of women writers who emerged in the second half of the nineteenth century to insist on the rights of women to a better education, to be heard in the public sphere, and to take up the pen in addition to motherhood. These women included the journalist Carolina Freyre de Jaimes, who directed the women's magazine *El Album* in Lima during the 1860s and 1870s (suggesting a female audience); the novelist Juana Manuela Gorriti, who was a regular contributor to the magazine and became an early feminist; and the *Cuzqueña* Clorinda Matto de Turner, the founder of the *indigenista* novel, but who also wrote a textbook for teaching literature to the "fair sex."

The mother of the modern women's movement in Peru, however, was the Aprista activist Magda Portal (1903–89). According to Castro-Klarén, "she defined a new profile for women as politican and writer." Her autobiography *Ser mujer en el Perú* (1979) recounts her struggles to incorporate important feminist issues, like the right to vote, into the party program in the 1930s. These struggles bore fruit in the 1950s, when women gained the right to vote and were granted entry into the military.

By the mid-1970s, as Blondet (1995) noted, the women's movement was being intellectually nourished from several new sources, including feminist discourse from the 1975 World Conference for International Women's Year in Mexico and liberation theology, particularly from the Puebla bishops' conference in 1979 as well as the continuing influence of various revolutionary movements in Cuba and China and the political Left in general. Working separately or together, women from the barios, middle-class feminists, and political activists began to agitate publically for change. Their protests were linked to the economic crisis during the second phase and involved demands for improved living conditions, subsidies and food supplies for their nascent organizations, and an end to domestic violence. In a larger sense they were also, of course, related to issues deriving from the broader societal changes associated with modernization that had been propelling women out of the home and their traditional domestic role and into the job market.

In particular, women were increasingly playing leading roles in grassroots civic organizations throughout the country. These organizations dealt mostly with the major practical issues of life, such as economic survival, human rights, and displacement and survival in a wartorn society, and took a number of forms such as mothers' clubs and federations, migrant associations, community employment workshops, and communal kitchens. Many were also assisted by NGOs and community projects. In time, the political parties took note of these gender-based grassroots groups and organizations, as did the state, and began establishing working relations with them.

As the economic and social crisis deepened after the midpoint of Belaúnde's term, the government faced a mounting challenge from the Shining Path (Sendero). Since it burst on the scene in 1980, the Shining Path had made considerable headway in gaining adherents and wreaking destruction in Ayacucho. Two years later, it had gained control of an estimated 85 percent of the northern and central provinces of the department. Demonstrating its increasing power in March 1982, Senderista guerrillas made a spectacular attack on the main prison in Ayacucho and liberated dozens of Senderista prisoners. Another indication of its progress was the turnout of over 10,000 sympathizers in Ayacucho city for the funeral in September of slain Senderista leader Edith Lagos, still another example of the growing number of women in the political sphere. Buoyed by its success, the Shining Path celebrated its second clandestine National Conference and began to develop the next stage of its "Guerra de las Guerrillas," to expand the revolution's base beyond Ayacucho and strengthen the guerrilla army.

This early success coincided with the "subsistence crisis" that was increasingly engulfing the peasantry of the most impoverished regions of the southern highlands. Long-term population pressures, together with the more recent disruptions in production caused by the agrarian reform and natural calamities, were forcing increasing numbers of peasants to leave their communities and join the migratory exodus in search of work. The spreading dislocation and deepening pauperization produced an "explosive pain and discontent" among sectors of the peasantry, making it increasingly receptive to the siren song of the Shining Path's message.

By now, a second wave of recruits was coming from the ranks of high school, and, in some cases, primary school students, mostly from peasant families. These recruits formed what one scholar called a "disposable mass," impressionable, in search of an identity, and critical of their parents' generation's "archaic ways." Caught between two worlds, "they [were] . . . now without a place in rural society, but . . . [could not] find a place either in 'modern' Peru, asphyxiated by the crisis and the unemployment" (Degregori, quoted in McClintock, 1998, p. 291). The Shining Path promised to sweep away the corrupt old order and replace it with a new Senderista state. Militancy in the party became a means of upward social mobility. As one former Senderista young man later put it:

> They said that Ayacucho was going to be a liberated zone in 1985. Many of us thought in 1981 that by 1985 it would be an independent republic. We asked ourselves "don't you want to be a minister or military chief or something in such a new state"? (Degregori quoted in Stern, 1996, p. 3)

The prospect of exercising power and settling old or imagined scores against their perceived "oppressors" proved highly intoxicating to potential recruits.

Growing signs of the Shining Path success finally prompted Belaúnde, in December 1982, reluctantly to suspend constitutional guarantees, declare a state of emergency, and place the department of Ayacucho under complete military control. Before then, the president had been slow to react to the threat of the Shining Path, defining the guerrilla movement as simply a criminal organization and hoping that the counterinsurgency division within the *Guardia Civil*, known as the *Sínchis*, could, together with the police, eliminate the guerrillas. Underfinanced, poorly trained, and riddled with corruption and political factionalism, however, the national police force was hardly up to the task.

In one sense, Belaúnde's reliance on the *Guardia Civil* also played into the hands of the insurgents, since it was generally reviled by the peasants as enforcers for local elites and therefore one of the main oppressors of the peasantry. Moreover, the *Sínchis* had no concept of the necessity of winning over the hearts and minds of the civilian population. They indiscriminately seized, tortured, and killed anyone who was suspected of being a Senderista or sympathizer, which had the effect of simply alienating the bulk of the peasant and civilian population.

The government's decision to send the army against the Shining Path marked a new stage in the counterinsurgency program that led to sharply higher civilian casualties. Led by General Clement Noel y Moral, who was appointed the first civil-military commander of the emergency zone, the army counterinsurgency forces essentially followed, but in a much more devastating and efficient manner, the indiscriminate repression practiced by the *Sínchis*. This repression, together with the rising number of attacks by the Senderistas, resulted in sharply higher casualties, mostly innocent civilians caught in the cross fire, which jumped from 2,800 in 1983 to 4,300 in 1984. General Noel also initiated the policy of organizing and arming peasant militias, called *rondas campesinas*, to arm and assist communities that were opposed to the Shining Path. Another of his strategies, modeled on those of the Vietnam War, was to relocate the peasant population from difficult-to-defend areas in the high *altiplano* to so-called strategic hamlets at lower elevations, fortified by the army.

Meanwhile, the Shining Path's terrorist campaign of assassination and bombing gathered momentum in other parts of the country. The targets were governmental officials, including mayors and governors; development workers and projects; transportation and communication facilities; mining centers; power-generating facilities; police stations; and army barracks. The number of attacks, according to Durand (1994, p. 114), increased from 219 in 1980 to 2,050 in 1985, totaling more than 6,000 over the period and causing an estimated $2,139,542 in economic losses. One indication of the spreading Senderista violence was the fact that by 1983, over half the reported terrorist acts were being committed outside the Ayacucho region.

The rising human costs of the military's campaign of repression ignited criticism by human rights groups and the Left, particularly after the massacre on January 26, 1983, of eight journalists in the remote village of Uchuraccay near Huanta. Widely reported in the national press; the subject of an official commission of investigation; and given international coverage by the famed Peruvian writer Mario Vargas Llosa, who was the head of the commission, the Uchuraccay massacre served to intensify the growing national debate over human rights violations by the army that included charges of racism and exploitation of the indigenous population. Even in military circles, influential voices raised questions about the government's antisubversive policy. For example, General Adrian Huamán, commander of the emergency zone who replaced General Noel in early 1984, declared in August that the military was unable to contain the insurgency without social, economic, and humanitarian aid from the government to assist the impoverished population of the region. Huaman was, in effect, an advocate of winning the war through stepped-up aid and development efforts, designed to win over the civilian population. Two days after his declaration, the government relieved the general of his command.

By the end of his term, Belaúnde's administration was in complete disarray, besieged by the collapsing economy, the spreading guerrilla insurgency, and the growing popular demoralization. Politically, the crisis provided an opening to APRA and the IU. APRA had been busy reorganizing and revising itself around the youthful figure of Alan García Pérez ever since its humiliating defeat in 1980. Alan García was born in 1949. His parents were both Aprista activists, and his father had served a prison sentence for his political militancy. At age eleven, Alan joined the party, and after attending school in Peru, was sent to Spain and France in the early 1970s for his higher education. At the Sourbonne in Paris, he studied with a prominent Andean scholar, who later described him as not intellectual, but clever, astute, and determined to succeed in politics. He returned to Peru to work for the party in 1977 when the aging Haya, now anxious to promote a new generation of potential party leaders, appointed him his personal secretary and then APRA secretary of organization. During the 1980 campaign, García, according to Graham (1996), supported Villanueva and then stayed out of the ensuing power struggle between the defeated candidate and Andrés Townsend Escurra.

The chance to advance his cause further came with the Fourteenth Party Congress, which met in 1982 to select a new secretary general. García became the popular choice of the younger and progressive delegates, who sought a break with the old guard and the violent, sectarian nature of the party's past. His strong APRA credentials and support from party patrician and personal godfather Luis Alberto Sánchez and other key leaders proved decisive in his election to the top party post. Shortly thereafter, having successfully assumed a centrist position between the Left and Right factions, García was overwhelmingly selected the party's standard bearer for 1985.

In the campaign that followed, García sought to revive and reshape the multiclass coalition that had sustained APRA during the classical period of Latin American and Peruvian populism (1930–60). Certainly, this seemed logical, since the international context of debt and severe economic recession and its effects on Peru were strikingly similar to the depression era of the 1930s. However, García realized that in the mid-1980s, the key to electoral success lay not in the organized working class, which Haya had courted and won in the early period of the party. Rather, it resided in the urban informal sector, which had almost doubled since the beginning of the decade, from 440,000 to 730,000 workers. This explosive growth came not only from continued migration from the interior, but from workers who had lost their jobs as a result of the massive contraction of industry and commerce. Indeed, while the deepening recession had weakened the industrial labor market and demobilized the trade unions, APRA had long since lost control of the labor movement to the Left and the IU. For example, the Aprista Confederación Trabajadora Peruana (CTP) now represented only 10 percent of organized labor. For this reason, García calculated that his party's best hope for an electoral comeback lay in appealing to the *informales*. Such a strategy would also serve to reverse APRA's historic weakness in Lima, where the party had never won even a plurality.

The young Aprista aspirant added another nontraditional sector to his revised populist coalition—the peasantry, which he saw as strategically linked through the phenomenon of migration to the urban-based informal sector. No longer locked into the now-defunct hacienda structure, the peasantry was also accessible to modern campaign techniques. Together with the *informales*, García calculated that they represented 70 percent of the population, but earned only 25 percent of the national income. In terms reminiscent of past populist rhetoric, García referred to this popular majority as "the forgotten ones" and "the future of the nation" and proposed to redress their condition through job creation, redistributive measures, and social assistance

(Cameron, 1994, pp. 42–46). Similarly, the Aprista candidate revived the favorite populist term *oligarchy*, which he claimed had survived the agrarian reform in the form of powerful elite financial groups allied with international banks.

At the same time, García sought to broaden his appeal to the middle class, particularly those who had formed the core of Belaúnde's support in 1980, but who were now disillusioned with the failed president. To accomplish this goal, García pushed the party to exorcise the image of its sectarian past and to open itself up to new strata and regions, particularly to non-Aprista sectors of the middle class. For example, APRA eliminated the left-handed, fascist-like Aprista salute and substituted the waltz "Mi Perú" for the martial-like Aprista "Marseillaise." Moreover, García made a point of emphasizing in his campaign speeches the party's commitment to *all* Peruvians, eliminating the manichean party slogan "solo el APRA salvará el Perú." Although García's reaching out to a wider public stirred some internal resentment among the party faithful, it proved highly successful when the party won an overwhelming victory in the 1983 municipal elections.

During the presidential campaign, which got under way in earnest in 1984, the thirty-five-year-old García blended an emphasis on pragmatism, technical capacity, and social conscience that was designed to appeal to a middle-class that was anxious for change but fearful of a more radical Marxist alternative. Toward this end, he presented APRA as a social democratic party, a moderately progressive force that was capable of moving Peru forward. In specific terms, he advocated integration of the Indian population, emphasis on rural development, decentralization of the government (always a popular issue outside Lima), and aid to the poor. To the crucial business-industrial sector, another populist part of the cross-class coalition, he advocated a turnaway from the failed neoliberal policies of the Belaúnde regime and greater state involvement in reactivating growth, but eschewed the old Aprista penchant for the nationalization of industry. At the same time, García identified the enemy as the IMF and called for limiting payment on the ballooning national debt to no more than 20–25 percent.

Although the revised APRA led by the energetic and charismatic García quickly became the favorite to win the election, the party faced an imposing challenge from the Left, now relatively united under Alfonso Barrantes and IU. While *"El Frijolito,"* or Little Bean, as Barrantes was affectionately known, represented the more moderate face of the Left, the stance brought him under strong pressure from the party's radical Left. Moreover, IU's platform was more specific than APRA's, explicitly calling for the nationalization of the Southern Peruvian Copper Company, the revision of foreign oil contracts, a selective moratorium on the debt, and nationalization of the banks. Such a program, while popular among its traditional clientele in the unions, shantytown grassroots organizations, and rural peasant federations, raised strong fears in the middle class and business sectors that Barrantes's moderation could not assuage. In the end, García's new APRA managed to win the political center and thus the election.

With a record 91 percent of the eligible population voting, García won 47 percent of the vote, against 22 percent for Barrantes, 12 percent for Bedoya (PPC), and only a little over 6 percent for Alva Orlandini (AP). Not only had the Center-Left won a resounding victory with almost 70 percent of the vote, but the Right had suffered a stunning setback with only 18 percent. García's appeal to the informal sector was remarkably successful, since his vote in the shantytowns doubled from 20 percent in 1980 to 40 percent in 1985. However, unable to win the required 50 percent majority, García avoided a runoff only when the second-place Barrantes withdrew. A postelection analysis revealed that García had succeeded in breaking out of APRA's customary regional limits in the north by winning decisively in Lima's *pueblos jóvenes*, Cuzco, Puno, and the *selva*.

The García Administration: From Orthodoxy to Heterodoxy, 1985–90

As he prepared to assume office in July 1985, García confronted a bleak economic picture. It was clear that Belaúnde's orthodox policies had completely failed. Overall, real living standards had fallen sharply on a per capita basis from $1,232 in 1980 to $1,055 in 1985. In the public sector alone, monthly wages had plummeted from $230 in 1980 to $97 in 1985. Moreover, unemployment and underemployment had soared, so that by some estimates only 35 percent of the workforce was considered adequately employed in 1984. Unemployment, cuts in food subsidies, and reductions in spending for health and education had all appreciably worsened the condition of the poor. One particularly telling statistic showed that per capita calorie consumption in the country in 1985 was only 1,781 calories versus the 2,400 daily recommendation by international health organizations. In Ayacucho, the figure was only 1,271, having worsened substantially after the 1983 drought in the southern highlands, so that cases of starvation among subsistence peasants were being reported by one ecumenical church group.

Meanwhile, the wealthy, more than survived by avoiding taxes, "dollarizing" their income to protect their assets against inflation, and sending their capital to safe havens out of the country. Likewise, the informal, or black market, economy continued to expand rapidly, with the downside effects of low wages, lack of benefits, and loss of governmental tax revenues. Perhaps the most notorious defensive strategy involved the surging illicit coca industry.

Coca production and consumption, of course, had been a traditional feature of Indian society for centuries. It was used not only for ritual purposes, but to assuage the effects of high-altitude work and hunger. Production had centered in the subtropical jungle valleys and eastern slopes of the Andes in the department of Cuzco, particularly in Lares and La Convención, and then moved farther to the north between the 1940s and 1960s. The boom in coca production, however, dates from the 1970s, when the sharply increased demand from the United States for cocaine brought Colombian narco-traffickers into the region of the Huallaga River Valley to organize production and exportation. The main centers of the booming industry came to be located in the Upper Huallaga and the city of Tingo María, some 250 miles northeast of Lima. By the late 1980s, fully half the world's supply of coca paste, the thick greenish compound of mashed coca leaves and kerosene from which cocaine is made, came from Peru.

The first official attempts to curtail the growth of the industry were taken during the Morales Bermúdez administration at the behest of the United States. A state monopoly, the Empresa Nacional de la Coca, was established to regulate the traditional sale of coca, whose production was confined to areas of Cuzco. Other governmental agencies, funded mostly by the United States, were set up to spur control-and-eradication efforts, as well as to promote the substitution of alternative crops and to carry out enforcement. Inefficient and underfunded, these measure did little to stem the boom in coca production, which spread, according to Crabtree (1992, pp. 115–117), from an estimated 10,000 hectares in 1980 to 195,000 hectares in 1986. By 1985, the Upper Huallaga was attracting a large number of migrants, primarily from the impoverished southern Andes, who were lured by relatively high wages and prospects for a better life. At the same time, coca had become a major source of national, if illicit, income and employment, serving to cushion the overall impact of the economic depression of the 1980s.

Seeing a lucrative potential source of funding, the Shining Path also began to move into the Upper Huallaga in 1984 to gain adherents among the small-scale, peasant growers. Its strategy was to defend the interests of the growers by protecting them from narco-traffickers, on the one hand, who sought, by intimidation and force, to buy coca at the lowest possible price and from governmental officials and police, on the other hand, who were trying to shut down and eradicate production. Soon the Shining Path had skillfully built a successful grassroots organization to defend the growers, who, besieged on two fronts, responded favorably to the guerrillas' unusually pragmatic message of assistance.

Although not part of the Shining Path's original strategy, the emergence of the coca industry in a frontier region, where the state's presence was notoriously absent, gave the party a golden opportunity to open a second important front in the guerrilla war outside Ayacucho. More important, it filled the party's coffers from taxes that it levied on the narco-traffickers to do business with the growers. At one point, it was estimated that the guerrillas collected upward of $30 million annually from these "taxes." This money enabled the Shining Path to increase substantially its military sophistication and its guerrilla army to an estimated 5,000–7,000 fighters. The Senderista militants received salaries of between $250 and $500 a month, well above the average monthly pay of schoolteachers in the country. By 1986 and thereafter, the Shining Path began attacking military installations and ambushing police and army patrols with impunity. It was now arguably the wealthiest guerrilla movement in history, a position it solidified when in early 1987 it seized the town of Tocache which had replaced Tingo María as the coca capital of the country. For the moment at least, the Upper Huallaga was *"tierra liberada" and* a veritable cash cow for the advancing Shining Path rebellion.

Meanwhile, high public expectations greeted García's receipt of the red-and-white presidential sash on Independence Day, 1985. At thirty-six, García was the youngest president in the country's history and had received the largest popular vote ever recorded. He also led the country's oldest party into power for the first time in its six-decade history. This victory created great anticipation among Aprista party faithful who stood poised to receive the spoils of government that had been so long denied to them. On the other hand, the challenges that the new president faced were unprecedented. The economy was mired in arguably the worst depression in a century, a situation that aided the rapid advance of the Shining Path. Moreover, Peru's population was not only the third poorest in South America (after Bolivia and Paraguay), but was, on average, younger, more impoverished, and more urban than a decade earlier. These conditions had led to a resurgence of the Left since 1980, which, coalesced in IU, represented a formidable opposition challenge to the new government in Congress.

And so it was with great anticipation that García addressed the Congress on inauguration day to outline his strategy and economic program. In his speech, the new president restated his conception of a social pyramid, first developed in his campaign tract *El Futuro Diferente*, that Peru was organized at the top by a privileged sector consisting of organized labor and state workers. The government's attention needed to be focused rather on the 70 percent of the population at the bottom of the pyramid: street vendors and shantytown residents, on the one hand, and poor, disadvantaged peasants composing what he called the Andean Trapezoid, on the other. Through a policy that he called "productive social reactivization," his government proposed to take measures to restart the economy to benefit this marginalized majority.

At the same time, García saw the need for the state to defend private property and individual initiative, so that the entrepreneurial classes would be encouraged to reinvest in the economy to achieve growth. In short, the new president boldly proposed to undertake social change and reform for the poor majority without alienating the business elites that were crucial for economic progress. He gambled that the latter would go along with such a reform program after having experienced the debacle of Belaúnde's orthodox policies and because they were clearly fearful of the advance of both the legal (IU) and subversive (Shining Path) Left.

The most stunning part of his speech, however, was the announcement that the new government would restrict payment on the foreign debt to only 10 percent of the country's exports. This nationalistic position, which took a defiant attitude toward the international financial community, served several economic and political purposes. On the one hand, it challenged the IMF and its policy of "conditionality," which demanded austerity for loans. García apparently believed that the banks' fear of the "contagion," or spread of Peru's position to other debtor countries, would improve the government's weak negotiating position. At the same time, his proposal was less radical than Fidel Castro's call for the Third World to stop paying its loans altogether. On the other hand, nonpayment could be counted on to be popular with the public at large, as well as with the business class, which, according to Mauceri (1996, p. 62), perceived that the savings would be invested in the promised measures to reactivate economic growth.

In the ensuing months, García moved quickly to implement what came to be known as a "heterodox" (as opposed to the previous "orthodox") economic program. Based on a policy of selective state intervention in the economy, the program provided governmental subsidies to both business and labor to stimulate the depressed economy and revive growth. It also contained anti-inflationary measures, such as a complex system of wage and price controls. Fiscal policy stressed employment, with the government establishing programs to hire workers on state projects that were designed to improve living conditions in the shantytowns and impoverished rural areas. For example, the Programa de Apoyo de Ingreso Temporal (PAIT) provided temporary employment at the minimum wage for over 150,000 workers in Lima alone. Economically, this and other governmental measures stimulated consumer demand, while politically, through a characteristically Aprista system of clientelism, they helped to consolidate the party's popular electoral support.

As for the other key segment of García's economic and political strategy—the business community—it received numerous governmental concessions and subsidies. Assistance included tax credits; multiple exchange rates, designed to help exporters and importers of industrial inputs (machinery, raw materials); and other incentives. García also embarked on a policy of *concertación*, or cooperation with the private sector, in which he consulted regularly with businessmen, dubbed the "twelve apostles," who headed the dozen largest enterprises in the country. In response to governmental assistance, the administration expected entrepreneurs to reinvest their profits from growth back into the economy and to provide the political support necessary for the regime's success. By limiting payment on the debt, "priming the pump," and reaching out to the private sector, García was clearly pinning his hopes on an internally, rather than externally (foreign loans and investments), generated economic recovery.

For the first half of his regime, García's heterodox policies paid off. Per capita income rose from −1.1 percent in 1985 to 7.3 percent and 5.1 percent in 1986 and 1987, respectively, raising internal demand and stimulating production. Real growth jumped from 1.5 percent in 1985 to 8.5 percent and 7 percent in 1986 and 1987, respectively. Growth came mainly from the manufacturing (+19 percent in 1986), construction (+30 percent) and agricultural sectors, but traditional exports remained relatively stagnant.

Agriculture benefited from the stronger urban demand, as well from the greater availability of credit, but those who gained tended to be producers who were the most integrated into the market, rather than the poorest, most disadvantaged peasants whom García had pledged to help in the so-called Andean Trapezoid. Unfortunately, his Plan Sierra, a five-year, $640 million program to aid 2,000 communities with a population of 2.5 million, was, according to Crabtree, 1992, pp. 53–59), slow in developing and did not begin to unfold until well into 1988, when the overall economy was again in a tailspin.

Nevertheless, these were the best couple of years of economic growth since the Odría administration and the Korean War-induced export boom of the early 1950s. Overall Peru's roughly 8 percent growth rate outpaced those of other Latin American countries by a substantial margin. At the same time, this "miniboom" occurred primarily in the urban and modern (formal and informal) sectors of the economy. As for inflation, it dropped over the same period, from an annual rate of 163 percent to 64 percent. Confidence in the *inti*, which had earlier replaced the *sol*, climbed as dollar-denominated holdings in the banking system plunged from 57 percent to 13 percent.

Yet even as the economic picture appeared to brighten, warning signs began to appear. For one thing, the government's fiscal condition deteriorated, not so much from increased spending, which actually fell as a percentage of the GNP, but from declining governmental income (from taxes and state enterprises). Despite substantial economic growth in 1986 and 1987, public-sector income as a percentage of the GDP fell sharply (from 46 percent in 1985 to 33.5 percent in 1986 to 26 percent in 1987).

The decrease in public-sector income was due to many technical reasons, but mainly to the García administration's failure to reform the country's notoriously narrow and lax tax system, one of the worst in South America. For example, only 800 large companies (out of 10,000) accounted for 75 percent of the tax receipts to the treasury in 1987. Moreover, three times as many Ecuadorians and twelve times as many Chileans (in relation to the total population) filed income tax returns as did Peruvians. One study estimated that in 1987, tax evasions amounted to 4.4 percent of the GDP, or the equivalent of 40 percent of total tax income. Businessmen regularly flaunted the tax laws, since none had ever been prosecuted and sent to prison or their enterprises shut down by the government.

Another sign of trouble to come was the administration's *concertación* with business, which was slow to get off the ground. As a result, by mid-1987 there was still no indication that private-sector investment, a crucial factor in extending the two-year-old recovery, was increasing. Furthermore, as expected, there was no net increase in the flow of external loans to Peru. García's limit on debt repayment had led U.S. banks to declare their Peruvian loans "value impaired" and the IMF to render Peru "ineligible" for future lending. It is interesting that the administration's 1986 debt repayment amounted to 13 percent, about the same amount that Belaúnde had paid in 1985. Finally, the balance of payments deteriorated, as imports surged while exports remained relatively stagnant.

Meanwhile, civil-military relations during the first two years of the García regime underwent some alterations. In general, the armed forces assumed a positive attitude toward the new president. The old animosities with APRA had been effectively buried with the rise of a new generation of officers, and during the electoral campaign, García's moderation seemed preferable to the prospects of a victory by Barrantes and the IU. At the same time, García's nationalistic stance on debt repayment and his announcement soon after his inauguration of a nonaligned foreign policy were well received by the military.

Reactions to his specific policies, however, were mixed. García was determined to try to assert civilian control over the armed forces, long an allusive dream for democrats in a country where military intervention in politics was endemic. The opportunity arose when evidence came to light of the army's involvement in a series of killings at Accomarca. García reacted swiftly by dismissing the head of the Armed Forces Joint Command, the commander in charge of the central region in Lima, and the commander of the Ayacucho Emergency Zone. Although this action was unprecedented by a civilian president, it did not significantly reduce the power of the armed forces or alter its fundamental relationship with civilian authority. The air force was also rankled by García's cutting a previous order for twenty-six Mirage-2000 fighters in half. This act explains the abortive coup by General Luis Abram Cavallerino in April 1987 from the air base at Las Palmas.

García also sought initially to stress the developmental and human rights side of the counterinsurgency strategy of the armed forces. However, much of the promised governmental aid for the Andean Trapezoid never materialized. And the emphasis on getting the military to show greater restraint on human Rights violations was undermined by the government's massacre of 250 rebellious Senderista prisoners held in the Lurigancho and El Frontón prisons on June 19, 1986.

Military opposition to García was further raised by his attempt, in March 1987, to create a single Ministry of Defense by merging the three service ministries into a single Cabinet post. In practice, this merger would have considerably reduced the power of the navy and air force, which vigorously opposed the proposal. Despite such opposition to García's policies, however, as long as the new president remained popular—his public approval ratings soared to 90 percent six months into his term—he was able to retain the upper hand in civil-military relations. At the same time, the military establishment under the García administration continued to command 20 percent of the national budget (5 percent more than education and 14 percent more than health services). This proportion amounted to $106 per capita, which was three times the average per capita spending of all other South American nations in 1988, according to Doughty (in Hudson, 1993).

In addition, García had some success in confronting a fundamental problem that had plagued Peru for much of its history—the dominance of Lima and the highly centralized system of the government. Although the problem can be traced back to the establishment of the viceregal court and colonial government in the sixteenth century, the centrality of Lima in Peruvian life was accentuated by the concentration of more than a third of the country's total population in the city since the mid-twentieth century. The dramatic expansion of the state during the Velasco period, combined with the concentration of commerce and industry in the capital (accounting for about two-thirds of the nation's industrial output and total wages), further contributed to the predominance of Lima in the country's life. For those living in the provinces, of course, the primacy of the capital has been both a blessing, in that Lima has attracted a steadily increasing flow of migrants in search of a better life, and a curse, in that the city has consumed and monopolized an overwhelmingly disproportionate share of the nation's wealth and resources.

Ever since its founding, the APRA party, although not alone, had sought to address this problem. Regionalization was part of its original 1924 program, while the constitution of 1979, written under the aegis of Haya de la Torre, stipulated the estabishment of regional governments throughout the country. So it was not surprising that in his campaign platform, García promised to undertake the administrative decentralization of the country. In March 1987 he fulfilled this pledge by promulgating a bold plan to reorganize the country's twenty-four departments into twelve larger regions with legislative, administrative and taxing powers (see map 1). Although elections to these regional legislatures were held, over the next few years, the functioning of these new administrative units was constrained by funding problems related, as I shall explain, to the sudden collapse of the economy.

Another challenge faced by the García administration came from the Shining Path, which, by the middecade, was expanding the radius of its operations. For example, the Shining Path had moved into the central and norther highlands, particularly the department of Pasco and the Upper Huallaga, as well as the south, principally in Puno. In Pasco it succeeded in establishing influence among the peasantry in the highest, most remote, and poorest communities. However, the rebels were less effective when they moved down toward Cerro de Pasco, hoping to gain adherents among the miners. In Cerro, their stridently doctrinaire appeal was less well received among a trade unionist population that was more concerned with collective bargaining over wage and working conditions in the copper mines.

In Puno, with a long tradition of conflicts over land distribution (even after the agrarian reform) and peasant rebellion, the Shining Path sought to gain a foothold among the mountainous Quechua-speaking population located near the Bolivian border in the provinces of Azángaro and Melgar. There the terrain and proximity to Bolivia, with its poorly guarded frontier, provided both a source of supply and a safe haven for the Senderistas' activities. However, the Shining Path encountered important obstacles in Puno. Well-developed local peasant federations and an activist and progressive Church with links to the legitimate Left were difficult to penetrate or win over to the party's message and resisted the Shining Path's operations.

The southern Andean Church's long-standing progressive stance went back at least to the establishment of the Andean Pastoral Institute in 1968, whose goal was to train pastoral workers and missionaries in the indigenous culture and languages of the south. A decade later, a pastoral letter in 1978 denounced injustices and human Rights violations against the region's predominantly peasant population. Much of the progressive thrust of the southern Andean Church came from foreign missionary orders, such as the Maryknoll order and Carmelites from the United State.

To counter the Church's successful pastoral efforts among the indigenous population, the Shining Path was forced to alter its established tactic of assassination and intimidation of local officials and to adopt more standard political means of persuasion to win over influential local supporters and the region. In the coca-growing Upper Huallaga of San Martín, on the other hand, the influence of Sendero continued to spread rapidly in 1985–86.

By 1985, the Shining Path had also moved into Lima with a campaign of sabotage that, among other things, caused numerous blackouts that, together with periodic bombings and assassinations, spread a growing sense of fear and apprehension among the general population. In May 1986 a series of assassinations, culminating in the killing of an admiral, led high-ranking officers to demand that the government should declare Lima an emergency zone. The Shining Path also began a concerted effort to infiltrate civic organizations, such as trade unions, teachers' organizations, and women's groups.

The Shining Path's appeal in Lima went beyond the increasingly pauperized popular classes, penetrating as well the frustrated and downwardly mobile sectors of the middle classes. This appeal was particularly strong among well-educated young people whose professional aspirations were increasingly frustrated by the economic crisis. Indeed, McClintock (1998) correlated the rapidly rising number of university-educated graduates during the 1980s with eroding employment opportunities commensurate with their qualifications. For example, the level of unemployment among this segment of the population, unlike in earlier economic crises, was double that of the rest of the population. Moreover, among increasingly poorly paid workers in the public sector, the Shining Path made large gains in recruits among teachers, whose monthly salaries had plummeted to only $90 by the late 1980s, two-thirds of what they had been a decade earlier. In this context, the

Senderistas were finding the universities especially fertile places for recruiting a generation of young people without hope.

In addition to the usual array of alienated teenagers attracted to such a movement, the Shining Path also recruited children as young as eight and women. The children, referred to as "orphans of the revolution," were so impressionable that they were easy prey to the Shining Path's sophisticated propaganda methods. As for women, they were often usefully employed as household servants and informants, providing, according to Masterson (1991, p. 278), the inside information necessary for the assassination attempts against high-ranking government, APRA, and army officials.

Nationalization of the Banks: From Boom to Bust, 1987–90

With the economy showing increasing signs of unraveling and the Shining Path continuing its steady advance, García's popularity began to wane as his five-year term passed the halfway point. In need of adjusting his heterodox economic plan and of reversing his now-declining public opinion polls, García cast about for a dramatic new initiative that, like his 1985 debt declaration or Velasco's 1969 agrarian reform decree, could inject new life into both the economy and his political fortunes. The solution was apparently hurriedly conceived in a two-week period, with no consultation or adequate preparation for effective implementation. On the second anniversary of his assumption of power, García announced, to a stunned Congress and nation, that he was nationalizing the remaining 20 percent of the country's private banking system (excluding foreign banks). Eighty percent of the nation's credit had been controlled by the state ever since the Velasco years. This announcement sent shock waves not only through the business community, on whom García's heterodox policy depended for investment, but through the general public at large, which, after the failures of the Velasco era, remained skeptical of such statist solutions. Although only a contributory, rather than a fundamental, cause of the country's subsequent economic collapse, the declaration to nationalize the banking system proved to be a colossal political blunder and a major turning point from which García was never able to recover.

In economic terms, the announcement ended what little confidence the president had been able to generate through his *concertación* with the "twelve apostles" of the business community (four of whom were among the most powerful bankers in the country). Already apprehensive of a possible lurch to the Left and socialism by the government, the disillusioned private sector began to disinvest through the flight of capital to safe havens abroad. García is known to have become increasingly impatient and angry over the slow response of business in carrying out its pledge to make major new investments in the economy. He knew that heterodoxy, in the absence of foreign loans, would not work without these investments.

García now struck back angrily at what he called the "financial oligarchy." He charged, in language infused with the rhetoric of class conflict, that it was the center of a nefarious system of links between banks, savings and loans associations, and insurance companies and the big economic interest groups dominating the economy. This charge had a ring of truth to it, since five of the largest banks, together with several big entrepreneurial groups, purportedly controlled 50 percent of the GDP. However, public opinion, which García had calculated would be highly favorable to the announcement, was generally negative. The announcement also engendered some fierce opposition, enabling the resuscitation of the political Right, which had been largely moribund since García's 1985 electoral landslide.

Unable to get the measure through a reluctant Congress and suffering a major loss of business confidence, García sustained a major political defeat at just the moment when the economy continued to deteriorate. For example, from January to December 1987, inflation rose from an annualized rate of 65 percent to 114.5 percent. Moreover, the demand-led boom of 1986 subsided during the course of 1987, so that the 7.5 percent annual rate of growth was much higher at the beginning than at the end of the year. More troubling was the sharp swing in the trade surplus, which was largely due to a surge in imports, so that the reserves went from a surplus of $1.2 billion in 1985 to a deficit of $521 million in 1987, the highest since 1981. The government's fiscal condition also worsened as tax receipts fell but spending declined only slightly.

To reverse these adverse trends, the government abandoned its heterodox policies for orthodox ones. Such radical policy changes, characteristic of Peruvian governments for more than a quarter century, have led economists to refer to the "pendulum effect" as an important contributing factor to Peru's poor economic performance during this period. Efforts were made to mend fences with the international financial community as governmental representatives met with the World Bank and talked of resuming payment on the debt in hopes of raising new loans. In October 1987, the government devalued the *inti* by 24 percent and announced the first of a series of progressively more severe austerity packages over the next eighteen months. However, worried about the political costs to his declining popularity and reacting to bureaucratic infighting and policy disputes in his administration, García moderated each package in an effort to make it more politically palatable. Such a policy of "gradualism" did little to stem the inflationary spiral, the economic slowdown, or falling wages. The rate of inflation, for example, soared from an annual rate of 360 percent in the first quarter of 1988 to almost 7,000 percent in the second, according to Graham (1992, p. 109), the highest in modern Peruvian history.

As conditions continued to deteriorate, García finally agreed, in September 1988, to abandon his policy of gradual austerity for a real shock treatment that included a massive 75 percent devaluation; fiscal adjustments, such as higher prices (gasoline prices quadrupled, pharmaceutical prices sextupled) and taxes; and a monetary squeeze consisting of a doubling of interest rates. Not even this shock treatment was enough, however, to detain the march of inflation that continued to surge and necessitated still another, even stronger, austerity package in November, which, among other things, devalued the *inti* to 500 to the dollar.

The social costs of these adjustment measures, which actually did little to contain the hyperinflationary spiral, were enormous. With prices now decontrolled, the annual rate of inflation reached a record 1,722 percent in 1988, only to be broken the following year at 2,776 percent. At the same time, the GNP contracted almost 9 percent and 12 percent in the same years. As a result, real income dropped 22 percent between 1987 and 1989, falling to the 1960s levels. Shortages of staples also occurred, along with long lines of housewives lining up for beef and chicken bones, pig fat, and the heads and tails of fish. Consumers simply could not afford other parts of animals, which then spoiled for the lack of buyers. By one measurement, annual household incomes in Lima contracted 64 percent in 1987–88. The employment index (1979 = 100 percent), which had risen in García's first eighteen months to 104.5 percent, plunged thereafter to 96.1 percent (and in manufacturing, from 101.3 percent to 88.2 percent). By 1990, fully 70 percent of the workforce was either unemployed or underemployed.

The situation in the rural areas was equally grave. Having undergone a modest revival (3 percent annual growth) during the first half of García's term, agriculture then experienced a collapse in markets and prices, causing farm incomes to plunge. As the demand for farm products dropped in the cities, the terms of trade in agriculture became sharply negative while the prices of inputs like fertilizer soared. Moreover, García's vaunted credit program to farmers contracted as governmental programs ran out of money. By 1989 agricultural production, after rising in the previous two years, declined sharply, producing shortages in the cities and necessitating costly governmental imports. Rice, for example, normally a surplus commodity, had to be imported from North Korea.

The deepening social crisis brought on by García's structural adjustment packages was revealed in the growing evidence of widespread malnutrition. According to one study, less than half the population earned enough ($48)in a month to purchase the minimum basket of goods necessary for adequate subsistence. Over 6.5 million persons did not earn enough ($31 per month) to consume the minimum calory levels necessary to avoid malnutrition. The incidence of malnutrition was particularly acute in young children, and the infant mortality rate increased substantially. Efforts by the government through its Social Compensation Program, initiated in April 1989, to alleviate the impact of the shock packages, had little effect because of bureaucratic inefficiency and the lack of funding. However, NGOs, with external financing, and grassroots self-help organizations (the communal kitchens and

"Glass of Milk" programs) stepped up their relief efforts in Lima's shanty-towns and elsewhere.

Popular reaction to the impact of the shock was relatively muted. The call by the Confederation of Peruvian Workers for a national strike in October and again in December received only limited support from labor. Many workers were so hard pressed that they were reluctant to sacrifice a day's wages, while others feared that they would lose their jobs if they failed to show up for work. There was also considerable fear that any labor demonstrations or marches would be violently repressed by the government. Nevertheless, the number of individual strikes in the country rose to 815 in 1988 from 579 in 1985. The most severe strikes occurred in the hard-hit public sector among municipal workers, teachers, hospital workers, and miners whose wages had declined because of the ongoing financial crisis of the state and economy.

A major beneficiary of this overall state of affairs, of course, was the Shining Path, which continued to expand its operations in both rural and urban areas. The Shining Path had the most success in the Upper Huallaga. By 1988 coca production in the region had reached an estimated 10,000 tons on more than 250,000 hectares, employing perhaps a quarter of a million people. The government's efforts to induce growers to substitute other crops, such as coffee, rice, maize, cacao, or fruit, had not worked, even when the price of coca fell because of an oversupply in the United States. And when agricultural prices declined in the recession of 1988–89, farmers actually switched from traditional crops to coca.

The late 1980s also saw a shift in coca processing from laboratories along the Colombian border to areas within the Huallaga that were closer to the sources of supply. By 1987, it was estimated that the region was producing $1 billion dollars annually—twice the value of copper exports. Indeed, coca accounted for approximately 40 percent of the value of exports and 20 percent of the agricultural GDP. For dollars to be converted into *intis*, the banking industry expanded rapidly into the Huallaga, with planeloads of dollars from the region, according to Crabtree (1992, p. 196), transported to Lima in exchange for their equivalent in *intis*.

For the Shining Path, control of the Huallaga had become a key to its overall strategy, providing a ready source of manpower, arms, and cash with which to contemplate a strategic "equilibrium," or parity, with the country's armed forces. However, before it could achieve this end, it had to confront the MRTA, led by former Aprista Víctor Polay Campos, an old university chum of García. MRTA had also targeted the potential riches in the Huallaga and established a presence there to try to cut in on the financial rewards of the coca industry. The two guerrilla forces collided in Tocache in early 1987, with the Shining Path inflicting a major military defeat on its rival.

A major modification in the Shining Path's guerrilla strategy occurred at its First Congress held in 1988. Declaring that sufficient progress had been made in the countryside, Guzmán concluded that the organization should now shift its focus to the cities, particularly Lima. The decision apparently was a controversial one, however, eliciting the opposition of a faction, led by Guzmán's wife Augusta La Torre, who argued that the Shining Path was not ready for such a bold move and that it would prematurely expose the organization's leadership.

Accordingly, the Shining Path stepped up its operations in Lima, particularly terror tactics, such as bombing attacks, which were a major feature of its psychological war aimed at demoralizing the population. Perhaps its greatest impact on the cities was the *paro armado* (armed strike), first developed in Ayacucho. The tactic relied on the threat of violence against anyone who tried to go to work after the organization declared a strike. It proved particularly effective against bus and *colectivo* (jitny) drivers, who were afraid to take their vehicles out on the streets, thereby frustrating workers' attempts to get to work.

As the Shining Path continued to advance and the economy continued to deteriorate, García's approval ratings in public opinion polls plummeted, dropping in one poll from 90 percent to less than 10 percent in December 1988. His standing in the APRA declined as well. García was heckled and booed, for example, at the sixteenth party Congress in 1988, and his main rival, Luis Alva Castro, who harbored presidential ambitions, was elected general secretary.

The president's precipitous decline in the public opinion polls, of course, created an opening for both the Left and the Right. IU held its First Congress in January 1989 amid high hopes for the upcoming municipal elections later in the year and the Congressional and presidential elections scheduled for 1990. These hopes were dashed, however, when a major division between the moderates and radicals, which had been developing since 1987, became unreconcilable. In general terms, the moderates, led by Barrantes, were more accommodating to the APRA and intransigently opposed to the Shining Path, while the radicals took the opposite position. Unable to agree on the composition of a national executive committee at the January Congress, the two factions fatally headed into the upcoming elections with separate lists of candidates.

This time, it was the Right that gained the most from the economic crisis. The galvanizing issue was García's declaration of his intention to nationalize the banking system. This announcement had triggered the largest protest demonstration by the forces of the Right in the history of the country. On August 21, 1987, the Plaza de San Martín in Lima filled to capacity with an estimated 30,000 protesters to hear the president and his proposal roundly denounced by Mario Vargas Llosa. In his speech, the internationally acclaimed writer argued that the nationalization of the banks was an arbitrary, unconstitutional act by a despotic, authoritarian government that was bent on destroying democracy and the free enterprise system. Only nine months after its disastrous showing in the municipal elections, the Right was miraculously revived by a new coalition of the main conservative parties—

FREDEMO, which consisted of Belaúnde's AP, Bedoya's PC, and the Movimiento Libertad. Although FREDEMO was backed by the Instituto Libertad y Democracia, headed by Hernando de Soto, author of *The Other Path*, Vargas Llosa, by virtue of his oppostion to the bank nationalization, was now the rising political star of the Right and early favorite to succeed the faltering García and the APRA government in the 1990 elections.

The first tangible electoral beneficiary of the government's collapse, however, was the election of the independent candidate Ricardo Belmont for mayor of Lima in November 1989. A wealthy, affable *Limeño* who controlled a major television station and had gained celebrity status by hosting a popular television talk show, Belmont effectively portrayed himself as an average person standing against the old, outmoded parties and politicians and ran for mayor on the promise of public works (*obras*), which became the name of his movement. Confessing that "although I am light-skinned, the mestizo, Indians and blacks in the shantytowns like me a lot," Belmont replicated García's multiclass success in 1985, sweeping to victory with strong support in Lima's working-class districts and shantytowns. His victory was the first sign of the looming importance a new political phenomenon in the country—the "independent" candidate—which, as Cameron (1996, pp. 48–49) noted, foreshadowed the astonishing "rise from nowhere" of Alberto Fujimori in the 1990 presidential elections.

13 Fujimori, Neoliberalism, and Peru's Progress, 1990–95

The 1990 Campaign

The leading candidate for the presidency in 1990 was the internationally acclaimed novelist Mario Vargas Llosa, whose popularity had soared as the spokesman for the Right against García's attempt to nationalize the banking system in 1987. A relative newcomer to Peruvian politics, Vargas Llosa was born into a middle-class family in Arequipa in 1936. Because of the separation of his parents, he spent his childhood in Cochabamba, Bolivia, and Piura, where his grandfather, a diplomat and governmental official, had received political appointments. Packed off as a teenager to the Leoncio Prado Military School in Lima, the young Vargas Llosa had experiences there and later at San Marcos University during the Odría dictatorship that made strong impressions on him.

At Leoncio Prado, he found a microcosm of Peruvian life, punctuated by prejudice, hypocrisy, and machismo, which he later captured in the novel *La Ciudad y los Perros* (1963). The unflattering portrait of the school led the authorities to ban the novel, and it was burned in a public ceremony. At San Marcos University, where Odría's spies kept the university and its Left-leaning students under constant surveillance, Vargas Llosa became involved with socialism. From his experiences during the oppressive Odría years, the aspiring writer also developed a deep admiration for the ideas of individual freedom and the state's potential to suffocate it.

Later Vargas Llosa won a scholarship to the University of Madrid, where he wrote his doctoral dissertation on the Colombian writer Gabriel García Márquez. For a time, he lived in Paris as a translator and journalist, sending articles to various newpapers and journals in Peru. By the early 1970s, having cemented his international reputation with the prize-wining novels *La Casa Verde* (1966) and *Conversación en la Catedral* (1969), Vargas Llosa broke with García Márquez, then the leading intellectual defender of the Latin American Left and the Cuban Revolution, and began to move steadily to the Right.

His early dalliance with Peruvian politics may be said to have begun during Belaúnde's second term, when the president asked him to head the official commission to investigate the massacre of eight journalists at Uchuraccay, near Ayacucho, in 1983. The following year, he was offered but turned down the portfolio of prime minister. It was not until the 1987 bank nationalization, however, that Vargas Llosa's political ambitions came to the fore. On the heals of the demonstration, he and a number of collaborators, including Hernando de Soto, author of *The Other Path* and founder of the Instituto de Democracia y Libertad (IDL), organized the Movimiento Libertad (ML) (Liberty Movement).

Libertad, as it came to be known, quickly became a vehicle for the Right and Vargas Llosa's potential presidential candidacy in the 1990 elections. In February 1988, ML formed a democratic front with Acción Popular (AP) and the Partido Popular Cristiano (PPC) under the banner of FREDEMO. For a time, the leadership of the new Right coalition was disputed by Belaúnde, still the head of AP, but in June 1989, Vargas Llosa was chosen the presidential nominee of the alliance. In the meantime, Soto had left ML in opposition to its strong antileftist stance. Vargas Llosa entered the presidential campaign as the overwhelming favorite. All his main declared opponents were weak. On the one hand, Luis Alva Castro, of the APRA, carried the burden of the failed García into the campaign, but without his charisma, while Alfonso Barrantes and Henry Pease García split the declining vote of the Left.

According to public opinion polls, the majority of Peruvians, racked by years of civil conflict and economic crisis, were now politically moving toward the moderate center, away from the extremes of the Right and Left. At the same time, as indicated by the election of Ricardo Belmont as Lima's new mayor, they manifested a profound antipathy and mistrust for the established political class. Afterall the traditional parties AP and APRA, after raising expectations, had not only failed miserably to stabilize the country during the 1980s, but had led it into a cycle of decline, disorder, and dispair.

Perhaps overconfident from polls showing his political strength against his rivals, Vargas Llosa and his advisers miscalculated this new political mood. Philosophically attuned to British Prime Minister Margaret Thatcher, whom he greatly admired, the FREDEMO candidate believed that Peru in the 1990s was ready for a "great conservative transformation," similar to the one that had swept the Anglo-American world during the 1980s. The outlines of this transformation were detailed in unusually specific terms for a candidate in a speech Vargas Llosa delivered at a forum for presidential candidates sponsored by the main association of business executives in December 1989.

In the speech, Vargas Llosa called for a harsh IMF-like stabilization program to reduce the soaring rate of inflation and promised to reintegrate the country into the international economy. Trade would be liberalized, full debt payments would be resumed, foreign investment would be encouraged, state enterprises would be privatized, price controls and subsidies would be eliminated, the tax structure would be overhauled, and legislation guaranteeing job security for workers would be overturned. Echoing Thatcher, as well as Soto, he called for a sweeping deregulation of the state and the construction of a free market economy that would replace the failed statism and mercantilism of the past.

The general public reaction to the program, however, was negative. The program was seen as an overly severe and extremist prescription to a public that was searching for candidates who would espouse more moderate and less painful solutions to the country's predicament. The speech frightened not only the poor majorities, who fully understood the implications for them of stabilization, but segments of the business and middle classes, who looked askance at the possibility of an end to the statist and mercantilist systems from which many had profited in the past.

Some observers believe that even though Vargas Llosa won the first round of the two-stage election process, he actually lost the election with this speech. By outlining the particulars of his intended program, he was painted as a radical, right-wing zealot by his rivals, who warned of wholesale layoffs and other social costs from his "shock" program. The fact that he also had chosen to ally himself with the two established parties of the Right, which were discredited in the public's eyes, along with the rest of the old political establishment, likewise worked to weaken his candidacy. Finally, the fifty-four-year-old writer's light complexion, cosmopolitan lifestyle, Eurocentric outlook, and aloof demeanor cast him in the popular mind as "the candidate of the rich," a portrait that the opposition successfully exploited. Only three weeks from the first round, with Alva Castro having narrowed somewhat Vargas Llosa's initial big lead, pollsters detected a steady shift in the electorate to a previously little-known university professor and administrator of Japanese descent by the name of Alberto Fujimori.

Fujimori was born in Lima in 1938, four years after his parents had arrived in the country from Japan to work as agricultural field hands. Japanese contract laborers had begun to come to Peru around the turn of the century to work on the sugar and cotton plantations. But as soon as their contracts were fulfilled, some left the countryside for the capital, where, according to Gardiner (1975), they settled in enclaves and entered petty commerce, often thriving because of their habits of saving, individual initiative, and hard work. The Fujimori family was no exception. They sent their son to public schools and then to study agricultural engineering at the National Agrarian University. After graduation, Fujimori received scholarships for postgraduate study in France and the United States and later returned to his alma mater to teach, rising eventually to become rector. During the late 1980s, he gained a wider public audience when he hosted a popular television talk program called *Getting Together*, which blended agricultural news and politics aimed at farmers.

With an eye toward politics and sensing an outsider's prospects in the

President Alberto Fujimori (1990–). Reproduced with the permission of the General Secretariat of the Organization of American States.

prevailing mood of antipolitics, Fujimori first tried to obtain a place on the senatorial list of Barrantes's Izquierda Socialista (IS) in the 1990 elections. Unsuccessful, he organized a political party called Cambio 90 (Change), composed of independent professionals and small businessmen, many of whom were Protestant evangelicals. Evangelicals constituted only 5 percent of

Peru's population but 40 percent of the fledgling Cambio 90 Party, and they brought to the party their missionary, door-to-door canvassing techniques. Although Fujimori had no previous political experience, he astutely read the electorate's desire for new faces. He would become the quintessential political outsider, untainted by association with Peru's discredited political class. When asked by a leftist leader during the campaign why she was holding a poster of the candidate, a market vendor replied simply, "because he hasn't done anything yet" (quoted in Roberts, 1995, p. 95, fn. 35).

After entering the campaign as a virtual unknown, Fujimori quickly denounced Vargas Llosa's shock therapy and called for a more gradualist approach to stabilization. His campaign slogan "Honesty, Technology, and Work," stood out from the usual demogoguery of the traditional politicians and conjured up positive images of probity and technocratic efficiency. In a population that admired the progress of hardworking Japanese immigrants who had succeeded through talent and perseverance, rather than through their family names and connections, Fujimori's ancestry and successful career became an advantage. Rumors soon circulated that as president his ancestry would give the Japanese-Peruvian ready access to loans and capital from Tokyo.

Such personal attributes resonated well among the country's mestizo and Indian masses, shantytown dwellers and campesinos alike. In particular, Fujimori targeted the huge popular or informal, sector in the sprawling Lima shantytowns, whose inhabitants were migrants, as his family had been, struggling to improve their lot. He later said that his "entire campaign was organized so that my message would reach my social base: the informal sector and the marginalized" (Salcedo, quoted in Cameron, 1997, p. 71). With an eye toward appealing to this constituency, Fujimori chose Máximo San Román, mestizo president of the country's most important small and medium-sized business association, as his vice presidental candidate. On the campaign trail, "El Chino," as Fujimori came to be known, deftly identified with the common people, drawing a folksy contrast with his urbane, aristocratic opponent Vargas Llosa and his Caucasian circle of advisers.

Fujimori seemed to revel in rubbing shoulders with the common people in city young towns or highland country markets, often donning a colorful Andean poncho and *chullo* (hat). In the shantytowns, he liked to tour in a tractor called the Fujimobile, from which he would invariably remind audiences that he would be "un presidente como tu" (a president like you) (Conaghan and Malloy, 1994, p. 227). This populist style was also reflected in his campaign promises, such as to make governmental credit easily available to *informales* and *campesinos* and to provide legal protection to street vendors. In contrast, the gentlemanly and formal Vargas Llosa felt uncomfortable campaigning in the slums, often appearing stiff, aloof, and even arrogant, so he rarely appeared there. All these images reached the population by television, by now the most important medium in the country.

Fujimori also scored points in a presidential debate when, referring to his opponent's declared intention to "Europeanize Peru," he remarked with a smirk, "It seems to me that you would like to make Peru into Switzerland, Doctor Vargas Llosa" (quoted in M. Vargas Llosa, 1991, p. 37). As a member of Vargas Llosa's public relations team accurately summed it up, "Fujimori became a dark-skinned Peruvian who had taken on the light-skinned and aristocratic Vargas Llosa. He may have been first generation Peruvian, but in the war of images he represented the polyglot Peru that had been exploited and marginalized by the European interlopers that Vargas Llosa symbolized" (quoted in Cameron, 1994, p. 118).

When the vote was finally cast, Fujimori came from seemingly nowhere to garner 25 percent of the ballots, only three points behind Vargas Llosa's 28 percent, with Alva Castro third, at 19 percent, and the combined two candidates of the Left last, at 11 percent. His remarkable showing was due, in great part, to his having received the lion's share of the vote of the informal sector in the shantytowns. Conversely, the failure of the Left could be attributed not only to its divisions, but to the fact that its classist approach had virtually ignored the social changes of the past fifteen years that had produced the bulging new strata of *informales*. To many on the Left, the informal sector represented a petty bourgeoisie that oscillated unpredictably in a reactionary or progressive way, depending on the circumstances.

As for the congressional vote, FREDEMO candidates managed to win a plurality of one-third of the seats in both houses of Congress (21 out of 62 senators and 83 of 180 deputies), while APRA won only slightly less than a third (17 senators and 70 deputies). The gains had been expensive, given the fact that FREDEMO had spent a whooping $12.8 million on the presidential and congressional campaigns, much of it on slick public relations media. On the other hand, Fujimori's Cambio 90 campaign spent under a quarter of million dollars and won less than a fifth of the seats in Congress (14 senators, and 32 deputies). Consequently, if Fujimori won the second round, as seemed probable, he faced a potential gridlock in Congress, hardly a promising circumstance for Peru's fledgling democracy.

Having passed through to the second round of voting, Fujimori steadfastly occupied the center of the political spectrum while he successfully boxed Vargas Llosa in on the Right. He had little difficulty picking up votes from the Center-Left APRA, for whom the FREDEMO and the novelist were an anathema, and from the Left, which had nowhere to go. As for Vargas Llosa, he was unable to shed the "richman" tag or breakdown the class cleavage that characterized much of Peruvian politics. The candidate of FREDEMO had won over 70 percent of the vote in the upper-class districts of San Isidro and Miraflores, but less than 20 percent in the popular districts of Independencia and Villa María del Triunfo/Villa El Salvador.

Little changed in the weeks leading up to the vote, although Fujimori rejected a proposal from Vargas Llosa to form a majority coalition government and avoid the second round. Vargas Llosa tried to soften his stabilization program, but the damage had already been done, even as Fujimori continued to project a moderate, pragmatic image. Religion became an issue when the Church, spurred by conservative members of the hierarchy, organized a rally on May 31, led by the new Archbishop Augusto Vargas Alzamora, protesting alleged insults by Fujimori's Protestant evangelicals. The archbishop's sensitivity over the subject was, in one sense understandable, since Protestantism had made substantial gains in Peru over the past half century. A 1981 census registered 4.7 percent of the population as "non-Catholic Christian," up from 3.2 percent in 1972. The greatest gains were made by the missionary churches, such as the Seventh Day Adventists, Pentecostals, and Baptists, as opposed to the main-line Protestant churches. During the first fifty years of the century, the Adventist church was the largest Protestant group in the country. However, in the past twenty years, the Pentacostals were the fastest growing Protestant group, with 212,822 members in 1982. Other nonmainstream sects, such as the Mormons and Jehovah's Witnesses, have also grown considerably in recent years.

Many of these groups viewed Latin America as an especially promising area for proselytizing, partly because of the unresponsiveness of the traditional Catholic Church to change. However, Klaiber (1992, p. 357) noted that the Church in Peru, particularly after Vatican II, had been particularly responsive in the young towns and the southern Andes, offering many of the same attractions as those provided by the Protestant sects. He attributed the expansion of non-Catholics to the population explosion, which simply overwhelmed the Catholic Church and opened up space for the newcomers.

The growth of Protestantism, particularly among the subaltern classes, can be attributed to other factors as well. For many, Protestantism seemed to fill a vacuum in the lives of the poor, in terms of community, participation, and security, that the Catholic Church had been unable or unwilling to address. This, along with the quick promotion of lay persons to positions of responsibility, contributed to a greater sense of personal self-esteem. Marzal (1972) also noted that some of the Protestant sects placed a greater emphasis on the Old Testament, which emphasizes a rigid code of conduct and preaches a messianic message that appeals to a similarly impoverished population. Other Protestant sects, such as the Mormons and Adventists, seem to have attracted a large following from the rising urban, lower middle classes.

If Archbishop Vargas's outburst about Protestantism did not succeed in swaying many voters in the second-round electioneering, it nevertheless, produced odd bedfellows in a Church divided, like most Peruvian institutions, between liberals and conservatives, some bishops supporting Vargas Llosa, a professed agnostic, against Fujimori, a practicing Catholic. Racism also raised its ugly head in the campaign, when a member of the Peruvian delegation to the United Nations, echoing an attitude widely held in the upper classes, declared that he doubted that the home of the Incas was ready to vote for a candidate who was a first-generation Peruvian. The result of the second-round vote belied such an assertion, however, since Fujimori picked up virtually most of the first-round votes for APRA and the Left and won a resounding victory—62 percent to Vargas Llosa's 38 percent.

Fujishock and the Autogolpe, 1990–92

Upon assuming office in July 1990, Fujimori declared that he had inherited a "disaster." Hernando de Soto, now a close adviser, elaborated: "This society is collapsing. . . . There is no respect for the state, the parliament, the laws, the judicial system, not even the traffic lights. Nothing works here" (quoted in *Current History*, 1992, p. 77). Although much of this "disaster" can be laid at the door of the García administration, in truth it was also the result of a longer-term crisis. For example, the GDP had grown a paltry 1 percent a year between 1976 and 1989, hardly enough to sustain a population that was growing at the rate of over 2.5 percent a year over the same period. Incomes had suffered accordingly, with real wages in 1990 half that of 1980 levels, which themselves were half the level of the mid-1970s.

Peru's economic decline had, according to Mauceri (1995), contributed to a severe weakening of the state during the same roughly fifteen-year period. Tax revenues during the 1980s, for example, declined by more than half as a result of the economic decline. With public resources shrinking, the country's basic infrastructure lapsed into a state of severe disrepair, aggrevated by the widespread destruction of roads, bridges, and other facilities by the Shining Path insurgency. Equally damaging to the capacity of the state was the 60 percent decline in the wages of public employees between 1985 and 1990, which, together with the layoffs, undermined both morale and the level of expertise of public administrators.

The crisis of the state can also be attributed to its politicization during the 1980s. Not only did the return of partisan politics come with redemocratization in 1980, but sound economic policy making suffered as well, driven by ideological or political concerns, rather than pragmatic ones. In a variation of the political pendulum effect of democracy then dictatorship, the country lurched from orthodox to heterodox economic prescriptions. Moreover, exchange rates were routinely manipulated for political reasons, and corruption ran rampant as the winning party proceeded to use the state apparatus to loot the treasury.

Much of the economy's downspin in the late 1980s, of course, was the result of García's heterdox experiment, which imploded with a bang. Between 1988 and 1990, the per capita GDP fell by 25 percent and would soon reach the 1950 level, the result of the general contraction of the economy, according to CEPAL (1991), by 8.4 percent in 1988, 11.4 percent in 1989, and 4.9 percent in 1990. In 1985, 60 percent of Lima's population had been "adequately" employed, but by 1990 less than 10 percent were. Real wages were now below the 1970 levels. Thus, it was not surprising that average household consumption fell 46 percent over the same period. Income distribution likewise became increasingly skewed. Whereas labor's share of the national income fell from 37.7 percent in 1980 to 28.8 percent in 1989, returns to capital rose from 38.1 percent to 42.5 percent. According to one reliable source, unemployment in 1989 reached levels "never before observed" (quoted in

Cameron, 1997, p. 59). State revenues also plummeted, with tax receipts falling to only 3 percent of the GDP by the end of García's term.

The social costs of García's failed economic policies were predictably severe. As poverty levels rose sharply throughout the country, spending on public health and education fell, 30 percent over the decade 1980–90. The crisis in public health was perhaps best symbolized by the outbreak of cholera in early 1991, a disease that had not been seen since the nineteenth century. Cholera struck more than a quarter of a million people, killing an estimated 2,500 people and subsequently spreading to other countries.

The economic collapse was accompanied by the continuation, indeed seeming intensification, of the bloody decade-long war between the Shining Path and the armed forces. Since its inception in 1980, the insurgency had claimed more than 20,000 lives, caused an estimated $15 billion in economic damage, and created upward of 200,000 internal refugees. Nearly 40 percent of the country and more than half its people were under martial law. In an effort to win the war, the military had become one of the world's worst human rights abusers, only to be more than matched by the savagry with which the revolutionaries attacked the civilian population. The general perception was that the Shining Path was steadily advancing toward its goal of bringing down the state.

Part of the problem in the state's inability to stem the tide of the Shining Path was, of course, the economic crisis that adversely affected the military, as it did other branches of the government. Salaries of officers had plummeted, so that a Peruvian general, to take one example, earned only a quarter of his Chilean counterpart in 1990. These low salaries, in turn, had led to an increase in drug-related corruption in the armed forces, as well as rising rates of desertion and declining morale. By the 1990s, the pride in the advances in professionalization during the 1950s and 1960s was, according to Mauceri (1995, p. 13), only a distant memory.

Also inhibiting the military's decade-long struggle to defeat the Shining Path was an unresolved policy connundrum. One school of thought in the armed forces advocated an "Argentine-style dirty-war solution" that would resort to massive repression no matter what the cost in human rights violations. The counteropinion, the so-called developmentalist solution, argued that only massive social assistance and economic development programs could root out the fundamental causes of the insurgency and win over "the hearts and minds" of the population. During the 1980s, the state ineffectually alternated between the two approaches and made little headway in ending the insurgency.

Confronted with such daunting problems, it did not take long for Fujimori to act. A few weeks after he assumed power, he decreed a truly draconian orthodox stabilization package, far harsher than anything that Vargas Llosa had contemplated. Attacking the runaway inflation, the government slashed price subsidies and social spending and raised interest rates and taxes. For example, gasoline prices rose 3,000 percent, while most foodstuffs rose 500 percent. Water rates rose eightfold and electricity fivefold. This "Fujishock," as it was called, was followed, in February 1991, by a series of measures that were designed to restructure the economy. These measures included the start of state privatization, the deregulation of financial and labor markets, tax and tariff reform, investment incentives, and the decentralization of some social services. In a move to restore international financial confidence and the reintegration of Peru into the world economy, Fujimori began making regular monthly payments of $60 million to international financial institutions on the country's now $21 billion foreign debt.

One effect of the austerity program, of course, was the further pauperization of the population. Overall between 1990 and 1992, the real income of Peruvians dropped by fully one-third. In Lima, overall consumption dropped 24 percent, and an estimated 1 million workers lost their jobs. For those who were able to retain their jobs, wages in the public sector dropped 60 percent, and those in the private sector fell 40 percent. A conservative estimate was that 54 percent of the total Peruvian population were living in poverty. Over the next few years, the proportion of under- or unemployed in the workforce increased from 81.4 percent in 1990 to 87.3 percent in 1993, while the informal sector swelled from 45.7 percent in 1990 to 57 percent in 1992. Levels of inequality rose accordingly.

Commenting on the impact of the Fujishock, one economist noted that "it is like performing heart, stomach, kidney and lung surgery all at the same time on a patient who hasn't eaten in three years" (quoted in *Current History*, 1992, p. 77). Although Fujimori promised to cushion the poorest segments of the population from the effects of his shock therapy with a $400 million social emergency program, only $90 million was actually spent. The only tangible gain was the reduction of hyperinflation, which came down sharply from 7,650 percent to an estimated 55 percent by the end of 1992.

Despite the severity of the the government's shock treatment and its negative material impact on the majority of the population, Fujimori's popularity, as measured in public opinion polls, continued to remain high. Cameron attributed his popularity to the fact that Peru under Fujimori became a "paradigmatic example" of what O'Donnell called a "delegative democracy" (Cameron and Mauceri, 1997, p. 48). In effect, this meant that the people had elected Fujimori to carry out in their name whatever measures he deemed to be in the national interest, in spite of the promises that he may have made in the heat of the campaign. For Cameron, Peruvians' yearning for political authority and economic stability was so great that they would accept whatever actions the new president took to resolve the crisis.

Roberts, who considers Fujimori a neopopulist, attributed his continued high popularity ratings to the president's clever manipulation of certain political and symbolic themes. For example, like previous populists, he deftly identified and targeted a domestic enemy for attack. However, instead of the oligarchy or plutocracy, the favorite enemy of past populists, he substituted the country's established political class and institutions. Cultivating his campaign image and theme as an outsider and antiestablishment politician, once he was in power, El Chino, practiced what has been called the "politics of anti-politics" (Roberts, 1995, p. 98).

Lacking his own institutional political base, Fujimori singled out the political parties, Congress, and the judiciary for increasing criticism. The country, he charged, had been ruled by a corrupt, inefficient, and sectarian "partyocracy" (*partidocracia*), run by entrenched bosses who had brought Peru to the edge of financial and political ruin. By denouncing the country's weak representative institutions (which were controlled by his opponents), Fujimori not only contributed to their delegitimation, but garnered widespread political support while setting himself up as the new arbiter of the political situation. Such a campaign of defamation is consistent, of course, with the notion of a delegative democracy, whereby Congress and the judiciary are viewed by the president as little more than "nuisances," unnecessary restraints on executive power to be tolerated only in courting international favor.

Moreover, as in the campaign, Fujimori continued to appeal directly to the people in a highly personalistic fashion without the mediation of institutions or corporatist organizations. Whereas past populists had mobilized labor, Fujimori bypassed the unions, which were largely under the control of the United Left anyway. More important, the catastrophic rise in unemployment during the 1980s had decimated labor's ranks and eviscerated its traditional organizational punch. At the same time, the economic collapse had swelled the informal sector, so that by the 1990s, it now comprised five times the number of workers as the formal sector.

Although labor had supported Fujimori in the second round, after he took office it angrily challenged the new president's shock program, which led to wage cuts, layoffs of workers, and the derogation of laws protecting the collective rights of workers. However, Fujimori easily endured three failed national strikes, which clearly revealed labor's impotence and political irrelevance. By 1991 union membership had fallen a third to only 12 percent of the workforce, while the informal sector in Lima represented nearly half the economically active population.

During the first twelve months of his term, Fujimori enjoyed tremendous policy-making power, despite the weak position of his Cambio 90 Party in Congress. Much of this policy-making power was derived from the Constitution of 1979, which had concentrated power in the chief executive. Moreover, because of his continued high public opinion ratings, the customary postelection political honeymoon, and FREDEMO's general concurrence with his stabilization package and neoliberal economic goals, Congress delegated the new president authority to issue decrees to implement his program. At the same time, at the outset of his regime, Fujimori had established a crucial pact with the all important armed forces, which would serve as the main institutional foundation of the new regime.

To accomplish this goal, he chose as his principal adviser on military affairs Vladimiro Montesinos, an obscure lawyer and former army captain with a murky past, but excellent knowledge of who was who in the armed forces. Discharged from the army for allegedly passing information to the

United States, Montecinos had defended Fujimori from tax evasion charges and specialized in defending drug traffickers. Fujimori's first move to consolidate control over the military came on the day of his inauguration when he replaced the commanding officers of the navy and air force. In late 1991, he managed to get Congress to pass a law changing the selection process for the chiefs of the armed forces. Congress gave the president power to make such apointments from among the highest-ranking officers, instead of strictly by rank, and to retire any officer without cause. This opened the process of promotion to political manipulation, as Fujimori proceeded to dismiss a number of service chiefs and to promote a new commander in chief, General Nicolás Hermoza Ríos, whose record was purportedly undistinguished.

Although this decision went against the "institutionalist" faction in the military, which advocated independence from political interference, it was nevertheless accepted in return for Fujimori's promise to expand and legitimate, that is, legalize, the armed forces' counterinsurgency effort against the Shining Path. Henceforth promotions and retirements were based not on professional merit, but on loyalty to Fujimori and Hermoza Ríos. Montesinos also gained control of the National Security Agency, which, according to Obando (1996), he used not only to track down subversives, but to exercise surveillance over opposition groups.

With military support and a momentarily compliant Congress, Fujimori was able to promulgate a series of decrees liberalizing the economy, encouraging foreign investment, slashing state expenditures, and cutting tariffs. On the revenue side, the president cracked down on tax evaders and eliminated subsidies and tax exemptions to large enterprises that had been obtained through political chicanery. To combat the Shining Path, Fujimori authorized the establishment of civil defense patrols, or *rondas*, in both cities and the countryside. Over the next few years, the army distributed more than 10,000 Winchester Model 1,300 shotguns to peasant *rondas*, often handed out in ceremonies by Fujimori himself or a general after being blessed by a priest as if for use in a holy war. Reversing a ban on arms to peasants that went all the way back to the postconquest period, Congress passed a law in 1992 legalizing the distribution of weapons and thereby cementing an unlikely alliance between the army and the peasantry in the war against the Shining Path.

This new alliance was the result of a significant shift in peasants' opinions against the Shining Path that had been developing over the past few years. Peasants' disenchantment stemmed from the insurgents' indiscriminate violence and inflexible tactics. Peasants, who generally relied on social interchange and income from sources outside the community, reacted negatively to the Shining Path's strategy to strangle the cities by closing off their access to markets to sell their products.

At the same time, the Shining Path often went way beyond community mores in implementing its "revolutionary justice" against so-called enemies.

It was one thing to execute an occasional cattle rustler or corrupt official, but quite another to engage in indiscriminate killings of supposed "collaborators" with ties of family and kinship in the community. This latter tactic ran counter to the tradition of compromise in Andean communities whereby transgressors were punished but usually integrated back into the village "family." Having yielded the governance of their communities to the rebels and experienced their harsh, arbitrary rule, the peasants now recoiled and sought to reestablish their original communal forms of government. For these reasons, "instead of a progressive consolidation of rural backing after the fashion of the Chinese Red Army or Viet Cong, the Shining Path laid the foundation for the explosion of armed revolt against its revolutionary design" (Quoted in Stern, ms. 1996, p. 17).

For its part, the army recognized peasants' changed sentiment and moved to exploit it. It adopted the so-called integrated strategy of promoting "sociopolitical development" and "civic action" in the countryside. It also adopted a policy of selective, rather than indiscriminate, killing of suspected Senderistas that had marked the "dirty war" approach during much of the 1980s. Wisely substituting Quechua-speaking recruits with peasant backgrounds for racially biased *costeños* (inhabitants of the coast) in its counterinsurgency operations, the army improved relations with villagers, fraternizing with them at community festivals, distributing food and tools, and assisting in development projects. This new approach proved popular in gaining the allegiance of the Andean civilian population and helped foster the spread of the *rondas*, which became crucial in rolling back the Shining Path in the 1990s.

The *rondas* had first appeared in the 1970s and 1980s in the northern departments of Cajamarca and Piura as autochthonous organizations in the communities that were designed to root out rustlers, resolve intercommunity disputes, and organize community self-help projects (Starn, 1999). Then in the early 1980s, the military adopted the term for its concept of forced peasant patrols to oppose the Senderistas' incursions into the communities. In time and with less coercive methods, the idea gained acceptance in the communities, with the peasants taking the initiative and the army providing "logistical" support in the form of tools, medicines, and food, in addition to guns.

By the early 1990s, these self-defense organizations had spread across the central and southern Andes at a startling rate and, in the process, had taken on the dimensions of a social movement. In 1994 a total of 4,205 *rondas*, comprising almost a quarter of a million members, existed throughout the country. Despite occasional disputes with local military commanders, the *rondas* proved highly effective against the Shining Path. They also helped to improve the military's negative human rights image, which had soared during the previous decade as Peru gained the dubious distinction of being the number one violator in the world.

During the first eighteen months of his term, the president also took measures to curtail the booming coca trade in the Upper Huallaga. Coca was Peru's most important export, amounting to $1 billion annually, a third of all exports combined, and employed up to 15 percent of the workforce. The inflow of dollars from Colombian traffickers found their way to the informal foreign exchange market in Lima, where they were purchased by the Central Bank to help pay for Peru's bloated foreign debt. Given the importance of the country's coca trade to the economy, it is no wonder that Fujimori, reflecting public opinion, was not anxious to follow U.S. initiatives to step up the "war on drugs."

At first, Fujimori balked at signing an accord with the United States to fight the war. He complained that U.S. aid was mainly for military assistance and did not include enough for economic aid. However, after protracked negotiations, the two sides finally agreed, in May 1991, to the accord. Fujimori calculated that his plan to reinsert Peru into the world financial system would be hindered without such a drug enforcement agreement with the Collossus of the North. The subsequent aid package amounted to $60 million, with the bulk of it in military assistance and only 2 percent allocated for alternative development projects. Most of the Peruvian military effort, however, went toward fighting the Shining Path insurgency, which as you have seen, protected peasant producers in the Upper Huallaga. In effect, this meant that United States aid was used mainly for counterinsurgency operations against the Shining Path, rather than for the eradication or interdiction of drugs. After objections were raised in Congress over Peru's soaring human rights abuses, however, the military portion of the assistance was reduced somewhat and made contingent on improvements in the country's human rights record.

As Fujimori pushed forward his policy solutions to the economy, the guerrilla war, and the drug trade, he displayed an increasing arrogance and authoritarian tendency that rankled the opposition and the media. For example, he showed little disposition to negotiate with opposition members of Congress, and he arbitrarily made promotions and dismissals in the military to consolidate his support. Insiders related that the president liked power, and he was increasingly portrayed satirically in the media as a would-be Japanese emperor. Congress also became exasperated over the president's propensity to exceed the decree-issuing powers that it had granted him and his frequent intemperate criticism of the country's civilian institutions.

By the end of 1991, tensions began to increase between Congress and the Executive. In November, Fujimori issued a cascade of 120 decree laws just before his congressional authority was about to run out. Aimed at liberalizing the economy and restructuring the state, many of them involved controversial issues and exceeded congressional authorization. For example, one decree modified the 1969 land reform law, removing restrictions on the sale of land and the operation of agricultural enterprises. Another, which Fujimori euphemistically labeled "labor flexibilization," significantly altered existing labor laws regulating the right to organize and strike and job security. Still another established a committee to oversee the privatization of state-owned enterprises called the Committee for the Promotion of Private Investment.

Finally, in the area of counterinsurgency, the president responded to pressure from the armed forces to create special military courts to try suspected terrorists. This decree was in reaction to a notoriously low conviction rate (10 percent) in the civilian courts of suspected terrorists who managed to bribe and threaten judges to secure their release. Fujimori also decreed that members of the military could not be tried in civilian courts for human rights abuses, thereby virtually granting immunity to members of the armed forces.

The decree that gave the military even greater authority against terrorism responded to the growing threat of the Shining Path. The number of assasinations of public officials, priests, and civic leaders continued to rise (there were over 400 between 1988 and 1992). Moreover, the Shining Path's growing presence in Lima, particularly in the shantytowns, began to bring the war directly to the urban population. In an especially notorious attack, a Senderista assasination team killed community activist María Elena Moyano during a celebration of the Glass of Milk program in Villa El Salvador in February 1992 and then dynamited her body in front of her children and other celebrants. By now, the Shining Path was boasting of having reached "strategic parity" with the state, and Lima was increasingly gripped by a pervasive climate of fear and dispair over the growing levels of violence and economic chaos, even as the inflation rate was sharply dropping.

In the midst of the deteriorating situation, Fujimori shocked the country once more by carrying out an *autogolpe* (self-coup) on April 5, 1992. Ending twelve years of democratic government, the president suspended the Constitution, closed Congress, and ordered the arrest of several opposition leaders. With the backing of business and military leaders, he announced the creation of a "Government of Emergency and National Reconstruction" that would prepare the way for "true democracy." Justifying his actions, Fujimori blamed Congress for its "irresponsible, sterile, antihistoric and antipatriotic" behavior "which favors the interests of small groups and party leaders over the interests of Peru" (quoted in Rochabrun, 1996, p. 16). Shortly after the coup, Fujimori was greeted enthusiastically by crowds as he walked through the downtown streets of Lima.

Cameron attributed the *autogolpe* to "a complex set of conditions, including economic distress and violence, the decay of institutions and the collapse of political parties, the assertion of the military, and the reaction of the international community" (Cameron and Manceri, 1997, p. 68). At the same time, however, he pointed out that it could not have been successful without the support of the Peruvian people. In this respect, the self-coup proved to be widely popular with most Peruvians, who seemed to agree that the country needed a stronger government to deal with the ongoing crisis. Public opinion polls indicated that an astonishing 70 percent of the population supported the self-coup.

Although Fujimori charged Congress with obstructing his economic program and the judiciary with hindering the fight against terrorism, political motives also lay behind his action. In addition to closing Congress, soldiers sought unsuccessfully to arrest Alan García, who the government feared would become the leader of the opposition by exploiting the social costs of the austerity program and thereby positioning himself for a return to the presidency in the 1995 elections. Having been accused of widespread corruption during his term in office, García nevertheless enjoyed the privilege of immunity from prosection as Senator-for-Life, a privilege granted to former presidents that the Senate had refused to overturn. Fujimori, blocked by the Constitution from seeking a second term, fully realized the potential of the charismatic García, now once again general secretary of his party, to obstruct his programs and make another bid to return to power in a scant thirty months.

While remaining popular at home, Fujimori was widely criticized abroad for his abrogation of democracy. Many countries, including the United States, suspended economic aid and withdrew their support, thereby jepordizing Peru's reintegration into the world economy on which Fujimori's economic recovery plan rested. As a result, Fujimori backtracked and agreed in a speech to the Organization of American States (OAS) in May to call elections for a constituent assembly to rewrite the Constitution and to hold municipal elections later in the year. This plan seemed to satisfy the international community, which seemed to be more concerned over the threat of the Shining Path, the progress of drug trafficking, and the prospects of economic liberalization than over the setback to democracy.

Despite his retreat on the matter of elections, the president proceeded, with the support of the armed forces, to rule by decree, concentrating all the powers of the state in his hands. One of his first acts was to dismantle the judiciary, which had remained packed with García appointees. Thirteen Supreme Court judges and more than 100 lower-court judges and prosecutors were replaced, and the president, despite considerable criticism from human rights organizations, moved ahead to establish secret military tribunals to try suspected terrorists. It may be said that, to a great extent Peruvian democracy had been undone by its inability to deal with counterinsurgency.

On the other hand, the Shining Path welcomed the *auto-golpe*, long believing that dictatorship would lead to intensified and indiscriminate state repression, thus increasing the polarization of the country from which it would ultimately benefit. In July it unleashed an offensive that included the bombing of a television station in Lima and a car bombing in an affluent suburb that killed 21 and injured 250, while nationwide the offensive left 179 people dead. Then just as its leader Abimael Guzmán was apparently preparing "Operation Conquer Lima," he was suddenly captured on September 12 in a suburban Lima safe house by the Peruvian national intelligence police (DINCOTE). Although Fujimori was quick to claim credit for Guzmán's capture, the operation was the culmination of intensified intelligence work since 1990 that had targeted the Shining Path's leadership for capture. In fact, it was directed by General Antonio Vidal, who had been appointed to head DINCOTE by former President García. Trailing a suspected Senderista who had been released from jail to Guzmán's hiding place, DINCOTE agents carried out a flawlessly executed stakeout, disguising themselves as city employees, street peddlers and "guests" at a nearby backyard barbecue. At a propitious moment, thirty-five agents burst into the house and peacefully apprehended the leader, who allegedly exclaimed to his captors, "Now it's my turn to lose."

DINCOTE agents also arrested two other top Shining Path leaders and, even more important, discovered the master computer files to the entire organization. This bonanza of information led to additional police roundups that netted more than 1,000 suspects within a few weeks. By the year's end, nine-tenths of the movement's high leadership had been captured, and Guzmán had been brought to trial before a hooded navy judge, who sentenced him to life in prison. The image caught on television weeks earlier of a paunchy middle-aged man with a scruffy beard and thick glasses, meekly zipping up his trousers, did much to dispel the mystique of invincibility that had grown around Guzmán and his movement.

The mystique was further punctured when the imprisoned Shining Path leader petitioned the president for peace, calling on his followers to lay down their arms and negotiate with the government. This act had the effect of virtually recognizing Fujimori as the victor in the long war and causing consternation and division among the remnants of the Shining Path's leadership. A hard-line faction proceeded to reorganize under new leaders and refused to recognize Guzmán's entreaties for peace. Nevertheless, a series of amnesties, or "repentance" laws, over the next two years decimated the ranks of the insurgency. The program offered a variety of benefits to guerrillas who surrendered and officially yielded some 5,500 defections from the Shining Path and over 800 from the MRTA between 1992 and 1994. Driven from the Upper Huallaga by the Shining Path, which had defeated its attempt to horn in on its lucrative "protection racket," MRTA had retreated to the cities and its urban roots. This retreat had exposed its organization to the security forces, and many of its cells were broken up and its leaders imprisoned. One MRTA leader, however, the former textile union official Néstor Cerpa Carolini, escaped to Ecuador.

Although the capture of Guzmán in September dealt a huge blow to the Shining Path, the level of violent terrorist attacks did not immediately abate. Moreover, the government was soon threatened from another quarter. On November 13, only weeks before the elections for the Constituent Assembly were to take place, retired General Jaime Salinas Sedo led an attempted coup against Fujimori. Salinas had been one of the victims of Fujimori's interference in the military's merit-based promotion-and-retirement process, having been forced into early retirement for political reasons. Proclaiming a desire to return the country to democratic rule, Salinas had counted on support among those in the armed forces who had seen little improvement in their economic condition. Salaries for a division general, for example, were only $283 per month, while a second lieutenant earned only $213 a month. There was also considerable dislike in military circles for Fujimori's national security adviser Vladimiro Montesinos, who orchestrated most of the decisions about high-level military personnel. Fujimori learned of the plot and managed to escape to the Japanese Embassy before the plotters, who planned to break into the National Palace, were arrested and the movement was foiled.

The capture of Guzmán had given a significant boost to Fujimori at the time of the November elections for the Constituent Assembly, or Democratic Constituent Congress (Congreso Constituente Democrático—CCD) as it was called. As announced in the details worked out in July and August, the CCD was to be a single chamber, composed of 80 members whose terms would last until the end of Fujimori's term on July 28, 1995. The CCD was charged with writing a new constitution, subject to approval by a national plebiscite, as well as proposing new legislation and exercising the power of oversight over the executive. How the latter would work in practice, however, remained vague and unspecified.

The government also tried to manipulate the outcome of the November elections, despite increased public support for Fujimori after the capture of Guzmán. The president's personal popularity, however, was not easily transferred to his party, which was renamed Nueva Mayoría/Cambio 90 and reorganized by Jaime Yoshiyama, an engineer and member of the president's cabinet. Several of the main opposition parties, including APRA, AP, and Vargas Llosa's Libertad abstained from the vote while the United Left and Socialist Accord were unable to participate because they had failed to receive the minimum 5 percent necessary to qualify in the previous election. Facing only the PPC and a number of other minor parties and groups, many of them lesser-known stand-ins for the traditional parties, Nueva Mayoría/Cambio 90 won a 38 percent plurality of the vote and a majority of 44 out of 80 seats. However, the vote could not be seen as truly representative. Although there was some opposition representation as the newly elected body set out to write a new constitution, Fujimori was able to use his party's majority, as well as his power of veto, to control the assembly and shape the final document to his liking.

Meanwhile, as the CCD began its work in late January 1993, the promised, but delayed municipal elections finally took place. This time, the traditional parties all participated in the elections, but with mixed results. In Lima independent Ricardo Belmont easily won reelection as mayor with an impressive 44 percent of the vote in a field of 40 candidates. His party

Obras swept to victory in most districts in the capital, whereas the Left won only one district and APRA and the PPC garnered only 3 percent and 2 percent of the vote, respectively. Nationally, the traditional parties did better, receiving approximately 40 percent of the vote, but with independents winning the majority of the municipalties. Significantly, Fujimori's party Nueva Mayoría/Cambio 90 fared badly, winning only one municipality.

The results of these elections, as well as data from polls suggest that more than halfway through his term, Fujimori continued to retain the overall support of the public. This support was based primarily on the *autogolpe*, the capture of Guzmán, and the sharp decline in inflation. However, there was dissatisfaction over the depth of the recession and the widening circle of poverty caused by the austerity program, which now claimed upward of two-thirds of the population. Still the opposition remained weak, divided, and essentially leaderless (García had managed to slip into exile), allowing Fujimori to continue to dominate the country and shape its political institutions.

This fact was confirmed in the plebiscite held in October 1993 on the proposed new Constitution. The CCD had done its work and produced a new constitutional document that was more than satisfactory to Fujimori. For one thing, it permitted the reelection of the president, clearing the way for Fujimori's candidacy in 1995. It also tightened the laws on terrorism by reinstituting the death penalty and institutionalizing the trial of suspected terrorists in secret military courts. In addition, the new Constitution did much to consolidate the institutional power at the top that Fujimori had acquired from his *autogolpe*. It created a more centralized state, dominated by a powerful chief executive who presided over a unicameral Congress with few checks on presidential authority. In short, the new Constitution that was about to be submitted to the voters was tailored to serve as the legal basis for a regime that was increasingly characterized as autocratic, arbitrary, and unrestrained by institutional constraints. In the words of Cameron, it "institutionalized a semi-authoritarian political system."

Calling for a straight yes-or-no vote by the public, the plebiscite on the new charter won approval by a 52 percent to 48 percent vote. This was a surprisingly close result, certainly not the 70–30 percent approval rating predicted by the president. The government won in Lima but lost in the provinces, causing a major magazine to proclaim Fujimore "the president of Lima." More important, the lower percentage of the urban poor and a higher percentage of the wealthy voted yes than in the 1990 elections. It appears that the social costs of stablilization without the promised safety net had hurt the government in both the provinces and Lima's shantytowns. On the other hand, the economic benefits of economic liberalization had almost immediately benefited the upper-income groups, which ironically had favored Vargas Llosa in 1990. Despite offical machinations to influence the vote, an OAS team that was sent to monitor the fairness of the elections concluded that no major fraud had occurred and certified the outcome.

The closeness of the plebiscite, however, caused Fujimori to reassess his program more than half way through his term and only two years from the 1995 elections in which he could now legally run. Indeed, postelection public opinion polls showed that support for the president was slipping among the lower-income groups. Opponents once again began criticizing the government's failure to generate growth or real income, which remained at 1988 levels. Clearly, the president needed to increase the level of social spending to alleviate the severe distress of the urban and rural poor who were the backbone of his support.

Fortunately for Fujimori, the opportunity to revive governmental social spending presented itself in the windfall revenues that suddenly materialized as a result of the program to sell off state-owned enterprises. This program had gotten off to a slow start after the passage of a new privatization law in 1991, which established a governmental commission (COPRI) to sell off or liquidate all state-owned enterprises. The initial reaction from the private sector was skeptical, as reflected in an editorial in Lima's most influential economic newsletter. "Who will invest in this terror-infested, low exchange rate, hugely high interest rate, volitile environment?" (quoted by Wise in Cameron and Mauceri, 1997, p. 102). Accordingly, over the next twelve months, only 12 out of a possible 135 to 182 publically owned firms had been sold. The program finally gained some momentum a year later, when in December 1992, the state-run iron mining company Hierroperú was sold to a Chinese firm for $311.8 million. Still, as late as early 1994, less than $500 million in state assets had been sold off.

Two factors accounted for the program's gradual success: Fujimori's *autogolpe* of April 5, which negated congressional opposition to the program, and a marked decline in the international perception of the risks of investing in Peru. Inflation was down, the Shining Path had been severely crippled by its leaders' arrests, and terrorist violence was beginning to show signs of diminishing. Moreover, the economy, after suffering a brief downturn after the *autogolpe* because of the flight of capital and the cutoff of foreign loans (upward of $2 billion) because of international displeasure, finally began to grow again. The GDP registered a 6.9 percent gain in 1993 and would be followed by a 12.9 percent gain in 1994, the first increases since 1991.

Then in February 1994, the privatization program scored a major success with the sale of the state-owned telephone and telecommunications companies to an international consortium headed by Telefónica of Spain. The favorable price of the sale, a whopping $2 billion, was more than four times the price set by the government. About $1.4 billion of the sale went immediately into the treasury, amounting to 57 percent of the annual value of exports and 5.2 percent of the GDP. This success had a favorable impact on the sale of other state-owned companies in the petroleum, mining, and electricity sectors. Thus, by the end of 1994, the government had sold or was set to sell most of the private companies that had been nationalized during the period of military rule from 1968 to 1980. The total inflow of these revenues to the treasury exceeded $3 billion by the middle of 1995.

While businesses clamored for tax relief and the IMF clamored for increased debt payments, political reasons largely dictated how this privatization dividend was to be used. However, how to use them without retriggering inflation was a concern, not to mention the fact that any decision would have to be cleared with the international lending agencies whose policy of conditionality controlled the flow of loans to Peru. Progress had been made on the debt, particularly after Fujimori responded to international criticism of the *autogolpe* and agreed to hold elections. In mid-1993, the government reached a highly favorable agreement with the Paris Club of Western creditors to reschedule and reduce some $8 billion in the country's debt. This agreement opened the way for $500 million in foreign direct investments that entered Peru over the next six months.

As financial conditions improved, Fujimori seized the opportunity to shore up his 1995 reelection chances while silencing his critics over the dearth of social spending. In February 1994, he went on television to announce that half the privatization dividend would be earmarked for that purpose. Three months later, the IMF was persuaded to authorize the government to spend $875 million on social programs. By midyear, with the economy continuing to grow, the president was promising to create a million new jobs in construction and public works and to build one school a day for the rest of the year and two to three per day in 1995.

In addition to revenues from privatization and improved debt-servicing arrangements, state finances were strengthened by tax reform during Fujimori's term. Peru's tax revenues had fallen to only 6.5 percent of GDP in 1989, well under the 10 percent that was generally considered adequate. Tax reform, therefore, was high on Fujimori's policy agenda when he took office in 1990. As a result, Fujimori reorganized the Superintendent of Tax Administration (SUNAT), revamped the customs administration (SUNAD), and began to revise the tax laws. The state of tax collection in Peru at the time was truly archane. There were some 200 different kinds of taxes and 33 different taxpayer classifications, and the rules governing taxes fluctuated sharply each year. To attack these problems, SUNAT and SUNAD were streamlined, the number of taxes were slashed, and individual and property taxes were raised.

As a result of these changes, the extractive capabilities of the state improved dramatically. The percentage of taxes collected to the GDP rose to 8 percent in 1991 and 10 percent in 1992. One of the effects of the reforms was to centralize further Executive control over fiscal policy at the expense of municipal governments. On one level, this move was seen as an effort by Fujimori to undermine the financial base of rival mayors, particularly the popular Daniel Estrada of Cuzco and Ricardo Belmont of Lima, as well as those who had organized a no vote on the plebiscite. It also revived the age-old dispute between regionalism and centralism in the country. On the other hand, as a result of the increased revenues from tax reforms, together with those from the privatization program, the Central Bank's reserves climbed from a deficit of $143 million left by the García government to over $6 billion by the end of 1994.

With adequate revenues under increased Executive control and a growing economy, Fujimori was able to undertake an effective populist campaign for reelection in 1995. Dipping into the Central Banks' reserves, the Ministry of Economy and Finance withdrew $500 million, or 6 percent, for governmental spending on infrastructural improvements and public works. The key to the political uses of the social spending program was the president's greater decision making and budgetary control over the ministries. Although power had always been concentrated in the Executive, during his first term Fujimori worked relentlessly to expand presidential control. This tendency accelerated after the *autogolpe* when budgetary allocations became more concentrated in the Ministry of the Presidency, which heretofore had access to only 1 percent of the budget, but by 1994 had access to 14 percent. The upshot was that Fujimori could now effectively micromanage the government's social programs, targeting specific areas and sectors of the population for maximum political impact. In effect, the Ministry of the Presidency had assumed a monopoly over public works and social projects.

The National Development and Social Compensation Fund (FONCODES) was one of the most important social development agencies, particularly on matters of employment, health, nutrition, basic education, and other areas benefiting the population in poverty. By mid-1994, fewer than nine months before the scheduled elections, the number of social assistance projects (4,760) and jobs (23,000 a month) that FONCODES funded and managed had increased dramatically. Geographically, they were targeted for the poorest departments in the country and those with the highest unemployment rates.

FONCODES was complemented by the National Housing Fund (FONAVI) and the National Nutritional Assistance Program (PRONAA), both also managed through the Ministry of the Presidency. FONAVI was responsible for a veritable explosion in the construction of low-cost housing, schools, and medical clinics in the urban shantytowns and elsewhere. PRONAA accelerated the distribution of food rations aimed at increasing the nutritional level of poor children. It bypassed both the grassroots *Vaso de Leche* program and the 7,000-odd communal kitchens with ties to the Catholic Church, which were considered "competitors" in a policial sense to the Fujimori government. As election day approached, Fujimori adopted a high-visibility "shuttle strategy," making daily personal visits, often by helicopter, to these projects and programs to maximize media and public relations exposure in behalf of his campaign.

That the air force assisted in moving the president around the country quickly to attend these ceremonial and public relations functions was significant. It highlighted the fact that the armed forces had become the principal institutional vehicle to deliver these services and the related political message. Indeed, as the threat of the Shining Path began to fade in the wake of the capture of Guzmán and much of the movement's high command, the military increasingly assumed a civic action role that the president could easily exploit politically.

In addition, in many parts of the highlands, the armed forces were the only functional arm of the state still in existence. This was particularly the case in the Emergency Zones, where military commanders were the maximum political authority and the effort at reconstruction was already under way. The existence and effectiveness at the community level of the *rondas*, organized to combat the Shining Path, could now be diverted by the government to assist in reconstruction and the delivery of social services. At the same time, Fujimori's grip on the armed forces tightened as a consequence of the *autogolpe*, so that in return for perks and benefits from the government, the institution could be mobilized by its leaders to play an important organizational role in the president's reelection.

Therefore, the military increasingly took on the governmental tasks of distributing food and services and managing infrastructural projects. It was, of course, an easy additional step to have soldiers take on some campaign functions—posters, propagandizing, and generally promoting Fujimori's political campaign. In effect, the armed forces became, according to Kay (1996, p. 31), a surrogate party in the highlands for the president's bid for reelection.

With his unique brand of "Fujipopulism" and the apparatus of the state firmly in his grasp, the president confidently approached the 1995 presidential elections. Such could hardly be said of the political opposition. Afterall, the traditional parties, under Fujimori's relentlessly effective attack for their alleged incompetance and corruption, were in a complete state of exhaustion and decomposition and were the objects of the voters' disdain. Moreover, most voters had, in Cameron's view (1994), rejected the class-based, ideologically polarized party affiliations of previous decades and declared themselves politically independent, that is, nonideological and pragmatic, as Fujimori had correctly divined.

Finally, it is clear that the voters in 1995, as in 1990 after the traumatic previous decade, craved order and economic stability over social justice and democracy, the twin themes of 1980 (Kay, 1996, p. 40). Fujimori had finally delivered on these demands, having crushed runaway inflation and defeated the Shining Path. Indeed, in some ways, Fujimori had, in Stern's view (1996, ms. p. 45) succeeded in assuming some of the mythic mantle of his now-vanquished revolutionary opponent Guzmán, who had also promised order and efficiency, albeit along the lines of a new, utopian communism, rather than neoliberal capitalism.

It is not surprising, then, that Fujimori's opponents in the election all described themselves as "independents" and "outsiders." The most well known, at least internationally, was former Secretary General Javier Pérez de Cuellar, who had just stepped down after a distinguished two terms as head of the United Nations. Also throwing their hats in the ring were popular Lima mayor Ricardo Belmont and economist Alejandro Toledo, whose main claim to the candidacy seemed to be his Indian origins and credentials as a former visiting professor at Harvard University. APRA, which Fujimori had managed to keep under a cloud by pursuing corruption charges against former President García, tried to regroup by nominating congresswoman Mercedes Cabanillas as its candidate. In retrospect, none of Fujimori's opponents had much of a chance of winning against the "institutional machinery of Fujipopulism."

Not that Fujimori took his reelection in any way for granted. On the one hand, he campaigned indefatigably in the highlands, shantytowns, and jungle regions of the country where his popular clientele resided. In doing so, he assumed the role of benefactor, bestowing the largesse of his cash-flush social program before large, appreciative crowds with the television cameras rolling. At the same time, the president used his huge powers of office to enhance his electoral chances for victory in other similarly traditional, if manipulative, ways. For example, he encouraged the number and proliferation of candidates, nineteen in all, to divide the opposition vote. He also had his name and picture strategically placed on the ballot to the disadvantage of his opponents.

When the votes were finally tallied on April 9, 1995, Fujimori had won 64 percent of the vote. However, this seemingly overwhelming victory was deceiving, for this time around the government calculated the percentage on the basis of excluding, rather than including, the number of votes that were null and void. This method increased his overall percentage substantially, for had the votes been calculated in the same manner as in 1990, Fujimori would have won only 52 percent of the vote. Nevertheless, the president did manage to put together the same winning coalition as in 1990, that is, the rural and urban popular classes, with support from the urban middle and upper classes. Everywhere that Fujimori targeted his social assistance and infrastructure spending, he won handily, including Puno (64 percent), which had rejected his Constitution only sixteen months earlier.

The election results for Congress revealed that the traditional parties were all but dead. Fujimori's Cambio 90/Nueva Mayoría narrowly won a majority of 52 percent, which translated into a surprising 67 out of 120 seats in the Congress. But the four established parties combined (APRA, AP, PC, IU) received only 12 percent of the vote. In fact, none received the necessary 5 percent required by the National Elections Tribunal to qualify as continuing parties. Although there was plenty of evidence of official manipulation and some "local irregularities" in the election, foreign observers who were invited to monitor the elections declared them essentially "free and fair."

The election campaign itself, however, was overshadowed by the brief border war that erupted between Peru and Ecuador on January 26, 1995. Although a declaration of peace was signed three weeks later, on February 17, the fighting claimed over 300 casualties on both sides, as well as a combined $500 million in costs. It was the most serious outbreak of violence between the the the two sides since the 1941 war. Needless to say, the combat news from the front tended to push the electoral campaign into the background, although there is no evidence that the war was provoked by the government to divert public attention from domestic problems.

Clashes along the fifty-mile portion of the Amazonian border area, which had never been officially adjudicated and demarcated, had occurred regularly over the past fifteen years. But none had led to serious hostilities, until January, when Ecuadorian incursions were unsuccessfully challenged by the Peruvian forces stationed in the area. Unlike previous incursions, this time the Ecuadorians were not only better equipped and prepared, but willing to press the fight, rather than retreat. Ecuador had also established permanent bases in the region of the Cenapa River, which had been undetected by Peruvian forces and could not be captured. The February cease-fire was agreed to by both sides on the basis of the Rio Protocol of 1942. It provided for the guarantor nations (Argentina, Brazil, Chile, and the United States) to provide military observers to oversee and monitor a demilitarized zone in the disputed border region.

While hostilities temporarily heated up in early 1995 along the Peru-Ecuador border, the internal war with the Shining Path was winding down. After the capture of Guzmán in 1992, the level and intensity of Senderista attacks began to wane noticeably by the middle of 1993. As Guzmán languished in jail under a life sentence, a hard-line faction that rejected his call for "peace talks" with the government tried to reorganize the movement as Sendero Rojo (Red Path), led by Oscar Ramírez Durán alias "Comrade Feliciano." Capable of carrying out occasional acts of bombing or assassination, Sendero Rojo nevertheless spent much of its energy avoiding the army—becoming little more than a shadow of the party's former self.

Fujimori's First Term Assessed

At the close of Fujimori's first five years in office, what can be said about his administration? Clearly, one of the president's greatest successes was the defeat of the Shining Path guerrilla insurgency, which in 1990 appeared to some observers to be on the verge of seizing power. The fifteen-year battle, dating from 1980, had cost the country some 35,000 lives and economic losses estimated at $25 billion. Now that Guzmán was behind bars and the movement was dispersed, the government was able to turn its attention to the reconstruction of the country.

Similarly, during his first term, Fujimori succeeded in stablizing an economy that was spiraling out of control. In 1989 the last year of the García government, the economy contracted 11.7 percent and inflation reached an all-time high of 7,649 percent. Shortly after his election, Fujimori chose to institute a harsh stabilization program, which succeeded in breaking the back of hyperinflation whose adverse effects were born most heavily by the poor. Nevertheless, the social costs of Fujishock were enormous, despite substantial grassroots and international efforts, with hunger, malnutrition, and even starvation prevalent in many parts of the country.

Over the next five years, Fujimori opened the country's closed, protected, and highly regulated economy to the free market and international trade and investment. Tariffs were reduced from 66 percent to 15.7 percent; 173 out of 183 state companies were privatized; and the number of public employees was cut in half, from 470,000 to 210,000. Economic liberalization and reform, together with the halt in inflation, defeat of terrorism, and renewed payments on the foreign debt, set the stage for the country's reentrance into the international economy and, by 1993, a resumption in economic growth.

These achievements, however, came at substantial human and institutional costs. For one thing, the president's *autogolpe* in 1992 and authoritarian style, which earned him the popular sobriquet Chinochet, although arguably needed to deal with the deepening economic crisis and terrorist threat, ended more than a decade of democratization. Since then, Fujimori has ruled largely by decree, subordinated the Congress to his authority, and increased the powers of the armed forces and the intelligence service. He has also purged the courts; ignored official corruption; attacked the country's democratic institutions, including the political parties; and consistently overlooked human rights violations by the armed forces. Indeed, the 1995 amnesty law allowed soldiers who were convicted of human rights crimes to go free.

As for improving the performance and efficiency of the state, Fujimori's record is mixed. He inherited a government that had already shrunk to less than one-quarter of its previous size, as measured by per capita spending, which, according to Webb (1991), fell by 83 percent between 1975 and 1990. The president continued to reduce the size of the government through layoffs and budget cuts, reformed and streamlined the tax system, and renegotiated the country's external debt. These and other selective reorganizational efforts led Cameron and Mauceri to conclude that there are now "developmental 'islands of efficiency' in an otherwise weak and ineffective public sector" (1997, conclusion).

Of course, by continuing to run the country from the Executive branch and delegating little power outside his tight circle of associates, Fujimori may have succeeded in "getting things done." But he has done so at the expense of undermining the country's representative institutions and marginalizing the civil society. In short, in assessing Fujimori's first term, one must say that the restoration of political and economic order in Peru has come at the expense of the "withering" of democracy, the weakening of the state, and the widespread social deterioration of the population.

Chronology

2500 B.C.	Beginnings of village farming and fishing
1800 B.C.	Introduction of corn, development of irrigation, and beginnings of ceramics
800 B.C.	Chavín, first Pan-Andean civilization
100 B.C.	Rise of the coastal cultures of Moche and Nasca
A.D. 600	Tiahuanaco (Tiwanaku) and Huari (Wari) Empires flourish in the southern Andes
A.D. 850–900	City of Chan-Chan constructed as the capital of the Chimor Empire near Trujillo
A.D. 1200–1400	Formative period of the Incas
A.D. 1400–1500	Inca imperial expansion
1492	Spanish reconquest completed, Jews expelled from the Iberian Peninsula, and Columbus encounters a "New World," inaugurating a biological and cultural exchange
1525	Death of Huayna Capac ignites Inca civil war
1532	Arrival of Spanish in Peru; Pizarro captures Atahualpa at Cajamarca
1532–72	Period of Spanish conquest
1533	Spaniards capture Cuzco
1534	Franciscan order arrives in Peru
1535	Pizarro founds the City of the Kings, or Lima
1536	Rebellion of Manco Inca; formation of neo-Inca state at Vitcos, Vilcabamba
1537	Almagro returns from Chile and rebels
1538	Pizarro defeats Almagro at the Battle of Salinas
1541	Pizarro is assassinated
1542	Audiencia established in Lima; the crown decrees New Laws to limit the enslavement of Indians and the *encomienda*
1543	Viceroyalty of Peru created with its capital in Lima
1544	Gonzalo Pizarro's coup kills Viceroy Blasco Núñez de Vela
1545	Discovery of silver mines at Cerro Rico (Potosí)

1548	Rebellion of Gonzalo Pizarro defeated and royal authority restored
1551	University of San Marcos founded in Lima
1555	Philip II succeeds Charles V as king of Spain
1564	Taki Onqoy "conspiracy" discovered at Huamanga
1569	Viceroy Toledo arrives in Peru
1570	Holy Office of the Inquisition established in Lima
1571–82	Toledo implements colonial reform program
1571	Patio silver-refining process introduced at Potosí; Indians ordered to congregate into *reducciones*
1572	Neo-Inca state at Vitcos, Vilcabamba conquered, and the last Inca, Túpac Amaru I, executed at Cuzco
1573	First *mita* labor recruits arrive at Potosí
1583	Arrival of first printing press in Lima
1609	Garcilaso de la Vega publishes *Comentarios reales de los Incas*
1610	Population of Lima estimated at 25,000
1610–60	Campaign to Extirpate Idolatry
1617	Isabel Flores de Oliva dies in Lima, later canonized as Santa Rosa de Lima
1630	New silver mine discovered at Cerro de Pasco
1633	Crown decrees the sale of imperial offices in the New World
1650	Population of Potosí peaks at 160,000
1650s	Beginning of century-long crisis in silver output at Potosí
1657–60	English pirate Sir Francis Drake plunders Peru's coast
1681	Four-volume *Recopilación de las leyes de Indias* published
1687	Severe earthquake devastates the central coast
1700	Last Hapsburg king Charles II dies and is succeeded by Philip V, the Bourbon grandson of Louis XIV
1701–13	War of Spanish Succession
1718–21	Pan Andean epidemic of the plague kills 300,000
1742	Juan Santos Atahualpa proclaims himself Inca and rises in rebellion in the Amazon
1750	Population of Potosí declines to 30,000
1759	Reforming Bourbon monarch Charles III ascends the throne of Spain
1767	Jesuit order expelled, and holdings estimated at 5.7 million pesos confiscated

1776	New Viceroyalty of the River Plate created; North American colonies win independence from England
1778	Spanish crown decrees "free trade" within the empire
1780–82	Massive Rebellion of Túpac Amaru II claims 100,000 lives
1784	Crown abolishes the hated *reparto de mercancía* and office of the *corregidor de indios*
1784–90	Viceroyalty divided into seven intendencies
1789	French Revolution
1792	Census estimates the population of Peru at around 1 million
1796	Spain goes to war against England, adversely affecting international trade
1808	Napoleon invades Spain, and the Royal Government collapses
1810	Local governing juntas replace peninsular governments in major South American cities, but not in Peru
1812	Spanish Cortes convenes in Cádiz and decrees a liberal constitution
1814	Ferdinand VII restored to the throne of Spain and abolishes the liberal Constitution of 1812
1814	Rebellion against the crown erupts in Cuzco
1820–21	General San Martín's army of liberation invades Peru, captures Lima, and declares Peru independent
1822	San Martín meets Bolívar in Guayaquil and later resigns as ruler
1824	Battle of Ayacucho; General Sucre defeats the royalist army commanded by Viceroy Serna, securing the independence of Peru and South America
1821–45	Early republic marked by extreme political instability during which there were twenty-four regime changes and the Constitution was rewritten six times
1836–39	Peru and Bolivia form a confederation led by General Santa Cruz
1845–1862	Era of General Castilla, who establishes a *pax An-dina* of relative political stability and economic progress based on guano and nitrate exports
1849–74	Arrival in Peru of some 100,000 Chinese coolies to work in the guano islands, railroad construction, and coastal plantations

1851	Tariffs lowered inaugurating a new era of free trade; first operative railroad in South America opened between Lima and Callao
1854	Castilla emancipates the slaves
1858	Castilla suppresses bloody protectionist riots by Lima artisans protesting the flood of inexpensive imported goods
1866	Spanish fleet bombards Callao, but is repulsed and eventually withdraws from the Pacific after a brief war (1865–68) with Peru, Chile, and Ecuador
1868	President Balta contracts with American Henry Meiggs to construct a railroad system
1869	Finance Minister Piérola shifts the contract for guano exports from national contractors to a French company headed by Auguste Dreyfus
1870	Bloody Chinese uprising of coolies, known as "the rebellion of the painted faces," erupts on a north-coast plantation
1872	Pardo is elected first civilian president
1873	Onset of the worldwide depression that severely affects Peru; President Pardo decrees the establishment of a state nitrate monopoly in the face of drastically falling guano prices and state revenues; Peru signs mutual defense treaty with Bolivia
1876	Peru forced to default on foreign debt
1879–83	The War of the Pacific in which Peru loses its southern provinces of Tarapacá and Arica to Chile
1885	Massive Indian rebellion in the northern highlands of Ancash, led by Atusparia
1886	Controversial Grace contract signed, which canceled foreign debt in return for major concessions to British bondholders
1895	Piérola assumes the presidency after a bloody civil war
1895–1919	Era of relative political peace and export-led prosperity based on elite rule known as the "Aristocratic Republic"
1912–14	Guillermo Billinghurst elected president on a populist platform; deposed in a military coup led by General Benavides
1914–18	World War I inaugurates a period of socioeconomic and political upheaval in Peru
1918–19	Series of worker-student strikes leading to the establishment of the eight-hour day and university reform
1919–30	*Oncenio*, eleven-year rule of President Leguía, marked by heavy foreign investment and curtailment of civil liberties

1923	Popular demonstrations against regime's attempt to dedicate Peru to the Sacred Heart of Jesus
1924	Founding in Mexico of the Alianza Popular Revolucionaria Americana (APRA Party) by Haya de la Torre
1930	Death of Mariátegui, leading intellectual and founder of the Peruvian Communist Party
1930	Coup led by Lieutenant Colonel Sánchez Cerro deposes Leguía, inaugurating a period of economic and political instability
1931	Peru suspends payment on the national debt
1932	Popular uprising in Trujillo severely repressed by the army, which leads to enduring political enmity between the armed forces and APRA
1932–33	Border war with Colombia fought over disputed territory in Leticia
1933	President Sánchez Cerro assassinated by Aprista militant, leading to the second presidency of General Benavides
1940	National census reveals a population of 6.2 million, up from 2.6 million in 1876 census
1941	Brief border war with Ecuador
1945–48	Bustamante y Rivera elected president with support from the APRA Party, legalized for the first time since 1932
1948	Callao naval revolt weakens Bustamante regime and leads to successful coup by General Odría
1950	Founding of the Centro de Altos Studios Militares (CAEM)
1955	Enfranchisement of women
1956	*Convivencia* (pact) between the APRA and the ruling elite legalizes the party for the first time since 1948
1962–63	Military coup in the wake of inconclusive national elections leads to rule by a junta representing the three branches of the armed forces
1963–68	Democratic rule restored with the election of Belaúnde Terry as president
1965	Armed forces violently suppress three highland guerrilla movements
1968–75	Coup led by General Velasco Alvarado deposes the Belaúnde regime and inaugurates an unprecedented period of social and economic reform
1969	Beginning of radical agrarian reform

1975	Bloody police strike and urban riots lead to a coup, led by General Morales Bermúdez, deposing Velasco
1975–80	Morales regime dismantles many of Velasco's reforms and leads a transition back to civilian rule
1980	Belaúnde Terry is reelected president; Sendero Luminoso, or Shining Path, guerrilla movement unleashes "Peoples' War"
1985	García Pérez elected first Aprista president in history amid economic decline and deepening guerrilla violence by the Shining Path
1990	Political unknown Alberto Fujimori is surprisingly elected president and undertakes a severe economic austerity program and army-led campaign against the Shining Path
1991	Outbreak of cholera, not seen since the nineteenth century, symbolizes the socioeconomic crisis of the past decade
1992	*Autogolpe* (self-coup) by President Fujimori suspends the Constitution and closes Congress; Shining Path leader Abimael Guzmán captured in Lima
1995	Fujimori reelected president

Tables and Charts

Table 1. Economic and Other Data

	1980	1985	1989	1990
GDP (millions, 1980 $)[a]	20,579	20,167	19,500	18,418
GDP per Capita (1980 $)[a]	1,190	1,039	924	854

GDP Growth Rates (1990 prices)[b]

	1991	1992	1993	1994	1995	1996	1997	Average 1981–90	Average 1991–97
Latin America	3.5	3.0	3.9	5.4	0.2	3.5	5.3	1.0	3.5
Peru	2.8	−0.9	5.8	13.8	7.8	2.5	7.0	−1.2	5.4

GDP per Capita Growth Rates[b]

	1991	1992	1993	1994	1995	1996	1997	Average 1981–90	Average 1991–97
Latin America	1.7	1.2	2.1	3.7	−1.5	1.9	3.6	−1.0	1.8
Peru	0.9	−2.6	4.0	11.9	6.0	0.7	5.1	−3.3	3.6

Structure of Production (% of GNP)[a]: Agriculture, 11%; Industry, 43%; Services, 46%

Export Composition ($6.8 billion, 1997)[a]
copper, zinc, fishmeal, crude petroleum and byproducts, lead, refined silver, coffee, cotton
Partners: U.S. 19%, Japan 9%, Italy, Germany (1995)

Import composition ($8.6 billion, 1997)[a]
machinery, transport equipment, foodstuffs, petroleum, iron and steel, chemicals, pharmaceuticals
Partners: U.S. 21%, Colombia, Chile, Argentina, Japan, Germany, Brazil (1995)

Table 1. *Continued*

Balance of Payments (millions of $)[e]

	Trade Balance	Exports	Imports
1987	−500.0	2715.0	3215.0
1988	−134.0	2731.0	2865.0
1989	246.0	3533.0	2286.0
1990	399.0	3321.0	2922.0
1991	189.0	3406.0	3595.0
1992	−340.0	3661.0	4001.0
1993	−599.0	3523.0	4123.0
1994	−972.0	4574.0	5545.0
1995	−2111.0	5576.0	7687.0
1996	−1996.0	5897.0	7893.0

External Debt: $23.4 billion (1996)

Average Real Wages (1990 = 100)

	Real Wages	Growth Rates[c]
1987		6.1
1988		−23.6
1989		−46.7
1990		−14.4
1991	115.2	15.2
1992	111.1	−3.6
1993	110.2	−0.8
1994	127.4	14.9
1995	116.7	−8.4
1996	111.2	−4.5
1997	111.0	

Poverty (% of population)[d]

Moderate		Extreme	
1990	1995	1990	1995
39.6	13.4	8.7	7.7

Income Distribution-Gini index (1994)
−44.9

Major Ethnic Groups[a]

Amerindian	45%
Mestizo (mixed Amerindian and white)	37%
White	15%
Black, Japanese, Chinese, and other	3%
Population (1997)	25,573,924

Educational Issues

Current literacy (over age 15)[a]:
total population 88.7%
(male, 94.5%; female, 83%)

Level of Education
Achieved (as % Population)[e]:

Illiteracy statistics:[e] 50% (1940), 38% (1961), 27% (1972), 18% (1981), 13% (1993), 11% (1996)

	1981	1996
No level	16.1	10.6
Primary	42.3	30.0
Secondary	31.4	40.7
University	10.2	18.7

Sources: [a]CIA World Factbook 1997
[b]ECLAC 1997
[c]IADB 1997
[d]World Bank 1998
[e]National Institute of Statistics and Information, Peru 1996

Table 2. Total Population and Annual Population Change in Peru, 1530–1995

Year	Total Population	Annual Population Change	
		Number	Percentage
1530[1]	16,000,000	−2,285,714	−7.1
1548	8,285,000	−428,611	−2.6
1570	2,738,500	−252,114	−3.0
1650	3,030,000	3,644	0.1
1796	1,076,122	−13,382	0.5
1825	2,488,000	48,685	4.5
1836	1,373,736	−97,660	−3.9
1850	2,001,203	44,819	3.2
1862	2,487,916	40,559	2.0
1876	2,651,840	11,709	0.5
1940	6,207,967	55,564	2.0
1961	9,906,746	176,132	2.8
1972	13,572,052	333,209	3.3
1981	17,005,210	381,462	2.5
1990[2]	22,332,100	743,996	3.4
1995[2]	23,532,000	1,199,900	5.4

[1]Estimates for the preconquest population of Peru vary widely, but in recent years have been greatly increased from the guesses of the 1950s of 3 million to 4 million based on the ethnohistorical study of the impact of epidemic diseases sweeping the region beginning in about 1524. Recent estimates for the population in the territory covering present-day Peru range from 12 million to 30 million.
[2]Estimated.

Sources: Rex A. Hudson (ed.), *Peru: A Country Study* (Washington, DC, 1993), 321; and Richard Webb and Graciela Fernández Baca (eds.), *Perú '96 en números: anuario estadístico* (Lima, 1996), 205.

Table 3. Total Population and Annual Population Change in Lima, 1614–1996

Year	Total Population	Annual Population Change	
		Number	Percentage
1614	24,441	N.A.	N.A.
1700	37,259	126	0.5
1796	52,627	160	0.4
1836	55,627	75	0.1
1857	94,195	1,837	3.3
1862	89,434	−952	−1.0
1876	100,156	766	0.8
1891	103,956	253	0.2
1898	113,409	1,350	1.3
1903	130,089	3,336	2.9
1908	140,884	2,159	1.7
1908[1]	172,927	N.A.	N.A.
1920	223,807	4,240	2.5
1931	373,875	13,642	6.1
1940	562,885	13,188	9.4
1961	1,632,370	50,928	9.0
1972	3,002,043	124,516	7.6
1981	4,164,597	129,516	4.3
1990[2]	6,414,500	249,989	6.0
1996[2]	6,914,000	N.A.	N.A.

N.A. = not available.

[1]Province of Lima. After 1908 population growth and settlement size made the province the unit for measurement.

[2]Estimated.

Sources: Rex A. Hudson (ed.), *Peru: A Country Study* (Washington, DC, 1993), 322; and Richard Webb and Graciela Fernández Baca (eds.), *Perú '96 en números: anuario estadístico* (Lima, 1996), 205.

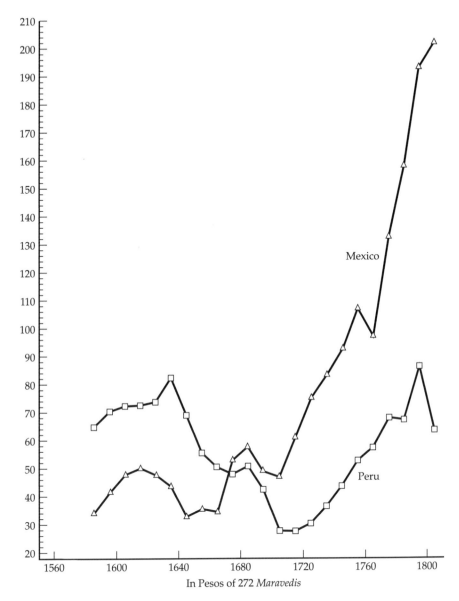

Chart 1. Registered Silver Production in Peru and Mexico, 1581–1810. *Source:* Mark
A. Burkholder and Lyman L. Johnson, *Colonial Latin America* (New York, 1998), 139.

Table 4. Export Quantum Index and Growth Rate, 1830–1989
(1900 = 100)

Years	Export Quantum	Average Annual Growth from Last Period (percentage)	Years	Export Quantum	Average Annual Growth from Last Period (percentage)
1830–39	16		1915–19	289	5.7
1840–49	31	6.9	1920–24	346	3.6
1850–59	64	7.6	1925–29	568	9.7
1860–69	84	2.7	1930–34	541	−1.0
1870–79	121	3.8	1935–39	699	5.2
1880–89	43	−18.9	1940–44	520	−5.8
			1945–49	570	1.9
			1950–54	736	5.2
1880–84	36		1955–59	1,111	8.6
1885–89	49	6.0	1960–64	2,278	15.4
1890–94	54	1.9	1965–69	2,746	3.8
1895–99	76	7.3	1970–74	2,597	−1.1
1900–04	110	7.7	1975–79	2,674	0.6
1905–09	158	7.4	1980–84	3,258	4.0
1910–14	215	6.7	1985–89	3,565	1.8

Source: Efraín Gonzáles de Olarte (ed.), *The Peruvian Economy and Structural Adjustment: Past, Present and Future* (Miami, 1996), 32.

Table 5. Long-Term Trends in Exports

Years	Export Quantum	Years	Number of Years	Average Annual Growth (percentage)
1831	12	1831–77	46	5.5
1877	139	1877–90	13	−7.8
1890	48	1890–1929	39	6.8
1929	622	1929–49	20	−0.8
1949	563	1949–61	12	11.4
1961	2,053	1961–88	27	2.0
1988	3,473			
		1949–88	39	4.8
		1831–1988	157	3.7

Source: Efraín González de Olarte (ed.), *The Peruvian Economy and Structural Adjustment: Past, Present and Future* (Miami, 1996), 32.

Table 6. Governments since Independence, 1821–1995

		Dates
1	José de San Martín	1821–1822
2	Junta: José de la Mar, Manuel Salazar y Baquijano, Felipe A. Alvarado	1822–1823
3	José de la Riva-Agüero	1823
4	José Bernardo de Torre Tagle	1823–1824
5	Simón Bolívar, Antonio José de Sucre	1824–1826
6	Andrés de Santa Cruz	1826–1827
7	José de la Mar	1827–1829
8	Agustín Gamarra	1829–1833
9	Pedro Pablo Bermúdez	1834
10	Luis José de Orbegoso	1833–1835
11	Felipe Santiago Salaverry	1835–1836
12	Andrés de Santa Cruz (Peru-Bolivia Confederation)	1836–1839
13	Agustín Gamarra	1839–1841
14	Francisco Vidal, Juan Crisostomo Torrico	1842–1843
15	Domingo Elías, Domingo Nieto	1843–1844
16	Justo Figuerola	1844
17	Ramón Castilla	1845–1851
18	José Rufino Echenique	1851–1855
19	Ramón Castilla	1855–1862
20	Miguel de San Román	1862–1863
21	Juan Antonio Pezet	1863–1865
22	Mariano Ignacio Prado	1865–1868
23	Pedro Diez Canseco (provisional)	1868
24	José Balta	1868–1872
25	Manuel Pardo*	1872–1876
26	Mariano Ignacio Prado	1876–1879
27	Nicolás de Piérola*	1879–1881
28	Francisco García Calderón*	1881
29	Lizardo Montero	1881–1883
30	Miguel Iglesias	1883–1886
31	Andrés A. Cáceres	1886–1890
32	Remigio Morales Bermúdez	1890–1894
33	Justiniano Borgoño	1894
34	Andrés A. Cáceres	1894–1895
35	Manuel Candamo (Junta)*	1895
36	Nicolás de Piérola*	1895–1899
37	Eduardo López de Romaña*	1899–1903
38	Manuel Candamo*	1903–1904
39	Serapio Calderón*	1904
40	José Pardo y Barreda*	1904–1908
41	Augusto B. Leguía*	1908–1912
42	Guillermo Billinghurst*	1913–1914
43	Oscar R. Benavides	1914–1915
44	José Pardo y Barreda*	1915–1919
45	Augusto B. Leguía*	1919–1930
46	Luis Miguel Sánchez Cerro	1930–1931
47	David Samanez Ocampo (Junta)	1931
48	Luis Miguel Sánchez Cerro	1931–1933
49	Oscar R. Benavides	1933–1939

Table 6. *Continued*

	Dates
50 Manuel Prado Ugarteche*	1939–1945
51 José Luis Bustamante y Rivero*	1945–1948
52 Manuel A. Odría (Junta)	1948–1950
53 Manuel A. Odría	1950–1956
54 Manuel Prado Ugarteche*	1956–1962
55 Ricardo Pérez Godoy, Nicolás Lindley	1962–1963
56 Fernando Belaúnde Terry*	1963–1968
57 Juan Velasco Alvarado	1968–1975
58 Francisco Morales Bermúdez	1975–1980
59 Fernando Belaúnde Terry*	1980–1985
60 Alan García Pérez*	1985–1990
61 Alberto Fujimori*	1990

*Civilian

Source: F. Pease G.Y. *Perú: hombre e historia*, Vol. 3 (Lima, 1993).

Bibliographical Essay*

General Surveys

The best, most comprehensive, and up-to-date survey is Nelson Manrique et al., *Nuestra historia*, 4 vols. (Lima, 1995). Also valuable is Duccio Bonavia and Franklin Pease G. Y., *Perú: hombre e historia*, 3 vols. (Lima, 1991–93). Older but still useful are Juan Mejía Baca (ed.), *Historia del Perú*, 12 vols. (Lima, 1980) and Julio Cotler, *Clases, estado y nación en el Perú* (Lima, 1978). The classic is Jorge Basadre's *Historia de la República del Perú, 1822–1933*, 10 vols. (10th ed., Lima, 1983). A superb recent interpretative analysis, which focuses on the twentieth century, is Sinesio López Jiménez, *Ciudadanos reales e imaginarios: concepciones, desarrollo y mapas de la ciudadanía en el Perú* (Lima, 1997).

There are numerous general histories in English, all somewhat dated. Magnus Mörner's *The Andean Past: Land, Societies and Conflicts* (New York, 1985) covers the three countries that formed the Inca Empire (Peru, Bolivia, and Ecuador) and is mainly social and economic in emphasis. See also various chapters in *The Cambridge History of Latin America* (*CHLA*), vols. 1–12, edited by Leslie Bethell (Cambridge, England, 1984–96). David Scott Palmer, *Peru: The Authoritarian Tradition* (New York, 1980) emphasizes mainly the twentieth century. Useful as well are David Werlich, *Peru: A Short History* (Carbondale, IL, 1978); Henry E. Dobyns and Paul L. Doughty, *Peru: A Cultural History* (New York, 1976); and Fredrick B. Pike, *The Modern History of Peru* (New York, 1967).

Two important works cast light on Peru in the late twentieth century: Maxwell A. Cameron and Phillip Mauceri (eds.), *The Peruvian Labrynth: Polity, Society, Economy* (University Park, PA, 1997), which serves as a worthy successor to Abraham Lowenthal's (ed.) highly influential *The Peruvian Experiment: Continuity and Change under Military Rule* (Princeton, NJ, 1975), and with Cynthia McClintock (eds.), *The Peruvian Experiment Reconsidered* (Princeton, NJ, 1983). Another excellent overview of the history, politics and economy by leading specialists is Rex Hudson (ed.), *Peru: A Country Study* (Washington, DC, 1993). Two useful, compact histories that also provide perspectives on the crisis of the late twentieth century are James D. Rudolph, *Peru: The Evolution of a Crisis* (Westport, CT, 1992), and Latin American Bureau, *Peru: Paths to Poverty* (London, 1985). Also valuable is Orin Starn et al., *The Peru Reader: History, Culture, Politics* (Durham, NC, 1995). Those who are interested in the Japanese presence and antecidents in Peru should consult Mary Fukumoto's comprehensive *Hacia un nuevo sol: Japoneses y sus descendientes en el Perú: historia, cultura e identidad* (Lima, 1997).

The most recent economic history is John Sheahan, *Searching for a Better Society: The Peruvian Economy since 1950* (University Park, PA, 1999). The standard economic history is Rosemary Thorp and Geoffrey Bertram, *Peru 1890–1977: Growth and Policy in an Open Economy* (New York, 1978). It should be consulted in tandem with Efraín Gonzáles de Olarte (ed.), *The Peruvian Economy and Structural Adjustment: Past, Present and Future* (Miami, 1996). Richard Webb and Graciela Fernández (eds.) provide the necessary statistical data in *Perú en números 1997: anuario estadístico* (Lima, 1997).

---

*Covers mainly books and important articles published in the last quarter century. For earlier titles see Henry E. Dobyns and Paul L. Doughty, *Peru: A Cultural History* (New York, 1976).

The standard history of the Catholic Church is Jeffrey Klaiber, S.J., *The Catholic Church in Peru, 1821–1985* (Washington, DC, 1992). On the military, see Daniel M. Masterson, *Militarism and Politics in Latin America: Peru from Sánchez Cerro to Sendero Luminoso* (New York, 1991). *The Foreign Policy of Peru* since independence is examined by Ronald Bruce St. John (Boulder, CO, and London, 1992). A broader treatment of United States–Peruvian relations, which reveals the long history of political, economic, social, and cultural interactions between the two countries, is Lawrence A. Clayton, *Peru and the United States: The Condor and the Eagle* (Athens, Georgia, 1999). See also Fredrick B. Pike, *The United States and the Andean Republics: Peru, Bolivia and Ecuador* (Cambridge, MA, 1977). A brief but incisive cultural history is Sara Castro-Klarén, "Lima: A Blurred Centrality," in Mario Valdez (ed.) *A Comparative Cultural History of Latin America* (Oxford University Press, 2000). See also James Higgins, *A History of Peruvian Literature* (Liverpool, England, 1987). Deborah Poole brilliantly explores the role that visual images and technologies have played in shaping modern understandings of race in *Vision, Race, and Modernity: A Visual Economy of the Andean Image World* (Princeton, NJ, 1997).

For an excellent recent historiographical essay, see Pease, *Peru* vol. 2, chap. 4, 93–128 as well as the bibliographical sections on Peru in *CHLA*, 11 (1995). Jorge Basadre, *Introducción a las bases documentales para la historia de la República del Perú*, 2 vols. (Lima, 1971) provides a more detailed historiographical reference for older titles. Readers should also consult the *Handbook of Latin American Studies*, edited by Dolores Moyano Martin. Published annually by the University of Texas Press, the *Handbook* surveys the latest scholarly literature on Peru (books and articles in English and Spanish), all carefully annotated. It is available online at the following Website: http://lcweb2.loc.gov/hlas/.

Incas and Pre-Incas

Craig Morris and Adriana Von Hagen wrote a sumptuously illustrated introduction to pre-Inca civilization entitled *The Inka Empire and Its Andean Origins* (New York, 1993). See also Michael E. Moseley, *The Incas and Their Ancestors: The Archaeology of Peru* (London, 1992), and Ian Cameron's very readable *Kingdom of the Sun: A History of the Andes and Their People* (New York, 1990). Two fine surveys by Peruvian scholars are Luis K. Watanabe, *Nuestra historia*, vol. 1, *Culturas preincas del Perú* (Lima, 1995), and Duccio Bonavia, *Perú: Hombre y historia. De los orígenes al siglo XV* (Lima, 1991). Citations of the more specific literature can be found in the bibliographies of these surveys.

On the Incas, readers should begin with María Rostworowski de Diez Canseco, *History of the Inca Realm*, translated by Harry B. Iceland (New York, 1998), as well as the essays in *Homenaje a María Rostworowski: arqueología, antropología e historia en los Andes*, edited by Rafael Varón Gabai and Javier Flores Espinoza (Lima, 1997). Three other excellent surveys of the Incas are Nigel Davies, *The Incas* (Boulder, CO, 1995); Thomas C. Patterson, *The Inca Empire: The Formation and Disintegration of a Pre-Capitalist State* (New York, 1991); and Moseley, *The Incas and Their Ancestors*. Also useful is George Collier, Renato Rosaldo, and John Wirth (eds.), *The Inca and Aztec States, 1400–1800: Anthropology and History* (New York, 1982). See also the pioneering works of R. T. Zuidema, including his *Inca Civilization in Cuzco* (Austin, TX, 1990), and John Murra, "Andean Societies before 1532," in *CHLA*, 1 (1984), 59–90. Susan Ramirez suggests a major reinterpretation in "Cuzco: A Reconsideration of Sovereignty, Territoriality and the Inca State," manuscript, 1999.

In numerous articles John Rowe laid the foundations of much later work on the Incas. Ann Kendall examined *Everyday Life of the Incas* (London, 1973), as did more recently Michael A. Malpass, *Daily Life in the Inca Empire* (Westport, CT, 1996). Marcia Ascher and Robert Ascher analyzed *The Code of the Quipu* (Ann Arbor, MI, 1981). The problem of writing is examined in Elizabeth Hill Boone and Walter D. Mignolo (eds.), *Writing without Words: Alternative Literacies in Mesoamerica and the Andes* (Durham, NC, 1994). The role of women is developed by Irene Silverblatt, *Moon, Sun and Witches: Gender Ideologies and Class in Inca and Colonial Peru* (Princeton, NJ, 1987). See also Constance Classen, *Inca Cosmology and the Human Body* (Salt Lake City, UT, 1993), and Gary Urton, *At the Crossroads of the Earth and Sky: An Andean Cosmology* (Austin, TX, 1981). Brian Bauer and S. P. Dearborn examine *Astronomy and Empire in the Ancient Andes* (Austin, TX, 1995).

There are numerous surveys by Peruvian scholars: the most notable are Jorge Silva S., *Nuestro Historia*, vol. 2, *El imperio de los cuatro suyos* (Lima, 1995); Fernando Silva Santisteban and Rogger Ravines, *Los incas: Historia y arqueología del Tawantinsuyu* (Lima, 1994); María Rostworowski, de Diez Canseco, *Historia del Tawantinsuyu* (Lima, 1988); Waldemar Espinoza Soriano, *Los Incas: economía, sociedad y estado en la era del Tahuantinsuyo* (Lima, 1987); and Franklyn Pease G.Y., *Del Tawantinsuyu a la historia del Perú* (Lima, 1978). See also Pease's more recent *Los incas: una introducción* (Lima, 1991). Rostworowski has been one of the most prolific and original writers on the Incas and pre-Hispanic civilizations in Peru. Her *Ensayos de historia andina: elites, etnías, recursos* was published in 1993 (Lima). A useful but older survey is Luis Guillermo Lumbreras, *The Peoples and Cultures of Ancient Peru* (Washington, DC, 1974). See also Louis Gaudin, *A Socialist Empire: The Incas of Peru* (Princeton, NJ, 1961).

The question of the origins of the Inca State is addressed by Brian Bauer, *The Development of the Inca State* (Austin, TX, 1992); Gary Urton, *Pacariqtambo and the Origins of the Incas* (Austin, TX, 1990) and Jonathan Haas, Sheila Pozorski, and Thomas Pozorski, *The Origins and Development of the Andean State* (Cambridge, England, 1987). Terrance D'Altroy examines *Provincial Power in the Inca Empire* (Washington, DC, 1992). Johann Reinhard has written on *Machu Picchu: The Sacred Center* (Lima, 1991) which would be read profitably along with the account of its discoverer Hiram Bingham, *Machu Picchu— A Citadel of the Incas* (New Haven, CT, 1930). The authoritative works on *The Inca Road System* (New York, 1984) and *Inca Settlement Planning* (Austin, TX, 1990) are by John Hyslop. Craig Morris and Donald E. Thompson examine *Huánuco Pampa: An Inca City and Its Hinterland* (London, 1985). Catherine Julien interprets the Incas from the perspective of *Hatunqolla: A View of Inca Rule from the Lake Titicaca Region* (Berkeley, CA, 1983). Geoffrey W. Conrad and Arthur Demarest compare *Religion and Empire: The Dynamics of Aztec and Inca Expansionism* (New York, 1984) and have written other important works.

In a seminal work R. T. Zuidema explains *The Ceque System of Cuzco: The Social Organization of the Capital of the Inca* (Leiden, the Netherlands, 1964). A more recent work is Brian S. Bauer, *The Sacred Landscape of the Inca: The Cuzco Ceque System* (Austin, TX, 1999). John Murra's major work is *The Economic Organization of the Inca State* (Greenwich, CT, 1955). See also his *La organización económica del estado Inca* (Lima, 1978) and *Formaciones económicas y políticas del mundo Andino* (Lima, 1976). Franklin Pease G. Y. has also written on *Los últimos Incas del Cuzco* (Lima, 1976). The authoritative biography on *Pachacutec Inca Yupanqui* (Lima, 1953) is by María Rostworowski de Diez Canseco. Ramiro Matos Mendieta examines *Pumpu: Centro administrativo inca de la puna de Junín* (Lima, 1994). Liliana Regalado de Hurtado has written on *Sucesión incaica* (Lima, 1993). Rogger Ravines has examined *Tecnología Andina* (Lima, 1978). See also Charles Gibson's classic *The Inca Concept of Sovereignty and the Spanish Administration in Peru* (Austin, TX, 1948), and Sally Falk Moore, *Power and Property in Inca Peru* (Westport, CT, 1973). Some of the leading Spanish chroniclers of the Incas are listed below under the conquest.

Conquest and Colony

SIXTEENTH CENTURY

Readers should begin with Steve J. Stern's penetrating interpretive overview "Paradigms of Conquest: History, Historiography, and Politics," *Journal of Latin American Studies (JLAS)* 24 (1992), 1–34, and John H. Elliott's "The Spanish Conquest and Settlement of America," in *CHLA*, 1, 149–206. The best recent history of the period is Luis Millones, *Peru colonial* (Lima, 1995), vol. 2 of Manrique, *Nuestra historia*. Nelson Manrique probes *El universo men-*

tal de la conquista de America (Lima, 1993). The standard narrative is John Hemming, *The Conquest of the Incas* (New York, 1970), the classic version being William H. Prescott, *The History of the Conquest of Peru*, (New York, 1998 [1847]). See also Hemming's *Search for El Dorado* (London, 1978).

James Lockhardt's *The Men of Cajamarca* (Austin, TX, 1972) profiles the conquerors. The most recent biography of the Pizarros is Rafael Varón Gabai, *Francisco Pizarro and His Brothers: The Illusion of Power in Sixteenth-Century Peru* (Norman, OK, 1997). Other biographies include José Antonio del Busto Duthurburu, *Francisco Pizarro: El Marques Gobernador* (2d ed., Lima, 1978); Guillermo Lohmann Villena, *Francisco Pizarro. Testimonio, documentos oficiales, cartas y escritos*. (Madrid, 1986); and Raúl Porras Barrenechea, *Pizarro* (Lima, 1978). All three authors have published extensively on the colony.

On the military aspects of the conquest see John F. Guilmartin, Jr., "The Cutting Edge: An Analysis of the Spanish Invasion and Overthrow of the Inca Empire, 1532–1539" in *Transatlantic Encounters: Europeans and Andeans in the Sixteenth Century*, edited by Kenneth J. Andrien and Rolena Adorno (Berkeley, CA, 1991), 40–69. Patricia Seed examines the requirement in the *Ceremonies of Possession in Europe's Conquest of the New World, 1492–1640* (Cambridge, England, 1995). See also her "The Conquest of the Americas, 1492–1650," in *Cambridge Illustrated History of Warfare*, edited by Geoffrey Parker, (Cambridge, England, 1995), and Sabine MacCormack, "Atahualpa and the Book," *Dispositio* 16:36/38 (1988), 141–168. The encounter is also given original treatment by Antonio Cornejo Polar, "El comienzo de la heterogeneidad en las literaturas andinas: voz y letra en el 'diálogo' de Cajamarca," *Revista de Crítica Literaria Latinoamericana* (1990).

The Indian perspective of the conquest has been reconstructed by Nathan Wachtel in *The Vision of the Vanquished: the Spanish Conquest of Peru through Indian Eyes, 1530–1570*, (New York, 1977). See also his "The Indian and the Spanish Conquest," in *CHLA*, 2 (1984), 207–248, as well as Edmundo Guillen, *Visión peruana de la conquista (la resistencia incaica a la invasión española)* (Lima, 1978). On the formation and importance of Indian allies, see Steve J. Stern, "The Rise and Fall of Indian-White Alliances: A Regional View of 'Conquest' History," *Hispanic American Historical Review* (*HAHR*) 61:3 (August 1981), 461–491.

Early Indian rebellions are considered in George Kubler, "The Neo-Inca State (1537–1572)," *HAHR* 27:2 (May 1947), 189–203, and Luis Millones, "Un movimiento nativista del siglo XVI: el Taki Onqoy," and "Nuevos aspectos del Taki Onqoy," in *Ideología mesiánica del mundo andino*, edited by Juan Ossio (Lima, 1973), 83–94; 95–102. See also Millones's edited *El retorno de las huacas. Estudios y documentos sobre el Taki Onqoy. Siglo XVI* (Lima, 1990), and Pedro Guibovich Pérez, "Cristóbal de Albornoz y el Taki Onquoy," *Histórica* 15:2 (1991), 205–236. A dissenting view that questions the idea of millenarianism as the driving force of Andean native rebellion can be found in Gabriela Ramos and Henrique Urbano, (eds.), *Catolicismo y extirpación de idolatrías, siglos XVI–XVIII: Charcas, Chile, México, Perú* (Cuzco, 1993). See also Ana María Lorandi, *De quimeras, rebeliónes y utopías: la gesta del Inca Pedro Bohorques* (Lima, 1997).

The civil wars are examined in José Antonio del Busto Duthurburu, *La pacificación del Perú* (Lima, 1984), while Teodoro Hampe provides a biography of *Don Pedro de la Gasca* (Lima, 1989). Edmundo Guillen Guillen chronicles *La guerra de reconquista inca: Vilcabamba: epílogo trágico del Tawantinsuyo* (Lima, 1994).

Anthony Pagden's *The Fall of Natural Man: The American Indian and the Origins of Comparative Ethnology* (New York, 1982) describes the famous debates in Salamanca in 1550 between Sepúlveda and Las Casas over the true nature of the Amerindian and shows how the Europeans seized on the Aristotelian notion of natural slavery to rationalize their treatment of the conquered Indians. See also Lewis Hanke's classic *The Spanish Struggle for Justice in the Conquest of America* (Philadelphia, 1949), and Bartolomé de Las Casas, *Los tesoros del Perú* (Madrid, 1958). Gustavo Gutiérrez has written on *Las Casas: In Search of the Poor of Jesus Christ* (New York, 1993), as has Isacio Pérez Fernandez, *Bartolomé de Las Casas en el Perú* (Cuzco, 1988).

There are numerous chronicles and contemporary accounts of the conquest and early colony. Some of the more noteworthy are Agustín de Zárate, *The Discovery and*

Conquest of Peru, translated by J. M. Cohen (Baltimore, 1968); Juan Betanzos, *Narrative of the Incas*, translated and edited by R. Hamilton and D. Buchanan (Austin, TX, 1996); Bernabé Cobo, *History of the Inca Empire*, translated by Roland Hamilton (Austin, TX, 1979); Martín de Murua, *Historia general del Perú* (Madrid, 1962); Pedro Sarmiento de Gamboa, *Historia de los Incas* (Buenos Aires, 1943); Father Pablo de Arriaga, *The Extirpation of Idolatry in Peru* [1621] translated by L. Clark Keating (Lexington, KY, 1968); Pedro Cieza de León, *History of the Inca Empire* (Austin, TX, 1979); Garcilaso de la Vega, "El Inca," *Royal Commentaries of the Incas* [1609] (Austin, TX, 1966); Felipe Huamán Poma de Ayala, *El primer nueva crónica y buen gobierno*, 3 vols., edited by John V. Murra and Rolena Adorno, translated from the Quechua Jorge L. Urioste (Mexico City, 1980) [*Letter to a King* (1613) translated by Christopher Dilke (New York, 1978)]; and Luis Millones (ed.), *La crónica de Tuti Cusi Yupanqui* (Lima, 1985), and *The Huarochirí Manuscript: A Testament of Ancient and Colonial Andean Religion*, translated from the Quechua by Frank Salomon and George L. Urioste (Austin, TX, 1991).

For a perceptive discussion of these and other native Andean chroniclers, see Franklin Pease G. Y., *Las cronistas y los Andes* (Lima, 1995). See also his "Las primeras versiones españoles sobre el Perú," *Colonial Latin American Review* (*CLAR*), 1 (1992), 65–76, and Raúl Porras Barrenechea, *Los cronistas del Perú y otros ensayos*, edited by Franklin Pease (Lima, 1986). See also the anthologies compiled by Francisco Carrillo, *Enciclopedia histórica de la literatura peruana*, vol. 2, *Cartas y cronistas del descubrimiento y conquista* (Lima, 1987), and *Cronistas del Perú antiguo*, vol. 4 (Lima, 1989). Also important is Tom Cummins, "Representation in the Sixteenth Century and the Colonial Image of the Inca," in *Writing without Words*, 188–219.

Noble David Cook has painstakingly estimated the pre-Columbian population at the time of the conquest and its precipitous drop over the next century in his *Demographic Collapse: Indian Peru, 1520–1620* (Cambridge, England, 1981) and in his more recent work, *Born to Die: Disease and New World Conquest (1492–1650)* (New York, 1998). See also his and W. George Lovell (eds.), *"Secret Judgments of God": Old World Disease in Colonial Spanish America* (Norman, OK, 1992). Cook's other works include *The People of the Colca Valley: A Population Study* (Boulder, CO, 1982); "Population Data for Indian Peru: Sixteenth and Seventeenth Centuries," *HAHR*, 62:1 (February 1982), 73–120; and the edited *Tasa de la visita general de Francisco de Toledo* (Lima, 1975).

Nicolas Sánchez-Albornoz provides an excellent overview of the population of the colonial Andes in "The Population of Colonial Spanish America," in *CHLA*, 2, 3–36. A dissenting view on the size of the pre-Columbian population can be found in Daniel E. Shea, "A Defense of Small Population Estimates for the Central Andes in 1520," in *The Native Population of the Americas in 1492*, edited by William M. Denevan (Madison, WI, 1976). See also Nicolas Sánchez-Albornoz's *Indios y tributos en el Alto Perú* (Lima, 1978). On the impact of European disease and epidemics in the demographic collapse, see Henry F. Dobyns, "An Outline of Andean Epidemic History to 1720," *Bulletin of the History of Medicine* 37 (1963), 493–515, and Alfred W. Crosby's classic *The Columbian Exchange* (Westport, CT, 1972), which examines the biological and cultural consequences of 1492 for the central Andes.

Information on Spanish immigration to the Andes can be found in Ida Altman, *Emigrantes y sociedad: Extremadura y América en el siglo XVI* (Madrid, 1992). See also Peter Boyd-Bowman, *Patterns of Spanish Emigration to the New World (1493–1580)* (Buffalo, NY, 1973) and Sánchez Albornoz, "The Population." James Lockhart's *Spanish Peru, 1532–1560* (Madison, WI, 1968, 1994) is the standard social history of the early Spanish population and society, while his *Letters and People of the Spanish Indies: Sixteenth Century*, with Enrique Otte, eds., (Cambridge, England, 1976) sheds light on the origins, motives and occupations of the early immigrants. See also Lockhart's "Social Organization and Social Change in Colonial Spanish America," in *CHLA*, 2, 265–320. Richard M. Morse examines, "The Urban Development of Spanish America," in *CHLA*, 2, 67–104. Insight into the attitudes, values, and mentality of the early Spanish invaders can be gleened in Alexandra Parma Cook and Noble David Cook, *Good Faith and Truthful Ignorance: A Case of Transat-*

lantic Bigamy (Durham, NC, 1991). See also Teodoro Hampe Martínez, "The Diffusion of Books and Ideas in Colonial Peru: A Study of Private Libraries in the Sixteenth and Seventeenth Centuries," *HAHR* 73:2 (1993), 211–233. Rosa María Acosta de Arias Schreiber writes on *Fiestas coloniales urbanas (Lima-Cuzco-Potosí)* (Lima, 1997).

The classic account on *The African Slave in Colonial Peru, 1524–1650* is by Fredrick Bowser (Stanford, CA, 1974). On the complex problem of colonial ethnic/racial stratification and identity, see David Cahill's important "Colour by Numbers: Racial and Ethnic Categories in the Viceroyalty of Peru, 1532–1824," *JLAS* 26:2 (1994), 325–346. The older Magnus Mörner, *Race Mixture in the History of Latin America* (Boston, 1967) is also useful. See also Hiroyasu Tomoeda and Luis Millones, *500 Años de Mestizaje en los Andes* (Osaka, 1992). On the meaning of the term *Indian*, see Irene Silverblatt, "Becoming Indian in the Central Andes of Seventeenth-Century Peru," in *After Colonialism: Imperial Histories and Postcolonial Displacements*, edited by Gyan Prakash (Princeton, NJ, 1995), 279–298.

Numerous works have appeared on early colonial society and economy. Two seminal studies that embrace the view of Indians as active not, as previously portrayed, passive, participants in the conquest who elaborated sophisticated strategies of resistance and adaptation are Steve J. Stern's, *Peru's Indian Peoples and the Challenge of Spanish Conquest: Huamanga to 1640* (Madison, WI, 1982), and Karen Spalding's *Huarochirí: An Andean Society under Inca and Spanish Rule* (Stanford, CA, 1984). Both works also offer important, but contrasting interpretations of the emerging colonial economy. Spalding characterizes colonial Peru as essentially feudal from the outset, while Stern rejects this view, referring to "aristocratic entrepreneurs" who exhibited strong commerical and productive characteristics. See also Spalding's numerous articles, including "Exploitation as an Economic System: The State and the Extraction of Surplus in Colonial Peru," in *The Inca and Aztec States, 1400–1800*, edited by George Collier et al. (New York, 1982), 321–344. Stern shows how the native peoples adroitly resorted to colonial law and the courts to protect their interests in "The Social Significance of Judicial Institutions in an "Exploitative Society: Huamanga, Peru, 1570–1640," also in Collier et al., 289–320. An earlier classic study is George Kubler, "The Quechua in the Colonial World," *Handbook of South American Indians*, edited by J. H. Steward, vol. 2 (New York, 1963), 331–410. More recently Susan Ramirez explores *The World Upside Down: Cross-Cultural Contact and Conflict in Sixteenth Century Peru* (Stanford, CA, 1996).

José de la Puente Brunke examines the *Encomienda y encomenderos en el Perú: estudio social y político de una institución colonial* (Seville, 1992). A comprehensive profile of a Peruvian *encomendero* can be found in Efraín Trelles Aréstegui's *Lucas Martínez Vegaso: Funcionamiento de una encomienda peruana inicial* (Lima, 1982). See also Fred Bronner, "Peruvian Encomenderos in 1630: Elite Circulation and Consolidation," *HAHR* 57:4 (1977), 633–659.

The silver mining industry has been the subject of exhaustive research by Peter Bakewell, who provides an excellent synthesis in "Mining in Colonial Spanish America," in *CHLA*, 2, 105–152. Gwendolyn Ballantine Cobb examines *Potosí y Huancavelica. Bases económicas del Perú, 1545–1640* (La Paz, 1977). For an earlier comparative perspective, see David H. Brading and Harry E. Cross, "Colonial Silver Mining; Mexico and Peru," *HAHR* 52:2 (1972). Carlos Contreras examines *La ciudad del mercurio: Huancavelica, 1570–1700* (Lima, 1982). See also Guillermo Lohmann Villena, *Las minas de Huancavelica en los siglos XVI y XVII* (Seville, 1949), and Arthur P. Whitaker, *The Huancavelica Mercury Mine* (Cambridge, MA, 1941).

The *mita* labor system has received considerable scholarly attention. Two important monographs are Jeffrey A. Cole, *The Potosí Mita, 1573–1700: Compulsory Indian Labor in the Andes* (Stanford, CA, 1985), and Peter Bakewell, *Miners of the Red Mountain: Indian Labor in Potosí, 1545–1650* (Albuquerque, NM, 1984). See also Thierry Saignes, "Notes on the Regional Contribution to the Mita in Potosí in the Early Seventeenth Century," *Bulletin of Latin American Research (BLAR)* 4:1 (1985). Steve J. Stern succinctly examines the *mita* and labor system at Potosí in his discussion of the debate over "Feudalism, Capitalism, and the World-System in the Perspective of Latin America and the Caribbean," *American His-*

torical Review (AHR) 93:4 (October 1988), 829–872 (reprinted in *Confronting Historical Paradigms: Peasants, Labor, and the Capitalist World System in Africa and Latin America,* edited by Frederick Cooper et al. [Madison, WI, 1993], 23–83). Numerous chronicles on Potosí have been edited and published, several by Lewis Hanke. See also *Tales of Potosí: Bartolomé Arzans de Orsua y Vela,* introduced and edited by R. C. Padden (Providence, RI, 1975).

A general survey of the transatlantic trade with references to Peru can be found in Murdo J. Macleod, "Spain and America: The Atlantic Trade, 1492–1720," in *CHLA,* 1, 341–388. See also James Lockhart, "Trunk Lines and Feeder Lines: The Spanish Reaction to American Resources" in Andrien and Adorno, *Transatlantic Encounters,* 90–120, as well as Fernando Iwasaki Cauti, *Extremo Oriente y Perú en el siglo XVI* (Madrid, 1992), and Woodrow W. Borah, *Early Colonial Trade between Mexico and Peru* (Berkeley, CA, 1954). The rise of the internal colonial Andean economy is analyzed in a path-breaking work by Carlos Sempat Assadourian, *El sistema de la economía colonial: Mercado interno, regiones y espacio económico* (Lima, 1982). Although Assadourian, unlike Karen Spalding, refuses to interpret the Andean colonial economy as either feudal or capitalist, he shows how the mining economy spawned the development of considerable internal production and exchange over a broad "economic space." See also his "The Colonial Economy: The Transfer of the European System of Production to New Spain and Peru," *JLAS* 24 (1992), 55–68; *Transiciones hacia el sistema colonial Andino* (Lima, 1994) and many other works. Assadourian's work is assessed in Steve J. Stern's "New Directions in Andean Economic History: A Critical Dialogue with Carlos Sempat Assadourian," *Latin American Perspectives* 12 (1985), 133–148.

The works of Assadourian and Stern stimulated new research on the indigenous participation in the colonial economy that can be found in *Ethnicity, Markets, and Migration in the Andes: At the Crossroads of History and Anthropology,* edited by Brooke Larson and Olivia Harris with Enrique Tandeter (Durham, NC, 1995), an updated and expanded edition of *La participación indígena en los mercados surandinos: estrategias y reproducción social, siglos XVI–XX* (La Paz, 1987). In this vein, two influential works are Brooke Larson, *Colonialism and Agrarian Transformation in Bolivia: Cochabamba, 1550–1900* (Princeton, NJ, 1988), and Luis Miguel Glave, *Trajinantes: caminos indígenas en la sociedad colonial, siglos XVI–XVII* (Lima, 1989). Glave, like Assadourian, explores the formation of the Andean internal market, emphasizing the ways that Andean socioeconomic structures were adapted to fit the new colonial order.

The best recent studies of *obrajes* are Miriam Salas de Coloma, *Estructura colonial del poder español en el Perú. Huamanga (Ayacucho) a traves de sus obrajes, siglos XVI–XVIII,* 3 vols. (Lima, 1998), and Neus Escandell-Tur, *Producción y comercio de tejidos coloniales: los obrajes y chorrillos del Cuzco 1570–1820* (Cuzco, 1997), based on her Ph.D. dissertation "Textile Production and Trade during the Colonial Period: Cuzco, 1570–1820," UCSD, 1993.

Luis Miguel Glave examines the origins and evolution of the Indian community in *Vida símbolos y batallas: creación y recreación de la comunidad indígena, Cusco, siglos XVI–XX* (Lima, 1992). On the migration of Indians (*forasteros*), see Ann M. Wightman's prize-winning *Indigenous Migration and Social Change: The Forasteros of Cuzco, 1520–1720* (Durham, NC, 1990), and David Robinson (ed.), *Migration in Colonial Spanish America* (Cambridge, England, 1990).

Magnus Mörner's "The Rural Economy and Society of Colonial Spanish America," in *CHLA,* 2, 189–218, provides an overview. See also Manuel Burga's important *De la Encomienda a la hacienda capitalista: el valle de Jequetepeque del siglo XVI al XX* (Lima, 1976), as well as Pablo Macera's classic "Feudalismo colonial americano: el caso de las haciendas peruanas," *Acta Histórica,* reprinted in Macera, *Trabajos de historia* (Lima, 1977). More recently see Jorge A. Guevara Gil, *Propiedad agraria y derecho colonial: los documentos de la hacienda Santotis, Cuzco (1543–1822)* (Lima, 1993).

The diversity of the hacienda and land tenure system throughout colonial Peru is noted in a number of studies that trace Peru's regional development in the colonial period. Susan R. Ramirez, *Provincial Patriarchs: Land Tenure and the Economics of Power in Colonial Peru* (Albuquerque, NM, 1986), covers the north coast, focusing on the landholding elite, as does Robert G. Keith's *Conquest and Agrarian Change* (Cambridge, MA, 1976), which offers an incisive analysis of the emergence of the hacienda system and its diversity. Also noteworthy on Upper Peru is Larson's *Colonialism*. Keith A. Davies examines the formation of Arequipa and its unique, smallholding development in the sixteenth and seventeenth centuries in *Landowners in Colonial Peru* (Austin, TX, 1984). Luis Miguel Glave and María Isabel Remy team up to construct a richly detailed, microhistory across several centuries of agrarian economy and society in Ollantaytambo (between Cuzco and Machu Picchu) in *Estructura agraria y vida rural en una región andina: Ollantaytambo entre los siglos XVI y XIX* (Cuzco, 1983).

Women in Andean society are receiving increasing attention. An overview is provided by Asuncion Lavrin, "Women in Spanish American Colonial Society," *CHLA*, 2, 321–356. For another overview see María Emma Mannarelli, "Sexualidad y desigualdades genéricas en el Perú del siglo XVI," *Allpanchis* 22: 35–36 (1990), 225–249. Methods of control over women are examined in Silverblatt's *Moon, Sun, and Witches*. See also her "Andean Women under Spanish Rule," in *Women and Colonization: Anthropological Perspectives*, edited by Mona Etienne and Eleanor Leacock (New York, 1980).

The most recent work is Kathryn Burns, *Colonial Habits: Convents and the Spiritual Economy of Cuzco, Peru* (Durham, NC, 1999). She argues, among other things, that nuns played a vital role in reproducing an Andean colonial order in which economic and spiritual interests were deeply intertwined. María Rostworowski de Diez Canseco has written a biography of *Doña Francisca Pizarro: una ilustre mestiza, 1534–1598* (Lima, 1989). See also Amaya Fernandez Fernandez et al., *La mujer en la conquista y la evangelización en el Perú (Lima 1550–1650)*, (Lima, 1996), Elinor C. Burkett, "Indian Women and White Society: The Case of Sixteenth-Century Peru," in *Latin American Women: Historical Perspectives*, edited by Asuncion Lavrin (Westport, CT, 1978), and her "Early Colonial Peru: The Urban Female Experience" (Ph.D. diss., University of Pittsburgh, 1975). An early survey is Judieth Prieto de Zegarra, *Mujer, poder, y desarrollo en el Perú* 2 vols. (Lima, 1980).

For a suscinct overview of Spanish colonial administration, see J. H. Elliott, "Spain and America in the Sixteenth and Seventeenth Centuries," in *CHLA*, 1, 287–340. A more recent analysis is John Lynch, "The Institutional Framework of Colonial Spanish America," *JLAS* 24 (1992), 69–81. John J. TePaske analyzed "The Costs of Empire: Spending Patterns and Priorities in Colonial Peru, 1581–1820" *CLAR*, 2:1 (1993), 1–33. See also Charles Gibson, who traces the transition from Inca to Spanish rule in his clasic work, *The Inca Concept of Sovereignty and the Spanish Administration in Peru* (2d ed., New York, 1969).

There is no recent biography of Viceroy Toledo. Thus, we must rely on Roberto Levillier's *Don Francisco de Toledo*, 4 vols. (Buenos Aires, 1935–40), and Arthur F. Zimmerman, *Francisco de Toledo, Fifth Viceroy of Peru, 1569–1581* (Caldwell, ID, 1938). Toledo's reforms were based on Juan de Matienzo's *Gobierno del Perú* (1567), reprinted in Guillermo Lohmann Villena (ed.), *Travaux de l'Institut Francais d'Etudes Andines*, 11 (Paris, 1967).

There are numerous studies on the *curacas*, or native ethnic chiefs. The most recent is Scarlett O'Phelan Godoy, *Kuracas sin sucesiones: del cacique al alcalde de indios, Perú y Bolivia, 1750–1835* (Cuzco, 1997). See also Franklin Pease G. Y. *Curacas, reciprocidad y riqueza* (Lima, 1992) and Rafael Varón Gabai *Curacas y encomenderos. Acomodamiento nativo en Huaraz, siglos XVI–XVII* (Lima, 1980). Other articles are Carlos Sempat Assadourian, "Los señores étnicos y los corregidores de indios en la conformación del estado colonial," *Anuario de Estudios Americanos* 44 (1987), 325–426; Karen Spalding, "Defendiendo el suyo. El kuraka en el sistema de producción andina," in *Reproducción y transformación de las sociedades andinas, siglos XVI–XX*, edited by Segundo Moreno Yáñez and Frank Salomon (Quito, 1991); Luis Miguel Glave, "Un curacazgo Andino y la sociedad campesina del siglo XVII: la historia de Bartolomé Tupa Hallicalla, curaca de Asillo," *Allpanchis* 33 (1989), 11–39; and Susan Ramirez, "The 'dueno de indios': Thoughts on the Consequences of the Shifting Bases of Power of the 'curaca de los viejos' under the Spanish in Sixteenth-Century Peru," *HAHR* 67:4 (November 1987).

A key article on the Catholic Church is Nuria Sala i Vila, "Gobierno colonial, iglesia y poder en Perú," *Revista Andina* 11:1 (1993), 133–161. A general survey of the Church with numerous references to Peru can be found in Josép M. Barnadas, "The Catholic Church in Spanish America," in *CHLA*, 1, 511–540. Also important is Sabine MacCormack's detailed *Religion in the Andes: Vision and Imagination in Early Colonial Peru* (Princeton, NJ, 1991), as well as her articles. Works on the Inquisition include Pedro Guibovich Pérez, *En defensa de Dios: estudios y documentos sobre la Inquisición en el Perú* (Lima, 1998); Teodoro Martínez Hampe, *Santo oficio e historia colonial: approximaciones al Tribunal de la Inquisición de Lima (1570–1820)* (Lima, 1998); María Emma Mannarelli, *Hechiceras, beatas y expositas: mujeres y poder inquisitorial en Lima* (Lima, 1998); and Fernando Ayllón, *El Tribunal de la Inquisición: de la leyenda a la historia* (Lima, 1997). See also Nicolas Griffith, "Inquisition of the Indians? The Inquisitorial Model and the Repression of Andean Religion in Seventeenth-Century Peru," *Colonial Latin American Historical Review* 3 (Winter 1994), 19–38, and his *The Cross and the Serpent: Religious Repression and Resurgence in Colonial Peru* (Norman, OK, 1996), which interprets extirpation in the context of a multifaceted power struggle in the villages among the local parish priest, the *curaca*, and the chief native magistrate.

The most recent treatment of *Idolatry and Its Enemies: Colonial Andean Religion and Extirpation, 1640–1750* is by Kenneth Mills (Princeton, NJ, 1997), who attempts, among other things, to reconstruct Andean religion as it was in the mid-colonial period. On the transition from Andean religious beliefs to Christianity, see Veronica Salles-Reese, *From Viracocha to the Virgin of Copacabana: Representation of the Sacred at Lake Titicaca* (Austin, TX, 1997). Also important are Ramos and Urbano, (eds.), *Catolicismo y extirpación*; Luis Millones, (ed.), *El retorno de las huacas* (Lima, 1990) and his *Historia y poder en los Andes centrales* (Madrid, 1987); and Pierre Duviols, *Cultura Andina y represión. Procesos y visitas de idolatrías y hechicerías, Cajatambo siglo XVII* (Cuzco, 1986). The older, standard source on the subject is Duviols, *La destrucción de las religiones andinas (durante la Conquista y la Colonia)* (Mexico City, 1977). The original account is Arriaga, *La extirpación* [1621]. See also Teodoro Hampe Martínez, *Cultura barroca y extirpación de idolatrías: la biblioteca de Francisco de Ávila (1648)* (Cuzco, 1996).

SEVENTEENTH CENTURY

The best work on the seventeenth century is Kenneth J. Andrien's *Crisis and Decline: The Viceroyalty of Peru in the Seventeenth Century* (Albuquerque, NM, 1985). Andrien contends that Peru did not enter a depression in the seventeenth century, but rather experienced a restructuring from silver mining to a more self-sufficient, diversified, and regionalized economy. The more traditional interpretation of a depressionary century is outlined in John J. TePaske and Herbert S. Klein, "The Seventeenth-Century Crisis in New Spain: Myth or Reality," *Past and Present* 90 (February 1981), 116–135. The same authors have compiled a data set of the accounts of the revenues and expenditures of the *The Royal Treasuries of the Spanish Empire in America*, vol. 1, Peru (Durham, NC, 1982). See also Peter Bakewell, *Silver and Entrepreneurship in Seventeenth-Century Potosí* (Albuquerque, NM, 1988) and Luis Miguel Glave, "El virreinato peruano y la llamada 'crisis general' del siglo XVII," in *Cuadernos de Historia*, 2 (Lima, 1986).

Early trade links between Peru and Mexico are described in Woodrow Borah, *Early Colonial Trade between Mexico and Peru* (Berkeley, CA, 1954), and Lawrence A. Clayton "Trade and Navigation in the Seventeenth-Century Viceroyalty of Peru," *JLAS* 7 (1975), 1–21. Clayton's *Caulkers and Carpenters in a New World: The Shipyards of Colonial Guayaquil* (Athens, OH, 1980) describes the rise of the Guayaquil shipyards that provided ships for both the treasure fleet and maritime traffic that plied the Pacific west coast. See also Fred Bronner, "Church, Crown and Commerce in Seventeenth-Century Lima: A Synoptic Interpretation," in *Jarbuch fur Geschichte von Staat, Wirtschaft und Gesellschaft Lateinamerikas*, 29 (Cologne, Germany, 1992).

Andrien also carefully describes and analyzes the decline in royal government in Peru during the seventeenth century, much of which he attributes to the sale of public offices beginning in 1633. See also John Parry, *The Sale of Public Offices in the Spanish In-*

dies under the Hapsburgs (Berkeley, CA, 1953). The decline of colonial government can also be attributed to the increased costs of imperial defense, which, along with foreign intrusion into the Pacific, is chronicled by Peter T. Bradley, *The Lure of Peru: Maritime Instrusion into the South Sea, 1598–1701* (New York, 1989). See also his *Society, Economy, and Defence in Seventeenth-Century Peru: The Administration of the Count of Alba de Liste, 1655–1661* (Liverpool, England, 1992); "The Defence of Peru, 1648–1700," in *Jahrbuch*, 29, 90–120; and with David Cahill, *Hapsburg Peru: Images, Imagination and Memory in Peru* (Liverpool, England, 1999). Jesuit estates and entrepreneurial prowess are examined by Nicolas P. Cushner's *Lords of the Land: Sugar, Wine and Jesuit Estates of Colonial Peru, 1600–1767* (Albany, NY, 1980) and *Farm and Factory: The Jesuits and the Development of Agrarian Capitalism in Colonial Quito, 1600–1767* (Albany, NY, 1982). See also Pablo Macera's classic *Instrucciones para el manejo de las haciendas Jesuitas del Perú (siglos XVII–XVIII)* (Lima, 1966), as well as other works such as the sugar industry in his *Trabajos de Historia*, 4 vols. (Lima, 1977).

Sources on the Church are Brian R. Hamnett, "Church Wealth in Peru: Estates and Loans in the Archdiocese of Lima in the Seventeenth Century," *Jahrbuch*, 10 (1973), 113–132; Antonine Tibesar, *Franciscan Beginnings in Colonial Peru* (Washington, DC, 1953); and Luis Martin, *The Intellectual Conquest of Peru: The Jesuit College of San Pablo, 1568–1767* (New York, 1968). A good survery of church-state relations is by Margaret E. Crahan, "Civil-Ecclesiastical Relations in Hapsburg Peru," *Journal of Church and State* 20:1 (Winter 1978), 93–111.

The life of Santa Rosa de Lima has received considerable attention: Luis Millones, *Una partecita del cielo* (Lima, 1993); Fernando Iwasaki Cauti, "Mujeres al borde de la perfección: Rosa de Santa María y las alumbradas de Lima," *HAHR* 73:4 (November 1993), 581–613; and Luis Miguel Glave, "Santa Rosa de Lima y sus espinas: la emergencia de mentalidades urbanas de crisis y la sociedad andina (1600–1630)" in *Manifestaciones religiosas en el mundo colonial americana*, vol. 1, edited by C. García Ayluardo and M. Ramos Medina (Mexico City, 1993), 53–70. The latter has been expanded into a book: *De Rosa y espinas: economía, sociedad y mentalidades andinas, siglo XVII* (Lima, 1998). See also Teodoro Hampe Martínez, *Santidad e identidad criolla: estudio del proceso de canonización de la Santa Rosa* (Lima, 1998). Forthcoming from Oxford University Press is Frank Graziano, *Wounds of Love: The Mystical Marriage of Santa Rosa de Lima.*

On San Martín de Porras, see Iwasaki Cauti, "Fray Martín de Porras: Santo, ensalmador y sacamuelas," *CLAR* 3:1–2 (1994), 159–184, and José del Busto, *San Martín de Porras* (Lima, 1992). Other useful works on the religious climate of colonial Peru are Armando Nieto, *Francisco del Castillo, el apóstol de Lima* (Lima, 1992); María Emma Mannarelli, *Pecados públicos* (Lima, 1993); and Nancy Van Deusen, *Dentro del cerco de los muros: el recogimiento de la época colonial* (Lima, 1987) and her recent articles "Defining the Sacred and the Worldly: *Beatas* and *Recogidas* in Late Seventeenth-Century Lima," *Colonial Latin American History Review* 6:4 (Fall 1997), 441–477, and "Determining the Boundaries of Virtue: The Discourse of *Recogimiento* among Women in Seventeenth-Century Lima," *Journal of Family History* 22:4 (October 1997), 373–389.

Intellectual and cultural developments of the viceroyalty can be found in Jacques Lafaye, "Literature and Intellectual Life in Colonial Spanish America," in *CHLA*, 2, 663–704. The evolution of creole nationalism is developed in D. A. Brading's stunning *The First America: The Spanish Monarchy, Creole Patriots and the Liberal State, 1492–1867* (Cambridge, England, 1991), which compares the creole quest for identity in the viceroyalties of New Spain and Peru. In a similar vein, but for Peru, Bernard Lavalle examines *Las promesas ambiguas: criollismo colonial en los Andes* (Lima, 1993). The structure and function of colonial ceremonies and celebrations, which were an important means of controlling and unifying a heterogeneous colonial population, are innovatively explored by Juan Carlos Estenssoro Fuchs, *Música y sociedades coloniales: Lima 1680–1830* (Lima, 1989) and in other articles. See also Thierry Saignes's important "Indian Migration and Social Change in Seventeenth-Century Charcas," in *Ethnicity, Markets, and Migration in the Andes: At the Crossroads of History and Anthropology*, edited by Brooke Larson and Olivia Haris (Durham, NC, 1995), 167–195.

J. G. Varner has a biography of *El Inca: The Life and Times of Garcilaso de la Vega, 1539–1616* (Austin, TX, 1968), author of the *Royal Commentaries of the Incas*. Similarly, *Guamán Poma: Writing and Resistance in Colonial Peru* (Austin, TX, 1986), by Rolena Adorno carefully analyzes the works of the author of *Letter to a King*. A highly provocative and influential work is Manuel Burga's *Nacimiento de una utopía: muerte and resurrección de los Incas* (Lima, 1987). On the School of Cuzco paintings, see Teresa Grisbert, *Iconografía y mitos en el arte* (La Paz, 1980).

Some important documentary collections for the period are Roberto Levillier, (ed.), *Gobernantes del Perú: cartas y papeles, siglo XVI*, 14 vols. (Madrid, 1921–26), and Lewis Hanke (ed.), with Celso Rodríguez, *Los virreyes españoles en América durante el gobierno de la casa de Austria. Perú*, 5 vols. (Madrid, 1978–79).

EIGHTEENTH AND EARLY NINETEENTH CENTURIES (TO 1830)

An excellent overview of the Bourbon reforms is David Brading's "Bourbon Spain and Its American Empire," in *CHLA*, 1, 389–440. John R. Fisher has written extensively on the period. See his *Commercial Relations between Spain and Spanish America in the Era of Free Trade, 1778–1796* (Liverpool, England, 1985), "Soldiers, Society, and Politics in Spanish America, 1750–1821," *Latin American Research Review* (*LARR*) 17:1 (1982), and *Government and Society in Colonial Peru: The Intendent System, 1784–1814* (London, 1970), as well as numerous other articles. The standard account of the disruptive impact on Lima as a result of the creation of the viceroyalty of Buenos Aires is Guillermo Céspedes del Castillo, *Lima y Buenos Aires* (Seville, 1956). See also Carmen Parrón Salas, *De las reformas borbónicas a la república: el consulado y el comercio marítimo de Lima, 1778–1821* (Murcia, Spain, 1995).

On creole participation in audiencias, see Mark A. Burkholder and D. S. Chandler, *From Impotence to Authority: The Spanish Crown and the American Audiencias, 1787–1808* (Columbia, MO, 1977), and Burkholder's *Politics of a Colonial Career: José Baquijano and the Audiencia of Lima* (Albuquerque, NM, 1980). Manuel Marzal examines *La utopía posible: indios y jesuitas en la América colonial* (Lima, 1992). On the influence of the Enlightenment, see Pablo Macera, *Tres etapas en el desarrollo de la conciencia nacional* (Lima, 1956), and Guillermo Lohmann Villena, "Criticismo e ilustración como factores formativos de la conciencia del Perú en el siglo XVIII," in *Problemas de la formación del estado y de la nación en hispanoamérica*, edited by Inge Buisson et al. (Bonn, 1994), 15–31.

The starting point for the economy in the eighteenth century is Nils Jacobsen and Hans-Jurgen Puhle's excellent edited volume *The Economies of Mexico and Peru during the Late Colonial Period, 1760–1810* (Berlin, 1986). Mörner's overview of Spanish America, "The Rural Economy and Society," also covers Peru in the eighteenth century. Alberto Flores Galindo provides a rich analysis of the economy and society of Lima in *Aristocracia y plebe, Lima 1760–1830* (Lima, 1984). See also Ileana Vegas de Cáceres, *Economía rural y estructura social en las haciendas de Lima durante el siglo XVIII* (Lima, 1996). Jorge Juan and Antonio de Ulloa report their ten-year mission to the viceroyalty of Peru in *Discourse and Political Reflections on the Kindgoms of Peru . . .*, edited by John J. TePaske (Norman, OK, 1978[1735]). D. G. Browning and D. J. Robinson examine "The Origin and Comparability of Peruvian Population Data: 1776–1815," in *Jahrbuch*, 14 (1977).

John R. Fisher's *Silver Mines and Silver Miners in Colonial Peru, 1776–1824* (Liverpool, England, 1977) is the standard source on late colonial mining. A more recent study is Enrique Tandeter, *Coercion and Market: Silver Mining in Colonial Potosí, 1692–1826* (Albuquerque, NM, 1993). See also his "Población y economía en los Andes" (siglo XVIII), *Revista Andina* 13:1 (July 1995), 7–22 and other articles. Carlos Contreras examines *Los mineros y el rey: Los Andes del Norte, Hualgayoc, 1770–1825* (Lima, 1995). See also Rose Marie Buechler, *The Mining Society of Potosí, 1776–1810* (Syracuse, NY, 1981). Magdalena Chocano examines *Comercio en Cerro de Pasco a fines de la época colonial* (Lima, 1982).

On prices, see the contributions by Kendall W. Brown (Arequipa), Enrique Tandeter and Nathan Wachtel (Potosí and Charcas), and Brooke Larson (Cochabamba) in Lyman L. Johnson and Enrique Tandeter (eds.), *Essays on the Price History of Eighteenth-Century Latin America* (Albuquerque, NM, 1990). See also Pablo Macera, *Los precios del Perú, siglos XVI–XIX: Fuentes* (Lima, n.d.). Carlos Sempat Assadourian and his colleagues hypothesize that the expansion of mining after 1750 in Upper and Lower Peru both reflected and acted as a stimulus to the general economic expansion of the late colonial period. See *Minera y espacio económico en los Andes: siglos XVI–XX* (Lima, 1980).

Two important recent works on colonial finance and credit are Herbert S. Klein, *The American Finances of the Spanish Empire: Royal Income and Expenditures in Colonial Mexico, Peru and Bolivia, 1680–1809* (Albuquerque, NM, 1998), and Alfonso W. Quiroz, *Deudas olvidadas: instrumentos de crédito en la economía colonial peruana, 1750–1820* (Lima, 1993). Earlier works are Javier Tord Nicolini, *Las cajas reales y la sociedad colonial peruana, 1700–1820* (Lima, 1983), and Nicolini with C. Lazo, *Hacienda, comercio, fiscalidad y luchas sociales (Perú Colonial)* (Lima, 1981).

A number of important regional and local studies reveal aspects of both the economy and society in the eighteenth century. Nils Jacobsen analyzes the "long" nineteenth-century economy and society of the southern *altiplano* in *Mirages of Transition: The Peruvian Altiplano, 1780–1930* (Berkeley, CA, 1993). Kendell W. Brown studies Arequipa in *Bourbons and Brandy: Imperial Reform in Eighteenth-Century Arequipa* (Albuquerque, NM, 1986). Cristóbal Aljovín de Losada's "Los compradores de temporalidades a fines de la colonia," *Histórica* 14:2 (1990), 183–233, examines the sale of Jesuit estates after the order's expulsion in 1767, while Jorge Polo and G. La Borda treat the former Jesuit hacienda Pachachaca's commercial fortunes in *La hacienda Pachachaca: autoabastecimiento y comercialización (segunda mitad del siglo XVIII)* (Lima, 1980). Magnus Mörner surveys rural society and production in Cuzco in *Perfil de la sociedad rural del Cuzco a fines de la colonia* (Lima, 1978). Olinda Celestino and Albert Meyers' *Las cofradías en el Perú: región central* (Frankfurt, 1981) suggests that the rising number of land disputes indicated a growing pressure of population on the land and deteriorating man–land relationships.

On Lima's economic structure, see also M. M. Haitin, "Late Colonial Lima: Economy and Society in an Era of Reform and Revolution," (Ph.D. Diss., University of California, Berkeley, CA, 1983), and "Prices, the Lima Market and the Agricultural Crisis of the Late Eighteenth Century in Peru," *JLAS* 22 (1985), 167–198. O. Febres Villaroel studies "La crisis agrícola en el Perú en el último tercio del siglo XVIII," *Histórica* 27 (1964), 102–199, and A. Moreno Cebrián examines *El corregidor de indios y la economía peruana en el siglo XVIII* (Madrid, 1977). Other regional studies previously cited on the earlier colonial period extend their analyses through the eighteenth century. They include Glave and Remy, *Estructura agraria*; Cushner, *Lords of the Land*; Spalding, *Huarochiri*; Ramirez, *Provincial Patriarchs*; Macera, *Trabajos de Historia*; and Larson, *Colonialism*. See also Scarlett O'Phelan Godoy and Yves Saint-Geours (eds.), *El Norte en la historia regional, siglos XVIII–XIX* (Lima and Piura, 1998).

The eighteenth-century upsurge in Indian and *casta* rebellions, culminating in the Túpac Amaru revolt of 1780, has produced a substantial literature and considerable controversy and debate over the years. On the revolt of Juan Santos Atahualpa, the most recent works are Arturo Enrique Torre y López, "Juan Santos: el invencible?" *Histórica* 17:2 (1993), 239–266, and Alonso Zarzar, *Apo Capac Huayna, Jesús Sacramentado* (Lima, 1989). The best account in English is Michael F. Brown and Eduardo Fernandez, *War of the Shadows: The Struggle for Utopia in the Peruvian Amazon* (Berkeley, CA, 1991).

There are four main interpretations of the Great Rebellion of Túpac Amaru that erupted in Cuzco in 1780: those who see it as a precursor to independence, as Inca revivalism and neo-Inca nationalism, as a traditional form of political negotiation for reform of the colonial state, and as an anticolonialist, proto-nationalist movement. The most recent analysis is Ward Stavig, *The World of Túpac Amaru: Conflict, Community, and Identity in Colonial Peru* (Lincoln, NE, 1999). See also Charles F. Walker's *Smoldering Ashes: Cuzco and the Creation of Republican Peru, 1780–1840* (Durham, NC, 1999), and his edited

Entre la retórica y la insurgencia: las ideas y los movimientos sociales en los Andes, Siglo XVIII (Cuzco, 1996), which has important contributions by Estenssoro Fuchs on popular ideologies and Sergio Serulnikov on Upper Peru peasants' understanding of just order. See also the latter's "Disputed Images of Colonialism: Spanish Rule and Indian Subversion in Northern Potosí, 1777–1780," *HAHR* 76:2 (May 1996), 189–226, which breaks new ground in interpreting eighteenth-century Andean rebellion which may be applicable to events in Lower Peru.

An important older overview is Steve J. Stern (ed.), *Resistance, Rebellion, and Consciousness in the Andean Peasant World: 18th to 20th Centuries* (Madison, WI, 1987). Alberto Flores Galindo critiques the various interpretations in "Las revoluciones tupamaristas: temas en debate," *Revista Andina* 7:1 (1989), 279–287, while Jean Piel asks "Como interpretar la rebelión pan-Andina de 1780–1783," in *Tres levantamientos populares: Pugachov, Túpac Amaru, Hidalgo*, edited by Jean Meyer (Mexico City, 1992), 71–80. Other edited volumes containing important contributions are Flores Galindo, *Túpac Amaru II—1780: Antología* (Lima, 1976) which includes John Rowe's seminal "El movimiento nacional inca del siglo XVIII," originally published in 1954; Flores Galindo, *Túpac Amaru y la Iglesia: Antología* (Cuzco, 1983); *Actas del coloquio internacional: Túpac Amaru y su tiempo* (Lima, 1982); and Luis Durand Flores (ed.), *La revolución de los Túpac Amaru: Antología* (Lima, 1981).

The causes of the uprisings are also explored by Scarlett O'Phelan Godoy in *La gran rebelión en los andes: De Túpac Amaru a Túpac Catari* (Cuzco, 1995), *Rebellions and Revolts in Eighteenth-Century Peru and Upper Peru* (Cologne, Germany, 1985), *Un siglo de rebeliónes anticoloniales. Perú y Bolivia 1700–1783* (Lima, 1988), as well as numerous other articles. Her latest book examines the decline of the *curacas* in *Kurakas sin sucesiones*. See also Ward Stavig, "Ethnic Conflict, Moral Economy, and Population in Rural Cuzco on the Eve of the Thupa Amaro II Rebellion," *HAHR* 68:4 (1988), 737–770; John Rowe, "Genealogía y rebelión en el siglo XVIII: Algunos antecedentes de la sublevación de José Gabriel Thupa Amaru," *Histórica* 6:1 (July 1982), 65–85; and David Cahill, "Crown, Clergy and Revolution in Bourbon Peru: The Diocese of Cuzco, 1780–1814," (Ph.D. diss., University of Liverpool, 1984), as well as several of his articles. Two other important studies are Jan Szeminski's *La utopía tupamarista* (Lima, 1984), and Jürgen Golte's *Repartos y rebeliónes. Túpac Amaru y las contradicciones de la economía colonial* (Lima, 1980).

Leon G. Campbell's, *The Military and Society in Colonial Peru* (Philadelphia, 1978) examines the suppression of the rebellion by royalist forces. See also his "Recent Research on Andean Peasant Revolts, 1750–1820," *LARR* 14:1 (1977), 3–49, and other articles. Other useful works are José Antonio del Busto, *José Gabriel Túpac Amaru antes de la rebelión* (Lima, 1981), Luis Durand Flores, *Independencia e integración en el plan político de Túpac Amaru* (Lima, 1973), and his edited *Colección documental del bicentenario de la revolución emancipadora de Túpac Amaru*, 5 vols. (Lima, 1980–82). The Comisión Nacional del Sesquicentenario de la Independencia del Perú published *Colección documental de la independencia del Perú* in 30 volumes (Lima, 1971–75), which includes vol. 3, *La rebelión de Túpac Amaru* (Lima, 1980). Kathryn Burns, "Amor y rebelión en 1782: el caso de Mariano Túpac Amaru y María Mejía," *Histórica* 16:2 (1992), 131–176, uncovers an interesting sidelight.

The roots of continuing native unrest and rebellion in the wake of the Great Rebellion are examined by Nuria Sala i Vila, *Y se armó el tole tole: tributo indígena y movimientos sociales en el virreinato del Perú, 1784–1814* (Lima, 1996). She shows how the crown's overhaul of the tribute system after the Túpac Amaru revolt worked to undermine the Indian communities by allowing outsiders to control its collection. Several works chronicle these subsequent revolts, particularly those of Cuzco in 1805 and 1814. See, for example, Luis Durand Flores, *El proceso de independencia en el sur Andino: Cuzco y La Paz 1805* (Lima, 1993); Alberto Flores Galindo's highly original *Buscando un Inca: identidad y utopía en los Andes* (Lima, 1987); and John Fisher, "Regionalism and Rebellion in Late Colonial Peru: The Aguilar-Ubalde Conspiracy of 1805," *Biblioteca Americana* 1:1 (1982), 44–59. The later revolt is the subject of Víctor Peralta Ruíz, "Elecciones, Constitucionalismo y Revolución en el Cuzco, 1809–1815" in Carlos Malamud (ed.), *Partidos políticos y elecciones en América*

Latina y la Península Ibérica, 1830–1930, 2 vols. (Madrid, 1995), 83–112; Sala i Vila, "La participación indígena en la rebelión de los Angulo y Pumacahua, 1814–1816," in Pilar García Jordan and Miguel Izard (eds.), *Conquista y resistencia en la Historia de América* (Barcelona, 1992), 273–288; David P. Cahill, "Una visión andina: el levantamiento de Ocongate de 1815," *Histórica* 12:2 (December 1988), 133–159; and Cahill with Scarlett O'Phelan Godoy, "Forging Their Own History: Indian Insurgency in the Southern Peruvian Sierra, 1815," *BLAR* 11:2 (1992), 126–167. The older study is Jorge Cornejo Bouroncle, *Pumacahua: la revolución del Cuzco de 1814, estudio documentado* (Cuzco, 1974). See also Luis Durand Flores, *Criollos en conflicto: Cuzco después de Túpac Amaru* (Lima, 1985).

The struggle for independence, as would be expected, has generated a considerable bibliography. Since Peru formed part of the larger process of independence throughout South America, students should begin with the excellent recent analysis by Brian R. Hamnett, "Process and Pattern: A Re-examination of the Ibero-American Independence Movements, 1808–1826," *JLAS* 29:2 (May 1997), 279–328. See also David Bushnell and Neill Macaulay, *The Emergence of Latin America in the Nineteenth Century* (New York, 1988, 1994); George Reid Andrews's incisive "Spanish American Independence: A Structural Analysis," *Latin American Perspectives* 12:1 (Winter, 1985), 105–132; and John Lynch *The Spanish American Revolutions, 1808–1826* (London, 1973). On the development and significance of creole nationalism, see Brading's *The First Americans*; Lavalle, *Las promesas ambiguas*; and Cecilia Méndez, *Incas Sí, Indios No: apuntes para el estudio de nacionalismo criollo en el Perú* (Lima, 1993). Méndez is the latest scholar (see Ramos and Serulnikov) to question the significance of the Andean utopia (Flores Galindo and Burga) as a major cause of native rebellion. In contrast to the work of the latter, she analyzes it as an intellectual discourse that reflects the nationalistic aspirations of Peruvian intellectuals, rather than a reliable account of the collective mentality or aspirations of the native Andean peasantry.

The most detailed account on Peru in English is by Timothy E. Anna, *The Fall of the Royal Government in Peru* (Lincoln, NE, 1979), which argues that the economic decline of Peru after 1812 led to the collapse of the royal regime. Anna's work, which examines the rebellion primarily from the perspective of Lima, is complemented by Walker's *Smoldering Ashes*. The provincial dimensions are examined in John Fisher's "Royalism, Regionalism, and Rebellion in Colonial Peru, 1808–1815," *HAHR* 59:2 (1979), 232–257.

The idea of "Indigenous Nationalism" was promoted by the Velasco Alvarado (1968–75) government's publication of the *Colección documental*. It is an amalgam of official documents, newspapers of the period, writings of ideologues, memoirs, and travel accounts. On the creole version, see Félix Dengri Luna, Armando Nieto Velez, S.J., and Alberto Tauro, *Antología de la independencia del Perú* (Lima, 1972), and *Quinto Congreso Internacional de Historia de América*, 5 vols. (Lima, 1972), both also issued by the Comisión Nacional del Sesquicentenario de la Independencia del Perú.

A revisionist, Marxist school, led by Heraclio Bonilla and Karen Spalding (eds.) in their *La independencia en el Perú* (Lima, 1972, 1981) challenged these views. They argue that Peru's independence was essentially the work of outside forces that lacked effective commitment by elites, widespread popular participation, and any sense of national consciousness. This contributed to a postindependence period characterized by a weak state, the persistence of traditional colonial social and economic structures of domination, and the rise of external dependence on British imperialism. Jorge Basadre also joined the debate in *El azar en la historia y sus límites* (Lima, 1973), while Scarlett O'Phelan Godoy challenges "El mito de la independencia concedida: los programas políticos del siglo XVIII y del temprano Siglo XIX en el Perú (1730–1814)" in *Problemas de la formación del estado.*

Other useful works include John R. Fisher, Allan J. Kuethe, and Anthony McFarlane (eds.), *Reform and Insurrection in Bourbon New Granada and Peru* (Baton Rouge, LA, 1990); Alberto Flores Galindo (comp.), *Independencia y revolución (1780–1840)*, 2 vols. (Lima, 1987); and Brian R. Hamnett, *Revolución y contrarrevolución en México y el Perú: liberalismo, realeza y separatismo (1808–1824)* (Mexico City, 1978).

Popular participation in the struggle for independence is the subject of numerous articles and books. Peter Guardino, "Las guerrillas y la independencia peruana: un ensayo de interpretación," *Pasado y Presente* 2:3 (1989), 101–117; Heraclio Bonilla, "Bolívar y las guerrillas indígenas del Perú," *Cultura: Revista del Banco Central del Ecuador* (May–August 1983), 81–95; Ezequiel Beltrán G., *Las guerrillas de Yauyos en la emancipación del Perú, 1820–1824* (Lima, 1977); and Raúl Rivera Serna, *Los guerrilleros del centro en la emancipación peruana* (Lima, 1958).

Independence and the Nineteenth Century

Long known as "the forgotten century," the nineteenth century is receiving more attention from historians. An excellent revisionist approach is Peter Guardino and Charles Walker, "The State, Society, and Politics in Peru and Mexico in the Late Colonial and Early Republican Periods," in *Latin American Perspectives* 19:2 (Spring 1992), 10–43. Various historians debate the problem of *Tradicion y modernidad en los Andes* in the nineteenth century (Henrique Urbano, comp., Cuzco, 1992). The larger Latin American context can be found in Frank Safford, "Politics, Ideology and Society in Post-Independence Spanish America, 1821–1870," in *CHLA*, 3 (1985), 347–421. A useful, short overview is Heraclio Bonilla, "Peru and Bolivia from Independence to the War of the Pacific," in *CHLA*, 3, 539–582. English antiquarian Clements Markham's *A History of Peru* (Chicago, 1892) is still valuable.

Two earlier interpretative essays on the formation and role of the state are Ronald H. Berg and Frederick Stirton Weaver, "Towards a Reinterpretation of Political Change in Peru during the First Century of Independence," *Journal of Interamerican Studies and World Affairs (JISWA)* 20:1 (February 1978), 69–84, and Stephen Gorman, "The State, Elite and Export in Nineteenth-Century Peru," *JISWA* 21:3 (August 1979), 395–418. For historiographical overviews, see Nelson Manrique, "La historiografía peruana sobre el siglo XIX," *Revista Andina* 9:1 (July 1991), 241–259, and Christine Hünefeldt, "Viejos y nuevos temas de la historia económica del siglo XIX," in *Las crisis económicos en la historia del Perú*, edited by Heraclio Bonilla (Lima, 1986), 33–60. Early and later approaches to the problem of *La decentralización en el Perú republicano (1821–1998)* are examined by Pedro Planas (Lima, 1998).

The idea of a collapsed state opening the way for the penetration of foreign imperialism is developed by the dependency school, particularly Bonilla, "Continuidad y cambio en la organización política del Estado en el Perú independiente," in *Problemas de la formación del estado*, 481–498, also reprinted in *Independencia y revolución: 1780–1840*, edited by Alberto Flores Galindo (Lima, 1987), 269–294, and Bonilla et al. (eds.), *La independencia*. See also John Fisher, "La formación del estado peruano (1808–1824) y Simón Bolívar," in *Problemas de la formación del estado*, 465–480; Flores Galindo, "El militarismo y la dominación británica (1825–1845)," in *Nueva historia general del Perú*, edited by C. Aranibar and H. Bonilla (Lima, 1979), 107–123; and Celia Wu Brading, *Generals and Diplomats: Great Britain and Peru, 1820–1840* (Cambridge, England, 1991).

In "Continuidad y cambio," Bonilla argues that colonial structures persisted well into the nineteenth century. The same theme is developed by Julio Cotler, *Clases, estado y nación en el Perú* (Lima, 1978), and Jesus Chavarria, "The Colonial Heritage of National Peru: An Overview," *Boletín de Estudios Latinoamericanos y del Caribe* 25 (1978), 37–49. See also Alberto Flores Galindo's provocative *Aristocracia y Plebe, Lima 1760–1830* (Lima, 1984) on class relations in the transition from colony to republic.

According to the traditional interpretation of rampant, postindependence *caudillismo*, political ideas were reduced to sterile debates in the drawing rooms of the urban, cosmopolitan elites and had little impact on political outcomes. These early ideological divisions are well treated in Gonzalo M. Portocarrero, "Conservadurismo, liberalismo y democracia en el Perú del siglo xix," in *Pensamiento político peruano* (Lima, 1987), 85–98, and Daniel M. Gleason, "Anti-Democratic Thought in Early Republican Peru: Bartolomé Herrrera and the Liberal-Conservative Ideological Struggle," *The Americas* 38 (1981),

205–217. See also Hugo Garavito Amezaga, *El Perú Liberal: Partidos e ideas políticas de la ilustración a la república aristocrática* (Lima, 1989), and Fernando Trazegnies' important *La idea del derecho en el Peru republicano del siglo XIX* (Lima, 1980), which examines changes in the law in the postindependence period and its evolution throughout the nineteenth century.

The church in the early republic is examined by Klaiber, *The Catholic Church and Religion and Revolution in Peru, 1824–1976* (Notre Dame, IN, 1977). A more detailed account is Pilar García Jordan, *Iglesia y poder en el Perú contemporaneo 1821–1919* (Cuzco, n.d.), and "Estado moderno, Iglesia y secularización en el Perú contemporaneo (1821–1919)," *Revista Andina* 6:2 (December 1988). Both see relations between the Church and the liberal state as relatively benign because of mutual needs to sustain their power.

Path-breaking work on this period has been done by economic historian Paul Gootenberg, who sees more behind the *caudillo* conflicts than mere personalistic struggles for power. His meticulous and revisionist *Between Silver and Guano: Commercial Policy and the State in Postindependence Peru* (Princeton, NJ, 1989) is a model of historical analysis on issues of trade and politics. Similarly, Walker focuses on the ignored program of Agustín Gamarra, a dominant *caudillo* figure during the early republic, in his seminal *Smoldering Ashes*, which also attributes a greater degree of agency to the subaltern classes in postindependence politics, but who are, in the end, denied citizenship in the new republic. Also focusing on Cuzco is Thomas Kruggeler, "Unreliable Drunkards or Honorable Citizens? Artisans in Search of Their Place in Cuzco Society (1825–1930)," (Ph.D. diss., University of Illinois, Urbana-Champaign, 1993).

Another revisionist work on the dynamics of *caudillismo* is Cecilia Méndez, "Rebellion without Resistance: Huanta's Monarchist Peasants in the Making of the Peruvian State, Ayacucho 1825–1850," (Ph.D. diss., SUNY, Stony Brook, 1996). Earlier Patrick Husson, in *De la guerra a la rebelión (Huanta, siglo XIX)* (Lima, 1992), had posited that this monarchist revolt pitted the old provincial elite allied with the native peasantry against emerging sociopolitical groups representing the new republic. See also Heraclio Bonilla, "La oposición de los campesinos indios a la República Peruana: Iquicha, 1827," in *Los pueblos campesinos de las Américas: etnicidad, cultura e historia en el siglo XIX*, edited by Bonilla and Amado A. Buerrero Rincón (Santander, Spain, 1996), 301–313.

Gootenberg pioneered the study of prices for the period in his "Carneros y Chuño: Price Levels in Nineteenth-Century Peru," *HAHR* 70:1 (February 1990), 1–57. His other works are "North-South: Trade Policy, Regionalism and Caudillismo in Post-Independence Peru," *JLAS* 25:2 (May 1991), 273–308; "Beleaguered Liberals: The Failed First Generation of Free Traders in Peru," in *Guiding the Invisible Hand: Economic Liberalism and the State in Latin American History*, edited by Joseph Love and Nils Jacobsen (New York, 1988), 63–97, and "The Social Origins of Protectionism and Free Trade in Nineteenth Century Lima," *JLAS* 14 (1982), 329–58. See also his *Tejidos y harinas, corazones y mentes: el imperialismo norteamericano del libre comercio en el Perú, 1825–1840* (Lima, 1989), and "Paying for Caudillos: The Politics of Emergency Finance in Peru, 1820–1845," in *Liberals, Politics and Power: State Formation in Nineteenth-Century Latin America*, edited by V. Peloso and B. Tenenbaum (Athens, GA, 1996), 134–165.

Additional important economic and quantitative studies have been published on the early republican period. In *Mirages of Transition*, Nils Jacobsen also argues that continuity, rather than change, was the hallmark of a process of conservative modernization during the "long" nineteenth century. Other valuable works are Shane Hunt, "Price and Quantum Estimates of Peruvian Exports, 1830–1962," discussion paper (Princeton, NJ, 1973); Heraclio Bonilla, "La coyuntura comercial del siglo XIX en el Perú," *Desarrollo Económico* 12:46 (July–September 1972), 305–331; and Bonilla, *Gran Britañia y el Perú. Los mecanismos de un control económico* (Lima, 1977). The adverse impact of free trade on Cuzco is examined by Bonilla, Lia del Rio, and Pilar Ortiz de Zevallos, "Comercio Libre y crisis de la economía Andina: El caso de Cuzco," *Histórica* 2:1 (1978). However, the recent work of Kruggeler disputes this dependency view. William L. Lofstrom foreshadows United States economic interest in Peru in *Paita: Outpost of Empire: The Impact of the New*

England Whaling Fleet on the Socioeconomic Development of Northern Peru, 1832–1865 (Mystic, CT, 1997).

The problem of foreign loans and debt is examined by Carlos Marichal, *A Century of Debt Crises in Latin America: From Independence to Great Depression, 1820–1930* (Princeton, NJ, 1989), and Carlos Palacios Moreyra, *La deuda anglo-peruana, 1822–1890* (Lima, 1983). See also W. M. Mathew, "The First Anglo-Peruvian Debt and Its Settlement, 1822–49," *JLAS* 2 (1970), 81–98.

The major work on mining is José Deustua, *The Bewitchment of Silver: The Social Economy of Mining in Nineteenth-Century Peru* (Athens, OH, 1999). Two other important works on mining for the period are José Deustua, *La minería peruana y la iniciación de la república, 1820–1840* (Lima, 1986), and Carlos Contreras, *Mineros y campesinos en los Andes: mercado laboral y economía campesina en la Sierra Central, siglo XIX* (Lima, 1987). See also Deustua's "Routes, Roads and Silver Trade in Cerro de Pasco, 1820–1860," *HAHR* 74:1 (1994), 1–31, and "Mining Markets, Peasants, and Power in Nineteenth-Century Peru," *LARR* 29:1 (1994), 29–54, which, like Assadourian for the colonial period, analyzes the ramifications of silver mining on the internal market in the early republic, as well as Nelson Manrique, *Mercado interno y región: la sierra central, 1820–1930* (Lima, 1987).

Pablo Macera treats a wide range of agrarian, economic, and social issues in his *Trabajos de Historia*, 4 vols. (Lima, 1977). For example, see his "Feudalismo colonial americano"; "Algodon y comercio exterior peruano en el siglo xix," in vol. 3, and "Las plantaciones azucareras andinas, 1821–1875" in vol. 4. Jean Piel has also written extensively on agrarian matters in *Capitalisme agraire au Perou*, 2 vols. (Paris, 1975–83). The best source on the wool trade is Jacobsen, *Mirages*. See also Rory Miller, "The Wool Trade of Southern Peru, 1850–1915," *Ibero-Amerikanisches Archiv* 8 (1982), 297–311, and W. S. Bell, *An Essay on the Peruvian Cotton Industry, 1825–1920* (Liverpool, England, 1985).

Indian Communities are treated by Mark Thurner in *From Two Republics to One Divided: Contradictions of Postcolonial Nationmaking in the Andes* (Durham, NC, 1997), and "'Republicanos' and 'la Comunidad de Peruanos': Unimagined Political Communities in Postcolonial Andean Peru," *JLAS* 27:2 (May 1995), 291–318. Nils Jacobsen examines "Liberalism and Indian Communities in Peru, 1821–1920," in *Liberals, the Church and Indian Peasants*, edited by R. H. Jackson (Albuquerque, NM, 1997), 123–170. See also Luis Miguel Glave, *Vida símbolos* and Christine Hünefeldt, *Lucha por la tierra y protesta indígena y las comunidades indígenas del Perú entre colonia y república, 1800–1830* (Bonn, 1982). Other useful articles are Henre Favre, "El mundo andino en tiempos de Bolívar: los Asto entre 1780–1830," *Revista del Museo Nacional* 47 (1983–85), 259–271, and "Bolívar y los indios," *Histórica* 10:1 (July 1986), 1–17.

Tristan Platt outlines his tributary-state model in *Estado boliviano y ayllu andino: tierra y tributo en el norte de Potosí* (Lima, 1982). Two attempts to apply this model to Peru are María Isabel Remy, "La sociedad local al inicio de la república: Cuzco, 1824–1850," *Revista Andina* 6:2 (December 1988), 451–484, and Luis Miguel Glave, "Demografía y conflicto social: historia de las comunidades campesinas en los Andes del sur" (Lima Instituto de Estudios Peruanos, Documento de Trabajo 23, 1988).

Víctor Peralta Ruíz carefully examines state finances in Cuzco in *En pos del tributo: burocracia estatal, elite regional y comunidades indígenas en el Cuzco rural, 1826–1854* (Cuzco, 1991). He posits a quid pro quo between the state and Indian communities based on the continued collection of the tribute while showing how an emergent mestizo class used the provincial bureaucracy to gain power and prestige in the countryside. Early tax policies are examined as well by Nils Jacobsen, "Taxation in Early Republican Peru, 1821–1851: Policy Making between Reform and Tradition," in *América Latina en la época de Simón Bolívar*, edited by Reinhard Liehr (Berlin, 1989), 324–330; Carlos Contreras, "Estado republicano y tributo indígena en la sierra central en la post-independencia," *Histórica* 13:1 (July 1989), 9–44; and Christine Hünefeldt, "Poder y contribuciones: Puno, 1825–1845," *Revista Andina* 7:2 (December 1989), 367–409.

Social developments in the early republic have also received increasing attention. Gootenberg's demographic study on "Population and Ethnicity in Early Republican Peru:

Some Revisions," *LARR* 3 (1991), 109–157, revises some of George Kubler's propositions (1952). The standard works on slavery are Christine Hünefeldt *Paying the Price of Freedom: Family and Labor among Lima's Slaves, 1800–1854* (Berkeley, CA, 1994), and Carlos Aguirre, *Agentes de su propia libertad: los esclavos y la desintegración de la esclavitud, 1821–1854* (Lima, 1993), both of which attribute greater agency to slaves in the process of manumission. See also Peter Blanchard's balanced *Slavery and Abolition in Early Republican Peru* (Austin, TX, 1992), which sees manumission more as an outcome of the civil war of 1854–55. Carlos Aguirre and Charles Walker (eds.) explore problems of criminality and social violence across time in *Bandoleros, abigeos y montoneros: criminalidad y violencia en el Perú, siglos xvii–xx* (Lima, 1990). See also Carlos Aguirre, "The Lima Penitentiary and the Modernization of Criminal Justice in Nineteenth-Century Peru," in *The Birth of the Penitentiary in Latin America: Essays on Criminology, Prison Reform, and Social Control, 1840–1940*, edited by Ricardo Salvatore and Aguirre (Austin, TX, 1996); and Christine Hünefeldt, "Cimarrones, bandoleros and milicianos: 1821," *Histórica* 3 (1979), 71–88.

Gender studies and women in the nineteenth century are receiving increasing attention. See Christine Hünefeldt, *Liberalism in the Bedroom: Quarreling Spouses in Nineteenth-Century Lima* (University Park, PA, 1999); Sarah C. Chambers, *From Subjects to Citizens: Honor, Gender and Politics in Arequipa, Peru, 1780–1854* (University Park, PA, 1999); and Gertrude M. Yeager, "Women and the Intellectual Life of Nineteenth-Century Lima," *Inter-American Review of Bibliography* 40:3 (1990), 361–393.

The guano era (1840–80) has been the focus of considerable scholarly inquiry and debate over the years. The most recent example is Paul Gootenberg's penetrating *Imagining Development: Economic Ideas in Peru's "Fictitious Prosperity" of Guano, 1840–1880* (Berkeley, CA, 1993). Gootenberg is the first historian to show that a sophisticated tradition of contrary, "developmentalist" thought competed with the advocates of the predominant liberal, outward-oriented growth model during the guano era. See also his *Between Silver and Guano*.

The mechanics of the guano trade and the considerable degree of autonomy maintained by the Peruvian government are carefully developed in W. M. Mathew's *The House of Gibbs and the Peruvian Guano Monopoly* (London, 1981) and several important articles, including "A Primitive Export Sector: Guano Production in Mid-Nineteenth-Century Peru," *JLAS* 9:1 (1977). Economist Shane Hunt disputes the enclave thesis of Jonathan Levin (1960) in "Growth and Guano in Nineteenth-Century Peru," in *The Latin American Economies: Growth and the Export Sector, 1830–1930*, edited by Roberto Cortes Conde and Shane Hunt (New York, 1985), 255–319, which supersedes his *Growth and Guano in Nineteenth-Century Peru* (Princeton, NJ, 1973) ["Guano y crecimiento en el Perú del siglo XIX," *HISLA* 4 (1984), 35–92]. See also Cecilia Méndez, "La otra historia del guano: Perú 1840–1879," *Revista Andina* 5:9 (1987), 7–46. The dependency view is developed by Heraclio Bonilla in *Guano y burguesía en el Perú* (3d ed., Quito, 1994); in this recent edition, he brings his thesis up to date and responds to his critics. The attempt of the government to shift from guano to nitrate exports is analyzed by Robert Greenhill and Rory Miller, "The Peruvian Government and the Nitrate Trade, 1873–1879," *JLAS* 5:1 (1973), 107–131.

The standard study on the importation of Chinese laborers to replace black slaves after manumission is Watt Stewart, *Chinese Bondage in Peru: A History of the Chinese Coolie in Peru, 1849–1874* (Durham, NC, 1951). The subject has been reexamined more recently by Fernando Trazegnies, *En el país de las colinas de arena: reflexiones sobre la inmigración china en el Perú del s. XIX* 2 vols. (Lima, 1994), and Humberto Rodríguez Pastor, *Hijos del celeste imperio en el Perú (1850–1900): migración, agricultura, mentalidad y explotación* (Lima, 1989). See also H. E. Maude, *Slavers in Paradise: The Peruvian Labour Trade in Polynesia, 1862–1864* (Canberra, Australia, 1981).

The problem of guano and the debt is analyzed by Alfonso W. Quiroz in his revisionist *La deuda defraudada: consolidación de 1850 y dominio económico en el Perú* (Lima, 1987). See also his important *Domestic and Foreign Finance in Modern Peru, 1850–1950: Financing Visions of Development* (Pittsburgh, PA, 1993). On guano and state formation, see Javier Tantaleán Arbulú, *Política económica-financiera y la formación del Estado: siglo xix* (Lima, 1983).

Watt Stewart is also the biographer of railroad builder *Henry Meiggs: Yankee Pizarro* (Durham, NC, 1946). On the significance of railroads and development, see Carlos Contreras, "Mineros, arrieros y ferrocarril en Cerro de Pasco, 1870–1904" *HISLA* 5 (1984); Guido Pennano, "Desarrollo regional y ferrocarriles en el Perú," *Apuntes* 5:9 (1979), 131–151; and Heraclio Bonilla, "El impacto de los ferrocarriles: algunas proposiciones," *Historia y Cultura* (1972), 93–120. Early industrial development is chronicled in Jorge M. Grieve, "El desarrollo de las industrias mecánicas en el Perú entre 1800 y 1880," *Historia y Cultura* 15 (1982), 23–69. On the reinvestment of guano profits in coastal agriculture, see Macera, "Las Plantaciones"; Engelsen, "Social Aspects"; and Burga, *De la encomienda.* Guano's impact on the development of commerce and agriculture in the central sierra is suggested by Florencia Mallon, *The Defense of Community in Peru's Central Highlands: Peasant Struggle and Capitalist Transition, 1860–1940* (Princeton, NJ, 1983), and Manrique, *Mercado interno y región.* See also Manuel Burga, "La hacienda en el Perú, 1850–1930: evidencias y método," *Tierra y sociedad* (1978), 9–38.

Carmen Mc Evoy's, *La utopía republicana: ideales y realidades en la formación de la cultura política Peruana (1871–1919)* (Lima, 1997), based on her UCSD dissertation, covers nineteenth- and early twentieth-century political history in broad strokes. She shows how the Civilistas, led by Manuel Pardo, overcame the authoritarian legacies of Ramón Castilla, only to fall back gradually into authoritarian ways themselves. See also her *Un proyecto nacional en el siglo XIX: Manuel Pardo y su visión del Perú* (Lima, 1994). Readers should also consult Ulrich Mucke's excellent *Der Partido Civil in Peru* (Stuttgart, Germany, 1998), which is rich in analyses of mechanisms of rule, both in the Executive and legislature, as well as the electoral process. Vincent Peloso examines "Liberals, Electoral Reform, and the Popular Vote in Mid Nineteenth Century Peru," in *Liberals, Politics, and Power*, 186–211. The elites' view of the Indian is analyzed by Efraín Kristal, *The Andes Viewed from the City: Literacy and Political Discourse on the Indian in Peru 1848–1930* (New York, 1987).

On European immigration during the guano era, see Pilar García Jordan, "Reflexiones sobre el darwinismo social: inmigración y colonización, mitos de los grupos modernizadores Peruanos, 1821–1919," *Bulletin de Institut Francais d'Etudes Andines* 21:3 (1992), 961–975. Italian immigration is examined in Giovanni Bonfiglio, *Los Italianos en la sociedad Peruana* (Lima, 1993), and Evelyn Worrall, *La inmigración Italiana: 1860–1914* (Lima, 1990). Also useful is Christine Hünefeldt, "Inserción socioeconómica de los extranjeros en el Perú: una interpretación de los datos censales entre 1840 y 1870," in *Primer seminario sobre poblaciones inmigrantes: actas* (Lima, 1986), 141–196. The early history of the Grace brothers in Peru can be found in Larry Clayton, *W. R. Grace & Co.: The Formative Years, 1850–1930* (Ottawa, IL, 1985), and Marquis James, *Merchant-Adventurer: The Story of W. R. Grace* (Wilmington, DE, 1993).

Francisco Quiroz Chueca has written on *La protesta de los artesanos: Lima-Callao, 1858* (Lima, 1988). See also Cecilia Méndez, "Importaciones de lujo y clases populares: un motin Limeño," *Cielo Abierto* 29:10 (July 1984). An arresting reinterpretation of the mob violence triggered by the 1872 aborted coup is *Masas urbanas y rebelión en la historia: golpe de estado: Lima 1872* (Lima, 1978) by Margarita Giesecke. On the upsurge of peasant revolts in the second half of the century, see Michael J. Gonzales, "Neo-colonialism and Indian Unrest in Southern Peru, 1867–1898," *BLAR* 6:1 (1987), 1–26. On the Bustamante rebellion, see Nils P. Jacobsen, "Civilization and Its Barbarism: The Inevitability of Juan Bustamante's Failure," in *The Human Tradition in Latin America, the Nineteenth Century*, edited by William Beezley and Judith Ewell (Wilmington, DE, 1989), 82–101, and Emilio Vásquez, *La rebelión de Juan Bustamante* (Lima, 1976). Humberto Rodríguez Pastor has examined *La rebelión de los rostros pintados* (Lima, 1979).

Some of the best nineteenth-century travel accounts are J. J. von Tschudi, *Travels in Peru (1838–42)*, translated by T. Ross (London, 1847); Basil Hall, *Extracts from a Journal Written on the Coast of Chile, Peru and Mexico in the Years 1820, 1821, and 1822*, 2 vols. (Edinburgh, 1824); Clements R. Markham, *Travels in Peru and India* (London, 1862); Thomas J. Hutchinson, *Two Years in Peru*, 2 vols. (London, 1873); and Flora Tristán, *Peregrinations of a Pariah, 1833–34: Flora Tristán*, translated by Jean Hawkes (Boston, 1986), and *Flora*

Tristán, Utopian Feminist: Her Travel Diaries and Personal Crusade, edited and translated by Paul and Doris Beik (Bloomington, IN, 1993).

Late Nineteenth and Early Twentieth Century

An overview of the period can be found in Peter F. Klarén, "The Origins of Modern Peru, 1880–1930," in *CHLA*, 5, 587–640. It is accompanied by an extensive bibliographical essay (891–896), which is updated in volume 11 (1994). See also Mc Evoy, *La utopía republicana.* David Nugent wrote a provocative regional study of the emergence of the modern state: *Modernity at the Edge of Empire: State, Individual and Nation in the Northern Peruvian Andes, 1885–1935* (Stanford, CA, 1997). Also useful on this period is Magnus Mörner, *The Andean Past: Land, Societies, and Conflicts* (New York, 1985). For informative essays on urban planning, religion, social structure, the labor movement, ethnicity, and culture, see Aldo Panfichi and Felipe Portocarrero S. (eds.), *Mundos interiores: Lima, 1850–1950* (Lima, 1995).

A comprehensive history of the Pacific War has yet to be written in either Spanish or English. Moreover, there is no Peruvian counterpart to William F. Sater's solid *Chile and the War of the Pacific* (Lincoln, NE, 1986) whose bibliography contains the relevant sources on both sides of the conflict, whereas a brief, but good diplomatic overview can be found in Ronald Bruce St John, *The Foreign Policy of Peru* (Boulder, CO, 1992). The best general Peruvian account can still be found in the works of Jorge Basadre, particularly his *Historia de la República del Perú* 6th ed., 17 vols. (Lima, 1968–69), vol. 8, and *Chile, Perú y Bolivia independientes* (Barcelona and Buenos Aires, 1948). On domestic politics and social mobilization in the aftermath of the fall of Lima, see Margarita Guerra Martiniere, *La ocupación de Lima 1881–1883: el gobierno de García Calderón* (Lima, 1991), and *La ocupación de Lima, 1881–1883: aspectos económicos* (Lima, 1996). Enrique Amayo has written on *La política británica en la Guerra del Pacífico* (Lima, 1988). See also Héctor López Martínez, *Guerra con Chile: episodios y personajes, 1879–1885* (Lima, 1989).

The centenary of the war did stimulate production on the subject, mainly edited works by Peruvian historians. The best of these works is Jorge Basadre (ed.), *Reflexiones en torno a la Guerra de 1879* (Lima, 1979), which contains original contributions from a number of well-known Peruvian historians. See also Wilson Reátegui Chávez et al., *La guerra del Pacífico*, 2 vols. (Lima, 1979, 1984); Percy Cayo Córdoba et al., *En torno a la Guerra del Pacífico* (Lima, 1983); and Fernando Lecaros (ed.), *La Guerra con Chile en sus documentos* (Lima, 1979). Retired General Edgardo Mercado Jarín has an interesting analysis of *Política y estrategia en la Guerra con Chile* (Lima, 1979).

The most important documentary source continues to be Pascual Ahumada Moreno (ed.), *Guerra del Pacífico: Recopilación completa . . .* , 8 vols. (Valparaiso, Chile, 1895–91). A more recent collection of documents and interpretive articles was published by the Ministry of War's Comisión Permanente de Historia del Ejército del Perú, *La resistencia de La Breña*, 3 vols. (Lima, 1982–84). Andrés A. Cáceres wrote his recollections in *La guerra del 79: sus campañas (Memorias)* (Lima, 1973), as did his wife Antonia Moreno de Cáceres, *Recuerdos de la campaña de la Breña (Memorias)* (Lima, 1974). On the Peruvian campaign of Chilean General Patricio Lynch, see his *Memoria . . .* (Lima, 1883–84). See also Ricardo Palma's pithy *Crónicas de la guerra con Chile (1881–1883)* (Lima, 1984). Celia Wu de Brading has translated the reports of two British naval officers in *Testimonios británicos de la ocupación chilena de Lima (enero de 1881)* (Lima, 1986).

The debate over the formation of an alternative popular nationalism as a result of the Chilean invasion was spurred by the highly original works of Mallon, *The Defense of Community,* and Manrique, *Campesinado y nación.* The debate was joined by Heraclio Bonilla, "The Indian Peasantry and 'Peru' during the War with Chile," in *Resistance, Rebellion, and Consciousness,* 219–231. See also Mallon's contribution "Nationalist and Antistate Coalitions in the War of the Pacific: Junín and Cajamarca, 1879–1902," in *Resistance Rebellion, and Consciousness,* 232–279, and *Peasant and Nation: The Making of Postcolonial Mexico and Peru* (Berkeley, CA, 1995). Bonilla's interpretation was originally put forward in "The War of the Pacific and the National and Colonial Problem in Peru," *Past and Present* (November 1978), 92–118, based on his doctoral dissertation at San Marcos University in 1977. See also his *Guano y burguesía* and *Un siglo a la deriva: ensayos sobre el Perú, Bolivia y la guerra* (Lima, 1980).

On the social dissolution engendered by the war, see Bonilla, "The War of the Pacific," and Henri Favre, "Remarques sur la lutte des classes au Perou pendant la Guerre du Pacifique," in *Litterature et societe au Perou du XIXe siecle a nos jours* (Grenoble, France, 1975), 54–81. Peter Blanchard attributes the proliferation of peasant revolts after the war to the general economic, political, and administrative disarray following Peru's defeat. See his "Indian Unrest in the Peruvian Sierra in the Late Nineteenth Century," *Americas* 38 (1982), 449–463. Like Mallon on the Pacific War, Thurner applies a postcolonial analysis of the Atusparia rebellion in *From Two Republics* and "Atusparia and Cáceres: Rereading Representations of Peru's Late Nineteenth-Century 'National Problem,'" *HAHR* 77:3 (August 1997), 409–442. See also William W. Stein's, *El levantamiento de Atusparia: el movimiento popular ancashino de 1885, un estudio de documentos* (Lima, 1988); C. Augusto Alba Herrera, *Atusparia y la revolución campesina de 1885 en Ancash* (Lima, 1985); and Wilfredo Kapsoli (ed.), *Los movimientos campesinos en el Perú: 1879–1965* (Lima, 1977), which includes a contribution on Atusparia by Manuel Valladares and Jean Piel. Peasant unrest in Huanta leading up to the salt rebellion in 1895 is examined by Husson, *De la guerra*.

The best source on the postwar economic recovery and growth is Thorp and Bertram, *Peru 1890–1977*. This work includes careful sectoral and regional analyses of export production and manufacturing and argues that a brief surge of autonomous growth occurred at the beginning of the century, only to fade after 1908. See also Gianfranco Bardella, *Un siglo de la vida económica del Perú, 1889–1989* (Lima, 1989). The standard dependency analysis is Ernesto Yepes del Castillo, *Perú 1820–1920: un siglo de desarrollo capitalista* (Lima, 1972). See also his "El desarrollo peruano en las primeras décadas del siglo XX," in *Nueva historia general del Perú* (Lima, 1979). Quiroz challenges Thorp and Bertram and Yepes in his revisionist *Domestic and Foreign Finance* and *Banqueros en conflicto: estructura financiera y economía Peruana, 1884–1930* (Lima, 1989). In both works he attributes greater importance to domestic financial and business groups for Peru's modernization and development during the Aristocratic Republic and beyond. See also his "Financial Development in Peru under Agrarian Export Influence, 1884–1950," *Americas* 47:4 (1991), 447–476. The tariff question is examined by Carlos Boloña, "Tariff Policies in Peru, 1880–1980," (Ph.D. diss., St. Anthony's College, Oxford, 1981). British councilar reports for the period can be found in Bonilla, *Gran Britañia y el Perú*, particularly vols. 2–4.

Valuable economic data and analyses on the period have been generated by Shane Hunt, *Real Wages and Economic Growth in Peru, 1900–1940* (Boston, 1977), and *Price and Quantum Estimates of Peruvian Exports, 1830–1962* (Princeton, NJ, 1973). Using these and other sources, Albert Berry analyzes "International Trade, Government, and Income Distribution in Peru since 1870," *LARR* 25:2 (1990), 31–60. Other quantitative data appear in P. E. Dancuart and J. M. Rodríguez (eds.), *Anales de la hacienda pública del Perú*, 24 vols. (Lima, 1902–08), and various works by Pablo Macera in his *Trabajos*.

The export economy for the period is also treated in a number of other specialized works. For example, Rory Miller has written several important articles, including "The Making of the Grace Contract: British Bondholders and the Peruvian Government, 1885–1890," *JLAS* 8:1 (1976), 73–100; "The Grace Contract, the Peruvian Corporation and Peruvian History," *Ibero-Amerikanisches Archiv*, vol. 9 (1983), 319–348, "Railroads and Economic Development in Central Peru, 1890–1930," in J. Fisher (ed.), *Social and Economic Change in Modern Peru* (Liverpool, England, 1976), "The Wool Trade of Southern Peru, 1850–1915," *Ibero-Amerikanisches Archiv* 8 (1982), 297–312; and "British Firms and the Peruvian Government, 1895–1930," in D. C. M. Platt (ed.), *Business Imperialism 1840–1930: An Inquiry Based on British Experience in Latin America* (London, 1977).

William Bollinger provides much useful information on "The Rise of United States Influence in the Peruvian Economy, 1869–1921" (unpublished MA thesis, UCLA, 1972), as does Heraclio Bonilla, "Emergence of U.S. Control of the Peruvian Economy, 1850–1930," in Joseph S. Tulchin (ed.), *Hemispheric Perspectives on the United States* (Westport, CT, 1978), 325–351. See also Bollinger's Marxist interpretation of "The Bourgeois Revolution in Peru: A Conception of Peruvian History," *Latin American Perspectives* 4:3 (Summer 1977), 18–54. For an antidote to these dependency views, see Clayton, *Peru and the United States*. Rodrigo Montoya Rojas contributes to the debate on economic transition in *Capitalismo y no capitalismo en el Perú: un estudio histórico de su articulación en un éje regional* (Lima, 1981), and *Lucha por la tierra, reformas agrarias y capitalismo en el Perú del siglo XX* (Lima, 1989).

The formation and development of the Aristocratic Republic is best interpreted by Manuel Burga and Alberto Flores Galindo, *Apogeo y crisis de la república aristocrática* (Lima, 1979). See also Pedro Planas, *La república Autocrática* (Lima, 1994), and his *El 900: balance y recuperación* (Lima, 1994), as well as McEvoy, *La utopía republicana*. Alicia del Aguila examines the social spaces of the elites and subalterns in *Callejones y mansiones: espacios de opinión pública y redes sociales y políticas en la Lima del 1900* (Lima, 1997). Miller challenges the idea of the formation of a cohesive oligarchy in "The Coastal Elite and Peruvian Politics, 1895–1919," *JLAS* 14:1 (1982), 97–120 and, "La oligarquía costera y la república aristocrática en el Perú, 1895–1919," *Revista de las Indias* 48:182–83 (January–August 1988), 551–566. For a response, see Michael J. Gonzalez, "Planters and Politics in Peru, 1895–1919," *JLAS* 23:3 (October 1991), 515–542, and Quiroz, "Financial Leadership and the Formation of Peruvian Elite Groups, 1884–1930," *JLAS* 20:1 (May 1988), 49–81. See also Nils Jacobsen, "Free Trade, Regional Elites and the Internal Market in Southern Peru, 1895–1932," in *Guiding the Invisible Hand*, 145–175. Nelson Manrique's *Yawar Mayu: Sociedades terratenientes serranas, 1879–1910* (Lima, 1988) provocatively argues that the War of the Pacific strengthened the traditional sierra landowning class while weakening the coastal elite, leading to a postwar alliance between the two groups for the purpose of reestablishing control over the country after the war.

Other important older studies on the formation of the oligarchy are Dennis Gilbert's *The Oligarchy and the Old Regime in Peru* (Ithaca, NY, 1977) and his *La oligarquía peruana: historia de tres familias* (Lima, 1982), as well as Sinesio López J., "El estado oligárquico en el Perú: un ensayo de interpretación," *Revista Mexicana de Sociología* 40:3 (1978), 991–1007. A more recent examination of the subject can be found in Felipe Portocarrero Suárez's important *El imperio Prado: 1890–1970* (Lima, 1995). A good analysis of elite, particularly Civilista, political thought can be found in Kristal, *The Andes Viewed from the City* and Luis Alberto Sánchez, *Balance y liquidación del novocientos* (Santiago, 1941), as well as the writings of Alejandro Deustua, Joaquín Copelo, Manuel González Prada, Javier Prado, Francisco García Calderón, Manuel Vicente Villarán, José de la Riva Agüero, and Víctor Andrés Belaúnde among others. See also Thomas Ward, *La anarquia inmanentista de Manuel González Prada* (New York, 1998).

A valuable sociohistorical portrait of *Lima en 1900* by Richard Morse (Lima, 1973) is based on the sociological work and observations of Capelo, Villarán, and other contemporaries. See also Marcos Cueto, *El regreso de las epidemias: salud y sociedad en el Perú del siglo XX* (Lima, 1997), which examines improvements in sanitation and public health after 1900 in contrast to their deterioration at the end of the century. David Parker offers an intriguing analysis of *The Idea of the Middle Class: White-Collar Workers and Peruvian Society, 1900–1950* (University Park, PA, 1998). He argues that Lima white-collar workers defined themselves as middle class as much on the basis of traditional values, such as family honor, education, and "lifestyle," as on the modern capitalist criteria of income and occupation. See also Gonzalo Portocarrero (ed.), *Las clases medias: entre la pretensión y la incertidumbre* (Lima, 1999). On Italian immigration, see Bonfiglio, *Los Italianos*, and Worrall, *La inmigración Italiana*.

There are a number of important regional studies that provide a new picture of social and economic developments outside Lima during this period. Nils Jacobsen's magisterial *Mirages of Transition* revises the standard dependency perspective on the period. Also focusing on the south are Luis Miguel Glave, "Aricultura y capitalismo en la sierra sur del Perú (fines del siglo XIX y comienzos del XX)," in *Estados y naciónes en los Andes*, edited by J. P. Deler and Y. Saint Geours, I (Lima, 1986), 213–243; Benjamin Orlove, *Al-*

pacas, Sheep, and Men: The Wool Export Economy and Regional Society in Southern Peru (New York, 1977); Alberto Flores Galindo, *Arequipa y el sur andino, siglo XVIII a XX* (Lima, 1977); and Manuel Burga and Wilson Reátegui Chávez, *Lanas y capital mercantil en el sur: la Casa Ricketts, 1895–1935* (Lima, 1981). See also Geoff Bertram, "Modernizacion y cambio en la industria lanera en el sur del Perú, 1919–1930, un caso frustrado de desarrollo," *Apuntes* 3 (1977), 3–22. A contemporary account is by the German traveller, Karl Kaerger, *Condiciones agrarias de la sierra peruana (1899)*, translated by Christine Hünefeldt (Lima, 1979).

Magnus Mörner assesses "The Extent and Limitations of Change: Cuzco, Peru, 1895–1920," in *The Transformation of Rural Society in the Third World*, edited by Mörner and Thommy Svensson (London, 1991), 98–119. On Cuzco, see also J. Tamayo Herrera, *Historia social del Cuzco republicano* (Lima, 1978). Mallon's *Defense of Community* analyzes the transition to capitalism in the central highlands, while Carmen Diana Deere does the same for Cajamarca in *Household and Class Relations: Peasants and Landlords in Northern Peru* (Berkeley, CA, 1990). On the north, see also Lewis Taylor's "Main Trends in Agrarian Capitalist Development: Cajamarca, Peru, 1880–1976" (Ph.D. diss., University of Liverpool, 1979); *Bandits and Politics in Peru: Landlord and Peasant Violence in Hualgayoc 1900–1930* (Cambridge, England, 1983); and "Enrique López Albújar and the Study of Peruvian Brigandage," *BLAR* 13:3 (1994), 247–280.

The development of Peruvian mining can be found in numerous works: Luis Jochamowitz, *Hombres, minas y pozos 1896–1996: un siglo de minería y petroleo en el Perú* (Lima, 1996); Carlos Contreras, *Mineros y campesinos en los Andes* (Lima, 1988); Josh DeWind, *Peasants Become Miners: The Evolution of Industrial Mining Systems in Peru, 1902–1974* (New York, 1987); Julian Laite, *Industrial Development and Migrant Labour in Latin America* (Austin, TX, 1981); Dirk Kruijt and Menno Vellinga, *Labor Relations and Multinational Corporations: The Cerro de Pasco Corporation in Peru (1902–1974)* (Assen, the Netherlands, 1979); and Alberto Flores Galindo, *Los mineros de la Cerro de Pasco, 1900–1930* (Lima, 1974). The Amazonian rubber boom and bust is recounted by Michael Edward Stanfield, *Red Rubber, Bleeding Trees: Violence, Slavery, and Empire in Northwest Amazonia, 1850–1933* (Albuquerque, NM, 1999), and by Guido Pennano, *La economía del caucho* (Limá, 1988).

Coastal export agriculture has received a good deal of scholarly attention. An important interpretive overview is Bill Albert, "External Forces and the Transformation of Peruvian Coastal Agriculture, 1880–1930," in *Latin America, Economic Imperialism and the State*, edited by Christopher Abel and Colin M. Lewis (London and Dover, NH, 1985), 231–249. On the development of the sugar industry on the north coast, see Michael J. Gonzales, *Plantation Agriculture and Social Control in Northern Peru, 1875–1933* (Austin, TX, 1984); Bill Albert, *An Essay on the Peruvian Sugar Industry, 1880–1920* (Norwich, England, 1976; and Peter F. Klarén, "The Social and Economic Consequences of Modernization in the Peruvian Sugar Industry, 1870–1930," in *Land and Labour in Latin America: Essays on the Development of Agrarian Capitalism*, edited by Kenneth Duncan and Ian Rutledge (Cambridge, England, 1977), 229–252. See also Burga's important *De la encomienda*. On the cotton industry, see Vincent Peloso, *Peasants on Plantations: Subaltern Strategies of Labor and Resistance in the Pisco Valley, Peru* (Durham, NC, 1999); Michael J. Gonzales, "The Rise of Cotton Tenant Farming in Peru, 1890–1920: The Condor Valley," *Agricultural History* 65:1 (1991), 51–71; and W. S. Bell, *An Essay on the Peruvian Cotton Industry, 1825–1920* (Liverpool, England, 1985).

The process of *latifundia* expansion, dynamized by international and national market forces in the early twentieth century, was first outlined by Francois Chevalier, "L'-Expansion de la grande propriete dans le Haut-Perou au XXe siecle," *AESC* 21 (1966), 815–831. The outcome was the enclosure and dislocation of peasant holdings, which led to increasing peasant migration and a number of agrarian uprisings, particularly in the wool-raising south. This process has been documented in a number of works, including Jacobson, Mallon, Manrique, Klarén, and others. A good analytical overview on peasant revolts is Michael J. Gonzales, "Neo-Colonialism and Indian Unrest in Southern Peru, 1867–1898," *BLAR* 6:1 (1987), 1–26. See also Peter Blanchard, "Indian Unrest"; Wilson Reátegui Chávez (ed.), *Documentos para la historia del campesinado peruano, siglo XX* (Lima, 1978); and Wilfredo Kapsoli, *Los movimientos*.

Peasant migrations from the sierra to the coast is the subject of Henri Favre's "The Dynamics of Indian Peasant Society and Migration to Coastal Plantations in Central Peru," in *Land and Labour in Latin America*, 253–268. *Enganche* as a mechanism of labor recruitment for the developing coastal plantations is interpreted and debated in a number of works: Michael Gonzales, "Chinese Plantation Workers and Social Conflict in Peru in the Late Nineteenth Century," *JLAS* 21:3 (October 1989), 385–424, and "Capitalist Agriculture and Labour Contracting in Northern Peru, 1880–1905," *JLAS* 12 (1980), 291–1933; Peter Blanchard, "The Recruitment of Workers in the Peruvian Sierra at the Turn of the Century: The *Enganche* System," *Inter-American Economic Affairs* 33:3 (1979); Albert, *An Essay*; and Klarén, "The Social and Economic Consequences." Japanese indentured labor in the sugar industry at the turn of the century has been examined by Harvey C. Gardiner in *The Japanese and Peru, 1873–1973* (Albuquerque, NM, 1975).

Peter Blanchard's "A Populist Precursor: Guillermo Billinghurst," *JLAS* 9:2 (1977), 251–273, is the best analysis of the reformist president. The background on the development of the armed forces prior to Benavides's overthrow of Billinghurst is outlined in Dan Masterson, *The Military and Politics in Latin America: Peru from Sánchez Cerro to Sendero Luminoso* (New York, 1991). See also Paquita Benavides de Peña et al., *El Mariscal Benavides: su vida y su obra*, 2 vols. (Lima, 1976–81).

The standard treatment of the impact of World War I on Peru is Bill Albert, *South America and the First World War: The Impact of the War on Brazil, Argentina, Peru and Chile* (Cambridge, England, 1988). Albert concludes that the war did not institute a process of Import Substituting Industrialization in Peru, largely because of the rapidity with which the country was able to reestablish and expand its export markets with the belligerents. Peruvian finance during and after the war is carefully examined by Quiroz, *Domestic and Foreign Finance*. He argues that Peruvian elite groups vigorously participated in the modernization and diversification of the economy during this period. This view stands in contrast to that of the dependency school, which argues that the economic behavior of the elites was tradition bound and "irrational," constituting a major obstacle to economic development. For the latter view, see Yepes del Castillo, *Peru 1820–1920*, and Julio Cotler, *Clase, estado y nación*.

The standard work on the labor movement is Peter Blanchard, *The Origins of the Peruvian Labor Movement, 1883–1919* (Pittsburgh, PA, 1982). On sugar workers, see Peter Kammann, *Von der Landarbeiterbewegung zur Angestelltengewerkschaft: Soziale Protestbewegungen im Tal des Chicama, Peru 1909–1968* (Frankfurt, 1990). See also Denis Sulmont, *El movimiento obrero en el Perú, 1900–1980* (Lima, 1980) and Ricardo Melgar Bao, *Burguesía y el proletariado en el Perú* (Lima, 1980). David Parker reexamines "Peruvian Politics and the Eight-Hour Day: Rethinking the 1919 General Strike," *Canadian Journal of History* 30 (December 1995), 417–438. See also the memoirs of Julio Portocarrero, *Sindicalismo Peruano: primera etapa, 1911–1930* (Lima, 1987). Several excellent essays on the culture of Lima's working class can be found in Steve Stein (ed.), *Lima obrera: 1900–1930*, 2 vols. (Lima, 1986–87). Particularly notable are those by Laura Miller, "La mujer obrera en Lima, 1900–1930," and Susan C. Stokes, "Ethnicidad y clase social: los afro-peruanos de Lima, 1900–1930" in vol. 2. See also Stein's "Popular Culture and Politics in Early Twentieth-Century Lima," *New World* 1:2 (1986), 65–46, and José Deustua, Steve Stein, and Susan Stokes, "Soccer and Social Change in Early Twentieth-Century Peru," parts 1 & 2, *Journal of Latin American Popular Culture* 4 (1984) and 6 (1985). Piedad Pareja develops the link between *Anarquismo y sindicalismo en el Peru* (Lima, 1978), while Luis Tejada examines Lima's bakers' syndicate in *La cuestión de pan: el anarchosindicalismo en el Perú, 1880–1919* (Lima, 1988).

There are numerous good studies of *indigenismo*, including José Tamayo Herrera's *Historia del indigenismo cusqueño, siglos XVI–XX* (Lima, 1980) and *Historia social e indigenismo en el altiplano* (Lima, 1982); and Nelson Manrique, "Clorinda Matto y el nacimiento del indigenismo literario (*Aves sin nido*, cien años despues)" in *Debate Agrario* 6 (June 1989). See Herrera's more recent *Liberalismo, indigenismo y violencia en los países andinos (1850–1995)* (Lima, 1998); and the works of Kristal (1987), Klaiber (1977), Rénique (1991), and Deustua and Rénique (1984). See also Thomas Davies, Jr., *Indian Integration in Peru*

(A Half Century of Experience 1900–1948) (Lincoln, NE, 1974); Wilson Reátegui, *Tres instituciones indigenistas del siglo XX* (Lima, 1978); Wilfredo Kapsoli, *El pensamiento de la asociación Pro-Indígena* (Cuzco, 1980); and *Ayllus del sol, anarquismo y utopía andina* (Lima, 1984). The *Memorias* of Luis E. Valcárcel, a leading *indigenista* and scholar from Cuzco, are indispensible (Lima, 1981). A more recent analysis by Marisol de la Cadena places the movement in its provincial context: "From Race to Class: Insurgent Intellectuals 'de provincia' in Peru, 1910–1970," in Stern (ed.), *Shining and Other Paths: War and Society in Peru, 1980–1995* (Durham, NC, 1998), 22–59. See also Clorindo Matto de Turner's classic *indigenista* novel *Torn from the Nest*, translated by John R. Polt and edited by Antonio Cornejo Polar (New York, 1998).

The literature on José Carlos Mariátegui is voluminous. His complete works were published in *Obras completas de José Carlos Mariátegui*, 20 vols. (Lima, 1957–70). His most well-known work is *Siete ensayos de interpretación de la realidad Peruana* (Lima, 1927), which appeared in an English version as *Seven Essays on Peruvian Reality*, translated by Marjory Urquidi (Austin, TX, 1971). A complete bibliography of works on and about Mariátegui, as well as a careful analysis of his thought, is Harry E. Vanden, *National Marxism in Latin America: José Carlos Mariátegui's Thought and Politics* (Boulder, CO, 1986). Charles Walker wrote a perceptive article on, "Lima de Mariátegui: los intelectuales y la capital durante el oncenio," *Socialismo y Participación* 35 (September 1986), 71–88. See also his "Bibliografía reciente sobre José Carlos Mariátegui," *Revista Andina* 4:1 (July 1986), 253–273.

Other notable works on Mariátegui include Sandro Mariátegui (ed.), *Simposio internacional: Amauto y su época* (Lima, 1998); Roland Forgues, *Mariátegui, la utopía realizable* (Lima, 1995); Gonzalo Portocarrero et al., *La aventura de Mariátegui: nuevas perspectivas* (Lima, 1995); Marc Becker, *Mariátegui and Latin American Marxist Theory* (Athens, OH, 1993); Robert Paris, *La formación ideológica de José Carlos Mariátegui* (Mexico City, 1981); Bruno Podestá (ed.), *Mariátegui en Italia* (Lima, 1981); Jesús Chavarria, *José Carlos Mariátegui and the Rise of Modern Peru, 1880–1930* (Albuquerque, NM, 1979); and Alberto Flores Galindo, *La agonía de Mariátegui: la polémica con la Komintern* (Lima, 1980). See also Pedro Planas, *El pensamiento social de Víctor Andrés Belaúnde: antología* (Lima, 1997), who was a main protagonist of Mariátegui, and José de la Riva Agüero, *Obras completas* (Lima, 1964).

Like Mariátegui, Víctor Raúl Haya de la Torre has been the subject of considerable scholarly attention. Haya's *Obras completas* was published in 6 vols. (Lima, 1976–77). For a selected compilation in English, see Robert J. Alexander (comp. and trans.), *Aprismo: the Ideas and Doctrines of Víctor Raúl Haya de la Torre* (Kent, OH, 1973). The best (intellectual) biography of Haya is Fredrick B. Pike, *The Politics of the Miraculous in Peru: Haya de la Torre and the Spiritualist Tradition* (Lincoln, NE, 1986). On the young Haya, see Pedro Planas, *Los orígenes del APRA: el joven Haya (mito y realidad de Haya de la Torre)*, (2d ed., Lima, 1986). See also Richard V. Salisbury, "The Middle American Exile of Víctor Raúl Haya de la Torre," *The Americas* 40 (1983), 1–16. On the origins of the APRA party, see Steve Stein, *Populism in Peru: Emergence of the Masses and the Politics of Social Control* (Madison, WI, 1980); Peter F. Klarén, *Modernization, Dislocation and Aprismo: Origins of the Peruvian Aprista Party, 1880–1932* (Austin, TX, 1973); and Jeffrey L. Klaiber, S.J., "The Popular Universities and the Origins of Aprismo, 1921–1924," *HAHR* 55:4 (1975), 693–715. See also his larger work *Religion and Revolution in Peru* (Notre Dame, IN, 1977). Liisa North also analyzes *Orígenes y crecimiento del Partido Aprista: el cambio socio-economico en el Perú* (Lima, 1975). On the differences and rupture between Mariátegui and Haya, see Ricardo Luna Vegas, *Mariátegui, Haya de la Torre y la verdad histórica* (Lima, 1978).

Karen Sanders probes the debate over the national question in the thoughts of González Prada, García Calderón, Víctor Andrés Belaúnde, Mariátegui, and Haya in her excellent *Nación y tradición: cinco discursos en torno a la nación peruana, 1885–1930* (Lima, 1997). See also Malgorzata Nalewajko, *El debate nacional en el Perú (1920–1933)* (Warsaw, 1995).

The best comprehensive treatment of the economy during and after the war, which includes a sector by sector analysis, is Thorp and Bertram, *Peru 1890–1977* as well as Quiroz's *Domestic and Foreign Finance*. On economy and society in the *altiplano*, see Nils

Jacobsen, *Mirages of Transition*, especially his interpretation of Indian unrest during and after the war. The decline and collapse of the Aristocratic Republic is interpreted by Stein, *Populism in Peru*, as are the social changes of the *Oncenio* during the 1920s.

José Luis Rénique brilliantly portrays *Los sueños de la sierra: Cuzco en el siglo XX* (Lima, 1991). See also his doctoral dissertation, "State and Regional Movements in the Peruvian Highlands: The Case of Cuzco, 1895–1985" (Columbia University, 1988; Ann Arbor, MI, 1993), and Jesús Guillén, *La economía agraria del Cuzco 1900–1980* (Cuzco, 1989). A number of interesting essays on Cuzco can be found in Juan Vega Ganoza and Jesús Guillén Marroquín (eds.), *Cuzco, problema y posibilidad* (Cuzco, 1981).

Information on the Church can be found in Jeffrey L. Klaiber, S.J., *The Catholic Church in Peru*, as well as the more detailed work by Jordan, *Iglesia y poder*. The best account of *The Foreign Policy of Peru* for the period is by St John.

Leguia's *Oncenio* is the subject of Planas, *La República Autocrática*. See also Clayton, *Peru and the United States* and Baltazar Caravedo Molinari, *Clases, lucha política y gobierno en el Perú (1919–1933)* (Lima, 1977). Leguía's speeches are contained in *Discursos, mensajes y programas*, 3 vols. (Lima, 1924–26), and *Mensaje* (Lima, 1928, 1929, 1930). The standard economic history of the *Oncenio* is Thorp and Bertram, *Peru 1890–1977*. For good accounts of his economic and financial policies, see Paul Drake, *The Money Doctor in the Andes: The Kemmerer Missions, 1923–1933* (Durham, NC, 1989), and Barbara Stallings, *Banker to the Third World: U.S. Portfolio Investment in Latin America, 1900–1986* (Berkeley, CA, 1987). See also Quiroz, "Lima como Centro financiero."

Post 1930

In general the period has not been well studied. The best overview is Geoffrey Bertram, "Peru, 1930–1960," in *CHLA*, 8 (1991), 385–450. See also Adam Andarle, *Los movimientos políticos en el Perú entre las dos guerras mundiales* (Havana, 1985); Masterson, *Militarism and Politics*, chaps. 2 and 3; and Cotler, *Clases*. José Carlos Huayhuaca has collected the photographs of *Martín Chambi, fotógrafo: Cuzco, 1920–1950* (Lima, n.d.), the master photographer of highland daily life and work in the South.

The fall of Augusto B. Leguía and the rise of Luis M. Sánchez Cerro are best analyzed by Stein, *Populism in Peru*. See also his "Populism in Peru: APRA and the Formative Years," in *Latin American Populism*, edited by Michael L. Conniff (Albuquerque, NM, 1981), 113–134, and Steven J. Hirsch's recent revisionist " 'We Want Social Justice': Union Workers, the Peruvian Aprista Party, and Populist Politics in Lima-Callao, 1931–48" (Ph. D. diss., George Washington University, 1996). Imelda Vega-Centeno B., *Aprismo Popular: cultura, religión y política* (Lima 1991) and Klaiber, *Religión y revolución* analyze the party's use of popular religion and culture to attract a mass political following. See also Orazio R. Ciccarelli, *Militarism, Aprismo and Violence in Peru: The Presidential Elections of 1931* (Buffalo, NY, 1971).

Víctor Villanueva recounts *Así cayó Leguía* (Lima, 1977). Pedro Ugarteche has collected *Sánchez Cerro: papales y recuerdos de un presidente del Perú*, 4 vols. (Lima, 1969–70). See also B. Loveday, *Sánchez Cerro and Peruvian Politics, 1930–1933* (University of Glasgow Institute of Latin American Studies, Occasional Paper no. 6, 1973). José Luis Rénique analyzes the role of "Los decentralistas arequipeños en la crisis del año 1930," *Allpanchis* 12 (1979).

See also Manuel Castillo Ochoa, "El populismo conservador: Sánchez Cerro y La Unión Revolucionaria," in *Pensamiento político peruano 1930–1960*, edited by Alberto Adrianzén (Lima, 1990), 47–76. Anti-Japanese sentiment during the 1930s is outlined in Orazio Ciccarelli's "Peru's Anti-Japanese Campaign in the 1930s: Economic Dependency and Abortive Nationalism," *Canadian Review of Studies in Nationalism* 9:1 (Spring 1982), 115–133, and Gardiner, *The Japanese*.

Ciccarelli has written authoritatively on "Fascism and Politics in Peru during the Benavides Regime, 1933–39: The Italian Perspective," *HAHR* (August 1990), 405–432, and

"Fascist Propaganda and the Italian Community in Peru during the Benavides Regime, 1933–1939," *JLAS* 20:2 (November 1988), 361–388. On fascism in Peru's ruling classes, see José López Soria (ed.), *El pensamiento fascista (1930–1945) Antología* (Lima, 1981), and Willy Pinto Bamboa, *Sobre fascismo y literatura (la guerra civil española en la Prensa, El Comercio y La Crónica 1936–39* (Lima, 1983). Thomas M. Davies, Jr., takes up the same theme in "Peru," in *The Spanish Civil War, 1936–39: American Perspectives*, edited by Mark Falcoff and Fredrick B. Pike (Lincoln, NE, 1982).

The Trujillo revolt of 1932 has not been adequately studied, although Guillermo Thorndike's *El año de la barbarie, Perú 1932* (Lima, 1969) provides some of the essentials, as do the works of Víctor Villanueva, a former military officer and Aprista. Two valuable works are Thomas M. Davies, Jr., and Víctor Villanueva (eds.), *Secretos electorales del APRA: Correspondencia y documentos de 1939* (Lima, 1982), and *300 documentos para la historia del APRA* (Lima, 1978). The former illustrates Haya's eagerness to strike deals in his quest for power, while the latter exposes the various plots and conspiracies hatched by the party during the period. Carmen Balbi examines *El Partido Comunista y el Apra en la crisis revolucionaria de los años treinta* (Lima, 1980), and with Laura Madalengoitia, *Parlamento y lucha política: Perú, 1932* (Lima, 1980). On the latter see Víctor Andrés Belaúnde, *El debate constitucional: discursos en la asamblea 1931–32* (Lima, 1966). José Deustua and Alberto Flores Galindo examine the question of "Los Comunistas y el movimiento obrero: Perú, 1930–1931," in *Historia: problema y promesa, homenaje a Jorge Basadre*, vol. 2, edited by Franklin Pease et al. (Lima, 1984).

Luis Alberto Sánchez was a political confidant of Haya, high party leader, and important political figure whose career, like Haya's, spans much of the century. His works include *Testimonio personal: memorias de un peruano del siglo XX*, 4 vols. (Lima, 1969–76); *Apuntes para una biografía del Apra*, 3 vols. (Lima, 1978–81); *Correspondencia, 1924–1976*, 2 vols. (Lima, 1983), as well as various other works on Peruvian literature, politics, and history. Some of his private papers are located at Pennsylvania State University and catalogued in *Literature and Politics in Latin America: An Annotated Calendar of the Luis Alberto Sánchez Correspondence, 1919–1980*, translated and compiled by Donald C. Henderson and Grace R. Pérez (University Park, PA, 1982). See also Henderson, *Perú visto por L.A.S.: historia y vida política* (Lima, 1990).

The economic history of the period can be found in Rosemary Thorp and Geoffrey Bertram, *Peru 1890–1977*, and Quiroz, *Domestic and Foreign Finance*. See also Rosemary Thorp and Carlos Londoño, "The Effect of the Great Depression on the Economies of Peru and Colombia," in *Latin America in the 1930s: The Role of the Periphery in World Crisis*, edited by Rosemary Thorp (New York, 1984), 81–116, as well as Thorp's *Economic Management and Economic Development in Peru and Colombia* (Pittsburgh, PA, 1991). Paul Drake adroitly analyzes the Kemmerer mission in *The Money Doctor*. On wages and prices, see Hunt (1977). For U.S. investments in Peru during the period, see Stallings, *Banker to the Third World*, chap. 6. On the emergence of an industrial class, see Baltazar Caravedo Molinari, *Burguesía e industria en el Perú, 1933–1945* (Lima, 1976), and *Clases, lucha política*. Several useful studies of the economy during the period can also be found in Heraclio Bonilla (ed.), *Las crisis económicas en la historia del Perú* (Lima, 1986).

Information on the evolution of rural society is relatively thin. A recent work by Alejandro Diez Hurtado, *Comunes y haciendas: procesos de comunalización en la sierra de Piura, siglos XVIII–XX* (Cuzco, 1998), shows that the dissolution of the hacienda in Piura began well before the 1930s, perhaps as early as the 1890s. See also Juan Martínez-Alier, *Haciendas, Plantations and Collective Farms: Agrarian Class Societies—Cuba and Peru* (London, 1977), and *Los huacchilleros del Perú* (Lima, 1973). Also important is Florencia Mallon, *The Defense of Community*, and Manrique, *Mercado interno*, both on the central highlands. The evolution of the northern highlands is examined in Deere, *Household and Class*. See also Taylor's dissertation (1979).

The best study of mining during this period is Elizabeth Dore, *The Peruvian Mining Industry: Growth, Stagnation, and Crisis* (Boulder, CO, 1988). See also Jochamowitz, *Hombres, minas y pozos*, and Dennis Sulmont, *Historia del movimiento obrero minero metalúrgico*

(Lima, 1980). On labor at Cerro de Pasco, see Krujit and Vellinga, *Labor Relations and Multinational Corporations*. Migrant labor to the mines is examined by Laite, *Industrial Development and Migrant Labour*, and "Migration and Social Differentiation amongst Mantaro Valley Peasants," in *Miners, Peasants and Entrepreneurs: Regional Development in the Central Highlands of Peru*, edited by Norman Long and Bryan R. Roberts (Cambridge, England, 1984). The process of peasant proletarianization is addressed by DeWind, Jr., *Peasants Become Miners*; Wilfredo Kapsoli, *Los movimientos campesinos en Cerro de Pasco, 1880–1963* (Lima, 1975); and Flores Galindo, *Los mineros de Cerro de Pasco*.

The figure of Oscar Benavides—military hero and two-time president (1914–15, 1933–39)—is treated in José Zárate Lescano, *El mariscal Benavides: Su vida y su obra* (Lima, 1976). Two-time president Manuel Prado (1940–45, 1956–62) has received little scholarly attention, but his *Mensajes presidenciales* (Lima, 1939–45) is useful. See also Portocarrero Suárez, *El imperio Prado*.

The best work on the military is Masterson, *Militarism and Politics*. See also the works of Víctor Villanueva. The war with Ecuador is capably covered in Clayton, *Peru and the United States*, and St John, *The Foreign Policy*. Older studies are Bryce Wood, *The United States and Latin American Wars, 1932–1942* (New York, 1966), and D. H. Zook, *Zarumilla-Marañón: The Ecuador-Peru Dispute* (New York, 1964). See also Ernesto Yepes del Castillo, *Tres días de guerra, ciento ochenta de negociaciones: Perú, Ecuador, 1941–42* (Lima, 1998), and Félix Denegri Luna, *Perú y Ecuador: apuntes para la historia de una frontera* (Lima, 1996).

The regime of José Luis Bustamante is skillfully examined by Gonzalo Portocarrero M., *De Bustamante a Odría: el fracaso del Frente Democrático Nacional, 1945–1950* (Lima, 1983), and Nigel Haworth's chapter on "Peru" in *Latin America between the Second World War and the Cold War, 1944–1948*, edited by Leslie Bethell and Ian Roxborough (Cambridge, England, 1992), 170–189. See also Carlos Monge, "If the People Are Sovereign, the People Must Be Fed: Agricultural Policies and Conflicts during the Bustamante y Rivero Administration, Peru, 1945–48" (Ph.D diss., University of Miami, 1993).

Manuel Odría's administration is ably analyzed by David Collier, *Squatters and Oligarchs: Authoritarian Rule and Policy Change in Peru* (Baltimore, 1976). On Belaúnde, see William Ascher, *Scheming for the Poor: The Politics of Redistribution in Latin America* (Cambridge, MA, 1984), particularly chap. 8; Jane S. Jaquette, "Belaúnde and Velasco: On the Limits of Ideological Politics," in *The Peruvian Experiment*, 402–437; and "The Politics of Development in Peru," Ph.D. dissertation (series), Latin American Studies Program, Cornell University, (Ithaca, NY, 1971). See also Cotler, *Clases*, and "Peru since 1960," in *CHLA*, 8, 451–459. Gilbert interprets *La oligarquía* and St John treats *The Foreign Policy* for the period. Electoral data can be found in R. Roncagliolo, *Quien gano? Elecciones, 1931–81* (Lima, 1980).

The incorporation of labor is detailed as part of the larger South American process in Ruth Collier and David Collier, *Shaping the Political Arena: Critical Junctures, the Labor Movement, and Regime Dynamics in Latin America* (Princeton, NJ, 1991), 316–330. See also Alberto Moya Obeso, *Sindicalismo Aprista y sindicalismo clasista en el Perú, 1920–1956* (Lima, n.d.), and Denis Sulmont, *El movimiento obrero*. Labor relations at Cerro de Pasco are examined by Krujit and Vellinga in *Labor Relations and Multinational Corporations* and others.

The major interpretation of Haya is Pike, *The Politics of the Miraculous*, which includes an examination of APRA's shift to the right after 1940. See also Mariano Valderrama, "La evolución ideológica del APRA: 1924–1962" in *El APRA: un camino de esperanzas y frustraciones*, edited by Valderrama et al. (Lima, 1980), and Grant Hilliker, *The Politics of Reform in Peru* (Baltimore, 1971). The struggle between APRA and the CP for control of the labor movement is debated in M. Lauer et al., *Frente al Perú oligárquico (1928–1968): Debate Socialista*, 1 (Lima, 1977).

The fundamental source on the economy for the period continues to be Thorp and Bertram, *Peru 1890–1977*, as well as Rosemary Thorp, "Stabilization Policies in Peru, 1959–1977," in *Inflation and Stabilization in Latin America*, edited by R. Thorp and L. Whitehead (London, 1979). Also extremely useful on the 1950s and 1960s are chaps. 2 and 3 in Richard Webb, *Government Policy and the Distribution of Income in Peru, 1963–1973* (Cambridge, MA, 1977), as are the appropriate chapters in Dore, *The Peruvian Mining Industry,* and Jochamowitz, *Hombres, minas y pozos*. See also W. Warren, *Inflation and Real Wages in Underdeveloped Countries: India, Peru and Turkey* (London, 1976). E. V. K. Fitzgerald covers the Prado and Belaúnde administrations in *The Political Economy of Peru, 1956–1978* (Cambridge, England, 1979); see also Shane Hunt, "Distribution, Growth and Government Economic Behavior in Peru," in *Government and Economic Development*, edited by Gustavo Ranis (New Haven, CT, 1971). For information on educational advances in the 1950s and 1960s, see Robert S. Drysdale and Robert G. Myers, "Continuity and Change: Peruvian Education," in *The Peruvian Experiment*, 254–301.

The process of industrialization is considered by John Weeks, *Limits to Capitalist Development: The Industrialization of Peru, 1950–1980* (Boulder, CO, 1985), Frits Wils, *Industrialization, Industrialists, and the Nation State in Peru: A Comparative Sociological Analysis* (Berkeley, CA, 1979), and M. Beaulnes *Industrialización por sustitución de importaciones, 1958–1969* (Lima, 1975). See also the works by Baltizar Caravedo, including "The State and the Bourgeoisie in the Peruvian Fishmeal Industry," *Latin American Perspectives* (1977) and *Desarrollo desigual*. Numerous bibliographical citations can be found in Francisco Durand, "La industrialización en el Perú: Bibliografía," *Estudios Andinos* 17–18 (1981), 195–246. See also Portocarrero Suárez, *El imperio Prado*, also treated in Gilbert, *La Oligarquía*. Teobaldo Pinzas critically reviews the literature in *La economía peruana, 1950–1978: un essayo bibliográfico* (Lima, 1981).

The basic study of the military is Masterson, *Militarism and Politics in Latin America*. See also the works by Víctor Villanueva. His works are critically discussed by James Malloy, "Dissecting the Peruvian Military: A Review Essay," *JISWA* 15:3 (August 1973), 375–382. The 1962 coup is also analyzed by Arnold Payne, *The Peruvian Coup d'Etat of 1962: The Overthrow of Manuel Prado* (Washington, DC, 1968). On the Church, see Klaiber, S.J., *The Catholic Church*, particularly chap. 8, and Milagros Peña, *Theologies and Liberation in Peru: The Role of Ideas in Social Movements* (Philadelphia, 1995).

The basic sources for the peasant movements of the late 1950s and 1960s are Howard Handelman, *Struggle in the Andes: Peasant Political Mobilization in Peru* (Austin, TX, 1975), and Manuel Burga and Alberto Flores Galindo, "Feudalismo Andino y movimientos sociales (1866–1965)," in *Historia del Perú*, edited by Juan Mejía Baca (Lima, 1980), 11–112. See also Diego García Sayán, *Toma de tierras en el Perú* (Lima, 1982); Peter Kammann, *Movimientos campesinos en el Perú, 1900–1968: Análisis cuantitativo y cualitativo preliminar* (Lima, 1982); Alberto Flores Galindo, "Apuntes sobre las ocupaciones de tierras y el sindicalismo agrario, 1945–1964," *Allpanchis* 11 (1978), 175–185; and Wilfredo Kapsoli E., *Los movimientos campesinos en el Perú, 1879–1965* (Lima, 1977). The leader of the movement in La Convención, Hugo Blanco, is the author of *Tierra or muerte: las luchas campesinas en el Perú* (Mexico City, 1974). Rural conflicts are also briefly surveyed in Colin Harding, "Land Reform and Social Conflict in Peru," in *The Peruvian Experiment*, 220–253.

Raúl Hopkins surveys the *Desarrollo desigual y crisis en la agricultura Peruana, 1944–1969* (Lima, 1981). See also A. Figueroa, "La agricultura y el desarrollo capitalista en el Perú," and Heraclio Bonilla, "Estudios sobre la formación del sistema agrario peruano: Logros y perspectivas," in *La cuestión rural en el Perú*, edited by J. Iguiñiz (Lima, 1983), 225–234, 235–260. For the northern highlands, see Deere, *Household and Class*; Lewis Taylor, "Main Trends"; and John S. Gitlitz, "Hacienda, Comunidad, and Peasant Protest in Northern Peru" (Ph.D. diss., University of North Carolina, Chapel Hill, 1975). See also C. Scott's important "Peasants, Proletarianization and the Articulation of Modes of Production: The Case of the Sugar-Cane Cutters in Northern Peru, 1940–1969," *Journal of Peasant Studies* (1976), 321–342. Two works edited by Norman Long and Bryan R. Roberts examine the process of economic change in the central highlands: *Miners, Peasants, and Entrepreneurs*; and *Peasant Cooperation and Capitalist Expansion in Central Peru*, (Austin, TX, 1978). See also Gerardo Rénique, *La agricultura del valle de Mantaro: estadísticas socio-económicas, 1950–1968* (Lima, 1978). On the southern highlands, see José Luis Rénique's important *Los sueños de la sierra*; Jesús Guillén, *La economía agraria del Cuzco: 1900–1980* (Cuzco, 1989); and Martínez Alier, *Los huacchilleros*. For sources on migration, see Hector

Martínez's critical assessment, *Migraciones internas en el Perú (aproximación crítica y bibliografía)* (Lima, 1980). See also A. Ortiz S., *Migraciones internas y desarrollo desigual: Perú, 1940–1972* (Lima, 1982).

Useful personal memoirs include José Luis Bustamante y Rivero, *Tres años de lucha por la democracia en el Perú* (Buenos Aires, 1949); Pedro Beltrán, *La verdadera realidad nacional* (Madrid, 1976); and Sánchez, *Testimonio personal*. See also Haya de la Torre, *Obras completas*, and Fernando Belaúnde Terry, *La conquista del Perú por los Peruanos* (Lima, 1959), translated as *Peru's Own Conquest* (Lima, 1965). Jorge del Prado, longtime head of the Peruvian Communist Party, wrote *Cuatro facetas de la historia del PCP* (Lima, 1987), and Valcárcel, *Memorias* (Lima, 1981). For a *Biografía del movimiento social-cristiano en el Perú (1926–1956), apuntes*, see Pedro Planas Silva (Lima, 1996).

The military "revolution" of 1968 stimulated an extensive bibliography. The best starting points for a comprehensive examination are Lowenthal's *The Peruvian Experiment*, its sequel *The Peruvian Experiment Reconsidered*, edited with Cynthia McClintock, and with Jane Jaquette, "The Peruvian Experiment in Retrospect," *World Politics* 39:2 (January 1987), 280–296. The most recent analysis, with new information gathered through extensive interviews of key governmental officials, is Dirk Kruijt, *Revolution by Decree: Peru, 1968–75* (Amsterdam, 1994). Also important is Masterson, *Militarism*. For good, short overviews, see Cotler, "Peru since 1960" and Luis Pásara, "La docena militar," in Juan Mejía Baca (ed.), *Historia del Perú*, 12 (Lima, 1980). George D. E. Philip examines the first phase in *The Rise and Fall of the Peruvian Military Radicals, 1968–1976* (London, 1978). Liisa North and Tanya Korovkin analyze the background and outlook of the leaders in *The Peruvian Revolution and the Officers in Power, 1967–1976* (Montreal, 1981). See also Frederick M. Nunn's *Time of the Generals: Latin American Professional Militarism in World Perspective* (Lincoln, NE, 1992), and "Professional Militarism in Twentieth-Century Peru: Historical and Theoretical Background to the *Golpe de Estado* of 1968," *HAHR* 59:3 (August 1979), 391–418.

The essentially authoritarian and corporatist character of the regime is developed by several authors: David Scott Palmer, *The Authoritarian Tradition* (New York, 1980); Alfred Stepan, *The State and Society: Peru in Comparative Perspective* (Princeton, NJ, 1978); David Chaplin (ed.), *Peruvian Nationalism: A Corporatist Revolution* (Princeton, NJ, 1976); and James M. Malloy, *Authoritarianism, Corporatism and Mobilization in Peru* (Pittsburgh, PA, 1973).

David G. Becker sees the rise of a "new bourgeoisie" during the *Docenio*, aided by favorable policies toward education and transnational corporations in his *The Bourgeoisie and the Limits of Dependency: Mining, Class, and Power in "Revolutionary" Peru* (Princeton, NJ, 1983). A Marxist interpretation can be found in William Bollinger, "The Bourgeois Revolution in Peru: A Conception of Peruvian History," *Latin American Perspectives* 4 (Summer 1977), 18–56. Other aspects of the *Docenio* are emphasized in Raúl P. Saba, *Political Development and Democracy in Peru: Continuity in Change and Crisis* (Boulder, CO, 1987), and David Booth and Bernardo Sorj (eds.), *Military Reformism and Social Classes: The Peru Experience, 1968–1980* (London, 1983). The fall from power of the oligarchy is chronicled by Henry Pease García, *El ocaso del poder oligárquico: lucha política en la escena oficial, 1968–1975* (Lima, 1977).

Sheahan discusses the economy in *Searching*, as does Carol Wise, "Peru Post 1968: The Limits to State-Led Economic Development" (Ph.D. diss., Columbia University, 1990). See also E. V. K. Fitzgerald, *The State and Economic Development: Peru since 1968* (Cambridge, England, 1976) and *The Political Economy*; see also Thorp and Bertram, *Peru 1890–1977*. Guido Pennano (ed.) and others chronicle the economic decline in *Crónica de un colapso económico: Perú 1974–1979*, 2 vols. (Lima, 1980). Barbara Stallings examines "Peru and the U.S. Banks: Privatization of Financial Relations," in Richard R. Fagen (ed.), *Capitalism and the State in U.S.–Latin American Relations* (Stanford, CA, 1979). See also R. Devlin, *Transnational Banks and the External Finance of Latin America: The Experience of Peru* (Santiago, 1985); Drago Kisic, *De la corresponsibilidad a la moratoria: el caso de la deuda externa peruana 1970–1986* (Lima, 1987); and John Sheahan, "Peru: Economic Policies and Structural Change, 1968–1978," *Journal of Developing Areas* 7 (1980). The redistributive implications of the revolution are discussed in Webb, *Government Policy*, and Adolfo Figueroa, "The Impact of Current Reforms on Income Distribution in Peru," in *Income Distribution in Latin America*, edited by Alejandro Foxley (London, 1976). On industrialization, see Weeks, *Limits to Capitalist Development*; Wils, *Industrialization*; and Hugo Cabieses et al., *Industrialization and Regional Development* (Amsterdam, 1982). The industrial communities are examined by Giorgio Alberti, Jorge Santistevan, and Luis Pásara (eds.), *Estado y clase: la comunidad industrial en el Perú* (Lima, 1977). Evelyne Huber Stephens examines *The Politics of Workers' Participation: The Peruvian Approach in Comparative Perspective* (New York, 1980), while Henry Dietz discusses the urban poor in *Poverty and Problem Solving under Military Rule: The Urban Poor in Lima, Peru* (Austin, TX, 1980), and, more recently, in *Urban Poverty, Political Participation and the State: Lima, 1970–1990* (Pittsburgh, PA, 1998).

On the role of U.S. corporations during the 1960s, see Charles T. Goodsell, *American Corporations and Peruvian Politics* (Cambridge, MA, 1974). The issue of nationalization is treated by Adalberto J. Pinelo, *The Multinational Corporation as a Force in Latin American Politics: A Case Study of the International Petroleum Company in Peru* (New York, 1973); George Ingram, *Expropriation of U.S. Property in South America: Nationalization of Oil and Copper Companies in Peru, Bolivia and Chile* (New York, 1974); and Dore, *The Peruvian Mining Industry*. Alan Angel has examined *Peruvian Labour and the Military Government in Peru since 1968* (London, 1979). The eonomic failures of the regime are astutely pointed out by Daniel Shydlowsky and Juan Wicht, *Anatomía de un fracaso económico: Perú, 1968–1978* (Lima, 1978), and "The Tragedy of Lost Opportunity in Peru," in *Latin American Political Economy*, edited by Jonathan Hartlyn and Samuel A. Morley (Boulder, CO, 1986), 217–242.

Perhaps the most studied aspect of the revolutionary government has been the agrarian reform program. A good assessment can be found in A. Fernández de la Gala and A. Gonzáles Zúñiga (eds.), *La reforma agraria peruana, 20 años después* (Chiclayo, Peru, 1990). See also Linda J. Seligman, *Between Reform and Revolution: Political Struggles in the Peruvian Andes, 1969–1991* (Stanford, CA, 1995); Elena Alvarez, *Política económica agricultura en el Perú, 1969–1979* (Lima, 1983), and *Política agraria y estancamiento de la agricultura, 1969–1977* (Lima, 1980); Tom Alberts, *Agrarian Reform and Rural Poverty* (Boulder, CO, 1983); Cristóbal Kay, "The Agrarian Reform in Peru: An Assessment," in *Agrarian Reform in Contemporary Developing Countries*, edited by A. K. Ghose (London, 1983); and Cynthia McClintock, *Peasant Cooperatives and Political Change in Peru* (Princeton, NJ, 1981), and "Post-Revolutionary Agrarian Politics" in *The Politics of Transformation*, edited by Stephen M. Gorman (Boulder, CO, 1982), 17–66.

Also valuable are José Matos Mar and José Manuel Mejía, *La reforma agraria en el Perú* (Lima, 1980); Peter S. Cleaves and Martin J. Scurrah, *Agriculture, Bureaucracy and Military Government in Peru* (Ithaca, NY, 1980); José María Caballero, *Economía agraria de la sierra antes de la reforma agraria de 1969, Agricultura, reforma agraria y pobreza campesina* (Lima, 1980), and with Elena Alvarez, *Aspectos cuantitativos de la reforma agraria (1969–79)* (Lima, 1980); Carlos Amat y León (ed.), *Realidad del campo peruano después de la reforma agraria: 10 ensayos críticos* (Lima, 1980); David Guillet, *Agrarian Reform and Peasant Economy in Southern Peru* (Columbia, MO, 1979); and Mariano Valderama, *Siete años de reforma agraria peruana 1969–1976* (Lima, 1976).

On sugar workers, see Santiago Roca, *Las cooperativas azucareras en el Perú: distribución de ingresos* (Lima, 1975). Also worthwhile are Cristóbal Kay, "Achievements and Contradictions of the Peruvian Agrarian Reform," *Journal of Development Studies* 18, (1982), 141–170, and Susana Lasarria-Cornhiel, "Agrarian Reform of the 1960s and 1970s in Peru," in *Searching for Agrarian Reform in Latin America*, edited by William C. Thiesenhusen (Boston, 1989), 127–155.

Various participants in the military government have written on the revolution. For example, see Héctor Béjar, *La revolución en la trampa* (Lima, 1976); Héctor Cornejo Chávez, *Socialcristianismo y la revolución de Velasco* (Lima, 1975); Carlos Delgado, *El proceso revolucionario peruano: testimonio de lucha* (Buenos Aires, 1972), and *Revolución y participación* (Lima, 1974); Carlos Franco, *La revolución participatoria* (Lima, 1975), *Perú participación pop-*

ular (Lima, 1979), and his edited *El Perú de Velasco*, 4 vols. (Lima, 1986); María del Pilar Tello, *Golpe o revolución? hablan los generales del 68*, 2 vols. (Lima, 1983); and Juan Velasco Alvarado, *La voz de la revolución: discursos . . .* (Lima, 1972).

An excellent analytical summary of the Second Phase of the *Docenio* can be found in Stephen M. Gorman, "The Peruvian Revolution in Historical Perspective," in his edited work *Post Revolutionary Peru: The Politics of Transformation* (Boulder, CO, 1982). Also included in this volume are a number of informative studies on the transition from military to civilian rule, including Sandra Woy-Hazelton, "The Return to Partisan Politics in Peru." The transition is also skillfully examined by Julio Cotler, "Military Interventions and 'Transfer of Power to Civilians' in Peru," in Guillermo O'Donnell, Philippe C. Schmitter, and Laurence Whitehead, *Transitions from Authoritarian Rule: Latin America* (Baltimore, 1986), 148–172. See also James M. Malloy and Mitchell A. Seligson (eds.), *Authoritarians and Democrats* (Pittsburgh, PA, 1988). More recently Federico Prieto Celi offers *Regreso a la democracia: entrevista biográfica al General Francisco Morales Bermúdez Cerrutti, Presidente del Perú (1975–1980)* (Lima, 1996).

There is no major study of the second Belaúnde administration, although Cotler covers it in his "Peru since 1960," in *CHLA*, as do James D. Rudolph, *Peru: The Evolution of a Crisis* (New York, 1992), and Michael Reid, *Peru: Paths to Poverty* (London, 1985). Alberto Flores Galindo provides a long-range historiographical perspective in "La imagen y el espejo: la historiografía peruana (1910–1986)," in *Márgenes* 4 (December 1988).

José Matos Mar's *Desborde popular y crisis del estado* (Lima, 1984) is the classic study of the widening breach between the state and society, as is Hernando de Soto's *El otro Sendero* (Lima, 1986), on the proliferation of the *informales* and the informal sector. See also Norman Adams and Nestor Valdivia, *Los otros empresarios: ética de migrantes y formación de empresas en Lima* (Lima, 1991), and D. Carbonetto et al., *Lima: sector informal* (Lima, 1988). See also D. Cotlear et al. *Perú: la población migrante* (Lima, 1987).

David Scott Palmer compares "The Changing Political Economy of Peru under Civilian and Military Rule," *JISWA* 37:4 (Spring 1984), 37–62. Peru's macroeconomic experiments during the 1980s are examined and interpreted by Manuel Pastor, Jr., *Inflation, Stabilization, Debt: Macroeconomic Experiments in Peru and Bolivia* (Boulder, CO, 1992), and with Carol Wise, "Peruvian Economic Policy in the 1980s: From Orthodoxy to Heterodoxy and Back," *LARR* 27:2 (1992), 83–118. See also Paul Glewwe and Dennis de Tray, *The Poor in Latin America during Adjustment: A Case Study of Peru* (Washington, DC, 1989).

The debt crisis of the early 1980s is analyzed in the context of Peruvian financial history by Kisic, *De la corresponsabilidad a la moratoria;* Thomas Scheetz, *Peru and the International Monetary Fund* (Pittsburgh, PA, 1986); and Óscar Ugarteche, *El estado deudor: economía política de la deuda, Perú y Bolivia 1968–1984* (Lima, 1986). Also important is Daniel M. Schydlowsky, "The Tragedy of Lost Opportunity in Peru," in *Latin American Political Economy: Financial Crisis and Political Change*, edited by Jonathan Hartlyn and Samuel A. Morley (Boulder, CO, 1986). Alfred H. Saulniers surveys *Public Enterprises in Peru: Public Sector Growth and Reform* (Boulder, CO, 1988), as does Carlos Zuzuñaga Flores (ed.), *Las empresas públicas en el Perú* (Lima, 1985).

On elections in the period of democratization, see Fernando Tuesta Soldevilla, *Partidos políticos y elecciones en el Perú (1978–1993)* (Lima, 1994), as well as several other earlier works on the same subject of elections. Henry A. Dietz examines "Electoral Politics in Peru, 1978–1986," *JISWA* 28 (Winter 1986–87). Eduardo Ferrero Costa surveys *Relaciones del Perú con los Estados Unidos* during this period (Lima, 1987).

A number of works confront the problems of democratic consolidation during the 1980s. See, for example, Julio Cotler, "Political Parties and the Problems of Democratic Consolidation in Peru," in *Building Democratic Institutions: Party Systems in Latin America*, edited by Scott Mainwaring and Timothy R. Scully (Stanford, CA, 1995), 323–353, and Cotler's edited work, *Para afirmar la democracia* (Lima, 1986), as well as Cynthia McClintock, "The Prospects for Democratic Consolidation in a 'Least Likely' Case: Peru," *Comparative Politics* 21:2 (1989), 127–148. Also useful are Luis Pásara and Jorge Parodi (eds.), *Democracia, sociedad y gobierno en el Perú* (Lima, 1988); Alberto Adrianzén et al., *Democra-*

cia: realidades y perspectivas (Lima, 1988); and Alberto Giesecke (ed.), *Burocracia, democratización y sociedad* (Lima, 1989). See also Patricia Wilson, "Lima and the New International Division of Labor," in *The Capitalist City: Global Restructuring and Community Politics*, edited by Michael Peter Smith and Joe R. Feagin (New York, 1987), 199–214. Michael Fleet and Brian H. Smith offer *The Catholic Church and Democracy in Chile and Peru* (Notre Dame, IN, 1997).

Nigel Haworth examines "Radicalization and the Left in Peru, 1976–1991," in *The Latin American Left: From the Fall of Allende to Perestroika*, edited by Barry Carr and Steve Ellner (Boulder, CO, 1993), 41–60, as does Cynthia Ann Sanborn, "The Democratic Left and the Persistence of Populism in Peru, 1975–1990" (Ph.D. diss., Harvard University, 1991). See also Lewis Taylor, "One Step Forward, Two Steps Back: The Peruvian Izquierda Unida, 1980–1990," *Journal of Communist Studies* 6 (1990), 108–119 and Ricardo Letts, *La izquierda peruana: organizaciónes y tendencias* (Lima, 1981).

Rural conditions are assessed, including an excellent evaluation of the agrarian reform, by R. F. Watters, *Poverty and Peasantry in Peru's Southern Andes, 1963–1990* (Pittsburgh, PA, 1994). See also J. M. Mejía, *La neoreforma agraria: cambios en la propiedad de la tierra 1980–1990* (Lima, 1990). Other works on agrarian society and economy are Fernando Eguren et al., *Perú: el problema agrario en debate* (Lima, 1988); R. Hopkins et al., *La lenta modernización de la economía campesina* (Lima, 1987); and Javier Iguíñiz (ed.), *La cuestión rural en el Perú* (Lima, 1986). See also M. Lajo Lazo, *La reforma agroalimentaria: antecedentes, estrategio y contenido* (Cuzco, 1986); A. Figueroa, *Capitalist Development and the Peasant Economy in Peru* (Cambridge, England, 1984); and J. M. Caballero, "Agriculture and the Peasantry under Industrialization Pressures: Lessons from the Peruvian Experience," *LARR* 19:2 (1984), 3–40.

The emergence of the Shining Path insurgency in 1980 and its rapid growth during the decade produced an explosion of scholarship and reporting of varying quality. The most recent to appear is Cynthia McClintock's excellent comparative study, *Politics, Economics, and Revolution: Explaining the Guerrilla Movements in Peru and El Salvador* (Washington, DC, 1998). A thought-provoking and perceptive overview, which contextualizes and grounds the movement in a historical perspective, is Steve J. Stern's introduction to his edited volume *Shining and Other Paths: War and Society in Peru, 1980–1995* (Durham, NC, 1998). The book was produced from a 1995 conference at the University of Wisconsin, which gathered a dozen or more top Peruvianists (mostly Peruvians) to examine the social origins, dynamics, and consequences of the war. An excellent overview and analysis is Lewis Taylor, "Counter-Insurgency Strategy, the PCP–Sendero Luminoso and the Civil War in Peru, 1980–1996," *BLAR* 17:1 (January 1998), 35–59. The deterioration in the condition of peasants is examined by W. P. Mitchell, *Peasants on the Edge: Crop, Cult, and Crisis in the Andes* (Austin, TX, 1991).

A useful complementary volume is the *Shining Path of Peru*, edited by David Scott Palmer (New York, 1992), which brings together an important collection of essays by leading analysts of the movement. Palmer was a teaching colleague of Abimael Guzmán while he was a Peace Corps volunteer at the University of Huamanga in the 1960s. In addition to this book, Palmer has written a number of articles on the movement, including "Rebellion in Rural Peru: The Origins and Evolution of Sendero Luminoso," *Comparative Politics* 18:2 (January 1986), 127–146, in which he interprets the insurgency as another chapter in the "historic pattern of periphery-center conflict" in Peru. See also his "The Revolutionary Terrorism of Peru's Shining Path," in *Terrorism in Context*, edited by Martha Crenshaw (University Park, PA, 1995), 249–308.

Sociologist Carlos Iván Degregori is the foremost Peruvian "Senderologist," as analysts of the movement came to be known. Degregori sees what was initially a small, violent vanguard trying unsuccessfully to trigger a broader-based peasant rebellion as evolving over time into a largely urban movement composed of intellectuals and "young people without hope." In "Why Peasants Rebel: The Case of Peru's Sendero Luminoso," *World Politics* 37:1 (October 1984), 48–84, McClintock views the insurgency as a broader-based, peasant rebellion arising from the sharply declining living standards of the Ayacucho peasantry during the 1970s and 1980s. See also her "Peru's Sendero Luminoso Rebellion: Origins and Trajectory," in *Power and Popular Protest: Latin American Social Movements*, edited by Susan Eckstein (Berkeley, CA, 1989), 61–101.

Degregori disputes the view of Sendero as the expression of yet another Andean millenarian movement. Rather, he emphasizes the party's "hyperclassism," that is the placing of class distinctions over other forms of inequality, such as race, region, or ethnicity, according to strict Marxist-Leninist doctrine. Degregori's major work is *Ayacucho 1969–1979: el surgimiento de Sendero Luminoso: del movimiento por la gratitud de la enseñanza al inicio de la lucha armada* (Lima, 1990). See also his *Que difícil es ser Dios: ideología y violencia política en Sendero Luminoso* (Lima, 1989), *Sendero Luminoso: los hondos y mortales desencuentros* (part 1), *Lucha armada y utopía autoritaria* (part 2) (Lima, 1985–86), and *Ayacucho, raíces de una crisis* (Lima, 1986). More recently he has written on the role of *Las rondas campesinas y la derrota de Sendero Luminoso* (Lima, 1996).

Another important work is Gustavo Gorriti, *The Shining Path: A History of the Millenarian War in Peru*, translated with an introduction by Robin Kirk (Chapel Hill, NC, 1999). Gorriti draws a particularly fascinating portrait of the movement's founder and maximum leader Abimael Guzmán in *The New Republic*, 18 June 1990. More general accounts are Deborah Poole and Gerardo Rénique's, *Peru: Time of Fear* (London, 1992), and Simon Strong's flawed *Shining Path: Terror and Revolution in Peru* (New York, 1992).

A compelling critique is Orin Starn, "Missing the Revolution: Anthropologists and the War in Peru," *Cultural Anthropology* 6:1 (1991), 63–91. In a similar but intemporate vein, see Deborah Poole and Gerardo Rénique's attack on "The New Chroniclers of Peru: U.S. Scholars and Their 'Shining Path' of Peasant Rebellion," *BLAR* 10:2 (1991), 133–191. See also Enrique Meyer's "Peru in Deep Trouble: Mario Vargas Llosa's 'Inquest in the Andes' Reexamined," *Cultural Anthropology* 6:4 (1991), 466–504. Vargas Llosa's account can be found in "The Story of a Massacre," *Granta* 9 (1983), 62–83.

On Guzmán's thought, see Luis Arce Borja (ed.), *Guerra popular en el Perú: el pensamiento Gonzalo* (Brussels, 1989), and Guzmán's interview with Arce Borja, "La entrevista del siglo: Presidente Gonzálo rompe el silencio," *El Diario*, 24 July 1988. Another leading strategist of the movement was Antonio Díaz Martínez, who was killed in the Lurigancho prison uprising in 1986. His ideas are outlined in Colin J. Harding, "Antonio Díaz Martínez and the Ideology of Sendero Luminoso," *BLAR* 7:1 (1987), 65–73. See also Díaz Martínez's *Ayacucho: hambre y esperanza* (Ayacucho, 1969; 2d ed., Lima, 1985) and other works. Official publications of Sendero include *Retomemos a Mariátegui y reconstituyamos su partido* (Lima, 1975); *Desarrollemos la guerra de guerrillas* (Lima, 1982); and *El desarrollo de las ideas marxistas en el Perú* (Lima, 1979).

Starn, like Degregori (1996) more recently, has also written on the grassroots *rondas campesinas*, which began in the northern sierra in the late 1970s as vigilante patrols organized by peasant communities to hunt down stock rustlers and were later turned against Sendero (not to be confused with the *rondas* or peasant civil-defense committees that were formed by the armed forces in the central and southern highlands to combat Sendero). See Starn's *Nightwatch: The Politics of Protest in the Peruvian Andes* (Durham, NC, 1999). See also his " 'I Dreamed of Foxes and Hawks': Reflections on Peasant Protest, New Social Movements and the *Rondas Campesinas* of Northern Peru," in *The Making of Social Movements in Latin America*, edited by A. Escobar and S. Alvarez (Boulder, CO, 1992); *Con los llanques todo barro: refleciones sobre rondas campesinas, protesta rural y nuevos movimientos sociales* (Lima, 1991); and his edited volume *Hablan los ronderos: La búsqueda por la paz en los Andes* (Lima, 1993). See also John Gitlitz and Telmo Rójas, "Peasant Vigilante Committees in Northern Peru," *JLAS* 15:1 (1983), 163–197.

Sendero's move beyond its initial base in Ayacucho into other parts of the country is the subject of several studies. For example, Brown and Fernández, in *War of Shadows*, argue that the Ashaninkas saw the guerrillas' arrival in the central *selva* as returning ancient culture heroes. For other areas, see José Luis Rénique, "La batalla por Puno: Violencia y democracia en la sierra sur," *Debate Agrario* 10 (1991), 83–108; José E. Gonzáles, "Guerrillas and Coca in the Upper Huallaga Valley," in Palmer, *Shining Path*, 123–143;

Lewis Taylor, "Agrarian Unrest and Political Conflict in Puno (1985–87)," *BLAR* 6:2 (1987); and Michael L. Smith, "Shining Path's Urban Strategy: Ate Vitarte, " in Palmer, *Shining Path*, 127–148. See also Nelson Manrique, "La década de la violencia," *Márgenes* 5–6 (1989), 137–182 for the Mantaro Valley.

The role of women in Sendero is perceptively examined by Robin Kirk, *Grabado en piedra: las mujeres de Sendero Luminoso* (Lima, 1993). On the other hand, Carol Andreas's *When Women Rebel: The Rise of Popular Feminism in Peru* (Westport, CT, 1985) is strongly pro-Sendero. On the larger issue of the impact of the war on women, see Isabel Coral Cordero, "Women in War: Impact and Responses," in Stern, *Shining and Other Paths*.

The radicalization of young people and their susceptibility to the siren song of Sendero is developed in Julio Cotler, "La radicalización política de la juventud popular en el Perú," *CEPAL* 29 (1986), and Carlos Iván Degregori, "Del mito de Inkarri al 'mito' del progreso: poblaciones andinas, cultura, e identidad nacional," *Socialismo y Participación* 66 (1986), 49–56. See also Nicolás Lynch, *Los jóvenes rojos de San Marcos: el radicalismo universitario de los años setenta* (Lima, 1990), and Denis Chávez de Paz, *Juventud y terrorismo: Características sociales de los condenados por terrorismo y otros delitos* (Lima, 1989). Gonzalo Portocarrero and Patricia Oliart offer insights in their important *El Perú desde la escuela* (Lima, 1989). The relationship of Sendero and the democratic Left is developed in Iván Hinojosa, "Sobre parientes pobres y nuevos ricos: las relaciones entre Sendero Luminoso y la izquierda radical Peruana," in Stern, *Shining and Other Paths*, and Sandra Woy-Hazleton and William A. Hazleton, "Shining Path and the Marxist Left" in Palmer, *The Shining Path*.

For the military's strategy and campaign to defeat the insurgency, see Taylor, "Counter-Insurgency Strategy"; Carlos Iván Degregori and Carlos Rivera, *Perú 1980–1990: fuerzas armadas, subversión y democracia. Redefinición del papel militar en un contexto de violencia subversiva y colapso de régimen democrático* (Lima, 1993); and Masterson, *Militarism*. Belaúnde's and García's delicate relationship with the armed forces is examined in Philip Mauceri, *Los militares en el Perú: su política en la insurgencia y democratización (1980–1989)* (Lima, 1989). General Roberto C. Noel Moral, who was the commander of the Ayacucho Emergency Zone, wrote his account in *Ayacucho: Testimonio de un soldado: Memorias* (Lima, 1989). The impact of the capture of Guzmán on Sendero is analyzed by Nelson Manrique, "La caida de la cuarta espada y los senderos que se bifurcan," *Márgenes* 13–14 (1995), 11–42.

Gabriela Tarazona-Sevillano examines *Sendero Luminoso and the Threat of Narcoterrorism* (New York, 1990), as does Gustavo Gorriti, "Democracia, narcotráfico y la insurrección de Sendero Luminoso," in Pásara and Parodi (eds.), *Democracia*, 193–212. See also David Scott Palmer, "Peru, the Drug Business and Shining Path: Between Scylla and Charybdis?" *JISWA* 34:3 (1992), 65–88.

The demographic displacement caused by the war against Sendero is poignantly described by Robin Kirk, *Decade of Chaqwa: Peru's Internal Refugees* (Washington, DC, 1991). As a journalist covering Peru during this period, see her observations in *The Monkey's Paw: New Chronicles from Peru* (Amherst, MA, 1998). On the general problem of human rights violations in Peru during the war, see various reports published by Americas Watch, Amnesty International, the U.S. State Department, and the Washington Office on Latin America, as well as by the Comisión Andina de Juristas in Lima. Susan C. Bourque and Kay B. Warren offer, "Democracy without Peace: The Cultural Politics of Terror in Peru," *LARR* 24:1 (1989).

Other valuable contributions to understanding Sendero are Harold O. Sklar, *Between Freedom-Fighting and Terrorism in Peru—The Issue of Sendero Luminoso* (Oslo, 1988); Gordon H. McCormick, *The Shining Path and Peruvian Terrorism* (Santa Monica, CA, 1987); James Anderson, *Sendero Luminoso: A New Revolutionary Model?* (London, 1987); Colin Harding, "The Rise of Sendero Luminoso," in *Region and Class in Modern Peru*, edited by Rory Miller (Liverpool, England, 1986); Vera Gianotten, Tom de Wit, and Hans de Wit, "The Impact of Sendero Luminoso on Regional and National Politics in Peru," in *The New Social Movements and the State in Latin America*, edited by David Slater (Amsterdam, 1985), 171–202; and Lewis

Taylor, *Maoism in the Andes: Sendero Luminoso and the Contemporary Guerrilla Movement in Peru* (University of Liverpool, Center for Latin American Studies, Working Paper no. 2, 1983). For *An Annotated Bibliography of the Shining Path Guerrilla Movement: 1980–1993*, see Peter A. Stern (Austin, TX, 1996), and John M. Bennett, *Sendero Luminoso in Context: An Annotated Bibliography* (Lanham, MD, 1998). On MRTA, see Gordon H. McCormick, *Sharp Dressed Men: Peru's Túpac Amaru Revolutionary Movement* (Santa Monica, CA, 1993).

On the general problem of violence during the 1980s, see Tina Rosenberg's gripping, *Children of Cain: Violence and the Violent in Latin America* (New York, 1991), and Alma Guillermoprieto's equally moving *The Heart that Bleeds: Latin America Now* (New York, 1994). The problem is examined in historical perspective by Deborah Poole (ed.), *Unruly Order: Violence, Power, and Cultural Identity in the High Provinces of Southern Peru* (Boulder, CO, 1994), and Henrique Urbano (comp.) and Mirko Lauer (ed.), *Poder y violencia en los Andes* (Cuzco, 1991). Also important is Nelson Manrique, *La piel y la pluma: escritos sobre la literatura, etnicidad y racismo* (Lima, 1999). Other studies include Juan Ossio, *Violencia estructural en el Perú* (Lima, 1990); DESCO, *Violencia política en el Perú, 1980–1988*, 2 vols. (Lima, 1989); Juan Ansión, *Pishtacos. De verdugos a sacaojos* (Lima, 1989); *Violencia y pacificación* (Lima, 1989); Denis Sulmont et al., *Violencia y movimiento sindical* (Lima, 1989); Rolando Ames (ed.), *Informe al congreso sobre los sucesos de los penales* (Lima, 1988); Rodrigo Montoyo et al., *La sangre de los cerros Urqukunapa Yawarnin* (Lima, 1987); Alberto Flores Galindo and Nelson Manrique, *Violencia y campesinado* (Lima, 1986); and Felipe McGregor et al., *Siete ensayos sobre la violencia en el Perú* (Lima, 1985).

The best works on the García administration and the rise to power of APRA are John Crabtree, *Peru under García: An Opportunity Lost* (Pittsburgh, PA, 1992), and Carol Graham, *Peru's APRA: Parties, Politics and the Elusive Quest for Democracy* (Boulder, CO, 1992). Also useful are Cotler, "Peru since 1960," in *CHLA*; Rudolph, *Peru: The Evolution*; and Reid, *Peru: Paths*. García outlines his own diagnosis and prescription in *Un futuro diferente: la tarea histórica del APRA* (Lima, 1985). His speeches can be found in his *A la inmensa mayoría, discursos (1985–1987)* (Lima, 1988).

García's controversial heterodox policy has drawn considerable scholarly attention. See Manuel Pastor, Jr., *Inflation, Stabilization, Debt*, and with Carol Wise "Peruvian Economic Policy in the 1980s"; Rosemary Thorp, *Economic Management and Economic Development in Peru and Colombia* (Pittsburgh, PA, 1991); and Ricardo Lago, "The Illusion of Pursuing Redistribution through Macropolicy: Peru's Heterodox Experience, 1985–1990," in *The Macroeconomics of Populism in Latin America*, edited by Rudiger Dornbusch and Sebastian Edwards (Chicago, 1991), 263–330. See also Eva Paus, "Adjustment and Development in Latin America: The Failure of Peruvian Heterodoxy, 1985–1988," *World Development* 19:5 (1991), 411–434; Pedro Pablo Kuczynski, "Peru," in *Latin American Adjustment: How Much Has Happened?* edited by John Williamson (Washington, DC, 1990); Germán Alarco, *Economía Peruana, 1985–1990: enseñanzas de la expansión y del colapso* (Lima, 1990); and Leonel Figueroa, "Economic Adjustment and Development in Peru: Towards an Alternative Policy," in *Adjustment with a Human Face: Protecting the Vulnerable and Promoting Growth*, edited by Giovanni Cornia, Frances Stewart, and Richard Jolly (Oxford, 1987). Daniel Carbonetto, an Argentine economist and one of the architects of the policy, collaborated with others in *El Perú heterodoxo: un modelo heterodoxo* (Lima, 1987). See also Carol Wise on "Democratization, Crisis, and APRA's Modernization Project in Peru," in *Debt and Democracy in Latin America*, edited by Barbara Stallings and Robert Kaufman (Boulder, CO, 1989). The economic crisis and a prescription for its resolution are presented by Felipe Ortiz de Zeballos, *The Peruvian Puzzle* (New York, 1989).

Francisco Durand inquires into *Business and Politics in Peru: The State and the National Bourgeoisie* (Boulder, CO, 1994). See also his *Empresarios y la concertación* (Lima, 1987), and *La burguesía: los primeros industriales; Alan García y los empresarios* (Lima, 1988). Carlos Malpica analyzes *El poder económico en el Perú*, 2 vols. (Lima, 1989), as does Eduardo Anaya Franco, *Los grupos de poder económico: un análisis de la oligarquía financiera* (Lima, 1990), and Ludovico Alcorta, *El nuevo capital financero: grupos financieros y ganancias monopólicas en el Perú* (Lima, 1992). On hyperinflation, see Jürgen Schuldt, *Hacia la hyperinflación en el Perú*

(Lima, 1988). See also Efraín Gonzáles de Olarte (ed.), *Economía para la democracia* (Lima, 1989), and *Crisis y democracia: el Perú en busca de un nuevo paradigma de desarrollo* (Lima, 1987), as well as Heraclio Bonilla and Paul Drake (eds.), *El Apra: de la ideología a la práxis* (Lima, 1989). Numerous studies on the economy during this period were also published by the Fundación Friedrick Ebert in Lima.

Grassroots social groups and movements, whose proliferation was a hallmark of the 1980s, are the subject of Susan C. Stokes, *Cultures in Conflict: Social Movements and the State in Peru* (Berkeley, CA, 1995). The leading Peruvian scholar on the increasing role of women in these groups and generally in Peruvian society is Cecilia Blondet whose works include "Out of the Kitchens and onto the Streets: Women's Activism in Peru," in *The Challenge of Local Feminisms*, edited by Amrita Basu (Boulder, CO, 1995), 251–275; with Carmen Montero *La situación de la mujer en el Perú, 1980–1994* (Lima, 1994); also with Montero, *Los comedores populares: Balance y lecciones de una experiencia* (Lima, 1994); *Las mujeres y el poder: Una historia de Villa El Salvador* (Lima, 1991); and numerous articles. Other useful works are Roselie Lenten, *Cooking under the Volocanoes: Communal Kitchens in the Southern Peruvian City of Arequipa* (Amsterdam, 1993); Amelia Fort, *Mujeres peruanas: La mitad de la población del Perú a comienzos de los 90* (Lima, 1993); Virginia Vargas, *Como cambiar el mundo sin perdernos: el movimiento de mujeres en el Perú y América Latina* (Lima, 1992); Patricia Portocarrero (ed.), *Mujer en el desarrollo: balances y propuestas* (Lima, 1990); Nora Qaler and Pilár Nuñez (eds.), *Mujer y comedores populares* (Lima, 1989); Patricia Córdova and Carmen Luz Gorbiti, *Apuntes para una interpretación del movimiento de mujeres: Los comedores comunales y los comités del vaso de leche en Lima* (Lima, 1989); and Susan Lobo, *Tengo casa propia: organización social de las barriadas de Lima* (Lima, 1984). See also Maruja Barrig, "The Difficult Equilibrium between Bread and Roses: Women's Organizations and the Transition from Dictatorship to Democracy in Peru," in *The Women's Movement in Latin America: Feminism and the Transition to Democracy*, edited by Jane S. Jaquette (Boston, 1989).

The situation of migrants in Lima is examined by Dietz, *Urban Poverty*, and Jean-Claude Driant, *Las barriadas de Lima: historia e interpretación* (Lima, 1991). See also Carlos Iván Degregori et al., *Conquistadores de un nuevo mundo: de invasores a ciudadanos en San Martín de Pórras* (Lima, 1986), and Jürgen Golte and Norma Adams, *Los caballos de Troya de los invasores: estrategias campesinas en la conquista de la Gran Lima* (Lima, 1987). Numerous other studies include Teófilo Altamirano, *Presencia andina en Lima Metroplitana* (Lima, 1984); Jorge B. Burga and Claire Delpech, *Villa El Salvador: la ciudad y su desarrollo, realidad y propuestas* (Lima, 1989); Romeo Grompone et al., *La Lima de los 80: crecimiento y segregación social* (Lima, 1983); and Denis Sulmont's study of labor's problems *Cuestionamiento y posibilidades de renovación en el movimiento sindical* (Lima, 1990). The deteriorating conditions of workers and other social groups such as urban slum dwellers, including women, are skillfully documented in Carmen Rosa Balbi et al., *Movimientos sociales: elementos para una relectura* (Lima, 1990).

Several studies address the problem of drug trafficking. For the historical context, see Joseph A. Gagliano, *Coca Prohibition in Peru: The Historical Debates* (Tucson, AZ, 1984), and Jonathan Cavanaugh and Rosemary Underhay, *Coca and Cocaine: An Andean Perspective* (Westport, CT, 1993). On trafficking, see Diego García Sayán (ed.), *Coca, cocaína y narco-tráfico: el laberinto en los Andes* (Lima, 1989); Rensselaer Lee, *The White Labyrinth* (New Brunswick, NJ, 1989); and Edmundo Morales, *Cocaine: White Gold Rush in Peru* (Tucson, AZ, 1989).

Alberto Fujimori's first administration has been the subject of considerable commentary and analysis. The best overview is Maxwell A. Cameron and Phillip Mauceri (eds.), *The Peruvian Labyrinth* (University Park, PA, 1997). See also *Los enigmas del Poder: Fujimori 1990–1996*, edited by Fernando Tuesta Soldevilla (Lima, 1996). Both volumes provide extensive bibliographical essays. Journalist Alfredo Barnechea trys to put Peru's problems into global perspective in *La república embrujada: un caso en la pobreza de las naciónes* (Lima, 1995).

For an analysis of Fujimori's electoral victories see José María Salcedo, *Terremoto: como ganó Fujimori?* (Lima 1995); Jeff Daeschner, *The War of the End of Democracy: Mario Vargas Llosa vs. Alberto Fujimori* (Lima, 1993); and Carlos Iván Degregori and Romeo

Grompone, *Elecciones 1990: demonios y redentores en el nuevo Perú* (Lima, 1991). Vargas Llosa's own analysis can be found in *A Fish in the Water* (New York, 1994), in Spanish *El pez en el agua: memorias* (Barcelona, 1993). See also Álvaro Vargas Llosa, his son, who managed the campaign, *El diablo en campaña* (1991) and *The Madness of Things Peruvian: Democracy under Siege* (New Brunswick, NJ, 1994).

Philip Mauceri incisively dissects the reasons for the weakening of the state over the past fifteen years in *State under Siege: Development and Policy Making in Peru* (Boulder, CO, 1996). He also provides a good overview and analysis of Fujimori's first term, as well as the 1992 self-coup in "State Reform, Coalitions, and the Neoliberal Autogolpe in Peru," *LARR* 30:1 (1995), 7–38. See also Henry Pease García, *Los años de la langosta: la escena política del Fujimorismo* (Lima, 1994). The thesis of the compatibility of Fujimori's neo-liberalism with populism is developed by Kenneth M. Roberts, "Neoliberalism and the Transformation of Populism in Latin America: The Peruvian Case," *World Politics* 48:1 (October 1995), 82–116, and Bruce H. Kay, "Fujipopulism and the Liberal State in Peru, 1990–1995," *JISWA* 38:4 (1996). See also Kurt Weyland, "Neopopulism and Neoliberalism in Latin America: Unexpected Affinities," *Studies in Comparative International Development* 31:3 (Fall 1996), 3–31. A useful biography of the president is Luis Jochamowitz, *Ciudadano Fujimori: la construcción de un político* (Lima, 1993). See also the following issues of *Current History*: February 1991, February 1992, March 1993, and February 1996.

On the economy in the 1990s see Sheahan, *Searching*; John Crabtree and Jim Thomas (eds.), *Fujimori's Peru: The Political Economy* (New York, 1998); and Efraín Gonzáles de Olarte (ed.), *The Peruvian Economy and Structural Adjustment: Past, Present and Future* (Miami, 1996). See also the latter's edited *Neoliberalismo y desarrollo humano: desafíos del presente y del futuro* (Lima, 1998), *El neoliberalismo a la Peruana: economía política del ajuste estructural, 1990–1997* (Lima, 1998), and *El péndulo peruano: políticas económicas, gobernabilidad y subdesarrollo, 1963–1993* (Lima, 1994). Daniel M. Schydlowsky and Jürgen Schuldt critique *Modelo económico peruano de fin del siglo: Alcances y limites* (Lima, 1996). See also Carol Wise, "The Politics of Peruvian Economic Reform: Overcoming the Legacies of State-Led Development," in the *JISWA* 36 (Spring 1994). The problem of providing an adequate safety net for the poor during the transition to neoliberalism under Fujimori is examined by Carol Graham in *Safety Nets, Politics, and the Poor: Transitions to Market Economies* (Washington, DC, 1994). See also Carlos Paredes and Jeffrey Sachs (eds.), *Peru's Path to Recovery: A Plan for Economic Stabilization and Growth* (Washington, DC, 1991), and J. Iguiñiz et al., *Los ajustes: Perú 1975–1992* (Lima, 1993).

The problem of the consolidation and breakdown of democracy under Fujimori is addressed by Maxwell A. Cameron, *Democracy and Authoritarianism in Peru: Political Coalitions and Social Change* (New York, 1994). Another perspective is Cynthia McClintock, "Presidents, Messiahs and Constitutional Breakdowns," in *The Failure of Presidential Democracy*, edited by Juan J. Linz and Arturo Valenzuela (Baltimore, 1994). On the same subject, see Cotler, who also puts the problem in historical context, in his "Political Parties." See also J. Tulchin and G. Bland (eds.), *Peru in Crisis: Dictatorship or Democracy?* (Boulder, CO, 1994). Also useful is Comisión Andina de Juristas, *Del golpe de estado a la nueva constitución* (Lima, 1993); *La constitución de 1993: análisis y comentarios* (Lima, 1993); and C. Kenny, "Por que el autogolpe? Fujimori y la opinión pública," in *La política bajo Fujimori: Partidos políticos y opinión pública*, edited by Fernando Tuesta (Lima, 1996). See also Gregory D. Schmidt's "The Evolution of Executive Decree Authority in Peru's 'Volcanic Democracy,' "in *Executive Decree Authority: Calling Out the Tanks, or Filling Out the Forms?*, edited by John M. Carey and Matthew Soberg Shugart (Cambridge, England, 1998). General Jaime Salinas Sedo, leader of an unsuccessful coup against Fujimori in the name of democracy, wrote *Desde el Real Felipe: en defensa de la democracia* (Lima, 1997). The plight of the Peruvian left in the post–Cold War era of neoliberalism is explored in Kenneth M. Roberts, *Deepening Democracy? The Modern Left and Social Movements in Chile and Peru* (Stanford, CA, 1999).

The defeat of the Shining Path is analyzed by Taylor, "Counter-Insurgency Strategy"; Carlos Iván Degregori, *La última tentación del Presidente Gonzalo y otros escritos sobre el auge y colapso de Sendero Luminoso* (Lima, 1996); and Carlos Tapia, *Del "Equilibrio Estratégico" a la derrota de Sendero Luminoso* (Lima, 1996). See also Manrique, "La caida de la cuarta," 11–42. On the importance of the *rondas campesinas* in this process, see Orin Starn, "Villagers at Arms: War and Counterrevolution in Peru's Andes," in Stern, *Shining and Other Paths*; Carlos Tapia, *Autodefensa armada del campesinado* (Lima, 1995); and Ludwig Huber, *Después de Dios y la virgen está las rondas: Las rondas campesinas en Piura* (Lima, 1995). Philip Mauceri examines "Military Politics and Counter-Insurgency in Peru," *JISWA* 33:4 (Winter 1991), 83–109.

The problem of human rights is addressed by Carlos Chipoco, *En defensa de la vida: ensayos sobre derechos humanos y derecho internacional humanitario* (Lima, 1992), and Beatriz Ramaciotti (ed.), *Democracia y derechos humanos en el Perú de los 90: los nuevos retos* (Lima, 1993). See also various reports on Peru by Americas Watch, Amnesty International, and the Washington Office on Latin America. David Scott Palmer examines "United States–Peru Relations in the 1990s: Asymmetry and Its Consequences," in *Latin America and Caribbean Contemporary Record, 1989–1990,* edited by E. Gamarra and J. Malloy (New York, 1992).

Index

Note: Page numbers in *italics* indicate illustrations. Page numbers following by *"m"* indicate maps.

Abascal, José Fernando de, 126, 129
Acción Popular (AP), 319, 322, 327, 360
  opposition to military, 362
  in 1980 elections, 364, 365
Africans. *See* Blacks
Agrarian reform. *See* Land reform
Agriculture, 2
  in colonial Peru, 46–47
  in Inca society, xii, 15, 28
  introduction of Spanish cattle and, 49–50
  in postcolonial Peru, 140–141, 142
  18th-century, 100–101, 107–108
  19th-century, 165–166
  mid 20th-century, 302–303, 304, 305, 310, 331
  late 20th-century, 348–349, 375, 389, 395
Aguilar, Gabriel, 125
Alcabala (sales tax), 114
Alianza Popular Revolucionaria Americana (APRA)
  appeal of, 274
  Bustamante's administration and, 289–290, 296, 298
  domination of, 271, 290–296
  factions within, 296, 318, 329
  formation of, 259–260
  García Pérez and, 364, 378, 383–384
  Haya's death and, 364, 365
  legalization of, 287
  loss of popularity, 336
  military's antipathy for, 275–276, 320–321, 337
  Morales Bermúdez and, 360
  Odría's efforts to undermine, 302
  outlawing of, 299, 300
  Prado's administration and, 282, 283–284, 286
  program of, 273
  realignment of, 282, 283, 287, 288, 291, 295–296
  repression and persecution of, 275
  urban orientation of, 295
  violence and subversion by, 275, 276, 287, 296, 298
  World War II and, 282, 283, 286
  and 1931 elections, 272–273
  and 1936 elections, 280
  and 1939 elections, 281
  and 1945 elections, 287, 288, 293
  and 1956 elections, 307
  and 1962 elections, 318, 319–320
  and 1978 elections, 364–365
  and 1980 elections, 377
  and 1983 elections, 377
  and 1990 elections, 404
  and 1995 elections, 422
Almagro, Diego, 34, 37, 40
  blacks in expedition of, 51
  conflict with Pizarro, 40–41
Alomia Robles, Daniel, 247
Altiplano (plateau), 2, 7
Alva Castro, Luis, 397, 400, 401
Alzamora, Isaac, 218
Amauta (journal), 255, 256–257, 259, 262
Amazonia, 4
Amazonian rubber boom, 211
Amerindians. *See* Indians
Anarchism, 221–222, 236
Andean insurrection, age of, 108–121
  factors leading to, 112–115
Andean mountains, 1, 2
Andean utopia, 92–93, 116
Andean worldview, 13
Angulo brothers, rebellion led by, 128
Anthony Gibbs and Company, 164, 167, 170
AP. *See* Acción Popular
APRA. *See* Alianza Popular Revolucionaria Americana
Aqllakuna (chaste girls), 26
Arbitrios, Ramo de, 160
Architecture
  colonial, 98
  Inca, 25
  Spanish, 39
Areche, Antonio de, 104, 114, 120
Argentina
  student reform movement in, 239
  war with Peru-Bolivian Confederation, 156
Arguedas, José María, 317
Aristocratic Republic, 203
  and cultural expansion, 232–235
  economy during, 203–212, 216–217
  and emergence of oligarchy, 212–218
  and formation of working class, 219–225
  government during, 205–206
  politics during, 203, 214–215, 217–218
  population growth during, 218–219

Army. *See* Military
Arriaga, Antonio de, 118
Arriaga, Pablo José de, 92
Artisan industries
  in 17th century, 81
  in 19th century, 154
    guano boom and destruction of, 159, 161
    War of the Pacific and revival of, 198
Aspíllaga, Antero, 223, 238
Aspíllaga, Ramón, 224, 241
Atacama Desert, 183, 185
Atahualpa
  capture by Pizarro, 31, 34–37, *36*
  in civil war, 29–30, 35
  death of, 38
Atahualpa, Juan Santos. *See* Santos
    Atahualpa, Juan, rebellion of
Atusparia, Pedro Pablo, 194, 195
Audiencias, 87, 103–104
Avalanches, 1
Ávila, Francisco de, 92
Ayllu (communities), Inca, xii, 14
Ayulo, Laos, 241

Balboa, Vasco Núñez de, 33
Balta, José, 166, 176
  military coup against, 179
  railroad-building program of, 176, 177
Bambaren, Luis, 351–352
Banco del Perú, 171, 172
Bandera Roja, 368, 369
Banks
  first, 170–171
  in late 19th century, 178
  nationalization of, proposal for, 393, 397
Baquijano y Carillo, José, 127
Barrantes, Alfonso, 377, 378
  in 1984 elections, 384, 385
  in 1990 elections, 397, 400
Barriadas (squatter settlements), 301–302, 325,
    350
Basadre, Jorge, 239
Bastidas Puyucahua, Micaela, 115, 118
Beaterios (religious communities), 96
Becerra, Manuel José, 190
Béjar, Héctor, 329
Béjar, José Gabriel, 128
Belaúnde, Víctor Andrés, 214, 232, 242,
    257–258
Belaúnde Terry, Fernando, 307
  developmental strategy of, 332–334
  first administration of, 326–335
  highway project of, 332, 375
  and International Petroleum Company,
    334–335
  and land reform, 327–328
  loss of popularity, 336, 337
  and military, relations with, 362, 373–374
  second administration of, 365, 372–378, 382
  and Shining Path, 381
  in 1962 elections, 319, 320

  in 1963 elections, 322
  in 1980 elections, 364–365
Belmont, Ricardo, 398, 400, 416, 419, 422
Beltrán, Pedro, 279, 281, 291, 319
  as head of Central Bank, 300, 301
  as prime minister, 308, 315
Benalcázar, Sebastian de, 34
Benavides, Oscar R., 225, *277*
  background of, 276–278
  coup led by, 224, 225
  dictatorship of, 280–281
  presidency of, 278–279
  World War I and, 226
  in 1936 elections, 280
  in 1945 elections, 286, 287
Billinghurst, Guillermo
  political career of, 222–223
  presidency of, 224
Bingham, Hiram, 246
Black market, late 20th-century, 372–373,
    385
Blacks
  in colonial society, 52, 53, 82
    percentage of population, 100
  free, 149, 154
  in independence movement, 123
  introduction to Peru, 51–52
  in postcolonial society, *153*
  valorization of, in 1920s, 252
  See also Slaves, African
Blanco, Hugo, 314, 319
Bolívar, Simón de, 122
  and Peruvian independence movement,
    132–133
  privatization decree of, 146
Bolivia
  defensive alliance with, 185
  trade with, 141
  unification with Peru, 155–156
  in War of the Pacific, 181, 183, 185–186,
    187
Bolognesi, Francisco, 187
Bonaparte, Joseph, 126
Bourbon reforms, 101–108
  and peasant rebellions, 112–113
Bourgeoisie, origins of, 125–126
Britain. *See* Great Britain
Bueno, Cosme, 105
Buenos Aires
  and independence movement, 126
  17th-century development of, 81–82
Bureaucracy
  Bourbon reforms and, 104
  colonial, 86, 88–89
  guano boom and, 169
  post-independence, 144
  early 20th-century, 242
Bustamante, Juan, rebellion led by, 176
Bustamante y Rivero, José Luis, 282, 287
  and APRA, 289–290, 296, 298
  presidency of, 289–299

Cabanillas, Mercedes, 422
Cabildo (town council), 46, 87–88
Cáceres, Andrés Avelino
  explanation for defeat in War of the
    Pacific, 198
  fraudulent reelection planned by, 200–201,
    202
  and postwar politics, 193
  presidency of, 194, 195, 200
  reconstruction efforts of, 196–197
  in resistance to Chilean occupation,
    189–190
CAEM. *See* Centro de Altos Estudios
  Militares
Callejón de Huaylas, 1, 2
Cambio 90 Party, 402–403, 409
  Nueva Mayoría, 416, 417, 422
Candamo, Manuel, 217, 218
CAPs. *See* Cooperativas Agrarias de
  Producción
Caqui, Diego, 47, 71
Carmen Marín, José Del, 305
Castilla, Ramón, 160, 161–162
  and debt consolidation, 164
  and emancipation of slaves, 151
  first term of, 162–164
  second term of, 168
Castro Pozo, Hildebrando, 247, 340
Catholic Church. *See* Church, Roman
  Catholic
Caudillos, 136, 137
  guano boom and, 160
  and politics, 154–157
  and slavery, 151, 152
Cavallerino, Luis Abram, 390
Cave dwellers, 5
CCD. *See* Congreso Constituente
  Democrático
CCP. *See* Confederación Campesina del Perú
Centro de Altos Estudios Militares (CAEM),
  305, 315, 330
Cerpa Carolini, Nestor, 415
Cerro de Pasco Copper Corporation, 207,
  264–265, 271, 304, 312
Cerro de Pasco silver mine, 99–100, 140,
  141–142
Chacras (small estates), 78
Chancas, 16–17
Chan Chan, 6*m*, 11–12
Charles II, 101
Charles III, 101, 114, 123
Charles IV, 126
Charles V, 39
Chavín de Huantar, cultural center at, 7–8
Chiappa, Anna, 255
Chile
  Almagro's expedition to, 40
  expansion after War of the Pacific, 184*m*, 191
  invasion of Peru, resistance to, 189–190
  San Martín's capture of, 130
  trade with, 77, 81, 141

  in War of the Pacific, 181, 183, 185–191
  war scare of 1976, 362
  war with Peru-Bolivian Confederation, 156
    19th-century, 186–187
Chimor Kingdom, 11–12
China
  demand for American silver, 84
  impact of Revolution in, 314
  leader of Shining Path and, 368, 369, 371
Chincha Islands, 158
  Spain's attempt to seize, 175
Chinese indentured coolies, 163–164, 231
  guano boom and, 158
  revolts of, 177, 192
  social impact of, 151
Cholera, outbreak of, 407
Chupachos (ethnic group), 11
Church, Roman Catholic
  and colonial economy, 72, 82, 90
  and European control, 53–54
  and independence movement, 138
  investment capital provided by, 82, 90
  and land reform of 1960s, 328
  and military regime of 1968, 342
  reducciones and, 62
  Sacred Heart ceremony proposed by, 253,
    254
  southern Andean, 392
  and Spanish *reconquista*, 32
  and Spanish unification, 54
  and Toledan reforms, 60
  in 16th century, 54–56
  in 17th century, 89–92
  in 18th century, 138–139
  in 19th century, 162
  in early 20th century, 253–254, 275, 280
  in mid 20th century, 316, 328
  in late 20th century, 351–352, 405
CIs. *See* Comunidades industriales
Cisneros, Luis Benjamín, 171–172
Civilista Party
  factions within, 218
  and military junta of 1930, 269
  and oligarchy, 213
  origins of, 172
  pact with Democratic Party, 203, 217
  personal loyalties and, 214
  rise of, 172–179
  after War of the Pacific, 193–194, 198
  in late 19th century, 201
  in early 20th century, 235, 241
Clement, Paul, 225
Climate, 2
Clothing, Inca, 25
COAP. *See* Comité de Asesoramiento de la
  Presidencia
Coast
  Europeanization of, 77
  geography of, 2–4
  pre-Inca inhabitants of, 5, 7–8, 11–12
Cobo, Bernabé, 74

Coca industry, 385–387, 396, 412
Cochachín, Pedro "Uchcu," 195
Cochrane, Thomas, 131
Coffee, 313
Collectivism of Inca society, 14
Colombia, border disputes with, 258, 276, 278
Colonial Peru
  blacks in, 51–52
  Bourbon reforms and, 101–108
  crisis of 1560s, 56–58
  and demographic collapse, 48–51
  economy of
    plunder, 43–48
    17th-century, 70–85
    18th-century, 100–101, 105–108
  establishment of, 39–43
  fiscal crisis in, 85, 88
  forced resettlements in, 59, 60, 61
  government/administration of, 46, 85–89
    18th-century reform of, 103–104, 119–120
  independence movement in, 121–133
  Indian resistance and adaptation to, 65, 71
  millenarian revivals in (Taki Onqoy), 57–58
  politics in, 64
  population of, 51–53
  reparto system in, 63–64
  silver mining in, 43–44
    17th-century, 69, 75–76
    18th-century, 99–100, 106
  Toledo reforms and, 62–63, 64, 66–68, 69
  social stratification in, 52, 53, 93–95, 134–136
  Toledan reforms and, 58–68
  tribute system *(encomienda)* in, 41–43, 44–48
Colonos (hacienda workers), 293, 313, 321
  land reform efforts of, 326–327
Columbus, Christopher, 33
Comasino guerrillas, 110
Comité de Asesoramiento de la Presidencia (COAP), 343
Communication. *See* Transportation
Communist Party (CP), 271
  versus APRA, 292
  Guzmán's alternative to, 368
  outlawing of, 300
  World War II and, 282
Comuneros (seasonal workers), 312, 313
  land reform efforts of, 326–327
Comunidades industriales (CIs), 353–354, 357
Condorcanqui, José Gabriel. *See* Túpac Amaru II
Confederación Campesina del Perú (CCP), 361
Confederación de Campesinos del Perú, 326
Confederación de Trabajadores del Perú (CTP), 286
Congreso Constituente Democrático (CCD), 416, 417
Conservatives, in postcolonial Peru, 137, 154–155, 156, 201

Constitutional Assembly, 363–364
Constitutionalist Party, 193, 214
Convivencia, policy of, 307, 318
Cooperativas Agrarias de Producción (CAPs), 346
Cooperatives, creation of, 346
Copper mining, 206–207
  World War I and, 227
  in 1920s, 264
  in 1950s, 301, 309
Coricancha, Temple of, 17
Cornejo, Mariano H., 198
Cornejo Chávez, Héctor, 316, 343
Corregidores de indios (Indian agents), 61
  abolition of, 120
  and *reparto* system, 63
Corregimiento (administrative subdivision), 87
Corruption
  in colonial period, 89
  in postcolonial period, 168
  in early 20th century, 266
  in late 20th century, 407
Cortes, reforms of, 127
Cosmology, Inca, 18, 20
Cotton industry
  World War I and, 227
  World War II and, 284
  in early 20th century, 210–211, 263
  in mid 20th century, 302, 303
Council of the Indies, 86, 87
Coya (queen), 20
CP. *See* Communist Party
Creoles, 56
  in colonial Peru, 94–95
    Andean insurgency and, 115, 121
    Bourbon reforms and, 104
    bureaucracy and, 89
    differentiation from peninsulars, 97
    18th-century, 123–124
  and independence movement, 123, 126, 150
  in postcolonial Peru, 134, 136, 147
Crime
  in colonial society, 91
  in late 20th century, 376
Cristobal, Diego, 119
Crops, 2, 4, 5, 7
  coastal, 18th-century, 108
  European, 77
  See also Agriculture
CTP. *See* Confederación de Trabajadores del Perú
Cuban Revolution, impact of, 314, 329, 336, 377
Culture
  colonial, 17th-century, 74–75, 97–98
  Hispanic
    adaptation to, 47–48, 93
    transmission of, 52
  Inca, 25
  indigenismo and, 246–247
  pre-Inca, 7–8

working-class, emergence of, 221–222
early 20th-century, 232–235, 252
mid 20th-century, 317, 333
Cumberland, William, 244
Curacas (ethnic lords), 24
abolition of, 119, 120
and *encomienda* system, 45
in Spanish colonies, 45, 61
Cuzco
capture by Pizarro, 38
colonial, 74
neo-Inca revivalism at, 116
rebellions at, 118, 128–129
in Inca empire, 6*m*, 17, 19
and independence movement, 125
and *indigenismo* movement, 246, 259
postcolonial, 157

Debt, national
default on, 271, 278
Fujimori's program for repayment of, 408,
419
García's limit on repayment of, 387–388,
389
Leguía's administration and, 243, 244, 258,
266
military government of 1970s and,
354–355
post-independence, 164, 178
War of the Pacific and, 195, 196–197
World War I and, 226
Debt consolidation, 164–165
long-term impact of, 167, 168
Decentralist Party, 268
De Gaulle, Charles, 339
Delegative democracy, Fujimori's, 408–409
Delgado, Carlos, 343
Democratic Party, 194, 214
pact with Civilista Party, 203, 217
in late 19th century, 201
in early 20th century, 235
Denegri, Aurelio, 194
Deng Xiaoping, 371
Depressions
late 19th-century, 201
early 20th-century, 267, 276, 278
Díaz Martínez, Antonio, 369
Diez Canseco, Pedro, 176
Docenio, 342–358
and Catholic Church, 352
control of press, 352–353
economy under, 354–355
foreign policy during, 344–345
government expansion during, 343–344
industrial reform during, 353
land reform during, 346–349
legacy of, 356–358
Doctrineros (parish priests), 60
Drake, Francis, 83
Dreyfus, Auguste, 166, 178
Durán, Augusto, 235

Echenique, José Rufino, 164, 167–168
Ecology, 1–2
Economy
Bourbon reforms and, 105–108
Castillian, 32
guano boom and, 158–160, 161, 165–167,
171
Inca, 28–29
independence and paralysis of, 131
informal, late 20th-century, 372–373, 385
Kemmerer's reform program for, 269–271
of plunder, 43–48
post-independence, 139–145
postwar recovery of, 197–198
railroad expansion and, 174, 181–182
silver production and, 69, 70, 75–76
Toledo reforms and, 62
War of the Pacific and, 191–192
World War I and, 211, 225–228
World War II and, 282, 284–285
17th-century, 70–85
18th-century, 100–101, 105–108
19th-century, 180–181, 203–205
20th-century
early, 203–212, 216–217, 250–251
1920s, 243–244, 250–251, 263–267
1930s, 278–279, 281
1940s, 282, 284–285, 290, 297
1950s, 302–305, 306, 308–311
1960s, 331–332
1970s, 348–349, 354–355, 359–360, 362,
372–373
1980s, 374–376, 385, 388–389, 394–395,
406–407
1990s, 408, 423–424
Ecuador, border wars with, 285–286,
422–423
Education
colonial, 74, 90
military, 305
popular universities, 254
18th-century, 105
19th-century, 180
early 20th-century, 232, 242, 254
mid 20th-century, 328, 333
late 20th-century, 367–368
Eguiguren, Luis Antonio, 268–269, 271,
280
Ejército de Liberación Nacional (ELN),
329–330, 360
Elections
1872, 176–177, 179
1876, 181
1912, 222, 223
1916, 238
1919, 236, 241–242
1931, 271–274
1936, 279–280
1939, 281
1945, 286–288, 293
1950, 301

Elections (*continued*)
  1956, 306–307
  1962, 318–320
  1963, 322
  1978, 362–363
  1980, 364–365
  1983, 377, 384
  1984, 384–385
  1990, 397, 400–401, 402–405
  1993, 416–417
  1995, 421–422
  revisions in law governing, 269, 307, 363
ELN. *See* Ejército de Liberación Nacional
El Niño, 7, 263, 375
Encomienda (trusteeship), 41, 44–48
  central functions of, 52
  debate on, 55–56
  demise of, 56, 61, 65
  and demographic collapse, 49
  reform of, 42–43
Enganche (contract labor), 230–231
  disappearance of, 303
Enlightenment, 105
  and Catholic Church, 138
  and independence movement, 123, 127
  and peasant rebellions, 116
Entradas (expeditions of discovery), 40
Entrepreneurship, in early colonial period,
  47, 71, 72
Epidemic diseases, 34, 49, 50–51
Estancia (ranch), 78
Estrada, Daniel, 419
Eventuales (nonresident farm workers),
  exclusion from land reform, 347, 348
Exports
  World War I and, 226–227
  post–World War II, 297
  early 20th-century, 209, 212–213, 263, 267
  mid 20th-century, 302–303

Fairs, Andean, 143
Family, in colonial period, 95
Fascism, 279–280, 281
FDN. *See* Frente Democrático Nacional
Federación de Trabajadores Campesinos
  (FTC), 313–314
Ferdinand VII
  capture of, 126
  restoration of, 127, 128, 129
Fernandini, Eulogio, 204
Financial system
  in Aristocratic Republic, 204–205
  postwar restructuring of, 196–197
Fiscal problems
  in colonial Peru, 85, 88
  post-independence, 144
  World War I and, 226
  early 19th-century, 129–130
  mid 19th-century, 144, 164–165
  late 19th-century, 178, 180–181
Fishing industry, 303, 308–309, 375

Floods, 1
Flores, Luis M., 279, 281
Flores de Oliva, Isabel. *See* Santa Rosa de
  Lima
Foco theory, 329, 369
Forasteros (migrants), 79, 93
Foreign investment
  after War of the Pacific, 197
  early 20th-century, 242–243, 244
  mid 20th-century, 304, 308
France, influence on Peru, 213–214, 225
Franciscans, 109, 110
FREDEMO, 398, 400, 404
Frente Democrático Nacional (FDN), 287,
  288, 289
Freyre de Jaimes, Carolina, 379
FTC. *See* Federación de Trabajadores
  Campesinos
Fujimori, Alberto, *402*
  assessment of first term of, 423–424
  attempted coup against, 415–416
  authoritarian tendency of, 412
  autogolpe (self-coup) by, xv, 413–414, 420
  background of, 401
  and drug enforcement, 412
  economic conditions inherited by, 406–407
  and military, 409–410, 413, 420–421
  perceived inscrutability of, xii
  popularity of, 408–409, 416, 417
  privatization program of, 418–419
  and Shining Path, program to combat,
    410–411
  social spending program of, 419, 420
  stabilization program of, 407–408
  tax reforms of, 419–420
  in 1990 elections, 402–405
  in 1995 elections, 421, 422

Gadea, Hilda, 329
Gálvez, José de, 104, 119, 123
Gamarra, Agustín, 137–138, 155, 156
Ganadera de Cerro de Pasco, 251
García Calderón, Francisco, 213–214, 232
García Calderón, Francisco (interim
  president), 189, 190
García Márquez, Gabriel, 399
García Pérez, Alan
  administrative decentralization plan of, 391
  and APRA, 364, 378, 383–384
  background of, 382–383
  and bank nationalization, proposal for,
    393, 397
  economic policy of, 388–389, 394–395
  versus Fujimori, 414
  loss of popularity, 397
  presidency of, 385, 387–391
  in 1984 elections, 384–385
Gasca, Pedro de la, 42–43
Gender
  in Inca society, 14, 20
  See also Women

Generation of 1900, 198, 232
Generation of 1909, 246
Generation of 1919, 232–235, 239, 256–257
Generation of 1950, 333
Geoglyphs, Nazca, 9
Geography, 1–4, 3*m*
Gildemeister, Augusto, 291
Glass of Milk Program, 378
Gold rush, 39
Gongorismo, 97
González Prada, Manuel, 198–200, 218, *199*
  and anarchism, 221, 222
  influence of, 246–247
  on José Pardo's first administration,
    214–215
  and labor movement, 222
  wife of, 214
Gorriti, Juana Manuela, 379
Government/administration
  APRA and, 290–296
  in Aristocratic Republic, 205–206
  colonial, 46, 85–89
  of Inca empire, 24–27
  independence, 131–132
  military juntas
    of 1930s, 268–269
    of 1960s, 320–322, 336–358
    of 1970s, 359–365
  nepotism in, 214–215
  oligarchy and, 212–218
  pax Andina, 162–163
  18th-century reform of, 103–104, 119–120
  19th-century, 136–138, 167–168
  20th-century
    expansion of, 332–333, 343–344
    García's decentralization plan for, 391
    reductions of 1980s, 374–375
    restructuring of 1970s, 353
  See also under specific leaders names
Goyeneche y Barreda, José Manuel de, 126
Grace, Michael A., 197
Grace, William Russell, 169–170
Grace & Co., 228, 303, 304
Graña Garland, Francisco, 296
Grau, Miguel, 179, 187
Graves, Ana Melina, 260
Great Britain
  postwar investment in Peru, 197
  relations with Chile, 186
Great Rebellion. *See* Túpac Amaru II,
  rebellion of
Grupo Resurgimiento, 246
Gualpa, Diego, 43
Guamán Poma de Ayala, Felipe, 98
  Primer nueva crónica y bien gobierno, 36, 73,
    98
Guano, 4, 158
  nitrates as alternative to, 183
Guano boom
  and debt consolidation, 164–165
  demographic impact of, 169

economic impact of, 158–160, 161, 165–167,
    171
  end of, 180–181
  failure to derive long-term benefits from,
    181–182
  and mobilization of workers, 220
  political impact of, 160–162, 167–168, 171–172
  and railroad building, 181–182
  social impact of, 162–163, 169–170
Guarantee Trust, 244
Guerrilla movements
  independence. *See Montoneras*
  of 1960s, 329–330, 369
Guevara, Che, 329, 369
Gutarra, Nicolás, 236, 238
Gutiérrez, Tomás, military coup led by, 179
Gutiérrez Cuevas, Teodomiro, 229
Gutiérrez Merino, Gustavo, 352
Guzmán Reynoso, Abimael, *367*
  background of, 366–367
  capture of, 414–415
  followers of, 368–369, 370–371
  teaching of, 368–371

Haciendas, 78
  agricultural production at, 46–47
  elimination of, 342, 346
  expansion of, 208–209
  guano boom and, 165
  origin of, 46
  in postcolonial Peru, 147
  slaves on, 150
Haya, Raúl, 233
Haya de la Torre, Víctor Raúl, 232, *234*
  appeal of, 274
  and APRA, 259–260
  arrest of, 276
  background of, 233–235
  and Bustamante, 290
  candidacy for presidency, 260
  confinement in Colombian Embassy, 300
  exile of, 255, 259, 260, 306
  increased influence of, 288
  and *indigenismo*, 246, 259
  and labor movement, 237
  leadership style of, 296
  versus Mariátegui, 260–262
  moderate shift of, 282, 287, 288
  and Morales, 360
  and Prado, 307
  as president of Constitutional Assembly,
    363–364
  return from exile, 272
  and Sacred Heart ceremony, opposition to,
    253, 254
  and university reform movement, 239
  during World War II, 282, 283
  in 1931 elections, 273
  and 1936 elections, 280
  in 1962 elections, 318, 319–320
  in 1963 elections, 322

Health, public
  in early 20th century, 219, 221, 294
  in late 20th century, 407
Heraud, Javier, 330
Hermoza Ríos, Nicolás, 410
Hidalgos, 32
Hilbck, Emilio, 263
Hinojosa, Pedro de, 44
Horses, in conquest of Americas, 35, 38
Huacas (holy sites), 18
Huamán, Adrian, 382
Huancas (ethnic group), 11
Huancavelica mines, 66, 67, 68, 75
Huarca, Domingo, 249
Huari (Wari) empire, 9, 10
Huáscar, 29–30
Huayna Capac, 29, 34, 49
Humbolt Current, 2, 4, 7

Iglesias, Miguel, 190–191, 193, 195
Immigration
  guano boom and, 169–170
  Spanish, 51, 52–53
Imperialism, Haya on, 260, 261
Imports
  in postcolonial Peru, 142, 162, 169, 179
  in early 20th century, 258, 267
  in mid 20th century, 304–305
Import substituting industrialization (ISI)
  after War of the Pacific, 197
  World War I and, 228, 265
  in mid 20th century, 331
Incas
  civil wars of, 29–30, 38
  culture of, 25
  demographic collapse of, 48–51
  economy of, 28–29
  empire of, 6m, 19, 29
  expansion of, 15–17
  governance system of, 24–27
  historical accounts of, 12–13
  labor system of, 19, 23–24
  legal code of, 26
  military organization of, 22–23
  origins of, 13–15
  and reciprocal exchange principle, 27–28
  recording system of, 12, 21
  religion of, 17–18
  road system of, 22
  society of, 14–15
  Spanish conquest of, 33–39, 59
  under Spanish rule, 39–51. *See also* Colonial
    Peru
  state organization of, 19–21
  18th-century nationalism, 116–117, 121
    attempts to eradicate, 119
  vertical archipelagos of, xii, 28
Independence movement, 122–130
  Bolívar and, 132–133
  origins of, historical interpretations of,
    121–122

popular participation in, 122–123
  San Martín and, 130–131
Indians
  demographic collapse of, 48–51
  millenarian revivals of, 57–58, 117, 229
  political organization of, 20th-century,
    248–249
  in postcolonial Peru, 136, 147–148
  psychological trauma of, 50
  resistance and adaptation to Spanish rule,
    65, 71
  revolts of
    World War I and, 228–229
    late 19th century, 175–176
    early 20th century, 245–249
  rubber boom and exploitation of, 211
  in War of the Pacific, *188*, 214
  See also Peasants
Indigenismo, 200, 245–247
  cultural impact of, 256, 257, 259
  official policy of, 247–248
Industrial Promotion Law (1956), 331
Informales, 372–373
  APRA and, 383
  Fujimori's campaign and, 403
Inkarrí, myth of, 117
Inquisition, Spanish, 33, 54, 92
Intellectuals
  generation of 1900, 198, 232
  generation of 1909, 246
  generation of 1919, 232–235, 239, 256–257
  generation of 1950, 333
  response to defeat in War of the Pacific,
    198–200
  after World War II, 317
Intendant system, 104, 120
Internal Security Law (1949), 301
International Petroleum Company (IPC),
    212, 227, 265
  dispute with, 334–335
  expropriation of holdings of, 344, 345
Inti (sun god), 18, 19–20, 24
Investment capital
  Catholic Church and, 82, 90
  guano boom and, 171
  See also Foreign investment
IPC. *See* International Petroleum Company
Iraola, José, 195
Irish immigrants, 169–170
Irrigation system, 5, 8
ISI. *See* Import substituting industrialization
Italian-Peruvians, 204
Izquierda Unida (IU), 377, 384

Japanese residents
  contract workers, 231, 401
  internment of, 283
Jesuits
  and education, 74, 105
  expulsion from New World, 103
Jiménez, Gustavo, 269, 275

Juan, Jorge, 105
Jungle, 4
  Indian population in, 109–110

Katarista insurgency, 119
Kemmerer, Edwin Walter, 244
  reform program of, 269–271
Korean War, 300–301

Labor force
  early 20th-century, 219–220
  See also Working class
Labor movement
  anarchism and, 221–222
  APRA/Bustamante government and,
    291–292
  great strikes of 1918–1919, 236–238
  guano boom and, 220
  military government of 1970s and, 354, 356
  Odría's government and, 302
  revival of 1970s, 360–361
  in rural areas, 326–327
  World War I and, 230–231
  World War II and, 283, 286, 290
  early 20th-century, 222–224
  mid 20th-century, 317
  late 20th-century, 360–361, 409
Labor system
  colonial, 78–79
  Inca, 14, 19, 23–24
  Toledo reforms and, 60, 62, 67
La Coalición, 334, 336
Lagos, Edith, 380
Lake Titicaca, 2, 6m
La Mar, José de, 155
La Marginal highway project, 332, 375
Lambayeque sugar plantations, 78
Landázuri Ricketts, Juan, 316
Land distribution
  in Andean society, 14
  in colonial Peru, 46, 77–78
  in Inca empire, 26–27
  in postcolonial Peru, 146
  19th-century consolidation, 175–176
  20th-century consolidation, 208–209
  in mid 20th century, 324
Land reform
  Belaúnde's administration and, 326–328
  military junta of 1960s and, 321
  Prado's administration and, 314–315
  Velasco's administration and, 342, 346–349,
    357
Languages
  in Inca empire, 25
  in modern Peru, 342
La Perricholi (Miqueta Micaela Villegas), 97
Las Casas, Bartolome de, 41
La Torre, Augusta, 368, 397
Lavalle, Hernando de, 306
Lavalle, José Antonio de, 186
Law of professional risk, 220

Ledesma Izquieta, Genaro, 312–313
Legal codes
  colonial, 65–66
  Inca, 26
Leguía, Augusto B.
  background of, 241
  and Billinghurst, 223
  coup led by, 239–240
  economic policies of, 243–244
  economy under, 250–251, 263–267
  as finance minister, 217, 218
  first administration of, 241
  foreign policy of, 258–259
  governmental corruption under, 266
  imprisonment of, 268
  Indian unrest and, 245
  indigenismo policy of, 247–248
  military coup against, 262–263, 267
  modernization program of, 249–251,
    252–253, 258
  political career of, 240
  second administration of, 242–244
  and Twenty-Four Friends, 213
  in 1919 elections, 238, 241–242
Leguía, Juan, 266
Lévano, Delfin, 222
l'Hermite, Jacques, 83
Liberalism
  in colonial Peru, 127, 168
  guano boom and, 160, 167
  in postcolonial Peru, 137, 155
Liberal Party
  personal loyalties and, 214
  in early 20th century, 235
Liberation Theology (Gustavo Gutiérrez), 352
Lima
  Bolívar's entry in, 133
  colonial, 73
    cultural life in, 74–75, 97–98
    economy of, 72–74, 76
  defense in War of the Pacific, 189
  earthquakes in, 81, 91
  founding of, 39
  guano boom and, 165, 169
  independence movement and, 124, 127, 128
  indigenismo school in, 246–247
  merchants of, 84, 108, 124
  occupation by Chile, 191
  during *Oncenio*, 250
  population growth in, 20th-century, 219, 301
  San Martín's entry in, 131
  shantytowns in, 350–351
  Shining Path in, 392
  slaves in, 148, 149, 152, 153–154
  strikes in, 222, 237
  working class in, 220
  17th-century, 72–74, 73, 81, 82, 89, 100
  18th-century, 103
  early 20th-century, 214, 219, 250, 251, 258
  mid 20th-century, 301, 316, 324–325
  late 20th-century, 350–351

Lissón, Emilio, 253, 254
Lobatón, Guillermo, 330
Lomas (meadows), 5
Lombardo Toledano, Vicente, 286
López, Nicolás Lindley, 322
López Albújar, Enrique, 247
López de Romaña, Eduardo, 217, 223
Loyola, Inigo de, 55
Lupacas (ethnic group), 11
Luque, Hernando de, 34
Lynch, Patricio, 187–188

Machu Pichu, rediscovery of, 246
Maize (corn), introduction of, 5
Maldonado, Diego, 45
Malnutrition, in 1980s, 395
Manco
  crowning of, 38
  rebellion of, 40, 41
Manila galleons, 84
Mantaro Valley, 140, 142, 156–157, 304,
    309–310
Manufacturing
  World War I and, 228
  World War II and, 284–285
  in 17th century, 80, 81
  in 19th century, 198, 204
  in early 20th century, 265
Manzanilla, José Matías, 198, 236
Mao Zedong, death of, 371
Mariátegui, José Carlos, 232
  background of, 235
  death of, 262
  exile of, 255
  versus Haya, 260–262
  and *indigenismo*, 246, 256, 257
  influence of, 369
  journal founded by, 255, 256–257
  and nationalism, 257
  newspaper founded by, 239
  return to Peru, 255–256
  and socialism, 256, 261
Markham, Clements, 149
Maroons, 150
Martínez Vegaso, Lucas, 47
Marxism, influence of, 255, 260
Matto de Turner, Clorinda, 200, 245–246, 379
Meiggs, Henry, 166, 177
Melgar, Mariano, 129
Mendoza Leyva, Abelardo, 276
Merel, Héctor, 236
Mestizo *(casta)*, 48, 53, 93–94
  Bourbon reforms and, 113
  in 1940 census, 285
  percentage of population, 18th-century, 100
  prejudice against, 94
Mexico, Haya de la Torre in, 259
Mezzich, Julio César, 369
Middle classes
  APRA and, 384
  Haya on, 261

Mariátegui on, 261–262
  in early 20th century, 231–232, 242, 267
  in mid 20th century, 292, 317, 325
Migrants
  in colonial society, 79
  in early 20th century, 251, 294
  in mid 20th century, 301–302
  in late 20th century, 365
  See also Immigration
Military
  anti-Aprismo stance of, 275–276, 320–321,
    337
  Aristocratic Republic and restructuring of,
    205
  Callao revolt (1948), 298–299
  Chilean, 186–187
  civic action role of, 421
  Civilistas and reform of, 179, 180, 183–185
  counterinsurgency training of, 330
  coup of 1914, 224–225
  coup of 1930, 262–263, 267
  coup of 1968, 336–338, 340–341
  and elections of 1962, 319–320
  Fujimori and, 409–410, 413, 420–421
  García's regime and, 390
  guerrilla movement of 1960s and, 338
  Inca, 22–23
  national security doctrine of, 318, 346
  Odría's regime and, 300
  postcolonial, 136–137
  professionalization of, 225, 305–306,
    315–316
  and revolution of 1968
    first phase of, 338–358
    second phase of, 359–365
  and Shining Path, counterinsurgency
    against, 381–382, 407, 410–411
  and war with Ecuador, 285–286
  20th-century
    reform of, 337–338
    in 1950s, 305–306
    in 1960s, 318, 319–320
    in 1970s, 373–374
    in 1990s, 407
Millenarianism
  16th-century, 57–58
  18th-century, 117
  20th-century, 229
Mining
  foreign control of, 207, 227, 304
  Korean War and, 301
  nationalization of, 345–346
  World War I and, 227
  mid 20th-century, 303–304
  See also Copper mining; Silver mining
MIR. *See* Movimiento de Izquierda
    Revolucionaria
Miró-Quesada, Antonio, 272, 278
Missionaries
  first, 54–56
  in *selva*, 109, 110

Misti (Quechua for white), in postcolonial Peru, 138
Mita system
in colonial Peru, 62–63
impact on communities, 67
silver mining and, 67–68
in Inca empire, 23–24
in postcolonial Peru, 146
Mitimae (settler groups), 19, 22, 25–26
ML. *See* Movimiento Libertad
MLR. *See* Movimiento Laboral Revolucionario
Moche civilization, 8–9
Monasteries, in colonial period, 90
Montaña society, 18th-century, 109–110
Monteagudo, Bernardo, 131
Montero, Lizardo, 189
Montesinos, Vladimiro, 409–410, 416
Montoneras (Indian guerrilla forces)
bourgeoisie and, 126
in independence movement, 123, 133
in postcolonial Peru, 156
and postwar politics, 193
in War of the Pacific, 190, 192
Moors, Spanish wars with, 31–33
Morales Bermúdez, Francisco, 335, 356
economic policy of, 359–360, 362
foreign policy of, 361–362
government of, 359–365
Morales Bermúdez, Remigio, 200–201
Moreno, Esther, 379
Morote, Osmán, 368
Morote Best, Efraín, 367
Movimiento de Izquierda Revolucionaria (MIR), 318–319, 329, 330, 360
Movimiento Laboral Revolucionario (MLR), 354
Movimiento Libertad (ML), 400
Movimiento Revolucionario Túpac Amaru (MRTA), 376–377, 415
versus Shining Path, 396
Movimiento Social Progresista (MSP), 340
Moyano, María Elena, 413
MRTA. *See* Movimiento Revolucionario Túpac Amaru
Mutual aid societies, 220

Napoleonic wars, 108, 126
Nationalism
generation of 1919 and, 257, 261
neo-Inca, 116–117, 121
attempts to eradicate, 119
Natural disasters, 1, 7, 12
in colonial period, 81, 91
in late 20th century, 375
Navala Huachaca, Antonio, 157
Nazca society, 6*m*, 9
Neo-Inca revivalism/nationalism, 18th-century, 116–117
New Left, 362, 363
origins of, 360–361

Newspapers
in early 20th century, 232
in late 20th century, 352–353
Nitrate production
first attempts at, 180
and War of the Pacific, 183, 185, 186
Noel y Moral, Clement, 381–382
Noriega, Francisco, 194
Nueva Mayoría/Cambio 90 Party, 416, 417, 422
Nuñez Vela, Blasco, 42, 86
Nunneries, in colonial period, 90, 96

Odría, Manuel A.
background of, 299
coup led by, 299
dictatorship of, 299–307
as minister of government, 296, 298
in War with Ecuador, 286
in 1962 elections, 319, 320
in 1963 elections, 322
Odría, María Delgado de, 301, 307
Offices, sale of, in colonial period, 88–89, 104, 112–113
Oil industry
nationalization of, 344, 345
World War I and, 227
World War II and, 283–284
early 20th-century, 211–212, 265
mid 20th-century, 304, 334–335
Oligarchy
counterattack on APRA/Bustamante government, 297–298
developmental program of, 216–217
emergence of, 212–218
fissures in, 279–280
Odría's rule and, 300
sources of disagreement within, 215–216
World War I and, 228
Olivares, Conde Duque de, 88
Oncenio, 242–244
culture during, 252
economy during, 250–251, 263–267
foreign policy during, 258–259
governmental corruption during, 266
Indian unrest during, 245–248
modernization during, 249–251, 252–253, 258
Orbegoso, Luis de, 155
Orejones (big ears), 21
Orientalism, xi
Ovando, Nicolás de, 33

Pachacuti Inca Yupanqui
and public works, 19
and religion, 17–18
and territorial expansion, 15–17
usurpation of power by, 20
Pact of Monterrico, 307
Painting, colonial, 55
Palacios, Alfredo, 239

Palma, Ricardo, 198
Paloma, pre-Inca inhabitants of, 5
Panama, founding of, 34
Panama Canal, impact of, 226, 228
PAP. *See* Partido Aprista Peruano
Pardo y Barreda, José, 204, 218
    first administration of, 214–215
    labor unrest and, 237
    second administration of, 226, 235
    and Twenty-Four Friends, 213
Pardo y Lavalle, Manuel, 171–172, *173*
    assassination of, 181
    campaign to end military rule, 178–179
    developmental agenda of, 179
    economic crisis and, 180–181
    military policies of, 179, 180, 183–185
    popular election of, 176–177, 179
    railroad-building program of, 172–175
Partido Aprista Peruano (PAP), 287
Partido Civil Independiente, 218
Partido Democrático Cristiano (PDC), 316,
    322, 327, 340
Partido Popular Cristiano (PPC), 362, 363,
    364
Partido Unión Nacional, 199–200
Partido Unión Revolucionario (UR), 271
Patio amalgamation process, 66, 68
Patronage, in postcolonial politics, 214–215
Pax Andina, 162–163, 168
PCP. *See* Peruvian Communist Party
PDC. *See* Partido Democrático Cristiano
Peasants, *295, 325*
    APRA and, 383
    in cooperatives, 346–347
    disenchantment with Shining Path,
        410–411
    introduction of term, 342
    labor organization of, 292–294
    revolts of 1950s and 1960s, 311–314, 321
Pease García, Henry, 400
Pérez de Cuellar, Javier, 421–422
Pérez Godoy, Ricardo, 320, 322
Perón, Juan, 300
    Odría compared with, 301, 302
Peru-Bolivian Confederation, 137, 141,
    155–156
    support for, 157
    war on, 156
Peruvian Communist Party (PCP), 329, 330,
    349
Peruvian Guano Company, 181
Petroleum industry. *See* Oil industry
Pezet, Juan Antonio, 175
Pezuela, Joaquín de la, 129, 131
Piérola, Nicolás de
    background of, 201
    and Billinghurst, 222–223
    coups led by, 188, 201–202
    death of, 235
    as finance minister, 176, 177, 178
    and military, professionalization of, 225

presidency of, 203–204
rivalry with Pardo, 180
and War of the Pacific, 189
Pizarro, Francisco
    arrival in Inca empire, 30, 31
    blacks in expedition of, 51
    capture of Atahualpa, 31, 34–37, *36*
    conflict with Almagro, 40–41
    conquest of Inca empire, 34–39
    early career of, 33–34
    founding of Lima, 39
Pizarro, Gonzalo, rebellion of, 42–43
Pizarro, Pedro, 38
Plan Inca, 340–341
Plantations, 78
    Chinese coolies on, 163
    cooperativization of, 346
    slaves on, 149
    workers on, in early 20th century, 230
Plutocracy
    guano-era, 165, 169, 170, 171
    See also Oligarchy
Polay Campos, Víctor, 396
Politics
    Aristocratic Republic and, 203, 214–215,
        217–218
    in colonial Peru, 64
    guano boom and, 160–162, 167–168,
        171–172
    liberalization of 1970s, 359–360
    in postcolonial Peru, 154–157
    after War of the Pacific, 193–194
    in early 20th century, 214–215, 217–218,
        222–224, 235–236
    in late 20th century, 359–360, 378–379
    See also specific political parties
Polygamy, 110
Population
    in colonial Peru, 51–53
    demographic collapse, colonization and,
        48–51
    guano boom and, 169
    in postcolonial Peru, 145–146
    17th-century, 82
    18th-century, 100, 113
    early 20th-century, 218–219
    mid 20th-century, 285, 294, 316, 323
    late 20th-century, 365
Porras Barrenechea, Raúl, 239
Portal, Magda, 379
Portocarerro, Julio, 236
Portugal, Latin American colonies of, 102,
    102m
Positivism, 198
Postcolonial Peru, *135m*
    Church in, 138–139
    contradictions underlying, 134, 136
    economy of, 139–145
        guano boom and, 158–160, 161, 165–167,
            171
    railroad expansion and, 174

foreign immigration to, 169–170
government in, 136–138
Indians in, 136, 147–148
politics in, 154–157
  guano boom and, 160–162, 167–168,
  171–172
  rise of Civilismo, 172–179
population in, 145–146
slaves in, 146–147, 152
social stratification in, 144, 146–147
Potato, Andean, 2
Potosí silver mines, 43–44
  decline in production, 66, 75
  economic impact of, 69, 70
  labor system at, 67, 68
  in 18th century, 99, 106
Poverty, late 20th-century, 407, 408
PPC. *See* Partido Popular Cristiano
Prada, González, 218
Prado, Javier, 198
Prado, Jorge del, 368
Prado, Mariano Ignacio, 175, 181, 281
  and War of the Pacific, 186, 188
Prado y Ugarteche, Jorge, 280
Prado y Ugarteche, Manuel, 281–282
  and agrarian reform, 314–315
  alliance with APRA, 283–284, 286
  first presidency of, 282–286
  peasant unrest and, 313, 314
  second presidency of, 307–308
  in 1939 elections, 281
  in 1956 elections, 307
Pre-Inca cultures, 5–12
Prialé, Ramiro, 300
Printing press, 74
Privatization
  of communal lands, in postcolonial Peru,
  146
  of state-owned enterprises, Fujimori's
  program for, 418–419
Protectionism
  guano boom and move away from, 160,
  161
  post-independence, 145, 155
Protestantism, 91–92, 405
Pueblos jóvenes (young towns), xiv, 350
  Church and, 351–352
  New Left and, 362
  and politics of 1980s, 378–379
Puente Uceda, Luís de la, 318, 329, 330
Puga, José Mercedes, 190
Pumacahua, Mateo García, 128
Puna (grassland), 1–2
  pre-Inca inhabitants of, 5

Quechua language, 25
  first grammar of, 55
  as second national language, 342
Quesada Larrea, José, 281
Quipu (recording device), 12, 21
  early form of, 10

Racial relations
  in colonial society, 94
  in early 20th century, 231, 252, 285
  in late 20th century, 405
Rafael contract, 181
Railroad building
  Balta's program of, 176, 177
  completion of, 219
  economic impact of, 174, 181–182
  financing of, 177, 178
  Meiggs and, 166, 177
  Pardo's program of, 172–175
  workers involved in, 270
Ramírez Durán, Oscar, 423
Ravines, Eudocio, 271
Rebellions, revolts, and revolutions
  post-independence, 157
  18th-century, 108–121
    causes of, 112–115
    crown's response to, 119–120
    of Juan Santos Atahualpa, 109–112
    of Túpac Amaru II, 109, 114, 115, 117–119
  19th-century, 128–129, 170
    of Chinese coolies, 177, 192
    Indian, 175–176
    protectionist (1858), 128–129
    tax on salt and (1896), 205
    after War of the Pacific, 194–195
  20th-century
    APRA-led, 275
    Indian, 245–249
    military juntas of 1930s and, 269, 271
    peasant (1950s and 1960s), 311–314, 321,
    326, 327
    popular protests (1970s), 356, 360
    World War I and, 228–229
  See also specific organizations
Reciprocal exchange, principle of, 27–28
Reconquista, Spanish (711–1492), 31–33
Reducciones (forced Indian settlements), 59,
  60, 61, 62, 79
Religions
  in colonial period, 90–91
  Inca, 17
  millenarian revivals, 57–58, 117, 229
  native
    as challenge to colonial rule, 60
    Church efforts to purge, 91, 92
    introduction of Christianity and, 54–55
  pre-Inca, 7–8
  See also Church, Roman Catholic
Repartimiento de mercancías (reparto), 63–64, 72
  abolition of, 106, 107, 119–120
  Bourbon reforms and, 112–113
Repúblicas de indios, 62, 93, 136
Resettlements, forced, in Andean colony, 59,
  60, 61. *See also Reducciones*
Revolution of 1895, 201
Rio Protocol, 286
Riva Agüero y Osma, José de la, 132, 232,
  280

Rivers, 4
Rodríguez Pastor, Carlos, 375
Rondas (civil defense patrols), 410, 411, 421
Rubber industry, 211, 264
Rumi Maqui Rebellion, 228–229
Russia. *See* Soviet Union

Sabogal, José, 246
Sacred Heart ceremony, proposal for, 253, 254
SAIS. *See* Sociedades Agrícolas de Interés Social
Salinas Sedo, Jaime, 415–416
Salt deposits, 109
Samanez Ocampo, David, 269
Sánchez, Luis Alberto, 239, 383
Sánchez Carrión, José Faustino, 127, 133
Sánchez Cerro, Luis M.
  assassination of, 276
  background of, 267–268
  military junta headed by, 268–269
  popular appeal of, 272
  presidency of, 274–276
  return from exile, 271
  in 1931 elections, 272, 273, 274
San Marcos University, 74, 105, 116
  and independence movement, 127
  and reform movement, 238–239
  in mid 20th century, 329
San Martín, José de, 122, 124
  capture of Chile, 130
  and Peruvian independence movement, 130–131
  republican government of, 131–132
  resignation of, 132
  on slavery, 150
San Martín de Porras(Saint), 91
San Román, Máximo, 403
San Román, Miguel, 175
Santa Cruz, Andrés, 137–138
  and Peru-Bolivian Confederation, 155, 157
Santa Rosa de Lima (Isabel Flores de Oliva), 91, 96–97
Santos Atahualpa, Juan, rebellion of, 109–112
Santo Tomás, Domingo de, 42, 55–56
Sapa Inca, 19–21, 27
School of the Americas, 330
Scientific expeditions, European, 105
SEC. *See* Sociedad Empleados de Comercio
Selva (tropical forest), 109–110
Sendero Luminoso. *See* Shining Path
Sendero Rojo, 423
Seoane, Edgardo, 336
Seoane, Manuel, 239
Serna, José de la, 131, 133
Shining Path, xv
  coca industry and, 386–387
  early success of, 380
  expansion of, 391–393, 396
  Fujimori's program to combat, 410–411
  Guzmán's capture and, 415, 423

military counterinsurgency against, 381–382
  versus MRTA, 396
  origins of, 329, 369–372
  second wave of recruits, 380–381, 393
  support for, 342
  terrorist campaign of, 376, 382, 407, 413, 414
  urban shift of, 392, 396–397
Shipbuilding, 17th-century, 80
Sierra (highlands), 1–2
  pre-Inca inhabitants of, 7, 9–11
Silver mining
  colonial, 43–44
  17th-century, 69, 75–76
  18th-century, 99–100, 106
  Toledo reforms and, 62–63, 64, 66–68, 69
  postcolonial, 140, 141–142
  after War of the Pacific, 197, 206
Sistema Nacional de Movilización Social (SINAMOS), 349–350, 353, 360
Slaves, African, 148–154
  arguments for maintaining, 151–152
  in *caudillo* wars, 151
  in colonial Peru, 51–52
  emancipation of, 149, 151, 162, 163
  in independence movement, 123, 150–151
  in postcolonial Peru, 146–147, 152
Smallpox, 34, 49
Soccer, 252
Socialism, generation of 1919 and, 256, 261
Socialist Party of Peru, 262
Social property, 355
Social stratification
  colonial, 52, 53, 134–136
  in Inca society, 19, 21
  postcolonial, 144, 146–147
  17th-century, 93–95
Sociedad Consignataria del Guano, 170
Sociedad Empleados de Comercio (SEC), 232
Sociedades Agrícolas de Interés Social (SAIS), 346–347
Solomón-Lozano Treaty of 1922, 258
Soto, Hernando de, 34, 64, 301, 372–373, 400, 406–407
Southern Peruvian Copper Corporation, 304
Soviet Union
  Haya in, 260
  junta of 1969 and, 345
  Revolution of 1917, impact of, 229, 237, 238
Spain
  colonial rule by. *See* Colonial Peru
  emigration from, 51, 52–53
  government over Peruvian colony, 85, 88–89
  independence from. *See* Independence movement
  late medieval society of, 32
  Latin American colonies of, 102*m*
  political unification of, 33
  recolonization of Peru, 99, 103

reconquista period in (711–1492), 31–33
reliance on Andean colony, 57
war with (1865), 175
17th-century, 91, 95
18th-century, 101–103
Speilbergen, Joris van, 83
Sports, popularization of, 252
Squatter settlements, 301–302, 325, 350. *See
also Pueblos jóvenes*
Strikes
for eight-hour day, 236–237
first, early 20th-century, 220, 222, 223, 224
by Guardia Civil, 356
to lower cost of living, 238
during World War I, 231
of 1918–19, 236–238
of 1930s, 271
of 1960s, 326
of 1970s, 360, 362–363
of 1980s, 396
of 1990s, 409
Sucre, Antonio José de, 133
Sugar industry
cooperativization of, 346
World War I and, 226
World War II and, 284
in 18th century, 107
in 19th century, 191, 196
in early 20th century, 209–210, 263
in mid 20th century, 302–303, 309
Sun, cult of, 17, 18, 19–20
Swayne, Henry, 241

Taki Onqoy sect, 57–58
campaigns against, 60
Tangüis, Fermín, 210, 263
Taxes
evasions of 1980s, 389
See also Tribute system
Tello, Julio C., 247
Terrorism, 376–377, 382, 407, 413, 414
Textile industry
19th-century, 204
early 20th-century, 221, 222
Tiwanaku (Tiahuanco), city of, 9–10
Toledo, Alejandro, 422
Toledo, Francisco de, 58–59, 88
reforms of, 59–68
Topa Inca Yupanqui, 16, *16*, 17
Toquepala copper mines, 309
Toro, David, 280
Torre Tagle, Marquis de, 130, 132, 133
Townsend Ezcurra, Andrés, 364
Trade
colonial, 46–47
with Chile, 77, 81
contraband, 84, 105
Napoleonic wars and, 108
reparto system and, 63–64
silver production and, 69, 70, 75–76
17th-century, 77, 80, 81, 83–84

18th-century, 105–106, 109
in Inca empire, 28–29
postcolonial, 139, 141, 144–145
conservative-liberal clash on, 155
coolie, 163, 164
guano, 158–159, 160, 161
Transportation
Inca road system, 22
La Marginal highway project, 332, 375
during *Oncenio,* 250
17th-century, 80
See also Railroad building
Treaty of Ancón, 191, 193
Treaty of Lima, 259
Trelles, Oscar, 327
Tribute system
in colonial Peru, 41, 42–43, 44–48
Bourbon reforms and, 113
Toledo reforms and, 62
in Inca empire, 27–28, 44
monetization of, 62
in postcolonial Peru, 138, 146, 147
Castilla's reforms and, 162, 163
late 19th-century reinstitution of, 176
Trotsky, Leon, 260
Tuna War, 345
Túpac Amaru, 59
Túpac Amaru II, *111,* 112, 115
capture and execution of, 119
ideological influences on, 115–116
rebellion of, 109, 114, 117–119
creole participation in, 115
legacy of, 120–121
reasons for defeat, 118
Túpac Huallpa, 38
Turpo, José María, 229
Twenty-Four Friends, 213

Ubalde, Juan Manuel, 125
Uchuraccay massacre, 382, 400
Ulloa, Antonio de, 105
Ulloa, Manuel, 336, 374, 375
Unanue, Hipólito, 105
memoirs of, 139–140
UND. *See* Unión Nacional Democrática
Unemployment
in mid 19th century, 170
in early 20th century, 267
in late 20th century, 363, 385, 395, 406
Unión Nacional Democrática (UND), 287
United States
and APRA, 292
direct investment in Peru, 242–243, 244
drug enforcement agreement with, 412
Fujimori's regime and, 414
increasing commercial presence of, 228,
244, 304
and junta of 1962–63, 321
and junta of 1969, 344–345
Leguía government and, 249–250
loans to Peru, 258, 266

United States (*continued*)
military assistance by, 306, 315–316, 330
and mining industry, 207
sugar exports to, 226, 303, 309
War of the Pacific and, 189, 190
World War II and relations with, 282–283
Universidades populares (UPs), 254
University students
and labor movement, 237
and land reform, 328–329
radicalization of, 237, 333
and reform movement, 238–239
UPs. *See Universidades populares*
UR. *See* Partido Unión Revolucionario
Urbanization
in early 20th century, 219
in mid 20th century, 302, 311, 316–317
Ureta, Eloy G., 285, 286
in 1945 elections, 287–288
Uriel García, José, 246
Utopia, Andean, 92–93, 116

Valcárcel, Luis, 246
Valle, José del, 119
Valle Caviedes, Juan del, 98
Vallejo, César, 233
Valverde, 36–37
Vanguardia Revolucionaria (VR), 361
Vargas Alzamora, Augusto, 405
Vargas Llosa, Mario, 382, 397
background of, 399
economic program of, 400–401
political involvement of, 399–400
in 1990 elections, 404
Vasconcelos, José, 259
Vega, Garcilaso de la, 44, 98
Royal Commentaries of the Incas, 116
Vegetation, 2, 4
Velasco Alvarado, Juan, xv, 335, *339*
background of, 338–339
and Catholic Church, 352
coup against, 356
in coup of 1968, 340–341
foreign policy of, 344–345
government expansion under, 343–344
health problems of, 355
and land reform, 342, 346–349
legacy of, 356–358
views of, 339–340
Velasco Revolution of 1968, 121–122
Vertical archipelagos, Inca, xii, 28
colonial reconstruction of, 71
Viceroyalty, 86–87
Vidal, Antonio, 415
Villanueva, Víctor, 286, 287, 298
Villanueva del Campo, Armando, 300, 364, 365
Villarán, Manuel Vicente, 198, 217, 279

Villegas, Miqueta Micaela (La Perricholi), 97
Vilque fair, 143
Violence, xv. *See also* Terrorism
Viracocha (Inca god), 18, 117
Vitarte textile factory, 221, 222
Vitcos, neo-Inca kingdom of, 41
capture of, 59
threat posed by, 58, 59
VR. *See* Vanguardia Revolucionaria

Wari (Huari) empire, 9, 10
War of the Pacific, 187–191
and Chilean expansion, 184*m*, 191
economic impact of, 191–192
explanations for defeat in, 198–200
Indians in, *188*, 214
naval engagements in, 187
origins of, 183, 185–187
outbreak of, 181
politics after, 193–194
reconstruction following, 195–198
revolts after, 194–195
White-collar workers, 231–232, 242
Wine industry, 17th-century, 80
Women
activism of 1980s, 378, 379
in colonial period, 78, 95–97
haciendas owned by, 78
in Inca society, 14, 20
right to vote, 307
in Shining Path, 368, 393, 397
slaves, 149, 152
Spanish immigrants, 52
workers, activism of, 236
Wool production
World War I and, 227
in 18th century, 107
in 19th century, 141, 143, 166–167
in 20th century, 208, 245, 263–264
Working class
formation of, 219–225
Mariátegui on, 262
reforms of 1970s and, 353–354
World War I and, 229–232
in early 20th century, 267
in mid 20th-century, 317, 325
World War I
economic impact of, 211, 225–228
social impact of, 228–235
World War II, impact of, 282–286
Writing/recording, Inca system of, 12, 21

Yanaconas (resident estate workers), 79
efforts to improve conditions of, 293
Yanas (serfs), 19, 21
Yoshiyama, Jaime, 416
Young towns. *See Pueblos jóvenes*

Zulen, Pedro, 246